Communications in Computer and Information Science 752

Commenced Publication in 2007
Founding and Former Series Editors:
Alfredo Cuzzocrea, Orhun Kara, Dominik Ślęzak, and Xiaokang Yang

More information about this series at http://www.springer.com/series/7899

Mohamed Sultan Mohamed Ali · Herman Wahid
Nurul Adilla Mohd Subha · Shafishuhaza Sahlan
Mohd Amri Md. Yunus · Ahmad Ridhwan Wahap
(Eds.)

Modeling, Design and Simulation of Systems

17th Asia Simulation Conference, AsiaSim 2017
Melaka, Malaysia, August 27–29, 2017
Proceedings, Part II

Springer

Editors
Mohamed Sultan Mohamed Ali
Universiti Teknologi Malaysia
Skudai
Malaysia

Shafishuhaza Sahlan
Universiti Teknologi Malaysia
Skudai
Malaysia

Herman Wahid
Universiti Teknologi Malaysia
Skudai
Malaysia

Mohd Amri Md. Yunus
Universiti Teknologi Malaysia
Skudai
Malaysia

Nurul Adilla Mohd Subha
Universiti Teknologi Malaysia
Skudai
Malaysia

Ahmad Ridhwan Wahap
Universiti Teknologi Malaysia
Skudai
Malaysia

ISSN 1865-0929   ISSN 1865-0937 (electronic)
Communications in Computer and Information Science
ISBN 978-981-10-6501-9   ISBN 978-981-10-6502-6 (eBook)
DOI 10.1007/978-981-10-6502-6

Library of Congress Control Number: 2017952391

Printed on acid-free paper

This Springer imprint is published by Springer Nature
The registered company is Springer Nature Singapore Pte Ltd.
The registered company address is: 152 Beach Road, #21-01/04 Gateway East, Singapore 189721, Singapore

Preface

The Asia Simulation Conference is an annual simulation conference organized by the following Asian simulation societies: the Korea Society for Simulation (KSS), the China Simulation Federation (CSF), the Japan Society for Simulation Technology (JSST), the Society of Simulation and Gaming of Singapore, and the Malaysia Simulation Society (MSS). This conference provides a forum for scientists, academicians, and professionals from around the world. With this goal in mind, the Federation of Asia Simulation Societies (ASIASIM) was formed in 2011. The main purpose of ASIASIM is to provide an Asian forum for regional and national simulation societies to promote the advancement of modeling and simulation. As a leading conference in the field of simulation, the 17th Asia Simulation Conference (AsiaSim 2017), held in Melaka, Malaysia, aimed to be the premier forum for researchers and practitioners from academia and industry in the Asia Pacific region to share their ideas, research results, and experiences, thus promoting research and technical innovation in these fields domestically and internationally.

The papers presented at this conference have been collected in this volume of the series Communications in Computer and Information Science. The papers contained in these proceedings address challenging issues in modeling and simulation in various fields such as embedded systems, symbiotic simulation, agent-based simulation, parallel and distributed simulation, high performance computing, biomedical engineering, big data, energy, society and economics, medical processes, simulation language and software, visualization, virtual reality, modeling and simulation for IoT, machine learning, as well as the fundamentals and applications of computing. This year, AsiaSim received 263 submissions. After a thorough reviewing process by the Technical Committee, 124 papers were selected for presentation as full papers, with an acceptance rate of 47.1%. This volume contains 64 full papers presented at AsiaSim 2017 and divided into 2 main tracks, namely: Advanced Modeling and Simulation; and Modeling and Simulation Technology.

The high-quality program would not have been possible without the authors who chose AsiaSim 2017 as a venue for their publications. We are also very grateful to the Program Committee members and Organizing Committee members, who put a tremendous amount of effort into soliciting and selecting research papers with a balance of high quality and new ideas and applications.

We hope that you enjoy reading and benefit from the proceedings of AsiaSim 2017.

August 2017

Mohamed Sultan Mohamed Ali
Herman Wahid
Nurul Adilla Mohd Subha
Shafishuhaza Sahlan
Mohd Amri Md. Yunus
Ahmad Ridhwan Wahap

Organization

AsiaSim 2017 was organized by the Universiti Teknologi Malaysia and the Malaysian Simulation Society.

Patron

Wahid Omar   Universiti Teknologi Malaysia, Malaysia

Advisor

Johari Halim Shah Osman   Universiti Teknologi Malaysia, Malaysia
Rubiyah Yusof   Malaysian-Japan International Institute of Technology, Malaysia

General Chairs

Yahaya Md. Sam   Universiti Teknologi Malaysia, Malaysia
Zaharuddin Mohamed   Universiti Teknologi Malaysia, Malaysia
Md Nazri Othman   Universiti Teknikal Malaysia Melaka, Malaysia

Secretariat Chairs

Nurul Adilla Mohd Subha   Universiti Teknologi Malaysia, Malaysia
Shafishuhaza Sahlan   Universiti Teknologi Malaysia, Malaysia
Rozaimi Ghazali   Universiti Teknikal Malaysia Melaka, Malaysia
Raihatul Jannah Abdullah   Universiti Teknikal Malaysia Melaka, Malaysia

Financial Committee

Anita Ahmad   Universiti Teknologi Malaysia, Malaysia
Khairul Hamimah Abas   Universiti Teknologi Malaysia, Malaysia

Technical Committee

Hazlina Selamat   Universiti Teknologi Malaysia, Malaysia
Zaharuddin Mohamed   Universiti Teknologi Malaysia, Malaysia
Norhaliza Abdul Wahab   Universiti Teknologi Malaysia, Malaysia
Fatimah Sham Ismail   Universiti Teknologi Malaysia, Malaysia
Mohamed Sultan Mohamed Ali   Universiti Teknologi Malaysia, Malaysia
Zool Hilmi Ismail   Malaysian-Japan International Institute of Technology, Malaysia

Publication Committee-Proceeding Editors

Mohamed Sultan Mohamed Ali	Universiti Teknologi Malaysia, Malaysia
Herman Wahid	Universiti Teknologi Malaysia, Malaysia
Nurul Adilla Mohd Subha	Universiti Teknologi Malaysia, Malaysia
Shafishuhaza Sahlan	Universiti Teknologi Malaysia, Malaysia
Mohd Amri Md Yunus	Universiti Teknologi Malaysia, Malaysia
Ahmad Ridhwan Wahap	Universiti Teknologi Malaysia, Malaysia

Publication Committee-Program

Herlina Abdul Rahim	Universiti Teknologi Malaysia, Malaysia
Sallehudin Ibrahim	Universiti Teknologi Malaysia, Malaysia
Mohd Ridzuan Ahmad	Universiti Teknologi Malaysia, Malaysia
Ahmad Ridhwan Wahap	Universiti Teknologi Malaysia, Malaysia

Local Arrangements Committee

Abdul Rashid Husain	Universiti Teknologi Malaysia, Malaysia
Shahdan Sudin	Universiti Teknologi Malaysia, Malaysia
Mohamad Amir Shamsudin	Universiti Teknologi Malaysia, Malaysia
Sophan Wahyudi Nawawi	Universiti Teknologi Malaysia, Malaysia
Mohd Ariffanan Mohd Basri	Universiti Teknologi Malaysia, Malaysia
Mohd Hafis Izran Ishak	Universiti Teknologi Malaysia, Malaysia
Mohd Amri Md Yunus	Universiti Teknologi Malaysia, Malaysia
Norazhar Abu Bakar	Universiti Teknikal Malaysia Melaka, Malaysia
Saifulza Alwi@Suhaimi	Universiti Teknikal Malaysia Melaka, Malaysia
Mohd Shahrieel Mohd Aras	Universiti Teknikal Malaysia Melaka, Malaysia
Ahmad Zaki Shukor	Universiti Teknikal Malaysia Melaka, Malaysia
Muhamad Khairi Aripin	Universiti Teknikal Malaysia Melaka, Malaysia

Publicity Committee

Herman Wahid	Universiti Teknologi Malaysia, Malaysia
Leow Pei Ling	Universiti Teknologi Malaysia, Malaysia
Salinda Buyamin	Universiti Teknologi Malaysia, Malaysia
Rosbi Mamat	Universiti Teknologi Malaysia, Malaysia
Muhammad Nizam Kamarudin	Universiti Teknikal Malaysia Melaka, Malaysia
Chong Shin Horng	Universiti Teknikal Malaysia Melaka, Malaysia
Afnizanfaizal Abdullah	Universiti Teknologi Malaysia, Malaysia
Mohd Adham Isa	Universiti Teknologi Malaysia, Malaysia

International Program Committee

Abdullah Alshehri	King Abdul Aziz University, Saudi Arabia
Abdul Ghapor	National University of Sciences and Technology, Pakistan
Abul K.M. Azad	Northern Illinois University, USA
Axel Lehmann	Universität der Bundeswehr München, Germany
Bidyadhar Subudhi	National Institute of Technology Rourkela, India
Bo Hu Li	Beihang University, China
Emiliano Pereira Gonzalez	University of Alcala, Spain
Fredrik Ekstrand	Malardalen University, Sweden
Gary Tan	National University, Singapore
Guoping Liu	University of South Wales, UK
Hemanshu R. Pota	University of New South Wales, Australia
Herman Parung	Hasanuddin University, Indonesia
Jie Huang	Beijing Institute of Technology, China
João Reis	University of Lisbon, Portugal
Jorge M. Martins	University of Lisbon, Portugal
Kang Sun Lee	Myongji University, South Korea
Kashif Ishaque	Mohammad Ali Jinnah University, Pakistan
Kyoko Hasegawa	Ritsumei University, Japan
Lin Zhang	Beihang University, China
Md Sohel Rana	Rajshahi University of Engineering and Technology, Bangladesh
Mehmet Önder Efe	Hacettepe University, Turkey
Mohammad Hasan Shaheed	Queen Mary University of London, UK
Moh Khairudin	Yogyakarta State University, Indonesia
Md Nazri Othman	Universiti Teknikal Malaysia Melaka, Malaysia
Mohd Rizal Arshad	Universiti Sains Malaysia, Malaysia
Mustapha Muhammad	Bayero University, Nigeria
Ngo Van Thuyen	Ho Chi Minh City University of Technology and Education, Vietnam
Nordin Saad	Universiti Teknologi Petronas, Malaysia
Osamu Ono	Meiji University, Japan
Quang Ha	University of Technology Sydney, Australia
Raymund Sison	De La Salle University, Philippines
Rini Akmeliawati	Islamic International University Malaysia, Malaysia
Sarvat M. Ahmad	Ghulam Ishaq Khan Institute, Pakistan
Sasikumar Punnekkat	Malardalen University, Sweden
Satoshi Tanaka	Ritsumei University, Japan
Stephen John Turner	King Mongkut's University of Technology Thonburi, Thailand
Sumeet S. Aphale	The University of Aberdeen, UK
Teo Yong Meng	National University of Singapore, Singapore
Thasaneeya R. Nopparatjamjomras	Mahidol University, Thailand

Victor Sreeram   University of Western Australia, Australia
Walid Aniss   Aswan University, Egypt
Yun Bae Kim   Sungkyunkwan University, South Korea

Regional Program Committee

Ahmad Jais Alimin   Universiti Tun Hussein Onn Malaysia, Malaysia
Azlina Aziz   Multimedia University, Malaysia
Edwin Tan   Monash University, Malaysia
Hairul Azhar Abdul Rashid   Multimedia University, Malaysia
Haziah Abdul Hamid   Universiti Malaysia Perlis, Malaysia
Hazimi Hamzah   Universiti Teknologi Mara Penang, Malaysia
Hazlina Mohd Yusof   International Islamic University, Malaysia
Hezri Fazalul Rahiman   Universiti Teknologi Mara, Malaysia
Iqbal Saripan   Universiti Putra Malaysia, Malaysia
Ismail Saad   Universiti Malaysia Sabah, Malaysia
Kamarul Hawari Ghazali   Universiti Malaysia Pahang, Malaysia
Khisbullah Hudha   Universiti Pertahanan Nasional Malaysia, Malaysia
Muhamad Fahezal Ismail   Universiti Kuala Lumpur, Malaysia
Muralindran Mariappan   Universiti Malaysia Sabah, Malaysia
Nooritawati Md. Tahir   Universiti Teknologi Mara, Malaysia
Norfaradila Wahid   Universiti Tun Hussein Onn Malaysia, Malaysia
Norimah Yusof   University of Malaya, Malaysia
Raja Ahmad Kamil Raja   Universiti Putra Malaysia, Malaysia
  Ahmad
Rosli Omar   Universiti Tun Hussein Onn Malaysia, Malaysia
Rosmiwati Mohd Mokhtar   Universiti Sains Malaysia, Malaysia
Rozaimi Ghazali   Universiti Teknikal Malaysia Melaka, Malaysia
Saiful Azrin Zulkifli   Universiti Teknologi Petronas, Malaysia
Sazli Saad   Universiti Malaysia Perlis, Malaysia
Shahnourbanun Sahran   Universiti Kebangsaan Malaysia, Malaysia
Shahrum Shah   Malaysian-Japan International Institute of Technology,
                                  Malaysia
Siti Norul Huda Sheikh   Universiti Kebangsaan Malaysia, Malaysia
  Abdullah
Yvette Shanli   Asia Pacific University, Malaysia
Zuwairie Ibrahim   Universiti Malaysia Pahang, Malaysia

Organizers

Organized by

In Cooperation with

 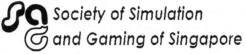

Contents – Part II

Modeling and Simulation Technology

Contents – Part I

Modeling and Simulation of Systems

Advanced Modeling and Simulation

Improvement of GPS Accuracy in Positioning by Using DGPS Technique

Hidhir Lutfi Isa, Sarah Aimi Saad, Amirah 'Aisha Badrul Hisham,
and Mohammad Hafis Izran Ishak[✉]

Department of Control and Mechatronics (CMED), Faculty of Electrical
Engineering, Universiti Teknologi Malaysia, 81310 Skudai, Johor, Malaysia
{hlutfi2, saimi2, aaisha2}@live.utm.my, hafis@fke.utm.my

Abstract. In today's world, Global Positioning System (GPS) for tracking
system plays an important role in tracking required locations. To obtain accurate
location in developing the proposed system, several issues. Although
Differential-GPS (DGPS) system is expensive, GPS module may have some
errors and does not provide the accurate position information of the location.
Therefore, the required location needs to have an accurate correction and
improvement which can be achieved using DGPS technique. In this research, the
proposed technique improves the position of the required location utilizing
U-blox Neo 6 M receiver GPS module. With the proposed method, the position
of the location is improved within 1–3 m.

Keywords: GPS · DGPS · Correction projection

1 Introduction

Differential Global Positioning System (DGPS) is an enhancement of Global Positioning System (GPS) [4]. The DGPS technique will be used as a reference station coordinate to correct the location of the user to be more accurate by giving the differential error of the position. There are two types of methods in DGPS technique which are 'Block Shift technique' and Range Correction technique. In Block Shift technique, it is made by comparing with the reference station position and instantly computing the corrected position. On the other hand, the 'Range Correction technique' will generate correction to all pseudorange by comparing the true to the observed range. It was based on the reference station coordinates. The block shift technique is the easiest technique to implement, but it is only available if both GPS receiver at remote and base station use the same satellite constellation to get the position. Other than that, the Range Correction technique can use any combination of corrected ranges, it can be used without reference station. So that, it is most effective in real-time to implement DGPS systems.

Currently, there are many type of GPS receivers and chip-sets are being developed and has been released. If the expensive GPS receiver which can provide raw observation in real-time or read the correction messages such as the Radio Technical Commission for Maritime Services (RTCM), Radio Technical Commission for Aeronautics (RTCA) or Satellite-Based Augmentation System (SBAS) [4], the user can

© Springer Nature Singapore Pte Ltd. 2017
M.S. Mohamed Ali et al. (Eds.): AsiaSim 2017, Part II, CCIS 752, pp. 3–11, 2017.
DOI: 10.1007/978-981-10-6502-6_1

developed a customized DGPS whose accuracy 1–3 m. Many manufacturers are still producing end devices which can operate only in a stand-alone positioning mode in which, do not apply any correction data or using DGPS technique. Moreover, there are many chip-sets that are been installed in vehicle navigation kits or mobile phones do not provide as accurate position as DGPS results. Even the market share of the DGPS-disabled GPS modules is still be a dominant. There is no adequate way to achieve the (approximately 1 m) accuracy of DGPS system. This is because of conventional DGPS corrections are based on the 'range correction' technique.

By using the block shift solution, the project was developed by constructing an equation to project the correction error to the rover position. Based on the technique proposes, this paper suggests a method to improve the positioning of the location, which can correct the GPS receiver of rover by giving it the corrected position.

2   System Architectural Design of DGPS Positioning System

The proposed architectural design consists two of GPS devices which interfaced to the ESPresso Lite V2.0 controller. The GPS module was set up at both Reference Station (RF) and Rover. The error of position at RF are sent to the Rover to improve the positioning of Rover location.

The design and function of each block is explained in Fig. 1:

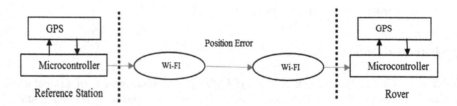

Fig. 1.   Block diagram of proposed DGPS technique for improved the position.

2.1   Global Positioning System

The Global Positioning System is an application in the field of positioning, it can give a fast, easy and accurate positioning [5]. The information was supported from the satellite. Firstly, the information was received by the signal that transmitted to the satellites and the time take for transmission is calculated. It will depends on the time it takes for latitude and longitude information that are fed into the receiver.

Each GPS satellite will transmits data that indicates its location and current time. It comprises of 24 satellites arranged in 6 orbital planes with 4 satellites per plane, terrestrial monitoring networks and GPS receivers operated by users [1, 4, 6, 10]. 2-D position of the user consists of latitude and longitude while 3-D position of the user consists of the latitude, longitude and altitude. To calculate a 2-D position, the user must be at a location where his or her receiver can lock on to at least three satellites' signals whereas to obtain the 3-D location of the user, the user's receiver must be at a location where it will be able to receive signal from at least 4 satellites [2, 7–9].

Fortunately, due to the way the satellites are positioned, it is always possible to obtain signals from at least four satellites at any given time. Other than that, GPS is also able to provide service to an unlimited number of users since the user received the signal passively [3].

2.2 Differential Global Positioning System

DGPS is an enhancement to GPS that will improve the location accuracy from 15 m for GPS accuracy to centimeter level in case of the best implementation [4, 7]. The accuracy can be improved further up to 1 m. The DGPS technique basically consists of two parts: Transmitter and Receiver. The transmitter will provide location with the supported from satellite. The satellite information are then sent to the receiver.

Firstly, the signals received at RF and the process of data collection is continued for four hours, then the average value is calculated to determine the known location. After that, location observed at the RF will be compared to the known location. Difference value between the two locations at current time are calculated, the value is also known as position error. The value of position error obtained is then be added to Rover location to improve its positioning.

On the earth, position of users may be up to 200 nautical miles (370 km) from the RF [4]. However, the errors will be affected by space like ionospheric and tropospheric errors [7]. At this case, the accuracy of position will decrease with distance of the RF. Other problem that may be encountered is RF's and rover's satellite count is different and therefor causing inconsistency in data collected.

3   Methodology

This section is divided into two parts. First, the algorithm used to apply DGPS technique and second part is the choice of hardware and software for the experiment.

3.1 Algorithm for DGPS Technique

Positioning by using domain DGPS is purely straightforward and simple to comprehend. Since the calculation of position different is easy to calculate between the known and observe position of Reference Station of GPS receiver. Thus, the difference will added to the Rover's measurement, which enhance its position.

In the position domain of DGPS, the computed coordinate, ARS will be subtract from known coordinate of the Reference station. With this position difference, it mean the correction of the position error of the GPS. It is marked as BX.

$$B_X = A_{RS,known} - A_{RS}. \tag{1}$$

The Reference Station this will correct the Rover position by using the Wi-Fi with internet provider. After that, the Rover Station (bus GPS) will be apply this correction to its measured coordinate. So that, it will be improve the position accuracy.

$$A_{Rover,DGPS} = A_{Rover,measured} + B_X. \tag{2}$$

With this simple mathematical model solution of DGPS system. It will involve both stations. Both stations need to coordinate the satellite selection with each other. This method does not require the raw details of GPS signal observation, which is an advantage for low-end receiver.

3.2   Choice of Hardware and Software

The device used in this experiment is U-blox Neo 6M as GPS sensor, ESPresso Lite V2.0 as the main board and the programming is done in Arduino IDE. The data obtained from the experiment is analyzed and mapped on OpenStreetMap for better visualization by using ArcGIS, a cloud based mapping software. The overview of the software is as shown in Fig. 2.

Fig. 2. Overview of ArcGIS software.

4   Results

The experiment is conducted to improve GPS positioning by using DGPS method. The device used in this experiment is as shown in Fig. 3. It is conducted in two parts. The first part is the setup of the reference station. The reference station is set up and data are collected continuously for four hours at the same location. Based on the data collected, the reference point coordinate is determine by calculating the average value. Data obtained is as shown in Fig. 4.

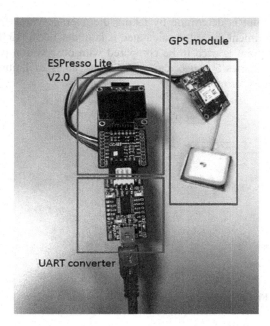

Fig. 3. Device used in the experiment.

1	Latitude	Longitude
2	1.558931589	103.641983
3	1.558931589	103.641983
4	1.558931589	103.641983
5	1.558931589	103.641983
6	1.558931589	103.641983
7	1.558931589	103.641983
8	1.558911705	103.6419601
9	1.558911705	103.6419601
10	1.558911705	103.6419601
11	1.558911705	103.6419601
12	1.558911705	103.6419601
13	1.558911705	103.6419601
14	1.558895016	103.6419449
15	1.558895016	103.6419449
16	1.558895016	103.6419449
17	1.558891678	103.6419449
18	1.558891678	103.6419449
19	1.558891678	103.6419449
20	1.558878422	103.6419449
21	1.558878422	103.6419449
22	1.558878422	103.6419449
23	1.558876753	103.6419449
24	1.558876753	103.6419449
25	1.558861732	103.6420212

Fig. 4. Coordinate values recorded at the same location.

The reference point is determine by taking the average value from the data collected. For this experiment the value calculated is latitude: 1.558813309 and longitude: 103.6419955. This point is used to be compared with observation point to determine the error position. Figures 5 and 6 shows different values of latitude and longitude obtained during the experiment.

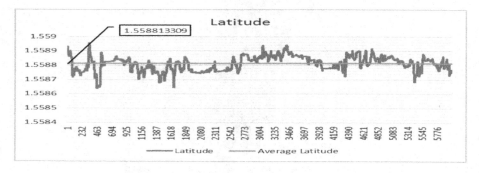

Fig. 5. Different values of latitude position obtained.

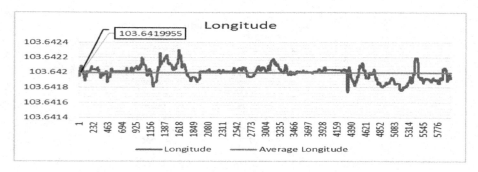

Fig. 6. Different longitude values obtained.

The second part of the experiment is positioning test using DGPS technique. The test was done in UTM Skudai campus area twice at the same route. The result is as shown in Figs. 7, 8 and 9.

Figure 7 shows that the point is nearer to the road, which indicates that the positioning has improved compared to the technique is applied. The scale of the map is 1 cm to 5 m.

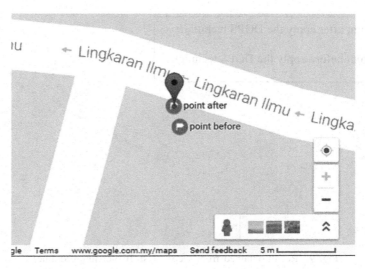

Fig. 7. The point on the route before and after DGPS technique is applied.

Figures 8 and 9 shows the experimental results for the technique approach in real time. The black dots show the coordinate before the correction point was added, while the red dot is the coordinate after the correction point was added. The dotted point is the coordinate signaled from the satellite for every 1 s. This experiments shows that this technique can be used to improve data in real time situation.

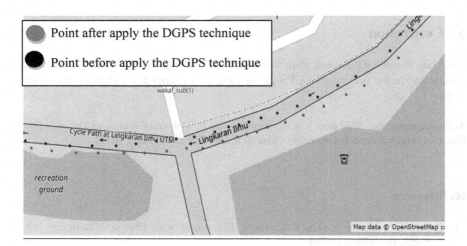

Fig. 8. Result obtained from the first test. (Color figure online)

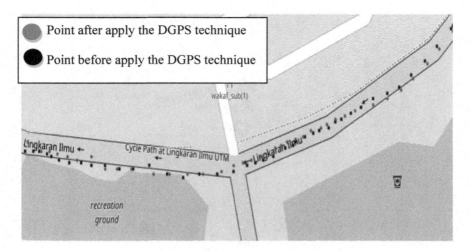

Fig. 9. Result obtained from second test. (Color figure online)

5 Discussion

The experiment is conducted separately and the simulation was not done in real time. The values for reference point was calculated manually. The processing was implemented on Microsoft Excel 2013 on Lenovo laptop with Intel i-5 core of 2.5 GHz processor. The software use to display the information is ArcGIS and mapped to OpenStreetMap. For future improvement, data processing can be done in real time.

6 Conclusion

Based on the result obtained from the experiment, it can be seen that DGPS technique does improve the accuracy of GPS positioning up to meter level. The error is reduced within 1–3 m.

Acknowledgments. This work was supported in part by Universiti Teknologi Malaysia (UTM), Malaysia, under Research University Grant Scheme GUP (Vote No. 13H86).

References

1. Crato, N.: Figuring It Out: Entertaining Encounters with Everyday Math, pp. 49–52. Springer, Heidelberg (2010)
2. Garmin: What is GPS? Garmin Ltd. http://www8.garmin.com/aboutGPS/
3. Kaplan, E.D., Hegarty, C.J.: Understanding GPS: Principles and Applications, 2nd edn, pp. 1–4. Artech House, London (2006)

4. Acosta, N., Toloza, J.: Techniques to improve the GPS precision. Int. J. Adv. Comput. Sci. Appl. **3**(8), 125–130 (2012)
5. Naveenkumar, M., Ranjith, R.: Border alert and smart tracking system with alarm using DGPS and GSM. Int. J. Emerg. Technol. Comput. Sci. Electron. **8**(1), 45–51 (2014)
6. Moaiied, M.M., Mosavi, M.R.C.A.: Increasing accuracy of combined GPS and GLONASS positioning using fuzzy Kalman filter. Iran. J. Electr. Electron. Eng. **12**(1), 21–28 (2016)
7. Seedat, M., Thusi, S., Gogobala, A., Zaca, M.: Types of GPS Technology, pp. 1–6 (2011)
8. Svaton, M.: Low-cost implementation of Differential GPS using Arduino Low-cost implementation of Differential GPS using Arduino Examensarbete utfört i Transportsystem Martin Svaton (2016)
9. Jin, L.E.: Bus Tracking and Ticket Payment System for UTAR, May 2015
10. Lin, J.Y., Yang, B.K., Do, T.A., Chen, H.C.: The accuracy enhancement of GPS track in google Map. In: Proceedings of 2013 8th International Conference on Broadband and Wireless Computing, Communication and Applications BWCCA 2013, pp. 524–527 (2013)

Structural Analysis of *Keropok Keping* Drying Machine

Mohamad Syazwan Zafwan Mohamad Suffian[1]([⊠]),
Muhammad Naim Leman[2], Shahrol Mohamaddan[1],
and Abang Mohamad Aizuddin Abang Mohamad Mohtar[1]

[1] Universiti Malaysia Sarawak (UNIMAS),
94300 Kota Samarahan, Sarawak, Malaysia
msmsyazwan@unimas.my
[2] Institut Latihan Perindustrian (ILP),
94300 Kota Samarahan, Sarawak, Malaysia

Abstract. In *keropok keping* industries, most of the production processes are implemented by semi-automated machines. However, the drying process is still conducted using a traditional method where the *keropok* is arranged under the sunlight. To improve the drying process, a new rotary type of *keropok keping* drying machine was invented. The new machine will undergo structural analysis via static analysis. The static analysis is only focusing on the vital parts of the new design machine.

Keywords: Static analysis · *Keropok keping* drying machine · Semi-automated machine · Rotating machine

1 Introduction

Keropok keping is a dried crispy food product relatively popular in South-east Asian countries [1]. Currently, its manufacturing is the mostly practised in small scale industry [4]. In Malaysia, the *keropok keping* industries are widely operated in the coastal areas in the state of Terengganu, Kelantan, Johor, Kedah and some parts of Pahang due to the high seafood supply, high temperature and windy area that contributed to the sustainability of the industries [2]. Ingredients for making the *keropok keping* are fillet fish, squid, prawn and shrimp as protein ingredients and seasonings such as pepper, garlic, salt, sugar and monosodium glutamate (MSG) as flavour to the *keropok*. The protein ingredients normally give its distinction to the name of the *keropok keping*. Flour is a principle ingredient for making *keropok keping* and technically the protein components can be altogether skipped and a less tasty puffed *keropok keping* is created.

In *keropok keping* making process, the flour is mixed with grinded fillet fish, squid or prawn and all the ingredients by using a mixer to obtain a dough. Typically, the diameter of dough formed is around 5 to 10 cm. The dough then is shaped into round, oblique, stick or longitudinal forms and gelatinized by boiling or steaming [5]. The gelatinized dough is then cooled, drained and cut into the thin slices with thickness around 3 mm and finally, the slices are dried under the sunlight until the moisture

© Springer Nature Singapore Pte Ltd. 2017
M.S. Mohamed Ali et al. (Eds.): AsiaSim 2017, Part II, CCIS 752, pp. 12–25, 2017.
DOI: 10.1007/978-981-10-6502-6_2

content reaches around 10%. The dried *keropok keping* obtained is considered as the half-finished product or intermediate product. The *keropok* is typically fried in hot oil to obtain the edible puffed cracker before eaten as a snack food or together with rice and other daily dishes [3].

In *keropok keping* industries, most of the production process activities are conducted by the semi-automated or automated machines such as grinding, mixing and slicing machine [2]. However, the drying process is still implemented using a traditional method as in Fig. 1. In this method, the slices of *keropok* are spread and arranged on the ground or a drying board called *pemidai* under the sunlight so that the *keropok* is exposed to the surrounding heating temperature and wind to be dried. At the moment, this method is considered the most convenient, suitable and practical due to the operating cost is considered much cheaper than the other method. However, this method is exposed to low level of hygiene and bad weather which can limit the potential of the *keropok keping* to be manufactured in high volume [2]. By using the *pemidai*, the keropok may be contaminated by surrounding dust and dirt from air pollution. Besides, it is also exposed to the animals and insects such as birds, mice, and flies [2]. From this situation, the quality level of the *keropok* product will decrease, caused by the products are dirty, cracked, failure and unattractive shape. Besides, contaminated the *keropok* can cause illness to the consumers and the product demand may be decrease affected by these problems. In order to meet the market demands which is tremendously increased, entrepreneurs need to increase the total amount of output. In furtherance of that, an enormous change needs to be done such as, extending the operating hours of production, and at the same time, the number of manpower also needs to be increased. Besides, entrepreneurs also need to find more space for drying process neither using their own property nor lending from others.

Fig. 1. Drying the keropok keping by using the traditional method

By recruiting more manpower and lending more space for the drying process, it will be incurring a more overhead cost to the entrepreneur. As a result, entrepreneurs need to increase the price of their products as they have to contra with the increasing of their overhead. Thus, entrepreneurs will be facing big business issues whereby the demand of the products in a market will definitely be decreased. Therefore, finding the drying process alternative is needed in order to solve the entire problems. The suitable method is to develop the drying machine for the *keropok keping* in order to improve the drying process in the *keropok keping* industries.

2   Design and Fabrication of *Keropok Keping* Drying Machine

A *keropok keping* drying machine was designed and fabricated. It consists of six main parts namely drying chamber, moving tray, transmission system, heating element, cooling fan, and control system. The no–load testing with two level of air velocity with 1.5 m/s and 2.0 m/s were experimented to the machine. The evaluation was conducted to determine the maximum temperature, the lowest of air humidity and the pattern of air velocity above the tray inside the drying chamber. Based on the results, the maximum temperature can be reached in the chamber is 39.8 °C and the trend shows, the highest air velocity blown inside the chamber, the lower temperature of the drying air. The lowest humidity is recorded in the chamber is around 47.6% and the pattern of the humidity shows, when the air velocity increases the humidity inside the chamber is slowly decreased. The pattern of air velocity above the tray is highest when the tray rotates nearly to the fan inlet with angle of rotation 135°. The air velocity recorded at this position is 0.29 m/s and 0.36 m/s with air inlet velocity 1.5 m/s and 2.0 m/s respectively. The machine is expected to improve the hygiene of drying process in the *keropok keping* industries.

2.1   Idea Generation and Conceptual Design

The critical solution designs for the machine can be determined into five elements are drying chamber, type of tray design, transmission system, air source, and heat source design. The solution for each problem is identified into sub problem as in Table 1. The number of possible combination ideas concepts can be calculated as $2 \times 2 \times 1 \times 1$ $1 = 4$ (based on the number of table row and column) that means four ideas concepts can be generated through this table.

Table 1. Morphological chart for *keropok keping* drying machine

Subproblems solution concept				
Drying chamber	Tray	Transmission system	Air source	Heat source
Drum type	Stationary tray	Roller chain type with sprocket	Fan	Heating element
Cabinet type	Moving tray			

The best idea concept for the *keropok keping* drying machine is selected by using Pugh selection matrix. The computer aided design software is utilized to develop 3D model for the selected idea. The machine design architecture is also developed in this stage. The machine is made up of six main parts namely drying chamber, moving tray, transmission system, heating element, cooling fan and control system. The CAD model and design architecture for the machine can be illustrated as in Figs. 2 and 3.

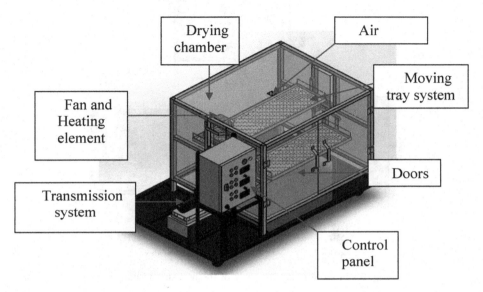

Fig. 2. 3D modelling of *keropok keping* drying machine

2.2 Structure Frame and Wall Design

The size of the structure frame is 95.08 cm length, 80.08 cm width, and 77 cm height. The main material used in the frame design is 2.54 cm × 2.54 cm hollow aluminum square steel because this type of material is a light weight and anti-corrosion. The machine structure plays an important role in supporting and withstanding all static and dynamic load condition in the machine and to investigate the Von-Mises stress and deformation on the frame. The machine is also covered with five side walls are top, left, right, back and a bottom wall. A pair of the door is also provided to ease the users to load and unload the trays in the drying chamber. The transparent polycarbonate sheet is selected as the main material for the dryer walls and door. The advantages of this material are it is not brittle, resists in high temperature, lightweight, low thermal conductivity and can trap the heat in a certain time. The structure and wall design for the machine can be illustrated in Fig. 4.

2.3 Structure Frame Analysis

The material properties and technical condition applied in the machine frame structure can be shown in Table 2. Tetrahedron mesh with refinement and structured hex-dominant mesh are applied to the geometry of the frame and shaft respectively and generated by FEA software. The mesh generated can be illustrated as in Figs. 5 and 6.

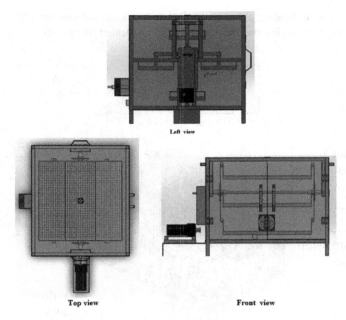

Fig. 3. Front, top and left view of the new drying machine

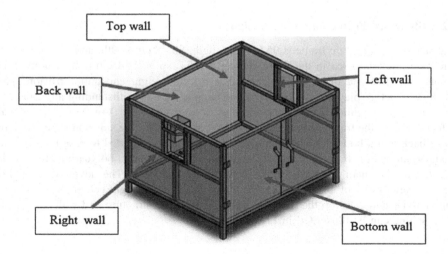

Fig. 4. Structure frame and wall design

Table 2. Material properties and technical condition of the structure frame

Material properties	Technical condition
Material	Aluminium alloy
Mass density	2770 kg/m^3
Elastic modulus	7.1e + 10 Pa
Poisson's ratio	0.33
Yield limit	2.8e + 08 Pa

Fig. 5. Mesh generation with refinement for the structure frame

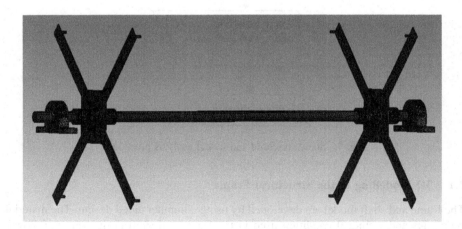

Fig. 6. Mesh generation of shaft

3 Static Analysis

The structural frame and shaft in the moving tray design can be considered as the critical parts in the machine. The frame and shaft play an important role to win stands all loads of bucket and tray during static condition. Therefore, the static analysis is carried out in order to understand the stress, deformation and dynamic characteristic of each part. In this study, the finite element analysis (FEA) software is utilized by using static structural and modal analysis. The static structure and modal analysis procedure can be shown in the flow chart as in Fig. 7.

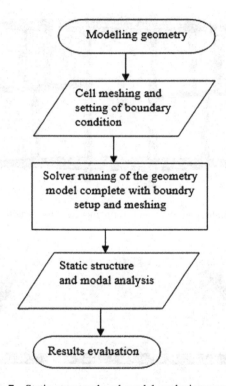

Fig. 7. Static structural and modal analysis procedure

3.1   3D Modelling of the Structural Frame

The frame and shaft model are developed by using computer aided design. The material properties and technical condition used in the frame and shaft design are as follows: Material: Aluminium alloy, Mass density: 2770 kg/m^3, Elastic modulus: 7.1e + 10 Pa, Poisson's ratio: 0.33 and Yield limit: 2.8e + 08 Pa.

3.2   Boundary Condition

The boundary condition set up for both structure frame and shaft can be shown in Figs. 8 and 9.

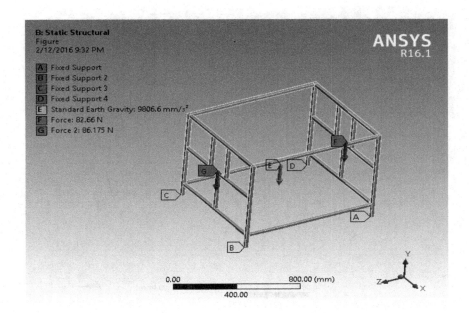

Fig. 8. Boundary condition for structure frame

Structure frame boundary condition

- Points A, B, C, and D are assumed fixed support.
- Standard earth gravity at point E is 9.81 m/s^2 in y-direction.
- Force at point G and F.

Force at Point G = Reaction force of the moving tray at point G + ½ weight of shaft + bearing self-weight

$$= 78.18\,N + 1.52\,N + 6.475\,N = 86.175\,N$$

Force at Point E = Reaction of the moving tray at point E + ½ weight of shaft + bearing self-weight

$$= 74.66\,N + 1.52\,N + 6.475\,N = 82.655\,N$$

Shaft boundary condition

- The bearing at point A and B are assumed as fixed support
- Standard earth gravity at point C is 9.81 m/s^2 in y-direction

- The force at point D, E, F, G, H, I, J and K is assumed as the half weight of bucket and tray is 17.85 N.

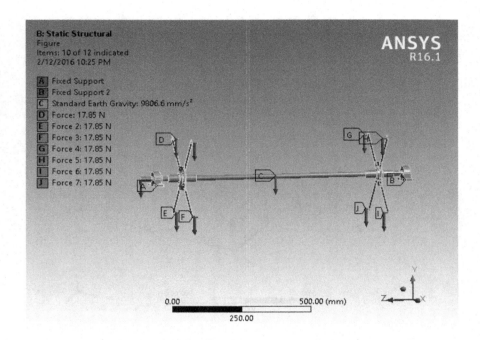

Fig. 9. Boundary condition for shaft

3.3 Static Analysis

Based on the structural frame analysis, the maximum convergence of Von-Mises stress occurs in the frame structure is 4.8177 MPa and the total deformation is 0.072055 mm in the y-direction with the number of elements is 645127. The results can be shown in Fig. 10.

In the frame structure design, the highest Von-Mises stress can be observed at the left and right of the structure frame. This is because both location need to support the distribution load of the moving tray system via pillow block bearing during the static condition. The total load of the moving tray system will be transferred from the bearing to the structure. In term of the structure deformation, the highest deformation can be observed at the same location with the deformation value is 0.072 mm in the y direction. The deformation result can be shown as in Fig. 11.

All the results are obtained after conducting the validation by convergence study to the structure. The study is done by tested the structure with difference size of element. The convergence graph for both results can be shown as in Figs. 12 and 13.

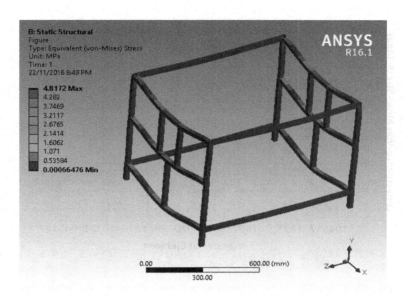

Fig. 10. Structure frame Von-Mises stress

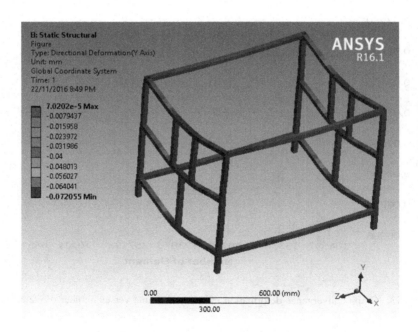

Fig. 11. Deformation of the structure frame

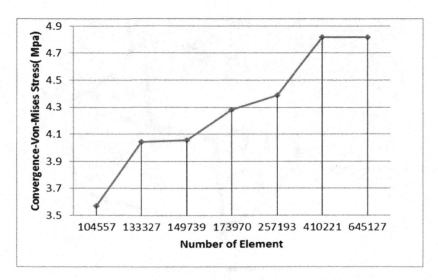

Fig. 12. Graph Von-Mises of the structure frame versus number of elements

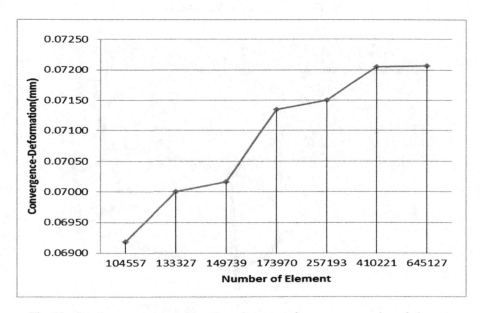

Fig. 13. Graph convergence deformation of structure frame verses number of elements

It can be concluded that the Von-Mises stress of the structure can be considered below the allowable stress of the material, which is approximately 200 MPa. The deformation of the structure from the simulation result is below 1 mm.

For the shaft, the maximum convergence Von-Mises stress is 11.892 MPa and the total deformation is 0.10765 mm in the y-direction with the number of elements is 211489. The results can be illustrated in Figs. 14, 15, 16 and 17.

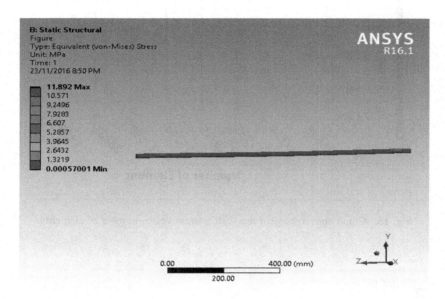

Fig. 14. Von-Mises stress of the shaft

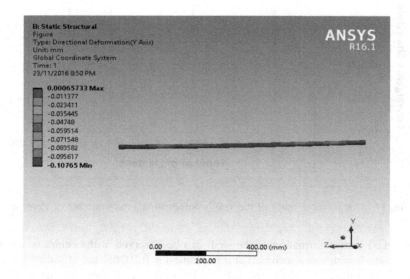

Fig. 15. Deformation of shaft (Color figure online)

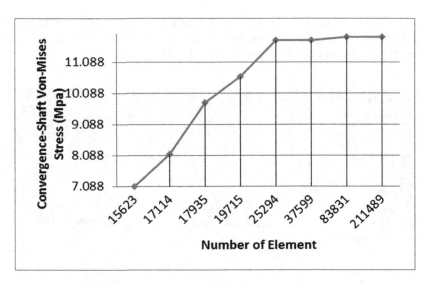

Fig. 16. Graph convergence of the shaft's stress versus number of elements

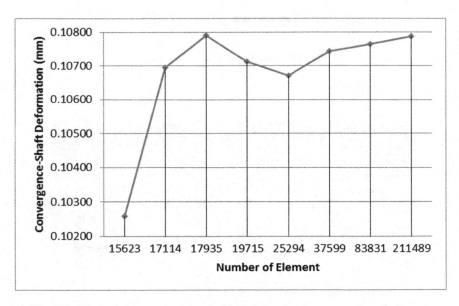

Fig. 17. Graph convergence of the shaft's deformation versus number of elements

The maximum deformation of the shaft can be observed at the center of the shaft (blue coloured) with value recorded at this position is 0.10765 mm at y-direction. The deformation result can be illustrated in Fig. 15 with the number of elements is 211489.

The convergence study is conducted to validate both results. The analysis result can be shown as in Figs. 16 and 17. The shaft is also tested with different size and number of element. The number of converge element is 211489.

The Von-Mises stress of the shaft is lower than the allowable stress of the material which is approximately 200 MPa. This shows that the strength of shaft meets the design requirement. The maximum deformation of the shaft is below than 1 mm. This shows that the stiffness of the shaft meets the design requirement. The shaft can be considered safe from the static load.

4 Conclusion

Based on both analysis, it can be concluded that the Von-Mises stress of the whole structure can be considered below the allowable stress of the material, which is approximately 200 MPa. The structure can be considered safe for assembly and operation as the deformation of the structure from the simulation result is below than 1 mm.

References

1. Kyaw, Z.Y., Yu, S.Y., Cheow, C.S., Dzulkifly, M.H., Howell, N.K.: Effect of fish to starch ratio on viscoelastic properties and microstructure of fish cracker ('keropok') dough. Int. J. Food Sci. Technol. **36**(7), 741–747 (2001)
2. Mohamaddan, S., Aizuddin, A.M., Mohtadzar, N.A.A., Mohamad Suffian, M.S.Z., Junaidi, N.: Development of Keropok Keping drying machine for small & medium enterprises (SMEs). In: IOP Conference Series: Materials Science and Engineering, vol. 114, no. 1, p. 12037 (2016)
3. Huda, N., Li Leng, A., Xian Yee, C.: Chemical composition, colour and linear expansion properties of Malaysian commercial fish cracker (keropok). Asian J. Food Agro-Ind. **3**(305), 473–482 (2010)
4. Taewee, T.K.: Cracker 'Keropok': a review on factors influencing expansion. Int. Food Res. J. **18**(3), 855–866 (2011)
5. Fellows, P.: Food Processing Technology: Principles and Practice. Elsevier, Amsterdam (2009)

Comparative Study Between Hourly and Daily Generation Maintenance Scheduling

Siti Maherah Hussin[✉], Mohammad Yusri Hassan,
Md. Pauzi Abdullah, Norzanah Rosmin,
and Muhamad Amzar Ahmad

Faculty of Electrical Engineering, Centre of Electrical Energy Systems,
Universiti Teknologi Malaysia, 81310 Skudai, Johor, Malaysia
maherah@fke.utm.my

Abstract. This paper compares daily and hourly based generation maintenance scheduling, that both solved using mixed integer linear programming (MILP). Scheduling the maintenance based on hourly gives more advantages as compared to the daily in terms of security and operating cost. In the daily basis, the loading and unloading characteristic of a generator may not be satisfied as it neglects the ramp rates constraints on the consecutive days, while in the hourly basis, these constrains have been considered. Numerical case studies were evaluated on the 6-bus system, IEEE 118-bus system, and practical system. A comparative study is carried out between hourly and daily basis. The result shows that the operating cost obtained was lower when scheduling the maintenance based on hourly as compared to the daily. It can be summarized that a global optimal solution could be achieved using hourly instead of only local optimal achieved in the daily basis.

Keywords: Mixed Integer Linear Programming (MILP) · Lagrangian Relaxation (LR) · Generation maintenance scheduling · Hourly operating cost

1 Introduction

There is an extensive literature discussing maintenance scheduling problem. The problem can be focused either for generation [1–5], transmission [6–8] or both systems [9–11]. The generation maintenance scheduling problem is more attractive as most of the overall operating cost comes from the production cost. Hence, by having proper generator maintenance scheduling, the production cost could be reduced effectively. For maintenance scheduling solutions, various optimization techniques are available, which can be classified as heuristic [12, 13], meta-heuristic [14–16], and mathematical programming techniques [17–20]. These techniques can be differentiated based on their searching mechanism and characteristics. Based upon the comparison made, the mathematical programming technique is the best option for solving maintenance scheduling problems compared to the heuristic and meta-heuristic techniques since it could provide an optimal solution and able to solve large-scale practical system. Dynamic programming (DP), integer programming (IP), lagrangian relaxation (LR) and mixed integer linear programming (MILP) are the examples of mathematical programming techniques.

© Springer Nature Singapore Pte Ltd. 2017
M.S. Mohamed Ali et al. (Eds.): AsiaSim 2017, Part II, CCIS 752, pp. 26–38, 2017.
DOI: 10.1007/978-981-10-6502-6_3

In [20–22], maintenance scheduling problem has been solved using LR technique. In their approach, they tackle the problem based on a daily basis with hourly time resolution. However, it is found that the schedules suggested by this approach do not satisfy ramp rates constraints of generators especially on the consecutive days. The result proposed in [21] shows that some of the generators have been switched off instantly which is not allowable in real practical system. The unloading of a unit must be done gradually within its rates and should generate at its minimum power before being totally off as indicated by the ramp rates constraints.

Based on the above shortcoming, comparative study is performed between hourly and daily basis generation maintenance scheduling using mixed integer linear programming (MILP). In hourly approach, maintenance problem is solved by considering an entire periods of planning interval. Thus, maintenance can be scheduled at any interval throughout the planning horizon and the interval that yields the lowest operating cost is selected to be an optimal solution. The maintenance start can be at any hour which does not restricted to the first hour of a day In contrast, in the daily approach, they evaluate the operating cost strictly interval by interval (one day interval) with hourly resolution (24 h) in which they neglected the ramp rate constraint of the consecutive days. The day that gave the lowest operating cost is considered an optimal period for scheduling the maintenance. The hourly-based maintenance scheduling approach could find the global optimal instead of the local optimal obtained in the daily approach.

The remaining of the paper is organized as follows. Section 2 describes the detailed strategy of the hourly-based maintenance scheduling. Section 3 provides detailed formulation of the problem. While, Sect. 4 discusses numerical case studies using 6-bus system, IEEE 118-bus system and utility system. Then, the conclusions are drawn in Sect. 5.

2 Hourly-Based Maintenance Scheduling

In this approach, maintenance is scheduled with respect to the total operating cost of the system while considering network security. Taking equipment out of service may affect unit generation as it will trigger the more expensive and/or inefficient unit to supply the demand and concurrently would increase the operation risk of the entire system. However, by having a good maintenance schedule, the operating cost can be minimized significantly. To schedule the maintenance during the period of the lowest possible operating cost, analysis of the cost is required in each time interval.

Figure 1 illustrates the process of finding minimal operating cost within the maintenance window. Here, the cost is analysed based on the hourly resolution. ES and LS in the flowchart represent the earliest and latest possible hour for maintenance to be started, respectively. The LS hour is determined based on the specified maintenance duration.

In a case of the maintenance window is of one week duration, the total hours of the time interval is 168 h (7 days × 24 h). In this example, the maintenance duration is

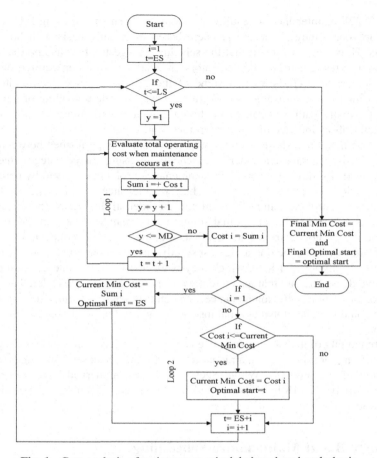

Fig. 1. Cost analysis of maintenance schedule based on hourly basis

assumed to be 24 h where it must be completed in consecutive hours. From the given example, the earliest possible hour is during hour 1, while the latest possible hour is during hour 144.

Loop 1 in the flowchart is mainly to evaluate the total operating cost if maintenance started at that hour. According to the above example, the total operating cost at the first iteration is obtained by adding up the cost at each hour for the first 24 h (1–24), since maintenance must be completed according to the specified duration once it is started. Meanwhile, at the second iteration, the summation of cost is computed between hours 2 to 25. The process continues for the following hours. Besides, loop 2 in the flowchart is purposely to identify the lowest total operating cost. Here, the cost will be compared iteratively. The process stops when the current hour is greater than the LS hour. Finally, an optimal period for scheduling the maintenance is obtained.

3 Problem Formulation of Generation Maintenance Scheduling

3.1 Objective Function

The objective of generation maintenance scheduling is to minimize the production, start-up and shut-down, and maintenance costs as stated in Eq. (1).

$$\sum_{j=1}^{J} C_{g,jt} \cdot p_{j,t} + C_j^u(t) + C_j^d(t)\} + C_{m,jt} \cdot X_{j,t} \tag{1}$$

3.2 Security-Constrained Unit Commitment

Scheduling generation maintenance is restricted to unit commitment constraints including of unit-wise and system-wise constraints. Unit-wise constraints consist of initial condition, generation limit, minimum up and down times, and ramping limit. Meanwhile, system-wise constraints consist of power balance and spinning reserve. The formulation of each constraint is stated in the following.

i. Generation capacity constraints: These limits indicate that an on-line unit must generate its power within these bounds.

$$P_{min,j} \cdot I_{jt} \leq p_{j,t} \leq P_{max,j} \cdot I_{jt} \tag{2}$$

ii. Power balance constraints: The total demand at each period must be fulfilled by all generators in the system.

$$\sum_{j=1}^{NG} p_{j,t} = D_t \tag{3}$$

iii. Minimum up and down time constraints: These constraints require a unit to stay in the ON/OFF condition according to its minimum pre-specified hours before it can change to another state.

$$\sum_{t=1}^{UT_j} (1 - I_{jt}) = 0 \tag{4}$$

$$where \ UT_j = \max\left\{0, min\left[NT, \left(T_j^{on} - q_{j0}^{on}\right) \cdot I_{j0}\right]\right\}$$

$$\sum_{\tau=t}^{t+T_j^{on}-1} I_{j\tau} \geq T_j^{on} \cdot \left(I_{jt} - I_{j(t-1)}\right) \tag{5}$$

$$\forall t = UT_j + 1, \ldots, NT - T_j^{on} + 1$$

$$\sum_{\tau=t}^{NT} I_{j\tau} - \left(I_{jt} - I_{j(t-1)}\right) \geq 0$$

$$\forall t = NT - T_j^{on} + 2, \ldots, NT \tag{6}$$

$$\sum_{t=1}^{DT_j} I_{jt} = 0 \tag{7}$$

where $DT_j = \max\left\{0, \min\left[NT, \left(T_j^{off} - q_{j0}^{off}\right).(1 - I_{j0})\right]\right\}$

$$\sum_{\tau=t}^{t+T_j^{off}-1} (1 - I_{j\tau}) \geq T_j^{off}.\left(I_{j(t-1)} - I_{jt}\right)$$

$$\forall t = DT_j + 1, \ldots, NT - T_j^{off} + 1 \tag{8}$$

$$\sum_{\tau=t}^{NT} 1 - I_{j\tau} - \left(I_{j(t-1)} - I_{jt}\right) \geq 0$$

$$\forall t = NT - T_j^{off} + 2, \ldots, NT$$

iv. Ramp rates constraints: These constraints ensure that in the successive periods, generation dispatch of a unit is within its rates.

$$p_{j,t} - p_{j,(t-1)} \leq RU_j\left(I_{j(t-1)}\right) + UP_j\left(I_{jt} - I_{j(t-1)}\right) + P_{j,max}(1 - I_{jt}) \tag{10}$$

$$p_{j,(t-1)} - p_{j,t} \leq RD_j\left(I_{jt}\right) + DP_j\left(I_{j(t-1)} - I_{jt}\right) + P_{j,max}\left(1 - I_{j(t-1)}\right) \tag{11}$$

v. Spinning reserve and non-spinning reserve constraints: These constraints ensure that the system reserve is enough for each hour of the entire period of study to cater for any loss of units.

$$\sum_{j=1}^{NG} SR_{jt} \geq R_{st} \tag{12}$$

$$\sum_{j=1}^{NG} OR_{jt} \geq R_{ot} \tag{13}$$

$$SR_{jt} \leq P_{max,j} \cdot I_{jt} - p_{jt} \tag{14}$$

$$OR_{jt} = SR_{jt} + \left(1 - I_{jt}\right) \cdot QSC_j \tag{15}$$

3.3 Maintenance Constraints

i. Maintenance window constraints: These constraints ensure that the unit is scheduled for maintenance between the starting time and the ending time.

$$
\begin{aligned}
&\textit{if } PS_j \leq t \leq PE_j, \quad X_{jt} = 0 \textit{ or } 1 \\
&\textit{if } t < PS_j \textit{ or } t > PE_j, \quad X_{jt} = 0
\end{aligned}
\tag{16}
$$

ii. Maintenance duration constraints: These constraints stated that maintenance must be completed according to its pre-specified duration.

$$
\sum_{t=PS_j}^{PE_j} X_{jt} = MD_j
\tag{17}
$$

iii. Maintenance continuity constraints: These constraints stated that maintenance must be completed in the consecutive hours once it is started.

$$
\sum_{t=k}^{k+MD_j-1} X_{jt} \geq MD_j \cdot \left[X_{jk} - X_{j(k-1)} \right]
\tag{18}
$$

$$
\forall j, k = PS_j, \ldots, PE_j - MD_j + 1
$$

$$
\sum_{t=k}^{PE_j} \left\{ X_{jt} - \left[X_{jk} - X_{j(k-1)} \right] \right\} \geq 0
\tag{19}
$$

$$
\forall j, k = PE_j - MD_j + 2, \ldots, PE_j
$$

iv. Crew constraint: This constraint is opposed when available manpower is limited. Here is an example when three generators are not allowed to schedule at the same time.

$$
X_{1t} + X_{2t} + X_{3t} \leq 1
\tag{20}
$$

3.4 Network Constraints

i. Transmission flow limits: These constraints ensure that power that flows in transmission line is always under its capacity limit.

$$
-PF_l^{max} \leq PF_l \leq PF_l^{max}
\tag{21}
$$

3.5   Coupling Constraints

i. Coupling constraints between generator maintenance X and unit commitment I. This constraint is purposely to certify the unit could not be in operation when it is scheduled for maintenance.

$$X_{jt} + I_{jt} \leq 1 \tag{22}$$

4   Comparative Study Between Hourly and Daily Maintenance Scheduling

The main purpose of this study is to show the differences of the generation maintenance schedule between hourly and daily approach. The hourly approach has solved the maintenance problem by considering an entire week of planning intervals Thus, any interval throughout the planning horizon that give the lowest operating cost is selected to be an optimal period for scheduling the maintenance. As a result, maintenance can be started at any hour throughout the maintenance window.

To demonstrate a maintenance scheduling that is based on a daily basis, maintenance is scheduled for each day sequentially throughout a week, and the operation cost is then observed on each day. In this approach, the day that gave the lowest operating cost is considered an optimal period for scheduling the maintenance. That is, maintenance will always start at the beginning of the day.

To see the effectiveness of the hourly basis compared to the daily basis, only one generator is selected for maintenance over a one-week planning horizon. The results for a 6-bus system, the IEEE 118-bus system and the utility system appear below.

4.1   6-Bus System

The 6-bus system consists of three generators, seven transmission lines, and three load demands as presented in Fig. 2. Chronological load profile over a one-week planning horizon is depicted in Fig. 3, in which the peak load is 270 MW. Tables 1, 2 and 3 show the generator information, and transmission network, respectively. For the purpose of this study, only G1 is optimized for maintenance scheduling over a one-week planning horizon, in which its maintenance duration is 24 h.

Table 4 tabulates the operating cost obtained when maintenance of G1 is scheduled sequentially on each day. From the evaluation, it is noted that the operating cost is at the lowest when scheduling G1 on Sunday. Thus, based on this approach, it can be concluded that the optimal maintenance period for G1 is during hours 145–168, with the operating cost yielded being \$520,280.17. However, in the hourly basis approach, G1 is optimally scheduled during hours 109–132, which gave an operating cost of about \$518,190.47, which is lower than for the daily approach. It can be emphasized that the global optimum can only be achieved by scheduling the maintenance on an hourly basis.

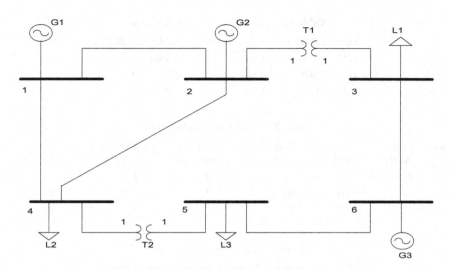

Fig. 2. The 6-bus system

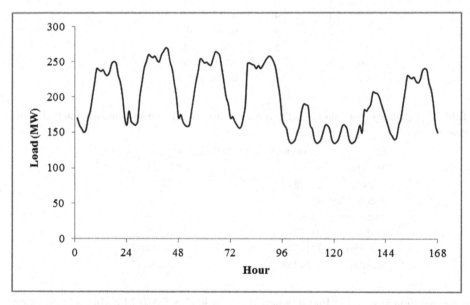

Fig. 3. Load profile over 168 h of the planning horizon (6-bus system)

4.2 IEEE 118-Bus System

The IEEE 118-bus system consists of 54 thermal units, 186 branches, and 91 loads. All network information can be referred to [21]. Spinning and non-spinning reserves of the system are set to be 5% and 7% of the load, respectively. The load profile used in this

Table 1. Generator cost coefficient data

Unit	a (MBtu/h)	b (MBtu/MWh)	c (MBtu/MW^{2}h)
G1	176.9	13.5	0.00045
G2	129.9	32.6	0.001
G3	137.4	17.6	0.005

Table 2. Generator operating data

Unit	Pmin (MW)	Pmax (MW)	Ramp rate (MW/h)	Min-up time (h)	Min-down time (h)	Initial state (h)
G1	100	220	55	4	4	4
G2	50	150	50	2	3	2
G3	20	100	40	1	1	1

Table 3. Transmission line data

Line	From bus	To bus	X (pu)	Line limit (MW)
1	1	2	0.170	200
2	2	3	0.037	100
3	1	4	0.258	200
4	2	4	0.197	80
5	4	5	0.037	100
6	5	6	0.140	100
7	3	6	0.018	100

Table 4. Operating cost with respect to a maintenance schedule with a one-day interval (6-bus system)

Day	Maintenance periods (hour)	Operating cost ($)
Monday	1–24	525045.16
Tuesday	25–48	530820.15
Wednesday	49–72	530203.79
Thursday	73–96	541572.19
Friday	97–120	524831.24
Saturday	121–144	530614.07
Sunday	**145–168**	**520280.17**

demonstration is stated in Fig. 4, where the peak load is 5,470 MW. In this evaluation, only G10 is selected for maintenance over a one-week planning horizon.

Table 5 tabulates the operating cost when maintenance is performed for each day sequentially throughout a week. From the observation, the highest operating cost is obtained when maintaining G10 on Tuesday, while the lowest cost is obtained when maintaining G10 on Friday. Based on this approach, the optimal period for performing the maintenance is during hours 97–120 (i.e. Friday), which gave an operating cost of about $9,194,791.55.

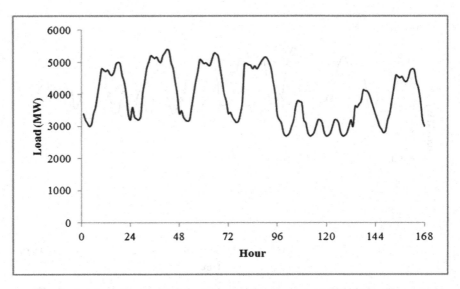

Fig. 4. Load profile over 168 h of the planning horizon (IEEE 118-bus system)

Table 5. Operating cost with respect to a maintenance schedule with a one-day interval (IEEE 118-bus system)

Day	Maintenance schedule (hour)	Operating cost ($)
Monday	1–24	9205196.93
Tuesday	25–48	9206603.23
Wednesday	49–72	9205494.36
Thursday	73–96	9205803.67
Friday	**97–120**	**9194791.55**
Saturday	121–144	9197304.79
Sunday	145–168	9202951.16

However, the optimal period for scheduling G10 is during hours 110–133 when based on the hourly approach. The operating cost obtained is $9,193,855.14. By comparing both results, it can be concluded that the hourly approach is superior to the daily approach as it provides a global optimal schedule with lower operating cost.

4.3 Validation Using Utility Data

The effectiveness of the hourly approach is further investigated by solving the maintenance scheduling problem for the real practical system. This system includes 99 generators, 663 transmission lines, and 326 load assets. The load profile over the study horizon is illustrated in Fig. 5, with the peak load of 14,529 MW which occurs at hour 42. Due to crew constraints, generators and transmission lines cannot be scheduled for

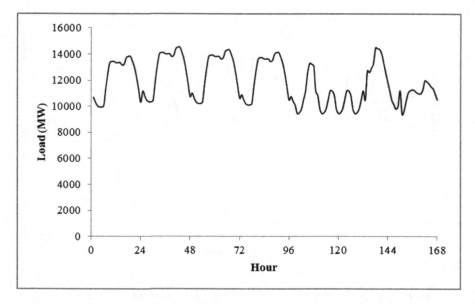

Fig. 5. Load profile over 168 h of the planning horizon (Utility system)

maintenance at the same time. According to the company practice, a fixed system operating reserve level of 900 MW is applied throughout the planning horizon. In this assessment, only G25 is maintained over a one week planning horizon with the duration of 24 h.

In the daily approach, maintenance of G25 is performed sequentially on each day and its operating cost is observed. The operating cost is then summarized in Table 6. According to this approach, the day with the lowest operating cost is considered the optimal period for scheduling the maintenance. Based on the results, G25 will be maintained on Friday which gives an operating cost of about $273,634,734.90. In contrast, by using the hourly approach, the optimal period for scheduling G25 is suggested during hours 109–132 with the operating cost of $273,588,993.74. Thus, it can be concluded that the operating cost is lower when scheduling the maintenance based on the hourly as compared to the daily approach.

Table 6. Operating cost with respect to a maintenance schedule with a one-day interval (Utility system)

Day	Maintenance periods (hour)	Operating cost ($)
Monday	1–24	273,784,432.60
Tuesday	25–48	274,471,313.14
Wednesday	49–72	274,019,145.14
Thursday	73–96	273,917,946.15
Friday	**97–120**	**273,634,734.90**
Saturday	121–144	273,955,787.30
Sunday	145–168	273,819,644.06

5 Conclusion

In this paper, a comparative study between hourly and daily based generation maintenance scheduling is highlighted. Simulation result showed that by using hourly approach, maintenance is scheduled at any hours which gave the lowest operating cost while in daily approach, maintenance is always start at the beginning of the day. Besides, the operating cost obtained is lower in hourly as compared to the daily approach. It can be concluded that by using the hourly approach, the global optimal schedule could be achieved instead of the local optimal schedule obtained in the daily approach.

Acknowledgement. The authors would like to thank Research Management Centre (RMC), Institute of Future Energy (IFE) and Centre of Electrical Energy Systems (CEES) for the financial support provided. The appreciation also goes to POWER Department, Faculty of Electrical Engineering, Universiti Teknologi Malaysia and the Ministry of Higher Education of Malaysia.

References

1. Kovacs, A., Erdos, G., Viharos, Z.J., Monostori, L.: A system for the detailed scheduling of wind farm maintenance. CIRP Ann. Manuf. Technol. **60**(1), 497–501 (2011)
2. Mohd Basri, M.A., Husain, A.R., Danapalasingam, K.A.: Enhanced backstepping controller design with application to autonomous quadrotor unmanned aerial vehicle. J. Intell. Robot. Syst. **79**(2), 295–321 (2014)
3. Suresh, K., Kumarappan, N.: Hybrid improved binary particle swarm optimization approach for generation maintenance scheduling problem. Swarm Evol. Comput. **9**, 69–89 (2013)
4. Zhan, J., Guo, C., Wu, Q., Zhang, L., Fu, H.: Generation maintenance scheduling based on multiple objectives and their relationship analysis. J. Zhejiang Univ. Sci. C **15**(11), 1035–1047 (2014)
5. Guedes, L.S.M., Vieira, D.A.G., Lisboa, A.C., Saldanha, R.R.: A continuous compact model for cascaded hydro-power generation and preventive maintenance scheduling. Electr. Power Energy Syst. **73**, 702–710 (2015)
6. Marwali, M.K.C., Shahidehpour, S.M.: Short-term transmission line maintenance scheduling in a deregulated system. IEEE Trans. Power Syst. **15**(3), 1117–1124 (2000)
7. Li, W., Korczynski, J.: A reliability-based approach to transmission maintenance planning and its application in BC hydro system. IEEE Trans. Power Deliv. **19**(1), 303–308 (2004)
8. Pandzic, H., Conejo, A.J., Kuzle, I., Caro, E.: Yearly maintenance scheduling of transmission lines within a market environment. IEEE Trans. Power Syst. **27**(1), 407–415 (2012)
9. Anders, G., Hamoud, G., Silva, A.M.L., Manso, L.A.: Optimal outage scheduling - example of application to a large power system. Electr. Power Energy Syst. **25**, 607–614 (2003)
10. El-Sharkh, M.Y., El-Keib, A.A.: An evolutionary programming-based solution methodology for power generation and transmission maintenance scheduling. Electr. Power Syst. Res. **65**, 35–40 (2003)
11. Billinton, R., Mo, R.: Composite system maintenance coordination in a deregulated environment. IEEE Trans. Power Syst. **20**(1), 485–492 (2005)
12. Basaran, U., Kurban, M.: The strategy for the maintenance scheduling of the generating units. In: Large Engineering System Conference on Power Engineering, pp. 172–176 (2003)

13. Garver, L.L.: Adjusting maintenance schedule to levelize risk. IEEE Power Appar. Syst. **PAS-91**(5), 2057–2063 (1972)
14. Mohan, C., Nguyen, H.T.: A controlled random search technique incorporating the simulated annealing concept for solving integer and mixed integer global optimization problem. Comput. Optim. Appl. **14**(1), 103–132 (1999)
15. Kim, H.K.: An algorithm for thermal unit maintenance scheduling through combined use of GA SA and TS. IEEE Trans. Power Syst. **12**(1), 329–335 (1997)
16. Kumarappan, N., Suresh, K.: Combined SA PSO method for transmission constrained maintenance scheduling using levelized risk method. Electr. Power Energy Syst. **73**, 1025–1034 (2015)
17. Yamyee, Z., Sidenblad, K.: A computationally efficient optimal maintenance scheduling method. IEEE Trans. Power Appar. Syst. **PAS-102**(2), 330–338 (1983)
18. Leou, R.C.: A flexible unit maintenance scheduling considering uncertainties. IEEE Trans. Power Syst. **16**(3), 552–559 (2001)
19. Pandzic, H., Conejo, A., Kuzle, I.: An EPEC approach to the yearly maintenance scheduling of generating units. IEEE Trans. Power Syst. **28**(2), 922–930 (2013)
20. Fu, Y., Shahidehpour, M., Li, Z.: Security-constrained optimal coordination of generation and transmission maintenance outage scheduling. IEEE Trans. Power Syst. **22**(3), 1302–1313 (2007)
21. Fu, Y., Li, Z., Shahidehpour, M.: Coordination of midterm outage scheduling with short-term security-constrained unit commitment. IEEE Trans. Power Syst. **24**(4), 1818–1830 (2009)
22. Wu, L., Shahidehpour, M., Fu, Y.: Security-constrained generation and transmission outage scheduling with uncertainties. IEEE Trans. Power Syst. **25**(3), 1674–1685 (2010)

Maximum Power Point Tracking (MPPT) Battery Charger for a Small Wind Power System

Mohd Nurhadi Mad Zain[1], Norzanah Rosmin[2(✉)],
Nor Khairunnisa Sidek[2], Aede Hatib Musta'amal@Jamal[3],
Maherah Hussin[2], and Dalila Mat Said[2]

[1] Suruhanjaya Tenaga, Tingkat 1, Bgnn KWSP,
Jalan Georgetown, 30450 Ipoh, Perak, Malaysia
[2] POWER Department, Faculty of Electrical Engineering,
Centre of Electrical Energy System (CEES), Universiti Teknologi Malaysia,
81310 Skudai, Johor, Malaysia
norzanah@fke.utm.my
[3] Faculty of Education, Universiti Teknologi Malaysia,
81310 Skudai, Johor, Malaysia

Abstract. This paper focuses on charging process of the battery charger for a small wind turbine system to track the highest power point in order to harvest the maximum output in the wide range of wind speed variations. The Maximum Power Point Tracking (MPPT) method with the assistance of classical Proportional-Integral-Derivative (PID) controller is used. The issue regarding how this charging process is managed was studied. Smart management during battery charging process is significantly required since the lack of charging management may affecting the battery's performance, particularly in terms of its lifetime and the degradation rate. Hence, in this paper, a battery charger with an effective performance is designed using the concept of controlling the pulsating charging current which is implemented by discontinuous conduction mode operation of a power converter. Results show that the efficiency of the charging process is good since the resulting pulsating current is working as expected and protection scheme worked well during the charging process by using buck-converter. This method enables the overcharging and overvoltage to be avoided. Besides that, it provides another feature where the self-discharging process can be avoided by providing small current flow in order to prolong the battery's lifetime.

Keywords: Maximum Power Point Tracking (MPPT) · Proportional-Integral-Derivative (PID) · Buck converter · Battery charger · Wind turbine

1 Introduction

Renewable energy sources derive their energy from ongoing natural processes such as sunshine, wind, flowing water, biological processes and geothermal heat flows. A general definition of renewable energy sources is that renewable energy is captured

© Springer Nature Singapore Pte Ltd. 2017
M.S. Mohamed Ali et al. (Eds.): AsiaSim 2017, Part II, CCIS 752, pp. 39–52, 2017.
DOI: 10.1007/978-981-10-6502-6_4

from an energy resource that is replaced rapidly by a natural process. The alternative energy has been developed to reduce the problem of the fossil-fuel exhaustion and environmental issues. One of the feasible energy is a wind-power system. For urban areas, wind power can be integrated with main grid. In contrast with the rural areas with weak grid, the stand-alone wind power system with the battery bank is essential in order for providing stable and reliable electricity.

Wind energy is one of the most promising alternative energy technologies of the future [1, 2]. Throughout recent years, the amount of energy produced by wind-driven turbines has increased due to the significant breakthrough in the wind energy system. It offers many advantages over the fossil based energy which explains why it becomes fast growing energy source in the world. Since the wind energy is clean and free, generating maximum energy from the wind is very important. It is due to the appreciation of the pollution-free source energy and not wasting the available chance. Even though wind energy has many environmental and supply advantages, there are several disadvantages that limit the usability of wind power. The main disadvantage to wind power is that it is unreliable because it does not blow at a constant rate. This will cause the changes in maximum power available at particular moments. Due to this intermittency problem, a smart energy storage device that able to overcome the fluctuations problem is required. This is important to ensure the continuity supply of service in wind power production.

Wind power can be stored in several ways, including transferring the generated electrical energy using the concept of compressed air, electrochemical energy, chemical energy, kinetic energy, magnetic field and electric field. As common, each of these storage options has some pros and cons in terms of life cycle, storage period, operating systems, energy density, self-discharge, efficiency, cost and etc. [3, 4]. Among the available storage options, electrochemical energy via battery storage is the most popular one. Improvements on battery technology are being performed aggressively in many years now [5]. For a smart wind power battery charger, it is necessary to be able to track the maximum power point at each wind speed variations. Due to this, many MPPT algorithms have been proposed to maximize the efficiency of the battery charger for wind power system.

In [6], the authors compared the performance of MPPT controller against the feedforward method. From their findings, MPPT presents better performance than feedforward method. Less power oscillations produced when MPPT is used. In addition, using MPPT, less parameter will be used. Using MPPT approach, advance technology must be used. The parameters and reading values will be stored in a memory or Digital Signal Processing (DSP) card system [6, 7]. To further improve the battery charging process, several methods have been proposed, for example, works that have been carried out in [6, 8]. In these works, the authors used voltage-oriented method. However, these approaches are quite complex and very costly.

For small power system, appropriate battery charger should be selected wisely for the economical purpose. For this system, lead acid batteries are commonly used for the purpose of energy storage system. It is quite cheap and well established compared to the others. However, lead acid battery has a drawback of having high degradation rate that may affect the system effectiveness. Hence, to improve the drawback of high degradation rate during charging and discharging process, pulsating current concept is introduced. Using this concept, system effectiveness (charging efficiency) can be increased; yet, the battery's lifetime also can be prolonged [1, 9, 10]. Though, over-speed protection, e.g. in terms of overvoltage and overcurrent [1] also can be much improved. This method has been proposed and proven work better on the battery charger in [11]. However, this method was designed for the general battery charger and not specific for wind power application.

Hence, in this study, a Maximum Power Point Tracking (MPPT) control strategy equipped with the pulsating charging current in order to improve the battery's per-formance is proposed. The design is focused for the application of a small-sized stand-alone wind power system. The simplicity of the electronic cuicuitary is also considered in this study, but the preference on the high reliability is also undertaken. To realize the proposed idea, buck converter with pulse-width modulation (PWM) switching will be used. The PWM is used to track the maximum power point by controlling the output process using duty cycle or its switching frequency. Focus will be paid on the three types of converter current; continuous current mode, dis-continuous current mode and zero current mode. These current modes will operate once at a time depends on the feedback input coming from the main battery charger circuit. In this paper, the content was structured as follows. Section 1 presents the background and the contribution of this study. In Sect. 2, the methodology of the carried study is presented. While Sect. 3 contains the simulation results and its discussion. Finally, some conclusions and suggestion are given in Sect. 4.

2 Wind Energy Conversion System

Wind turbine is a machine that can convert the wind power via a shaft that connected to an electrical generator before supplying the power to the load. When wind hits the turbine blades, the pressure difference between upper and lower sides of the blade enable the blades to rotate and then supplying electrical power. Wind power is fluc-tuated and therefore the output power also variable depends on the captured wind towards the blades. Figure 1 shows the schematic diagram of a 2-bladed wind turbine

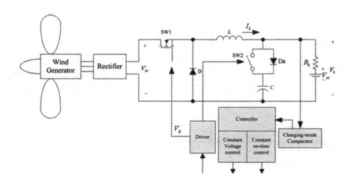

Fig. 1. Power converter application in wind energy system

connected to a power converter. In the power converter diagram, a rectifier with current and voltage control are depicted [12].

By considering that blades are frictionless and its rotation perpendicular to the airflow, the output power of wind turbine can be estimated using Eq. (1) [13, 14]:

$$P = (1/2)\rho\pi R^2 C_{p-opt} U^3 \tag{1}$$

where P_m is the output power of the wind turbine, ρ is the air density, C_p (λ,β) is the power conversion coefficient that is related to a tip-speed ratio (λ) and pitch angle (β), R is the radius of blade, and V_ω is the wind speed. The power conversion coefficient affected by a variety of aerodynamics factors such as number of blades, aerofoil sections, surface finish and angle of blades attack the airflow.

The mechanical power in the shaft can be converted to electricity by using fixed-speed or variable speed generator. In this study, permanent magnet synchronous generator (PMSG) is adopted because of this generator has high reliability and structurally simpler. The behaviour of rotor power versus the generator rotor speed for each wind speed is shown in Fig. 2. From the figure, it can be seen that when wind speed is increasing, power also keep increasing. But, it also can be observed that every wind speed has its optimum rotor speed to enable the wind power can be generated at maximum values. Hence, it is important to ensure blade rotor speed can rotate at the optimum speed to track the maximum power point. Voltage must be generated at its optimum one (to obtain maximum power) before feeding the voltage to the battery charger. Using MPPT approach, the MPPT controller will search the optimum rotor speed at each wind speed. To achieve MPPT function, optimum voltage range must be determined. This can be done by identifying the local wind speeds information.

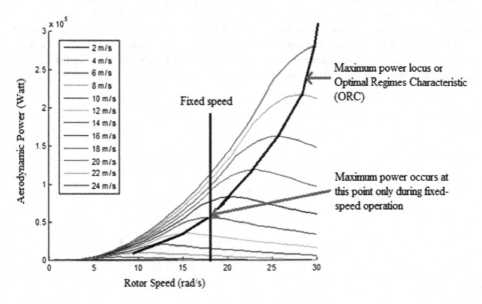

Fig. 2. Wind power against wind rotor speed

3 Description of the Proposed MPPT Control Scheme for Battery Charger

Battery charger may operate at two conditions; charging and discharging process. For battery charger of a wind turbine system, the charging process occurs when wind turbine generates mechanical power. For a lead acid battery, the electrons in the battery will move from positive to the negative terminal during the charging process. This will lead to the increment of voltage reading at the electrodes. For the discharging process, it occurs when the chemical reactions in the battery change the mechanical power from the generator shaft to the electrical power before supplying it to the loads. During this condition, the connection between battery and loads enables electrons flows from the negative to the positive terminal. Voltages at the electrodes will also be reduced.

For a lead acid battery, there are two issues that were commonly occurred during battery charger operation; overcharging and over-discharging situations. To prolong the battery lifetime, these two situations should be avoided. To solve these problems, a pulse current concept is proposed in this study. To perform this, a buck-converter is used. The most common charging method is performed using constant-current or constant–voltage control strategy. Using constant-current mode, the charging time can be shortened and charging current also can be limited at a certain optimal value. Smaller charging current is good because this could prolong the battery's lifetime but it implies to the longer charging time.

For the proposed buck-converter, the inductor current (in the buck-converter) can be controlled in two modes; continuous conduction mode (CCM) and discontinuous conduction mode (DCM). With assistance of 'ON' and 'OFF' switching signal, current can be controlled either in CCM or DCM operations. When the switch of the gate signal is set at 'ON' state, current will be increased meanwhile when the gate signal is set at 'OFF' state, current will be decreased. The typical waveforms of the gate signal and the inductor current during DCM and CCM operations are shown in Fig. 3(a) and (b), respectively.

In DCM, when the gate signal is at 'ON' state, inductor current will be increased until the gate signal is changed to be 'OFF' state. When the gate signal turned from 'ON' to 'OFF' state, current will be decreased until reaches zero value and then remains at this zero value for a certain moments. Current will increase again once the gate signal is 'ON' again. However, in CCM, current pattern is same as in DCM when the gate signal is set at 'ON' state where current will be increased until the 'ON' state is changed to be 'OFF' state. When the gate signal is set at 'OFF' state, current will be reduced and will reach zero at one time only. Then, current will be increased again when the gate signal is 'ON' again.

When the wind turbine output voltage V_{in} is greater than the threshold/boundary voltage (V_{bth}), the battery charger will enter the CCM operation as can be depicted in Fig. 4. When the battery charger is operating at the boundary condition (between DCM and CCM), this moment will be referred as rest duty period. During this rest duty period, current signal becomes zero while the charging period d_1 and discharging period d_2 equal to 1. For the current signal shown in Fig. 3, the amplitude of the charging current can be calculated using Eq. (2). Meanwhile, for the V_{in} voltage signal shown in Fig. 4, the voltage can be estimated using Eq. (3) [13–15].

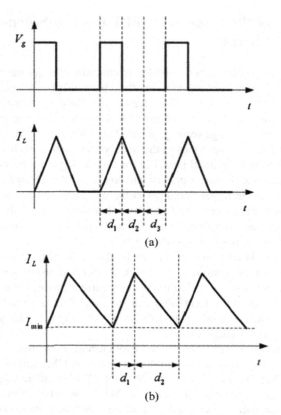

Fig. 3. Typical waveforms of the gate signal and inductor current in (a) DCM and (b) CCM

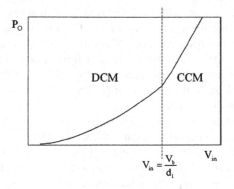

Fig. 4. Output power against wind turbine output voltage V_{in}

$$\Delta i = \frac{(V_{in} - V_b)d_1}{fL} = \frac{V_b d_2}{fL} \tag{2}$$

$$V_{in} = \frac{V_b}{d_1} \tag{3}$$

When the battery reaches its maximum charging voltage limit, the pulsating current mode operation with MPPT function should be combined together in order to prevent the overcharging situation of the battery. Battery charger needs to enter the constant voltage mode operation as the way to protect the battery from the overcharge damage.

The schematic diagram of the proposed battery charger in this study is shown in Fig. 5. Pulse width modulation (PWM) technique is used to supply the 'ON' and 'OFF' switching state. There are two modes during battery charger operation; pulsating current mode (PCM) and constant voltage mode (CVM). When the battery voltage (V_b) is below the threshold value (V_{bth}), the battery charger will be operated in PCM. During this mode, switch_2 is opened. Meanwhile, when the battery voltage (V_b) is greater than the threshold value (V_{bth}), the battery charger is operated in CVM, and the switch_2 is closed during this mode.

PCM is conducted in discontinuous conduction mode (DCM) where when the input voltage (V_{in}) is less than the rated voltage (V_{rated}). Constant on-time control is applied to generate the pulsating current. For a wind turbine system, when the speed of the wind increases, the output voltage of the wind turbine also increases. At this condition,

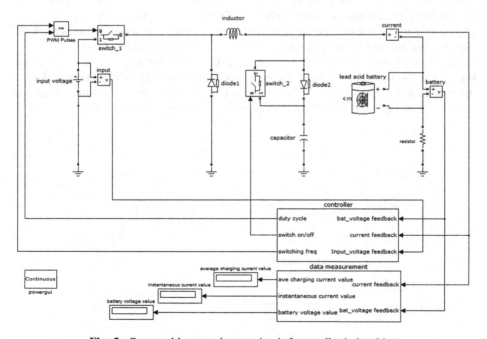

Fig. 5. Proposed battery charger circuit for small wind turbine

battery charger may enter the continuous conduction mode (CCM) zone where the input voltage (V_{in}) is greater than the rated voltage (V_{rated}). When the input voltage increases, current also increase. Hence, the blade rotor speed needs to be restrained and the battery voltage needs to be reduced and maintained at a nominal value. To limit the voltage at a constant value, capacitor is used (as shown in Fig. 5). By applying capacitor in parallel to the battery, the output voltage can be regulated to be at a nominal value. This is important for the elimination of overcharging condition.

As can be depicted in Fig. 5, a main controller is used to control the output voltage and output current. In this study, proportional-integral-derivative (PID) tuning method was chosen for the controller. PID controller maintains the output such that there is zero error between process variable and desired output by closed loop operations. PID uses three basic control behaviors; Proportional, integral and derivative. Proportional controller gives output which is proportional to current error. It compares desired with reference value or feedback process value. The resulting error is multiplied with proportional constant to get the output. If the error value is equal to zero, then this controller output will be zero. Due to limitation of this P-controller where there always exists an offset between the process variable and refrence point, integral controller is needed, which provides necessary action to eliminate the steady state error. It integrates the error over a period of time until error value becomes to zero. It holds the value to final control device at which error becomes zero. Integral control decreases its output when negative error takes place. It limits the speed of response and affects stability of the system. By decreasing integral gain, speed of the response could be increased. Integral controller doesn't have the capability to predict the future behavior of error. So it reacts normally once the reference point is changed. Derivative controller overcomes this problem by anticipating future behavior of the error. Its output depends on rate of change of error with respect to time, multiplied by derivative constant. It gives the kick start for the output thereby increasing system response. This main controller is comprising two internal controllers; voltage control and current control, as depicted in Fig. 6. For the main control loop, the measured battery voltage will be compared with the voltage reference of 28 V. Then, the main control system will determine either the circuit will be operated in voltage control mode or current control mode.

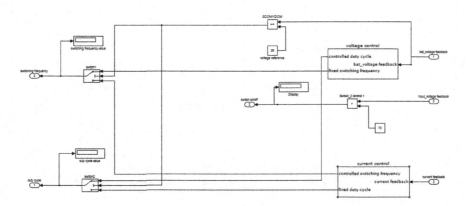

Fig. 6. Controller circuit for battery charger

Current control mode is a mode where feedback from the charging current is taken before comparing with the reference value of 18 A. PID controller is functioning to adjust the switching frequency to the suitable value. The duty cycles is remains fixed in current control mode, thus PWM switching cycle for switch1 also remains constant. Due to this, it is referred as constant on-time control [2]. For voltage control mode, feedback from the battery is taken before comparing with the reference value of 28 V. The proportional constant contributes more changes to the rise time of the signal.

In this study, the proposed battery charger circuit using buck converter is designed by considering a battery charger specification as listed in Table 1.

Table 1. Battery charger specifications [2]

No	Specification	Value
1	Wind turbine rated voltage, $V_{in\,rated}$	70 V
2	Full charge voltage, V_o	28 V
3	Charger input voltage, V_{in}	30–100 V
4	Duty cycle, d_1	0.4
5	Switching frequency, f_{sw}	22 kHz
6	Inductor, L	23 μH
7	Capacitor, C	1.347 mF
8	I_{rated}	80 A
9	$I_{charging}$	18 A

4   Results and Discussions

In this section, results will be divided into three subsections; continuous current mode (CCM), discontinuous current mode (DCM) and zero current mode (ZCM).

4.1   Continuous Current Mode (CCM)

The continuous current modes (CCMs) occur when the battery is not fully charged and when the input voltage (V_{in}) is exceeded the rated voltage (V_{rated}). The rated voltage is 70 V and for this study the optimum charging current (I_{opt}) is determined as 18 A. In CCM mode, the charging current will exceed the value of the I_{opt}. Figure 7 shows the steady-state response of the CCM operation mode of the simulated program. As shown in the figure, when the switch (gate signal) is set to 'ON' state, current will be increased. Conversely, when the switch (gate signal) is set to 'OFF' state, current will be decreased. Figure 7(a), shows the response of the CCM when the V_{in} is set at 80 V, meanwhile in Fig. 7(b), CCM response is shown when the V_{in} is set to 90 V. This comparison is done to show the behaviour of the CCM operation when V_{in} is set close (80 V) and farther (90 V) to the V_{rated}. As can be seen from the figure, higher peak charging current is generated when the V_{in} is set higher. When the V_{in} is set at 90 V, the charging current can reach maximum peak of around 32 A. But, when the V_{in} is set to

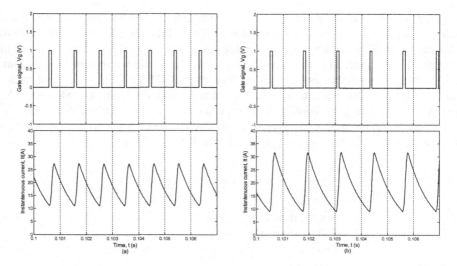

Fig. 7. Simulation of the gate signal and battery charging current under CCM operation at input voltage (a) 80 V and (b) 90 V

be 80 V, the charging current is reduced where the maximum peak charging current reduced to be 27.5 A. From the figure also, it can be observed that the output CCM signal shaped as sawtooth wave. This sawtooth current is actually shaped by the existence of inductor in the circuitry. The current slew rate is also influenced or controlled by this inductor as well.

4.2   Discontinuous Current Mode (DCM)

The discontinuous current mode (DCM) occurs when the battery is in the condition of not fully charged and V_{in} is less than or equal to 70 V. The steady-state response of the DCM charging process is shown in Fig. 8. As in CCM, current will increase when switch 1 is set at 'ON' state, meanwhile current is decreased until reaches zero condition and then remains at zero state for certain times when switch 1 at 'OFF' state. Obviously seen that, in contrast to the CCM, the DCM signals (as shown in Fig. 8) will remain at zero state for a few moments when the gate signal is set at 'OFF' state or before enter the next cycle. During this time, the electrons from the previous charging process have a rest time to achieve the equilibrium state inside the lead acid battery. In CCM, current will reduce to zero for one time only. In DCM, it can be seen that the charging process will response a bit slower or not too fast compared to CCM. However, in terms of efficiency, DCM presents better performance as in DCM resting time at equilibrium state is applied. As occurred in CCM charging process, in DCM, higher V_{in} will cause a greater peak charging current. As can be seen in Fig. 8(a), when the input voltage is set at 70 V, peak current may reach up to 58 A meanwhile peak current may reach 45 A when V_{in} is set lower (50 V), as depicted in Fig. 8(b), respectively.

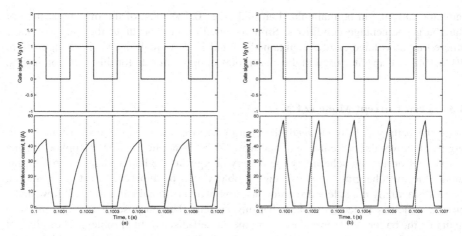

Fig. 8. Simulation of the gate signal and battery charging current under DCM operation at input voltage (a) 50 V and (b) 70 V

Another observation that has been considered during executing this study is the behaviour of the inductor current signal when the battery is not fully charged. Table 2 shows the inductor current response comparison when battery is at 85% charged and 70% charged. For both charging conditions, it can be observed that the value of

Table 2. Inductor current when battery is not fully charged

85% charged			70% charged		
Input voltage (V)	Output voltage (V)	Inductor current (A)	Input voltage (V)	Output voltage (V)	Inductor current (A)
40	26.28	18.02	40	26.01	18.04
50	26.21	18.07	50	26.01	18.04
60	26.21	18.06	60	26.17	18.08
70	26.41	18.12	70	26.17	17.99
80	26.26	18.05	80	26.09	18.04
90	26.25	17.89	90	26.10	18.07
100	26.28	18.14	100	26.11	18.05
55% charged			40% charged		
Input voltage (V)	Output voltage (V)	Inductor current (A)	Input voltage (V)	Output voltage (V)	Inductor current (A)
40	25.78	18.01	40	25.27	17.99
50	25.78	18.01	50	25.31	18.09
60	25.84	18.01	60	25.20	18.07
70	25.72	18.10	70	25.41	18.08
80	25.76	18.10	80	25.24	17.94
90	25.82	17.86	90	25.24	18.06
100	25.76	18.00	100	25.27	17.91

inductor current can be maintained around 18 ± 0.5 A most of the time regardless of the charge percentage conditions. Similar condition also occur to the output voltage where output voltage can be maintained around 26 V though the V_{in} is changed from 40 to 100 V. Capacitor used in the circuit plays important role for this state conditions.

4.3   Zero Current Mode (ZCM)

Once the battery is fully charged, the charging process will be stopped or terminated. Figure 9 shows the current behaviour when ZCM is applied. ZCM is applied for the purpose of protection scheme by the battery charger to the battery bank. Through this mode, the overcharging or overvoltage problems can be avoided. In actual operation, current is actually not solely discarded at zero but a very small current is still flow in the circuit, which is called as trickle charging current. The purpose of this current is to maintain the battery voltage and to overcome the self-discharging problem. The values of this trickle charging current are tabulated in Table 3. It can be seen from the table that the output voltage can be maintained at 28.05 V when V_{in} is changed from 30 V to 100 V. The trickle charging currents is very small, in which the currents flow in the range between $1.92e^{-5}$ to $7.18e^{-4}$ A. When these current values are plotted in a graph plot, it is found that it has a direct proportional relationship with V_{in}, as can be seen in Fig. 10.

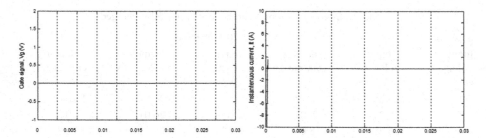

Fig. 9. Simulation of the gate signal and charging current under ZCM operation at input voltage is 28 V

Table 3. Inductor current when battery is fully charged

Input voltage (V)	Output voltage (V)	Inductor current (A)
30	28.05	$1.92e^{-5}$
40	28.05	$1.23e^{-4}$
50	28.05	$2.22e^{-4}$
60	28.05	$3.19e^{-4}$
70	28.05	$4.18e^{-4}$
80	28.05	$5.18e^{-4}$
90	28.05	$6.22e^{-4}$
100	28.05	$7.18e^{-4}$

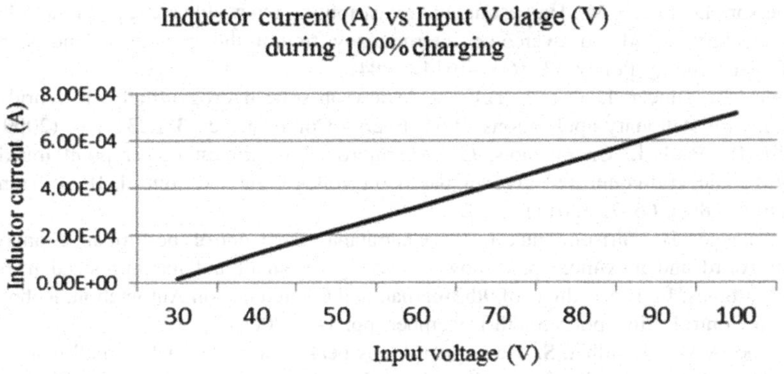

Inductor current (A) vs Input Volatge (V)
during 100% charging

Fig. 10. Graph of inductor current when battery is fully charged

5 Conclusion

With assistance of PID tuning method, charging current can be controlled successfully to operate at ¼ of the rated current (18 A), in both CCM and DCM charging process. During discharging process, self-discharging is successfully avoided by supplying a small current to the battery which is less than 72 mA. During ZCM charging process, the proposed protection scheme works well during the charging process. From these results, it can be summarised that the proposed MPPT battery charger for the considered small wind power system is successfully designed and tested in the software environment. Based on the presented results, overcharging and overvoltage problem can be avoided during battery charging process. Therefore, battery charger lifetime can be potentially prolonged.

Acknowledgement. The authors would like to thank Research Management Centre (RMC), Centre of Electrical Energy System (CEES), POWER Department, Faculty of Electrical Engineering, Universiti Teknologi Malaysia and the Ministry of Higher Education of Malaysia for the financial support provided under Fundamental Research Grant Scheme FRGS (4F794) and Research University Grant (RUG Tier1) 12H00 to carry out this research.

References

1. Lo, K.-Y., Chen, Y.-M., Chang, Y.-R.: MPPT battery charger for stand-alone wind power system. IEEE Trans. Power Electron. **26**(6), 1631–1638 (2011)
2. Li, Y., Xu, Z., Wong, K.P.: Advanced control strategies of PMSG-based wind turbines for system inertia support. IEEE Trans. Power Syst. **99**, 1 (2016)
3. Lu, M., Wen, J., Xie, H., Yue, C., Lee, W.-J.: Coordinated control strategy of wind turbine generator and energy storage equipment for frequency support. IEEE Trans. Ind. Appl. **51** (4), 2732–2742 (2015)

4. Anderson, D., Leach, M.: Harvesting and redistributing renewable energy: on the role of gas and electricity grids to overcome intermittency trough the generation and storage of hydrogen. Energy Policy **32**, 1603–1614 (2004)
5. Yilanci, A., Dincer, I., Ozturk, H.K.: A review on solar-hydrogen/fuel cell hybrid energy systems for stationary applications. Prog. Energy Combust. Sci. **35**, 231–244 (2009)
6. Kadri, R., Paul, J., Champenois, G.: An improved maximum power point tracking for photovoltaic grid-connected inverter based on voltage-oriented control. IEEE Trans. Ind. Electron. **58**(1), 66–75 (2011)
7. Neammanee, B., Sirisumranukul, S., Chatratana, S.: Control performance analysis of feedforward and maximum peak power tracking for small-and medium-sized fixed pitch wind turbines. In: Proceedings of 9th International Conference on Automation, Robotics and Vision Control, Singapore, 5–8th December, pp. 1–7 (2006)
8. De Broe, A.M., Drouilhet, S., Gevorgian, V.: A peak power tracker for small wind turbines in battery charging applications. IEEE Trans. Energy Convers. **14**(4), 1630–1635 (1999)
9. Li, J., Murphy, E., Winnick, J., Kohl, P.A.: The effect of pulse charging on cycling characteristics of commercial lithium-ion batteries. J. Power Sources **102**, 302–309 (2001)
10. Zhang, J., Yu, J., Cha, C., Yang, H.: The effects of pulse charging on inner pressure and cycling characteristics of sealed Ni/MH batteries. J. Power Sources **136**, 180–185 (2014)
11. Gamboa, G., Elmes, J., Hamilton, C., Baker, J., Pepper, M., Batarseh, I.: A unity power factor, maximum power point tracking battery charger for low power wind turbines. In: Proceedings of 25th Annual IEEE on Applied Power Electronics Conference and Exposition (APEC), Palm Springs, CA, pp. 143–148, February 2010
12. Lo, K.-Y., Chen, Y.-M., Chang, Y.R.: MPPT battery charger for stand-alone wind power system. IEEE Trans. Power Electron. **26**(6), 1631–1638 (2011)
13. Jiang, Z., Dougal, R.A.: Synergetic control of power converters for pulse current charging of advanced batteries from a fuel cell power source. IEEE Trans. Power Electron. **19**(4), 1140–1150 (2004)
14. Rosmin, N., Rahman, H.A., Mustaamal, A.H.: A performance comparison of three micro-sized blade rotor designs for Malaysia wind speed condition. Appl. Mech. Mater. **785**, 310–314 (2015)
15. Electricity Storage Association, Technology Storage. http://www.electricitystorage.org/technology/storage_technologies/technology_comparison
16. Pistoia, G.: Battery categories and types. In: Battery Operated Devices and Systems, chap. 2, pp. 17–73 (2009)
17. Pistoia, G.: Battery industrial applications. In: Battery Operated Devices and Systems, chap. 4, pp. 163–319 (2009)

Differential Search Algorithm in Deep Neural Network for the Predictive Analysis of Xylitol Production in *Escherichia Coli*

Siti Noorain Mohmad Yousoff[(✉)], 'Amirah Baharin, and Afnizanfaizal Abdullah

Synthetic Biology Research Group, Faculty of Computing, Universiti Teknologi Malaysia, 81310 Johor Bahru, Johor, Malaysia
ainyousoff@gmail.com, ami.b2525@gmail.com, afnizanfaizal@utm.my

Abstract. Xylitol is one of the bio-based chemical products that received well recognition and highly demanded from both food and pharmaceutical industries which led to various experiment to be carried out on various organism to produce xylitol. Recently, *E. coli* has become the spotlight to be one of the organisms that can be metabolically engineered to produce xylitol by using gene knockout strategy. However, gene knockout strategy required laborious, expensive and time-consuming when conducted *in vivo*. Motivated by this, *in silico* experiment has been done to simulate and manipulate the model of *E. coli* to construct a new *E. coli* model that will focus on producing xylitol by using Flux Balance Analysis (FBA). In this paper, a new hybrid method called DNNDSA is proposed which consists of both Deep Neural Network (DNN) method and Differential Search Algorithm (DSA) to do the predictive analysis on a newly constructed model of *E. coli* to predict which gene knockout condition is the best to be applied in metabolic pathway of *E. coli* to improve the xylitol production.

Keywords: Xylitol · *Escherichia Coli* · Flux Balance Analysis · Deep Neural Network · Differential Search Algorithm

1 Introduction

Recently, a bio-based chemical product such as xylitol has become the spotlight and has caught attention of many researchers due to the advantages offered by xylitol. Xylitol has been highly demanded in food, odontological and pharmaceutical industries. Xylitol has been widely used in sugar free chewing gum as a sugar substitute and it is also has possibility to be used as a sweetener in tonics, syrups and vitamin formulations in the food industries [1]. Besides that, it is widely used in odontological industry due to its anticariogenecity, tooth rehardening and remineralization properties. Moreover, it is also believed that due to its tooth friendly nature, xylitol can prevent the tooth decay problem as well as the ear infection. Xylitol has also been highly recommended to be taken by diabetic patients as it will not increase the blood sugar level and insulin in blood [2]. With these advantages, xylitol has received well recognition and highly demanded from both food and pharmaceutical industries which led

© Springer Nature Singapore Pte Ltd. 2017
M.S. Mohamed Ali et al. (Eds.): AsiaSim 2017, Part II, CCIS 752, pp. 53–67, 2017.
DOI: 10.1007/978-981-10-6502-6_5

researchers to produce more xylitol. This is proven when the market value of xylitol is increasing day by day and is estimated to be around $340 million per year with selling price of $4–5 kg^{-1} [1].

As a result from the highly demanded of xylitol from various industries, researchers put a lot of effort in producing more xylitol within short time. *Escherichia Coli* or widely known as *E. coli* has been one of the microbial host used by researchers to be metabolically engineered to produce xylitol. *E. coli* often used by researchers as a microbial host as well as acts as an ideal organism for industrial production of chemical due to their flexible conditions which are easy to grown, manipulate, culture in laboratory setting and inexpensive growth medium requirements [3]. With these flexible conditions, it has become one of the most suitable organisms to be used for metabolic engineering purpose to produce more xylitol as it is believed that by using metabolic engineering *E. coli* with the mixture of glucose and xylose, *E. coli* can produce xylitol at the high level [3].

One of the strategies often used to simulate and manipulate *E. coli* is by using gene knockout strategy. Gene knockout strategy is the strategy used to investigate effect of each gene in the metabolic pathway of an *E. coli* by deactivates certain genes function to observe their effect. Gene knockout strategy often uses due to the complexity of the metabolic network in an organism which always makes the effect of genetic modification is hard to predict [4]. Gene knockout strategy is a very powerful tool in industry [5] to study the function of a gene in the most effective way and can be relatively easily achieved in most cell types by using either *in vivo* or *in silico* methods. However, using gene knockout strategy in wet lab (*in vivo*) often faces the issues of highly cost and time-consuming. Therefore, *in silico* technique for metabolic engineering has been developed to overcome this problem as it is usually has computing power which has grown exponentially [6].

In accordance to this, advanced computational technologies is required to manipulate and simulate *E. coli* metabolic pathway in order to investigate certain genes functions towards the production of xylitol in *E. coli* and to find the best way to produce more xylitol in *E. coli*. Therefore, advanced computational technology such as Flux Balance Analysis (FBA) can be used as a simulation tool to observe and manipulate the metabolic pathway of *E. coli*. Meanwhile, deep learning method such as Deep Neural Network (DNN) can be used as an analysis tool to predict the production value of xylitol in *E. coli*. Despite the successfulness of DNN, this method still suffers from several limitations that may limit the prediction analysis result. One of the limitations that always occur in DNN is stuck at local minima which may result in lower performance and high computational time [7]. In order to solve these problems, global optimization technique such as Differential Search Algorithm (DSA) can be taken into consideration to help and assist DNN in order to get better prediction result.

The main focus of this paper is to conduct simulation on the *E. coli* metabolic pathway in order to observe function of genes in *E. coli* and manipulate the metabolic pathway of *E. coli* by adding and deleting certain genes (gene knockout strategy) that may led to the high production of xylitol in *E. coli*. DNN also will be used as an analysis tool to predict the best condition of gene knockout strategy that can help *E. coli* to produce xylitol. At the end of this paper, DSA will be implemented in the

DNN in order to get better prediction results as DSA is believed to have capability in overcoming the limitation that still occur in DNN.

2 Related Work

Over these past few years, artificial intelligence methods such as deep learning has been used to solve growing problems in various research field as it offer an efficient and powerful approaches to be used [7]. Besides that, optimization algorithm also has caught attention of many computer scientists to be used to enhance and optimize their experimental results. As the era of rapidly developing technologies take place, modifications of the computational technologies also take place. It is either modified the algorithms or combine (hybrid) the algorithms to overcome the limitations that occurred before.

One of the widely used optimization algorithm is Particle Swarm Optimization (PSO). Although it has achieved remarkable attentions due to its capability to solve diverse global optimization problems, PSO still suffer from the trap in the global optimum problem and required high computational cost to solve high dimensional problems. Motivated by this, Abdullah *et al.* [8] took initiative to modified PSO to overcome these limitations. To improve the local best particles searching in PSO, Abdullah *et al.* has implemented Differential Evolution (DE) mutation and crossover operations. Several analyses have been carried out and compared with the standard PSO and DE methods, and the result shows that the proposed method has the capability to escape local optimum effectively in highly dimensional problems. Not only that, result also shows that the proposed method has relatively fast convergence speed.

In other work, Abdullah *et al.* [9] proposed a new hybrid evolutionary spatial fuzzy clustering method to overcome the partial volume effect in the MRI images. MRI also known as Magnetic Resonance Imagining is a prominent tool to measure substantial changes in cerebrospinal fluid (CSF) flow dynamics, pressure and volume gradient. Unfortunately, MRI often hampered with the presence of partial volume effect in the image which led to this new proposed method by Abdullah *et al.* to solve the problem. They implemented Expectation Maximization (EM) method and improved it by using the evolutionary operations of Genetic Algorithm (GA) to distinguish CSF from the brain tissues. Result that has been validated using MRI image of Alzheimer's disease patient shows that the new proposed method able to filter the CSF regions from brain tissues efficiently compared to standard EM, FCM and SFCM methods.

On the other hand, Ismail *et al.* [10], proposed an *in silico* optimization method to deal with the difficulty of optimization process when steady state and the constraints of the components in the metabolic pathway are involved. The proposed method is a hybrid method called Newton Cooperative Genetic Algorithm (NCGA) which consists of Newton method to deal with the metabolic pathway, Cooperative Co-Evolutionary (CCE) and Genetic Algorithm (GA). Experiment has been carried out using this proposed method and the result shows that NCGA can achieved better result compared to the existing method.

3   Research Method

This research has been conducted according to three main phases which are phase 1 is the simulation process by using flux balance analysis (FBA), phase 2 is the predictive analysis by using DNN method and lastly is the phase 3 which is the optimization phase where better predictive analysis result can be observed. All the processes occur in these three phases has been summarized and visualized as in the Fig. 1 below for better understanding of the flow for this research.

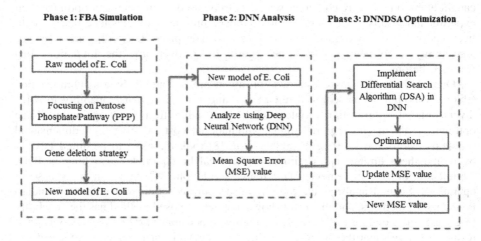

Fig. 1. Flowchart work for this experiment

3.1   Phase 1: Simulation by Using Flux Balance Analysis (FBA)

In this research, experiment has been conducted by using the dataset of *Escherichia Coli* organism with K-12 MG1655 strain version iJO1366 [11] that can be obtained from the system biology website http://systemsbiology.ucsd.edu/InSilicoOrganisms/OtherOrganisms [12]. The dataset provided is in the form of System Biology Markup Language (SBML) file format which required COBRA toolbox in MATLAB to encode the dataset. Once the dataset has been encoded, all the information contains in the dataset will be revealed and all the function of each gene in the metabolic pathway of *E. coli* can be observed and studied in further. As can be seen from the Fig. 1 above, this experiment will be focusing only on Pentose Phosphate Pathway (PPP). PPP will be used as the main pathway in *E. coli* to produce xylitol as it is actually a major route of intermediary carbohydrate metabolism in enteric bacteria as well as it also fulfill various roles in these organisms [13]. Besides that, PPP also plays an important role in breaking down the carbon sources such as glucose and also gluconate. In *E. coli*, there are two main pathways that occurred in PPP which are (i) the oxidative branch where pentose phosphate is formed from glucose 6-phosphate and (ii) a non-oxidative branch where fructose 6-phosphate and glyceraldehyde 3-phosphate are formed.

This experiment will only focus on PPP because the path in which xylitol can be produced in *E. coli* is contained in the PPP. Main strategy that will be used in this experiment is the gene knockout strategy where the genes that involved are phosphoglucose isomerase (pgi) and transketolase (tkt). Both of these genes have been selected to be used in this experiment as it is believed that both of these genes will give effect towards the production of xylitol in *E. coli*. The gene deletion strategy has been done by considering these three conditions which are:

   i. Deletion of pgi and tktA
  ii. Deletion of pgi and tktB
 iii. Deletion of pgi, tktA and tktB

All of these genes have been deleted according to these three conditions to observe their effects towards the production of xylitol in *E. coli*. These genes will be deleted by assuming that once these genes absence all the desired carbon flux will go to the pathway that will produce xylitol only and so that there will be less competitiveness between the pathway to produce xylitol. Besides deleting certain genes, xylitol phosphate dehydrogenase (XPDH) enzyme also has been added in the pathway so that *E. coli* that originally cannot produce xylitol can produce xylitol with the help of XPDH enzyme. XPDH has been found to have the highest selectivity towards D-xylose-5-phosphate and has the ability to convert D-glucose into xylitol at around 23% [14]. By the end of this simulation using FBA stage, new model of *E. coli* has been constructed to be used for the next stage purpose which is the analysis by using DNN.

3.2 Phase 2: Predictive Analysis Using Deep Neural Network (DNN)

Deep neural network (DNN) is one of the examples of deep learning method that will be used in this experiment to analyze and predict the best gene knockout condition. Recently, DNN has shown impressive, state-of-the-art and sometimes human-competitive results in various research fields [15–18]. DNN is a feed-forward, artificial neural network that usually contains more than one hidden layer between its input and output [19]. Typically, logistic function of each hidden layer, h in DNN will be used to map the total input from the layer below, m_h, to the scalar state, n_h that sends to the layer above.

$$n_h = \text{logistic}(m_h) = \frac{1}{1 + e^{-m_h}}, \ m_h = b_h + \sum_i p_i q_{ih} \tag{1}$$

Where b_h is the bias unit for h, i is the index over units in the layer below and q_{ih} is the weight on a connection to the unit h from unit i in the layer below. One of the advantages of DNN is it has flexible condition with a very large number of parameters when it has many units per layer and many hidden layers which make them capable to model the highly nonlinear and complex relationship between inputs and outputs [20]. By the end of this stage, DNN will give the mean square error (MSE) values as an output to predict which gene knockout condition is the best to be applied in *E. coli* metabolic pathway so that the production of xylitol can be boosted up to higher level. MSE usually uses to calculate the error or differences between predicted values and the observed actual values. Therefore, this means that the smallest the MSE value, the better it is, as it actually indicates that the smallest MSE value means the smallest the error is. Figure 2 below visualize how DNN train the input data by using backpropagation algorithm.

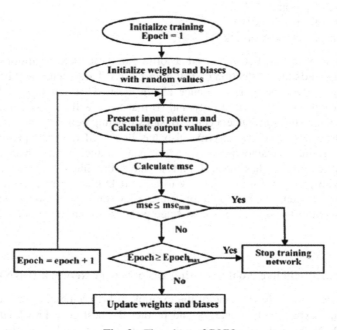

Fig. 2. Flowchart of DNN

One unique characteristic of DNN is that, this method used backpropagation algorithm to train the input data. As shown in Fig. 2 above, the training process take place by initializing the weights and biases with any random values. Then, it will compare the expected output value and actual output value of the data which then will give us the initial MSE value. A solution with the most minimum MSE value will be selected as the initial solution. This training process will be repeated until the new MSE value is smaller than current MSE value or when the epoch has achieved the given epoch at the beginning of the experiment. The main highlight that differentiates between DNN and DNNDSA which is the proposed method in this study is that, DNN only has training process while DNNDSA contain training, optimization and validation processes.

3.3   Phase 3: Optimization by Implementing Differential Search Algorithm (DSA) into DNN

Despite all the successfulness achieved by DNN, it still suffers from several other limitations especially stuck at local minima problem that has haunted artificial intelligence committee for many years. Motivated by this, we proposed a new hybrid method which is the combination of both differential search algorithm (DSA) and DNN into a new hybrid method called DNNDSA. DSA was chosen as it has several advantages which we believed can help DNN to overcome their problems. DSA is the global optimization technique which is good at locating the region of global minima and good at exploring the search space [21]. Moreover, according to [22], global optimization technique is required in order to avoid local minima problem. In accordance to this, DSA can be taken into consideration to help and assist DNN to get better finding result.

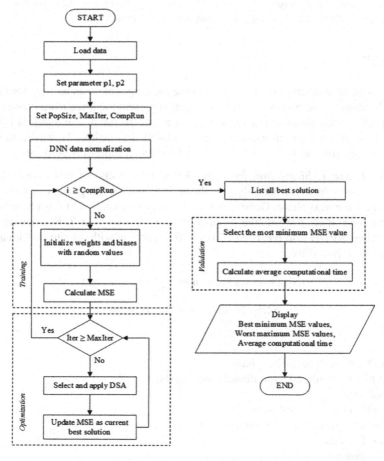

Fig. 3. Flowchart of DNNDSA

Figure 3 above is the flowchart of DNNDSA. It shows how DNNDSA works in this experiment. At the beginning of the experiment, all values for each of the parameters will be initialized. As for the iteration, different values of iteration will be used throughout the experiments which are 50, 100, 150 and 200. As can be seen from Fig. 3 above, there are three main processes will happen in this new method which are training process, optimization process and validation process. In the training process, weight and biases will be initialized with random values. After that, the MSE values will be generated as an initial solution. A solution with the most minimum MSE value will be selected as the initial solution. From here, optimization process will be carried out to search for any possible best solution which in this case to find the most minimum MSE value. If there is any minimum value that found, the new MSE will be saved and updated as current best solution. Otherwise, the initial solution will remain as the current best solution. In the validation process, *k-fold* cross-validation will be used to analyze the best MSE values given. The validation process involved the calculation of standard deviation that will represent the consistency of the algorithm for finding the best solution and the average computational times. By the end of this process, we will get better prediction result of the best gene knockout condition.

4 Result

For this experiment, each of the phases will give the output that can be used for the next phase. Therefore, there will be three main results represent the three main phases which are (i) result for simulation by using FBA, (ii) result for predictive analysis by using DNN and (iii) result for optimization by using DNNDSA method. However, the result for both phases (ii) and (iii) will be combined for the comparison purpose.

Result for Phase 1, Simulation by Using FBA: by the end of this phase, the new model of *E. coli* which consist only glycolysis, PPP and certain genes was constructed to be used for the next phase. Gene knockout strategy was applied in this phase in order to observe their effect towards the production of xylitol in *E. coli*. Besides that, new enzyme called XPDH also has been added in the pathway with an aim that it can help *E. coli* to produce xylitol.

$$\text{xu5p-D} + \text{nadh} + \text{h} \Leftrightarrow \text{xyli5p-D} + \text{nad} \tag{2}$$

$$\text{xyli5p-D} + \text{h2o} \Leftrightarrow \text{xyli-D} + \text{pi} \tag{3}$$

where:

xu5p-D: D-xylulose 5-phosphate
nadh: nicotinamide adenine dinucleotide (reduced)
h: hydrogen
xyli5p-D: D-xylitol 5-phosphate
nad: nicotinamide adenine dinucleotide
xyli-D: D-xylitol
pi: phosphate

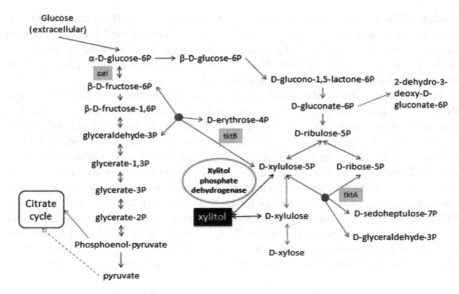

Fig. 4. New model of *E. coli* used in this experiment

Both equations above shows the new reaction that involved in the new pathway model to produce xylitol in *E. coli* after XPDH has been added in the pathway.

After simulation has been done towards the raw model of *E. coli*, the new model of *E. coli* was constructed for this research purpose which only focusing on certain pathways and genes that suitable with the aim of this research and the Fig. 4 above shows the overall pathways, genes and reactions that consist in the new model of *E. coli* that will be used in this research.

Table 1. Predictive analysis result for both DNN and DNNDSA

Gene knockout condition	Iteration	DNN		DNNDSA	
		MSE	Time (s)	MSE	Time (s)
PGITKT*a*	50	1.1066	**0.25876**	**1.0714**	120.8622
	100	1.1118	**0.51379**	**1.0723**	500.5953
	150	1.1226	**0.77896**	**1.0701**	1130.8387
	200	1.0896	**10.0379**	**1.0796**	2020.1287
PGITKT*b*	50	1.0948	**0.25783**	**1.0817**	120.7992
	100	1.2285	**0.52091**	**1.0755**	500.9543
	150	1.1154	**0.76671**	**1.0823**	1140.1544
	200	1.1381	**10.0231**	**1.0807**	2020.5533
PGITKT*a,b*	50	1.0969	**0.25776**	**1.0818**	130.2030
	100	1.1161	**0.50806**	**1.0739**	500.4391
	150	1.0945	**0.77197**	**1.0695**	1110.6470
	200	1.1218	**10.0101**	**1.0807**	2030.9046

Result for Phase 2 and Phase 3, Predictive Analysis by Using DNN and DNNDSA: by the end of these phases, predictive analysis on which best gene knockout condition can be observed by referring to the smallest MSE value for each of the iteration used which are 50, 100, 150 and 200. Not only that, the computational time for both methods also can be observed in the unit second (s).

Table 1 above shows the result of the predictive analysis for both DNN and DNNDSA methods. Three gene knockout conditions have been taken into consideration in this experiment and several iterations which are 50, 100, 150 and 200 will be used to run in each of the gene knockout conditions. It is important to recall that the smallest the MSE value, the better it is, as it is indicates that less error occur. Therefore, from the Table 1 above, we can see that by using DNNDSA method, we can get the smallest MSE values for each gene knockout condition as compared to DNN method. However, the computational time taken for each of the experiment shows that, by using DNN method, the result can be generated faster compared to DNNDSA method. After the overall result was observed from the Table 1 above, the best gene knockout condition can be predicted by calculating the average minimum MSE values for each of the gene knockout conditions used in this experiment by using the formula below:

$$\text{average minimum MSE value} = \frac{\sum (MSE_a)}{\sum (i)} \tag{4}$$

where MSE_a represents the MSE values of iterations that contains in each of the conditions and i indicates the number of iteration that has been used in this experiment.

Table 2. Average minimum MSE value for both DNN and DNNDSA

Gene knockout condition	Average minimum MSE value	
	DNN	DNNDSA
PGITKT*a*	1.10765	**1.07335**
PGITKT*b*	1.14420	1.08005
PGITKT*a,b*	**1.10733**	1.07648

Table 2 above shows the average minimum MSE values for both DNN and DNNDSA methods. The smallest the average of MSE value shows that, it is the best gene knockout condition where the absence of these genes may boost up the xylitol production in *E. coli*. As can be seen from the Table 2 above, both methods has predicted different best gene knockout conditions. DNN has predicted that with an absence of PGI, TKTa and TKTb (PGITKTa,b) from the pathway can help *E. coli* to produce more xylitol with 1.10733 average minimum MSE value. On the other hand, DNNDSA has predicted that with an absence of both PGI and TKTa (PGITKTa) from the pathway can help *E. coli* to produce more xylitol with 1.07335 average minimum MSE value.

DNN is a method where it trains the input data and search the optimal solution by searching at the local minima space only. Therefore, the optimal solution which in this case is the most minimum MSE value that DNN can get is only within the local minima space only and not to forget that DNN always suffer from the stuck at local minima problem. In contrast, DNNDSA is a new hybrid method where it has DSA as an optimization algorithm to search for the other best optimal solution outside from the local minima space which is the global minima space. Therefore, the result given by DNNDSA can be said as close to accurateness as it has the best optimal solution by searching at both local and global minima space. This explains why the results given by both DNN and DNNDSA are different. DNN may stop when it find the best optimal solution at local minima space however DNNDSA method will continue to search the best optimal solution at the global minima space.

To verify either the predicted gene knockout condition by DNNDSA is correct or not, total amount of xylitol that can be produced by each of the gene knockout conditions used in this experiment can be calculated. In this experiment, the total amount of xylitol was given in the concentration unit which is mmol gDW^{-1} h^{-1}, therefore conversion unit need to be done in order to observe the actual xylitol amount that has been produced. The xylitol production unit must be in g/L unit and the results are as follow:

Table 3. The total xylitol production in g/L unit

Gene knockout condition	Xylitol concentration (mmolgDW^{-1} hr^{-1})	Xylitol production (g/L)
PGITKTa	**4.51071428571501**	**8.667793989**
PGITKTb	0.167307692307347	0.321498662
PGITKTa,b	0.274193548387668	0.526890651

As discussed before, DNNDSA has predicted that with the absence of both PGI and TKTa genes from the metabolic pathway of *E. coli* may help *E. coli* to produce more xylitol with the presence of XPDH enzyme. This has been proven right when the highest xylitol production can be produced in *E. coli* when both PGI and TKTa were absent from the pathway with total xylitol production is 8.667793989 g/L as shown in Table 3 above.

5   Discussion

At the beginning of this experiment, simulation and manipulation processes are required in order to construct a new model of *E. coli* to be used in this experiment. The new constructed model of *E. coli* consists of only several pathways which are glycolysis and PPP. Even without glycolysis itself, *E. coli* still can survive with PPP pathway only. This is as stated by [23], where they mentioned that PPP can be used as a bypass pathway which is the pathway that can be used with additional reactions when the typical glycolysis pathway is not available. Main reason on why PPP has been the only focus pathway in this experiment is because the pathway that will produce xylitol in *E. coli* contains in PPP only. As stated by [13, 24], PPP is the only pathway that permits *E. coli* to utilize sugars such as D-ribose, L-arabinose and D-xylose which cannot be catabolized by the other routes. Since the pathway to produce D-xylose was in PPP which is the main pathway that is needed to produce xylitol, therefore PPP has been chosen to be used to construct the new model of *E. coli* in this experiment.

After the new model of *E. coli* has been constructed with several modifications, the predictive analysis by using DNN was conducted in order to predict which gene knockout condition is the best to be applied in the *E. coli* so that it can produce more xylitol. The experiment has been conducted using several iterations which are 50, 100, 150 and 200 in order to measure and observe the consistency of the predicted values for each of the gene knockout conditions. By the end of this process, DNN method has predicted that with an absence of PGI, TKTa and TKTb from *E. coli* metabolic pathway, xylitol can be produced at the high level. In contrast, when experiment has been carried out by using DNNDSA, the predicted best gene knockout condition is when only both PGI and TKTa absent from the *E. coli* metabolic pathway, xylitol can be produced at the high level. However, by the end of this process, when verified with the expected total amount of xylitol that can be produced by *E. coli*, it shows that with an absence of both PGI and TKTa from the metabolic pathway of *E. coli*, xylitol can be produced at the high level with total amount 8.667793989 g/L, the highest amount of xylitol production as compared to the other two gene knockout conditions. This is because, as stated by [25], when there is a disruption of PGI in the pathway, it will likely to increase the flux through PPP, thus all the desired carbon flux can be given to the PPP only. Moreover, when there is no PGI in the pathway, it will also automatically deactivate the glycolysis pathway in which can reduce the competitiveness of carbon flux between glycolysis and PPP. This is as mentioned by [23], where PPP will be maximized once glycolysis pathway is inactivated. As for the case of TKT gene, both TKTa and TKTb genes involved in the non-oxidative part of PPP alongside with other genes called RPI, RPE and TAL. In non-oxidative part, it is more reasonable to divide the non-oxidative part into RPI/RPE and TAL/TKT. For TAL gene, it also consists of TALa and TALb. The division of TAL/TKT genes has been done by pairing TALa/TKTb and TALb/TKTa. In accordance to this, deleting one of these genes from the metabolic pathway of *E. coli* will not affect the cell as *E. coli* still can survive with the remaining genes which in this case if TKTa was deleted from the pathway, *E. coli* still have TALb to support the pathway as well as it still has TKTb to back up the function of deleted TKTa. This is proven when Tan *et al.* [26], used this method to observe the effect towards succinate production in *E. coli*. When either TAL or TKT was deleted from the pathway, the cell still can survive and produce succinate from the pathway. Therefore, it is possible to apply this concept in this experiment as other researchers had already done so.

Despite of the successfulness of DNNDSA to predict the best gene knockout condition, it still lacks in computational time aspect. As can be seen from the result between DNN and DNNDSA, DNN method can give the output within short time period compared to DNNDSA where it takes longer time to give the output. DNNDSA may require longer time compared to DNN because it is a hybrid method which consists both DNN and DSA. Therefore, the complexity of the algorithm is bigger compared to DNN as well as their search space. It requires longer time to complete the searching process in order to find the best optimal solution because it needs to search for the best solution in both local and global minima space. The search space is double wider compared to DNN where DNN only required to find the optimal solution within local minima search space only. This explains why the computational time of DNNDSA is longer compared to DNN method.

6   Conclusion

Gene knockout strategy commonly used to study the effect of certain genes in organisms and traditionally used *in vivo* experimental setup. However, *in vivo* experimental setup commonly suffered from several imperfections which required the computational modeling to be exploited as it has the ability to represent the dynamic behaviors of the biological systems [27]. Therefore, advance computational technologies (*in silico*) are required to elucidate this limitation which led to the experiment in this paper to be carried out.

In this paper, simulation and manipulation have been done towards the metabolic pathway of *E. coli* in order for the *E. coli* to produce xylitol. Gene knockout strategy was implemented in this experiment in order to observe the effect of both PGI and TKT genes towards production of xylitol in *E. coli*. The new constructed model then be analyzed by using DNN method and it will give the prediction result on which gene knockout condition is the best to be applied in *E. coli* so that it can produce more xylitol. However, DNN still suffer from the stuck at local minima problem which required another global optimization technique to overcome this problem. DSA is one of the global optimization techniques that are used in this experiment to help and assist DNN to get better prediction result. By the end of the experiment, the best gene knockout condition has been predicted and total amount of xylitol that can be produced also has been predicted.

However, this new hybrid method called DNNDSA still lacks in term of the computational time. So, it is even better if in the future, there should be many future works that can overcome this limitation so that the computational time taken by DNNDSA can be faster as compared to other methods as it is already can give better prediction result as compared to DNN method.

Acknowledgement. We would like to express our appreciation to Malaysian Genome Institute (MGI) for supporting this project under Research Grant Scheme with Project Code No. FP0813B029(K2).

References

1. Prakasham, R.S., Rao, R.S., Hobbs, P.J.: Current trends in biotechnological production of xylitol and future prospects. Curr. Trends Biotechnol. Pharm. 3(1), 8–36 (2009)
2. Hassinger, W., Sauer, G., Cordes, U., Krause, U., Beyer, J., Baessler, K.H.: The effects of equal caloric amounts of xylitol, sucrose and starch on insulin requirements and blood glucose levels in insulin-dependent diabetics. Diabetologia 21(1), 37–40 (1981)

3. Cirino, P.C., Chin, J.W., Ingram, L.O.: Engineering Escherichia Coli for xylitol production from glucose-xylose mixtures. Biotechnol. Bioeng. **95**(6), 1167–1176 (2006)
4. Wah Tang, P., San Chua, P., Kee Chong, S., Saberi Mohamad, M., Wen Choon, Y., Deris, S., Abdul Rahim, R.: A review of gene knockout strategies for microbial cells. Recent Patents Biotechnol. **9**(3), 176–197 (2015)
5. Langsanam, S., Meechai, A., Cheevadhanarak, S., Bhumiratana, S.: In silicoGene Knockout using a Yeast Metabolic Model. In: The 15th Annual Meeting of the Thai Society of Biotechnology, pp. 1–5 (2204)
6. Khaled, K.F., Amin, M.A.: Dry and wet lab studies for some benzotriazole derivatives as possible corrosion inhibitors for copper in 1.0 M HNO 3. Corros. Sci. **51**(9), 2098–2106 (2009)
7. Yousoff, S.N.M., Baharin, A., Abdullah, A.: A review on optimization algorithm for deep learning method in bioinformatics field. In: 2016 IEEE EMBS Conference on Biomedical Engineering and Sciences (IECBES), pp. 707–711. IEEE, December 2016
8. Abdullah, A., Deris, S., Hashim, S.Z.M., Mohamad, M.S., Arjunan, S.N.V.: An improved local best searching in particle swarm optimization using differential evolution. In: 2011 11th International Conference on Hybrid Intelligent Systems (HIS), pp. 115–120. IEEE, December 2011
9. Abdullah, A., Hirayama, A., Yatsushiro, S., Matsumae, M., Kuroda, K.: Cerebrospinal fluid image segmentation using spatial fuzzy clustering method with improved evolutionary expectation maximization. In: 2013 35th Annual International Conference of the IEEE Engineering in Medicine and Biology Society (EMBC), pp. 3359–3362. IEEE, July 2013
10. Ismail, M.A., Deris, S., Mohamad, M.S., Abdullah, A.: A Newton cooperative genetic algorithm method for in silico optimization of metabolic pathway production. PLoS ONE **10** (5), e0126199 (2015)
11. Orth, J.D., Conrad, T.M., Na, J., Lerman, J.A., Nam, H., Feist, A.M., Palsson, B.Ø.: A comprehensive genome-scale reconstruction of Escherichia coli metabolism—2011. Mol. Syst. Biol. **7**(1), 535 (2011)
12. Feist, A.M., Herrgård, M.J., Thiele, I., Reed, J.L., Palsson, B.Ø.: Reconstruction of biochemical networks in microorganisms. Nat. Rev. Microbiol. **7**(2), 129–143 (2009)
13. Frankel, D.G.: Glycolysis, pentose phosphate pathway, and enter-doudoroff pathway. In: Escherichia Coli and Salmonella Typhimurium-Cellular and Molecular Biology. American Society for Microbiology, Washington, DC (1987)
14. Povelainen, M., Miasnikov, A.N.: Production of xylitol by metabolically engineered strains of Bacillus subtilis. J. Biotechnol. **128**(1), 24–31 (2007)
15. Krizhevsky, A., Sutskever, I., Hinton, G.E.: Imagenet classification with deep convolutional neural networks. In: Advances in Neural Information Processing Systems, pp. 1097–1105 (2012)
16. Dahl, G.E., Yu, D., Deng, L., Acero, A.: Context-dependent pre-trained deep neural networks for large-vocabulary speech recognition. IEEE Trans. Audio Speech Lang. Process. **20**(1), 30–42 (2012)
17. Taigman, Y., Yang, M., Ranzato, M., Wolf, L.: Deepface: closing the gap to human-level performance in face verification. In: 2014 IEEE Conference on Computer Vision and Pattern Recognition (CVPR), pp. 1701–1708 (2014)
18. Le, Q.V., Zou, W.Y., Yeung, S.Y., Ng, A.Y.: Learning hierarchical invariant spatio-temporal features for action recognition with independent subspace analysis. In: 2011 IEEE Conference on Computer Vision and Pattern Recognition (CVPR), pp. 3361–3368 (2011)

19. Hinton, G., Deng, L., Yu, D., Dahl, G.E., Mohamed, A.R., Jaitly, N., Kingsbury, B.: Deep neural networks for acoustic modeling in speech recognition: The shared views of four research groups. IEEE Sig. Process. Mag. **29**(6), 82–97 (2012)
20. Yousoff, S.N.M., Baharin, A., Abdullah, A.: Deep neural network method for the prediction of xylitol production. In: International Conference of Electrical, Electronic, Communication and Control Engineering (ICEECC), March 2017
21. Liu, B.: Composite differential search algorithm. J. Appl. Math. **2014**, 1–15 (2014). Article ID 294703
22. Dai, C., Chen, W., Zhu, Y.: Seeker optimization algorithm for digital IIR filter design. IEEE Trans. Industr. Electron. **57**(5), 1710–1718 (2010)
23. Ishii, N., Nakahigashi, K., Baba, T., Robert, M., Soga, T., Kanai, A., Hirasawa, T., Naba, M., Hirai, K., Hoque, A.: Multiple high-throughput analyses monitor the response of E. coli to perturbations. Science **316**(5824), 593–597 (2007)
24. Lin, E.C.: Dissimilatory pathways for sugars, polyols, and carboxylates. In: Escherichia Coli and Salmonella: Cellular and Molecular Biology, 2nd edn, pp. 307–342. ASM Press, Washington, DC (1996)
25. R Poulsen, B., Nøhr, J., Douthwaite, S., Hansen, L.V., Iversen, J.J., Visser, J., Ruijter, G.J.: Increased NADPH concentration obtained by metabolic engineering of the pentose phosphate pathway in Aspergillus niger. Febs J. **272**(6), 1313–1325 (2005)
26. Tan, Z., Chen, J., Zhang, X.: Systematic engineering of pentose phosphate pathway improves Escherichia Coli succinate production. Biotechnol. Biofuels **9**(1), 262 (2016)
27. Abdullah, A., Deris, S., Mohamad, M.S., Anwar, S.: An improved swarm optimization for parameter estimation and biological model selection. PLoS ONE **8**(4), e61258 (2013)

Xylitol Production of *E. coli* Using Deep Neural Network and Firefly Algorithm

'Amirah Baharin[(⊠)], Siti Noorain Yousoff,
and Afnizanfaizal Abdullah

Synthetic Biology Research Group, Faculty of Computing,
Universiti Teknologi Malaysia, 81310 Johor Bahru, Johor, Malaysia
ami.b2525@gmail.com, ainyousoff@gmail.com,
afnizanfaizal@utm.my

Abstract. The emergence of deep learning as a technique forms a part of artificial intelligence give a huge contribution in machine learning towards the development of powerful tools. Deep learning is potentially being well suited in genomics representations which enable distributed representations' data from multiple processing layers. Practically, deep learning is capable in demonstrating abstraction within the cell in genomic analysis with high predictive power reinforces leads this research. The enhancement of deep neural network in representing genome-scale data into mathematical model allows predictive analysis to be conducted. This work aims to investigate biological process within *E. coli* to explore genomics representation in identifying target microbial production. Furthermore, the use of firefly algorithm prevents it from getting stuck at local optima in finding optimal solution during network training. The outcome of this study contributes in identifying the effects of genetic perturbation towards xylitol production of selective metabolic pathway in metabolic network of *E. coli*.

Keywords: Deep neural network · Firefly algorithm · Metabolic engineering · Gene deletion · Xylitol

1 Introduction

In the past few years, metabolic engineering became major attention to adopt biological information inside cellular microorganisms. Several studies have been conducted to genetically modify cellular metabolism of host organisms in order to produce renewable chemicals and fuels. Xylitol is the main focused in this research to be extracted as it is commercially used in the industry over wide range of applications. The consumption of xylitol in the industrial field can be used as sweetener as well as food additive in food industry and any chewing gums or confectionary [1]. In addition, xylitol usage as sugar substitutes for diabetics [2] are highly benefited as xylitol consist of low glycaemic index and insulin responses. Furthermore, xylitol inhibits the growth of dental caries and promotes oral health [3, 4]. Normally, extractions of target compounds are modified using microbial metabolic system to fulfil the profitable industrial scale production. *In Silico* analysis in metabolic engineering is indispensable in generating testable

© Springer Nature Singapore Pte Ltd. 2017
M.S. Mohamed Ali et al. (Eds.): AsiaSim 2017, Part II, CCIS 752, pp. 68–82, 2017.
DOI: 10.1007/978-981-10-6502-6_6

predictions from the whole-cell computational modelling. This can be achieved through the integration between information of biochemical and biological intuition [5]. Experimental attempts in computational modelling used to guide the genetic modification in cellular metabolism. This analysis is conducted to ensure optimization of microbial strains by maximizing production of obtained chemical interest.

Genome-scale metabolic network models need to undergo metabolic reconstruction to predict the optimal growth, substrate preferences, consequences of gene deletions and yield of adaptive evolution. To date, these predictions can be implemented using constraint-based methods to enforce cellular limitations of biological network. Those limitations include topological, physio-chemical, gene regulatory or environmental constraints [6]. In this study, flux balance analysis is used as the constraint-based method to analyse the behavioral characteristics of *E. coli* towards the genetic perturbation in producing xylitol. Despite of this well-known constraint-based method, the optimal gene knockout hardly to be determined. This is due to the interaction between components, size and complexity of the metabolic network. Furthermore, the arguments arise in wild-type bacterium for such *E. coli* might be invalid when a long-term evolutionary pressure of genetically engineered knockout or any bacterial strains are not being exposed [7].

Thus, integration of deep neural network and firefly algorithm in this study aims to conduct prediction towards implementation of gene deletion in order to obtain high amount of xylitol production in *E. coli*. Due to the advantages of deep neural network in capturing high level of abstraction in cellular genomic for pathway analysis, this can be well adapted to analyse biological network of microorganisms. As well as identifying behavioral characteristics of respected metabolic network. It is a powerful approach to learn complex patterns from a lower level into a higher levels of network architectures. Moreover, multiple levels of information processing can be captured throughout multiple learning layers. Integration of various data types at high layers is permitted due to the modular structure and ability in generating data summarization of low dimensional representations in each layer [8]. Furthermore, in previous work Firefly Algorithm successfully develop accurate biological model. The combination of this method with other optimization algorithm performed in finding reliable parameters to generate valid model output according to experimental data [9]. However, deep neural network is facing difficulties due to overfitting and high tendency in getting stuck at local optima which results to undesirable performance [10]. Thus, firefly algorithm is useful in finding the model that gives best fit for the data. The use of optimization method employs exploration and exploitation in solutions space to be used in obtaining optimal output. The randomization nature allows solution searching from getting stuck at local minima. However, proper parameter adjustment required to obtain a good parameter value and stability between exploration and exploitation.

The rest of this paper organized as follows. Section 1 discuss the contribution of metabolic engineering towards the production of target metabolite in microorganisms. Section 2 provides brief explanation on the main method that are used which are Deep Neural Network and Firefly Algorithm. Meanwhile, Sect. 3 describes the implementation and experimental results. The last part of this paper includes, the conclusion and future works for this research.

2 Presented Methods

In this section mainly discussed about architectural representation of deep neural network and basic preliminaries for the implementation of firefly algorithm. Brief discussion for the newly proposed method of deep neural network firefly algorithm (DNNFA) is provided in this section together with the pseudo code of this method accordingly.

2.1 Deep Neural Network

Functional inspiration of deep neural network (DNN) architecture is adapted via biological cortex which forms hierarchical layer of arrangement interconnected neurons. This architectural representation will undergo transformation from the input received in layer below and propagated into the layer above. DNN forming feedforward architecture as it contains the input and output which are separated by multiple hidden layers. As the input layer is attached with given input sample, other unit inside the hidden layers are then computed the value of the output in each layer in accordance with the activity of the units connected from layer below. This topological concept is proven by full interconnection of input layer towards the first hidden layer, proceed towards the second layer until it reached into the output layer. The main interpretation of deep neural network propagation is depicted as follows;

$$y_k = f(x_k) = \frac{1}{1 + e^{-x_k}}, x_k = b_k + \sum_k y_l w_{lk} \tag{1}$$

where each hidden unit of k, all the input values will be used to map towards scalar state of y_k that passed from the previous layer x_k which is then being fed into the upper layer. This can be achieved by the used of non-linear activation function $f(\cdot)$ to obtain the non-linear hypothesis towards the whole network structure with the right architectural definition. The usage of logistic function as an activation function which in this case using sigmoidal function. In order to compute for such activation function, the input parameter is required with the combination of bias and respective weight. Here, the input of y_l which is passed from the previous layer for the computation of output in hidden layer x_k until the output layer is reached. The addition between of b_k bias of unit k and resultant multiplication between y_k and w_{lk} as the weight that connecting unit k in current layer from unit l from the layer below [11].

Back-propagation is used to train deep neural network using discriminative probabilistic model in order to calculate the discrepancy between actual and target outputs. Back-propagation is used in artificial neural network which applies supervised learning method to train the network. The simplicity and computational efficient of this learning algorithm make it widely used in the neural network field. In order to measure the discrepancy in each training phases, this will require the use of cost function. The cost function that needs to be minimized in this case is the mean squared error. Normally, standard networks are using back-propagation algorithm to compute the gradient for the error function with respect to parameters. This can be obtain by propagating in the backward manner (top to bottom layer in all modules).

$$C = \frac{1}{2T} \sum_{t=1}^{T} ||(f(x_k)^{(t)}) - (y^{(t)})||^2 \qquad (2)$$

Where the cost function C is minimized by given a fixed training set of $\{(x^{(l)}, y^{(l)}), \ldots, (x^{(T)}, y^{(T)})\}$ with training examples, T. In order to increase the network performance, the weight should be minimized after the calculation of the cost function takes place. This can be done by calculating the gradient of the cost function [10]. Afterwards the weights must be appropriately adjusted in obtaining weight optimization. The optimization is implemented by using mini batch stochastic gradient descent algorithm.

$$w_{lk}(s) = \alpha w_{lk}(s-1) + \varepsilon \frac{\partial c}{\partial w_{lk}} \qquad (3)$$

Where ε is the learning rate and the used of momentum coefficient can be further improved the training method by declaring the momentum, α in the range between 0 and 1 for smoothening the gradient of mini-batch, s. The value of weight must always be in the state of one to implement derivation of biases update rule.

2.2 Firefly Algorithm

Firefly algorithm can be classified into metaheuristics algorithm as it used randomization for a better way in providing global search scale. The implementation of metaheuristic algorithm emphasized between intensification and diversification. On one hand, the intensification involved local region searching that will exploit information based on the best current solution which can be found in that region. On the other hand, diversification will result in diverse solutions as the exploration in the search space based on the global scale. These combinations are important in obtaining global optimal solution.

This algorithm is created based on the characteristics of the fireflies itself that produce flashing lights which are then creating a unique pattern of lights between different species. The main function of creating those flashlights for the potential prey to be attracted and serves as communication to attract the partners. At a particular distance, r the light intensity is decreases from the origin of the light source that are inversely proportional to a square distance. Another factor that limit the light intensity is the absorption of light from air becomes weaker due to travels distances aspects. Thus, the formulation of firefly algorithm is directly associated between light intensity and respected objective function to be optimized. Precisely, there are three rules that must be considered in firefly algorithm which are (i) the fireflies are unisex; one will attracted to another fireflies without takes into account of their sex, (ii) attractiveness is directly proportional to the brightness; the movement will take place from less bright towards brighter fireflies and (iii) the landscape involved in objective function is directly affected towards the brightness of fireflies [12]. The whole structure of firefly algorithm is summarized in flowchart based on Fig. 1.

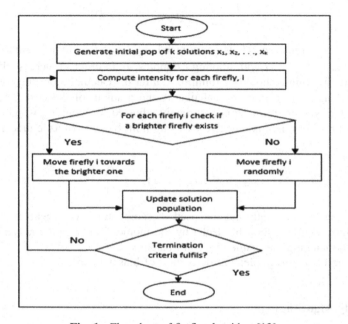

Fig. 1. Flowchart of firefly algorithm [13].

The movement of firefly i towards the brighter firefly j is determined by Eq. 4 below:

$$x_i = x_i + \beta_0 e^{-\gamma r_{i,j}^2}(x_j - x_i) + \alpha(rand - \frac{1}{2}) \tag{4}$$

Where the second term is related to the attraction and the third term referred to randomization parameter of α as the value is uniformly distributed between [0, 1]. Whereas β_0 is the attractiveness at $r = 0$ and its value is always 1. The γ annotation characterized the attractiveness of variations. This value is important in identifying the speed of convergence and behaviour of the algorithm. Practically, the length characteristics Γ will determine $\gamma = O(1)$ for the system to be optimized.

$$r_{ij} = ||x_i - x_j|| = \sqrt{\sum_{k=1}^{d}(x_{i,k} - x_{j,k})^2} \tag{5}$$

Meanwhile, the distance between firefly i and j at x_i and x_j is determined by Cartesian distance as shown Eq. 5 above. The value of $x_{i,k}$ represents k component of x_i spatial coordinate of respected firefly i^{th}. The whole structure of firefly algorithm is summarized in flowchart based on Fig. 2.

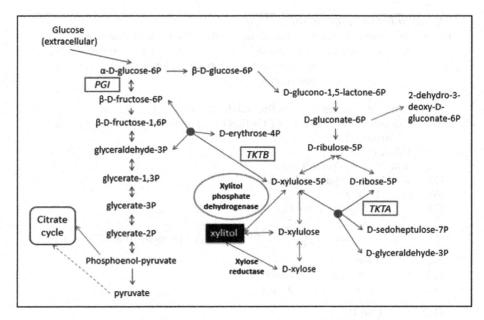

Fig. 2. Schematic representation for the deletion of PGI, TKTA and TKTB.

2.3   Deep Neural Network Firefly Algorithm (DNNFA) Method

The implementation of DNNFA is based on pseudocode is provided in Fig. 3 which combine DNN architecture and meta-heuristics algorithm. The implementation of FA acts as evolutionary of population-based of global optimization algorithm. In terms of DNN, the implementation of backpropagation involved fast local search, but suffer in finding global optimum in a complex search space. The combination in both algorithms is implemented by dividing into 2 parts algorithm 1 and algorithm 2.

At the initial stage, the population of fireflies are randomly generated. Each of the fireflies represents the set of weights involved in DNN. The fitness value of each firefly is calculated based on algorithm 2 as shown in line (1–2). Based on Eq. 2 shows the formulation of fitness to be computed in terms of mean squared error (MSE) value. The output of hidden layer and the network output is computed based on the Eq. 1.

The network training is conducted using backpropagation algorithm with the gradient descent learning during the computation of the fitness takes place. The set of weight is updated by Eq. 3. This weight change is adapted using additional parameters which include learning rate, α and momentum, ε. Learning rate is used to control the step size of the weight changes, whereas the momentum is needed to ensure the accelerations towards the convergence in the error surface. These process is implemented based on algorithm 2 presented in line (23–31).

The searching process is continued by finding other solutions in the population based on the intensity of fireflies is implemented in line (3–16). The steps are repeated until all fireflies in the population are calculated. This can be done by comparing the

---

Algorithm I: Firefly algorithm
Input: Objective function $f(w)$, Population size n, Maximum iteration, m,
Parameter setting : Network architecture, learning rate, momentum rate,
range of distance between solutions λ, crossover α and
mutation β.
Begin:
(1)   Initialize population of fireflies randomly, w_1, $i = \{1,2,3,...n\}$
(2)   Calculate light intensity I of fireflies based on the objective function in
        Algorithm 2
(3)   **While** ($t = 1 < m$)
(4)   **For** $i = 1{:}n$ (all n solutions)
(5)   **For** $j = n$ (all n solutions)
(6)   **If** $I_i < I_i$
(7)   Move firefly i to j
(8) $$w_i = w_i + \beta_0 e^{-\gamma r^2 \beta(y)}(w_i - w_j) + \alpha(rand - 0.5)$$
(9)   **Else**
(10)   Move w_1 randomly
(11) $$w_i = w_i + \alpha(rand - 0.5)$$
(12)   **End If**
(13)   Evaluate new fireflies in $f(w_i)$ using **Algorithm 2**
(14)   Update new $f(w_i)$
(15)   **End For** j
(16)   **End For** i
(17) $m = m+1$
(18)   List $f(w_i)$ per population
(19)   Select $f(w_i)$ from the whole populations
(20)   List all $[f(w_i)]^t$
(21)   **If** stopping condition is met, go to **step 22**
(22)   **Else** go to **step 3**
(23)   **End While**
        Output: $[f(w_i)]^m$
        End Begin

Algorithm 2: Deep neural network
Training using the fitness function
(24)   **For** $k = 1{:}\, l$, where l is length of data
(25)   Calculate the output of hidden layer
(26)   Calculate the network output
(27)   **End For**
(28)   Compute the mean squared error (MSE)
(29)   Weight change in back-propagation algorithm
(30)   **If** maximum epoch reach and training error is satisfied, go to **step 32**
(31)   **Else** repeat **step 24-30**
(32)   **End**

Fig. 3. Pseudo-code of DNNFA

fitness value of each firefly in the search space. In this situation, less bright firefly will change its position if there is a presence of best firefly with high score. In other words, if firefly *j* has lower MSE than firefly *i*, move firefly *i* towards firefly *j* as shown in line (8). The current best solution is updated saved as depicted in line (11). Top score is selected based on the lists of best solution is generated in overall iterations as the final output. The best firefly can be considered with the lowest MSE as the global best solutions.

3 Related Works

In this section elaborates about previous works which implementing optimization method, quantitative analysis and graph partitioning to improve the prediction of complex pattern and clustering process regarding for the extraction of biological information. For the prediction purpose, computational systems biology facing great attention that will lead to biochemical production in metabolic pathway of cell. Metabolic pathway can be known as nonlinear equation system as it can be described as a mathematical model. Thus, in silico optimization method is implemented to overcome this situation [14]. The combinatorial optimization approach is applied in several studies in finding optimal solutions from finite set of objects. Several approaches have been proposed that contain several sets of hybridizations of optimization algorithms. There are Newton Cooperative Genetic Algorithm (NCGA; newton methods and cooperative genetic algorithm) [14], LEPSO (particle swarm optimization and differential evaluations) [15], and S-CRO (swarm-based chemical reaction optimization; firefly algorithm and CRO) [16]. These methods required fine-tuning of parameters in order to perform robust searching capability. The NCGA enhance metabolic pathway prediction, minimize the concentration of total components involved [14]. Meanwhile LEPSO improved the resultant accuracy, the exploitation of neighborhood solution is increases and effectively escape from local optima in high dimensionality [15]. Whereas, in S-CRO parameter estimation is improved, better fitness values are consistently found, able to select appropriate model and estimates reliable parameters in experimental data [16].

4 Results

To address the effectiveness of the proposed method, genome-scale metabolic model of *E. coli* was used to predict the effect of genetic perturbation for such gene deletion towards the production of xylitol. The utilization of *E. coli* genome-scale metabolic model K-12 MG1655 which form stoichiometric matrix [17] is used to define the capabilities and system characteristics of *E. coli* metabolism. First of all, the whole metabolic network of this model should be interpreted with respect to selective pathways involved and corresponding enzymatic reaction in producing xylitol. Flux balance analysis is the constraint based-method which allows the representation of the whole metabolic network is defined into mathematical form. The results obtained from this simulation will be used as a benchmark for the training process involved in

DNNFA. In this section, the whole process in conducting this experimental analysis, dataset and parameter setting are briefly discussed to generate analytical results for this experiment.

4.1 Experimental Setup

In this phase, the procedure starts with analysing related components such as pathway and genes that contribute to xylitol production and growth in *E. coli* in great details. Based on the existing pathway metabolic model, important reactions are added into the model to produce xylitol with the use of enzymatic reactions in xylose reductase (XR) [3] and xylitol phosphate dehydrogenase (XPDH) [1]. Several nutritional consumptions are tested by using glucose, glycerol and xylose as carbon sources. Furthermore, several sets of gene deletion have been implemented using FBA to identify the effects towards xylitol production and respected growth rate. Thus, the results generated from gene deletion analysis by using FBA will produce several sets of pathways in matrix representation. In which several set of new models based on new pathways are generated from gene deletion process.

In total, only 3 sets of genes have been chosen to be deleted as it produced the highest production of xylitol. The genes involved are *PGI*, *TKTA* and *TKTB* are deleted from the model. The deletion process is implemented based on the gene list which contributed only in the pentose-phosphate pathway. This is due to the existence of biochemical reaction for the xylitol conversion exists in this pathway. Thus, these sets of gene deletions may increase the flux into the pentose-phosphate pathway in producing high amount of xylitol. Figure 3 shows a parts of metabolic pathway involved for the biochemical conversion of xylitol in pentose-phosphate pathway with corresponding sets of gene deletion.

The results generated from FBA consist of respected values represents the xylitol production rate and also the growth rate for each deleted gene model. In this case, several combination of genes has been deleted from *E. coli* model simultaneously. The training process of the proposed method is conducted by creating a lookup-table of xylitol production rate and the growth rate separately. These tables are generated based on the conditional value for each constraints added into the *E. coli* model which acted as carbon sources to produce target metabolites. In the final stage, comparative analysis and evaluation of the results have been implemented. The performance of the proposed method is compared with deep neural network. The performance measurement are calculated based on the best solution (MSE), mean, standard deviation of best solution. Figure 2 shows the overall flow for the implementation of experimental procedure.

4.2 Parameter Setting

Experimental analysis was carried out using three types of *E. coli* model which are the deletion of (i) *PGITKTA*, (ii) *PGITKTB* and (iii) *PGITKTATKTB*. This training data is to compute the prediction towards production of xylitol and its growth rate respectively. In order to evaluate the effectiveness of DNNFA, the model is trained with varying iterations. More specifically, the network training set up into 250 and 500 iterations. All of these iterations are conducted under 10 differential run. Several parameters are initialized before the training process is conducted. The parameters used are (i) alpha, $\alpha = 0.5$, (ii) beta, $\beta = 0.95$, (iii) gamma, $\lambda = 50$, (iv) momentum = 0.8 and (v) number of hidden layer = 4. Performance evaluation of DNNFA is based on the quality of resultant solutions and its consistency in finding solutions per independent run. Furthermore, this analysis is conducted by varying the value of learning rate in order to find solutions. The values of learning rate are 0.7, 1.7 and 2.7 respectively.

4.3   Xylitol Production and Growth Rate

Several set of deleted gene models has been set up in a lookup table as the input for the proposed method. The results will analyse which set of deleted genes that give the outmost production of xylitol. Tables 1, 2, 3 and 4 shows the results in term of MSE to measure the effectiveness of DNNFA and compared with DNN method with maximum number of iterations 250 and 500 accordingly.

Based on Table 1, DNNFA performs better compared to DNN in terms of best score, mean and standard deviation for MSE. This will proved the ability of DNNFA in avoiding from getting tuck at local minima in the analysis of xylitol production itself. DNNFA shows the effectiveness at learning rate 2.7 for all input model (*PGITKTA, PGITKTB, PGITKTATKTB*) since the best, mean and standard deviation having the

Table 1. Comparison performance between DNNFA and DNN for the prediction of gene deletion to increase xylitol production with learning rate 0.7, 1.7 and 1.7 in 250

Gene deletion	Learning rate	DNNFA			DNN		
		Best score	Mean	Std. dev	Best score	Mean	Std. dev
PGITKTA	0.7	0.03477	0.04007	0.00524	0.12846	0.16703	0.02694
	1.7	0.01161	0.01704	0.00503	0.10038	0.16493	0.03503
	2.7	0.00785	**0.01017**	0.00247	0.13504	0.17654	0.03576
PGITKTB	0.7	0.02989	0.03862	0.00573	0.06127	0.10536	0.02259
	1.7	0.01168	0.01649	0.00548	0.05878	0.10701	0.03632
	2.7	0.00532	**0.01063**	0.00324	0.05820	0.09874	0.02869
PGITKTATKTB	0.7	0.04159	0.05285	0.00849	0.14607	0.19969	0.03020
	1.7	0.01536	0.02475	0.00567	0.13991	0.19725	0.04082
	2.7	0.00731	**0.01895**	0.00672	0.14486	0.21615	0.03604

lowest score of MSE. However, the outmost score with the lowest average MSE is at the deletion of PGI and TKTA respectively with the score 0.01017. Further investigation has been implemented to analyze xylitol production towards the changes of iteration run with respected learning rate.

The results shown in Table 2 shows in all of the criteria, DNNFA proved that the use give the outmost results in terms of best score, mean and standard deviation of

Table 2. Comparison performance between DNNFA and DNN for the prediction of gene deletion to increase xylitol production with learning rate 0.7, 1.7 and 1.7 in 500 iteration.

Gene deletion	Learning rate	DNNFA			DNN		
		Best score	Mean	Std. dev	Best score	Mean	Std. dev
PGITKTA	0.7	0.01506	0.01725	0.00196	0.04651	0.13288	0.04998
	1.7	0.00381	0.00677	0.00216	0.06993	0.09735	0.02085
	2.7	0.00249	**0.00529**	0.00223	0.11321	0.18016	0.04934
PGITKTB	0.7	0.01275	0.01682	0.00284	0.06003	0.07769	0.01426
	1.7	0.00344	0.00633	0.00246	0.03982	0.06684	0.01924
	2.7	0.00223	**0.00451**	0.00380	0.03864	0.07901	0.02599
PGITKTATKTB	0.7	0.01453	0.01971	0.00337	0.12099	0.16073	0.02049
	1.7	0.00478	0.01043	0.00406	0.14472	0.18327	0.03333
	2.7	0.00354	**0.00817**	0.00585	0.1377	0.20371	0.05993

Table 3. Comparison performance between DNNFA and DNN for the prediction of gene deletion with respect to growth rate at learning rate 0.7, 1.7 and 1.7 in 250 iteration.

Gene deletion	Learning rate	DNNFA			DNN		
		Best score	Mean	Std. dev	Best score	Mean	Std. dev
PGITKTA	0.7	0.11208	0.13746	0.01081	0.21458	0.22435	0.00757
	1.7	0.12728	0.13536	0.00690	0.21001	0.22417	0.01140
	2.7	0.11527	**0.12992**	0.00672	0.20164	0.23555	0.02906
PGITKTB	0.7	0.09507	**0.12244**	0.01570	0.19887	0.21735	0.01278
	1.7	0.09864	0.13451	0.01461	0.18726	0.22513	0.01910
	2.7	0.12948	0.13833	0.00520	0.20763	0.23131	0.01653
PGITKTATKTB	0.7	0.03420	0.04513	0.00553	0.13085	0.16865	0.03204
	1.7	0.01376	0.02214	0.00656	0.11240	0.15492	0.03832
	2.7	0.00740	**0.01565**	0.00557	0.09999	0.17328	0.05121

MSE over DNN. DNNFA shows the ability in avoiding the local minima in predicting the xylitol production. Furthermore, at the learning rate 2.7, for all input model shows a great advantage by having the lowest mean for MSE. The deletion of PGI and TKTA is the chosen model for having the outmost score compared to the other gene deletion model correspondingly with 0.00451. Previously, for the iteration of 250, the deletion of *PGI* and *TKTA* is selected which having the score 0.01017. However, in overall cases the deletion of *PGI* and *TKTB* is the chosen genes to be the most optimal gene to be deleted since it shows the lowest mean value. This will prove the results obtained from the FBA previously which analyze xylitol production for respected gene deletion model with 5.66, 7.50, and 4 (mmol/gDW/hr) for *PGITKTA*, *PGITKTB* and *PGITKTATKTB*.

On the other hand, the ability of *E. coli* to survive should be preserved by linearly examined the value of the growth rates apart from predicting the xylitol production

Table 4. Comparison performance between DNNFA and DNN for the prediction of gene deletion with respect to growth rate at learning rate 0.7, 1.7 and 1.7 in 500 iteration.

Gene deletion	Learning rate	DNNFA			DNN		
		Best score	Mean	Std. dev	Best score	Mean	Std. dev
PGITKTA	0.7	0.07928	**0.095768**	0.01465	0.21289	0.22378	0.00722
	1.7	0.11043	0.12366	0.00693	0.21882	0.22858	0.00940
	2.7	0.11271	0.12490	0.00721	0.20709	0.23535	0.02759
PGITKTB	0.7	0.06418	**0.07671**	0.00900	0.19163	0.21369	0.01485
	1.7	0.09004	0.12738	0.01410	0.18977	0.2108	0.01403
	2.7	0.11528	0.13244	0.00781	0.18977	0.2108	0.01403
PGITKTATKTB	0.7	0.01642	0.02323	0.00451	0.09838	0.13454	0.02349
	1.7	0.00559	0.01154	0.00387	0.07969	0.14172	0.03912
	2.7	0.00323	**0.00806**	0.00480	0.06946	0.12703	0.03739

itself. This is to ensure in each sets of gene deletions, the cell can survive by carefully analysed the growth rate of the cell from getting dead. Furthermore, the consumptions for each carbon sources are added into the model in previous steps to boost up the production of xylitol and also for the growth of the cell. The value of the growth rate is analysed using the proposed methods DNNFA and compared with MSE value generated using DNN. Tables 3 and 4 shows the results obtain with respect to the growth rate in 250 and 500 iteration to run.

Table 4 DNNFA shows the results of the best performance in terms of the best score, mean and standard deviation of MSE over 250 independent runs. These results will ensure that DNNFA is used to avoid local minima in predicting the growth rate of *E. coli* towards the deletion of selective genes. For the best results, the deletion of *PGI*, *TKTA* and *TKTB* gene model is highly selected because of the lowest mean by 0.01565 MSE. Meanwhile, the mean value for the deletion of *PGIT* and *TKTA* is at the worst which having the high MSE for respected mean value of 0.12992. As far as learning rate is concerned, 2.7 is considered as the best learning rate since the results generated in *PGITKTATKTB* model has better results in terms of best score, mean and standard deviation for MSE. Further investigation has been implemented to analyze the prediction of growth rate with the changes of iteration run of 500 on the difference learning rate.

The results shown in Table 4 proved the ability of DNNFA in producing better results in terms of the best score, mean and standard deviation of MSE. This will prove the ability of DNNFA in avoiding getting tuck at local minima for the analyzation of the growth rate over DNN. For all deleted gene models, the results shows that the deletion of *PGI*, *TKTA* and *TKTB* gives the outmost value of growth rate as the MSE obtained is 0.00806 in terms of mean value. In this case, the worst MSE for mean value is at the deletion of *PGI* and *TKTA* with 0.095768. Furthermore, at the learning rate 2.7 can be considered as the best learning rate since the value of the best score, mean and standard deviation of MSE is at the lowest in the *PGITKTATKTB* gene deletion model as compared to the results obtained in other deletion models. Thus, based on this two test case using 250 and 500 independent run, the deletion of *PGI*, *TKTA*, and *TKTB* genes are the chosen genes to maintain the cell growth towards the deletion of selective genes. Previously, the analysis is conducted using FBA where the value of growth rate is carefully analyzed in producing excessive amount of xylitol in *E. coli* model. The chances of survival for *E. coli* are quite low since the values of growth rate are 3.48166E-29, 1.98068E-26 and 3.961359E-12 (1/hr) for PGITKTA, PGITKTB and PGITKTATKTB gene deletion models.

4.4   Discussion

Based on the two cases conducted which include the prediction of xylitol production and the growth rate in *E. coli* models are analyzed using DNNFA. The results are compared with DNN in order to investigate the effectiveness of the proposed method. In both of the cases, it can be said that at learning rate 2.7 is considered as the best learning rate in order to have the best scoring value. There are particular reasons on this behavioural characteristic due to the minimum point is situated in a long distance away. Thus, the increase of step size is required to allow the searching process to move faster and significantly speed up the learning. Furthermore, the existence in abundance of high error with low curvature saddle point in deep network, required high learning rate in order to escape from this situation. Such saddle point may consist of high number of plateaus will result to a slow learning process [18]. Usually in stochastic gradient descent for backpropagation, it follows down low curvature with small eigenvalue that causing small learning step and result in slow learning. However, in terms of computational time, DNNFA is required high computational time for the network training.

The deletion of PGI and TKTB is the most preferable to boost the excretion of xylitol as the results shown the lowest MSE in terms of xylitol production. The deleted genes unable to maintain the cell growth since mainly due to the flux is directed into pentose-phosphate pathway only since the absence of competitive pathway such glycolysis is avoided. This will increased the expression of XPDH to produce xylitol via biochemical conversion of D-xylulose-5-phosphate into xylitol. However, PGITKTB model shows the second best result in maintaining the cell growth compared to the PGITKTA model. Whereas, even though the deletion of PGI, TKTA and TKTB is considered as the best combination in providing the highest growth, however this model unable to produce high amount of xylitol itself. This factor is due to the released of pentose sugars for such D-ribose, D-ribulose and D-xylulose. The released of these sugars allow *E. coli* to use any available carbon sources to sustain for growth.

Overall, DNNFA provides great advantage towards the prediction of xylitol production and the growth rate in *E. coli* model by combining DNN and firefly algorithm for network training. Here, network formed from training data sets to develop DNN are collected from linear-programming problem related to steady-state metabolic modelling of FBA for the behaviour of *E. coli*. Whereas, meta-heuristic algorithm performed optimization by conducting search strategies based on the iteration concept. Each iteration will be heuristically modified in order to find a high quality of solution [19]. This will help DNN to improve the performance involved during the training process in finding optimal solutions. Furthermore, firefly algorithm offers a great opportunity during the search process to balance between exploration and exploitation. In fact, the behaviour of fireflies towards the finding of better and brighter firefly allow the value of best fitness function to be obtained inside deep neural network. This can be done by parameter tunings to learn good parameter values. Too much exploration in finding global optimality may decreased the rate of convergence.

5 Conclusion

The simulation of the results indicate 2.7 is the best learning rate value for the production of xylitol and growth rate with the lowest mean value of training MSE 0.00817 and 0.00806 respectively. Performance of DNNFA is analyzed in terms of best score, mean and standard deviation of MSE which are outperformed as compared to results of DNN. Furthermore, DNNFA managed to identify the selective gene list to increase the production of xylitol as well as maintaining the growth of the cell. In this case, the deletion of PGI and TKTB genes fulfill the criteria in both of the cases. For the future works, several criteria should be considered in order to improve the performance of proposed method. Firstly, adaptive learning rate should be implemented as this research is currently using constant learning rate which required manual curation. Secondly, the time complexity of DNNFA is highly complex due to the requirement of selective number of hidden neurons and the dual loop usage in firefly algorithm. Thus, the outer loop of firefly algorithm should be reduced [20] and optimal numbers of hidden neurons need to be identified accordingly.

Acknowledgments. This project was supported by Malaysian Ministry of Higher Education (MOHE), managed by University Technology Malaysia Research Management Centre (RMC) under Fundamental Research Grant Scheme (FRGS) vote number R.J130000.78 28.4F481.

References

1. Povelainen, M., Miasnikov, A.N.: Production of xylitol by metabolically engineered strains of bacillus subtilis. J. Biotechnol. **128**(1), 24–31 (2007)
2. Pepper, T.: Xylitol in sugar-free confections. Food Technol. **10**, 98–106 (1988)
3. Cirino, P.C., Chin, J.W., Ingram, L.O.: Engineering escherichia coli for xylitol production from glucose-xylose mixtures. Biotechnol. Bioeng. **95**(6), 1167–1176 (2006)
4. Emodi, A.: Xylitol: its properties and food applications. Food Technol. **32**, 20–32 (1978)
5. Kim, J.H., Han, K.C., Koh, Y.H., Ryu, Y.W., Seo, J.H.: Optimization of fed-batch fermentation for xylitol production by candida tropicalis. J. Ind. Microbiol. Biotechnol. **29**(1), 16–19 (2002)
6. Kauffman, K.J., Prakash, P., Edwards, J.S.: Advances in flux balance analysis. Curr. Opin. Biotechnol. **14**(5), 491–496 (2003)
7. Segre, D., Vitkup, D., Church, G.M.: Analysis of optimality in natural and perturbed metabolic networks. Proc. Nat. Acad. Sci. **99**(23), 15112–15117 (2002)
8. Park, Y., Kellis, M.: Deep learning for regulatory genomics. Nat. Biotechnol. **33**(8), 825–826 (2015)

9. Abdullah, A., Deris, S., Mohamad, M.S., Anwar, S.: An improved swarm optimization for parameter estimation and biological model selection. PLoS ONE **8**(4), e61258 (2013)
10. Tirumala, S.S.: Implementation of evolutionary algorithms for deep architectures. In: AIC, pp. 164–171 (2014)
11. Qian, Y., Fan, Y., Hu, W., Soong, F.K.: On the training aspects of deep neural network (DNN) for parametric TTS synthesis. In: 2014 IEEE International Conference on Acoustics, Speech and Signal Processing (ICASSP), 4 May 2014, pp. 3829–3833. IEEE (2014)
12. Yang, X.-S.: Firefly algorithms for multimodal optimization. In: Watanabe, O., Zeugmann, T. (eds.) SAGA 2009. LNCS, vol. 5792, pp. 169–178. Springer, Heidelberg (2009). doi:10. 1007/978-3-642-04944-6_14
13. Tilahun, S.L., Ong, H.C.: Vector optimisation using fuzzy preference in evolutionary strategy based firefly algorithm. Int. J. Oper. Res. **6**(1), 81–95 (2013)
14. Ismail, M.A., Deris, S., Mohamad, M.S., Abdullah, A.: A newton cooperative genetic algorithm method for in silico optimization of metabolic pathway production. PLoS ONE **10** (5), e0126199 (2015)
15. Abdullah, A., Deris, S., Hashim, S.Z., Mohamad, M.S., Arjunan, S.N.: An improved local best searching in particle swarm optimization using differential evolution. In: 2011 11th International Conference on Hybrid Intelligent Systems (HIS), 5 December 2011, pp. 115–120. IEEE (2011)
16. Abdullah, A., Deris, S., Mohamad, M.S., Anwar, S.: An improved swarm optimization for parameter estimation and biological model selection. PLoS ONE **8**(4), e61258 (2013)
17. Orth, J.D., Conrad, T.M., Na, J., Lerman, J.A., Nam, H., Feist, A.M., Palsson, B.Ø.: A comprehensive genome-scale reconstruction of escherichia coli metabolism. Mol. Syst. Biolo. **7**(1), 535 (2011)
18. Singh, B., De, S., Zhang, Y., Goldstein, T., Taylor, G.: Layer-specific adaptive learning rates for deep networks. In: 2015 IEEE 14th International Conference on Machine Learning and Applications (ICMLA), pp. 364–368. IEEE (2015)
19. Fister, I., Yang, X.S., Brest, J.: A comprehensive review of firefly algorithms. Swarm Evol. Comput. **13**, 34–46 (2013)
20. Kalpana, G., Amalarethinam, D.G.: Algorithm for managing uncertainty in job and data aware scheduling in grid computing. Int. J. Appl. Eng. Res. **10**, 82 (2015)

A Review of Deep Learning Architectures and Their Application

Jalilah Arijah Mohd Kamarudin[1(✉)], Afnizanfaizal Abdullah[1],
and Roselina Sallehuddin[2]

[1] Synthetic Biology Research Group, Faculty of Computing,
Universiti Teknologi Malaysia, 81310 Johor Bharu, Johor, Malaysia
jalilaharijah@gmail.com, afnizanfaizal@utm.my
[2] Soft Computing Research Group, Faculty of Computing,
Universiti Teknologi Malaysia, 81310 Johor Bharu, Johor, Malaysia
roselina@utm.my

Abstract. Deep Learning is a new era of machine learning research that are making major advances in solving problem with powerful computational models. Currently, this new machine learning method is widely used in object detection, visual object and speech recognition and also for making prediction of regulatory genomic and cellular imaging. Here, we review the methodology and applications of deep learning architectures including deep neural network, convolutional neural network and recurrent neural network. Next, we review several existing prediction tools in genomic sequences analysis that use deep learning architectures. In addition, we discuss the future research directions of deep learning.

Keywords: Machine learning · Deep learning · Deep neural network · Convolutional neural network · Recurrent neural network

1 Introduction

Machine learning has been widely used to extract knowledge from big data. Training data in machine learning algorithm is used for constructing models, uncovering underlying pattern and make predictions. Support vector machine (SVM), Bayesian networks, Gaussian network, hidden Markov models and others machine learning algorithms have been applied in various fields [1]. The performance of machine learning algorithms is depending on data representation known as features [2]. Typically, features are designed by human engineers and to identify the most suitable features for given task still remains difficult.

However, one of machine learning algorithm's type called as deep learning is use an representation learning to identify effective features for given tasks. The important aspect of deep learning is compatibility of the features however it learns from data themselves. Thus, deep learning integrates the simple features that learned from data in order to learn complex features. Deep learning also use artificial neural network of several non-linear layers. Besides, deep learning able to learn and identify hierarchical representations of data with higher level of abstraction [1].

© Springer Nature Singapore Pte Ltd. 2017
M.S. Mohamed Ali et al. (Eds.): AsiaSim 2017, Part II, CCIS 752, pp. 83–94, 2017.
DOI: 10.1007/978-981-10-6502-6_7

Deep learning has clear potential to make analysis in high-dimensional data by training complex networks with various layers that represent their internal structure. This new big terns in machine learning is making major improvement especially in object detection, visual object recognition, speech recognition, drug discovery and other area such as genomics.

Meantime, in bioinformatics field, the rapid growth of research in this area since early 2000s and solving problems in others field for many years. There are some cases in bioinformatics where researcher use evolutionary algorithm and optimization method in different area such as medical image clustering and analysis [3, 4], and biological network inference and selection [5, 6]. The best attempt of deep learning has been made in image and speech recognition [7–13], natural language processing [14, 15] and language translation [16].

2 Deep Learning Architecture

Deep learning consists of several types of architectures such as deep neural network (DNN), convolutional neural network (CNN) and recurrent neural network (RNN). These three architectures are used based on characteristic of input data and research objective.

DNNs are architectures that refer to multilayer perceptron (MLP) [17], stacked-auto-encoder (SAE) [18] and deep belief networks (DBNs) [19, 20] that use auto-encoders (AEs) [18], perceptrons [21] and restricted Boltzmann machines (RBMs) [22, 23] as building blocks of neural networks. CNNs is consists of convolutional layers, pooling layers and non-linear layers and it is particularly successive in image recognition. Meanwhile, RNNs are developed with cyclic connection with building blocks such as perceptrons, gated recurrent units (GRUs) [24] and long short-term memory units (LSTMs) [25, 26] to use sequential information from input data.

2.1 Deep Neural Network (DNN)

Deep Neural Network (DNN) is ideally inspired by neural networks in the brain [27–29] contains of several layers of interconnected compute unit or called as neurons. Neural network's depth is corresponding to the number of hidden layers and the width to the maximum number of neurons in one of its layers. Deep neural network is classified as deep network because of its capability to train network using higher number of hidden layers.

In DNN the first stage is input layer of the network receives the data. Next, data then transformed into non-linear by multiple hidden layers then final outputs are calculated in the output layer. All the neurons of the previous layer are connected with neurons in hidden and output layer. A weighted sum and output f(x) of inputs for each neuron are calculated. The output is calculated using selected non-linear activation function which is rectified linear unit (ReLU) [13]. ReLU threshold negative signal to zero then pass over positive signal that triggered faster learning. Regarding to the types

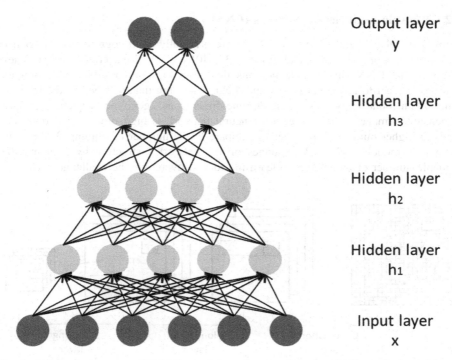

Output layer
y

Hidden layer
h3

Hidden layer
h2

Hidden layer
h1

Input layer
x

Fig. 1. The basic structure of DNN that contains of input unit x, three hidden units in each layer including h_1, h2, h_3 and output units y [30]. The weighted sum and non-linear function of its inputs at each layer are calculated as a result, the hierarchical representations can be achieved.

of layer used in Deep Neural Network and the corresponding learning method, it can be categorized as DBN, MLP and SAE (Fig. 1).

Since DNN has been widely applied in computational biology application specifically in analysis of regular genomics and cellular imaging, Heffernan *et al.* [31] using SAE in prediction of secondary structure, torsion angle and accessible surface area in protein amino acid sequences. Another example of DNN application is applies MLP in microarray and RNA-seq based gene expression data by Chen *et al.* [32] to detect subtle non-canonical splicing signals. But, different with Fakoor *et al.* [33] that applies SAE in classification of several cancers such as acute myeloid leukemia, breast cancer and ovarian cancer.

Deep neural network has been applied in several areas in biomedical imaging such as brain decoding [34, 35], segmentation [36] and recognition [37]. Plis *et al.* [38] using DBN on brain MRIs to classify schizophrenia patients while, Xu and his group [37] are using SAE for histopathology images in cell nuclei detection.

2.2   Convolutional Neural Network (CNN)

Convolutional Neural Network or CNN were originally from cognitive neuroscience and seminal work of Hubel and Wiesel [39, 40] on the visual cortex of cat. They discover that CNN have simple neurons that react to small motifs while complex neurons is react to large motifs in visual field. The input data of CNN in the form of multidimensional arrays for example one-dimensional genomic sequence or two dimensional images. The challenge of neural network is high dimensional data that leads to higher number of parameters compare to the number of training data that fit them in a model. CNN make changes on the network's structure by reducing the valuable number of parameters to learn in order to overcome the challenge (Fig. 2).

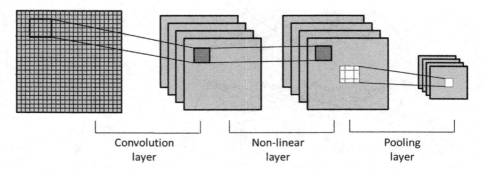

| Convolution | Non-linear | Pooling |
| layer | layer | layer |

Fig. 2. Basic structure of CNN that consists of convolutional layer, non-linear layer and pooling layer.

A convolutional layer in CNN composes of various maps of neurons known as feature maps or filters [41]. The size of feature maps is equivalent with the dimension of the input image. To reduce the number of model parameters CNN use concept of parameter sharing and local connectivity. In these concepts, each neuron in feature maps is only connected with local patch of neurons in the previous layer or receptive field. Next, all neurons in feature map share the same parameters and scan for the same feature in previous layer but at different locations. The weighted sum of input neurons and activation function is computing using discrete convolution to obtain the activity of neuron [20].

Usually, the frequency and exact position of features is irrelevant for final prediction for example, to identify objects in an image. By that, pooling layer summarizes adjacent neurons by calculating the average or maximum of their activities for representation of features activities. This pooling operation effectively enables to reduce the number of model parameters and down-sampled the input image. Mostly, CNN includes of several convolutional and pooling layer that enable to learn various number of abstract features from small edges to whole objects. The number of convolutional layers, size of receptive fields and number of features maps are dependently follows the application. Besides, the validation data set also need to strictly select.

CNN also is widely used in computational biology application similar to DNN. Recently, most of the researchers using CNN in their work especially to train data on DNA sequence with no need to define features. The CNN approach having the ability to directly train the model on high scale input sequence. Alipanahi *et al.* [19] has been use CNN architecture to predict DNA and RNA binding proteins. Their model called as DeepBind was able to discover the functional SNVs, to recover known sequence motifs and quantify the sequence alterations effect.

Other researcher such as Zhou and Troyanskaya [20] using these architecture to identify chromatin marks from DNA sequence. To determine the model performance, they observed the size of input sequence. If larger an input sequence, various convolutional layers are needed to capture the sequence features in divergent genomic length scales. Furthermore, a multitasking neural network or various output variables is use to identify diverse chromatin states within parallel.

An open-source deep learning framework known as Basset was developed by Kelley *et al.* [42] using a convolutional architecture to identify Dnase I hypersensitivity in various types of cell and the effect of SNVs onto the accessibility of chromatin. However, the convolutional neural network architecture is popular for image analysis compared to sequence analysis. A CNN use convolution operation for pattern matching while pooling operation is use as aggregation. The image is scan with a particular pattern and the strength of the match for each position is calculated using convolution operation art pixel level. Meanwhile, pooling operation is applied to discover the existence of the pattern in a region called as max pooling. The convolutional and pooling is the main reason of successful application of image analysis.

2.3   Recurrent Neural Network (RNN)

Recurrent Neural Network (RNN) was designed with cyclic connection in the basic structure and used sequential information. Since cyclic connection exists, RNN performed in hidden unit and process input data sequentially. Thus, past information is stored in the hidden units known as state vectors [13].

Although RNN is not to be deep DNNs and CNNs based on their number of layers but they can be consider as deeper structure if unrolled in time. However, researchers is facing up disappear gradient problem and learning long-term dependency of data during training RNNs. The solution to resolve this problem by replaces the simple perceptron hidden units with complex units including GRU and LSTM that running as memory cells (Fig. 3).

RNNs still provide effective analysis methods particularly in sequential information even it has been less explored compared to DNNs and CNNs. In addition, they are promising in fixed size prediction and for mapping a variable-length input sequence with another sequence.

As it expert in natural language processing, most of the researchers applies RNN architectures in this research area for example, Sutskever *et al.* [43] using two multi-layer LSTMs as translation model to translate from English to French. First layer of LSTM is used to encode input phase from source language and the second layer for

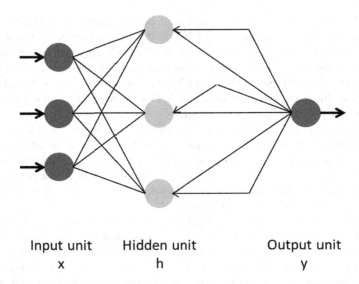

Input unit   Hidden unit   Output unit
x   h   y

Fig. 3. RNN has their basic structure with three types of elements which consists of input unit x, hidden unit h and output unit y.

encoding the output phase in target language. In handwriting recognition, Liwicki *et al.* [44] and Graves *et al.* [45] use bidirectional LSTMs to achieve state of art results.

RNN also commonly used in predicting biological sequences as their architecture is requires sequential information. Baldi *et al.* [46] use bidirectional recurrent neural networks (BRNNs) with perceptron hidden units for prediction of protein secondary structure. Besides that, Park *et al.* [47] and Lee *et al.* [48] was identify microRNA and target prediction by using RNNs and hidden units LSTM. This existing work makes the improvement of RNNs in analyzing biological sequences and others fields.

3   Discussion

In the previous section, there are three deep learning architectures including deep neural networks, convolutional neural network and recurrent neural network has been discussed. Table 1 shown the summary of those three deep learning architectures based on their methodology and application.

Researchers taking further steps by constructing the prediction tools based on the deep learning architectures. There are several existing prediction tools being discussed in this review such as DanQ [49], DeepSEA [20], DeepLNC [50] and Deep Motif [51] that has been used to predict functional DNA sequences, functional non-coding variants and long non-coding variants and classification of genomic sequences on the transcription factor binding site respectively. Table 2 summaries the purpose and method used all of these predicting tools.

Quang and Xie [49] propose DanQ as a predicting model for the function of non-coding DNA. This model uses a combination of convolutional and recurrent neural

Table 1. Summary of deep learning architectures.

Architecture	Description	Application
Deep neural network	Basic structure consists of input layer, multiple hidden layer and output layer	Biomedical imaging, detect splicing signals, cancer classification, cell nucleic detection, protein structure prediction
Convolutional neural network	Basic structure consists of convolutional layers, pooling layers and non-linear layers	Image analysis, predicting DNA and RNA binding protein, identify chromatin marks, identify Dnase I hypersensitivity
Recurrent neural network	Basic structure is designed with cyclic connection and having three elements such as input unit, hidden unit and output unit	Language translation, handwriting recognition, predicting biological sequence, predicting protein secondary structure

Table 2. Summary of existing deep learning prediction tools.

Architecture	Purpose	Method used	Reference
DanQ	Predicting the functional DNA sequences	Convolutional neural network and recurrent neural network model	[49]
DeepSEA	Predicting effect of non-coding variant	Convolutional neural network model	[20]
DeepLNC	Predicting a long non-coding variants	Deep neural network classifier	[50]
DeepMotif	Prediction of transcription factor binding sites (TFBs)	Convolutional neural network	[51]

network as framework. This framework consists of the convolutional layer to capture regulatory motifs and recurrent layer to capture long-term dependencies between motifs. In other words, recurrent layer is used to learn a regulatory grammar in order to advance predictions.

Apart from that, predicting tool related to predicting of non-coding sequences is called as DeepSEA was focusing to identifying functional effects of non-coding variants [20]. But, this predicting approach uses convolutional neural network (CNN) as their framework different with DanQ. DeepSEA is designed to learn regulatory sequence code from high-scale chromatin-profiling data and allowing identification of chromatin effects of sequence alterations with single nucleotides sensitivity. DeepSEA uses three main features in their deep learning-based approach includes integrating sequence information from a wide sequences context, learning sequence code at several spatial scales with hierarchical architecture and multitask joint learning of different chromatin factors sharing predictive features. Data release from Encyclopedia of DNA Elements (ENCODE) and Roadmap Epigenomics is used as a data training for DeepSEA. Training and testing datasets are divided by chromosomes and severely non-overlapping.

Meanwhile, another predicting tool known as DeepLNC was developed by Tripathi *et al.* [50] for the identification of long non-coding RNAs (lncRNAs). This prediction tool is use fast and accurate deep neural network (DNN) classifier for predicting compared to other classifiers. The DNN classifier uses information content stored in k-mer pattern and applied as a sole feature to annotate manually training datasets from LNCipedia and RefSeq databases. DeepLNC using the DNN as the major classifier to train the data set and also k-mer frequencies of lncRNAs and coding transcript sequences as computational features. Specifically, the training dataset from LNCipedia database consists of human annotated lncRNAs and testing dataset consists of mRNA transcripts from REqSeq [50].

Lanchantin *et al.* [51] were developing Deep Motif (DeMo) to generate motifs or interpretable patterns that represent the important transcription factor binding patterns. This computational tool uses a convolutional or highway MLP network that surpasses the state-of-art baseline for 92 diverse transcription factor binding sites (TFBS) datasets [51].

As being discussed in this review, the major issue need to be highlight is demanding of powerful prediction tools. There are limited numbers of computational tools that suitable for genomic sequence prediction. This is due to the difficulty of genomic interpretation and hidden information in genomic sequences [52]. Besides that, most of available data used commonly noisy and incomplete therefore, developer should integrate with the optimization approach to get effective computational tool [53, 54].

4 Conclusion

In era of big data, deep learning is high demanding for learning in high-dimensional data and useful in develop many applications in various field. Deep learning are artificial neural network composed of multiple non-linear layers and have been proposed based on characteristic of input data and research objectives. In this review, we provided general architectures of deep learning that consists of deep neural network (DNN), convolutional neural network (CNN) and recurrent neural network (RNN) based on their methodology parts and applications. We further summaries these three architectures as listed in Table 1. Besides, several existing prediction tools that using deep learning architectures also being discussed and summaries in Table 2.

We think that deep learning can achieve more success in near future because it required a little expertise to handle it. But, it still new in biological fields and the number of application are still limited. We expect in growing and increasing number of software infrastructure especially to handle biological problems can be continued developed and improved.

Other than that, the remaining challenges such as limited data, interpretation of deep learning and selection of a suitable models and hyperparameters are still need to be enhanced [41]. The hybrid architectures in deep learning architectures for example, a hybrid CNN and RNN model is need to be further study and this is a key for future progress of deep learning in various research fields.

Acknowledgments. We would like to express gratitude to the editor and reviewers for helpful suggestions and Malaysian Ministry of Higher Education (MOHE) for sponsoring this research. This research was supported by Fundamental Research Grant Scheme (FRGS), vot number 4F738 and managed by Research Management Centre (RMC), Universiti Teknologi Malaysia (UTM).

References

1. LeCun, Y., Bengio, Y., Hinton, G.: Deep learning. Nature **521**(7553), 436–444 (2015)
2. Larranaga, P., Calvo, B., Santana, R., Bielza, C., Galdiano, J., Inza, I., Lozano, J.A., Armañanzas, R., Santafé, G., Pérez, A., Robles, V.: Machine learning in bioinformatics. Brief. Bioinform. **7**(1), 86–112 (2006)
3. Abdullah, A., Deris, S., Hashim, S.Z.M., Jamil, H.M.: Graph partitioning method for functional module detections of protein interaction network. In: International Conference on Computer Technology and Development, ICCTD 2009, vol. 1, pp. 230–234. IEEE, November 2009
4. Ismail, M.A., Deris, S., Mohamad, M.S., Abdullah, A.: A Newton cooperative genetic algorithm method for in Silico optimization of metabolic pathway production. PLoS ONE **10** (5), e0126199 (2015)
5. Hayashi, N., Matsumae, M., Yatsushiro, S., Hirayama, A., Abdullah, A., Kuroda, K.: Quantitative analysis of cerebrospinal fluid pressure gradients in healthy volunteers and patients with normal pressure hydrocephalus. Neurol. Med. Chir. **55**(8), 657–662 (2015)
6. Abdullah, A., Hirayama, A., Yatsushiro, S., Matsumae, M., Kuroda, K.: Cerebrospinal fluid image segmentation using spatial fuzzy clustering method with improved evolutionary expectation maximization. In: 2013 35th Annual International Conference of IEEE Engineering in Medicine and Biology Society (EMBC), pp. 3359–3362. IEEE, July 2013
7. Farabet, C., Couprie, C., Najman, L., LeCun, Y.: Learning hierarchical features for scene labeling. IEEE Trans. Pattern Anal. Mach. Intell. **35**(8), 1915–1929 (2013)
8. Szegedy, C., Liu, W., Jia, Y., Sermanet, P., Reed, S., Anguelov, D., Erhan, D., Vanhoucke, V., Rabinovich, A.: Going deeper with convolutions. In: Proceedings of IEEE Conference on Computer Vision and Pattern Recognition, pp. 1–9 (2015)
9. Tompson, J.J., Jain, A., LeCun, Y., Bregler, C.: Joint training of a convolutional network and a graphical model for human pose estimation. In: Advances in Neural Information Processing Systems, pp. 1799–1807 (2014)
10. Liu, N., Han, J., Zhang, D., Wen, S., Liu, T.: Predicting eye fixations using convolutional neural networks. In: Proceedings of IEEE Conference on Computer Vision and Pattern Recognition, pp. 362–370 (2015)
11. Hinton, G., Deng, L., Yu, D., Dahl, G.E., Mohamed, A.R., Jaitly, N., Senior, A., Vanhoucke, V., Nguyen, P., Sainath, T.N., Kingsbury, B.: Deep neural networks for acoustic modeling in speech recognition: the shared views of four research groups. IEEE Sig. Process. Mag. **29**(6), 82–97 (2012)
12. Sainath, T.N., Mohamed A.-R., Kingsbury, B., et al.: Deep convolutional neural networks for LVCSR. In: IEEE International Conference on Acoustics, Speech and Signal Processing (ICASSP), p. 8614–8. IEEE (2013)
13. Min, S., Lee, B., Yoon, S. Deep learning in bioinformatics. Brief. Bioinform. bbw068 (2016)

14. Kiros, R., Zhu, Y., Salakhutdinov, R.R., Zemel, R., Urtasun, R., Torralba, A., Fidler, S.: Skip-thought vectors. In: Advances in Neural Information Processing Systems, pp. 3294–3302 (2015)

15. Li, J., Luong, M.T., Jurafsky, D.: A hierarchical neural autoencoder for paragraphs and documents. arXiv preprint arXiv:1506.01057 (2015)

16. Luong, M.T., Pham, H., Manning, C.D.: Effective approaches to attention-based neural machine translation. arXiv preprint arXiv:1508.04025 (2015)

17. Zhang, S., Zhou, J., Hu, H., Gong, H., Chen, L., Cheng, C., Zeng, J.: A deep learning framework for modeling structural features of RNA-binding protein targets. Nucl. Acids Res. **44**(4), e32–e32 (2016)

18. Suk, H.-I., Shen, D.: Deep learning-based feature representation for AD/MCI classification. In: Mori, K., Sakuma, I., Sato, Y., Barillot, C., Navab, N. (eds.) MICCAI 2013. LNCS, vol. 8150, pp. 583–590. Springer, Heidelberg (2013). doi:10.1007/978-3-642-40763-5_72

19. Alipanahi, B., Delong, A., Weirauch, M.T., Frey, B.J.: Predicting the sequence specificities of DNA-and RNA-binding proteins by deep learning. Nat. Biotechnol. **33**(8), 831–838 (2015)

20. Zhou, J., Troyanskaya, O.G.: Predicting effects of noncoding variants with deep learning-based sequence model. Nat. Methods **12**(10), 931–934 (2015)

21. Hua, K.L., Hsu, C.H., Hidayati, S.C., Cheng, W.H., Chen, Y.J.: Computer-aided classification of lung nodules on computed tomography images via deep learning technique. OncoTargets Ther. **8**, 2015–2022 (2014)

22. Roth, H.R., Lu, L., Liu, J., Yao, J., Seff, A., Cherry, K., Summers, R.M.: Improving computer-aided detection using <? Pub _newline ?> convolutional neural networks and random view aggregation. IEEE Trans. Med. Imaging **35**(5), 1170–1181 (2016)

23. Roth, H.R., Yao, J., Lu, L., Stieger, J., Burns, J.E., Summers, R.M.: Detection of sclerotic spine metastases via random aggregation of deep convolutional neural network classifications. In: Yao, J., Glocker, B., Klinder, T., Li, S. (eds.) Recent Advances in Computational Methods and Clinical Applications for Spine Imaging. LNCVB, vol. 20, pp. 3–12. Springer, Cham (2013). doi:10.1007/978-3-319-14148-0_1

24. Baldi, P., Pollastri, G., Andersen, C.A., Brunak, S.: Matching protein b-sheet partners by feedforward and recurrent neural networks. In: ISMB, pp. 25–36 (2000)

25. Ogawa, S., Lee, T.M., Kay, A.R., Tank, D.W.: Brain magnetic resonance imaging with contrast dependent on blood oxygenation. Proc. Natl. Acad. Sci. **87**(24), 9868–9872 (1990)

26. Hsieh, J.: Computed Tomography: Principles, Design, Artifacts, and Recent Advances, vol. 114. SPIE Press, Bellingham (2003)

27. McCulloch, W.S., Pitts, W.: A logical calculus of the ideas immanent in nervous activity. Bull. Math. Biophys. **5**(4), 115–133 (1943)

28. Farley, B.W.A.C., Clark, W.: Simulation of self-organizing systems by digital computer. Trans. IRE Prof. Group Inf. Theory **4**(4), 76–84 (1954)

29. Rosenblatt, F.: The perceptron: a probabilistic model for information storage and organization in the brain. Psychol. Rev. **65**, 386 (1958)

30. Svozil, D., Kvasnicka, V., Pospichal, J.: Introduction to multi-layer feed-forward neural networks. Chemometr. Intell. Lab. Syst. **39**(1), 43–62 (1997)

31. Heffernan, R., Paliwal, K., Lyons, J., Dehzangi, A., Sharma, A., Wang, J., Sattar, A., Yang, Y., Zhou, Y.: Improving prediction of secondary structure, local backbone angles, and solvent accessible surface area of proteins by iterative deep learning. Sci. Rep. **5**, 11476 (2015)

32. Chen, Y., Li, Y., Narayan, R., Subramanian, A., Xie, X.: Gene expression inference with deep learning. Bioinformatics **32**(12), 1832–1839 (2016)

33. Fakoor, R., Ladhak, F., Nazi, A., Huber, M.: Using deep learning to enhance cancer diagnosis and classification. In: Proceedings of International Conference on Machine Learning (2013)

34. van Gerven, M.A., de Lange, F.P., Heskes, T.: Neural decoding with hierarchical generative models. Neural Comput. **22**(12), 3127–3142 (2010)

35. Koyamada, S., Shikauchi, Y., Nakae, K., Koyama, M., Ishii, S.: Deep learning of fMRI big data: a novel approach to subject-transfer decoding. arXiv preprint arXiv:1502.00093 (2010)

36. Li, Q., Feng, B., Xie, L., Liang, P., Zhang, H., Wang, T.: A cross-modality learning approach for vessel segmentation in retinal images. IEEE Trans. Med. Imaging **35**(1), 109–118 (2016)

37. Xu, J., Xiang, L., Liu, Q., Gilmore, H., Wu, J., Tang, J., Madabhushi, A.: Stacked sparse autoencoder (SSAE) for nuclei detection on breast cancer histopathology images. IEEE Trans. Med. Imaging **35**(1), 119–130 (2016)

38. Plis, S.M., Hjelm, D.R., Salakhutdinov, R., Calhoun, V.D.: Deep learning for neuroimaging: a validation study. arXiv preprint arXiv:1312.5847 (2013)

39. Hubel, D.H., Wiesel, T.N.: Shape and arrangement of columns in cat's striate cortex. J. Physiol. **165**(3), 559 (1963)

40. Hubel, D.H., Wiesel, T.N.: The period of susceptibility to the physiological effects of unilateral eye closure in kittens. J. Physiol. **206**(2), 419 (1970)

41. Angermueller, C., Pärnamaa, T., Parts, L., Stegle, O.: Deep learning for computational biology. Mol. Syst. Biol. **12**(7), 878 (2016)

42. Kelley, D.R., Snoek, J., Rinn, J.: Basset: learning the regulatory code of the accessible genome with deep convolutional neural networks. Genome Res. (2016). doi:10.1101/gr.200535.115

43. Sutskever, I., Vinyals, O., Le, Q.V.: Sequence to sequence learning with neural networks. In: Advances in Neural Information Processing Systems, pp. 3104–3112 (2014)

44. Liwicki, M., Graves, A., Bunke, H., Schmidhuber, J.: A novel approach to on-line handwriting recognition based on bidirectional long short-term memory networks. In: Proceedings of 9th International Conference on Document Analysis and Recognition, vol. 1, pp. 367–371 (2007)

45. Graves, A., Liwicki, M., Fernández, S., Bertolami, R., Bunke, H., Schmidhuber, J.: A novel connectionist system for unconstrained handwriting recognition. IEEE Trans. Pattern Anal. Mach. Intell. **31**(5), 855–868 (2009)

46. Wulsin, D.F., Gupta, J.R., Mani, R., Blanco, J.A., Litt, B.: Modeling electroencephalography waveforms with semi-supervised deep belief nets: fast classification and anomaly measurement. J. Neural Eng. **8**(3), 036015 (2011)

47. Luong, M.T., Pham, H., Manning, C.D.: Effective approaches to attention-based neural machine translation. arXiv preprint arXiv:1508.04025 (2015)

48. Vincent, P., Larochelle, H., Bengio, Y., Manzagol, P.A.: Extracting and composing robust features with denoising autoencoders. In: Proceedings of 25th International Conference on Machine Learning, pp. 1096–1103. ACM (2008)

49. Quang, D., Xie, X.: DanQ: a hybrid convolutional and recurrent deep neural network for quantifying the function of DNA sequences. Nucl. Acids Res. **44**(11), e107–e107 (2016)

50. Tripathi, R., Patel, S., Kumari, V., Chakraborty, P., Varadwaj, P.K.: DeepLNC, a long non-coding RNA prediction tool using deep neural network. Netw. Model. Anal. Health Inform. Bioinform. **5**(1), 1–14 (2016)

51. Lanchantin, J., Singh, R., Lin, Z., Qi, Y.: Deep motif: visualizing genomic sequence classifications. arXiv preprint arXiv:1605.01133 (2016)

52. Leung, M.K., Delong, A., Alipanahi, B., Frey, B.J.: Machine learning in genomic medicine: a review of computational problems and data sets. Proc. IEEE **104**(1), 176–197 (2016)

53. Abdullah, A., Deris, S., Mohamad, M.S., Anwar, S.: An improved swarm optimization for parameter estimation and biological model selection. PLoS ONE **8**(4), e61258 (2013)
54. Abdullah, A., Deris, S., Hashim, S.Z.M., Mohamad, M.S., Arjunan, S.N.V.: An improved local best searching in particle swarm optimization using differential evolution. In: 2011 11th International Conference on Hybrid Intelligent Systems (HIS), pp. 115–120. IEEE, December 2011

The Enhancement of Evolving Spiking Neural Network with Dynamic Population Particle Swarm Optimization

Nur Nadiah Md. Said, Haza Nuzly Abdull Hamed[(✉)],
and Afnizanfaizal Abdullah

Faculty of Computing, Universiti Teknologi Malaysia,
Johor Bahru, Johor, Malaysia
nnadiah35@live.utm.my, {haza,afnizanfaizal}@utm.my

Abstract. This study presents an integration of Evolving Spiking Neural - Network (ESNN) with Dynamic Population Particle Swarm Optimization (DPPSO). The original ESNN framework does not automatically modulate its parameters' optimum values. Thus, an integrated framework is proposed to optimize ESNN parameters namely, the modulation factor (mod), similarity factor (sim), and threshold factor (c). DPPSO improves the original PSO technique by implementing a dynamic particle population. Performance analysis is measured on classification accuracy in comparison with the existing methods. Five datasets retrieved from UCI machine learning are selected to simulate the classification problem. The proposed framework improves ESNN performance in regulating its parameters' optimum values.

Keywords: Evolving · Spiking · Neural network · Dynamic · Population · Particle swarm · Optimization · Parameter

1 Introduction

Neural network inspired by the human brain is gaining popularity nowadays due to its capability in solving various problems. Artificial neural network (ANN) is a group of processing components in a collective network resembles the features of a biological neural network [1]. The characteristic of an early neural network is restricted to a single layer, which inspires researchers in improving the neural network architecture. It leads to the creation of a new generation of neural network [2]. Spiking neural network is the third generation of a neural network model. Evolving Spiking Neural Network (ESNN) is one of the well-known SNN categories that evolves from the latest spiking neurons [3].

However, ESNN is dependent on parameter tuning. Thus, an optimizer is needed to help automate the process of determining the ESNN's parameters combination [4]. Few studies integrate ESNN with several optimizers [4, 5]. However, some of the optimizers known today require a large computational cost which has driven researchers to establish more effective methods.

Particle Swarm Optimization (PSO) introduced by Kennedy and Eberheart [6, 7] based on swarm population is inspired by the nature of birds' flocking behavior. PSO

© Springer Nature Singapore Pte Ltd. 2017
M.S. Mohamed Ali et al. (Eds.): AsiaSim 2017, Part II, CCIS 752, pp. 95–103, 2017.
DOI: 10.1007/978-981-10-6502-6_8

has the ability to solve various issues of optimization [8–11]. However, despite the recognition received by PSO, this optimizer also has drawbacks. This study proposes a dynamic population concept in PSO known as Dynamic Population Particle Swarm Optimization (DPPSO), which will be implemented as an ESNN parameter optimizer. ESNN-DPPSO improve classification accuracy compared to the other ESNN integrated techniques.

2   Evolving Spiking Neural Network

Evolving spiking neural network (ESNN) was originally proposed as a visual pattern identification system. The earliest ESNN was derived from Thorpe's neuron model whereby the earlier spikes represent the significance of the output generated [12, 13].

ESNN evolves its form whereby for each input pattern, a new neuron is created and linked to the connectivity of neurons [12]. ESNN classifier determines the mapping by computing the distance between neurons to a particular class marker. Hence, it is appropriate to be utilized for time-invariant information categorization [14].

A single input value is encoded to multiple neurons by calculating the intersection of a Gaussian function [5] using the following mathematical equations.

$$\mu = lmin + ((2 * i - 3)/2) * ((lmax - lmin)/(M - 2)) \tag{1}$$

$$\sigma = (1/(\beta(lmax - lmin)))/M - 2 \text{ where } 1 \le \beta \le 2 \tag{2}$$

where:

μ = The center of a Gaussian intersection
σ = The width of variable interval $[lmin, lmax]$

There are three parameters for ESNN consisting of modulation factor (*mod*), similarity factor (*sim*), and threshold (*c*). The *mod* shows how the sequence of temporal spike's arrival time affects the neuron, whereas *sim* regulates the neuron distance and cluster in the output and the *c* determines when a neuron should produce an output spike. Details on ESNN can be found in [13].

3   Dynamic Population Particle Swarm Optimization

Although PSO has been widely used, there are a few drawbacks encompassing being trapped in a local optima and premature convergence [15]. This has influenced researchers to further improve the algorithm [16–19].

The proposed dynamic population PSO is implemented with a dynamic number of particles instead of a fixed population. The basic PSO element is retained to leverage its ability on fast convergence [15]. Algorithm 1 explains the details of DPPSO.

```
Algorithm 1: DPPSO
```

```
initialize DPPSO parameters
calculate reduction cycle
initialize particle with random value
initialize Pbest and Gbest with the lowest value
while not reaching the maximum iteration do
        get particle fitness
        if particle fitness > Pbest
            Pbest= particle fitness
        end if
        if Pbest> Gbest
            Gbest= Pbest
        end if
        if current iteration == reduction cycle value
            remove lowest fitness
        end if
        update particle based on PSO equation
  end while
```

The DPPSO has four parameters; inertia weight (ω), velocity towards global best (C_1), velocity towards particle best (C_2) and reduction cycle. First, the parameters are initialized. Next, the reduction is calculated. The particle is initialized with a random value. Particle best (P_{best}) is the best solution obtained by the particle itself while the global best (G_{best}) is measured by the best solution achieved globally. P_{best} and G_{best} are initialized each with the lowest value. If the particle fitness value is greater than P_{best}, the P_{best} value is updated. If the P_{best} value is greater than G_{best}, the G_{best} value is updated. If the current iteration value is equal to the reduction cycle value, particle with the lowest fitness value is removed. The particle position value is updated using the PSO rule in Eq. 3.

$$v_p(i,j) = \omega v_p(i,j) + C_1(P_{best}(i,j) - x(i,j)) + C_2(G_{best} - x(i,j)) \tag{3}$$

4 Integration of ESNN-DPPSO

The integrated ESNN-DPPSO is described in Algorithm 2. The algorithm begins with the initialization of particles and its fitness at the lowest value which is −9999. The iteration is set to 2000. The fitness is updated throughout the iteration. The reduction cycle (reductionCycle) removes a particle with the lowest fitness value and is set according to Eq. 4.

$$\text{Reduction cycle} = \text{Iteration}/(\text{reductionCycle} + 1) \tag{4}$$

If the current fitness value is better than the P_{best} value, the P_{best} is updated. The ESNN parameters are updated by training the fitness value of each particle with DPPSO. PSO rule is implemented to update the position of particles.

Algorithm 2: ESNN-DPPSO

```
for all particles do
        initialize all DPPSO parameters
        initialize fitness
end for
while not reaching maximum iteration do
        for all particles do
                calculate reduction cycle
                get fitness from ESNN
                if current fitness > PBest fitness then
                        PBest = current particle
                end if
                for all ESNN parameters do
                        update parameter
                end for
                if iteration == reduction cycle
                        remove lowest particle
                end if
        end for
end while
```

The proposed integrated framework is illustrated in Fig. 1.

4.1 Experiment Setup

In this study, five standard datasets retrieved from UCI machine learning repository [20] are selected to simulate the classification problems and are implemented to the proposed framework. The datasets are Iris, heart, breast cancer, Pima Indian diabetes, and wine datasets. The datasets are normalized using Eq. 5.

$$X = (Xi - Xmin)/(Xmin - Xmax) \tag{5}$$

where,

X = initial value of variable
Xi = variable value after normalization
$Xmax$ = variable maximum value
$Xmin$ = variable minimum value

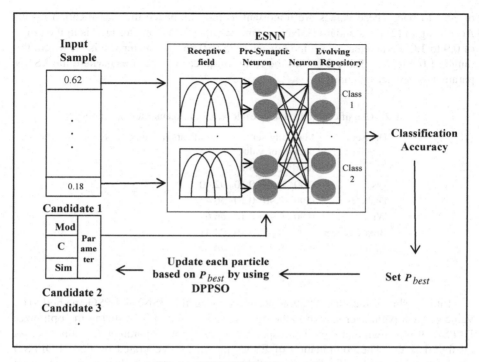

Fig. 1. ESNN-DPPSO framework

In addition, DPPSO has its own parameters. Table 1 shows the respective value of each selected DPPSO parameter.

Table 1. DPPSO parameter

Parameter	Value
Inertia weight	2.0
Velocity global best	2.0
Velocity best particle	2.0
Reduction cycle	4

5 Results and Discussion

The datasets are separated into two categories, training and testing. A 10-fold cross validation technique is used for these datasets. 90% of the datasets are used for training to avoid overfitting while the remaining datasets are used for testing. Overfitting can occur if the size of training is small. Next, each dataset is normalized followed by the training phase for classification. The training process for the integrated ESNN-DPPSO is shown in Algorithm 2. Three ESNN parameters; *mod*, *sim* and *c* are set in the range of zero to one. These values are important as they influence the classification result. According to [21], a standard ESNN parameter value for parameter *mod* is in the range of 0.9 to 1.0. Parameter *c* is set in between 0.55 to 0.85. Parameter *sim* is set within the range of 0.3 to 0.6. Table 2 shows the result of an early experiment where the ESNN parameters are set manually.

Table 2. Classification accuracy result based on manual tuning of ESNN

Dataset	Manually set parameter value			Classification accuracy %
	Mod	C	Sim	
Iris	0.90	0.90	0.10	92.00
Diabetes	0.90	0.90	0.10	56.41
Wine	0.90	0.95	0.10	66.67
Breast cancer	0.90	0.35	0.10	94.41
Heart	0.85	0.75	0.10	74.44

Table 3 shows the classification accuracy using the ESNN-DPPSO method. The value of each parameter shown is the optimum value found by utilizing the optimizer DPPSO. It is known that there is no specific combination of parameters' values across all five datasets. The combination of ESNN parameters generated by ESNN-DPPSO produces a better classification result than the manually set values of the standard ESNN parameters.

Table 3. Classification accuracy result using ESNN-DPPSO

Dataset	Manually set parameter value			Classification accuracy %
	Mod	C	Sim	
Iris	0.85	0.70	0.52	92.00
Heart	0.98	0.97	0.45	70.37
Diabetes	0.74	0.61	0.53	75.23
Breast cancer	0.99	0.87	0.54	95.48
Wine	0.98	0.91	0.58	85.40

In ESNN-DPPSO, the best *mod* value found is within the range of 0.7 to 1.0. This value should not be low as it depicts the ESNN connection weight. On the other hand, parameter *c* influences the PSP threshold value within the range of 0.6 to 1.0. Meanwhile, the best *sim* value is within the range of 0.4 to 0.5 as it controls the evolving neurons where a lower value shows less neurons in the same range are being merged.

Thus, ESNN-DPPSO assists the search of best ESNN parameters' values combination automatically and reduces computational time. Next, a comparison study is

Table 4. Comparison between ESNN-DPPSO classification result with other methods

Dataset	Algorithm	Classification accuracy %
Iris	Standard ESNN parameter	89.33
	ESNN Modified parameter	92.00
	ESNN-DPPSO	92.00
	DE-ESNN	**93.33**
Breast cancer	Standard ESNN parameter	66.18
	ESNN Modified parameter	94.41
	ESNN-DPPSO	**95.48**
	DE-ESNN	91.18
Diabetes	Standard ESNN parameter	38.46
	ESNN Modified parameter	56.41
	ESNN-DPPSO	**75.23**
	DE-ESNN	–
Heart	Standard ESNN parameter	66.30
	ESNN Modified parameter	**74.44**
	ESNN-DPPSO	70.37
	DE-ESNN	62.71
Wine	Standard ESNN parameter	44.45
	ESNN Modified parameter	66.67
	ESNN-DPPSO	**85.40**
	DE-ESNN	–

carried out to evaluate the performance of the proposed ESNN-DPPSO with other methods. Table 4 shows the comparison of the results of various ESNN methods such as a standard ESNN [21], standard ESNN using manually set parameters' values, ESNN-DPPSO, and DE-ESNN.

Based on Table 4, ESNN-DPPSO shows the best accuracy results for breast cancer, diabetes, and wine datasets with the accuracy of 95.48%, 75.23%, and 85.40% respectively compared to other methods. The proposed method has improved ESNN method by at least one percent better classification accuracy compare the other techniques. The DE-ESNN has the best classification accuracy for iris dataset with the score of 93.33% because DE-ESNN uses different parameter suitable for DE such as mutation constant and crossover constant. The DE-ESNN classification accuracy result for diabetes and wine dataset are absent since it use different dataset; appendicitis and ionosphere.

6   Conclusion

In this study, a new ESNN-DPPSO optimizer technique is proposed. This simulation optimizer shows a promising result in parameter optimization. The proposed optimizer, ESNN-DPPSO, searches for optimum ESNN parameters' values. The experiment result shows that ESNN-DPPSO has a better performance result in comparison to the standard ESNN and ESNN-DE for most datasets. For future work, more improvements on DPPSO could be carried out in order to obtain a better classification accuracy result.

Acknowledgment. This research work was supported by Universiti Teknologi Malaysia under the Research University Grant with vot. Q.J130000.2528.11H80.

References

1. Yegnanarayana, B.: Artificial Neural Networks. PHI Learning Pvt. Ltd., New Delhi (2009)
2. Huang, W., Hong, H., Song, G., Xie, K.: Deep process neural network for temporal deep learning. In: International Joint Conference on Neural Networks (IJCNN), pp. 465–472 (2014)
3. Dhoble, K., Nuntalid, N., Indiveri, G., Kasabov, N.: Online spatio-temporal pattern recognition with evolving spiking neural networks utilising address event representation, rank order, and temporal spike learning. In: The 2012 International Joint Conference Neural Networks (IJCNN), pp. 1–7 (2012)
4. Saleh, A.Y., Shamsuddin, S.M., Hamed, H.N.B.A.: Parameter tuning of evolving spiking neural network with differential evolution algorithm. In: International Conference of Recent Trends in Information and Communication Technologies, p. 13 (2014)
5. Hamed, H.N.A., Kasabov, N., Shamsuddin, S.M.: Quantum-inspired particle swarm optimization for feature selection and parameter optimization in evolving spiking neural networks for classification tasks. In: InTech (2011)
6. Kennedy, J., Eberhart, R.C.: Particle swarm optimization. In: Proceeding of IEEE International Conference on Neural Network, vol. 4, pp. 1942–1948 (1995)
7. Eberhart, R., Kennedy, J.: A new optimizer using particle swarm theory. In: IEEE Proceedings of the Sixth International Symposium on Micro Machine and Human Science, pp. 39–43 (1995)
8. Mao, C., Lin, R., Xu, C., He, Q.: Towards a trust prediction framework for cloud services based on PSO-driven neural network. IEEE Access 5, 2187–2199 (2017)
9. Chen, Y.C., Jiang, J.R.: Particle swarm optimization for charger deployment in wireless rechargeable sensor networks. In: 26th International Telecommunication Networks and Applications Conference (ITNAC), pp. 231–236 (2016)
10. Kaur, H., Prabahakar, G.: An advanced clustering scheme for wireless sensor networks using particle swarm optimization. In: 2nd International Conference on Next Generation Computing Technologies (NGCT), pp. 387–392 (2016)
11. Pal, D., Verma, P., Gautam, D., Indait, P.: Improved optimization technique using hybrid ACO-PSO. In: 2nd International Conference on Next Generation Computing Technologies (NGCT), pp. 277–282 (2016)
12. Kasabov, N.: Evolving spiking neural networks for spatio- and spectro-temporal pattern recognition. In: 2012 6th IEEE International Conference on Intelligent Systems (IS), pp. 27–32 (2012)
13. Wysoski, S.G., Benuskova, L., Kasabov, N.: Adaptive learning procedure for a network of spiking neurons and visual pattern recognition. In: Blanc-Talon, J., Philips, W., Popescu, D., Scheunders, P. (eds.) ACIVS 2006. LNCS, vol. 4179, pp. 1133–1142. Springer, Heidelberg (2006). doi:10.1007/11864349_103
14. Schliebs, S., Defoin-Platel, M., Kasabov, N.: Analyzing the dynamics of the simultaneous feature and parameter optimization of an evolving spiking neural network. In: The 2010 International Joint Conference on Neural Networks (IJCNN), pp. 1–8 (2010)

15. Saxena, N., Tripathi, A., Mishra, K.K., Misra, A.K.: Dynamic-PSO: an improved particle swarm optimizer. In: 2015 IEEE Congress on Evolutionary Computation (CEC), pp. 212–219 (2015)
16. Kaur, R., Arora, M.: A novel asynchronous Mc-Cdma multiuser detector with modified particle swarm optimization algorithm (MPSO). In: 2nd International Conference on Next Generation Computing Technologies (NGCT), pp. 420–425 (2016)
17. Soni, N., Bhatt, R., Parmar, G.: Optimal LFC system of interconnected thermal power plants using hybrid particle swarm optimization-pattern search algorithm (hPSO-PS). In: 2nd International Conference on Communication Control and Intelligent Systems (CCIS), pp. 225–229 (2016)
18. Song, K., Li, C., Yang, L.: Parameter estimation for multi-scale multi-lag underwater acoustic channels based on modified particle swarm optimization algorithm. In: IEEE Access (2017)
19. M'hamdi, B., Teguar, M., Mekhaldi, A.: Optimal design of corona ring on HV composite insulator using PSO approach with dynamic population size. IEEE Trans. Dielectr. Electr. Insul. **23**, 1048–1057 (2016)
20. UCI Machine Learning Repository. http://archive.ics.uci.edu/ml/
21. Hamed, H.N.B.A., Nuzly, H.: Novel integrated methods of evolving spiking neural network and particle swarm optimisation. Ph.D. dissertation, Auckland University of Technology (2012)

The Effects of Pressure Variation in Sliding Mode Controller with Optimized PID Sliding Surface

Chong Chee Soon[1], Rozaimi Ghazali[1(✉)], Hazriq Izzuan Zaafar[1],
Sahazati Md. Rozali[2], Yahaya Md. Sam[3], and Mohd Fua'ad Rahmat[3]

[1] Faculty of Electrical Engineering, Universiti Teknikal Malaysia Melaka,
Hang Tuah Jaya, 76100 Durian Tunggal, Melaka, Malaysia
rozaimi.ghazali@utem.edu.my
[2] Faculty of Engineering Technology, Universiti Teknikal Malaysia Melaka,
Hang Tuah Jaya, 76100 Durian Tunggal, Melaka, Malaysia
[3] Department of Control and Mechatronics Engineering,
Faculty of Electrical Engineering, Universiti Teknologi Malaysia,
81310 Skudai, Johor, Malaysia

Abstract. The high demands in the control of force and position implemented
in diverse applications have led to the increasing usage of Electro-Hydraulic
Actuator (EHA) system. However, the EHA system is commonly exposed to the
parameter variations, disturbances, and uncertainties, which are caused by the
changes in the operating conditions. Hence, this paper attempts to analyses the
impact of changes during the operating condition and a robust control strategy is
then formulated based on the control law of the Sliding Mode Control (SMC),
where the design of the sliding surface is integrated with the Proportional-
Integral-Derivative (PID) controller. Then, the Particle Swarm Optimization
(PSO) technique has been utilized to seek for the optimum PID sliding surface
parameters. The findings indicate that the proposed robust SMC with PSO-PID
sliding surface is preserved to ensure the actuator robust and stable under the
variation of the system operating condition, which produce 26% improvement in
terms of its robustness characteristic.

Keywords: Electro-Hydraulic Actuator · Sliding Mode Control · PID sliding
surface · Particle Swarm Optimization · Robustness analysis

1 Introduction

The power distribution by fluid power is historical and well acknowledge discipline,
which is an energy transmitted through the medium of pressurized fluid. The growing
of fluid power technology has fulfilled the demand in the control of an increased
quantities of mass with higher precision and acceleration through the lowest power
consumption implemented to various engineering applications.

In the areas of manufacturing assembly line, machining tools, and aerodynamic
control, quick response with accurateness at the high power level are the crucial
factors that yielding the integration of the electronic components into the hydraulic

© Springer Nature Singapore Pte Ltd. 2017
M.S. Mohamed Ali et al. (Eds.): AsiaSim 2017, Part II, CCIS 752, pp. 104–115, 2017.
DOI: 10.1007/978-981-10-6502-6_9

servomechanism. In the field of electronics, the data and information can be easily processed and transduced [1], while the demand in high force and high speed can be delivered by the hydraulic servomechanism [2]. Thus, an integration that absorbs the features of both electronic and hydraulic servomechanism forming the Electro-Hydraulic Actuator (EHA) system, which produces more reliable, more efficient, and better performance that could meet one expectations [3]. However, the EHA system is highly nonlinear, time varying, and have many uncertainties in nature, which resulting in more challenging tasks in the controller design and the development of an accurate dynamic model. These issues occurred in the hydraulic system have been discovered by many researchers in the past several decades [4–8].

In the study of [9], they have emphasized that various types of robust and adaptive control strategies have been developed over the years to overcome the issues occurred in this system [10, 11]. The issues discovered in the past including valve overlapping [12], directional changes in valve opening [13], and the non-smooth nonlinearities [14] during the control input saturation. However, in the recent study by [15], they have underlined that the unstructured uncertainties are always exist in the hydraulic system, which have become a main obstacle in the development of the controller design, especially in the development of high-accuracy tracking control. Further encouragement has been given to academia and researchers in the development of the high-accuracy control strategy in order to enhance the hydraulic actuator performance.

In the past, numerous control approaches have been suggested to enhance the tracking capabilities of the hydraulic actuator. These control strategies may be loosely classified into linear control, nonlinear control, and intelligent control approaches [16]. However, a linear control strategies might be facing the robustness issues towards the significant variations in the system's parameter. In addition, in the control of the positioning tracking in the EHA system, although the intelligent techniques have presented acceptable performances, but a potential stability problem has been governed by these techniques [17]. Generally, the discussions on the stability factors in the controller design were ignored. Therefore, in order to overcome the stability issues, and increase the robustness towards the changes occurred in the system, the nonlinear control strategy, which is SMC robust control that using different approaches is found to be potential in dealing with these issues [18–25].

Through the study of the literature, it is realized that recent trend has shifted towards the computational tuning method to dealing with the issues existed in the EHA system. With the evolutionary, high efficient, and cost effective computational optimization algorithm, extensive control issues have been solved and improved particularly in the engineering apparatus. The rapid improvements in computational technologies simultaneously enhance the robust control approaches, which has been implemented in the EHA system. In the metaheuristic optimization techniques such as PSO, GA, and DE, the PSO was found to be potential in solving the positioning tracking control issue especially in the EHA system employed to various types of controller [26–31].

Therefore, in this study, an evaluation regarding the robustness analysis of the proposed SMC with PID sliding surface control strategy implemented to the EHA system has been carried out. The mathematical modelling of the EHA system, and also the derivation of the PID sliding surface will be adopted from [32]. Then, the PSO algorithm will be employed to obtain the other variables value of the PID controller, which was later integrated into the sliding surface of SMC controller. Finally, the simulation exercises are presented to illustrate the effectiveness of the proposed method.

2 Physical Model of EHA System in Simulink

The development of the physical model for the EHA system will be done by using MATLAB/Simulink 2013 software. In this study, the EHA system will be first modelled according to the mathematical modelling of the EHA system based on the first principles of the physical law as discussed in [32]. After the formation of EHA system, the sliding mode controller will be integrated with the PID sliding surface, which is particularly applied to control the displacement of the EHA system. Figure 1 indicates the Simulink block diagram EHA system implemented in this study.

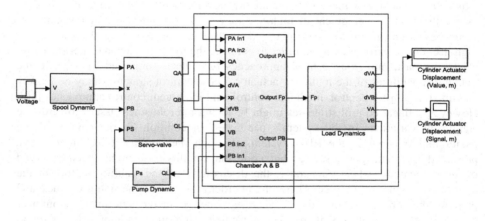

Fig. 1. Simulink block diagram of the EHA system

2.1 Integration of PSO to the SMC with PID Sliding Surface

PSO is an algorithm based on the inspiration of a swarming behaviour of insects, animals, or even humans, which was introduced by James Kennedy and Russell C. Eberhart, who is a social psychologist and an electrical engineer at America in 1995. A group of agents known as particles, which is the composition of insect like ants, animal like birds, or humans that randomly walking around the wide range area to looking for food, treasure, or resources supposedly. The searching activity will always start from random search, then these creatures will communicate and share their current best information among each other. Finally, the summarized or computed current best information will be formed into a global best information, which will usually end up with a quality global best information.

Two important operators that will manipulate in the searching process are the velocity and position update. During the searching process, each of the current particles will accelerate to the new position or searching point, by according to the velocity value that composed of previous velocity and position information. The general velocity and position update have a formation of the equations as denoted below [33]:

$$v_{id}^{k+1} = v_{id}^k + c_1 rand_1^k (pbest_{id}^k - s_{id}^k) + c_2 rand_2^k (gbest_{id}^k - s_{id}^k) \qquad (1)$$

$$s_{id}^{k+1} = s_{id}^k + v_{id}^{k+1} \qquad (2)$$

The description of the equation above is tabulated in Table 1. The searching process will be repeated until the stopping condition and criteria is met. The condition and criteria included fixed maximum for the number of iterations, or the error measurement of the function approximate or reached the minimum.

Table 1. List of terms and descriptions for the general equation of PSO

Terms	Descriptions
i	The value of particle or agent, where $i = 1, 2, 3, ..., n$
d	The dimension of the problem, where $d = 1, 2, 3, ..., n$
k	The iteration of particle or agent, where $k = 1, 2, 3, ..., n$
$k + 1$	The future iteration of particle or agent
v	The velocity of the algorithm
s	The searching point of the algorithm
$c_{1/2}$	c_1 represents the self-coefficient, c_2 represents the group/swarm-coefficient
$rand_{1/2}$	$rand$ = random numbers ranged from 0 to 1 $rand_1$ is the random value of self-coefficient $rand_2$ is the random value of group-coefficient
$pbest$	The particle's self or personal best value
$gbest$	The particle's group/swarm or global best value

In the development of the PSO algorithm in this study, the procedure of the development has been summarized into the flow chart as depicted in Fig. 2. The searching process will be started by a random distribution of the particle's velocity and position in the wide range area that consists of local and global region or problem space. The randomly distributed particles will then occupy the problem space and perform the execution in searching for the best solution, or in other terms known as fitness in the local region. Each of the particles will keep tracking their best coordinates, which were associated with the current velocity and the achieved current best fitness value so far that was known as local best, *lbest* value. The fitness value will be stored in the memory array with the given name of personal best, *pbest* value. Through the repetition of the searching process, the best *pbest* value among each of the particles will be judged as the global best, *gbest* value. Commonly, the development of the PSO algorithm as depicted in the flowchart in Fig. 2 will follow the procedures as stated below:

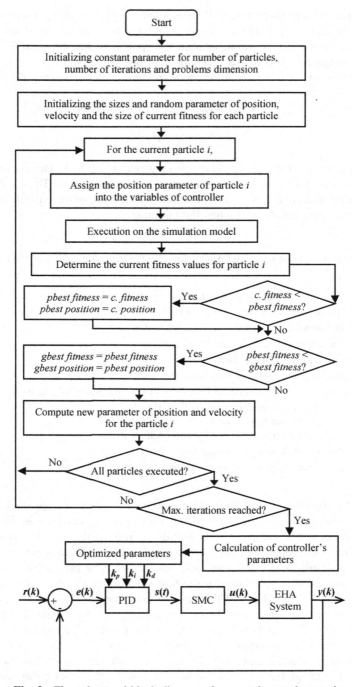

Fig. 2. Flow chart and block diagram of proposed control strategies

i. Initializing a constant value for the sizes of the swarm, numbers of iteration, and problems dimension (d),

ii. Initializing swarm of particles in an array according to the d with random set of velocities and positions,

iii. For each of the particles, start the execution in searching for the fitness information in the d variable,

iv. Evaluate the fitness information for the current particle with the *pbest* particle. If the current particle solution is better than *pbest* particle, *pbest* value will be replaced by the current particle value, and the location of the current particle will be transformed into the *pbest* location in the d dimension,

v. Compare the current fitness information with overall swarm fitness information. If the current fitness value is better than *gbest* fitness value, replacing the *gbest* fitness value with current fitness value,

vi. Updating the velocity and position information according to the Eqs. (1) and (2) respectively,

vii. Repeat the loop to Step iii until the stopping criterion is met.

where $r(k)$ denotes the reference or desired input signal, $e(k)$ is the errors produced by the system, $s(t)$ represents the sliding surface of the SMC, $u(k)$ is the control signal of the SMC, and $y(k)$ is the output response of the EHA system.

With the assistance of PID controller on the sliding surface of the SMC, the control signal is expected to be reached to the desired point faster and smoother than the conventional SMC approach. Finally, the PSO algorithm will be used to obtained an optimal value for the PID sliding surface of the SMC, which will significantly improve the control performance and reduce the control effort as demonstrated in the coming chapter.

2.2   Robustness Index

The robustness test is conducted with the purpose to evaluate the robustness of the developed controller. Generally, robustness test for EHA system is conducted by reducing or increasing the supply pressure to represent the parameter variations [3, 28]. The investigations under the changes of the operating conditions and robustness study of the implemented controllers are crucial in the control performance assessment. Thus, a practical way to measure the robustness of the controllers is to determine the Root Mean Square Error (RMSE) obtained for the nominal operating condition ($RMSE_{nom}$) and the changed of plant parameters ($RMSE_{var}$) condition. The quantitative measure which known as the robustness index (RI) for a reference trajectory (RT), under a particular plant condition over a tracking process of period (T) is given as:

$$RI(T, RT) = \frac{|RMSE_{nom} - RMSE_{var}|}{RMSE_{nom}} \tag{3}$$

The robustness index has been used in the comparative evaluation on the tracking performance of the EHA system by using the robust control scheme. This metric will show the capability of the proposed control scheme for the system under the disturbances and uncertainties circumstances.

3 Results and Discussion

Before the evaluation of the proposed method, the step reference input signal has been first employed to the EHA system that is operated without the assistant of the controller in order to observe the capability of the proposed control approach. The system has been connected in two different circumstances, which are open-loop and closed-loop, and executed in 60 s as demonstrated in Fig. 3.

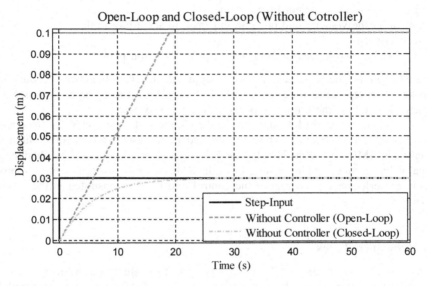

Fig. 3. The response of the EHA system in open-loop and closed-loop without the assistant of the controller (Color figure online)

As clearly depicted in Fig. 3, the EHA system will be operated in a static way, where the hydraulic actuator will be extended to the maximum stroke of the cylinder without follow the step reference signal that has been fed to the system as represented in green dash line. The times taken to reach to the maximum stroke are almost 18 to 20 s. When the system is connected in a closed-loop circumstance, the actuator has been clearly followed the desired trajectory. However, the actuator took a very long time to reach to the desired trajectory, which are between 20 to 25 s. Thus, in can be inferred that the assistant of the controller is needed in order to achieve our desired performance, which including efficiency, accuracy, fast and stable response.

The controller that is capable to perform without sacrificing the limitation of the EHA system is another issue to be concerned. Therefore, the controller robustness analysis based on the step input reference signal has been conducted. As the discussion that has been made in the article [34], the effect occurred during the changes in the EHA system parameters has been carefully evaluated. It is observed in that study, the most influential parameters are including the servo-valve gain (K), supply pressure (P_s), and the total moving mass (M_p). The Ps has been chosen in the evaluation of the controller robustness characteristic due to its practical application to the real-time EHA system. It is also observed in that study, the variation of ±25%, and ±75% doesn't contribute much to the effect occurred in the EHA system, but only at the settling time of the system. In order to assess the performance of the control scheme with the deduction of 25%, 50%, and 75% on the P_s, the parameters of the PSO algorithm have been applied to the PID controller, and the PID sliding surface of the SMC, which produced the performances as shown in Figs. 4 and 5 respectively.

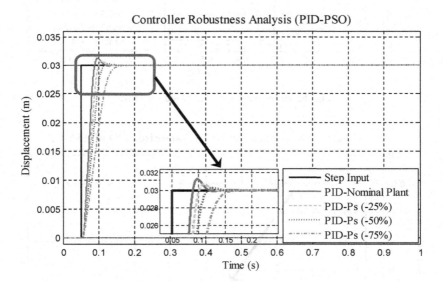

Fig. 4. Robustness analysis based on PID controller

Hence, the variation on the P_s with the deduction of 50% from the nominal supply pressure has been set in the scope of the study, which represent the changes occurred in the system parameters, that will be used to analyse the controller robustness charac-teristics. Figure 6 depicts the response of the SMC and the PID controller. The PID-PSO applied to the nominal plant is represented in red colour dash-dot line, and the PID-PSO applied to the varied plant denotes in green colour dot line, while the SMC-PID-PSO applied to the nominal plant demonstrated in magenta colour dash line, and the SMC-PID-PSO implemented to the varied plant indicated in blue colour solid line.

As clearly shown in the zoomed-in figure in Fig. 6. It is clearly seen that the response produced by the PID-PSO applied to the nominal EHA plant generated slower rise time and settling time depicted in red colour dash-dot line as compared to the SMC-PID-PSO that illustrated in magenta colour dash line. When the supply pressure

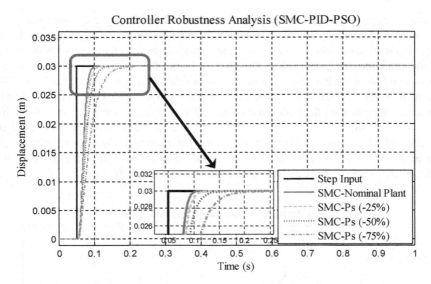

Fig. 5. Robustness analysis based on SMC

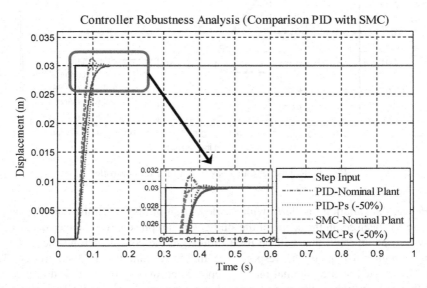

Fig. 6. Controllers robustness analysis implemented in nominal plant and pressure variation for the EHA system (Color figure online)

has been varied for the purpose of controller robustness analysis, the rise time and settling time of PID-PSO even worse as represented in green colour dot line, while the response of the SMC-PID-PSO result in better performance as shown in blue colour solid line.

To produce a much clearer view in the robustness characteristic of the SMC and the PID controller when employed to the nominal EHA plant and the variation on the EHA supply pressure, Table 2 tabulated the RMSE analysis and the robustness index for both controllers respectively. It can be seen in Table 2, the robustness index generated by SMC is smaller as compared to the PID controller, which indicated that the SMC controller has a better robustness characteristic compared to the PID controller when there is a change in system parameters. As compared with the PID controller, 26% improvement of the robustness characteristic has been obtained when the SMC is implemented to the EHA system. This phenomenon is crucial when dealing with the systems that have problems such as disturbances, nonlinearities, and uncertainties since these problems are hard to be captured and handle in the real world.

Table 2. Robustness analysis for SMC and PID controller

Controller	Plant	Controller robustness analysis	
		RMSE	Robustness index value
PID-PSO	Nominal	3.9671×10^{-3}	0.1629
	P_s, (−50%)	4.6132×10^{-3}	
SMC-PID-PSO	Nominal	3.7549×10^{-3}	0.1212
	P_s, (−50%)	4.2099×10^{-3}	

4 Conclusion

This paper has presented an optimization on the developed controller variables, which is the sliding mode controller based on PID sliding surface structure, implemented in the position tracking control of the EHA system. It is well-known that the EHA system is commonly exposed to the parameter variations, disturbances, and uncertainties. Therefore, an optimization is required to reduce the controller's effort and improve its robustness towards the changes and uncertain operating conditions. Compared to the conventional PID controller, the proposed robust control strategy outperforms without sacrificing the limitation of the EHA system, which was analysed in term of the robustness quality and the positioning tracking accuracy. In conclusion, it is demonstrated that the proposed robust SMC with the optimized PID sliding surface is preserved to keep the actuator robust and stable under the variation of the system operating condition.

Acknowledgement. The support of Universiti Teknikal Malaysia Melaka (UTeM), Universiti Teknologi Malaysia (UTM), and Ministry of Education (MOE) are greatly acknowledged. The research was funded by Fundamental Research Grant Scheme (FRGS) Grant No. FRGS/1/2014/ TK03/FKE/02/F00214 and High Impact Short Term (PJP) Grant No. PJP/2017/FKE/HI11/ S01534.

References

1. Maskrey, R.H., Thayer, W.J.: A brief history of electrohydraulic servomechanisms. Moog Tech. Bull. **100**, 141 (1978)
2. Soon, C.C., Ghazali, R., Jaafar, H.I., Hussien, S.Y.S., Rozali, S.M., Rashid, M.Z.A.: Position tracking optimization for an electro-hydraulic actuator system. J. Telecommun. Electron. Comput. Eng. **8**(7), 1–6 (2016)
3. Soon, C.C., Ghazali, R., Jaafar, H.I., Hussien, S.Y.S., Sam, Y.M., Rahmat, M.F.: Controller parameter optimization for an electro-hydraulic actuator system based on particle swarm optimization. J. Teknol. **78**(6–13), 101–108 (2016)
4. Merritt, H.E.: Hydraulic Control Systems. Wiley, New York (1967)
5. Bonchis, A., Corke, P.I., Rye, D.C.: Experimental evaluation of position control methods for hydraulic systems. IEEE Trans. Control Syst. Technol. **10**(6), 876–882 (2002)
6. Ursu, I., Ursu, F., Iorga, L.: Neuro-fuzzy synthesis of flight control electrohydraulic servo. Aircr. Eng. Aerosp. Technol. **73**(5), 465–472 (2001)
7. Ghazali, R., Sam, Y.M., Rahmat, M.F., Jusoff, K., Zulfatman, Hashim, A.W.I.M.: Self-tuning control of an electro-hydraulic system. Int. J. Smart Sens. Intell. Syst. **4**(2), 189–204 (2011)
8. Ghazali, R., Soon, C.C., Jaafar, H.I., Sam, Y.M., Rahmat, M.F.: System identification of electro-hydraulic actuator system with pressure and load effects. In: IEEE International Conference on Control System, Computing and Engineering, pp. 256–260 (2014)
9. Yan, J., Li, B., Ling, H.F., Chen, H.S., Zhang, M.J.: Nonlinear state space modeling and system identification for electrohydraulic control. Math. Probl. Eng. **2013**, 1–9 (2013)
10. Mohanty, A., Gayaka, S., Yao, B.: An adaptive robust observer for velocity estimation in an electro-hydraulic system. Int. J. Adapt. Control Signal Process. **26**(12), 1076–1089 (2012)
11. Yao, J., Jiao, Z., Yao, B.: Robust control for static loading of electro-hydraulic load simulator with friction compensation. Chin. J. Aeronaut. **25**(6), 954–962 (2012)
12. Papadopoulos, E., Mu, B., Frenette, R.: On modeling, identification, and control of a heavy-duty electrohydraulic harvester manipulator. IEEE/ASME Trans. Mechatron. **8**(2), 178–187 (2003)
13. Yao, B., Bu, F., Reedy, J., Chiu, G.T.C.: Adaptive robust motion control of single-rod hydraulic actuators: theory and experiments. IEEE/ASME Trans. Mechatron. **5**(1), 79–91 (2000)
14. Yu, H., Feng, Z., Wang, X.: Nonlinear control for a class of hydraulic servo system. J. Zhejiang Univ. Sci. **5**(11), 1413–1417 (2004)
15. Yao, J., Jiao, Z., Ma, D., Yan, L.: High-accuracy tracking control of hydraulic rotary actuators with modeling uncertainties. IEEE/ASME Trans. Mechatron. **19**(2), 633–641 (2014)
16. Pedro, J.O., Dangor, M., Dahunsi, O.A., Ali, M.M.: Differential evolution-based PID control of nonlinear full-car electrohydraulic suspensions. Math. Probl. Eng. **2013**, 1–13 (2013)
17. Kaddissi, C., Kenne, J.-P., Saad, M.: Identification and real-time control of an electrohydraulic servo system based on nonlinear backstepping. IEEE/ASME Trans. Mechatron. **12**(1), 12–22 (2007)
18. Shen, G., Zhu, Z.C., Li, X., Tang, Y., Hou, D.D., Teng, W.X.: Real-time electro-hydraulic hybrid system for structural testing subjected to vibration and force loading. Mechatronics **33**, 49–70 (2016)
19. Ghazali, R., Sam, Y.M., Rahmat, M.F., Soon, C.C., Jaafar, H.I., Zulfatman: Discrete sliding mode control for a non-minimum phase electro-hydraulic actuator system. In: 2015 10th Asian Control Conference (ASCC), pp. 1–6 (2015)

20. Has, Z., Rahmat, M.F., Husain, A.R., Ishaque, K., Ghazali, R., Ahmad, M.N., Sam, Y.M., Rozali, S.M.: Robust position tracking control of an electro-hydraulic actuator in the presence of friction and internal leakage. Arab. J. Sci. Eng. **39**(4), 2965–2978 (2014)
21. Gdoura, E.K., Feki, M., Derbel, N.: Sliding mode control of a hydraulic servo system position using adaptive sliding surface and adaptive gain. Int. J. Model. Identif. Control **23** (3), 248–259 (2015)
22. Soon, C.C., Ghazali, R., Jaafar, H.I., Hussien, S.Y.S., Rozali, S.M., Rashid, M.Z.A.: Optimization of sliding mode control using particle swarm algorithm for an electro-hydraulic actuator system. J. Telecommun. Electron. Comput. Eng. **8**(7), 71–76 (2016)
23. Ghazali, R., Sam, Y.M., Rahmat, M.F., Hashim, A.W.I.M., Zulfatman: Performance comparison between sliding mode control with PID sliding surface and PID controller for an electro-hydraulic positioning system. Int. J. Adv. Sci. Eng. Inf. Technol. **1**(4), 447–452 (2011)
24. Ghazali, R., Sam, Y.M., Rahmat, M.F., Zulfatman, Hashim, A.W.I.M.: Simulation and experimental studies on perfect tracking optimal control of an electrohydraulic actuator system. J. Control Sci. Eng. **2012**, 1–8 (2012)
25. Ghazali, R., Sam, Y.M., Rahmat, M.F., Hashim, A.W.I.M., Zulfatman: Sliding mode control with PID sliding surface of an electro-hydraulic servo system for position tracking control. Aust. J. Basic Appl. Sci. **4**(10), 4749–4759 (2010)
26. Fateh, M.M., Zirkohi, M.M.: Adaptive impedance control of a hydraulic suspension system using particle swarm optimisation. Veh. Syst. Dyn. **49**(12), 1951–1965 (2011)
27. Wonohadidjojo, D.M., Kothapalli, G., Hassan, M.Y.: Position control of electro-hydraulic actuator system using fuzzy logic controller optimized by particle swarm optimization. Int. J. Autom. Comput. **10**(3), 181–193 (2013)
28. Yao, J., Jiang, G., Gao, S., Yan, H., Di, D.: Particle swarm optimization-based neural network control for an electro-hydraulic servo system. J. Vib. Control **20**(9), 1369–1377 (2014)
29. Pedro, J.O., Dangor, M., Dahunsi, O.A., Ali, M.M.: Intelligent feedback linearization control of nonlinear electrohydraulic suspension systems using particle swarm optimization. Appl. Soft Comput. **24**, 50–62 (2014)
30. Rozali, S.M., Rahmat, M.F., Husain, A.R.: Performance comparison of particle swarm optimization and gravitational search algorithm to the designed of controller for nonlinear system. J. Appl. Math. **2014**, 1–9 (2014)
31. Soon, C.C., Ghazali, R., Jaafar, H.I., Hussien, S.Y.S., Rozali, S.M., Rashid, M.Z.A.: Optimal PID sliding surface for sliding mode control based on particle swarm optimization algorithm for an electro-hydraulic actuator system. In: Proceedings of Mechanical Engineering Research Day 2016, pp. 64–65 (2016)
32. Soon, C.C., Ghazali, R., Jaafar, H.I., Hussien, S.Y.S.: Sliding mode controller design with optimized PID sliding surface using particle swarm algorithm. Procedia Comput. Sci. **105**, 235–239 (2017)
33. Eberhart, R.C., Shi, Y.: Particle swarm optimization: developments, applications and resources. In: Proceedings of the 2001 Congress on Evolutionary Computation, vol. 1, pp. 81–86 (2001)
34. Soon, C.C., Ghazali, R., Jaafar, H.I., Hussien, S.Y.S., Sam, Y.M., Rahmat, M.F.: The effects of parameter variation in open-loop and closed-loop control scheme for an electro-hydraulic actuator system. Int. J. Control Autom. **9**(11), 283–294 (2016)

A New Local Search Algorithm for Minimum Span Frequency Assignment in Mobile Communication

Ser Lee Loh[1(⊠)], Seik Ping Lim[1], Shin Horng Chong[1],
and Dennis Ling Chuan Ching[2]

[1] Universiti Teknikal Malaysia Melaka, Hang Tuah Jaya,
76100 Durian Tunggal, Melaka, Malaysia
{slloh, horng}@utem.edu.my, happypink_5848@hotmail.com
[2] Universiti Teknologi Petronas, Seri Iskandar, 32610 Teronoh, Perak, Malaysia
dennis.ling@utp.edu.my

Abstract. Recent years, the use of mobile communication has been steadily increases. An important process in mobile communication is the assignment of frequency spectrum called channel to each of the caller and receiver pair in order to communicate. This headed to some problems faced by mobile communication on how to distribute the large number of users efficiently with the limited capital of radio frequency spectrum. Zero interference between channels assigned may contributed to a high quality call service between users. In mobile communication one of the ways to solve the problem is dividing a geographical area into a number of cells in order to reuse the limited frequencies with the aim of supporting more users and also to minimize interference. Hence, a local search method is proposed in this project to solve the channel assignment problem with the minimum span of frequency and zero interference between the channels assigned.

Keywords: Channel assignment · Minimum span of frequency · Interference

1 Introduction

In a cellular communication system, the geographical area is logically divided into small region called cells. Each cell has a cell site or a base station. A given transmission capacity can be classified into a set of non-interfering radio channels for the communication purpose. All channels can be used at the same time at different cells, provided these frequencies are sufficiently separated in difference, so that there is no interference between them.

Recently, as mobile phones become distinctly universal, there is a constantly developing requirement in mobile communication and their popularity guaranteed its high development rate. In any case, the frequency spectrum that can be used for communication purpose limited. Therefore, of the efficient utilization of channel frequencies turns into more and more important. The allocated spectrum has been separated into a number of channels depends on service requirement. Optimal assignment of frequency channels is an approach to solve the problem on limited usable

© Springer Nature Singapore Pte Ltd. 2017
M.S. Mohamed Ali et al. (Eds.): AsiaSim 2017, Part II, CCIS 752, pp. 116–125, 2017.
DOI: 10.1007/978-981-10-6502-6_10

frequencies and thus gives inspiration for the research on channels assignment problem (CAP). The purpose of CAP is to allocate of channels to every base station in such a way that the radio spectra is efficiently used and the interference among calls is avoided.

There are three constraints of the channel assignment that must be fulfilled due to the wireless interference between frequency spectrums. The cells assigned with the same channel are known as co-channel cells. Co-channel interference occurs when the signals at the same frequencies reach the receiver from the co-channel cells. Thus, certain pairs of radio cells cannot use the same channel simultaneously. Signals with nearby frequencies from adjacent cells cause the adjacent channel interference. Hence, certain pair of cells cannot use an adjacent frequency at the same time. The channels allocated in the same cell are known as co-site channels. The distance between any co-site channels must have a minimal separation of frequency between each other.

The channel allocation schemes can be divided into two types which are fixed channel allocation (FCA), where the channels are assigned to every cell permanently, and dynamic channel allocation (DCA), where all vacant channels are accessible for every cell. Insert FCA strategy in DCA strategies, firstly all channels are put in a central pool. When there have call requests, they are assigned to the new calls dynamically. When the call is done, they will be assigned back to the central pool. To avoid the interference, the selection of the most appropriate channel for any call is straightforward if it is only depend on current allocation and current traffic.

This project scoped at minimum span frequency assignment in mobile communication under the fixed channel allocation scheme. Interference is not allowed but channels may be reused as long as the minimal frequency separation constraint is fulfilled. The coding algorithms of the proposed local search will be developed using Matlab software.

1.1 Related Works

Recently, many researches of Channel Assignment Problem (CAP) have been carried out by using graph-theoretic method, heuristic approaches, and different optimization methods. The algorithms can be divided into two categories which are non-iterative algorithms and iterative algorithms. Calls ordering, cell ordering or heuristic frequency assignment techniques are used by most of non-iterative algorithms. Examples of iterative procedures are neural-network algorithms, genetic algorithms [1, 2], simulated annealing, other approaches and local search methods. A brief introduction of these iterative procedures will be presented in the following sections.

The authors solve the problem by using a hyper-heuristic method depends on the immense deluge algorithm [3]. However, a different method is used where the showed algorithms to figure the CAP in a case where the coverage is separated into different sizes of circular cells [4, 5]. A meta-heuristic with two stages, which is named *Greedy Randomized Adaptive Search Procedure* (GRASP) is proposed in [6] to solve the CAP. A set of starting solutions is constructed in the first stage. The neighborhood of constructed solution is carried out by local search in the second stage. A typical local search method is known as Frequency Exhaustive Assignment (FEA) which allocates calls to the least available frequency, while achieving the interference constraints. Optimal solution that achieves all benchmark occurrences considered is proposed by a hybrid GRASP-FEA in [7]. In [8], the authors solved the CAP by using the GRASP method, and both utilizing a graph coloring model.

In [9], the CAP as a hexagonal cellular system and violating the symmetry of the system were considered by the authors, a few of channel assignment system for a case constant demand on each node has been proposed. As demonstrated by these schemes, assign the channels are allocated to the nodes in a highly consistent and systematic way. Therefore, operation of GA utilizing these plans led to close-optimal assignment in a little number of iteration. A research introduced the non-constant requests on hexagonal cellular system, a clever idea of *critical block*, a fraternity whose minimum bandwidth demand is maximum with all other such clique for working out the CAP [10]. The non-constant requirements on the critical block followed by apportioned (by a linear integer programming formulation) into constant request of few littler sub-systems which gives an exquisite method of allocating frequency to critical block utilizing the system is proposed [9]. This apportioning followed by drawn-out for allocating frequency to the remaining system.

In [11], an algorithm is exhibited which is pertinent to the regular non-hexagonal network too. In this method, the first issue is changed to an identical smaller issue demanding smaller pursuit space. Then the smaller issue has been determined by using proper estimate algorithm rapidly. At last, the solution for the first issue have been acquired from the arrangement of the exchanged problem by using an altered Forced Assignment with Rearrangement (FAR) operation described in [12]. Furthermore, as a final-product of this method, there are some vacant or excess channels in some cell, as a rule. The particular excess channels may effectively use to address the transients request changes will emerge in actuality situation.

A local search method is the earliest strategies proposed to adapt to the computational obstinacy of NP-hard combinatorial advancement issues. Given a minimization issue with objective function f and feasible place R, a standard local search algorithms accomplice with every point $x_p \in R$ and neighborhood $N(x_p) \in R$. A present solution point $x_p \in R$ is given, the set $N(x_p)$ is finding for a point x_{p+1} with $f(x_{p+1}) < f(x_p)$. If the sort of point exists, it will become the new solution point, and the method is iterated. In any other case, x_p is remaining as a neighborhood best inside $N(x_p)$. To begin the technique, a set of feasible solution points is produce and every of them are the locally stepped forward inside its neighborhood.

1.2   Problem Statement

This project aims to minimize the span frequency assignment in mobile communication. From the past experience, the demand for channels or the number of calls in cell i is recorded and denoted by m_i. Based on this demand information, frequency or channel is assigned without violating the frequency separation constraint. Span frequency refers to the difference between the values of the maximum and the minimum frequencies assigned. To maximize the usage of limited channels, frequencies are reused in such a way the assignment gives zero interference.

The minimum span frequency assignment consists of the following five components [13]:

1. The number of cells in the system is represented by N.
2. The number of channel required in cell i is represented by m_i for $i = 1, \ldots, N$.
3. The frequency separation demand between a call in cell i and a call in cell j is represented by c_{ij} for $i, j = 1, \ldots, N$.
4. The frequency allocated to the kth call in the ith cell is represented by f_{ik} for $= 1, \ldots, N, k = 1, \ldots, m_i$. All frequency has been represented by a positive integer.
5. The set of frequency-separation requirement is represented with the compatibility matrix C, where $|f_{ik} - f_{jl}| \geq c_{ij}$ for all $i, j, k, l (i \neq j), (k \neq l)$.

The compatibility matrix C, has been used to make sure interference does not occur by giving enough frequency separation distance among channels. The linear programming of the problem is presented as follows:

Minimize

$$\left(\max_{i,k} f_{ik} \right)$$

subject to

$$|f_{ik} - f_{jl}| \geq c_{ij}, i, j = 1, \ldots, N, k, l = 1, \ldots, m_i$$

This problem can be represented in a connected graph where a call is represents by each node of the graph, and while the identical calls cannot use the similar frequency, an edge has been connected from two vertices. The minimum demand frequency separate distance between the two calls at its endpoints is represented with an edge. Frequency f_{ik} is the frequency allocated to the kth call in the ith cell.

The channel assignment problem is similar to allocating positive integers that represent frequencies to the vertices of the graph by satisfying the following two criteria:

1. The absolute difference value of the integers allocated to these nodes is greater than or equivalent to the edge value if they are joined by an edge.
2. The maximum number of allocated integer is as low as possible.

2 Proposed Local Search Algorithm

Next, a local search algorithm will be proposed and coding algorithms will be developed using Matlab software. There are 3 stages involved in developing the proposed local search algorithm. Firstly in stage 1, matrix E, which is the minimal separation of frequency between the calls, is formed. Next in stage 2, the range of infeasible solution is identified and finally in stage 3, the channels are assigned in the range of feasible solution. The minimum span frequency is obtained from the channel assignment. The proposed algorithm is refined and improved until the satisfactory simulation result is obtained.

2.1   Development of Proposed Local Search Method

From the problem statement, given a number of cells, N, separation matrix C and demand of channels, D, where $D = m_i$ and $M = \sum m_i$ for $i = 1, \ldots, N$. The frequency span assigned to all calls in N cells is being minimized.

An illustrative example is given as follows:

Given number of cells, $N = 5$, separation matrix $C = \begin{pmatrix} 6 & 5 & 1 & 0 & 0 \\ 5 & 6 & 4 & 2 & 0 \\ 1 & 4 & 6 & 3 & 1 \\ 0 & 2 & 3 & 6 & 2 \\ 0 & 0 & 1 & 2 & 6 \end{pmatrix}$ and the

demand of channels or number of calls in each of the cells, $D = \begin{pmatrix} 2 \\ 1 \\ 2 \\ 3 \\ 2 \end{pmatrix}$. This problem

is then represented by a connected graph where the nodes and arcs represent the calls and the minimal frequency separation between the two calls, respectively.

From the connected graph, nodes f_{11} and f_{21} are connected since the minimum frequency separation between cells 1 and 2 is non-zero ($C_{12} = 5$). In addition, the frequency assigned to f_{11} and f_{21} must have a minimum difference of 5 units. Nodes f_{11} and f_{41} is not connected because the minimum frequency separation between cells 2 and 3 is zero ($C_{14} = 0$). In other words, f_{11} and f_{41} may be assigned the same frequency.

2.1.1   Stage 1: Form the Matrix E

In this project, a new local search algorithm will be developed to solve the minimum span frequency problem. The calls are assigned in order starting from the first cell to the last cell. The minimal separation of frequency between the calls is given by matrix E, where the entries E_{ij} represent the minimal separation frequency between the calls i and j. For example, the minimum frequency separation between call 1 and call 2 is equal to 6.

$$E = \begin{bmatrix} 0 & 6 & 5 & 1 & 1 & 0 & 0 & 0 & 0 & 0 \\ 6 & 0 & 5 & 1 & 1 & 0 & 0 & 0 & 0 & 0 \\ 5 & 5 & 0 & 4 & 4 & 2 & 2 & 2 & 0 & 0 \\ 1 & 1 & 4 & 0 & 6 & 3 & 3 & 3 & 1 & 1 \\ 1 & 1 & 4 & 6 & 0 & 3 & 3 & 3 & 1 & 1 \\ 0 & 0 & 2 & 3 & 3 & 0 & 6 & 6 & 2 & 2 \\ 0 & 0 & 2 & 3 & 3 & 6 & 0 & 6 & 2 & 2 \\ 0 & 0 & 2 & 3 & 3 & 6 & 6 & 0 & 2 & 2 \\ 0 & 0 & 0 & 1 & 1 & 2 & 2 & 2 & 0 & 6 \\ 0 & 0 & 0 & 1 & 1 & 2 & 2 & 2 & 6 & 0 \end{bmatrix}$$

2.1.2   Stage 2: Identify the Range of Infeasible Solution

With the formation of matrix E, the set of frequency channel separation constraint is transformed to the difference between frequencies f_i and f_j must be greater than the entries, E_{ij}, from matrix E, where f_i represents the channel assigned to ith call in the list.

$$|f_i - f_j| \geq E_{ij}, \quad i,j = 1, \ldots, M$$

To find for f_i, firstly, the initial channel is assigned to the first call in the first cell, which is $f_j = f_1 = 1$. Then the values of all $f_j \pm E_{ij}$, where f_j is all calls that have been assigned with channel and have a nonzero minimal separation with ith call, are calculated. The range of $f_j \pm E_{ij}$ is the range for infeasible solutions since the f_i within the range of $(f_j - E_{ij}) < x < (f_j + E_{ij})$ violates the minimal separation constraint. Hence, f_i must be assigned a channel which is outside the range of x. Finally, the lowest available channel outside the range of x is assigned to f_i.

For example, f_1, f_2 and f_3 are assigned with channel 1, 7 and 12, respectively. Then, three ranges need to be computed to assign f_4 as shown by solid lines in Fig. 1:

1. The frequency different between call 1 and call 4 must be greater than 1 which is $|f_4 - f_1| \geq 1$. As the frequency allocated to the call 1 is equal to 1 ($f_1 = 1$), hence the f_4 cannot be in the range of $0 < f_4 < 2$.
2. The frequency different between call 2 and call 4 must be greater than 1 which is $|f_4 - f_2| \geq 1$. As the frequency allocated to the call 1 is equal to 1 ($f_2 = 7$), hence the f_4 cannot be in the range of $6 < f_4 < 8$.
3. The frequency different between call 3 and call 4 must be greater than 4 which is $|f_4 - f_1| \geq 4$. As the frequency allocated to the call 1 is equal to 1 ($f_3 = 12$), hence the f_4 cannot be in the range of $8 < f_4 < 16$.

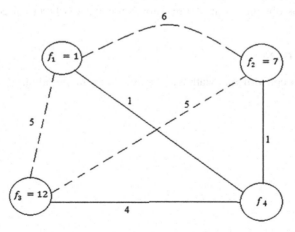

Fig. 1. A graphical representation of minimum span frequency assignment for f_4

2.1.3 Stage 3: Assigned the Channel in the Range of Feasible Solution

The 3 ranges are drawn as shown in Fig. 2. From these 3 ranges of infeasible solutions, the f_4 will be set as 2 since channel number 2 is the lowest feasible available channel that is not in the ranges of $0 < f_1 < 2$, $6 < f_2 < 8$ and $8 < f_3 < 16$ as shown in Fig. 2.

1 2 3 4 5 6 7 8 9 10 11 12 13 14 15 16

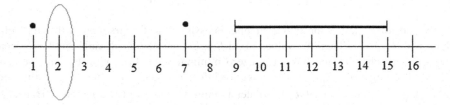

Fig. 2. A graphical representation of the frequency allocated to the *4*th call

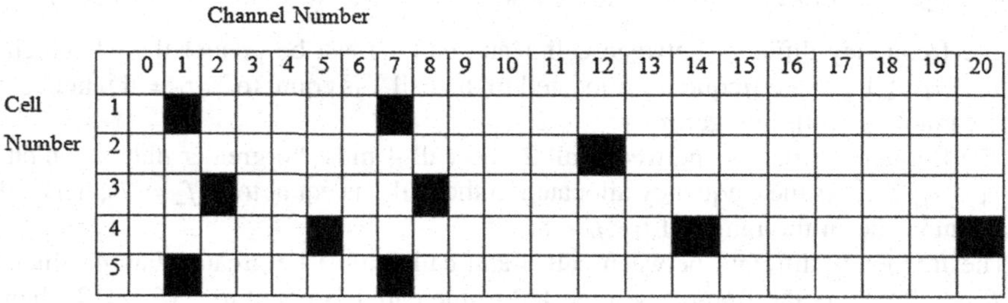

Channel Number
0 1 2 3 4 5 6 7 8 9 10 11 12 13 14 15 16 17 18 19 20
Cell
Number
1
2
3
4
5

Fig. 3. Interference free assignment for 4-cell and 13-channel system

The rest of the calls are assigned with channels using the same flow and finally, minimum span is obtained from the maximum number of channel used.

2.2 Program Code

The algorithm is coded using Matlab software to run the iteration.

```
for i=1:N
        for j=1:M(i)
            a=a+1, b=0;
            for k=1:N
                for l=1:M(k)
                    b=b+1;
                    if (k==i && l==j)
                        E(a,b)=0;
                    else
                        E(a,b)=C(i,k);
                    end
                end
            end
        end
    end

    P=100;
    f(1)=1;
    for i=1:a
        A=ones(1,P);
        for j=1:i
            if(E(i,j)>0)
                e=f(j)-E(i,j)
                for k=1:E(i,j)*2-1
                    e=e+1;
                    if (e>0)
                        A(e)=0;
                    end
                end
            end
        end
        for l=1:P
            if (A(l)==1)
                f(i)=1;
                break;
            end
        end
    end
```

3 Result and Discussion

The result is the channel assigned to each of the call where the minimum span of frequency is the maximum number of channels used. Based on the illustrative example, the following result is obtained and shown in Fig. 3.

$$f_{11} = 1$$
$$f_{12} = 7$$
$$f_{21} = 12$$
$$f_{31} = 2$$
$$f_{32} = 8$$
$$f_{41} = 5$$
$$f_{42} = 14$$
$$f_{43} = 20$$
$$f_{51} = 1$$
$$f_{52} = 7$$

There are 3 calls demand in cell 4 and channels 5, 14 and 20 are assigned to cell 4. Cells 2 have only 1 call demand and channel 12 is assigned. Cells 1, 3 and 5 have 2 call demands, respectively. Hence, channels 2 and 8 are assigned in cell 3 and channels 1 and 7 are assigned in cell 1 and cell 5, respectively. The minimum frequency separation constraint is fulfilled. For example, $C_{44} = 6$ restricts the minimum difference of frequencies assigned in cell 4 is 6. Hence, the difference between any of f_{41}, f_{42} and f_{43} is all at least 6. From this example, channel 1 and 7 are reused at cells 1 and 5, and the minimum span frequency is 20.

4 Conclusion and Recommendations

Recent years the evolution of mobile telecommunication raised the expansion of cellular users significantly. The number of vacant frequencies needed in mobile communication is much lower than the popularity of mobile usage increasing rate. Channels are assigned in such a way overall interference is zero, channel demand requirements are met and the span frequency assigned is being minimized. Zero interference may contribute to high quality calls. In this project, a new local search method is developed to solve the minimum span frequency problem in cellular network. The algorithm is efficient in searching for the minimum span of frequency. In overall, an optimal assignment of channels may increase the efficiency of mobile communication. This proposed method may be improved by changing the initial solution from one call to another and it will be carried out by authors in near future.

Acknowledgments. The authors would like to thank the Malaysian Ministry of Higher Education and Universiti Teknikal Malaysia Melaka for their financial funding through RAGS grant RAGS/2014/TK03/FKE/B00047.

References

1. Wang, L., Arunkumaar, S., Gu, W.: Genetic algorithms for optimal channel assignment in mobile communications. In: Proceedings of the 9th International Conference on Neural Information Processing, ICONIP 2002, vol. 3, pp. 1–33 (2002)
2. Beckmann, D., Killat, U.: A new strategy for the application of genetic algorithms to the channel-assignment problem. Veh. Technol. IEEE Trans. 48(4), 1261–1269 (1999)
3. Kendall, G., Mazlan, M.: Channel assignment in cellular communication using a great deluge hyper-heuristic. In: Proceedings of IEEE International Conference on Networking, pp. 769–773 (2004)
4. Wu, L.C., Wey, L.Y.: Channel assignment for cellular mobile networks with nonuniform cells. IEEE Proc. Commun. 145, 451–456 (1998)
5. Chavez-Santiago, R., Gigi, E., Lyandres, V.: Channel assignment for cellular mobile networks with nonuniform cells an improved heuristic algorithm. IEEE Proc. Commun. 153, 61–68 (2006)
6. Resende, M.G.C.: Greedy randomized adaptive search procedures (GRASP). AT&T Labs Research, Technical report, vol. 41, no. 1, pp. 1–11 (1998)
7. Vieira, C.E.C., Gondim, P.R.L., Rodrigues, C.A., Bordim, J.L.: A new technique to the channel assignment problem in mobile communication networks. In: Proceedings of IEEE 19th International Symposium on Personal, Indoor and Mobile Radio Communications, pp. 1–5 (2008)
8. Liu, X., Pardalos, P.M., Rajasekaran, S., Resende, M.G.C.: A GRASP for frequency assignment in mobile radio networks. DIMACS Ser. Discret. Math. Theor. Comput. Sci. 52, 195–201 (2000)
9. Ghosh, S.C., Sinha, B.P., Das, N.: Channel assignment using genetic algorithm based on geometric symmetry. IEEE Trans. Veh. Technol. 52(4), 860–875 (2003)
10. Ghosh, S.C., Sinha, B.P., Das, N.: A new approach to efficient channel assignment for hexagonal cellular networks. Int. J. Found. Comput. Sci. World Sci. 14(3), 439–463 (2003)
11. Ghosh, S.C., Sinha, B.P., Das, N.: Coalesced CAP: an improved technique for frequency assignment in cellular networks. IEEE Trans. Veh. Technol. 55(2), 640–653 (2006)
12. Tcha, D.-W., Kwon, J.-H., Choi, T.-J., Oh, S.-H.: Perturbation-minimizing frequency assignment in a changing TDMA/FDMA cellular environment. IEEE Trans. Veh. Technol. 49(2), 390–396 (2000)
13. Sivarajan, K.N., McEliece, R.J., Ketchum, J.W.: Channel assignment in cellular radio. In: IEEE 39th Vehicular Technology Conference, vol. 42, no. 4, pp. 846–850 (1989)

Underwater Target Tracking of Offshore Crane System in Subsea Operations

Hooi-Siang Kang[1,2], Yun-Ta Wu[3], Lee Kee Quen[4],
Collin Howe-Hing Tang[1(✉)], and Chee-Loon Siow[1,2]

[1] Faculty of Mechanical Engineering, Universiti Teknologi Malaysia (UTM),
81310 Johor Bahru, Johor, Malaysia
{kanghs,tangh,scloon}@utm.my
[2] Institute for Vehicle Systems and Engineering (IVeSE),
Universiti Teknologi Malaysia (UTM), 81310 Johor Bahru, Johor, Malaysia
[3] International Wave Dynamics Research Center,
National Cheng-Kung University,
No.1, University Road, Tainan City 701, Taiwan, ROC
ytwu@mail.ncku.edu.tw
[4] Department of Mechanical Precision Engineering,
Malaysia-Japan International Institute of Technology (MJIIT),
Universiti Teknologi Malaysia Kuala Lumpur,
54100 Kuala Lumpur, Wilayah Persekutuan, Malaysia
lkquen@utm.my

Abstract. Accurate underwater target tracking during subsea lowering is a complex technological problem in offshore installation and deep ocean mining. It involves the real-time motion compensation of both combined effects from flow-induced vibration on the cable-payload and wave-induced motions on the host vessel. A target tracking mechanism for a planar motion was theoretically derived and simulated in this paper under both regular and irregular wave motions. The simulation results have shown that the proposed target tracking system, by using PID controller integrated with hydrodynamic effects of both surface vessel and subsea payload, has followed the movable subsea target with small vicinity. The findings of this paper can be further implemented in the development of automatizing the subsea operations of the offshore crane system.

Keywords: Target tracking · Subsea mining · Wire rope cable · Offshore installation

1 Introduction

Subsea operations such as lifting and lowering subsea equipment in offshore oil and gas field installation, ocean mining, and underwater surveillance require accurate positioning method of the host vessel to the targeted location. The floating host vessel on the water surface is linked to the subsea targets, such as wellhead connector, anchoring point, submersible cans, and mineral rocks, via end effector which is connected to the host vessel through steel cable. The steel cable has dynamic behavior which can be regarded as a space curve [1, 2]. The combined dynamic behavior of offshore steel

© Springer Nature Singapore Pte Ltd. 2017
M.S. Mohamed Ali et al. (Eds.): AsiaSim 2017, Part II, CCIS 752, pp. 126–137, 2017.
DOI: 10.1007/978-981-10-6502-6_11

cable is highly complex motion with respect to the loads' excitation from the wind [3–6], wave [7, 8], current [9–11], host vessel's motion [12] and self-excitation [13, 14]. The dynamic behavior of an offshore crane cable when it is subjected to a flow field, and wave motion, is an important problem in subsea operation because the position of end effector could be significantly deviated from the desired coordinate. One of the most important factors to contribute to position deviation is caused by the combined effects of the ocean wind and currents. Offshore crane cable in the long span is exposed to the flow-induced vibration (FIV) when it is subjected to wind and currents. The formation of FIV is due to the pressure differences around a cylindrical body, forming vortices at the boundary layer which tend to separate at the downstream of the cable and result in the cable oscillation which is normal to the flow [9]. A large number of analytical and experimental studies have been conducted on flow induced vibrations (FIV) [3, 5, 6, 9, 10]. Another significant factor to the dynamic position variations during subsea operation is due to the motions of the surface vessel. According to [15], the wave-induced dynamic force is one of the most important excitations to be dealt with in the motion of offshore structures. Complex nonlinear hull/tendon/riser coupled dynamic analyses of a motion of offshore floating structure for the first-order and second-order sum- and difference-frequency wave loads and other hydrodynamic coefficients had been conducted in [16–18].

The majority of these previous research works in subsea cable operation only focused on either single factor by assuming the effects of other contributor is under certain restrictions. However, as the technology of subsea lowering operation facing more challenges in deep water condition, especially in the dynamic positioning and motion compensation issues [19–22], the researchers are now required to focus on an active control approach to track the subsea target in deep water. It is a complex problem because it must include both surface vessel motions and flow induced motions of the subsea target. In order to complete this research gap, this paper is aiming to develop an underwater target tracking system of offshore crane system for subsea lowering operation. The objectives of this paper are (i) to model target tracking system of offshore crane cable for subsea operations; and (ii) to numerically simulate the response of underwater target tracking under both regular and irregular wave motions.

2   Methodology

2.1   Equation of Motion

The schematic diagram of an offshore crane cable during subsea operation is illustrated in Fig. 1. The target tracking system is installed on the surface vessel to compensate the relative motions in between the surface vessel and the subsea target. In this paper, the motion compensation of target tracking was studied in X-Z planar motions. The displacement deviations will be calculated and a linear cart actuator will move on the rail dynamically to compensate the magnitude in X-direction. On the other hand, a winch is attached to the movable cart and it will interactively adjust the submerged length of steel wire cable, which is lowered down through the moonpool into the water column,

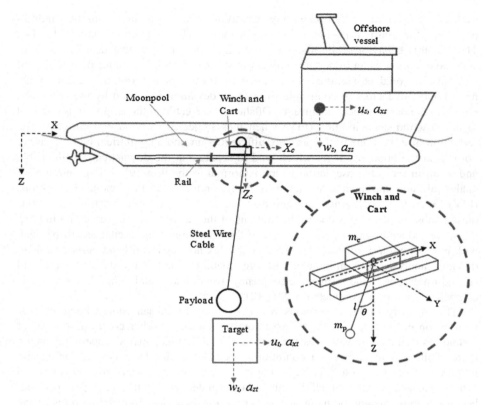

Fig. 1. Schematic diagram (non-scale) of subsea target tracking system.

according to the inputs to be calculated by target tracking controller to compensate the gaps in between the payload and target.

The dynamic behavior of the subsea target tracking system can be characterized by using Euler-Lagrange formulation L as follows [19]

$$L = \frac{1}{2}\left(m_c\dot{x}_c^2\right) + \frac{1}{2}m_p\begin{pmatrix} \dot{x}_c^2 - 2\dot{x}_c l \sin\theta - 2\dot{x}_c l\dot{\theta} \cos\theta + \\ l^2 \sin^2\theta + l^2\dot{\theta}^2 \cos^2\theta + \\ l^2 \cos^2\theta + l^2\dot{\theta}^2 \sin^2\theta \end{pmatrix} + \frac{1}{2}\left(I\dot{\theta}^2\right) + m_p gl \cos\theta$$

(1)

where m_c is the mass of cart actuator, m_p is the mass of payload, I is moment inertia of the payload, l is the cable length, x_c is the displacement of cart actuator in the horizontal direction, θ is the inclined angle of steel wire cable with respect to z-axis, $(\cdot)$ is first-time derivative of variables, and g is the gravitational acceleration.

By rewriting (1) into state space form, the generalized dynamic model of the target tracking system for offshore subsea operation in X-Z planar, as shown in Fig. 1, can be represented as

$$\mathbf{M}(q)\ddot{q} + \mathbf{V_m}(q,\dot{q})\dot{q} + \mathbf{G}(q)q = \mathbf{u} \tag{2}$$

where $\mathbf{M}(q)$ is the inertia matrix of the offshore crane (cart actuator) system and submerged payload, which can be defined as

$$\mathbf{M}(q) = \begin{bmatrix} m_c + m_p & -m_p l \cos\theta & -m_p \sin\theta \\ -m_p l \cos\theta & m_p l^2 & 0 \\ -m_p \sin\theta & 0 & m_p \end{bmatrix} \tag{3}$$

and the effects of centripetal-Coriolis factor $\mathbf{V_m}$ on the offshore crane system is

$$\mathbf{V_m}(q,\dot{q}) = \begin{bmatrix} 0 & m_p l\dot{\theta} \sin\theta & -2m_p\dot{\theta} \cos\theta \\ 0 & 0 & 2m_p l\dot{\theta} \\ 0 & -m_p l\dot{\theta} & 0 \end{bmatrix} \tag{4}$$

and the gravitational function, $\mathbf{G}(q)$ is defined as

$$\mathbf{G}(q) = \begin{bmatrix} 0 & m_p gl \sin\theta & -m_p g \cos\theta \end{bmatrix}^{\mathrm{T}} \tag{5}$$

On the right-hand-side of (2), the forces exerted from cart actuator and winch $\mathbf{u}$ to compensate the gaps for target tracking is defined as

$$\mathbf{u} = \{ F_x \quad 0 \quad F_l \}^{\mathrm{T}} \tag{6}$$

where F_x is referred to force input to cart and F_l is force input to the winch respectively. The state variables of the target tracking system is defined as

$$q = \{ x_c \quad \theta \quad l \}^{\mathrm{T}} \tag{7}$$

Wave force acting on the offshore surface vessel, lowering payload and movable target can be determined from the motion of neighboring water particles around these structures. By assuming linear wave theory and deep water conditions, the velocity potential is represented as

$$\phi = \frac{ag}{\omega} e^{kz} \sin(kx - \omega t) \tag{8}$$

where a is the amplitude of the wave, ω is the circular frequency of the wave motion, k is the wave number, z is the submerged depth from mean water level (MWL), x is the horizontal position, and t is the time. The velocities of water particles in both horizontal u and vertical direction w are

$$\begin{cases} u = \frac{d\phi}{dx} = \frac{d}{dx}\left(\frac{ag}{\omega} e^{kz} \sin(kx - \omega t) \right) = \omega a e^{kz} \cos(kx - \omega t) \\ w = \frac{d\phi}{dz} = \frac{d}{dz}\left(\frac{ag}{\omega} e^{kz} \sin(kx - \omega t) \right) = \omega a e^{kz} \sin(kx - \omega t) \end{cases} \tag{9}$$

and the accelerations of water particles in both horizontal a_x and vertical direction a_z are

$$
\begin{cases}
a_x = \frac{\partial}{\partial t}\left(\frac{\partial \phi}{\partial x}\right) = \omega^2 a e^{kz} \sin\left(kx - \omega t\right) \\
a_z = \frac{\partial}{\partial t}\left(\frac{\partial \phi}{\partial z}\right) = -\omega^2 a e^{kz} \cos\left(kx - \omega t\right)
\end{cases} \tag{10}
$$

The relative motion between the surface vessel, payload, and targeting point is determined based on the following assumptions: (a) the system is under deep water condition, where the radius of circular motion of water particles is decreasing exponentially when the submerged water depth z is increased; (b) sea current is assumed to be negligible in this study, hence, the nonlinear cable dynamics such as vortex induced vibration on cable are assumed to be negligible as well; (c) the cable is assumed to be massless, un-stretchable, and no bending throughout the control process; (d) the response amplitude operators (RAOs) of surface vessel are assumed to be 1:1 in both heave and surge motions with respect to the wave elevation; (e) the dynamic motion of payload is identical to the motion of surface vessel throughout the simulation. Based on these assumptions, the relative velocities between the surface vessel and the target in both horizontal and vertical directions are represented as

$$
\begin{cases}
\dot{X}_d = u_s - u_t \\
\dot{Z}_d = w_s - w_t
\end{cases} \tag{11}
$$

$$
\begin{cases}
\ddot{X}_d = a_{xs} - a_{xt} \\
\ddot{Z}_d = a_{zs} - a_{zt}
\end{cases} \tag{12}
$$

where u_s and w_s are the velocities of the surface vessel in horizontal and vertical directions, u_t and w_t are the velocities of the target in horizontal and vertical directions, respectively. While a_{xs} and a_{zs} are the accelerations of the surface vessel in horizontal and vertical directions, a_{xt} and a_{zt} are the accelerations of the target in horizontal and vertical directions, respectively. The relative velocities in (11) and relative accelerations in (12) are calculated as the desired magnitudes for the target tracking system to compensate the gaps in between the payload and the targeting point during the subsea operations.

The wave forces acting on the surface vessel, payload and target are identified as the external disturbances to the controlled target tracking system because wave forces will vary the actual F_x and F_l, as defined in (6), to be employed to compensate the gaps. By using Morison Equation, the total wave forces can be approximated as [2]

$$
\begin{cases}
F_{mx} = C_m \rho_w V_p \ddot{X}_c - (C_m - 1)\rho_w V_p \ddot{X}_d + \frac{1}{2}\rho_w C_d S_x \left(\dot{X}_c - \dot{X}_d\right)\left|\left(\dot{X}_c - \dot{X}_d\right)\right| \\
F_{mz} = C_m \rho_w V_p \ddot{Z}_c - (C_m - 1)\rho_w V_p \ddot{Z}_d + \frac{1}{2}\rho_w C_d S_z \left(\dot{Z}_c - \dot{Z}_d\right)\left|\left(\dot{Z}_c - \dot{Z}_d\right)\right|
\end{cases} \tag{13}
$$

where F_{mx} and F_{mz} are wave forces (which are regarded as disturbances) acting on the cart actuator, payload, and target in horizontal and vertical direction, respectively. X_c and Z_c are the displacements of cart actuator, X_d and Z_d are the relative displacements in between surface vessel and the target, $(\cdot)$ is time derivative of variables, C_m is the inertia coefficient of payload, ρ_w is the density of seawater, V_p is the volume of payload, C_d is the drag coefficient, S_x and S_z are the projected areas of payload in the horizontal and vertical directions respectively.

2.2 Simulation Conditions

In the simulation, the properties of target tracking system are listed in Table 1. A 250 kg spherical payload was initially to be lowered across the water column until 50 m below MWL, where the targeting tracking mechanism will be activated at this initial condition. There are several assumptions in the simulation [19]: (a) the payload and cart are connected through a rigid cable, which is assumed to be inextensible, massless, and frictionless; (b) the inclined angle of cable are assumed to be measured perfectly in the feedback mechanism; (c) the motions of payload and subsea target point are restrained in X-Z plane only; and (d) the maximum allowable swinging angle of the payload is bounded within $\pm\pi$ radian.

Table 1. Properties of the target tracking system.

Part	Properties	Magnitude
Payload	Mass	250 kg
	Shape	Sphere
	Volume	0.5 m^3
	Moment inertia	625,000 kgm^2
	Inertia coefficient	1.5
	Drag coefficient	0.47
	Projected area (vertical)	2 m^2
	Projected area (horizontal)	2 m^2
	Initial position	−50 m (below MWL)
Cable	Mass	Massless
	Length	100 m
	Initial length in water column	50 m
Cart and Winch	Mass	500 kg

The target tracking system is controlled by two classical PID controllers, as shown in Fig. 2, for controlling cart and winch respectively. The PID controller coefficients are listed in Table 2. In order to achieve the subsea target tracking system, cart and winch on the surface vessel are utilized to control the position of submerged payload. The control inputs are F_x an F_l, which actuate the cart in the X-direction and steel wire cable position in Z-direction respective. Meanwhile, the inclined angle of submerged cable remains uncontrolled in this case.

The target tracking system was simulated under both regular and irregular wave motions, as shown in Table 3. For regular wave input, the amplitude of $A = 1.75$ m was selected to generate wave force to the system. On the other hand, under the irregular wave motion, JONSWAP spectrum with significant wave height of $2A$ and peak enhancement factor $\gamma = 2.5$ was selected in the simulation.

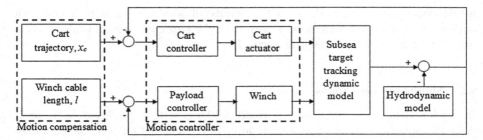

Fig. 2. Control block diagram for targeting tracking system.

Table 2. PID controller coefficients.

Coefficient	Horizontal direction	Vertical direction
K_p	20000	20000
K_I	200	200
K_D	500	1000

3   Results and Discussion

The simulation of target tracking system for subsea operations was conducted under both regular and irregular wave motions as shown in Table 3. The desired displacement in surge and heave directions was calculated by considering the motions of the surface vessel, payload, and target respectively. As shown in Fig. 3, the surge and heave motions were referred to the relative motions in between surface vessel and subsea target, which was integrated from (11). The wave elevation was varying in amplitude A of 1.75 m with respect to MWL under the regular wave inputs, whereas the wave amplitude was highly nonlinear under the irregular motion which has the significant wave height of $2A$.

Table 3. Input motions for target.

Input motion	Properties	Magnitude
Regular	Wave height	1.75 m
	Wave period	4 s
Irregular	Spectrum	JONSWAP
	Significant wave height	3.5 m
	Wave period	4 s
	Gamma	2.5
RAO	Surge	1.0
	Heave	1.0
Sea water	Density	1029 kg/m^3

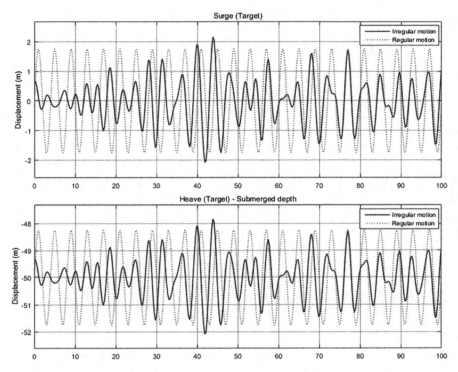

Fig. 3. Desired surge and heave to compensate the motions of target under regular and irregular wave inputs.

Since the RAO of the surface vessel is assumed to be 1:1 in both heave and surge motions with respect to the wave elevation, the relative displacements in both directions are identical in pattern. In the irregular wave motion, the deviations of displacement in between surface vessel and subsea target are varying from −2.1 m to 2.1 m in the horizontal direction, and with the same range of vertical displacement about −50 m below MWL. It is noteworthy that the motions of the target at such water depth could be very small as predicted by linear wave theory; hence, the relative displacements in this study were mainly due to the motions of the surface vessel which was subjected to the surface wave motions.

The response of target tracking system for subsea operations as derived from (7) after considering the influences of wave forces in (13), under regular wave motion, is shown in Fig. 4. The displacement of cart actuator x_c in the horizontal direction was traveling back and forth in the range of −2 m to 2 m to compensate the relative surge gaps between the surface vessel and the subsea targeting point. It can be found that the responses of the cart after considering the hydrodynamic forces followed the desired inputs into the cart. Similarly, the simulation results for actual submerged cable length l are in the regular mode, which is in accordance with the desired inputs to the winch. The deviations between the *actual* and *desired* motions can be further reduced by optimizing the PID controller coefficients.

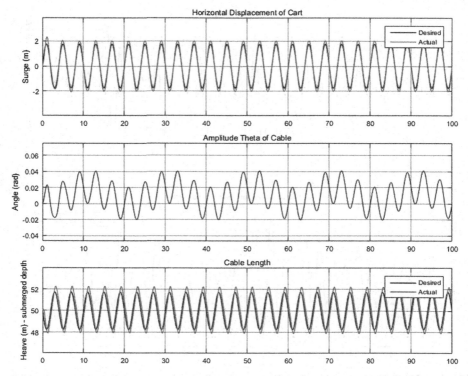

Fig. 4. Target tracking system responses in regular wave motion for horizontal displacement of cart actuator, inclined angle of cable, and submerged length of cable.

The inclined angle of steel wire cable θ can be used to verify the stability of target tracking system. In the simulation for regular wave motion, the inclined angle is varying from −0.02 rad to 0.04 rad, which means the inclined angle to be induced by the motion of cart actuator and the inertia of payload is less than 3° in this regular simulation.

On the other hand, the response of target tracking system for subsea operations as derived from (7) after considering wave forces in (13), under irregular wave motion, is shown in Fig. 5. The simulation of horizontal displacements for cart actuator x_c was well-matched with the desired inputs. The value of desired surge motion input to the cart actuator is highly non-linear in this case, which was varying irregularly in the range from −2 m to 2 m. The simulation results for submerged cable length l in the irregular mode were in accordance with the desired inputs to the winch too. It is noteworthy that the actual dynamic responses of cart and winch can be further modified by optimizing the corresponding PID controller's coefficients. The inclined angle of steel wire cable θ under the irregular wave condition is varying from −0.025 rad to 0.035 rad in the simulation, which means the inclined angle to be induced by the motion of cart actuator and the inertia of payload is less than 2° in this irregular simulation.

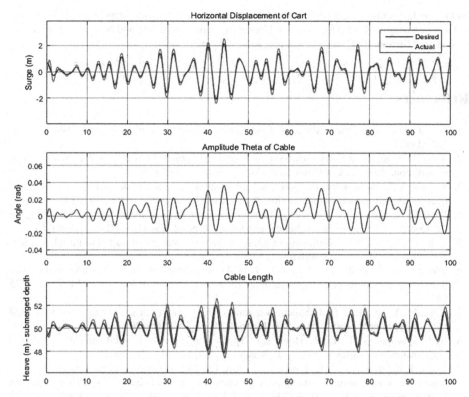

Fig. 5. Target tracking system responses in irregular wave motion for horizontal displacement of cart actuator, inclined angle of cable, and submerged length of cable.

4 Conclusion

Subsea target tracking of offshore crane cable is significant to assure cable's position integrity during subsea lowering operation. The dynamic positioning of hoisted payload can be adequately adjusted by using PID controller with respect to relatively feedback motions. From the study in this paper, it can be concluded that:

- the position of the submerged payload can be adjusted in close proximity to the movable target by using subsea target tracking method;
- the planar motion compensation can be achieved by using cart actuator and winch. However, the actual size of target tracking system is highly related with the amplitude of excitation wave motions to be compensated;
- the actual dynamic responses of cart and winch can be further modified by optimizing the corresponding PID controller's coefficients.

Acknowledgements. The authors would like to appreciate the full supports from Universiti Teknologi Malaysia (UTM) for Research University Grant Vot 4F789, and National Cheng-Kung University (Taiwan, ROC) for 2016 SATU Joint Research Scheme.

References

1. Garrett, D.L.: Dynamic analysis of slender rods. J. Energy Resourc. Technol. **104**(4), 302–306 (1982)
2. Ran, Z.: Coupled dynamic analysis of floating structures in waves and currents. Ph.D. dissertation, Texas A&M University, College Station (2000)
3. Tzanov, V.V., Krauskopf, B., Neild, S.A.: Vibration dynamics of an inclined cable excited near its second natural frequency. Int. J. Bifurcat. Chaos **24**(9), 1430024 (2014)
4. Pospisil, S., Fischer, C., Naprstek, J.: Experimental analysis of the influence of damping on the resonance behavior of a spherical pendulum. J. Nonlinear Dyn. **78**, 371–390 (2014)
5. Zulli, D., Egidio, A.D.: Galloping of internally resonant towers subjected to turbulent wind. J. Continuum Mech. Thermodyn. **27**, 835–849 (2015)
6. Warminski, J., Zulli, D., Rega, G., Latalski, J.: Revisited modelling and multimodal nonlinear oscillations of a sagged cable under support motion. J. Meccanica **51**, 2541–2575 (2016)
7. Xiao, F., Yang, H.Z.: Probabilistic assessment of parametric instability of a top tensioned riser in irregular waves. J. Mar. Sci. Technol. **19**(3), 245–256 (2014)
8. Radhakrishnan, S., Datla, R., Hires, R.I.: Theoretical and experimental analysis of tethered buoy instability in gravity waves. J. Ocean Eng. **34**(2), 261–274 (2007)
9. Quen, L.K., Tang, C.H.H., Kang, H.-S., Ma, G.: Neural-network prediction of riser top tension for vortex induced vibration suppression. In: 6th IEEE International Conference on Underwater System Technology: Theory and Applications (USYS 2016), Penang, Malaysia (2016)
10. Vandiver, J.K., Swithenbank, S.B., Jaiswal, V., Jhingran, V.: Fatigue damage from high mode number vortex-induced vibration. In: 25th International Conference on Ocean, Offshore and Arctic Engineering, Hamburg, Germany (2006)
11. Lucor, D., Triantafyllou, M.S.: Parametric study of a two degree-of-freedom cylinder subject to vortex-induced vibrations. J. Fluids Struct. **24**, 1284–1293 (2008)
12. Wang, Z., Yang, H.: Parametric instability of a submerged floating pipeline between two floating structures under combined vortex excitations. J. Appl. Ocean Res. **59**, 265–273 (2016)
13. Yang, H., Xiao, F., Xu, P.: Parametric instability prediction in a top-tensioned riser in irregular waves. J. Ocean Eng. **70**, 39–50 (2013)
14. Akcabay, D.T., Young, Y.L.: Parametric excitations and lock-in of flexible hydrofoils in two-phase flows. J. Fluids Struct. **57**, 344–356 (2015)
15. Patil, K.C., Jangid, R.S.: Passive control of offshore jacket platforms. J. Ocean Eng. **32**, 1933–1949 (2005)
16. Kim, M.H., Tahar, A., Kim, Y.B.: Variability of TLP motion analysis against various design methodologies/parameters. In: 11th International Offshore and Polar Engineering Conference, Stavanger, Norway (2001)
17. Bae, Y.H., Kim, M.H., Shin, Y.S.: Rotor floater mooring coupled dynamic analysis of mini TLP type offshore floating wind turbines. In: 29th ASME International Conference on Ocean, Offshore and Arctic Engineering, pp. 491–498. American Society of Mechanical Engineers, Shanghai (2010)

18. Kang, H.-S., Kim, M.-H., Bhat Aramanadka, S.S.: Tension variations of hydro-pneumatic riser tensioner and implications for dry-tree interface in semisubmersible. Int. J. Ocean Syst. Eng. **7**(1), 21–38 (2017)

19. Wong, T.T., Tang, C.H., Mailah, M.: Winch driven active heave compensation for load transfer in overhead crane system. In: 4th IEEE International Conference on Intelligent and Advanced Systems (ICIAS), Kuala Lumpur, Malaysia, pp. 34–39 (2012)

20. Jia, D., Agrawal, M.: Fluid-structure interaction: lowering subsea structure/equipment in splash zone during installation. In: Offshore Technology Conference, Houston (2014)

21. Nam, B.W., Kim, N.W., Choi, Y.M., Hong, S.Y., Kim, J.W.: An experimental study on deepwater crane installation of subsea equipment in waves. In: 25th International Ocean and Polar Engineering Conference. International Society of Offshore and Polar Engineers, Kona (2015)

22. Kang, H.-S., Tang, C.H.H., Quen, L.K., Steven, A., Yu, X.: Prediction on parametric resonance of offshore crane cable for lowering subsea structures. In: 6th IEEE International Conference on Underwater System Technology: Theory and Applications (USYS 2016), Penang, Malaysia (2016)

Design of a High Force Density Tubular Linear Switched Reluctance Actuator (TLSRA) Without Permanent Magnet

Chin Kiat Yeo, Mariam Md. Ghazaly[(✉)], Shin Horng Chong,
and Irma Wani Jamaludin

Center for Robotics and Industrial Automation (CeRIA),
Faculty of Electrical Engineering, Universiti Teknikal Malaysia Melaka,
Melaka, Malaysia
mariam@utem.edu.my

Abstract. A novel tubular linear switched reluctance actuator (TLSRA) without permanent magnet that has 7:7 stator-to-mover pole pairs ratio is presented in this paper. A detailed analysis of the effect of mover parameters on the performances of proposed TLSRA is presented to determine the optimized actuator parameters. As comparison, the performances of the conventional TLSRA with 7:5 stator-to-mover pole pairs ratio is also designed and compared with the proposed TLSRA using the identical dimensions. The differences between the proposed and conventional TLSRA is number of available working pole pairs. The proposed TLSRA has four working pole pairs for a three phases actuator instead of two working pole pairs for conventional TLSRA. The additional working pole pairs in the proposed TLSRA exhibit force improvement, approximate two times higher compared to the conventional TLSRA. The static force characteristics for the proposed TLSRA is calculated and computed by using the three-dimensional finite element method (FEM) with ANSYS Maxwell software.

Keywords: Linear actuator design · TLSRA · Thrust force · Mover optimization · Working pole pairs · FEM analysis

1 Introduction

Linear Switched Reluctance Actuators (LSRA) have been the subject of increasing interest to the field of engineering and technology. LSRA regardless the issues on high force ripples and acoustic noise are being focus of increasing demand due to several advantages over other type of linear actuators such as simple in structure, absence of permanent magnet, low manufacturing cost, lack of mechanical gears and capability to operate in elevated temperature [1–3]. LSRA are an attractive alternative actuator to the other types of linear actuator due to the concentrated windings can be located on either stator or mover part. Moreover, linear actuators such as piezoelectric actuator operate in short working range [4] and electrostatic actuator generate low output thrust force [5, 6] have cause the research of linear actuator focuses on design and development of LSRA. In recent years, LSRA have attract the attention of researchers due to the advancement

© Springer Nature Singapore Pte Ltd. 2017
M.S. Mohamed Ali et al. (Eds.): AsiaSim 2017, Part II, CCIS 752, pp. 138–148, 2017.
DOI: 10.1007/978-981-10-6502-6_12

in the power electronics technology, digital signal processing and control strategy which capable to overcome the weakness and improve the performance of the actuator [7]. Hence, LSRA have been proposed for various of applications such as active vehicle's suspension system [8], precision motion control [9], direct-drive wave energy conversion [10], left ventricular assist device [11] and propulsion railway transportation system.

In general, the typical design of LSRA can be characterized as three topologies: (i) Planar Single Sided; (ii) Planar Double Sided; (iii) Tubular. By comparison, the tubular topology of LSRA provide greater force density compare to planer topology actuator due to lesser flux leakage and the tubular topology LSRA minimized the stray magnetic field in the direction of travel along the stator and mover part [12]. Other than that, the configurations of LSRA are categorized into transverse flux and longitudinal flux configuration according to the relation between the flux lines and direction of the actuator move [13]. Longitudinal flux configuration occurred when the flux lines and movement of the actuator is in parallel while transverse flux configuration occurred when the plane with flux lines is perpendicular to the motion of the actuator.

The structure of TLSRA seems to be attractive for industrial purpose due to both closed form and the inherently absence of attractive force between the stator and mover. Even though there are many research done on force ripples [14, 15] and acoustic noise minimization [16, 17], low force density is another weaknesses of TLSRA need to overcome [18, 19]. In order to increase the diversity of applications, it is important to improve the force density of TLSRA. Optimization of TLSRA parameters is the most common approach used to maximized the generated thrust force of the actuator [20, 21]. In order to increase the magnetic flux of TLSRA, the hybrid TLSRA is introduced with the used of permanent magnets. The used of the permanent magnets have an obvious improvement on the thrust force for approximately 60% compare to the conventional TLSRA but leads to the increasing of manufacturing cost [8]. In addition, the applied of a thin layer of laminated steel on TLSRA has improved the magnetic field strength and force density of actuator while helps to reduce eddy current [22, 23]. Furthermore, the modification of the geometrical structure of TLSRA such as skewed pole [24, 25], tapered pole [26] and pole shoes [27] has improved the thrust force and reduced the force ripples of the actuator.

With the purpose of maximizing the performance of TLSRA, this paper proposes a TLSRA design which consists of 7:7 stator-to-mover pole pairs ratio. In addition, the mover parameters are optimized to obtain the optimum performance which covered the variation of mover tooth width, mover tooth height and mover tooth pitch. The simulation focuses on the influence of variation of some constructive parameters of the TLSRA on the thrust force generation involves the application of finite-element method (FEM) base simulation analysis.

The remainder of this paper is organized as follows. The conceptual design related with the proposed TLSRA is presented in Sect. 2, followed by the working principle. A Finite Element Method (FEM) tool is used in Sect. 3 to analyze and obtain the characteristic of the actuator such as thrust force and inductance. Finally, in Sect. 4 conclusions are drawn.

2   Concept Design and Working Principle

2.1   Concept Design

The schematic structure of the proposed TLSRA with 7:7 stator-to-mover pole pairs ratio is shown in Fig. 1. The actuator is a three phase TLSRA with longitudinal configuration which consists of stator and mover made up of medium carbon steel (AISI 1045). The coil windings are embedded on the each stator slot and two coils are connected in series for each phase. In other words, there are six windings on six stator slots to form a three phase actuator due to the minimum number of phases to provide a continuous movement is three. Generally, the conventional design of linear electric actuator made up of 8:6 or 12:10 stator-to-mover pole pairs ratio. This conventional design usually has two working pole pairs of stator and mover for each phase. The introduction of proposed TLSRA with 7:7 stator-to-mover pole pairs ratio enhances the performance and thrust force of this actuator. Even though the increment of the mover poles lead to higher mover weight, the introduction of the proposed TLSRA can produce higher force density due to the designed actuator has four working pole pairs for each phase. Moreover, the parameters of the mover are optimize in order to maximize the thrust force of the designed actuator.

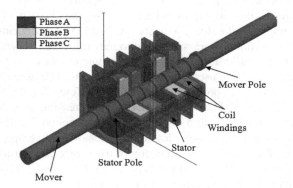

Fig. 1. Schematic structure of the proposed TLSRA.

2.2   Operating Principle

The operation of TLSRA base on the principle of minimum reluctance. The thrust force and motion of the actuator is generated due to the tendency of the mover to reach a position where the inductance of the actuator is maximized and the reluctance is minimum. The actuator is in the state of maximum reluctance when the energized pole pairs between stator and mover is fully unaligned. On the other hand, the actuator is in the state of minimum reluctance when the energized pole pairs between stator and mover is fully aligned. As shown in Fig. 2, when Phase A of the actuator is excited, the stator teeth 1, 2, 4 and 5 are energized. On the mover path, only mover teeth 1 is in the fully aligned position and mover teeth 2, 4 and 5 is not in fully aligned position with the stator teeth. Since there are three mover teeth in not fully aligned position, the mover tend to move toward right side in order to minimize the reluctance in the magnetic flux loop. As compare to the conventional design, the proposed actuator has 4 energized pole pairs instead of two which increase the thrust force of the TLSRA.

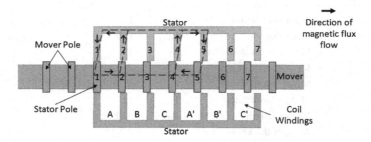

Fig. 2. Operating principle and flux pattern of proposed TLSRA.

2.3 Structure Parameter Optimization

The structure parameters of TLSRA has significant influence on the performance of the designed actuator. The proposed TLSRA will undergo the optimization on the mover which covered the mover tooth pitch, mover tooth height and mover tooth width in order to maximize the performance of the designed actuator. The TLSRA structure design presented in this paper is shown in Fig. 3 and the major TLSRA parameters are shown in Table 1.

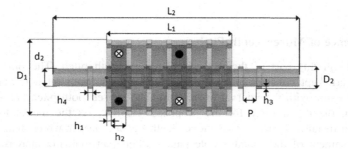

Fig. 3. Operating principle and flux pattern of proposed TLSRA.

Table 1. Parameters of the proposed TLSRA.

Parameter	Symbol	Value (mm)
Number of winding turns	n	300
Number of phases	P_n	3
Number of coil per phase	N	2

(*continued*)

Table 1. (*continued*)

Parameter	Symbol	Value (mm)
Stator outer diameter	D_1	63
Stator inner diameter	D_2	20
Stator tooth width	h_1	4
Stator slot width	h_2	12
Stator length	L_1	100
Mover outer diameter	d_2	19
Mover tooth height	h_3	2
Mover tooth width	h_4	4
Mover tooth pitch	P	11
Mover length	L_2	320
Air gap thickness	g	0.5
Coil diameter	D_c	0.5
Type of steel		AISI 1045

3 Simulation Results

In this section, the results of the simulation for TLSRA are presented. The results are focuses on optimizing the mover part of TLSRA. The results of variation three actuator parameters are obtained: mover tooth pitch, mover tooth height and mover tooth width. The thrust force results which are computed by ANSYS Maxwell 3D used to analyze the performance of the designed actuator and determine the optimize parameters of TLSRA.

3.1 Influence of Mover Tooth Pitch

The variable in this part of the analysis is mover tooth pitch. The other actuator parameters are kept constant as in Table 1. The mover tooth pitch is varied from 10 mm to 14 mm with the interval of 0.5 mm. The mover tooth pitch has significant influence on the thrust force for the proposed TLSRA. As the mover tooth pitch increase, the distance between two mover teeth become larger which will affect the position alignment of the actuator pole pairs. Other than that, the increasing of the mover tooth pitch also will cause the working pole pairs to be reduced which decrease the magnetic field strength of the actuator. Figure 4 depicted the influence of mover tooth pitch on the TLSRA thrust force.

When the applied current is 2 A, the thrust force reaches 7.14 N for 11 mm of mover tooth pitch follow by mover tooth pitch of 13 mm which generate 6.74 N of thrust force. As the mover tooth pitch is 12 mm, the thrust force is at the minimum and reaches almost 0 N due to all the pole pairs are in aligned position with minimum reluctance. Hence, the mover tends to maintain stationary at the aligned position. Therefore, the optimum mover tooth pitch is 11 mm due to mover tooth pitch with 11 mm provide the best performance in term of thrust force compare to other variables.

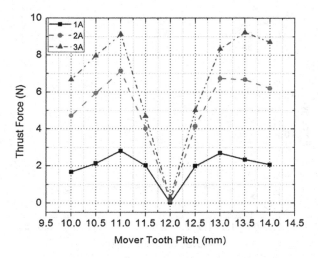

Fig. 4. Sensitivity of mover tooth pitch.

3.2   Influence of Mover Tooth Height

In this part of the analysis, the variation is mover tooth height. The other actuator parameters are kept constant as in Table 1. The mover tooth height is varied from 0 mm to 5 mm with the interval of 0.5 mm. The influence of the mover tooth height on the thrust force generated for the proposed TLSRA is shown in Fig. 5. As indicated in Fig. 5, the thrust force of the actuator has improved by increasing the mover tooth height up to 2 mm. However, the thrust force starts to decrease when the mover tooth height is 2.5 mm or larger. A lower thrust force is generated when the mover tooth height is smaller than 2 mm due to part of the magnetic flux directly flow to the mover stack which cause the lower reluctance and thrust force even at fully unaligned position. Meanwhile, mover tooth height larger than 2 mm also produced lower thrust force because the magnetic flux only able to flow through between the end surface of the stator and mover tooth only where the magnetic field strength is reduced. Instead, mover tooth width of 2 mm has stronger magnetic field strength as the magnetic flux able to flow through the end surface and side of the mover tooth.

When the applied current is 2 A, the thrust force reaches 12.96 N for mover tooth height of 2 mm follow by 12.78 N for mover tooth height of 1.5 mm. Figure 6 depicted the influence of mover tooth height on force per unit volume of the actuator. The results shows that mover tooth height with 2 mm can provide the highest thrust force and the force per unit volume of the TLSRA which indicate the mover tooth height with 2 mm is the optimum parameter.

3.3   Influence of Mover Tooth Width

The variable in this part of the analysis is mover tooth width. The other actuator parameters are kept constant as in Table 1. The mover tooth pitch is varied from 2 mm

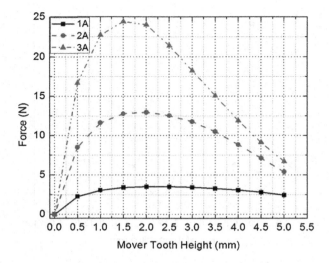

Fig. 5. Sensitivity of mover tooth height.

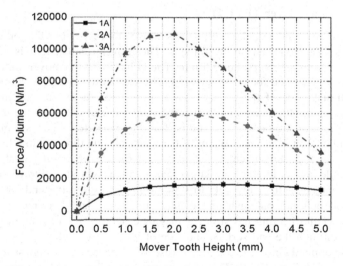

Fig. 6. Influence of mover tooth height on force per unit volume.

to 5 mm with the interval of 0.5 mm. The influence of the mover tooth width on the thrust force is shows in Fig. 7. As indicated in Fig. 7, the increasing of the mover tooth width up to 4 mm has significant improvement on the thrust force of the designed actuator. This is because the larger mover tooth surface area leads to stronger magnetic field strength at unaligned position as the mover tooth width increase.

When the applied current is 2 A, the thrust force reaches 12.96 N for mover tooth width of 4 mm which is the highest. However, as the mover tooth width is 4.5 mm and above, the thrust force generated started to reduce. The reduction in the generated thrust

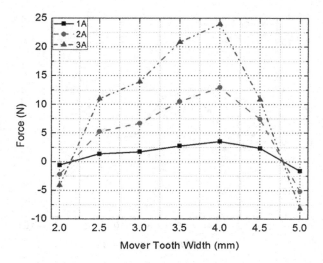

Fig. 7. Sensitivity of mover tooth width.

force is due to the large overlapping area occurred between the pole pairs even at fully unaligned position which cause the thrust force of the TLSRA lower compare to other parameters due to smaller reluctance.

3.4   Comparison Between Proposed and Conventional TLSRA

The comparison between the electromagnetic thrust force generated by conventional and proposed TLSRA is shown in Fig. 8. A conventional TLSRA used in this simulation has 7:5 stator-to-mover pole pairs ratio with 2 working pair poles. In addition, the stator to mover ratio for a single three phases TLSRA usually obtained by using the Eq. (1).

$$P_m = P_s - 1 \tag{1}$$

P_s is number of stator teeth and P_m is number of mover teeth for a complete single three phases equivalent circuit. Meanwhile, the proposed TLSRA has 7:7 stator-to-mover pole pairs ratio which has 4 working pair poles. As indicated in Fig. 8, the maximum thrust force generated by the conventional TLSRA is 6.45 N. Meanwhile, the proposed TLSRA generated two times higher the thrust force compare to the conventional design where it reaches 15.27 N. The proposed TLSRA generated higher thrust force due the additional two working pair poles compare to the conventional actuator. The proposed TLSRA with four working pair poles have stronger magnetic field strength as three working pair poles are in unaligned position even there is a working pole pair in aligned position. Therefore, the proposed TLSRA has better performance compare to conventional TLSRA due the designed actuator has higher force density.

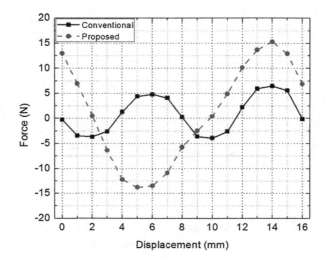

Fig. 8. Comparison performance between conventional and proposed TLSRA at 2A.

4   Conclusion

In this paper, a tubular linear switched reluctance actuator (TLSRA) without permanent magnet that has 7:7 stator-to-mover pole pairs ratio is proposed. The relations between actuator parameters and TLSRA output were investigated to optimum the performance of the designed actuator. The actuator parameters such as mover tooth pitch, mover tooth height and mover tooth height are the variables that usually will influence the performance of the TLSRA. The performance of the proposed TLSRA is compared to the conventional TLSRA in term of generated thrust force. Design studies shows that the proposed TLSRA with four working pair poles generated higher thrust force compared to the conventional TLSRA with two working pair poles for approximately two times. In order to improve the performances of TLSRA, the influence between more actuator parameters should be optimized depending on the applications. Therefore, the proposed TLSRA is more attractive and can be subject of future study.

Acknowledgement. Authors are grateful to Universiti Teknikal Malaysia (UTeM) and UTeM Zamalah Scheme for supporting the research. This research and its publication are supported by Ministry of Higher Education Malaysia (MOHE) under the Fundamental Research Grant Scheme (FRGS) no. FRGS/1/2016/TK04/FKE-CERIA/F00305, Research Acculturation Collaboration Effort (RACE) no. RACE/F3/TK5/FKE/F00249, Center for Robotics and Industrial Automation (CeRIA) and Center for Research and Innovation Management (CRIM).

References

1. Pan, J.F., Meng, F.J., Jiang, W.L., Cheung, N.C.: Fuzzy PID control for the linear switched reluctance machine. In: 5th International Conference on Power Electronics Systems and Applications, Hong Kong, pp. 1–4. IEEE Press (2013)
2. Lin, J., Cheng, K.W.E., Zhang, Z., Cheung, N.C., Xue, X., Ng, T.W.: Active suspension system based on linear switched reluctance actuator and control schemes. IEEE Trans. Veh. Technol. **62**(2), 562–572 (2013)
3. Yusri, I., Ghazaly, M.M., Rahmat, M.F., Chong, S.H., Abdullah, Z., Tee, S.P., Yeo, C.K.: Effects of varying arc angles and poles numbers on force characteristics of switched reluctance (SR) actuator. Int. J. Mech. Mechatron. Eng. **16**(5), 41–47 (2016)
4. Ghazaly, M.M., Sato, K.: Basic characteristics of a multilayer thin electrostatic actuator supported by lubricating oil for a fine-motion stage. Precis. Eng. **36**(1), 77–83 (2012)
5. Ghazaly, M.M., Sato, K.: Open-loop characteristics of a multilayer thin electrostatic actuator supported by lubricating oil for a fine-motion stage. In: Proceedings of the 4th International Conference on Mechatronics Technology, Osaka (2010)
6. Ghazaly, M.M., Sato, K.: Control performances of a fine motion stage using a multilayer electrostatic actuator without precise balls for lubrication. In: Proceedings of the 4th International Conference on Mechatronics Technology, Osaka (2010)
7. Sau, S., Vandana, R., Fernandes, B.G.: A new direct torque control method for switched reluctance motor with high torque/ampere. In: 39th Annual Conference of the IEEE Industrial Electronics Society, Vienna, pp. 2518–2523. IEEE Press (2013)
8. Garcia, J., Andrada, P., Blanque, B.: Assessment of linear switched reluctance motor's design parameters for optimal performance. J. Electr. Power Compon. Syst. **43**(7), 810–819 (2015)
9. Commins, P.A., Moscrop, J.W., Cook, C.M.: Synchronous reluctance tubular linear motor for high precision applications. In: Australasian Universities Power Engineering Conference: Challenges for Future Grids, Wollongong, pp. 1–6. IEEE Press (2015)
10. Mendes, R.P.G., Calado, M.R., Mariano, S., Cabrita, M.P.: Design of a tubular switched reluctance linear generator for wave energy conversion based on ocean wave parameters. In: International Aegean Conference on Electrical Machines and Power Electronics, Istanbul, pp. 146–151. IEEE Press (2011)
11. Llibre, J.F., Martinez, N., Nogarede, B., Leprince, P.: Linear tubular switched reluctance motor for heart assistance circulatory: analytical and finite element modeling. In: 10th International Workshop on Electronics, Control, Measurement and Signals, Liberec, pp. 1–6. IEEE Press (2011)
12. Jamaludin, A.H., Ghazaly, M.M., Yahya, T.A., Amran, A.C., Abdullah, Z., Ali, M.A.M., Ali, N.M.: Force optimization of a tubular linear reluctance actuator (TLRA) and tubular linear permanent magnet actuator with halbach array (TLPM). In: Proceeding of Mechanical Engineering Research Day, pp. 52–53. Centre for Advanced Research on Energy, Malacca (2016)
13. Amoros, J.G., Andrada, P., Blanque, B.: Design procedure for a longitudinal flux flat linear switched reluctance motor. Electr. Power Compon. Syst. **40**(2), 161–178 (2011)
14. Gan, W.C., Cheung, N.C., Qiu, L.: Position control of linear switched reluctance motors for high-precision applications. IEEE Trans. Ind. Appl. **39**(5), 1350–1362 (2003)
15. Pestana, L.M., Calado, M.R., Mariano, S.: Experimental force characterization of linear switched reluctance machine. In: 16th International Conference on Environment and Electrical Engineering, Florence, pp. 1–4. IEEE Press (2016)

16. Sekhara, R.E.V.C.: Torque ripple minimization of switched reluctance motor using fuzzy logic control. Int. J. Recent Innov. Trends Comput. Commun. **3**(7), 4335–4342 (2015)
17. Dowlatshahi, M., Saghaiannejad, S.M., Ahn, J.W., Moallem, M.: Minimization of torque-ripple in switched reluctance motors over wide speed range. J. Electr. Eng. Technol. **9**(2), 478–788 (2014)
18. Vattikuti, N., Vandana, R., Fernandes, B.G.: A novel high force density linear segmented switched reluctance machine. In: 34th Annual Conference of IEEE Industrial Electronics, Florida, pp. 1083–1088. IEEE Press (2008)
19. Zhao, S.W., Wang, W.X., Yang, X.Y., Cheung, N.C.: Analysis and design of a linear switched reluctance motor with force improvement. In: 5th International Conference on Power Electronics Systems and Applications, Hong Kong, pp. 1–4. IEEE Press (2013)
20. Amoros, J.G., Andrada, P., Blanque, B., Ganesca, M.M.: Influence of design parameters in the optimization of linear switched reluctance motor under thermal constraints. IEEE. Trans. Ind. Electron. **PP**(99), 1–8 (2017)
21. Teixeira, V.S.C., Oliveira, D.N., Cunha, H., Reis, L.L.N., Pontes, R.S.T.: Influence of the project parameters on the LSRM-Project optimization. In: Proceedings of IEEE International Electric Machines and Drives Conference, Antalya, pp. 554–558. IEEE Press (2007)
22. Llibre, J.F., Martinez, N., Leprince, P., Nogarede, B.: Analysis and modeling of linear switched reluctance for medical application. Actuators **2**(2), 27–44 (2013)
23. Myo, M.T.: Design and calculation of 75W three-phase linear switched reluctance motor. World Acad. Sci. Eng. Technol. **48**, 108–113 (2008)
24. Sampath, V.G., Elavarasan, R., Lenin, N.C., Arumugan, R.: A novel skewed linear switched reluctance motor-analysis and design. Appl. Mech. Mater. **787**, 874–877 (2015)
25. Lenin, N.C., Amurugam, R.: Design and experimental verification of linear switched reluctance motor with skewed poles. Int. J. Power Electron. Drive Syst. **6**(1), 18–25 (2015)
26. Sampath, V.G., Elavarasan, R., Lenin, N.C., Amurugam, R.: Design and experimental verification of linear switched reluctance motor with tapered poles. Appl. Mech. Mater. **787**, 878–882 (2015)
27. Lenin, N.C., Amurugam, R.: A novel linear switched reluctance motor: investigation and experimental verification. Songklanakarin J. Sci. Technol. **33**(1), 69–78 (2011)

CM NCTF with Velocity Feedforward Controller Design for Tracking Control of an AC Driven X-Y Ball Screw Mechanism

Norhaslinda Hasim, Shin-Horng Chong$^{(\boxtimes)}$, and Zulkifilie Ibrahim

Center for Robotics and Industrial Automation (CeRIA), Faculty of Electrical
Engineering (FKE), Universiti Teknikal Malaysia Melaka, Melaka, Malaysia
horng@utem.edu.my

Abstract. This paper presents an improved practical controller for enhancing the tracking performance of a ball screw mechanism. Essentially, a controller with practical and easy to design has been preferred for high motion control performance. The existing continuous motion nominal characteristic trajectory following (CM NCTF) controller demonstrates a low accuracy achievement at high frequency motion, where at 5 Hz, the percentage of error are higher than 10% and 15% for amplitude of 1 mm and 10 mm respectively. The NCTF controller comprises of a nominal characteristic trajectory (NCT) and a PI compensator where the controller parameters are easily determined and it is free from exact modeling. In this paper, the CM NCTF controller with velocity feedforward compensator has been proposed in order to enhance the tracking motion accuracy. The simulation results shown that the CM NCTF controller with velocity feedforward compensator achieves better tracking performances than that the CM NCTF controller alone by showing more than three times smaller motion error.

Keywords: Tracking performance · AC ball screw mechanism · Practical control · CM NCTF controller

1 Introduction

Ball screw mechanism are the most frequent machine used in industry to convert rotational to linear motion, especially to position or move a machine components to the specific location. Therefore, their accuracy and speed are very crucial where it determines the quality and productivity of the machine tools [1]. The ball screw mechanism can be driven by DC or AC servo motor. Ball screw with AC driven are widely used for industrial applications due to its less maintenance, less stability problems, and has higher efficiency over the DC driven mechanism. On the other hand, more difficult to be controlled and always suffers from its nonlinearities are frequently be the major obstacles in implementing the AC driven mechanism. Hence, this research focuses on the controller design of such mechanism.

PID controllers are established as the most widely used for ball screw mechanism due to its simplicity, high adaptability, and easy to understand the design with its tuning technique. Regardless of its reputation, the performance of PID controllers is bounded

© Springer Nature Singapore Pte Ltd. 2017
M.S. Mohamed Ali et al. (Eds.): AsiaSim 2017, Part II, CCIS 752, pp. 149–159, 2017.
DOI: 10.1007/978-981-10-6502-6_13

by the uncertainties and nonlinearities in the control structure. [2, 3] agree that tuning of PID control systems not always easy due to its simple control structure for wide classes of industrial control and by using PID alone cannot satisfy the need of the rising complexity and precision of control systems.

Therefore, in order to compensate its limitation, several researchers has studied the effectiveness of the conventional PID control and make some modifications in the control structure. Recently, [4–6] has proposed an integrated PID-based controller with feedforward to further improved the tracking performance of ball screw system and AC servo motor.

Advanced controllers have been introduced to achieve better positioning performance in ball screw mechanism. A disturbance observer with filtered variable control structure has compensate the effect of friction and disturbances [7]. Besides that, a backstepping sliding mode controller has been proposed to improve the tracking control and problem of modeling of the system used [8, 9]. An adaptive backstepping sliding mode controller is suggested with minimum tracking error prefilter to actively suppress for the vibrations and achieve high positioning performance. The proposed controller in [9] has been validated to achieve higher tracking accuracy, bandwidth and stability as compared with P/PI controller with velocity and acceleration feedforward. Reinforcement learning has been recommended by [10] as an option to typical controller approaches such as PID controllers. Even though these advanced controllers are able to perform well in positioning and tracking, but the determination of the unknown in the model parameters are necessary. The performance of these controllers is based on the accuracy of the known model and parameters used in the design procedures, which will affect the design process in terms of time consuming and labor required to identify the exact parameters. This will definitely limits their practical ability.

Authors in [11] have proposed the first NCTF control for point-to-point positioning system and examined with a rotary mechanism. Later in 2009, the continuous motion nominal characteristic trajectory following (CM NCTF) controller has been recommended by Sato and Maeda [12] as a high performance and simple control structure to a DC ball screw mechanism. The major advantage of this controller is its simple control structure as compared to other advanced controllers. Furthermore, the design procedure of a NCTF controller is much simpler and easy to understand. It does not require parameter identification or exact model of the plant which usually troublesome the researcher. In 2010, the CM NCTF controller was validated with a non-contact mechanism [13]. It shows that the procedure of the NCTF controller is independent of the friction characteristic. CM NCTF controller was proposed by [14] as a practical approach to perform positioning control on a DC driven one mass rotary system. In 2014, the AR-CM NCTF control was introduced by [15] for a linear motion mechanism with friction characteristics. The summary of the applicability of the NCTF controllers for several typical positioning systems that widely used in industries has been reviewed by [16].

X-Y ball screw mechanism has several sources of friction that makes it tedious for the controller design because the characteristics of mechanism with friction are nonlinear, thus simple controllers such as PID controllers do not offer the best possible performance. Furthermore, the friction compensation usually requires the identification of friction characteristics, which may vary. These characteristics made the process of system modelling and parameters identification are necessary for those advanced controller that requires accurate model for high positioning performance.

The existing CM NCTF controller demonstrates a significant low accuracy achievement at high frequency motion, where at 5 Hz, the percentage of error are higher than 10% and 15% for amplitude of 1 mm and 10 mm respectively. Therefore, the main goal of this paper is to improve the accuracy of the system at higher frequency. In this paper, the CM NCTF with velocity feedforward compensator will be proposed to examine the tracking performance. Simulation of tracking motion in single axis will be conducted in order to clarify the effectiveness of the CM NCTF and velocity feedforward control system.

The rest of the paper is written as follows: Sect. 2 describes the system description and dynamic model of the research. In Sect. 2.3, the controller design procedure is discussed. The performance of the CM NCTF with velocity feedforward compensator is validated and explained in Sect. 3. Finally, the remark conclusion and future studies are made.

2 Control Strategy

2.1 CM NCTF Control System Structure

CM NCTF controller is a second generation of NCTF based controller where it has a simple structure and easy to design. The CM NCTF controller consists of a nominal characteristic trajectory (NCT) element and a Proportional and Integrator (PI) compensator as depicted in Fig. 1. The NCT is designed from the object responses in open loop experiment and the inclination of the NCT near origin is denoted as β. Theoretically, the NCT plays an important role as a virtual error rate for the object to follow and it is expressed on the phase plane. The actual error rate, $(\dot{e})$ is comprises of $(\dot{x}_r - \dot{x})$, where the reference rate, $(\dot{x}_r)$ helps the mechanism to move rapidly. On the other hand, the PI compensator controls the velocity of the ball screw mechanism and make it follows the NCT and end at the origin. This will make the mechanism reaches the reference quickly without significant overshoot. When the object stops at the origin, it means the end of the object motion. Signal $U_p(t)$ shown in Fig. 1 represents the difference between the actual error rate $(\dot{e})$ and virtual error rate $(\dot{e}_{nct})$ by NCT. If the value of $U_p(t)$ is equal to zero, then object motion is perfectly following the NCT.

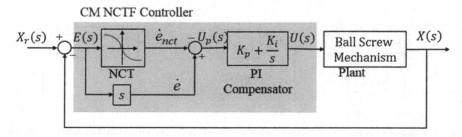

Fig. 1. Control structure of continuous motion NCTF (CM NCTF) controller.

In NCTF control system, the object motion is divided into two phases as shown in Fig. 2, which are reaching phase and following phase.

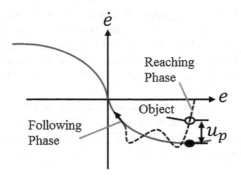

Fig. 2. Reaching phase and following phase in NCT.

2.2   Improvement for Tracking Motion

Figure 3 shows the improved CM NCTF control structure for tracking motion. Theoretically, when the position output, X(s) abruptly changes, the velocity feedforward path immediately shuttles that change to the velocity command (reference rate, $\dot{x}_r$). This greatly speeds the system response when compared to relying solely on the position loop. Based on the CM NCTF with a velocity feedforward compensator control structure, the control signal, U(s) is obtained by considering the reference rate ($\dot{x}_r$). The reference rate ($\dot{x}_r$) helps the mechanism to move rapidly.

The feedforward gain, K_{ff} is obtained from the inclination near origin, β and it is the largest gain of the control system. Practically, β refers to the following characteristic of the controller. Therefore, in this research K_{ff} used is 0.022, where it refers to $2/\beta$ value. The bandwidth of the CM NCTF with velocity feedforward compensator is larger than using CM NCTF controller only as can be depicted in Fig. 4.

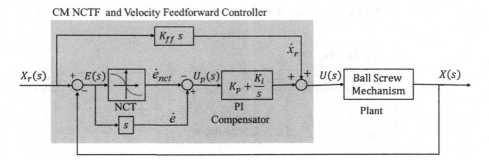

Fig. 3. Control structure of continuous motion NCTF (CM NCTF) controller with a velocity feedforward compensator.

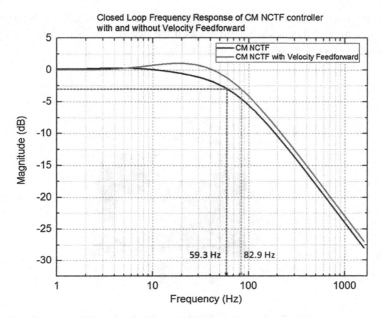

Fig. 4. Closed-loop frequency response of CM NCTF controller with and without velocity feedforward in simulation.

2.3 Design Procedure

In general, the design of the CM NCTF controller is similar with a conventional NCTF controller as presented in [13], where it involves in three simple steps:

    I. **Open-loop response,** where the ball screw mechanism is driven in open loop and the displacement and velocity responses are measured.

    II. **Construction of NCT,** where the NCT is constructed on the phase plane using the displacement and velocity of the mechanism during deceleration motion.

    III. **Design of PI compensator,** where it is designed based on the open-loop responses and NCT information.

The constructed NCT with inclination near origin, β equals to 87 s^{-1} is used in this research. The values of K_p and K_i of the PI compensator are 0.08 Vs/mm and 1.34 V/mm respectively. The details design procedures for the CM NCTF controller is discussed in [17]. It should be noted that this procedure can be completed without any previous information about the model parameters.

3   Performance Evaluation

3.1   Experimental Setup

In this research, the CM NCTF controller with and without velocity feedforward will be examined using an AC driven X-Y ball screw mechanism. The mechanism with the large additional mass is referred to as X-axis mechanism, and the other is referred as Y-axis mechanism. The mechanism is driven as if the two-mechanism were conceptually stacked as in X-Y configuration as shown in Fig. 5.

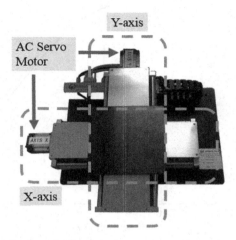

Fig. 5. AC driven X-Y ball screw mechanism.

Its dynamic model is represented in Fig. 6. This common configuration is similar as those of many positioning mechanism used in industry.

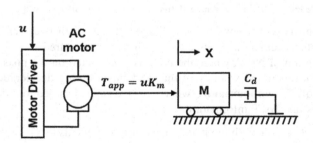

Fig. 6. Dynamic model of an AC driven ball screw mechanism.

The NCTF based controller parameter is derived based on a linear macrodynamic model, known as simplified object model, as shown in (1),

$$M\ddot{x}(t) + C_d\dot{x}(t) = K_m u(t) \tag{1}$$

where M is the mass, C_d is the damping coefficient, and K_m is the force constant of the motor. Since $K = \frac{K_m}{M}$ and $\alpha = \frac{C_d}{M}$, rewrite (1) as,

$$\ddot{x}(t) + \alpha\dot{x}(t) = Ku(t) \tag{2}$$

which leads to the transfer function of the simplified object model as:

$$\frac{X(s)}{U(s)} = \frac{K}{s(s+\alpha)} \tag{3}$$

The simulated model of the system is obtained by using experimental open-loop frequency response method. The obtained transfer function is:

$$G_{plant}(s) = \frac{4400}{s(s+100)} \tag{4}$$

Figure 7 shows the comparison open-loop responses that commanded by the designed input signal. The designed input signal is the combination of a step and exponential signals. In this research, the exponential signal (e^{-at}) makes the mechanism attenuated smoothly at deceleration part.

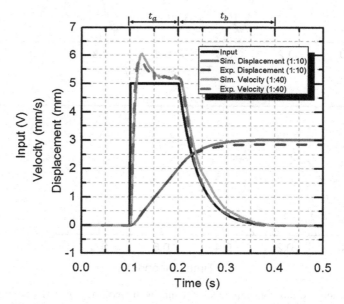

Fig. 7. Open-loop response with Y-axis of ball screw mechanism.

3.2 Results

The CM NCTF controller with and without velocity feedforward will be simulated to an AC driven X-Y ball screw mechanism model as obtained in Eq. (4). In this research, only the tracking performance of Y-axis mechanism will be considered.

In this section, the tracking performances of CM NCTF controller with and without velocity feedforward gain are examined through simulation. The frequency of the sinusoidal input used is 5 Hz, with sampling time of 1 ms. The amplitude of the sinusoidal input in Fig. 8 is 1 mm. The maximum peak error of the CM NCTF controller and CM NCTF with velocity feedforward controller are 105 μm and 30 μm respectively.

When the amplitude of the sinusoidal input is increased to 10 mm as shown in Fig. 9, the CM NCTF controller has a maximum peak error of 1592 μm, whereas CM NCTF with velocity feedforward controller has a maximum peak error of 475 μm. The maximum error and percentage of error for both controller is tabulated in Table 1.

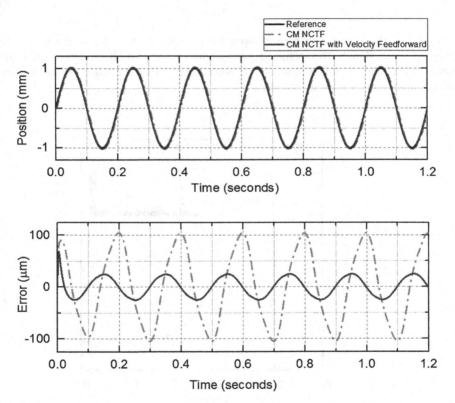

Fig. 8. Simulation results for amplitude of 1 mm with frequency of 5 Hz using CM NCTF controller with and without velocity feedforward.

Since the CM NCTF with velocity feedforward controller has a much smaller maximum peak error as the sinusoidal input supplied, it shows that the CM NCTF with velocity feedforward controller has a faster response as compared to the CM NCTF controller as expectation.

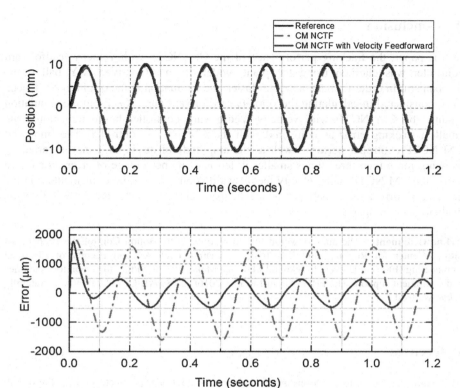

Fig. 9. Simulation results for amplitude of 10 mm with frequency of 5 Hz using CM NCTF controller with and without velocity feedforward.

Table 1. Maximum error, E_{max} of the CM NCTF controller with and without velocity feedforward compensator in Y-axis with variation of amplitude.

Frequency (Hz)	Amplitude (mm)	Max error, E_{max} (μm)	
		CM NCTF controller only	CM NCTF with velocity feedforward compensator
5	1	105	30
5	10	1592	475

Therefore, the simulation results shows that the CM NCTF with velocity feedforward has less influence in tracking performance as the amplitude of the sinusoidal is varied. It managed to compensate the variation and has the smallest motion error.

4   Conclusion

In this paper, the tracking performance of the CM NCTF with velocity feedforward controller was clarified using the plant model of an AC driven X-Y ball screw mechanism. In order to make a system faster, the inclination at the origin in NCT need to be considered in calculating the velocity feedforward gain, K_{ff}. From the simulation results, the CM NCTF with velocity feedforward controller has demonstrated the smallest tracking error as compared with the CM NCTF controller. The improved CM NCTF controller performs well as the amplitude of the input signal is varied by showing more than three times smaller in terms of its percentage of error. For future work, the CM NCTF with velocity feedforward controller will be implemented on the actual AC driven X-Y ball screw mechanism, and the performance will then be evaluate and compare.

Acknowledgments. The authors would like to be obliged to Motion Control Research Laboratory, Center for Robotics and Industrial Automation (CeRIA), and Faculty of Electrical Engineering (FKE) in Universiti Teknikal Malaysia Melaka for providing the laboratory facilities and equipment support. The FRGS Grant FRGS/1/2016/TK08/FKE-CeRIA/F00308 is gratefully acknowledged.

References

1. Mauro, S., Pastorelli, S., Johnston, E.: Influence of controller parameters on the life of ball screw feed drives. Adv. Mech. Eng. **7**(8), 1–11 (2015)
2. Shigemasa, T., Negishi, Y., Baba, Y.: A TDOF PID control system design by referring to the MD-PID control system and its sensitivities. In: European Control Conference, no. 1, pp. 3937–3942 (2013)
3. Guo, J., Wu, G., Guo, S.: Fuzzy PID algorithm-based motion control for the spherical amphibious robot. In: IEEE International Conference Mechatronics Automation, ICMA, pp. 1583–1588 (2015)
4. Abdullah, L., Jamaludin, Z., Maslan, M.N., Jamaludin, J., Halim, I., Rafan, N.A., Chiew, T. H.: Assessment on tracking performance of cascade P/PI, NPID and NCasFF controller for precise positioning of XY table ballscrew drive system. Procedia CIRP **26**, 212–216 (2015)
5. Zhang, C., Chen, Y.: Tracking control of ball screw drives using ADRC and equivalent-error-model based feedforward control. IEEE Trans. Ind. Electron. **63**(12), 7682–7692 (2016)
6. Xu, J., Qiao, M., Wang, W., Miao, Y.: Fuzzy PID control for AC servo system based on Stribeck friction model. In: Proceedings of 6th International Forum on Strategic Technology, IFOST 2011, vol. 2, pp. 706–711 (2011)
7. Lin, C.J., Lee, C.Y.: Observer-based robust controller design and realization of a gantry stage. Mechatronics **21**(1), 185–203 (2011)
8. Lu, C.H., Hwang, Y.R.: Hybrid sliding mode position control for a piston air motor ball screw table. ISA Trans. **51**(3), 373–385 (2012)
9. Dong, L., Tang, W.: Control of ball screw drives using adaptive backstepping sliding mode controller and minimum tracking error prefilter. In: IEEE International Conference on Control and Automation, ICCA, pp. 995–1000 (2014)

10. Fernandez-Gauna, B., Ansoategui, I., Etxeberria-Agiriano, I., Graña, M.: Reinforcement learning of ball screw feed drive controllers. Eng. Appl. Artif. Intell. **30**, 107–117 (2014)
11. Wahyudi, Sato, K., Shimokohbe, A.: Characteristics of practical control for point-to-point (PTP) positioning systems. Precis. Eng. **27**(2), 157–169 (2003)
12. Sato, K., Maeda, G.J.: A practical control method for precision motion—improvement of NCTF control method for continuous motion control. Precis. Eng. **33**(2), 175–186 (2009)
13. Chong, S.H., Sato, K.: Practical controller design for precision positioning, independent of friction characteristic. Precis. Eng. **34**(2), 286–300 (2010)
14. Foo, J.E., Chong, S.H., Nor, R.M., Loh, S.L.: Positioning control of a one mass rotary system with CM-NCTF controller. J. Telecommun. Electron. Comput. Eng. **8**(11), 125–129 (2016)
15. Chong, S.H., Sato, K.: Practical and robust control for precision motion: AR-CM NCTF control of a linear motion mechanism with friction characteristics. IET Control Theory Appl. **9**, 745–754 (2014)
16. Chong, S.H., Sato, K.: Nominal characteristics trajectory following control as practical controller: a review, pp. 4790–4795 (2015)
17. Hee, W.K., Chong, S.H., Aliza, C.A.: Selection of PI compensator parameters for NCTF controller based on practical stability limit. In: IEEE International Conference on Control System, Computing and Engineering, pp. 674–679 (2014)

Modelling Electrophysiological Data in Persistent Atrial Fibrillation Studies Using the Evolution of 3-Dimensional Dominant Frequency Mapping

Priscilla Sim Chee Mei[1], Nurul Adilla Mohd Subha[2],
and Anita Ahmad[2(✉)]

[1] Electronic and Computer Engineering Department,
Universiti Teknologi Malaysia, 81310 Skudai, Johor, Malaysia
[2] Control and Mechatronic Engineering Department,
Universiti Teknologi Malaysia, 81310 Skudai, Johor, Malaysia
anita@fke.utm.my

Abstract. The dominant frequency (DF) of atrial electrogram was claimed by researchers as to be correlated to the electrical activation of the atrial fibrillation (AF). By assessing the DF of AF data of 5 patients with persistent AF, this paper presented some AF signal analysis done to study the performance of the raw data, which is the data without QRS-T subtraction, data with QRS-T subtraction and rectification. The resultant data were mapped in 3-dimensional shapes of respective patients left atrium (LA), showing the DF activity changes during 21 s data recorded. The maps are useful for further analysis to justify which of the mentioned signal processing step is more reliable and also to study the relation between particular sites on the LA with the source (sites) of activation of AF.

Keywords: Atrial fibrillation · Atrial electrogram · Dominant frequency

1 Introduction

Atrial fibrillation (AF) is a common arrhythmia which more often than not leads to stroke [1, 2]. AF happens when the heart beats abnormally, in fast and irregular rhythm in the atria [3]. There are three types of AF: paroxysmal, persistent and permanent [4–6]. Paroxysmal AF only occurs once in a while, i.e. spontaneously terminated within 7 days, while persistent AF is one that does not stop by itself, i.e. sustained more than 7 days, but will stop if medication or cardioversion is given to help the heart return to its normal rhythm [7]. The permanent AF is however present all the time and cannot be fixed with either medication or cardioversion [7]. Hence, AF increases in criticality from paroxysmal to persistent and finally the permanent type.

1.1 AF Treatment

There are three main methods for AF treatment today. The first one is medication. This is simply done by giving antiarrhythmic drugs to the patient to regulate the heart

© Springer Nature Singapore Pte Ltd. 2017
M.S. Mohamed Ali et al. (Eds.): AsiaSim 2017, Part II, CCIS 752, pp. 160–171, 2017.
DOI: 10.1007/978-981-10-6502-6_14

activity into normal rhythm [7, 8]. The second treatment is through surgical procedure. AF patients will be implanted with pacemaker or implantable defibrillator which invasively helps the patient heart to regulate normally [1, 9]. The third main treatment for AF is by non-surgical procedures. This type of treatment includes electrical cardioversion and the catheter-based radiofrequency (RF) ablation. Electrical cardioversion is commonly done by applying a certain amount of electricity on the patient chest by using a paddles or patches to help reset the electrical conduction of the heart [5].

In this research, we are interested on the catheter ablation procedure. Catheter ablation has widely been used in the treatment procedure for paroxysmal or persistent AF [4, 10, 11]. However, the ablation is considerably a random burnt of patient left atrium (LA) tissue if it is done by delivering the RF energy throughout the cardiac tissue of the left atrium (LA) wall with no accurately identifiable site of AF activation source on the atrium wall as the specific ablation target. Furthermore, to minimize the risk of infection or death to the patients, the sites for ablation should be determined accurately within a short time [4, 12]. Hence, extended study on the signal of the atrial electrogram data is requisite to help improve the current treatment procedure.

1.2   AF Activation Sites and Correlation with Dominant Frequency

Researchers believed that AF is maintained by sites with high frequency, thus known as the activation source of AF [4, 13–16]. The main sites of activation include the left atrium (LA) roof, LA septum, LA posterior wall as well as the pulmonary vein's area [16, 17]. Since AF activity consists of signal which is random and often chaotic, the frequency domain analysis is preferable compare to the time domain analysis [4, 13, 15]. Dominant frequency (DF) is the commonly determined parameter in the frequency domain analysis which defined as the frequency with highest magnitude or power [4, 13, 18].

This paper will present the signal processing of the atrial electrogram to obtain the 3-dimensional mapping of the AF data using the raw data, data after QRS-T subtraction, and data after QRS-T subtraction being rectified. The study is significant to evaluate the signal processing steps which might contribute to time reduction in selecting the sites for ablation by understanding the correlation between the electrical activation of AF and its dominant frequency estimation.

2   Methodology

Figure 1 shows the methodology flow chart for the research. We proposed the raw data undergo QRS-T subtraction and rectification processing steps before the 3D DF mapping.

2.1   Subjects and Data Collection

The research focused on data of a total of five patients with persistent AF. The raw data were collected when the subjects underwent catheter ablation guided by contact

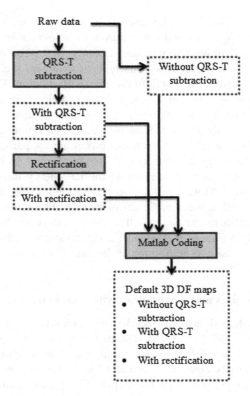

Fig. 1. Methodology flowchart

mapping using Ensite, NavX 6.0, St. Jude Medical (Glenfield Hospital, University of Leceister), performed in 20-s long continuous segments of each of the 2048 non-contact unipolar electrograms during AF.

The raw data collected for the research consist of wave (ECG) and virtual (atrial electrogram) signal recorded for a total of 21 s (7 s per recoding). The subjects' data files were named as a1, a2, a3, a4 and a5 respectively.

2.2 QRS-T Subtraction

The QRS-T components are signals caused by the ventricular activity of the heart which range between 10–30 Hz [19–22]. Hence, it is somehow irrelevant in this study of AF which mainly occurred in the left atrium. Meanwhile, studies show that AF range between 5–12 Hz [21]. Therefore, subtracting the QRS-T components from the atrial electrogram data might help improve the result of the analysis because the frequency overlapping will be eliminated [21, 23].

In this study, the interest data is the atrial electrogram (labeled as virtual) data. However, the ECG data recorded is useful as a reference to initially identify the location of the frequency of the QRS-T components to be subtracted later from the atrial electrogram data. This is because the normal ECG waveform is a basic repeating signal pattern with P, Q, R, S and T waves as shown in Fig. 2, therefore allowed easier detection of QRS and T components to be subtracted. Conversely, the AF waveform is rather random and irregular, so it is difficult to identify the QRS and T components from the AF graph.

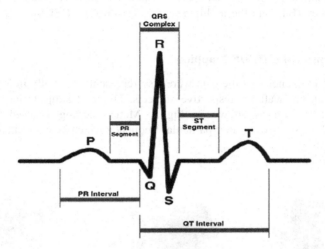

Fig. 2. General waveform for ECG signal

Flat interpolation method has been applied to replace the subtracted QRS-T waves with a base value.

2.3 Rectification

Rectification is another proposed signal processing for the data. This enables justification on the necessary of rectification on the data to improve the signal analysis. Rectification is used to transform biphasic waveform into monophasic waveform by using the absolute value function in Matlab [15]. According to some researchers, rectification can cause the peak and troughs of a signal become correspond with a sinusoid signal [15]. This information is essential especially for local recording of atrial electrogram which either using unipolar or bipolar electrode, because of its typical sharp biphasic waveform which requires signal preprocessing steps [15, 20, 24]. The more similar a signal pattern is to the sinusoid signal (in time domain), the lesser the error existed when using Fourier transform method for frequency domain analysis [15]. Similarly, the closer the atrial electrogram waveform being approximated to a sinusoidal function, the better the DF analysis could reflect the activation rate of AF.

2.4   Fast Fourier Transform

As mentioned earlier, DF is the main parameter determined to study the nature of the electrical activation of AF in frequency domain. Fast Fourier Transform (FFT) method has been chosen to obtain the dominant frequency of each of the 2048 point data for 21 s after the QRS-T subtraction and rectification. FFT method is claimed as fast and accurate in estimating the DF compare to methods such as autoregressive (AR), Blackman Tukey (BT) and the multiple signal classification (MUSIC) method [12].

2.5   3-Dimensional (3D) DF Mapping

The dominant frequencies of the data were also represented visually in 3-dimensional maps of left atrium wall for respective subjects. Different subjects have distinctive shapes of left atrium as shown in Fig. 3. Matlab coding is used to plot the 3-dimensional maps showing their particular frequency which keep on changing during the 21 s recording.

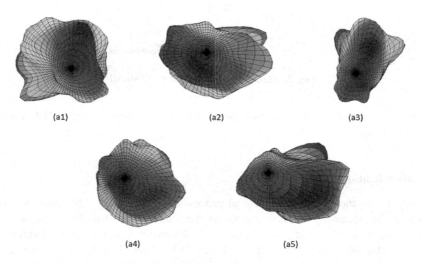

Fig. 3. Subjects *(a1)*, *(a2)*, *(a3)*, *(a4)* and *(a5)* respective 3D LA shapes

3   Result and Continuous Work

3D maps in default view were obtained as the result after the 3D DF mapping procedure. For each subject, 21 figures were obtained and saved to visualize the changes of DF on the maps per second. This will be used for visual observation and comparison of the DF changes for the raw data, data with QRS-T subtraction as well as the one with rectification. Figure 4 shows the example of 3D DF maps obtained for subject a1 for the 21 s consecutive AF.

These resultant 3D DF maps will further being used for proving relation between sites of LA (PV, MV, LAA and non DF areas) with the existence of electrical activation sources and also to study the reliability of QRS-T subtraction and rectification steps for better study of the AF electrogram data. For instance, DF activity on the known sites on LA such as the pulmonary veins (PV), left atrium appendage (LAA), and mitral valve (MV) areas might show significant irregular DF activity within the 21 s recording. If this happens, it can be inferred that the particular site do contribute or act as the main activation sites for AF as claimed by some researchers.

Another method to study the 3D DF maps is by using the organization index (OI) calculation. OI is defined as the ratio between power of DF and its harmonics (area of graph under the DF and its harmonics) to the total power. By knowing the OI value, we can relate the organization of particular sites on the LA with DF variability and thus

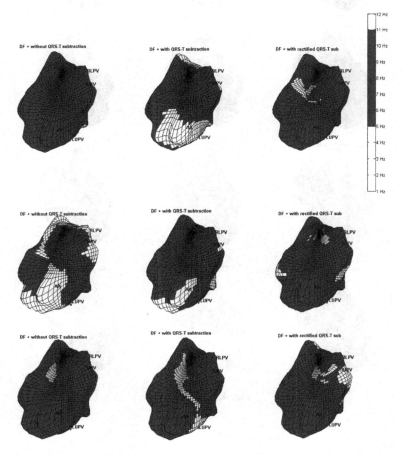

Fig. 4. (a) Subjects a1 3D DF maps for 1–3 s, (b) subjects a1 3D DF maps for 4–8 s, (c) subjects a1 3D DF maps for 9–13 s, (d) subjects a1 3D DF maps for 14–18 s, (e) subjects a1 3D DF maps for 19–21 s

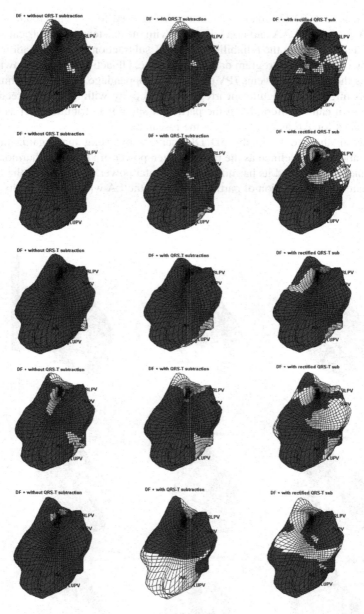

Fig. 4. (continued)

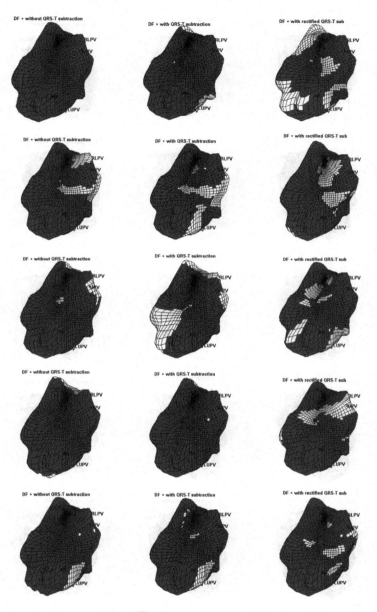

Fig. 4. (continued)

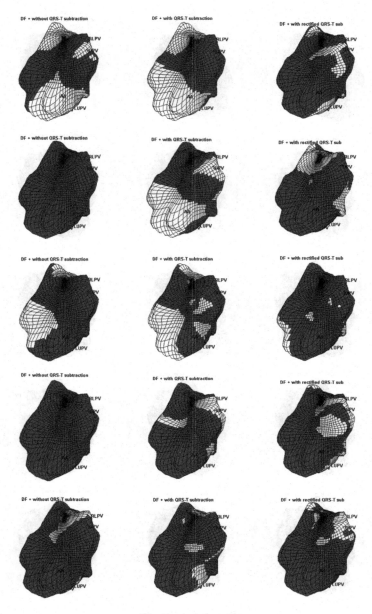

Fig. 4. (continued)

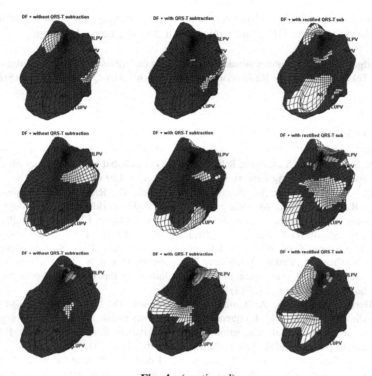

Fig. 4. (continued)

the electrical activation of DF. The higher the OI value (>0.5), the more regular the frequency activity of the particular sites, and hence indicates low DF variability or low possibility of electrical activation source for AF on that particular area of LA.

The evaluation of sites on LA can be compared with OI analysis to justify their relatability as the sites of electrical activation source for AF. Similarly, OI analysis result will also be used together with visual observation of the 3D DF maps to infer the importance of using the preprocessing steps: QRS-T subtraction and rectification, on AF electrogram data studies.

4   Conclusion

This research is exploring pre-processing approaches which included both with and without rectification and filtering using QRS-T subtraction for DF estimation. The modelling of the electrophysiological data of AF in 3D DF maps form is a credible method to study the correlation between the DF activity of AF and its electrical activation attributes.

We believed that the QRS-T subtraction is a significant preprocessing step for the AF data. It is also expected that the DF activity in particular sites of LA, such as the PV, MV and LAA sites are more relevant to the AF electrical activation source compare to the non DF sites. However, in order to accurately study the behavior of AF and its relation with the DF, more subjects and data are desired in future.

Acknowledgement. The authors would like to thank the Ministry of Higher Education and Universiti Teknologi Malaysia for supporting this research under Q.J130000.2523.15H29.

References

1. Chugh, S.S., Roth, G.A., Gillum, R.F., Mensah, G.A.: Global burden of atrial fibrillation in developed and developing nations. Global Heart **9**, 113–119 (2014)
2. Chugh, S.S., Havmoeller, R., Narayanan, K., Singh, D., Rienstra, M., Benjamin, E.J., Gillum, R.F., Kim, Y.-H., McAnulty, J.H., Zheng, Z.-J.: Worldwide epidemiology of atrial fibrillation: a global burden of disease 2010 study. Circulation **129**, 837–847 (2013)
3. Nattel, S., Shiroshita-Takeshita, A., Brundel, B.J., Rivard, L.: Mechanisms of atrial fibrillation: lessons from animal models. Progress Cardiovasc. Dis. **48**, 9–28 (2005)
4. Colilla, S., Crow, A., Petkun, W., Singer, D.E., Simon, T., Liu, X.: Estimates of current and future incidence and prevalence of atrial fibrillation in the U.S. adult population. Am. J. Cardiol. **112**, 1142–1147 (2013)
5. Zoni-Berisso, M., Filippi, A., Landolina, M., Brignoli, O., D'Ambrosio, G., Maglia, G., Grimaldi, M., Ermini, G.: Frequency, patient characteristics, treatment strategies, and resource usage of atrial fibrillation (from the Italian Survey of Atrial Fibrillation Management [ISAF] study). Am. J. Cardiol. **111**, 705–711 (2013)
6. Fukaya, H., Niwano, S., Sasaki, T., Kiryu, M., Kurokawa, S., Hatakeyama, Y., Sato, D., Yumoto, Y., Moriguchi, M., Niwano, H.: Attenuating effects of anti-arrhythmic agents on changes in fibrillation cycle length in very early phase paroxysmal atrial fibrillation—spectral analysis of fibrillation waves in surface ECG. J. Arrhythm. **25**, 135–141 (2009)
7. Omar, R., Teo, W.S., Foo, D., Han, C.K., Jamaluddin, A.N., Low, L.P., Ong, T.K.: Atrial fibrillation in Singapore and Malaysia: current trends and future prospects. J. Arrhythm. **27**, 171–185 (2011)
8. Kim, Y.H., Lim, H.E., Pak, H.N.: Use of three-dimensional mapping systems in the catheter ablation of atrial fibrillation. J. Cardiovasc. Electrophysiol. **17**, S16–S22 (2006)
9. Ching, C.K., Patel, D., Natale, A.: Catheter ablation of atrial fibrillation. J. Arrhythm. **23**, 85–101 (2007)
10. Ahmad, A., Schlindwein, F.S., Ng, G.A.: Comparison of computation time for estimation of dominant frequency of atrial electrograms: fast fourier transform, blackman tukey, autoregressive and multiple signal classification. J. Biomed. Sci. Eng. **3**, 843 (2010)
11. Ahmad, A., Buyamin, S., Senin, N.: Frequency analysis for surface electrocardiogram of atrial fibrillation. J. Teknol. **64** (2013)
12. Traykov, V.B., Pap, R., Sághy, L.: Frequency domain mapping of atrial fibrillation-methodology, experimental data and clinical implications. Curr. Cardiol. Rev. **8**, 231 (2012)
13. Ng, J., Goldberger, J.J.: Understanding and interpreting dominant frequency analysis of AF electrograms. J. Cardiovasc. Electrophysiol. **18**, 680–685 (2007)
14. Sanders, P., Berenfeld, O., Hocini, M., Jaïs, P., Vaidyanathan, R., Hsu, L.-F., Garrigue, S., Takahashi, Y., Rotter, M., Sacher, F.: Spectral analysis identifies sites of high-frequency activity maintaining atrial fibrillation in humans. Circulation **112**, 789–797 (2005)
15. Jalife, J.: Rotors and spiral waves in atrial fibrillation. J. Cardiovasc. Electrophysiol. **14**, 776–780 (2003)

16. Lin, Y.-J.: The frequency analysis and the atrial fibrillation. J. Biocatal. Biotransform. (2012)
17. Saini, I., Singh, D., Khosla, A.: QRS detection using K-Nearest Neighbor algorithm (KNN) and evaluation on standard ECG databases. J. Adv. Res. **4**, 331–344 (2013)
18. Corino, V.D.A., Sassi, R., Mainardi, L.T., Cerutti, S.: Signal processing methods for information enhancement in atrial fibrillation: spectral analysis and non-linear parameters. Biomed. Signal Process. Control **1**, 271–281 (2006)
19. Ahmad, A., Salinet Jr., J.L., Brown, P., Tuan, J.H., Stafford, P., Ng, G.A., Schlindwein, F.S.: QRS subtraction for atrial electrograms: flat, linear and spline interpolations. Med. Biol. Eng. Comput. **49**, 1321–1328 (2011)
20. Yeh, Y.-C., Wang, W.-J.: QRS complexes detection for ECG signal: the difference operation method. Comput. Methods Programs Biomed. **91**, 245–254 (2008)
21. Corino, V.D., Rivolta, M.W., Sassi, R., Lombardi, F., Mainardi, L.T.: Ventricular activity cancellation in electrograms during atrial fibrillation with constraints on residuals' power. Med. Eng. Phys. **35**, 1770–1777 (2013)
22. Ng, J., Kadish, A.H., Goldberger, J.J.: Technical considerations for dominant frequency analysis. J. Cardiovasc. Electrophysiol. **18**, 757–764 (2007)

Enhanced Probabilistic Roadmap for Robot Navigation in Virtual Greenhouse Environment

Mohd Saiful Azimi Mahmud, Mohamad Shukri Zainal Abidin[(✉)],
Zaharuddin Mohamed, Muhammad Khairie Idham Abd Rahman,
and Salinda Buyamin

Department of Control and Mechatronics, Faculty of Electrical Engineering,
Universiti Teknologi Malaysia, Skudai, Malaysia
{msazimi2,mkidham}@live.utm.my,
{shukri,zahar,salinda}@fke.utm.my

Abstract. Inefficient navigation capability in dynamic agricultural field limits the application of agricultural robot in the field. Probabilistic roadmap however has the robustness for outdoor navigation. A path planning algorithm was established upon an enhanced probabilistic roadmap and this was implemented in a virtual greenhouse environment. A smoothing algorithm for the robot's navigation has been proposed to improve the existing algorithm in producing an optimal path. A simulation was conducted using a crop inspection mobile robot and tested with suitable turning trajectories for lane changing. Several trajectories were initiated and compared based on travel time, distance and controller error in order to choose the best trajectories for crop inspection. The proposed smoothing algorithm was able to smooth out the initial paths in order to create an optimal path for the robot with error less than 0.1 m.

Keywords: Crop identification · Optimal path · Probabilistic roadmap · Robot navigation

1 Introduction

In agricultural robot development, navigational design is the major challenges faced by developers. Farming works, such as harvesting, weeding, spraying, and transportation, performed by mobile robots depend heavily on precise navigational system for its path in agricultural field [1]. An optimal path is defined as the shortest and smoothest path. In mobile robot path planning methods such as probabilistic roadmaps [2], artificial potential field [3], cell decomposition [4] and Voronoi roadmap [5] have been widely implemented to solve path planning problems. Voronoi roadmap approach computes path based on midpoint of obstacles thus unable to find a shortest path. Artificial potential field is a good path planner but it will be easily fall into local minimum as it does not have much information regarding the environment. Probabilistic roadmap is a method that usually implemented in path planning. It is a simple and has high success rate in solving path planning problem [6]. However, because of the randomness of particle generation, the computed path for this algorithm is not very smooth.

© Springer Nature Singapore Pte Ltd. 2017
M.S. Mohamed Ali et al. (Eds.): AsiaSim 2017, Part II, CCIS 752, pp. 172–182, 2017.
DOI: 10.1007/978-981-10-6502-6_15

Several methods have been introduced to produce a smoother path of Probabilistic Roadmap. A smoothing method called Cutting-triangle's-edge algorithm and Cubic Smoothing algorithm for Probabilistic Roadmap has been introduced by [7]. It reduces the distance travelled by removing the triangle shaped path and smoothing the edges using cubic polynomial. A smoothed polynomial upper bound on the number of required node samples to produce an accurate and smooth probabilistic roadmap was also introduced in [8]. Those methods are proven to improve the performance of probabilistic roadmap in terms of smoothness of the path edge. However, in agriculture, the generated path needs to minimise the robot turning in order to preserve the soil surface condition. Therefore, a better smoothing algorithm needs to be designed in order to fulfil the requirements of agricultural workspace.

This paper proposed an optimal path for a mobile robot's navigation using an enhanced probabilistic roadmap simulated in a virtual greenhouse environment. A unicycle like mobile robot model and a kinematics feedback motion tracking controller proposed in [9] is used in the simulation. Two smoothing techniques called repeated path algorithm and straight-line estimation algorithm were proposed. An approach of crop tagging using image processing by using Mahalanobis Distance [10–13] in order to filter out the YCbCrcolor channel from the image. The tagged crop coordinates will then become an input into the probabilistic roadmap for motion planning. Different types of turning methods were compared based upon the time taken, distance travelled and mean square controller error for the optimal path design.

2　Materials and Methods

Figure 1 shows the system overview for the robot navigation simulation. The system environment is divided into two sections: SolidWorks and MATLAB. The model for robot and environment were designed by using SolidWorks.

Based on Fig. 1, the robot model was transferred into MATLAB by using SimMechanics. For the environment model, SolidWorks design was converted into

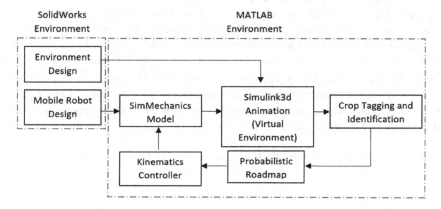

Fig. 1. Robot navigational system overview

Virtual Reality Modelling Language (VRML) file and transferred into Simulink3d Animation as the virtual environment. The aerial view from the virtual environment was captured and processed using Mahalanobis distance for crop identification and tagging. The tagged crop coordinates were used to generate a set of goal points for generating the navigation path by using Probabilistic Roadmap. From the computed path, the trajectory for each goal point was fed into the kinematics controller to control the mobile robot motion in the virtual environment.

2.1   Unicycle Like Mobile Robot Model

Unicycle like mobile robot model introduced in [9] was used due to its good mobility and simple configuration. Based on Eq. (1), u and ω denotes the linear and angular velocities that were developed by the robot. ψ is the robot orientation and a is the distance between the point of interest and the central point of the virtual axis linking the traction wheel. The kinematics law proposed in [14] is used. The control equation is given by:

$$\begin{bmatrix} u^c_{ref} \\ \omega^c_{ref} \end{bmatrix} = \begin{bmatrix} cos\psi & sin\psi \\ -\frac{1}{a}sin\psi & \frac{1}{a}cos\psi \end{bmatrix} \begin{bmatrix} x_d + l_x tanh\left(\frac{k_x}{l_x}\tilde{x}\right) \\ y_d + l_y tanh\left(\frac{k_y}{l_y}\tilde{y}\right) \end{bmatrix} \tag{1}$$

Based on Eq. (1), $\tilde{x} = x_d - x$ and $\tilde{y} = y_d - y$ are the error in current position in XY axes respectively. k_x and k_y are the gains of the controller, $l_x \in \mathcal{R}$ and $l_y \in \mathcal{R}$ are the saturation constants, (x, y) and (x_d, y_d) are the current and desired coordinates of the point of interest. Kinematics controller was designed for robot trajectory tracking based on robot kinematics.

2.2   Robot Turning Type

Several turning methods such as sharp turn, U turn and π turn were used for the robot navigation. Figure 2 shows the sharp turn, U turn and π turn respectively.

In designing robot turning, many approaches have been developed to optimize the field operation that focusing on minimizing operational time, cost and maundering over field area [15]. The coordinate of turning center was computed based on the midpoint between turning point, (x_{turn}, y_{turn}) and also crop point (x_{crop}, y_{crop}). x_{crop} was computed based on the furthest obstacles in x-coordinate in the current lane. y_{crop} was obtained based on midpoint between crop in Row A and Row B in y-coordinate. U turn and π turn was computed based on trigonometry formula. The formula for U turn:

$$x = x_{center} + rcos(\theta), y = y_{center} + rsin(\theta), \theta = 0, \ldots, 180. \tag{2}$$

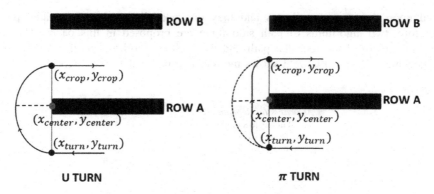

Fig. 2. Robot turning trajectories

And for π turn:

$$x = x_{center} + \frac{r}{2}cos(\theta) + \frac{r}{2}, y = y_{center} + \frac{r}{2}sin(\theta) + \frac{r}{2}, \theta = 0, \ldots 90$$
$$x = x_{center} + \frac{r}{2}cos(\theta) - \frac{r}{2}, = y_{center} + \frac{r}{2}sin(\theta) - \frac{r}{2}, \theta = 91, \ldots 180$$

(3)

Based on Eqs. (2) and (3), x_{center} and y_{center} denoted the centre of the curve that was calculated based on the coordinate between two crops in the different turning row. In agriculture, sharp turn is rarely used as it can cause severe damage to the soil structure. Therefore, soft turning type is needed which reduces the soil damage over headlands area [16].

2.3 Probabilistic Roadmap

A probabilistic roadmap (PRM) was one of the methods used to solve the motion planning problem. It had two phases: a learning phase and a query phase. In the learning phase, the roadmap was formed in the C-space of the robot and this information was stored as an undirected graph R [2]. A random free configuration was generated and was added to a node, N. For every new node, a number of nodes from the current N were selected and an attempt was made to connect each of them by using a local planner. The new node N_c tried to connect to c in order to increase its distance from c.

During the query phase, paths were found between the arbitrary input start and the goal configuration, when using the roadmap that was constructed during the learning phase. When the start configuration s and the goal configuration g was given, we tried to connect s and g to the two nodes of R, $\tilde{s}$ and $\tilde{g}$, with the feasible paths, P_s and P_g. In this paper, the feasible path was computed by using Dijkstra's search algorithm. Then, the path was improved by running a smoothing algorithm.

A smoothing algorithm was required to improve the path efficiency. For this paper, the navigational system used a sequence of start and goal configurations that were based upon the crop coordinates and they unexpectedly produced repeated paths. Therefore, two algorithms of path smoothing are proposed in this paper. The first algorithm removed the repeated path and the second algorithm predicted the path's straight-line behavior. Figure 3 shows the repeated path smoothing algorithm.

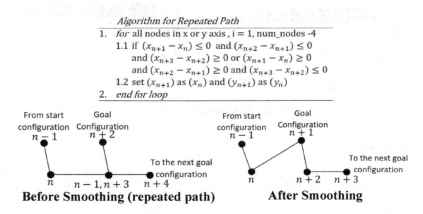

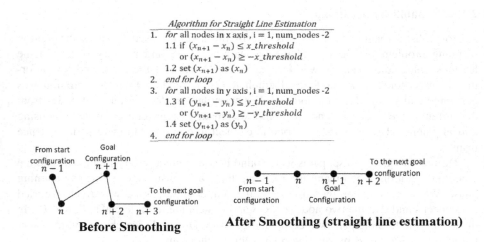

Fig. 3.   Repeated path smoothing algorithm

Figure 4 shows the estimation of a straight-line path's behavior and the algorithm proposed. Based on the algorithms as shown in Figs. 3 and 4, n denotes the number of nodes that were generated by the roadmap, x_n denotes the x coordinates of the nth node, and y_n denotes the y coordinates of the nth node, respectively.

Fig. 4.   Straight line estimation algorithm

3   Result and Discussion

3.1   Mobile Robot Model and Virtual Environment

Figure 5(a) shows the mobile robot model that was designed when using SolidWorks based upon the existing mobile robot system as shown in Fig. 5(b). Figure 5(c) shows the aerial view of the environment. In this view, the virtual camera was placed at the center of the environment in order to capture the overall environment that consisted of 4 crop rows and had a field view of 0.784.

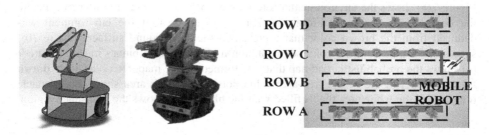

Fig. 5. Mobile robot and virtual environment design (a) robot design (b) real robot model (c) aerial view (from environment)

3.2   Mobile Robot Model and Virtual Environment

In order to identify the crops in the environment, the aerial view image was captured and the crop color was extracted by using color segmentation. The crops were then tagged based upon the color detection. They were marked with a blue box and named based on the rows and columns. For the color segmentation, the Cb and Cr parameters used 55 and 30, respectively. Figure 6(a) shows the aerial image and Fig. 6(b) shows the tagged crop from identification.

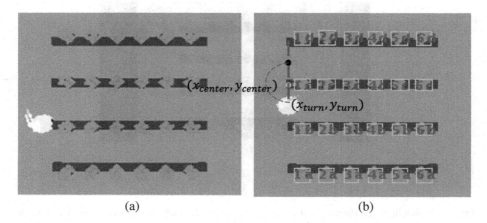

(a)   (b)

Fig. 6. Crop identification process (a) aerial image (b) identified crop (Color figure online)

Based on Fig. 6(b), the turning point, (x_{center}, y_{center}) was measured based on the end point of crop stand and the midpoint between crop distance in different row respectively. The goal point, $x_{goal(n)}$ for x-coordinate was selected based on x-coordinate of the tagged crop. For y-coordinate in each goal point, $x_{goal(n)}$ the midpoint between each row was selected. Then, a set of 24 different goal points was fed into probabilistic roadmap to plan the path in the environment.

3.3   Virtual Environment Probabilistic Roadmap

Figure 7(a) shows the environmental aerial view that was captured in order to generate the probabilistic roadmap. From Fig. 7(a), the free area of the environment was deduced from the brown color that represented the free ground surface. Figure 7(b) shows the output from the color segmentation in the form of a binary image. Figure 7 (c) shows the probabilistic roadmap that was formed. In the map, the nodes were drawn for each pixel in the map's free area (blue dots). The black area shows the obstacle regions and the white area that is filled with the blue nodes shows the free space region.

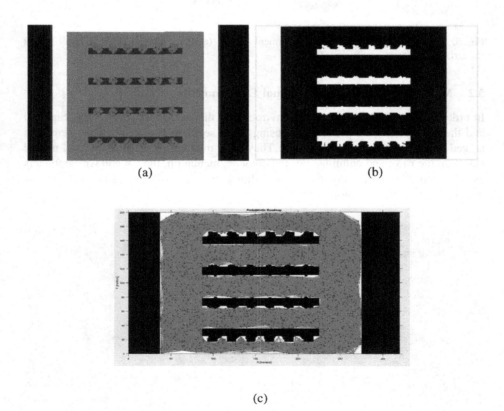

(a)   (b)

(c)

Fig. 7. Probabilistic roadmap generation process (a) aerial view (b) processed (binary) image (c) probabilistic roadmap produced (Color figure online)

The scale used between the probabilistic roadmap and the real parameters was 0.02239 as the computed roadmap's size of 200 m × 320 m was not based on the actual environment.

The connection distance between the nodes of 0.67 m and number of nodes of 2000 has been chosen because of the roadmap large size. Those measurements were also chosen as to improve the possibility of finding the shortest and the smoothest path in the map. The identified crop coordinates were then fed into the probabilistic roadmap. Then, a feasible path was computed by using Djikstra's search algorithm. For mobile robot's turning method, the navigational algorithm initialized the turning if there was a major difference between the present y-coordinate goal value and the next y-coordinate goal value. It computed the turning based upon the chosen turning type, whether it was a U turn, a π turn, or a default turn by probabilistic roadmap itself.

Figure 8 shows the path that was generated. Based on the figure, the generated path produces a repeated path that does not comply with an optimum path requirement. The generated path will stop at the closest node before arrived at the goal point. Then, in order to generate the path for next goal destination, it will use a previous closest node to navigate into the next node and it will produce a repeated path. The red dot line shows the generated path by using default Probabilistic Roadmap Algorithm. The path then was improved by the smoothing algorithm and The blue line shows the output from the algorithm. Based on the figure, the generated repeated path has been eliminated and the path has been further smoothed into a straight line path. The purpose of this smoothing algorithm is to generate a path that will optimize the mobile robot operation in the environment. Therefore, it was proven that the path had been smoothed and the straight line estimation had been successfully implemented. The parameters used for the smoothing algorithm were 2 and 5 for the $x\_threshold$ and the $y\_threshold$, respectively.

Figure 9 shows the trajectory that was formed based on different algorithm implementation. Based on the figure, the red dot line shows the pure PRM, green line

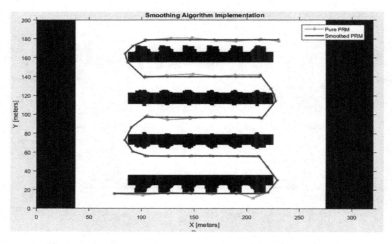

Fig. 8. Smoothing algorithm implementation (Color figure online)

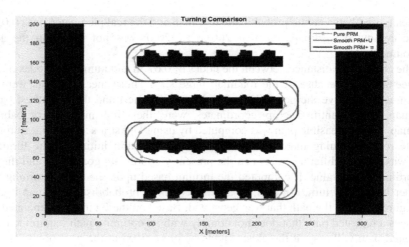

Fig. 9. Generated navigation trajectories (Color figure online)

represents the smooth PRM + U turn and the blue line represents the smooth PRM + π turn. The figure also shows that the addition of smooth turn indirectly adding some distances in robot path as it needed some space to make a softer turn.

Figure 10 shows the trajectory tracking error comparison between various algorithm implementation. For the trajectory tracking controller, the value of parameters used were 2 for k_x, 2 for k_y, 0.5 for l_x and 1 for l_y, respectively. Based on the figure, the maximum error that was produced from the implemented controller is about 0.12 m.

Table 1 shows the trajectories comparison for the Pure PRM, Smooth PRM, Smooth PRM + U Turn and Smooth PRM + π turn.

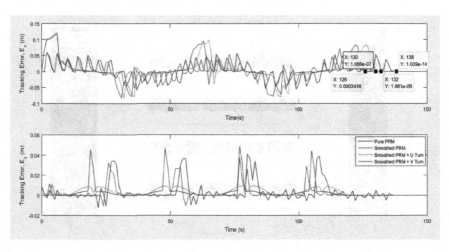

Fig. 10. Trajectory tracking error comparison

Table 1. Navigation trajectory type comparison

Trajectory type	Completion time (s)	Distance travelled (m)	Mean square error (m)
Pure PRM	138	19.6105	x = 0.0468, y = 0.0060
Smoothed PRM	132	18.9221	x = 0.0463, y = 0.0053
Smoothed PRM + U Turn	130	22.8269	x = 0.0789, y = 0.0008
Smoothed PRM + π Turn	126	22.8272	x = 0.0836, y = 0.0048

Based on Table 1, the comparison was conducted based upon the completion time, distance traveled and controller mean square error. Based on the comparison, the Smooth PRM + π Turn shows the best performance for field operation instead of having higher travel distance and controller error. The main reason behind this statement is that π Turn produces lower time consumption compared to other methods. It is due to the lower turning radius as the mobile robot speed will decrease during soft turns. Based on the table, although the Pure PRM shows lower distance travelled, it produces higher completion time. Generally, the Pure PRM algorithm produced a crooked and branched path. Therefore, the mobile robot will take time to turn based upon those branches and in the end, will increase the travel time. In Table 1, it is clear that the Pure PRM algorithm has been improved by using the proposed smoothing algorithm. The completion time, distance travelled and controller error has been improved and it provides better performance compared to the Pure PRM algorithm.

4 Conclusion

In summary, we have introduced a Probabilistic Roadmap based robot navigation in a virtual greenhouse environment. The navigation goal point system has been designed based on the crop identification process by using image processing algorithm. In this paper, a novel smoothing algorithm for Probabilistic Roadmap has also been introduced. Based on the simulation result, the performance of the Probabilistic Roadmap in robot navigation has been improved by using a proposed novel smoothing algorithm. The simulation results show that the Smooth PRM + π Turn has the best navigation performance in mobile robot navigation inside the greenhouse. Therefore, it is recommended to be implement in mobile robot navigation inside the greenhouse environment.

Acknowledgements. The authors are grateful to the Universiti Teknologi Malaysia and the Ministry of Higher Education (MOHE) for their partial financial support through their research fund, Vote no. R.J130000.7823.4F759 entitled 'A Study on Adaptive Control Strategies for Infiltration Process in Fibrous-capillary System for Precision Water-saving Agriculture'.

References

1. Longo, D., Mustaco, G.: Design and simulation of two robotics systems for automatic artichoke harvesting. Robotics **2**, 217–230 (2013)
2. Claude Overmars, L., Kavraki Lydia, E., Svestka, P., Jean, M.H.: Probabilistic roadmap for path planning in high-dimensional configuration spaces. IEEE Trans. Rob. Autom. **12**, 566–579 (1996)
3. Bence, K., Geza, S., Ferenc, T., Mauricio, B., Peter, K.: A novel potential field method for path planning of mobile robots by adapting animal motion attributes. Rob. Autom. Syst. **82**, 24–34 (2016)
4. Filliat, D., Meyer, J.A.: Map-based navigation in mobile robots: II. A review of map-learning and path-planning strategies. Cogn. Syst. Res. **4**, 283–317 (2003)
5. Tian, S., Cui, X., Gong, Y.: A general vector-based algorithm to generate weighted Voronoi diagrams based on ArcGIS Engine. Int. J. Comput. Inf. Technol. **3**, 737–742 (2014)
6. Daee, P., Taheri, K., Moradi, H.: A sampling algorithm for reducing the number of collision checking in probabilistic roadmaps. In: The 22nd Iranian Conference on Electrical Engineering, pp. 1313–1316. Tehran, Iran (2014)
7. Belhocine, M., Guername, R.: A smoothing strategy for PRM paths applications to six-axes MOTOMAN SV3X manipulator. In: Intelligent Robot and System, Alberta, Canada, pp. 4155–4160 (2005)
8. Siddharta, C., Vladlen, K.: Smoothed analysis of probabilistic roadmaps. Comput. Geom. **42**, 731–747 (2009)
9. Carelli, R., Celeste Wanderly, C., Martins Felipe, N.: An adaptive dynamic controller for autonomous mobile robot trajectory tracking. Control Eng. Pract. **16**, 1354–1363 (2008)
10. Sakarya, O.: Applying fuzzy clustering method to colour image segmentation. In: Proceedings of the Federated Conference on Computer Science and Information System, Lodz, Poland, pp. 1049–1054 (2015)
11. Bo, D., Zhangguan, L., Cuixiao, L.: An algorithm of image matching based on Mahalanobis distance and weighed KNN graph. In: 2015 2nd International Conference on Information Science and Control Engineering, Shanghai, China, pp. 116–121 (2014)
12. Eddarouich, S., Hammouch, A., Meriem, T., Touahni, R., Sbihi, A.: Unsupervised neural-morphological color image segmentation using Mahalanobis criteria of resemblance. In: Multimedia Computing and Systems (ICMCS) International Conference, Marrakesh, Morocco, pp. 314–320 (2014)
13. Zhijun, Y.: Visual saliency detection based on Mahalanobis distance and feature evaluation. In: 10th International Conference on Fuzzy System and Knowledge Discovery, Shenyang, China, pp. 251–255 (2013)
14. Carelli, R., Filho Mario, S., Martins Felipe, N., Teodiano, B., F.: Dynamic modelling and adaptive dynamic compensation for unicycle-like mobile robots. In: Advanced Robotics International Conference, Munich, Germany, pp. 1–6 (2009)
15. Hameed, I.A., la Cour-Harbo, A., Hansen, K.D.: Task and motion planning for selective weed control using a team of autonomous vehicles. In: 13th International Conference on Control, Automation, Robotics and Vision, Marina Bay, Singapore, pp. 1853–1857 (2014)
16. Jin, J.: Optimal field coverage path planning on 2D and 3D surfaces. Ph.D. thesis, Iowa State University, United States (2011)

Modeling and Simulation for Defect Depth Estimation Using Pulsed Eddy Current Technique

Muhammad Zamir Kamaruzzaman[1](✉),
Ilham Mukriz Zainal Abidin[2], and Ab Razak Hamzah[1]

[1] Fabrication and Joining Section, University Kuala Lumpur – Malaysia France
Institute (UniKL-MFI), 43600 Bangi, Selangor, Malaysia
zamirkamaruzzaman@gmail.com
[2] Leading Edge NDT Technology (LENDT) Group, Malaysian Nuclear Agency,
43000 Bangi, Selangor, Malaysia

Abstract. A finite element simulation for defect depth estimation using the pulsed eddy current (PEC) technique is presented in this paper. In this work, we investigate PEC inspection on defect with different depths, through the transient magnetic flux density profile from eddy current and defect interaction in a stainless steel sample. The investigation is implemented via time-stepping finite element method (FEM) modelled in 3D using COMSOL. The estimation of defect depth was made possible by the peak amplitude feature of the differential magnetic flux density profile acquired by the PEC coil. The underlying phenomena of the acquired results is then observed and discussed through the visualisation of the resultant eddy current density for different defect depths obtained from the simulation. The simulation results indicate the potential of detection and quantitative evaluation of defect using the PEC technique. It is expected the investigation will help in the future work of PEC in terms of sensor development and inversion models for defect characterisation.

Keywords: Pulsed eddy current · Non-destructive testing · Numerical modeling · 3D FEM

1 Introduction

Eddy current testing (ECT) is one of the Non Destructive Testing (NDT) methods that works on electromagnetic principles and is widely used for the inspection of electrically conductive samples. It allows the inspection of surface breaking as well as subsurface discontinuities, which are not too deep, due to the skin effect. The eddy current frequency directly affects the probability of detection of flaws that are located below surface and hence subsurface discontinuities [1]. In ECT, the excitation coil are fed with alternating current which generates eddy current in the conductive samples. In contrast to most eddy current technique, pulsed eddy current (PEC) uses transient waveforms for their coil excitation. The wideband pulse consists of a series of frequency components leading to richness of information [2–5].

© Springer Nature Singapore Pte Ltd. 2017
M.S. Mohamed Ali et al. (Eds.): AsiaSim 2017, Part II, CCIS 752, pp. 183–190, 2017.
DOI: 10.1007/978-981-10-6502-6_16

The interaction between the primary magnetic field generated by the coil and the secondary magnetic field generated by the eddy currents resulted in decreasing net flux and is monitored by pick up coils or magnetic sensing devices such as magneto-resistive devices to give an indication of defects or any variations in the material's properties [6]. ECT uses the excitation coil as the detection sensor and measures the impedance change of the coil. Unfortunately, sensors that uses coil as a detection sensor has less sensitivity at low frequencies which is needed in detecting deep flaws. To overcome this problem, PEC utilizes magnetic field sensors which measure directly the magnetic field intensity. These magnetic sensors or commonly called magnetometers measure directly the net magnetic field from the interaction of the primary and secondary magnetic fields.

In order to get better understanding of the PEC results especially in the case of different defect depths, numerical simulation of finite element is used to undertake the study. Using numerical simulation, we can obtain the visualisation of the eddy current distribution and interaction at the defect area which can help in understanding the PEC phenomena. The investigation is implemented via time-stepping [7, 8] finite element method (FEM) modelled in 3D using COMSOL. Such simulation investigations would be very helpful in understanding and interpreting the PEC response to different depths through the transient profiles of the magnetic flux density from the eddy current and defect interaction in the sample.

This paper is organised as follows: Sect. 2 presents the simulation work setup and the basic characteristics of eddy current distribution; Sect. 3 exhibits the simulation results and discussion on defect depths characterisation by means of PEC. Section 4 summaries the outcome of the work and conclusion are drawn afterwards.

2   Modeling and Simulation Setup

In PEC, it is essential to build the relationship between magnetic field distribution and different defect geometrical characteristics such as depth for the quantitative evaluation of the defect. This not only facilitates forward problems related to PEC, but also the inverse process involving sensor configuration, pattern recognition, defect quantification and reconstruction of 3D defects. Consequently, a series of numerical modelling simulations with regards to magnetic flux density under different defect depths are conducted.

In the simulation, the coil used has the dimensions of 10 mm inner diameter, 15 mm outer diameter, 40 mm height and 1000 turns of wire, and is current driven with a rectangular waveform of 1 A amplitude to generate a varying magnetic field. Figure 1 illustrates the excitation current input waveform used to drive the coil. Stainless steel samples with different defect depths of 1 mm, 3 mm, 5 mm, 7 mm and 9 mm were modelled and the resulting magnetic flux density along the coil axis, which is vertical to the surface of the sample, were acquired for the quantitative evaluation of the defect, as illustrated in Fig. 2.

In the time-stepping finite element analysis (FEA), the transient magnetic flux density profiles were acquired when the coil is positioned above the defect opening. The time step of the pulse waveform is 0.001 ms with a 1 ms excitation pulse width

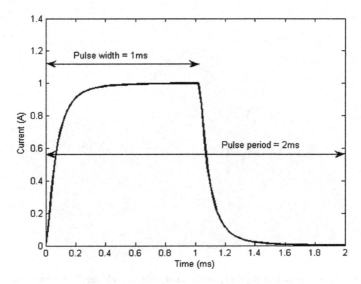

Fig. 1. Coil excitation current input waveform

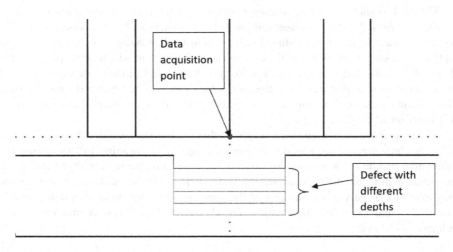

Fig. 2. Illustration of defect with different depths in the stainless steel sample and the data acquisition point for the investigation

and pulse repetition frequency is 200 Hz. All simulations were performed using COMSOL. Figure 3 shows the layout of the coil and the stainless steel sample having a defect, modelled as a 3D problem.

3D FEM simulation for the PEC testing were conducted in transient mode. The simulation was intended to visualise the underlying phenomena of PEC testing with regards to the change of induced current density which leads to the resultant magnetic flux density acquired with different defect depths.

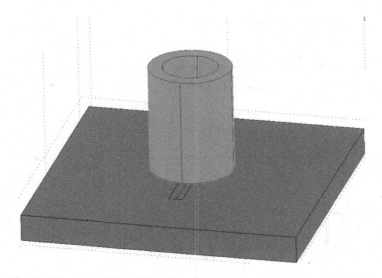

Fig. 3. 3D model of the PEC coil and stainless steel sample having defect

Figure 4(a) shows the visualisation (top view) of the induced eddy current density distribution from the stainless steel sample at 1 ms excitation. The visualisations shown are an absolute value of the induced current density distribution. As we can see, the eddy current density induced by the coil shows a distribution which corresponds to the shape of the coil itself. The region near the coil shows a high magnitude of density and drops abruptly with distance from the coil, which can also be observed from the slice view of the magnetic flux density in Fig. 4(b). This shows the induced current density is a function of radius of the coil.

The magnitude of change in the magnetic flux density from sample with defect with different characteristic such as depth, can be made to be meaning full by taking the differential profile of the results. To observe the change of the field with the change of the defect depths, the differential profile was made by taking the difference between the magnetic flux density of air and that of the stainless steel sample at each defect depth. The differential magnetic flux density for all defect depths can be mathematically defined as follows:

$$\Delta B_{Zm} = B_{Zref} - B_{Zm} \tag{1}$$

where B_{Zref} is the magnetic flux density for reference (air), B_{Zm} is the magnetic flux density for the stainless steel sample and m represents the defects with depths $m = 1$ mm, 3 mm, 5 mm, 7 mm, ..., N mm.

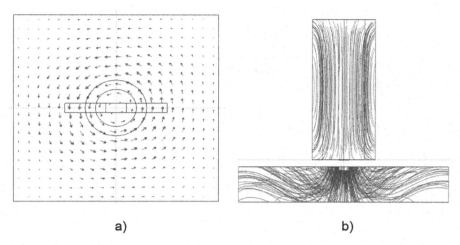

a)   b)

Fig. 4. Visualisation of (a) induced eddy current density distribution from top view, and (b) the slice view of the magnetic flux density

3   Simulation Results and Magnetic Flux Density Analysis

Transient profiles for the magnetic flux density when the coil was placed on air and above the stainless steel sample having defects with depths of 1 mm, 3 mm, 5 mm, 7 mm and 9 mm were simulated and shown in Fig. 5. Figure 5(a) shows the magnetic flux densities acquired at 1 ms excitation. Figure 5(b) shows the differential magnetic flux densities with regards to air.

From Fig. 5(a) it can be observed that the magnetic flux density when the coil is placed in air has the highest amplitude profile compared to when it is placed above the stainless sample with defects. In air, the magnetic flux density is coming directly from the excitation coil. However, when the coil is placed above the stainless steel sample, the induced eddy currents will generate its own magnetic field which will always oppose the magnetic field coming from the coil of the PEC probe. Thus, the net magnetic flux density will be reduced due to this interaction between the magnetic field from the coil and the magnetic field from the induced eddy currents. The differential results in Fig. 5(b) also shows that for different defect depths, the amplitude of the transient profiles of the differential magnetic flux density are reducing with the increase of defect depths. The peak amplitude of the differential magnetic flux density profile is the feature that can be used to estimate the depth of the defect.

To visualise the underlying phenomena for the results shown in Fig. 5, the slice view of the stainless steel sample for every defect depths were acquired from the simulation. Figure 6(a)–(d) show the resultant induced eddy current densities for each defect depth. The slice view for the visualisations were made at a single time point at the steady state region of the transient i.e. 1 ms.

As we can see from the slice view shown in the figures, the eddy current density is changing with different defect depths. The presence of defect inside the stainless steel sample will perturb the flow of the induced eddy currents. This will weaken the

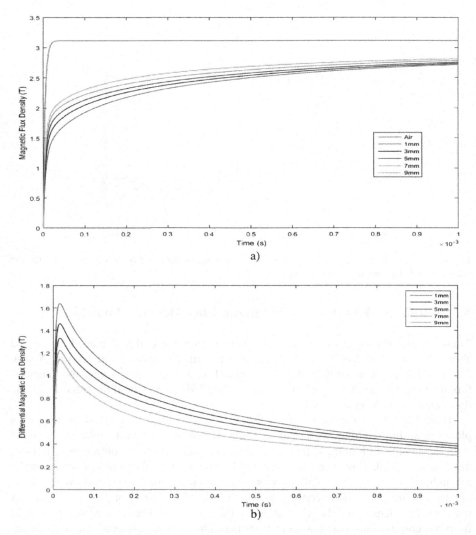

Fig. 5. Transient profiles for (a) magnetic flux density, and (b) differential magnetic flux density

magnetic field produced by the eddy currents and subsequently its density, since it has to divert itself to complete its path in a presence of a defect. As a result, the net magnetic flux density will be reduced. With the increase of defect depths, the flow of the eddy currents will increasingly be perturbed, thus reduced in eddy current density as shown in Fig. 6 and results in the increase in net magnetic flux density as presented in Fig. 5(a).

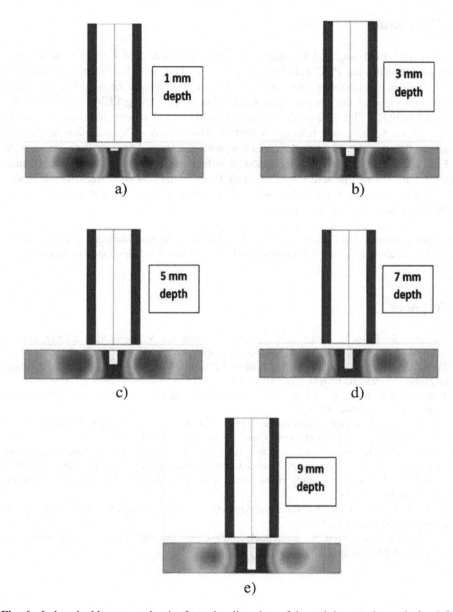

Fig. 6. Induced eddy current density from the slice view of the stainless steel sample for defect with depth of (a) 1 mm, (b) 3 mm, (c) 5 mm, (d) 7 mm and (e) 9 mm

4   Conclusion

In this paper, modeling and simulation for the estimation defect depth in a stainless steel sample using the PEC technique is presented. The study has been made through the simulation of transient profiles of the magnetic flux density from eddy current and defect interaction in the sample implemented via time-stepping FEM modelled in 3D using COMSOL. The results show that as depth of the defect increases, the eddy current tends to be more heavily perturbed which causes the increase in the net magnetic flux density. The simulation in this work discloses the underlying phenomena of PEC technique in the characterisation of defect particularly its depth. The quantitative evaluation of the defect by PEC may benefits the real-time quantitative evaluation since the inverse algorithm for defect detection and characterisation can be applied in one excitation process.

Acknowledgement. The authors would like to thank the Malaysian Nuclear Agency especially the staff of Leading Edge NDT Technology (LENDT) Group for their support of this work.

References

1. Grimberg, R., Udpa, L., Savin, A., Steigmann, R., Palihovici, V., Udpa, S.S.: 2D eddy current sensor array. NDT & E Int. **39**(4), 264–271 (2006)
2. Tian, G.Y., Sophian, A., Taylor, D., Rudlin, J.R.: Pulsed eddy current system for dynamic inspection of defects. Insight 256–260 (2004)
3. Tian, G.Y., Sophian, A.: Defect classification using a new feature for pulsed eddy current sensors. NDT & E Int. **38**(1), 77–82 (2005)
4. Smith, R.A., Hugo, G.R.: Transient eddy current NDE for ageing aircraft – capabilities and limitations. Insight: Non-Destr. Test. Cond. Monit. **43**(1), 14–25 (2001)
5. Fan, M., Cao, B., Sunny, A.I., Li, W., Tian, G., Ye, B.: Pulsed eddy current thickness measurement using phase features immune to liftoff effect. NDT & E Int. **86**, 123–131 (2017)
6. Tian, G.Y., Sophian, A.: Study of magnetic sensors for pulsed eddy current techniques. Insight **47**(5), 277–280 (2005)
7. Li, Y., Tian, G.Y., Ward, S.: Numerical simulations on electromagnetic NDT at high speed. Insight **48**(2), 103–108 (2006)
8. Li, Y., Tian, G.Y., Ward, S.: Numerical simulation on magnetic flux leakage evaluation at high speed. NDT & E Int. **39**(5), 367–373 (2006)

Mathematical Modelling and Quadratic Optimal Tuning Based PID Scheme for an Inverted Pendulum-Cart System

Mohd Fakhrurrazi Mohd Salleh and Mohamad Amir Shamsudin[✉]

Faculty of Electrical Engineering, Universiti Teknologi Malaysia,
81310 Johor Bahru, Johor, Malaysia
Razi.salleh@gmail.com, amir@fke.utm.my

Abstract. An Inverted Pendulum (IP) is one of pendulum-cart laboratory setup consisted of a pole mounted on a cart. The system encompasses complex control problems and greatly challenges the researchers in designing a better and optimal controller. This paper aims to model the IP and to design a PID control that using Quadratic Optimal Tuning (QOT) scheme for stabilization and position control of a single link IP. Firstly, a nonlinear model of IP is derived using Newtonian method. Then an augment model that include PID scheme is formulated. Lastly, the gains of PID scheme is tuned using QOT. Matlab-Simulink environment is utilized to simulate the balancing and position control performance of IP. The results show that the stability of the system had been confirmed and the system had a comparable performance with the one which controlled by LQR controller.

Keywords: Single link inverted pendulum · Quadratic Optimal Tuning Based PID

1 Introduction

Controlling an IP is a major challenge to researchers. Due to its high nonlinearity in nature. The dynamics of the IP system is highly non-linear [1, 2] and involves complex control problems. Various types of IP-based robot have been developed and model [3–5]. The system is kinetostatically and dynamically unstable. In the upright position, a small deviation of the pendulum bar from it results in an unstable motion; therefore, the system needs to dynamically balance its pendulum bar by actuating its motors in preventing the pendulum bar from toppling.

Thus, various control schemes such as linear [6, 7], nonlinear [8, 9], adaptive [10, 11] and hybrid [12, 13] controllers had been proposed to stabilize the robot. With an objective to achieve a real-time control for inverted pendulum, the researchers proposed a simpler control scheme for the derived dynamic of IP system [14]. Controlling using a conventional PID controller will results in acceptable responses and stability performance for both angle of pendulum bar and cart movement. This linear control scheme had a low computational burden, but the control performance degraded due to the nonlinearity effects.

© Springer Nature Singapore Pte Ltd. 2017
M.S. Mohamed Ali et al. (Eds.): AsiaSim 2017, Part II, CCIS 752, pp. 191–202, 2017.
DOI: 10.1007/978-981-10-6502-6_17

Moreover, the controlling accuracy and performance can be further improved by introducing a Linear Quadratic Regulator (LQR) controller. Quadratic tuning scheme is proved to be effective and able to improve the performance of inverted pendulum by 20% compared controller modelled from a known properties and measurement [15]. Thus, this paper proposes Quadratic Optimal Tuning Based PID control scheme to improve the control performance of PID controller on IP system.

2   Inverted Pendulum-Cart Setup and Dynamic Model

One Stage Pendulum-Cart system (OSPCS) can be used to demonstrate position control problem of single link robotics arm, missile stabilization problems, crane control problems and other relevant engineering problems. For stabilization problem, the system consists of an inverted pendulum mounted to a motorized cart. It is an unstable system where the pendulum bar will fall over if a control input is not applied to move the cart to balance the pendulum bar. The main objective of control scheme is to balance the inverted pendulum and the second objective is to move the cart within a specified length of rail by applying a force to the cart.

The system can be considered as two-dimensional problem where the pendulum bar is constrained to move in the vertical plane shown in Fig. 2. For the system, the control input u that move the cart horizontally and the output are the angular position of the pendulum bar $\cong \phi$ and the horizontal position x of the cart. The important parameters of physical quantities for OSPCS are shown in Table 1 (Fig. 1).

Table 1. Parameters for 1-stage inverted pendulum system.

Symbol	Physical quantity	Value
M	Cart mass	1.096 kg
m	Pendulum bar mass	0.109 kg
b	Cart friction force	0.1 N
l	The length from the rotation axis to the centroid of the pendulum bar	0.25 m
g	Acceleration of gravity	9.81 m/s^2

2.1   Dynamic Models

As shown in Fig. 2, OSPCS consists of two bodies: the pendulum bar and the cart. The important quantities are the length l which measured from the origin of rotation axis to the centroid of the pendulum bar, the angular position ϕ of the pendulum bar $\cong$ and the cart position coordinate x. N and P are the interaction forces between the cart and the pendulum bar, u is the actuated input from the motor to the pendulum-cart system. Further, Newton's equation of the OSPCS will be developed to derive its mathematical model.

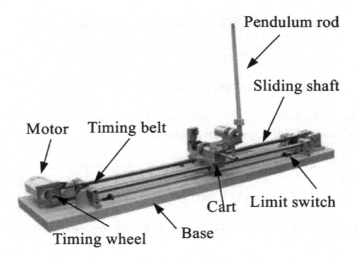

Fig. 1. A laboratory setup of a single-stage inverted pendulum-cart system

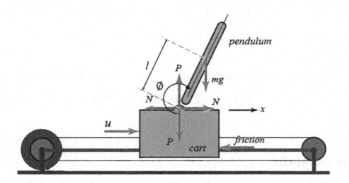

Fig. 2. Free body diagram of single-stage inverted pendulum-cart system

2.2 Mathematical Model of IP

Summing the forces in the free-body diagram of the cart and the pendulum in the horizontal direction, then the following equations are obtained.

$$M\ddot{x} + b\dot{x} + N = u. \tag{1}$$

$$N = m\ddot{x} + ml\ddot{\theta}\cos\theta - ml\dot{\theta}^2\sin\theta. \tag{2}$$

Secondly, summing the moment about the centroid of the pendulum due to the perpendicular forces that acted on the pendulum, one will obtained.

$$Pl \sin \phi + Nl \cos \phi - mgl \sin \phi = ml^2 \ddot{\phi} + m\ddot{x}l \cos \phi. \tag{3}$$

Where

$$-Pl \sin \phi - Nl \cos \phi = I\ddot{\phi}. \tag{4}$$

and $I = \frac{1}{3}ml^2$. Substituting Eq. (2) into (1) and Eq. (4) into (3), the first and second equations of motion for the system are obtained.

$$(I + ml^2)\ddot{\phi} + mgl \sin \phi = -ml\ddot{x} \cos \phi. \tag{5}$$

$$(M + m)\ddot{x} + b\dot{x} + ml\ddot{\phi} \cos \phi - ml\dot{\phi}^2 \sin \phi = u. \tag{6}$$

Solve Eqs. (5) and (6) for variables $\ddot{x}$ and $\ddot{\phi}$, then the equation for variable $\ddot{x}$ and $\ddot{\phi}$ are

$$\ddot{x} = \frac{(I + ml^2)\left(u - b\dot{x} + ml\dot{\phi}^2 \sin \phi\right) + (ml)^2 g \sin \phi \cos \phi}{I(M + m) + ml^2 (M + m \sin^2 \phi)}. \tag{7}$$

and

$$\ddot{\phi} = \frac{ml\left(-u \cos \phi + b \cos \phi \dot{x} - ml\dot{\phi}^2 \sin \phi \cos \phi - (M + m)g \sin \phi\right)}{I(M + m) + ml^2 (M + m \sin^2 \phi)}. \tag{8}$$

2.3   Linearized Model

To design PID control, at first the Eqs. (7) and (8) are linearized. Specifically, the system is linearized about the vertical upward position $\phi = \pi$ and due the employed control signal, the system stays at this equilibrium position within small deflection angle θ. Let $+\theta$ represent the deviation angle of pendulum from equilibrium, thus following assumptions of nonlinear function can be defined:

$$\begin{aligned} \cos \phi &= \cos(\pi + \theta) \approx -1 \\ \sin \phi &= \sin(\pi + \theta) \approx -\theta \\ \dot{\phi}^2 &= \theta^2 \approx 0. \end{aligned} \tag{9}$$

Thus, the n order linearized model of the system is

$$\dot{\mathbf{x}}(t) = \mathbf{A}\mathbf{x}(t) + \mathbf{B}u(t)$$

$$\begin{bmatrix} \dot{x} \\ \ddot{x} \\ \dot{\phi} \\ \ddot{\phi} \end{bmatrix} = \begin{bmatrix} 0 & 1 & 0 & 0 \\ 0 & A_{22l} & A_{23l} & 0 \\ 0 & 0 & 0 & 1 \\ 0 & A_{42l} & A_{43l} & 0 \end{bmatrix} \begin{bmatrix} x \\ \dot{x} \\ \phi \\ \dot{\phi} \end{bmatrix} + \begin{bmatrix} 0 \\ B_{2l} \\ 0 \\ B_{4l} \end{bmatrix} u. \tag{10}$$

where

$$A_{22l} = \frac{-(I + ml^2)b}{D_n} ; A_{23l} = \frac{(ml)^2 g}{D_n} ; B_{2l} = \frac{(I + ml^2)}{D_n} ;$$

$$A_{42l} = \frac{-mlb}{D_n} ; A_{43l} = \frac{ml(M + m)g}{D_n} ; B_{4l} = \frac{ml}{D_n} ;$$

$$D_n = I(M + m) + Mml^2 .$$

Here $\mathbf{A}$, $\mathbf{B}$ and $\mathbf{C}$ are state constant system matrix, system input matrix and system output matrix with appropriate dimension. $\mathbf{x} \in R^n$ and $u \in R$ are defined as state variable and control input with n number of state variables.

2.4 Transfer Function

To obtain transfer function of the system, using assumption of Eq. (9), Laplace transformation of the linearized equations of motion (5) and (6) are derived. The Laplace transforms are.

$$(I + ml^2) \Phi(s)s^2 - mgl\Phi(s) = mlX(s)s^2. \tag{11}$$

$$(M + m)X(s)s^2 + bX(s)s - ml\Phi(s)s^2 = U(s). \tag{12}$$

Solve Eq. (11), then an equation that relates angular of the pendulum and cart position is shown

$$X(s) = \left[\frac{(I + ml^2)}{ml} - \frac{g}{s^2} \right] \Phi(s). \tag{13}$$

Substitute Eqs. (13) to (12) and then rearrange the equation, and lastly a transfer function of pendulum angle and input force acting on the cart is obtained.

$$G_\Phi(s) = \frac{\Phi(s)}{U(s)} = \frac{ml/q^{s^2}}{s^4 + b(I + ml^2)/q^{s^3} + (M + m)mgl/q^{s^2} - bmgl/q^s} \tag{14}$$

Where $q = (M + m)(I + ml^2) - (ml)^2$. Both a pole and a zero at the origin and later, they can be cancelled. A transfer function of cart position and pendulum angle also can be derived from Eq. (13).

$$G_{X\Phi}(s) = \frac{X(s)}{\Phi(s)} = \frac{(I + ml^2)s^2 - gml}{mls^2}. \tag{15}$$

3 IP with PID Controller

The IP system with proposed PID controller is formulated and analyzed in s and time domain. In s domain analysis, the place of close loop poles is shown which depend on the selected system gains. The close loop system transient response property is closely related with the system close loop poles. Further in time domain, the controlled system with proposed controller is retransformed so that the PID gains can be tuned using QOT scheme.

3.1 PID-QOT Formulation

Figure 3 shows the closed loop control structure for IP system with proposed PID scheme.

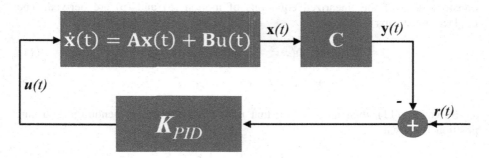

Fig. 3. State space model of single-stage inverted pendulum-cart system with PID control scheme

The applied input **r**, and proposed PID controller are

$$\mathbf{r}(t) = \begin{bmatrix} r_X & 0 & r_\Phi & 0 \end{bmatrix}^T,$$

$$\mathbf{K_{PID}} = \begin{bmatrix} \mathbf{K_P} \\ \mathbf{K_I} \\ \mathbf{K_D} \end{bmatrix} = \begin{bmatrix} K_{P1} & 0 & K_{P3} & 0 \\ K_{I1} & 0 & K_{I3} & 0 \\ K_{D1} & 0 & K_{D3} & 0 \end{bmatrix} = \begin{bmatrix} \mathbf{K_{PIDX}} & 0 & \mathbf{K_{PID\Phi}} & 0 \end{bmatrix}. \tag{16}$$

Where r_X and r_Φ are respectively the position and angle input variables, $\mathbf{K_P}$, $\mathbf{K_I}$, and $\mathbf{K_D}$ are proportional, integral and derivative gains vector of PID controller. Based on Eq. (18), the position and balancing PID controllers are $\mathbf{K_{PIDX}} = [\, K_{P1} \quad K_{I1} \quad K_{D1} \,]^T$ and $\mathbf{K_{PID\Phi}} = [\, K_{P3} \quad K_{I3} \quad K_{D3} \,]^T$. The control input $u(t)$ is

$$u(t) = -\mathbf{K_{PD}}\mathbf{x}(t) - \mathbf{K_I}\varsigma. \tag{17}$$

The second term in Eq. (19) can be simplified to a scalar by a following formulation

$$\mathbf{K_I}\varsigma = K_{I1}\varsigma_1 + K_{I3}\varsigma_3 = K_I'(\beta_1\varsigma_1' + \beta_3\varsigma_3') = K_I'\rho. \tag{18}$$

It can be indicated that $\rho = \boldsymbol{\beta}\varsigma$ and thus

$$\dot{\rho} = \mathbf{C}_\beta\mathbf{x}. \tag{19}$$

where $\mathbf{C}_\beta = [\beta_1 \quad 0 \quad \beta_3 \quad 0]$ is a coefficient with arbitrary selected value. The equivalent $n + 1$ order system dynamic can be formulated as the combination of original system state (10) and additional state (19). Thus, the dynamic of IP with PID controller can be rewritten as

$$
\begin{aligned}
\bar{\mathbf{x}}_e(t) &= \mathbf{A}_e\mathbf{x}_e(t) + \mathbf{B}_e u_e(t), \\
\begin{bmatrix} \dot{\mathbf{x}}(t) \\ \dot{\rho}(t) \end{bmatrix} &= \begin{bmatrix} \mathbf{A} & 0 \\ \mathbf{C}_\beta & 0 \end{bmatrix} \begin{bmatrix} \mathbf{x}(t) \\ \rho(t) \end{bmatrix} + \begin{bmatrix} \mathbf{B} \\ 0 \end{bmatrix} u_e(t), \\
u_e &= -\mathbf{K}_e\mathbf{x}_e(t) = \begin{bmatrix} K_{e1} & K_{e2} & \cdots & K_{e(n+1)} \end{bmatrix} \\
&= \begin{bmatrix} K_{P1} & K_{D1} & K_{P13} & K_{D3} & K_I' \end{bmatrix}\mathbf{x}_e(t).
\end{aligned}
\tag{20}
$$

To apply QOR tuning method, system (20) in firstly transform into Frobenius Canonical form using following transformation.

$$\mathbf{x}_f = \mathbf{T}\mathbf{x}_e, \tag{21}$$

where $\mathbf{x}_f(m \times 1)$ and $\mathbf{T}(m \times m)$ are transformation state variable vector and transformation matrix. Index $m = n+1$, and $\mathbf{T}$ matrix define as

$$
\mathbf{T} = \begin{bmatrix} \mathbf{q}_1 \\ \mathbf{q}_1 A_e \\ \vdots \\ \mathbf{q}_1 A_e^{n-1} \end{bmatrix} ; \mathbf{q}_1 = \mathbf{e}_n^T \mathbf{W}_c^{-1}, \tag{22}
$$

$\mathbf{q}_1$ is $1 \times m$ vector, $\mathbf{W}_c = [\, \mathbf{B}_e \quad \mathbf{A}_e\mathbf{B}_e \quad \cdots \quad \mathbf{A}_e^m\mathbf{B}_e \,]$ and unit vector $\mathbf{e}_n = [0 \quad 0 \quad \cdots \quad 1]$, the Frobenius canonical form of IP systems can be express as

$$\mathbf{x}_f = \mathbf{A}_f \mathbf{x}_f + \mathbf{B}_f u_f, \tag{23}$$

where

$$\mathbf{A}_f = \mathbf{T}\mathbf{A}_e\mathbf{T}^{-1} = \begin{bmatrix} 0 & 1 & 0 & \cdots & 0 \\ 0 & 0 & 1 & \cdots & 0 \\ \vdots & \vdots & \ddots & \ddots & \vdots \\ 0 & 0 & 0 & \cdots & 1 \\ -\alpha_m & -\alpha_{(m-1)} & -\alpha_{(m-2)} & \cdots & -\alpha_1 \end{bmatrix}, \tag{24}$$

$$\mathbf{B}_f = \mathbf{T}\mathbf{B}_e = \begin{bmatrix} 0 & 0 & \cdots & 1 \end{bmatrix}^T, \mathbf{x}_f = \begin{bmatrix} x_{f1} & x_{f2} & \cdots & x_{fm} \end{bmatrix}^T.$$

The input signal is

$$\begin{aligned} u_f &= -\mathbf{K}_f \mathbf{x}_f; \\ \mathbf{K}_f &= \begin{bmatrix} K_{f1} & K_{f2} & \cdots & K_{fm} \end{bmatrix}, \end{aligned} \tag{25}$$

and, the relationship between feedback gain of Eq. (25) and feedback gain of Eq. (20) is

$$\mathbf{K}_f = \mathbf{K}_e\mathbf{T}^{-1}. \tag{26}$$

As shown, system (24) is completely controllable, then $\mathbf{K}_f$ can be tuned by QOR method. The performance index function J is a quadratic performance of continuous-time linear time-varying function.

$$J = \frac{1}{2}\mathbf{x}_f^T(t_f)\mathbf{P}\mathbf{x}_f(t_f) + \frac{1}{2}\int_0^{t_f} \left(\mathbf{x}_f^T(t)\mathbf{Q}\mathbf{x}_f(t) + u_f^T(t)\mathbf{R}u_f(t) \right)dt. \tag{27}$$

Where the final time, t_f, is fix. $\mathbf{P}$, $\mathbf{Q}$, are chosen to be symmetry positive semidefinite, and $\mathbf{R}$ to be symmetry positive definite. The QOR optimal control problem is to drive the state vector $\mathbf{x}_f(t)$ to the origin from any nonzero initial values of states. The problem objective is to find $u_f(t)$; $0 \le t \le t_f$, such that the objective function (27) is minimized by choosing the appropriate weighting matrix $\mathbf{Q} = diag(Q_{11}, \ldots, Q_{mm})$ and $\mathbf{R} = R_{11}$. Finally, optimal gains of PID controller (16) is directly obtained. The formulation ensures the proposed controller has both advantages of PID and QOR schemes.

3.2   IP System with Optimal PID Scheme

Figure 4 shows the structure of PID-based feedback control for systems (14) and (15). In this structure, angle control of the pendulum located in inner loop and position control located in outer loop.

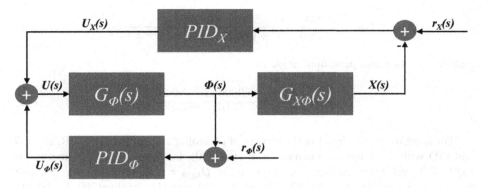

Fig. 4. Transfer function of single-stage inverted pendulum-cart system with PID control scheme

Define G_{KX} and $G_{K\Phi}$ as transfer function of PID controller (16) which can be written as

$$G_{KX}(s) = PID_X = K_{P1} + K_{D1}s + \frac{K_{I1}}{s},$$
$$G_{K\Phi}(s) = PID_\Phi = K_{P3} + K_{D3}s + \frac{K_{I3}}{s}. \tag{28}$$

Referring to Eq. (14) and when $G_{K\Phi}$ of (28) applied to the system, the open-loop transfer function for the inner loop for system in Fig. 4 is:

$$G_\Phi(s)G_{K\Phi}(s) = \frac{b_{2\Phi}K_{D3}\left(s^2 + \frac{K_{P3}}{K_{D3}}s + \frac{K_{I3}}{K_{D3}}\right)}{s^3 + a_{1\Phi}s^2 + a_{2\Phi}s + a_{3\Phi}}. \tag{29}$$

The PID feedback adds two null points with variable location to the pendulum system and the system would have two null points and three poles. The tuned PID with QOT will locate the pole and zero of the system which will characterize the stability, transient and steady state responses of the system.

4 Result and Discussion

Using data in Table 1, thus the n order linearized model of the system is

$$\begin{bmatrix} \dot{x} \\ \ddot{x} \\ \dot{\phi} \\ \ddot{\phi} \end{bmatrix} = \begin{bmatrix} 0 & 1 & 0 & 0 \\ 0 & -0.089 & 0.7132 & 0 \\ 0 & 0 & 0 & 1 \\ 0 & -0.2671 & 31.5397 & 0 \end{bmatrix} \begin{bmatrix} x \\ \dot{x} \\ \phi \\ \dot{\phi} \end{bmatrix} + \begin{bmatrix} 0 \\ 0.8903 \\ 0 \\ 2.6708 \end{bmatrix} u. \tag{30}$$

The transfer function of pendulum angle and input force acting on the cart is

$$G_\Phi(s) = \frac{\Phi(s)}{U(s)} = \frac{2.49s}{s^3 + 0.08299s^2 + 29.4s - 2.44}. \tag{31}$$

and cart position and pendulum angle is

$$G_{X\Phi}(s) = \frac{X(s)}{\Phi(s)} = \frac{0.009083s^2 - 0.2671}{0.02725s^2}. \tag{32}$$

For system describe by (30), three types of controller are employed – LQR, and PD and PID with QOT tuning scheme. For system (30), the chosen Q and R matric for LQR, PD and PID schemes are respectively Q_{LQR} = diag(400, 40, 60, 20) and R_{LQR} = 1, Q_{PD} = diag(500, 30, 50, 10) and R_{PD} = 1, and Q_{PID} = diag(500, 30, 50, 10, 5) and R_{PID} = 1. Based on the chosen Q and R matric, the obtained LQR, PD and PID controller are respectively

$$\mathbf{K} = [-20 \quad -17.5164 \quad 76.3229 \quad 14.558]. \tag{33}$$

$$\mathbf{K_{PD}} = \begin{bmatrix} \mathbf{K_P} \\ 0 \\ \mathbf{K_D} \end{bmatrix} = \begin{bmatrix} -22.3607 & 0 & 74.5478 & 0 \\ 0 & 0 & 0 & 0 \\ -17.8852 & 0 & 13.9019 & 0 \end{bmatrix}. \tag{34}$$

$$\mathbf{K_{PID}} = \begin{bmatrix} \mathbf{K_P} \\ \mathbf{K_I} \\ \mathbf{K_D} \end{bmatrix} = \begin{bmatrix} -2.2369 & 0 & 32.7292 & 0 \\ -0.8543 & 0 & -0.8543 & 0 \\ -3.1192 & 0 & 5.9715 & 0 \end{bmatrix}. \tag{35}$$

The closed loop poles for balance system (inner feedback loop) based on the obtained parameters of LQR (33) are −31.6245, −7.4319 and 0, PD (34) are −26.6108, −8.0941 and 0, and PID (35) are −7.4954 ± 7.4375i and 0. According the position of poles for the controlled balance system, the LQR and PD will produce critically damped balancing output response. But, due the position of dominant poles (−7.4954 ± 7.4375i) for the system with PID, the system will have under damped balancing output response. The expected result is shown as in Fig. 5. Figure 5 shows that system with LQR and PD controllers had quite similar balancing response. Meanwhile, system with PID controller took two times longer which about 5 s in stabilizing the pendulum at vertical position compared to the system with LQR or PD controller.

On the other hand, the closed loop poles for position system (outer feedback loop) based on the obtained parameters of LQR (33) are −10.2780 ± 7.6423i and −1.2407 ± 1.1980i, PD (34) are −8.6884 ± 8.6206i and −1.2371 ± 1.4531i, and PID (35) are −5.8611 ± 8.1649i, −0.0837 ± 0.6560i and −0.4718. According to the position of poles for the controlled position system using LQR, PD and PID, the controlled position system will slide fluctuation of position output response in transient state. The expected result is shown as in Fig. 6.

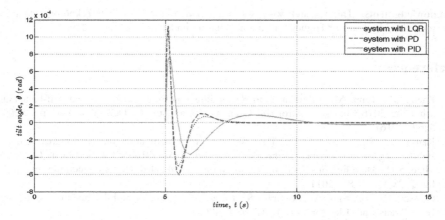

Fig. 5. The stabilization (angle) performance of the controlled single-stage inverted pendulum-cart system with LQR, PD and PID control schemes.

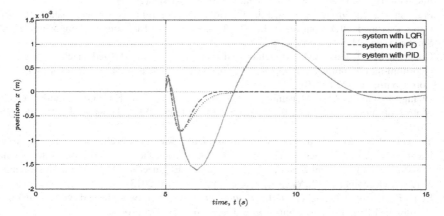

Fig. 6. The position performance of the controlled single-stage inverted pendulum-cart system with LQR, PD and PID control schemes.

5   Discussion

The mathematical model of 1-stage IP system has been derived and PID based control scheme using QOT method has been designed. Through the proposed formulation, PID and PD controller can be tuned using Q and R matrices that is normally used to tune LQR controller. The results show that using proposed formulation, the stability of the controlled system with PID based controller had been confirmed. All the poles of the system would be in the left-hand side of s-plane. The angle and position responses of the controlled IP with PID are comparable with the one which controlled by LQR controller. Further study using root locus on the controlled system with PID scheme can be conducted to further retune the PID parameters and improve the response of the system.

Acknowledgments. This research work was supported by the Universiti Teknologi Malaysia and funded by Ministry of Higher Education Malaysia under RUG Grant 14J19.

References

1. Zheng, Z., Teng, M.: Modeling and decoupling control for two-wheeled self-balancing robot. In: 2016 Chinese Control and Decision Conference (CCDC), Yinchuan, pp. 5263–5267 (2016)
2. Kausar, Z., Stol, K., Patel, N.: The effect of terrain inclination on performance and the stability region of two-wheeled mobile robots. Int. J. Adv. Rob. Syst. **9**(218), 1–11 (2012)
3. Miao, S.H.: Modeling of self-tilt-up motion for a two-wheeled inverted pendulum. Ind. Rob. Int. J. **38**(1), 76–85 (2011)
4. Grasser, F., D'Arrigo, A., Colombi, S., Rufer, A.C.: JOE: a mobile, inverted pendulum. IEEE Trans. Ind. Electron. **49**(1), 107–114 (2002)
5. Li, J., Gao, X., Huang, Q., Du, Q., Duan, X.: Mechanical design and dynamic modeling of a two-wheeled inverted pendulum mobile robot. In: Automation and Logistics, 2007 IEEE International Conference on, Jinan, China, pp. 1614–1619 (2007)
6. Pratama, D., Binugroho, E.H., Ardilla, F.: Movement control of two wheels balancing robot using cascaded PID controller. In: 2015 International Electronics Symposium (IES), Surabaya, pp. 94–99 (2015)
7. Goher, K.M., Tokhi, M.O.: Modeling and control of a two wheeled machine: a genetic algorithm-based optimization approach. Cyber J.: Multidiscip. J. Sci. Technol. J. Sel. Areas Rob. Control 19–22 (2010)
8. Huang, J., Guan, Z.H., Matsuno, T., Fukuda, T., Sekiyama, K.: Sliding-mode velocity control of mobile-wheeled inverted-pendulum systems. IEEE Trans. Rob. **26**, 750–758 (2010)
9. Ye, D.P., Yu, J.M., Zhou, Y.Z.: Control simulation for two-wheeled self-balancing robot linear move based on active disturbance rejection controller. In: 2012 2nd International Conference on Intelligent Materials and Mechanical Engineering, MEE 2012, 22 December 2012–23 December 2012, Yichang, China, pp. 129–136 (2013)
10. Ren, T., Chen, T.C., Chen, C.J.: Motion control for a two-wheeled vehicle using a self-tuning PID controller. Control Eng. Pract. **16**, 365–375 (2008)
11. Chiu, C.-H., Lin, Y.-W., Lin, C.-H.: Real-time control of a wheeled inverted pendulum based on an intelligent model free controller. Mechatronics **21**, 523–533 (2011)
12. Tanaka, Y., Ohata, Y., Kawamoto, T., Hirata, Y.: Adaptive control of 2-wheeled balancing robot by cerebellar neuronal network model. In: 2010 32nd Annual International Conference of the IEEE Engineering in Medicine and Biology Society, EMBC 2010, 31 August 2010–4 September 2010, Buenos Aires, Argentina, pp. 1589–1592 (2010)
13. Chiu, C.H., Lin, C.H.: A WIP control based on an intelligent controller. World Acad. Sci. Eng. Technol. **54**, 656–661 (2011)
14. Qianlai, S., Zhiyi, S.: A simple computer control method of inverted pendulum. J. Theor. Appl. Inf. Technol. **50**(3), 657–662
15. Trimpe, S., Millane, A., Doesseger, S., D'Andrea, R.: A self-tuning LQR approach demonstrated on an inverted pendulum. In: 19th IFAC World Congress, Cape Town, SA (2013)

PSO-Tuned PID Controller for a Nonlinear Double-Pendulum Crane System

Hazriq Izzuan Jaafar[1,2] and Zaharuddin Mohamed[1(✉)]

[1] Faculty of Electrical Engineering, Universiti Teknologi Malaysia (UTM),
81310 Johor Bahru, Johor, Malaysia
`hazriq@utem.edu.my`, `zahar@fke.utm.my`
[2] Faculty of Electrical Engineering, Universiti Teknikal Malaysia Melaka,
Hang Tuah Jaya, 76100 Durian Tunggal, Melaka, Malaysia

Abstract. This paper proposes an efficient PID controller for control of a double-pendulum crane system. Two different fitness functions of a particle swarm optimization (PSO) algorithm are used for the purpose of designing a controller. An accurate positioning with minimum hook and payload oscillations are tested with or without considering the parameters of the payload into the fitness function based on the horizontal distance sways of the crane. To test the effectiveness of the both approaches, extensive simulations are carried out under various crane operating conditions involving different payload masses. Their performances are examined based on the trolley positioning response and hook and payload oscillations reductions. Reductions of mean squared error (MSE) in the oscillations with a better trolley positioning response is obtained. It is envisaged that the appropriate fitness function can be very useful for determining satisfactory responses for double-pendulum crane system.

Keywords: Double-pendulum crane · Fitness function · Payload motion reduction · PID · PSO

1 Introduction

The control objective of cranes is to transport massive payloads to desired positions accurately as well as to suppress and eliminate the payload oscillation rapidly. To increase transportation efficiency and decrease payload oscillation, various control methods have been proposed. Most of the control methods treat the payload oscillation as a single-pendulum without considering a hook mass and additional cable as variables. However in practical, there are cases where double-pendulum is used. In industrial environments, a fast and accurate positioning with minimum hook and payload oscillations are desirable for an efficient and safe operation of the crane systems. This can directly increase the industrial productivity. In addition, it was reported that due to improper control, crane contributed to one-third of all construction accidents resulted to fatalities and injuries [1]. Dynamics of a double-pendulum crane is complicated and therefore control design is challenging. The double-pendulum crane system is an under-actuated nonlinear system with one control input (trolley force) and three control variables (trolley position, hook and payload oscillation angles). Hence, it

© Springer Nature Singapore Pte Ltd. 2017
M.S. Mohamed Ali et al. (Eds.): AsiaSim 2017, Part II, CCIS 752, pp. 203–215, 2017.
DOI: 10.1007/978-981-10-6502-6_18

is very interesting and meaningful to be studied and explored on double-pendulum crane system due to real industrial applications.

Research involving a double-pendulum crane started in 1998 [2]. Since then, many researchers investigated various control techniques for the double-pendulum cranes and has becoming an attractive benchmark that involve decoupling control [3], delayed feedback controller [4], passivity-based control [5], linear quadratic regulator-extension control [6], wave-based control [7] and sliding mode control [8]. In fact, iterative learning control was tested by Alhazza et al. to generate acceleration profiles of double-pendulum overhead crane maneuvers involving hoisting but measurement of payload oscillation was not discussed in [9]. Other work includes energy-based control [10], super-twisting-based control [11], online motion planning method [12] and amplitude-saturated nonlinear output feedback antiswing control [13]. In addition, a time optimal trajectory planning with upper and lower bounds of two pendulum angles and the allowable trolley velocity and acceleration consideration was designed [14, 15]. The first adaptive control method was proposed in [16] for a double-pendulum overhead crane system and successfully suppressed the maximum hook and payload oscillation, less maximum control force and lower transportation time. Nevertheless, all these control methods are based on rigorous mathematical analysis.

Despite the advent of many control theories and techniques, proportional-integral-derivative (PID) control is still one of the most widely used control in a number of practical systems and industries due to easy implementation, effective and low cost [17]. In [17], PID controllers were used to move the trolley and rail of a three dimensional crane with a reduced motion-induced sway. In another work, a hybrid collocated proportional-derivative (PD) with a non-collocated PID was designed for controlling the sway angles and the input tracking capability at the resonance mode of the pendulum sway [18]. In fact, some researchers also implemented PD-type controllers to suppress the swing oscillation of a gantry crane system [19–22]. In using the PID-type controllers for control of crane systems, a separate PID controller was used to achieve each objective. Thus, for the case of a single-pendulum crane, two PID controllers were located in the forward path and feedback loop for the positioning and sway control respectively. Similarly, for a double-pendulum crane, three PID controllers are required for positioning, hook and payload oscillations control.

It is known that a properly tuned PID controller resulted in a satisfactory system performance. A particle swarm optimization (PSO) algorithm was used to tune optimal PID parameters of a single-pendulum crane [17, 19, 21, 22]. The PSO performance is significantly affected by a fitness function and in [17], a common fitness function that based on minimising a payload angle was used. By using the PID controller, one possible way is to define the fitness function of PSO in a new way that include both the hook and payload signal feedback. In the best of authors knowledge, this approach using PSO has not been reported in literatures for double-pendulum crane system.

2 Dynamic Model of a Nonlinear Double-Pendulum Crane

The most popular technique for modelling of a double-pendulum crane system was the Lagrangian method [12, 13, 16, 23, 24]. The method which is based on finding the Lagrange equation is suitable for such a system. In this paper, a brief formulation for modelling of an overhead crane using the Lagrangian method is given.

A schematic diagram of a double-pendulum overhead crane system is illustrated in Fig. 1. The crane consists of three independent generalised coordinates namely the trolley position, x, the hook angle, θ_1, and the payload angle, θ_2. m, m_1, m_2, l_1 and l_2 represent the trolley mass, the hook mass, the payload mass, the cable length between the trolley and the hook, and the cable length between the hook and the payload respectively. F is an external force applied to the crane, which is the only control input for this system.

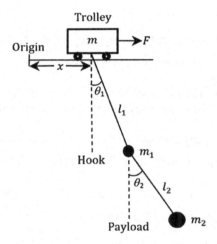

Fig. 1. A double-pendulum crane system.

The Lagrangian equation with respect to the generalised coordinate, q_i can be obtained as:

$$\frac{d}{dt}\left(\frac{\partial L}{\partial \dot{q}_i}\right) - \frac{\partial L}{\partial q_i} = T_i \tag{1}$$

where L, q_i ($i = 1,2,3$) and T_i represent the Lagrangian function, generalised coordinates (q_1, q_2 and q_3 represents x, θ_1 and θ_2 respectively) and a non-conservative force respectively. The Lagrangian function can be written as:

$$L = K - P \tag{2}$$

where K and P are kinetic and potential energies respectively. The system kinetic energy can be obtained as:

$$
\begin{aligned}
K = \frac{1}{2}m\dot{x}^2 + \frac{1}{2}m_1\left[\dot{x}^2 + 2\dot{x}l_1\dot{\theta}_1\cos\theta_1 + l_1^2\dot{\theta}_1^2\right] \\
+ \frac{1}{2}m_2\left[\dot{x}^2 + 2\dot{x}l_1\dot{\theta}_1\cos\theta_1 + 2\dot{x}l_2\dot{\theta}_2\cos\theta_2 + l_1^2\dot{\theta}_1^2 + l_2^2\dot{\theta}_2^2 + 2l_1l_2\dot{\theta}_1\dot{\theta}_2\cos(\theta_1 - \theta_2)\right]
\end{aligned} \tag{3}
$$

On the other hand, the potential energy can be obtained as:

$$
P = m_1g[l_1(1 - \cos\theta_1)] + m_2g[l_1(1 - \cos\theta_1) + l_2(1 - \cos\theta_2)] \tag{4}
$$

where g is the gravitational acceleration. By using the kinetic and potential energies of the system, the Lagrangian function can be written as:

$$
\begin{aligned}
L = \frac{1}{2}m\dot{x}^2 + \frac{1}{2}m_1\left[\dot{x}^2 + 2\dot{x}l_1\dot{\theta}_1\cos\theta_1 + l_1^2\dot{\theta}_1^2\right] \\
+ \frac{1}{2}m_2\left[\dot{x}^2 + 2\dot{x}l_1\dot{\theta}_1\cos\theta_1 + 2\dot{x}l_2\dot{\theta}_2\cos\theta_2 + l_1^2\dot{\theta}_1^2 + l_2^2\dot{\theta}_2^2 + 2l_1l_2\dot{\theta}_1\dot{\theta}_2\cos(\theta_1 - \theta_2)\right] \\
- m_1g[l_1(1 - \cos\theta_1)] - m_2g[l_1(1 - \cos\theta_1) + l_2(1 - \cos\theta_2)]
\end{aligned} \tag{5}
$$

By differentiating Eq. (5) and obtaining terms as in Eq. (1), the nonlinear dynamic model of the double-pendulum overhead crane system can be obtained as:

$$
\begin{aligned}
(m + m_1 + m_2)\ddot{x} + (m_1 + m_2)l_1\ddot{\theta}_1\cos\theta_1 + m_2l_2\ddot{\theta}_2\cos\theta_2 \\
- (m_1 + m_2)l_1\dot{\theta}_1^2\sin\theta_1 - m_2l_2\dot{\theta}_2^2\sin\theta_2 = F
\end{aligned} \tag{6}
$$

$$
\begin{aligned}
(m_1 + m_2)l_1\ddot{x}\cos\theta_1 + (m_1 + m_2)l_1^2\ddot{\theta}_1 + m_2l_1l_2\ddot{\theta}_2\cos(\theta_1 - \theta_2) \\
+ m_2l_1l_2\dot{\theta}_2^2\sin(\theta_1 - \theta_2) + (m_1 + m_2)gl_1\sin\theta_1 = 0
\end{aligned} \tag{7}
$$

$$
\begin{aligned}
m_2l_2\ddot{x}\cos\theta_2 + m_2l_1l_2\ddot{\theta}_1\cos(\theta_1 - \theta_2) + m_2l_2^2\ddot{\theta}_2 \\
- m_2l_1l_2\dot{\theta}_1^2\sin(\theta_1 - \theta_2) + m_2gl_2\sin\theta_2 = 0
\end{aligned} \tag{8}
$$

Equations (6)–(8) are the dynamic equations for the nonlinear crane with a trolley force, F. The control aim is to achieve a precise position, x and low angles of θ_1 and θ_2.

3 PID Control Scheme

In this work, three separate PID controllers are structured as shown in Fig. 2. Each control variable (the position, the hook and payload oscillation) signals are used as the feedback signals.

Block #1 represents the nonlinear double-pendulum crane system model based on Eqs. (6)–(8). Block #2 generates a reference input as a reference trolley position for the

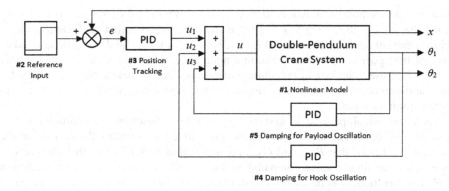

Fig. 2. A control structure with 3 PID controllers.

system. Then, the position error, e is fed into Block #3 that responsible to minimise the error and drive the trolley to the desired destination with a minimal induced sway. As a fast trolley movement induces high oscillations for the hook and payload, Blocks #4 and #5 are used as positive feedback loops to minimise the maximum and overall hook and payload oscillations.

Designs of these controllers are challenging as all the optimal parameters of the PID controllers have to be tuned concurrently. Nine PID parameters (K_p, K_i, K_d, K_{ps}, K_{is}, K_{ds}, K_{pd}, K_{id} and K_{dd}) need to be obtained for the control approach. As PSO has been shown to be effective in optimisations, PSO was used to find the optimal PID gains in this work. Implementation of the PSO algorithm as a meta-heuristic technique can be helpful to provide optimal solutions.

4 Particle Swarm Optimization

PSO was invented by Kennedy and Eberhart in the mid-1990s and is still being used to solve various engineering problems [25]. The concept of PSO was developed based on the ability of flocks of birds and schools of fish to search and move in their environment to find rich sources of food with certain speed and position by implementing an information sharing among all members of the swarm [22, 25, 26, 27]. A set of randomly initial particle spreads in the design space towards the optimal solution over a number of iterations.

Two initial parameters namely position, X_k^i and velocity, V_k^i of the particles are introduced in the optimisation process. The new velocity, V_{k+1}^i of the particles are depended on the current, X_k^i local best, P_{Best} and global best, G_{Best} values. The new position, X_{k+1}^i will be updated accordingly based on the new velocity as:

$$V_{k+1}^i = wV_k^i + c_1 r_1 \left(P_{Best} - X_k^i \right) + c_2 r_2 \left(G_{Best} - X_k^i \right) \tag{9}$$

$$X_{k+1}^i = V_{k+1}^i + X_k^i \tag{10}$$

where i is the number of iterations ($i = 1, 2, 3, \ldots, N$). c_1 and c_2 are positive learning factors that control the strength of cognitive and social acceleration coefficient while r_1 and r_2 represent random function values, $r_1, r_2 \in U(0,1)$. P_{Best} and G_{Best} are defined as personal best position and best position among P_{Best} respectively. w is called inertia weight (decrease from 0.9 to 0.4 during iterations) that influence particle for exploration and exploitation. A higher w implies better exploration while lower w leads to better exploitation [28].

Each individual particle is assessed by a fitness function. All particles try to replicate their historical success and in the same time try to follow the success of the best agent. It means that P_{Best} and G_{Best} are updated at each ith iteration if the particle has a minimum fitness value compared to the current P_{Best} and G_{Best} until maximum number of iteration, N is reached. Nevertheless, only particles that within the range of the system's constraint are accepted.

As the performance of the PSO algorithm depends on the fitness function, this work investigates two fitness functions for efficient control of the trolley positioning, hook and payload oscillations:

- Fitness Function 1: Based on the previously implemented fitness function [17] using the hook oscillation.
- Fitness Function 2: Considering both parameters, the hook and the payload.

For a comparative assessment, the fitness function in [17] was extended to suit with a double-pendulum crane system as the form in Eq. (12), and used in finding the PID parameters using the PSO. Figure 3 shows the horizontal distances, z_1 and z_2 of the hook and payload respectively where less z_1 and z_2 indicate low sways.

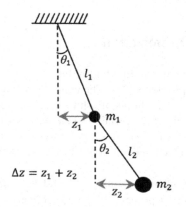

Fig. 3. Horizontal distances of hook and payload movement.

The horizontal distances were commonly used as they were directly related to the sway angles. Utilising $\Delta z = z_1 + z_2$ and to achieve a satisfactory input tracking with low sway, the fitness function can be obtained as:

$$Fit\_func = \sum_{i=1}^{N} \left| x_{ref} - x_{trolley}^{(i)} + \Delta z \right| \tag{11}$$

and can be expanded as:

$$Fit\_func = \sum_{i=1}^{N} \left| x_{ref} - x_{trolley}^{(i)} + l_1 \sin \theta_1^{(i)} + l_2 \sin \theta_2^{(i)} \right| \tag{12}$$

By reducing Δz, hook and payload oscillations can be minimised to achieve a maximum stability for the system.

5 Results and Discussion

The effectiveness of the controllers based on the fitness functions in achieving fast trolley motion and low oscillation was investigated within the simulation environment of a double-pendulum crane system. In addition, the capability of the controller to suppress the sways was also studied. Simulink and MATLAB were used as a simulation platform and the exercises were conducted with Intel Core i7-5500U Processor, 2.4 GHz and 12 GB RAM. The double-pendulum crane as used in [13] with nominal parameters was considered. The parameter values are: $m = 6.5$ kg, $m_1 = 2$ kg, $m_2 = 0.6$ kg, $l_1 = 0.53$ m, $l_2 = 0.4$ m and $g = 9.8$ m/s^2. The nonlinear model of the system can be obtained by substituting the parameters into Eqs. (6)–(8).

The fitness functions computed at each iteration were utilised to obtain nine optimal control parameters for the case with 3 PID controllers. For a fair comparison between both fitness functions, the PSO parameters were set to the same values. The population size of particle was 20 with maximum iterations of 100. The cognitive and social coefficients (c_1 and c_2) values were set as 2. The initial value, w was 0.9 and was linearly decreased to 0.4 at some stages in iteration for global and local searching. This is to reduce the risk of trapping into the local optimum and to enhance the convergence speed. The nine optimal PID parameters obtained using PSO with the two fitness functions are listed in Table 1.

Table 1. Nine optimal PID parameters via difference fitness functions of PSO.

	Parameters	Fitness Function 1	Fitness Function 2
PID 1 (trolley position)	K_p	19.7443	19.8320
	K_i	0.0046	0.0060
	K_d	15.9720	19.0922
PID 2 (hook oscillation)	K_{ps}	0.9709	0.8064
	K_{is}	29.5439	0.7613
	K_{ds}	7.2471	8.6851
PID 3 (payload oscillation)	K_{pd}	0.6627	0.5052
	K_{id}	1.5400	2.1890
	K_{dd}	0.1484	0.3776

The control scheme with 3 PID controllers as shown in Fig. 2 was utilised with the obtained optimal parameters as in Table 1. The aim is to move the trolley to a desired position of 0.6 m with low oscillation. Figure 4 shows the trolley position, hook and payload oscillations respectively with the control scheme. Table 2 summarises the overshoot (OS) and settling time (T_s) for the trolley movement. For the oscillations, maximum angles of hook (θ_{1_max}), payload (θ_{2_max}) and mean squared error (MSE) for both oscillations, MSE_{θ_1} and MSE_{θ_2} were considered. For the trolley position response in Fig. 4(a), the Fitness Function 2 provided a better performance with a less overshoot and a faster settling time. As the trolley motion and payload oscillation are coupled, a better transient response of the trolley will result in a less maximum oscillation of the hook and payload. According to [29], both θ_1 and θ_2 should be in the closed interval of -0.5 rad and 0.5 rad to guarantee that the double-pendulum oscillations are acceptable in the small range of maximum oscillations. With Fitness Function 2, the controller successfully suppressed the maximum oscillations of the hook and payload to 5.5921^0 and 9.8606^0, respectively. The overall oscillations with the MSE values shown in Table 2 where Fitness Function 2 provided up to 7.72% and 25.52% reductions in the hook and payload oscillations, respectively as compared to the other fitness function. In contrast, the previously developed fitness function (Fitness Function 1) resulted in higher oscillations.

To further evaluate the capability of the controller to suppress the sways, the double-pendulum crane under various operating conditions were simulated. In construction industries, the hook, m_1 is constant, but the payload, m_2 may change in several conditions. In this work, a case where m_2 is increased up to twice (2 kg and 4 kg) of m_1 were considered. Using the optimal PID parameters, overall performance for hook and payload oscillation are shown in Fig. 5.

With a similar $m_1 = m_2$, the differences in the maximum and overall oscillation was between 5–15% while higher m_2, the differences in the maximum and overall oscillations using PID control schemes were between 2–10%. Simulation results with a higher payload mass show less hook and payload oscillations. Table 3 summarises simulation results with difference control scheme and payload mass.

The fitness function using both parameters (Fitness Function 2) can be used and applicable to control double-pendulum crane with considering the parameters involving both the hook and the payload for the purpose of designing a controller. Indirectly reduce the maximum hook and payload oscillations. This was as expected as the all the states were used for the fitness function. The simulation results under various operating conditions showed that the controllers with Fitness Function 2 can provide a satisfactory and acceptable responses in controlling trolley position and minimising both sway oscillations.

Table 2. Performances of a double-pendulum crane system with difference fitness functions.

	Trolley position		Hook oscillation		Payload oscillation	
	OS (%)	T_s (s)	θ_{1_max}	MSE_{θ_1}	θ_{2_max}	MSE_{θ_2}
Fitness Function 1	4.2333	3.7467	6.0364^0	1.4553	11.8842^0	4.7846
Fitness Function 2	3.9527	3.5568	5.5921^0	1.3510	9.8606^0	3.8117

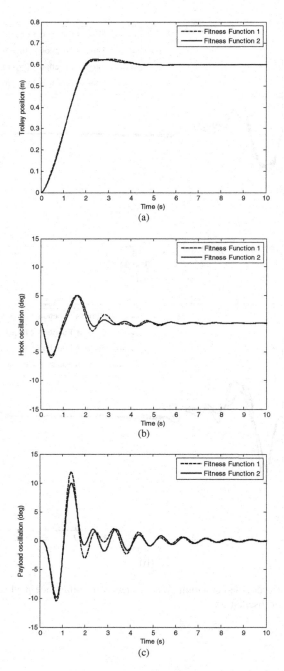

Fig. 4. Response of a double-pendulum crane system: (a) trolley position (b) hook oscillation (c) payload oscillation.

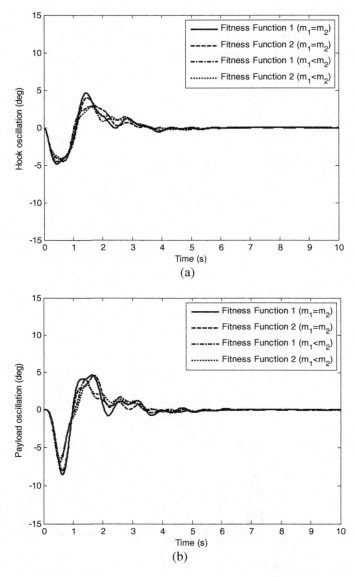

Fig. 5. Response of a double-pendulum crane system with difference payload mass: (a) hook oscillation (b) payload oscillation.

Table 3. Performances of a double-pendulum crane system with difference payload mass.

	Payload mass	Hook oscillation		Payload oscillation	
		θ_{1_max}	MSE_{θ_1}	θ_{2_max}	MSE_{θ_2}
Fitness Function 1	$m_1 = m_2$	4.8444^0	2.2926	8.5866^0	3.9385
Fitness Function 2		4.5270^0	2.1528	8.0488^0	3.4165
Fitness Function 1	$m_1 < m_2$	4.5202^0	1.7040	6.9111^0	2.3353
Fitness Function 2		4.3931^0	1.6246	6.4854^0	2.1213

6 Conclusion

Two fitness functions were tested to achieve optimal performance control scheme with an efficient hook and payload motion of an under-actuated nonlinear double-pendulum crane system using PSO algorithm. Performances analysis by using PID control schemes with both fitness functions based on horizontal distance were presented. The extended simulations under difference operating conditions were also investigated. The simulation results demonstrated that the fitness function that considers both the hook and the payload for the purpose of designing a controller provided better responses and improve the overall trolley position, hook and payload oscillations performance as compared to the other fitness function.

Acknowledgments. The authors gratefully acknowledged the Universiti Teknologi Malaysia for the financial support through The Research University Grant (Vote No. 14J06).

References

1. Ramli, L., Mohamed, Z., Abdullahi, A.M., Jaafar, H.I., Lazim, I.M.: Control strategies for crane systems: a comprehensive review. Mech. Syst. Sig. Process. 95, 1–23 (2017)
2. Singhose, W.E., Towell, S.T.: Double-pendulum gantry crane dynamics and control. In: Proceedings of the IEEE International Conference Control Applications, Trieste, Italy, pp. 1205–1209 (1998)
3. Lahres, S., Aschemann, H., Sawodny, O., Hofer, E.P.: Crane automation by decoupling control of a double pendulum using two translational actuators. In: Proceedings of the American Control Conference, Chicago, USA, pp. 1052–1056 (2000)
4. Masoud, Z.N., Nayfeh, A.H.: Sway reduction on container cranes using delayed feedback controller. Nonlinear Dyn. 34, 347–358 (2003)
5. Guo, W.P., Liu, D.T., Yi, J.Q., Zhao, D.B.: Passivity-based-control for double-pendulum-type overhead cranes. In: Proceedings of the IEEE Region 10 Conference, Chiang Mai, Thailand, pp. 546–549 (2004)
6. Yang, G., Zhang, W., Huang, Y., Yu, Y.: Simulation research of extension control based on crane-double pendulum system. Comput. Inf. Sci. 2(1), 103–107 (2009)
7. O'Connor, W., Habibi, H.: Gantry crane control of a double-pendulum, distributed-mass load, using mechanical wave concepts. Mech. Sci. 4, 251–261 (2013)

8. Tuan, L.A., Lee, S.G.: Sliding mode controls of double-pendulum crane systems. J. Mech. Sci. Technol. **27**(6), 1863–1873 (2013)
9. Alhazza, K.A., Hasan, A.M., Alghanim, K.A., Masoud, Z.N.: An iterative learning control technique for point-to-point maneuvers applied on an overhead crane. Shock Vib. **2014**, 1–11 (2014)
10. Sun, N., Fang, Y., Chen, H., Lu, B.: Energy-based control of double pendulum cranes. In: The 5th Annual IEEE International Conference on Cyber Technology in Automation, Control and Intelligent Systems, Shenyang, China, pp. 258–263 (2015)
11. Sun, N., Fang, Y., Chen, H., Fu, Y.: Super-twisting-based antiswing control for underactuated double pendulum cranes. In: IEEE International Conference on Advanced Intelligent Mechatronics, Busan, Korea, pp. 749–754 (2015)
12. Zhang, M., Ma, X., Chai, H., Rong, X., Tian, X., Li, Y.: A novel online motion planning method for double-pendulum overhead cranes. Nonlinear Dyn. **85**, 1079–1090 (2016)
13. Sun, N., Fang, Y., Chen, H., Lu, B.: Amplitude-saturated nonlinear output feedback antiswing control for underactuated cranes with double-pendulum cargo dynamics. IEEE Trans. Ind. Electron. **64**(3), 2135–2146 (2017)
14. Chen, H., Fang, Y., Sun, N., Qian, Y.: Pseudospectral method based time optimal trajectory planning for double pendulum cranes. In: Proceedings of the 34th Chinese Control Conference, Hangzhou, China, pp. 4302–4307 (2015)
15. Chen, H., Fang, Y., Sun, N.: A time-optimal trajectory planning strategy for double pendulum cranes with swing suppression. In: Proceedings of the 35th Chinese Control Conference, Chengdu, China, pp. 4599–4604 (2016)
16. Zhang, M., Ma, X., Rong, X., Tian, X., Li, Y.: Adaptive tracking control for double-pendulum overhead cranes subject to tracking error limitation, parametric uncertainties and external disturbances. Mech. Syst. Sig. Process. **76–77**, 15–32 (2016)
17. Maghsoudi, M.J., Mohamed, Z., Husain, A.R., Tokhi, M.O.: An optimal performance control scheme for a 3D crane. Mech. Syst. Sig. Process. **66–67**, 756–768 (2016)
18. Ahmad, M.A., Ramli, M.S., Zawawi, M.A., Raja Ismail, R.M.T.: Hybrid collocated PD with non-collocated PID for sway control of a lab-scaled rotary crane. In: Proceedings of the 5th IEEE Conference Industrial Electronics Application, Taichung, Taiwan, pp. 707–711 (2010)
19. Solihin, M.I., Kamal, M.A.S., Legowo, A.: Optimal PID controller tuning of automatic gantry crane using PSO algorithm. In: Proceeding of the 5th International Symposium Mechatronics Its Application, Amman, Jordan, pp. 1–5 (2008)
20. Solihin, M.I., Wahyudi, Legowo, A.: Fuzzy-tuned PID anti-swing control of automatic gantry crane. J. Vib. Control **16**(1), 127–145 (2010)
21. Jaafar, H.I., Hussien, S.Y.S., Ghazali, R., Mohamed, Z.: Optimal tuning of PID + PD controller by PFS for gantry crane system. In: 10th Asian Control Conference, Sabah, Malaysia, pp. 1–6 (2015)
22. Jaafar, H.I., Mohamed, Z., Abidin, A.F.Z., Ghani, Z.A.: PSO-tuned PID controller for a nonlinear gantry crane system. In: Proceedings of the IEEE International Conference on Control System, Computing and Engineering, Penang, Malaysia, pp. 515–519 (2012)
23. Qian, D., Tong, S., Lee, S.: Fuzzy-logic-based control of payloads subjected to double-pendulum motion in overhead cranes. Autom. Constr. **65**, 133–143 (2016)
24. Qian, D., Yi, J.: Hierarchical Sliding Mode Control for Under-actuated Cranes, pp. 1–199. Springer, Berlin (2015)
25. Kennedy, J., Eberhart, R.: Particle swarm optimization. In: Proceedings of the IEEE International Conferences Neural Networks, Perth, Australia, pp. 1942–1948 (1995)
26. Eberhart, R.C., Shi, Y.: Comparison between genetic algorithms and particle swarm optimization. In: Porto, V.W., Saravanan, N., Waagen, D., Eiben, A.E. (eds.) EP 1998. LNCS, vol. 1447, pp. 611–616. Springer, Heidelberg (1998). doi:10.1007/BFb0040812

27. Hassan, R., Cohanim, B., De Weck, O.: A comparison of particle swarm optimization and the genetic algorithm. In: Proceedings 46th AIAA/ASME/ASCE/AHS/ASC Structures, Structural Dynamics and Materials Conference, Austin, Texas, pp. 1–13 (2005)

28. Eberhart, R., Shi, Y.: Comparing inertia weights and constriction factors in particle swarm optimization, In: Proceedings of the 2000 Congress on Evolutionary Computation, California, USA, pp. 84–88 (2000)

29. Mar, R., Goyal, A., Nguyen, V., Yang, T., Singhose, W.: Combined input shaping and feedback control for double-pendulum systems. Mech. Syst. Sig. Process. **85**, 267–277 (2017)

Choice of Cumulative Percentage in Principal Component Analysis for Regionalization of Peninsular Malaysia Based on the Rainfall Amount

Shazlyn Milleana Shaharudin[1(✉)] and Norhaiza Ahmad[2]

[1] Department of Mathematics, Faculty of Science and Mathematics,
Universiti Pendidikan Sultan Idris, 35900 Tanjong Malim, Perak, Malaysia
shazlyn@fsmt.upsi.edu.my
[2] Department of Mathematics, Faculty of Science,
Universiti Teknologi Malaysia, UTM, 81310 Johor Bahru, Johor, Malaysia
norhaiza@utm.my

Abstract. Principal Component Analysis (PCA) is a popular method used for reduction of large scale data sets in hydrological applications. Typically, PCA scores are applied to hierarchical cluster analysis to redefine region. However, the choice of cumulative percentage of variance for PCA scores and identifying the best number of clusters can be difficult. In this paper, we investigate the effect of determining the number of clusters by comparing (i) standardized and unstandardized PCA scores on different cumulative percentages of variance (ii) to determine number of clusters using Calinski and Harabasz Index. We have found that Calinski and Harabasz Index is most appropriate to determine the best number of clusters and that standardized PCA scores within the range of 65% to 70% cumulative percentage of variance give the most reasonable number of clusters.

Keywords: Principal component analysis · Hierarchical analysis · Calinski and Harabasz Index

1 Introduction

Several researchers have used a variety of methods to define climatic types and delineate zones of similar climate. One of the methods that is popular among researchers to define region is through the combined use of principal component analysis (PCA) and cluster analysis. PCA is a data reduction technique where it allows the researcher to reorient the data, thus the first few dimensions account as much of the available information as possible. When working with less dimensions of the data set, this makes it easier to visualize the data and identify interesting patterns [1]. In defining region, the fundamental modes of PCA are considered for the clustering process [2]. Typically, in extracting components, one of the three rules, scree plot, Kaiser's rule and proportion of explain variance are taken as guideline [3, 4]. Scree plot proposed by [5] is a graphical approach which involved plotting the variance accounted for by each

© Springer Nature Singapore Pte Ltd. 2017
M.S. Mohamed Ali et al. (Eds.): AsiaSim 2017, Part II, CCIS 752, pp. 216–224, 2017.
DOI: 10.1007/978-981-10-6502-6_19

principal component in the order of descending eigenvalues from the largest to the smallest. For a large dimension data set especially rainfall data set, this approach is unsuitable to be used. This is due to the steep curve followed by a bend which are not clearly visible to get the cutoffs of the number of principal components. When the scree plot is not diagnostic, Kaiser's rule may come in handy. This method retains regarding the amount of variance accounted for those components. In this rule, eigenvalues greater than average eigenvalue (i.e. $\lambda > 1$) are retained because these axes summarize more information than any single original variable [17]. Hence, those components with $\lambda > 1$ is obtained to determine the number of principal components. Occasionally in the data set, some eigenvalues are close to 1, thus it also might be consider as a significance of principal components to obtain. As a result, this method has been criticized by [18, 19]. For high dimensional data set, [5] recommended using 70% cumulative percentage of variance as a rough guide to cutoff the number of principal components. To test whether 70% cumulative percentage of variance is appropriate in defining region, the range of the cumulative percentage (65% until 90%) is tested to choose a suitable range to cutoff the principal components to define climate region. However in defining region, extracting the correct number of component is crucial because it dictates the true regional boundaries. As far as we know, there is no literature showing how to choose the appropriate number of components based on the break-down point of the number of clusters.

The cutoffs of the number of components depends on the structure of the data set. In climate data, especially rainfall data set in Peninsular Malaysia, it involves many zero bound data which signifies that the observation is less than 1.0 mm [7]. These zero bound data might influence the choice of cumulative percentage of variance. It can be seen clearly when cluster analysis is employed to standardized and unstandardized principal component score, it demonstrates that the number of clusters are sensitive to the standardization data.

In this study, we establish a procedure to choose the best cumulative percentage of variance to obtain in defining region. We also need to investigate the effect of standardized and unstandardized principal component score to mitigate the effect of zero bound data.

2   Data

Daily rainfall totals for 33 years period 1975–2007 were obtained from 75 stations across Peninsular Malaysia. The rainfall data set considered for the purpose of this study is a matrix, comprising data from 75 stations and 365 days which constitute enough data to allow for defining region. In this present study, a wet day is defined as a day with at least 1 mm of rainfall [7]. Figure 1 shows the geographical coordinates of the stations in this study.

Before clustering process were employed, the needed standardization of the daily rainfall data was examined. Standardization is an important part in this analysis since mean and variance are likely to be small in consequence of zero bound data. The standardization will affect the result of clustering analysis where the rainfall stations are likely to be clustered together even if the stations are poorly correlated. Some

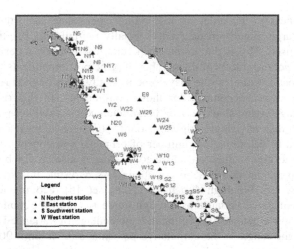

Fig. 1. The location of 75 rainfall stations in Peninsular Malaysia

adjustments are required in the usual standardization method due to a problem in zero bound data where the data were standardized by dividing the daily mean for that station, as given by

$$x_{ij}^* = \frac{x_{ij}}{\frac{365}{p} \sum_{j=1}^{p} x_{ij}} \tag{1}$$

where the denominator represents the daily mean rainfall at station i, calculated from the $p = 365 \times 33$ that is the daily observations. Daily rainfall is then expressed as a proportion of the mean of the daily total [6].

To validate the results in this study, we analyze another rainfall data set from other country which has same characteristic of rainfall data in Peninsular Malaysia. Daily rainfall data from 11 rainfall stations were obtained from Indonesia. The data were recorded from 2003 until 2005. The data set was assembled as data matrix of Peninsular Malaysia where the rows in the matrix represent the rainfall observation i.e. 365 rainfall days and 11 stations were represented in the columns of the data matrix. Standardization is also necessary to overcome the problem in dealing with zero bound data which is similar to the rainfall data in Peninsular Malaysia.

3   Methods

3.1   Principal Component Analysis

Principal components of the scaled rainfall data were computed based on the correlation matrix in order to extract the main modes of variation of the data and to reduce the from large dimension to low dimension. This procedure requires that several decisions be made in obtaining the best cumulative percentage of variance or in other words, the best number of extracted components to retain. As mentioned previously in the introduction, several methods have been obtained in extracting the number of components to retain. In this study, we used explained variance to determine the best number of components to obtain. When using this method, the challenge lies in selecting an appropriate threshold percentage. If we choose the higher percentage such as 90% and above, we may encounter difficulties such as inflating the importance of noise and results in poorly defined regions. On the contrary, if we choose low variation of cumulative percentage, the observations that are not well represented will be clustered together due to low scores for all of the components. Therefore, we construct this study in order to determine the best range of cumulative percentage of variance in the defined region.

3.2   Calinski and Harabasz Index

Cluster analysis using k means method was then performed on principal component score matrix. The drawback of the k means method is the requirement for the number of clusters must be specified before the algorithm is applied. To counter this issue, we apply Calinski and Harabasz Index as a guide for us in quantifying the best number of clusters for our data set. Calinski and Harabasz Index is computed as

$$[\text{trace}\, B/(k-1)]/[\text{trace}\, W/(n-k)] \tag{2}$$

where:

n = total number of items   k = number of clusters
B = between pooled within cluster sum of square
W = cross product matrix

The maximum value of the index was used to indicate the correct number of partitions in the data set.

4   Results and Discussion

In this section, we will discuss on the choice of cumulative percentage to cut off the number of principal components and the sensitivity of the number of cluster to the choice of cumulative percentage. We also show the effect of clustering result when using standardized and unstandardized principal component score. To validate the results of defining region in Peninsular Malaysia, we had compared the results with the rainfall data of Indonesia that has similar characteristic with Peninsular Malaysia.

The choice of cumulative percentage of variance will reflect the number of components to retain. As an example, we can see clearly in Table 1 where when 65% cumulative percentage was chosen, the number of components to retain is nine while when we chose 70% cumulative percentage, the number of components to retain is 13. The most significant effects shown on the choice of cumulative percentage of variance where it is sensitive to the number of cluster obtained. For instance, in Fig. 2, when we had selected effect 65% cumulative percentage, the number of cluster to retain was

Table 1. Results of standardized principal component score and number of clusters obtained using Calinski and Harabasz Index for Peninsular Malaysia

Eigenvalues	Cumulative percentage (%)	No. of component	No. of cluster	Calinski & Harabasz Index (max.value of index)
1.09	65	9	3	250.58
0.89	70	13	5	224.32
0.70	75	18	4	201.32
0.60	80	23	2	185.55
0.48	85	30	2	171.84
0.38	90	39	2	160.63

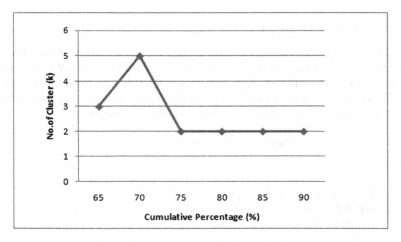

Fig. 2. Determined number of cluster for standardized principal component score for Peninsular Malaysia

three. When 5% additional cumulative percentage of variance is retained, the number of cluster changed from three to five. If we look through the Fig. 3, it gave the same result where 65% cumulative percentage of variance obtained two number of cluster. Meanwhile when 70% cumulative percentage of variance was retained, the number of cluster became six. However, the defined regions the selection of cumulative percentage above than 70% was not a good decision as a cut off for the number of principal components. As clearly presented in Figs. 1 and 2, the resulting number of cluster remained the same even with the additional 5% of the variance in every phase. Moreover, the number of cluster obtained from Figs. 1 and 2 is too small because in the defined region, we need more clusters to allow regions to benchmark their cluster against other regions [20]. This result is supported by [14] which stated that a few number of clusters i.e. two clusters would be insufficient to define region when dealing with analysing considerable extent of regions. This statement is proved by [11] where a sensitivity of the clustering results to the number of principal components retained has been noted elsewhere [21, 22].

Table 2. Results of standardized principal component score and number of clusters obtained using Calinski and Harabasz Index for Indonesia

Eigenvalues	Cumulative percentage (%)	No. of component	No. of cluster	Calinski & Harabasz Index (max.value of index)
0.98	65	5	4	108.68
0.86	70	6	6	93.13
0.74	75	7	2	83.90
0.72	80	8	2	69.75
0.68	85	9	2	69.60
0.58	90	10	2	60.20

Because of the sensitivity of the clustering results to the number of retained principal components, the correct number of components to retain needs to be identified. It is important that the variation between the clusters is represented in the direction of at least one of the principal components [12]. Accordingly, it is best to err towards retaining significantly more principal components rather than too few [13]. If there are too few components to retain, the observations that are not well represented will cluster together because they have low scores for all the components meanwhile inclusion of too many principal components inflates the importance of noise and results in poorly defined regions [6]. Clustering results are not as sensitive to the choice of cumulative percentage of variance when the component scores are left unstandardized compared to when they are standardized. If we look through Tables 3 and 4, the number of cluster remains the same even though we have increased 5% cumulative percentage of variance in every phase. This situation happened due to the lowest-order modes, which define the noise element of the data, are given minimal weighting. Therefore, we need standardized principal component score to ensure all the temporal modes are given equal weight and rainfall distribution patterns that occur frequently are treated as equal to unusual patterns and to noise components.

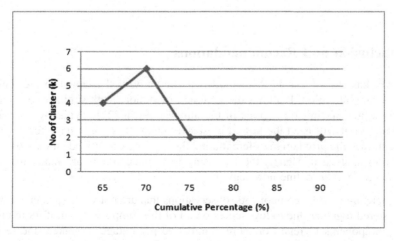

Fig. 3. Determined number of cluster for standardized principal component score for Indonesia

In order to obtain the best number of cluster, Calinski and Harabasz index was employed in principal component score matrix. According to Table 1 for Peninsular Malaysia, the values for cluster numbers run from two to five while for Indonesia in Table 2, the cluster was obtained from two to six. The optimum number of cluster was established as three for Peninsular Malaysian and four for Indonesia where each recorded the maximum value of index among the others.

Table 3. Results of unstandardized principal component score and number of clusters obtained using Calinski and Harabasz Index for Peninsular Malaysia

Eigenvalues	Cumulative percentage (%)	No. of component	No. of cluster	Calinski & Harabasz Index (max.value of index)
1.09	65	9	2	265.78
0.89	70	13	2	229.45
0.70	75	18	2	208.46
0.60	80	23	2	167.49
0.48	85	30	2	154.28
0.38	90	39	2	150.20

Table 4. Results of unstandardized principal component score and number of clusters obtained using Calinski and Harabasz Index for Indonesia

Eigenvalues	Cummulative percentage (%)	No. of component	No. of cluster	Calinski & Harabasz Index (max.value of index)
0.98	65	5	2	265.78
0.86	70	6	2	229.45
0.74	75	7	2	208.46
0.72	80	8	2	167.49
0.68	85	9	2	154.28
0.58	90	10	2	150.20

5 Conclusion and Recommendations

This study has shown that PCA method is particularly well adapted to the regionalization of rainfall region. It allows the grouping of stations with similar characteristics and recognition of climatic regions in the alpine domain [21]. Typically, in defining climate region, it will need the largest cluster to retain. If we only have fewer groups, we have to face the problem in differentiating the new region defined and it will give us difficulty to analyze it. Hence, the following recommendations are made for cluster analysis cum PCA to define new region:

(1) If there are too few components, observations that are not well represented will be clustered together due to low scores on all of the components but if more number of components to retain or more cumulative percentage are taken, the result of

defining region become poor as it will inflate the importance of noise. Therefore, the most suitable cumulative percentage to define region is between 65% until 70%.

(2) The principal component scores should be standardized as it will make the clustering result become sensitive to the number of component to retain.

(3) Validity index is recommended to be used when determining the best number of cluster to define region.

Generally, we have a lot of methods in defining region such as modeling method and regression method. Our proposed method may also be used by researchers to define climate region in their countries. All of the recommendations above can be used as guideline for other researchers with similar topics related to this paper. Having mentioned this, it is not a claim that all of the result is entirely accurate for all cases as it is based on rainfall data in Peninsular Malaysia and Indonesia. Both of these countries are part of the Asia, hence the weather and seasons are different compared to the other zones.

Acknowledgments. The authors would like to thank Universiti Pendidikan Sultan Idris for their financial funding.

References

1. Lattin, J.: Analyzing Multivariate Data. Curt Hinrichs, Canada (2003)
2. Romero, R., Ramis, C., Guijarro, J.A.: Daily rainfall patterns in the spanish mediterranean area: an objective classification. Int. J. Climatol. **19**, 95–112 (1999)
3. Alvin, C.R.: Methods of Multivariate Analysis. Wiley, Hoboken (2002)
4. Cliff, N.: Analyzing Multivariate Data. Harcourt Brace, San Diego (1987)
5. Cattell, R.B.: The scree test for the number of factors. Multivar. Behav. Res. **1**, 245–276 (1966)
6. Jollieffe, I.T.: Discarding variables in principal component analysis. I: artifical data. Appl. Stat. **21**, 160–173 (1972)
7. Mimmack, G.M., Mason, S.J., Galpin, J.S.: Choice of distance matrices in cluster analysis: defining region. J. Clim. **14**, 2790–2797 (2000)
8. Suhaila, J., Deni, S.M., Wan Zin, W.Z., Jemain, A.A.: Sains Malays. **39**(4), 533–542 (2010)
9. Wilks, D.S.: Statistical Methods in the Atmospheric Sciences, p. 467. Academic Press, Cambridge (1995)
10. Aldenderfer, M.S., Blashfield, R.K.: Cluster Analysis. Sage Publications, Inc., Beverly Hills (1984)
11. Mielke, P.W.: J. Atmos. Sci. **42**, 1209–1212 (1985)
12. Bunkers, M.J., Miller, J.R., DeGaaetano, A.T.: J. Clim. **9**, 130–146 (1996)
13. Jolliffe, I.T.: Principal Component Analysis. Springer Series in Statistics, p. 271. Springer, Heidelberg (1986)
14. Chang, W.C.: On using principal components before separating a mixture of two multivariate normal populations. J. Appl. Stat. **32**, 267–275 (1983)
15. Pelczer, I.J., Cisnerous-Iturbe, H.L.: Identification of rainfall patterns over the valley Mexico. In: 11th International Conference on Urban Drainage, pp. 1–9 (2008)
16. Fovell, R.G., Fovell, M.Y.C.: J. Clim. **6**, 2103–2135 (1993)

17. Donald, A.J.: Stopping rules in principal components analysis: a comparison of heuristical and statistical approaches. Ecology **74**(8), 2204–2214 (1993)
18. Grossman, G.D., Nickerson, D.M., Freeman, M.C.: Principal component analyses of assemblage structure data: utility of tests based on eigenvalues. Ecology **72**, 341–347 (1991)
19. Rexstad, E.A., Miller, D.D., Flather, C.H., Anderson, E.M., Hupp, J.W., Anderson, D.R.: Questionable multivariate statistical inference in wildlife habitat and community studies. J. Wildl. Manag. **52**, 794–798 (1988)
20. Mercedesm, D., Michael, E.P, Scott, S.: Defining Clusters of Related Industries (2013)
21. Baeriswyl, P.A., Rebetez, M.: Regionalization of precipitation in switzerland by means of principal component analysis. Theor. Appl. Climatol. **58**, 31–41 (1997)
22. Bunkers, M.J., Miller, J.R., DeGaetano, A.T.: Definition of climate regions in the northern plains using an objective cluster modification technique. J. Clim. **9**, 130–146 (1996)
23. DeGaetano, A.T.: Delineation of mesoscale climate zones in the Northeastern United States using a novel approach to cluster analysis. J. Clim. **9**, 1765–1782 (1996)

Modeling and Simulation Technology

Design Simulations of Odd-Order Variable Filters Utilizing the Stabilized Mathematical Model

Tian-Bo Deng$^{(\boxtimes)}$

Department of Information Science, Faculty of Science, Toho University,
Miyama 2-2-1, Funabashi, Chiba 274-8510, Japan
deng@is.sci.toho-u.ac.jp

Abstract. This paper first shows how to model an odd-order variable filter (OOVF) such that its stability is absolutely guaranteed under any variable circumstances, and then conducts computer simulations on the optimal design of an odd-order variable bandpass filter by employing the stable mathematical model. Finally, computer simulation results are provided to show the design performance as well as the guaranteed stability. The primary objective of this paper is to demonstrate that the presented mathematical model is useful in the computer design simulations that will never violate the stability conditions. As a result, numerical computer simulations can be conducted without concerning the stability issue. That is, the computer simulations utilizing the stabilized mathematical model will absolutely produce a stable OOVF.

Keywords: Odd-order variable filter (OOVF) · Bandpass OOVF · Stable mathematical model · Stability · Design formulation · Design simulation

1 Introduction

Digital filtering is one of the most fundamental operations in the digital signal processing (DSP) areas, and it plays an important rule in most DSP applications. The conventional fixed digital filters only have fixed characteristics and their characsersitics cannot be changed in the process of DSP applications. However, many DSP applications require that the digital filter being used should have changeable characteristics during the course of DSP applications. Such changeable characteristics include changeable group delay [1–3] and changeable bandwiths [4–10]. Due to the variability of those characteristics, such filters are named as variable filters. As is well known, variable filters are more flexible than the conventional fixed filters.

Although variable filters can be modeled as either a digital circuit with feedback loop (recursive model) or the one without feedback loop (non-recursive model), more attention must be paid to the stability issue of the recursive model. This is due to the fact that the feedback loop of a recursive model may easily

© Springer Nature Singapore Pte Ltd. 2017
M.S. Mohamed Ali et al. (Eds.): AsiaSim 2017, Part II, CCIS 752, pp. 227–236, 2017.
DOI: 10.1007/978-981-10-6502-6_20

become unstable. In [5–10], the stability problem has been addressed for the even-order designs, but this paper deals with the stability problem of an odd-order variable filter (OOVF). More specifically, the recursive designs in [5–10] use recursive models of even orders, where various transformation schemes are validated for solving the stability problem.

In [11], a stable mathematical model for the recursive OOVF has been proposed and its stability under any variable circumstances has been rigorously proved. This stable mathematical model enables the designer to conduct design simulations on the optimal design of an OOVF without any concern about the stability issue and this model-based simulations will definitely produce a stable recursive OOVF. Based on the theoretically-proved stability of the recursive OOVF, this paper adopts the stable mathematical model to the L_2-norm design. That is, this paper utilizes the stabilized model to conduct computer simulations for optimally designing a recursive OOVF. The design simulations aim to find an accurate mathematical model that approximates a given filter specification while keeping the resultant OOVF stable. Design simulation results are provided to demonstrate the performance of the designed recursive OOVF as well as the numerically verified stability. Therefore, this paper provides an effective way to design a recursive variable filter for the odd-order case and the stabilized model ensures that the stability condition will never be violated. As a consequence, the OOVF design can be viewed as generalized computer simulations from the even-order design simulations [10].

2   Odd-Order Stable Model

In this paper, we utilize the recursive mathematical model

$$H(z, \psi) = \frac{C(z, \psi)}{D_0(z, \psi) \displaystyle\prod_{k=1}^{N_2/2} D_k(z, \psi)}$$

$$= \frac{\displaystyle\sum_{k=0}^{N_1} c_k(\psi) z^{-k}}{[1 + d_{01}(\psi) z^{-1}] \displaystyle\prod_{k=1}^{N_2/2} [1 + d_{k1}(\psi) z^{-1} + d_{k2}(\psi) z^{-2}]} \tag{1}$$

where N_2 is an even integer, $D_0(z, \psi)$ and $D_k(z, \psi)$ are the first-order section and second-order sections, respectively,

$$C(z, \psi) = \sum_{k=0}^{N_1} c_k(\psi) z^{-k}$$

$$D_0(z, \psi) = 1 + d_{01}(\psi) z^{-1} \tag{2}$$

$$D_k(z, \psi) = 1 + d_{k1}(\psi) z^{-1} + d_{k2}(\psi) z^{-2}.$$

Thus, the mathematical model $H(z, \psi)$ in (1) has odd $(N_2 + 1)$ order.

By assuming

$$d_{02}(\psi) = 0$$

we get the unified model

$$H(z, \psi) = \frac{\displaystyle\sum_{k=0}^{N_1} c_k(\psi) z^{-k}}{\displaystyle\prod_{k=0}^{N_2/2} [1 + d_{k1}(\psi) z^{-1} + d_{k2}(\psi) z^{-2}]}. \tag{3}$$

This model represents a recursive odd-order variable filter (OOVF) whose coefficients are defined as the functions of the parameter ψ, where ψ tunes a given amplitude specification $A_d(\omega, \psi)$. In other words, design simulations are done in order to find $c_k(\psi)$, $d_{k1}(\psi)$, $d_{k2}(\psi)$ such that the specification $A_d(\omega, \psi)$ is accurately approximated. However, the design simulations directly using (3) may produce an unstable OOVF. Thus, a stable mathematical model for the OOVF is proved in [11] for performing the design simulations without any stability concern.

As mentioned in [11], the OOVF is stable if and only if

$$\begin{cases} |d_{k2}(\psi)| < 1 \\ |d_{k1}(\psi)| < 1 + d_{k2}(\psi) \end{cases} \tag{4}$$

is satisfied. Before conducting design simulations to get an OOVF, it is wise to represent the original $d_{k2}(\psi)$ and $d_{k1}(\psi)$ as

$$\begin{cases} d_{k2}(\psi) = \gamma \cdot T[x_{k2}(\psi)] \\ d_{k1}(\psi) = \gamma \cdot T[x_{k,1}(\psi)][1 + d_{k2}(\psi)] \end{cases} \tag{5}$$

by utilizing the transformation function $T(\chi)$, where γ is a scaling factor $\gamma \in (0, 1)$. As long as the function $T(\chi)$ is bounded within

$$T(\chi) \in [-1, 1] \tag{6}$$

it has been rigorously proved in [11] that the recursive OOVF is definitely stable regardless of the values of $x_{k2}(\psi)$, $x_{k1}(\psi)$. In [8,10], design simulations have been carried out for designing even-order variable filters on the basis of this principle. This paper extends this principle to the OOVF case and designs a stable OOVF using the stabilized OOVF model in (3).

3   Design Methodology and Design Simulations

This section first describes how to get the functions $c_k(\psi)$, $d_{k1}(\psi)$, and $d_{k2}(\psi)$, and then conducts design simulations to design an OOVF approximating a given bandpass amplitude specification $A_d(\omega, \psi)$. Finally, computer simulation results are used to show the design performance and verify the stability.

3.1   Design Methodology

The functions $c_k(\psi)$, $x_{k2}(\psi)$, and $x_{k1}(\psi)$ are assumed to be the polynomial functions, which can be found by employing the two-step schemes [4–10]. Here, we briefly summarize the design methodology.

Once the amplitude specification $A_d(\omega, \psi_i)$ is given, Table 1 demonstrates the process of the first step. The first step is to discretize $A_d(\omega, \psi)$ by sampling ψ, which yields the samples ψ_i, $i = 1, 2, \cdots, L$. Those samples in turn correspond to the specification samples $A_d(\omega, \psi_i)$. Then, a fixed filter is found to separately approximate each $A_d(\omega, \psi_i)$. More specifically, approximating $A_d(\omega, \psi_i)$ produces the ith fixed filter

$$
H_i(z) = \frac{\displaystyle\sum_{k=0}^{N_1} c_k z^{-k}}{\displaystyle\prod_{k=0}^{N_2/2} [1 + d_{k1} z^{-1} + d_{k2} z^{-2}]}
\tag{7}
$$

where the same transformation $T(\chi)$ for d_{k2} and d_{k1} is used, which results in x_{k2} and x_{k1}. Therefore, designing each fixed filter yields a set of values of $\{c_k, x_{k2}, x_{k1}\}$. This is explained in Table 1. The cost function to be minimized is the weighted sum of the squared error of the amplitude response.

The second step is to fit the resulting values of each coefficient by using a different polynomial, which is explained in Table 2. For instance, all the values of c_0 are fitted by using the polynomial $c_0(\psi)$. As a result, we can obtain all the

Table 1. First-step: design of fixed-coefficient filters

$\psi \in [\psi_{\min}, \psi_{\max}]$	Coefficients of each fixed filter
ψ_1	$A_d(\omega, \psi_1) \longrightarrow c_0, c_1, c_2, \cdots, c_{N_1}, x_{k2}, x_{k1}$
ψ_2	$A_d(\omega, \psi_2) \longrightarrow c_0, c_1, c_2, \cdots, c_{N_1}, x_{k2}, x_{k1}$
ψ_3	$A_d(\omega, \psi_3) \longrightarrow c_0, c_1, c_2, \cdots, c_{N_1}, x_{k2}, x_{k1}$
$\vdots$	$\vdots$
ψ_L	$A_d(\omega, \psi_L) \longrightarrow c_0, c_1, c_2, \cdots, c_{N_1}, x_{k2}, x_{k1}$

Table 2. Second-step: each polynomial fitting to respective values

ψ	$c_0(\psi)$ $\downarrow$	$c_1(\psi)$ $\downarrow$	$c_2(\psi)$ $\downarrow$	$\cdots$ $\downarrow$	$c_{N_1}(\psi)$ $\downarrow$	$x_{k2}(\psi)$ $\downarrow$	$x_{k1}(\psi)$ $\downarrow$
ψ_1	c_0	c_1	c_2	$\cdots$	c_{N_1}	x_{k2}	x_{k1}
ψ_2	c_0	c_1	c_2	$\cdots$	c_{N_1}	x_{k2}	x_{k1}
$\vdots$	$\vdots$	$\vdots$	$\vdots$	$\vdots$	$\vdots$	$\vdots$	$\vdots$
ψ_L	c_0	c_1	c_2	$\cdots$	c_{N_1}	x_{k2}	x_{k1}

polynomial functions $c_k(\psi)$, $x_{k2}(\psi)$, and $x_{k1}(\psi)$. Combining the above two steps completes the OOVF design using the stabilized model.

3.2   Design Simulations

Based on the above design methodology, this section conducts the computer simulations to approximate the bandpass amplitude specification

$$A_d(\omega, \psi) = \begin{cases} 0, & |\omega| \in [0, 0.26\pi + \psi] \\ 1, & |\omega| \in [0.32\pi + \psi, 0.64\pi - \psi] \\ 0, & |\omega| \in [0.70\pi - \psi, \pi]. \end{cases} \tag{8}$$

The design sets the orders $N_1 = 6$, $N_2 = 6$. Evidently, this is the seventh-order OOVF. To tune the bandwiths, ψ is allowed to take arbitrary value in

$$\psi \in [\psi_{\min}, \psi_{\max}]$$
$$\psi_{\min} = -0.10\pi \tag{9}$$
$$\psi_{\max} = 0.10\pi.$$

The entire range in (9) is sampled to get $L = 21$ sampled values, and the frequency $\omega \in [0, \pi]$ is sampled to get 601 points. Figure 1 shows the discretized bandpass specifications.

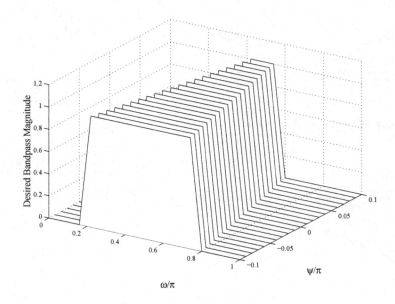

Fig. 1. Discretized bandpass specifications ($L = 21$)

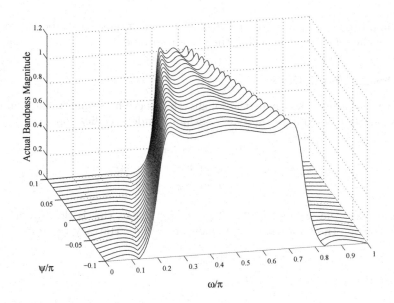

Fig. 2. Bandpass responses of the designed $L = 21$ fixed filters

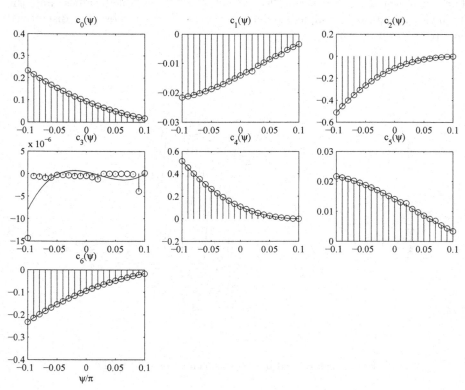

Fig. 3. Approximating polynomials for the numerator coefficients c_k

In this paper, we employ the transformation function

$$T(\chi) = \cos(\chi).$$

By setting $\gamma = 0.9999$, we design the first fixed bandpass filter $H_1(z)$ corresponding to $\psi_1 = \psi_{\min} = -0.10\pi$, and the initial coefficients are

$$\begin{bmatrix} c_0 \\ c_1 \\ c_2 \\ c_3 \\ c_4 \\ c_5 \\ c_6 \\ x_{12} \\ x_{22} \\ x_{32} \\ x_{01} \\ x_{11} \\ x_{21} \\ x_{31} \end{bmatrix} = \begin{bmatrix} -1.00911552434079 \\ -0.01951066953029 \\ -0.04822078914531 \\ 0.00004319184163 \\ -0.31785945124769 \\ 1.09500373878749 \\ -1.87399025764096 \\ 0.42818327304516 \\ 0.89563847121175 \\ 0.73095733842945 \\ 0.57785734633080 \\ 0.04031403161844 \\ 0.67708918759730 \\ 0.56890020520072 \end{bmatrix}. \tag{10}$$

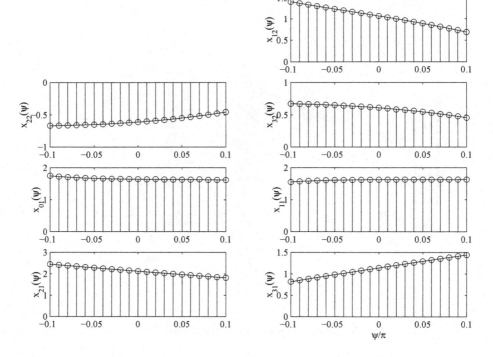

Fig. 4. Approximating polynomials for x_{k2} and x_{k1}

The MATLAB function *fminsearch* is employed to search for the sub-optimal coefficients iteratively. Furthermore, the simulation design ignores the amplitude errors in the transition bands.

Figure 2 depicts the actual bandpass amplitude responses of the designed $L = 21$ fixed filters. The average of the normalized root-mean-square (RMS) error and that of the maximum error are respectively

$$\bar{e}_2 = 4.5509\%, \quad \bar{e}_{\max} = 0.1072.$$

After designing the $L = 21$ fixed filters, each coefficient is fitted with the third-order polynomial. Figure 3 plots the approximating polynomials for the numerator coefficients, and Fig. 4 plots the approximating polynomials for the denominator coefficients. Moreover, Fig. 5 plots the actual bandpass responses of the designed OOVF, and Fig. 6 plots the stability triangles along with the denominator coefficients. As all the coefficient pairs (d_{k1}, d_{k2}) are within the triangles, the designed seventh-order OOVF is definitely stable. The average of the normalized RMS error and that of the maximum error are

$$\bar{e}_2 = 4.6043\%, \quad \bar{e}_{\max} = 0.1096$$

respectively.

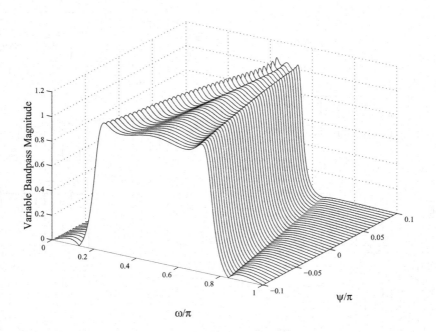

Fig. 5. Bandpass responses of the designed OOVF

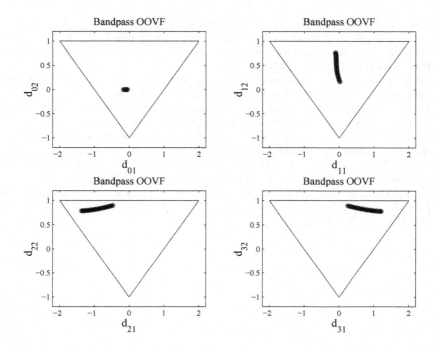

Fig. 6. Stability triangles for the designed seventh-order OOVF

4 Conclusion

This paper has utilized the stable odd-order mathematical model to design a stable bandpass OOVF with tunable amplitude (gain). After briefly describing the two-step design methodology using Tables 1 and 2, this paper has shown that a recursive OOVF can be designed without worrying about the stability problem, and the resultant recursive OOVF is certainly stable. Design simulations have demonstrated the effectiveness of the stable-model-based design methodology and the numerically verified stability.

References

1. Soontornwong, P., Chivapreecha, S.: Pascal-interpolation-based noninteger delay filter and low-complexity realization. Radioengineering **24**(4), 1002–1012 (2015)
2. Deng, T.-B.: Discretization-free design of variable fractional-delay FIR digital filters. IEEE Trans. Circ. Syst. II Analog Digit. Sig. Process. **48**(6), 637–644 (2001)
3. Deng, T.-B., Lian, Y.: Weighted-least-squares design of variable fractional-delay FIR filters using coefficient-symmetry. IEEE Trans. Sig. Process. **54**(8), 3023–3038 (2006)
4. Zarour, R., Fahmy, M.M.: A design technique for variable digital filters. IEEE Trans. Circ. Syst. **36**(11), 1473–1478 (1989)

5. Deng, T.-B.: Design of recursive 1-D variable filters with guaranteed stability. IEEE Trans. Circ. Syst. II Analog Digit. Sig. Process. **44**(9), 689–695 (1997)
6. Deng, T.-B.: New method for designing stable recursive variable digital filters. Sig. Process. **64**(2), 197–207 (1998)
7. Deng, T.-B.: An improved method for designing variable recursive digital filters with guaranteed stability. Sig. Process. **81**(2), 439–446 (2001)
8. Deng, T.-B.: Stability trapezoid and stability-margin analysis for the second-order recursive digital filter. Sig. Process. **118**(1), 97–102 (2016)
9. Deng, T.-B.: Generalized stability-triangle for guaranteeing the stability-margin of the second-order digital filter. J. Circ. Syst. Comput. (JCSC) **25**(8), 1–13 (2016)
10. Deng, T.-B.: Design of recursive variable-digital-filters with theoretically-guaranteed stability. Int. J. Electron. **103**(12), 2013–2028 (2016)
11. Deng, T.-B.: Stability-constrained variable mathematical model for odd-order recursive variable filters. In: Proceedings of 2017 IEEE ECTI-CON 2017, Phuket, Thailand, 27–30 June 2017

Driver Behavior Injection in Microscopic Traffic Simulations

Manuel Lindorfer[1]([✉]), Christian Backfrieder[1], Christoph Mecklenbräuker[2], and Gerald Ostermayer[1]

[1] Research Group Networks and Mobility, FH Upper Austria, Hagenberg, Austria
{manuel.lindorfer,gerald.ostermayer}@fh-hagenberg.at
[2] Christian Doppler Lab Wireless Technology for Sustainable Mobility, Vienna University of Technology, Vienna, Austria
cfm@nt.tuwien.ac.at

Abstract. The individual behavior of drivers has a significant influence on the characteristics of vehicular transportation systems such as safety, capacity or traffic flow. Apparently, considering such behaviors in the scope of microscopic traffic simulations is inevitable in order to accomplish simulations close to reality. In recent years, considerable efforts have been put into modeling longitudinal and lateral movements of vehicles or their lane-change behavior, respectively. However, sometimes it is necessary to deviate from the standard behavior prescribed by these models in order to study the effects of exceptional situations in road traffic such as sudden braking maneuvers. This paper addresses this specific use case by introducing a generic behavior injection model, allowing for the integration of predefined driver behaviors into microscopic traffic simulations. Furthermore, it enables the reconstruction of real traffic scenarios by incorporating data gathered from vehicular measurement campaigns. The result is a simple, yet flexible model applicable to a wide range of microscopic traffic simulators.

Keywords: Microscopic traffic simulation · Driver behavior · Computer modeling

1 Introduction

The area of traffic simulation has gained more and more importance in recent years, playing a crucial role in the development of technologies and applications designed for Intelligent Transportation Systems (ITS). Simulations are a widespread and frequently used tool to model complex transportation networks and to investigate scenarios that cannot be studied in a real experiment or by any other analytical method. Throughout the years, numerous simulation frameworks have been developed by researchers in the field, designed for the simulation of vehicular traffic at different levels of abstraction [1–5]. In contrast to macroscopic simulators, which describe entire traffic flows in their collectivity,

© Springer Nature Singapore Pte Ltd. 2017
M.S. Mohamed Ali et al. (Eds.): AsiaSim 2017, Part II, CCIS 752, pp. 237–248, 2017.
DOI: 10.1007/978-981-10-6502-6_21

microscopic traffic simulators provide the highest level of detail, as the movements of every single vehicle and its characteristics are modeled individually. Frameworks belonging to the class of the latter make use of a variety of models which encapsulate single tasks of the driver, including but not limited to behavioral models, such as lane-change models and longitudinal models, and fuel consumption models.

In the last decades, considerable efforts have been put into modeling driver behavior in various aspects, resulting in a vast number of behavior models available in literature (e.g. [6–15]). Although most of these models describe vehicular traffic adequately, they do not allow for simulating situations that deviate from their prescribed behavior. This, however, is sometimes useful, if not required, especially when studying the effects of exceptional situations in road traffic such as sudden braking maneuvers or the impacts of individual driving behavior on both traffic flow and safety.

In order to overcome this deficiency, we introduce a generic behavior injection model, which is capable of enriching microscopic traffic simulations by a number of predefined, customizable driver behaviors. Furthermore, it allows for the reconstruction of real traffic scenarios by integrating data gathered from vehicular measurement campaigns or driving simulator studies such as speed or acceleration traces. The model makes use of a flexible and decoupled data structure, allowing for a straightforward extension and modification of the very same.

The remainder of this paper is organized as follows. The next section gives an overview of related projects in the scope of this work. In Sect. 3, the developed behavior injection model is introduced, including a detailed description of its individual components and their interactions. Subsequently, we demonstrate the model's applicability by integrating it with the microscopic traffic simulator TraffSim [1]. Section 5 concludes the paper and gives a short overview of planned future work.

2 Related Work

The importance of microscopic traffic simulation and driver behavior modeling in particular is increasing continuously. Starting already in the 1960s, a multiplicity of behavioral models have been developed for that reason. While several models have been proposed allowing for the accident-free simulation of vehicular traffic under idealized conditions (e.g. [6–8]), others incorporate behavior such as a delayed response (e.g. [9–11]) or perceptual limitations (e.g. [12]) in order to model the impacts of human driving on traffic flow to a more copious extent. Additionally, various models try to capture the dynamics concomitant with lane-changes, e.g. [13–15]. Due to the ever growing demand for a even more realistic simulation of vehicular traffic, several efforts have been put into the coupling of traffic simulation frameworks and driving simulators in recent years. All these systems aim for integrating specific driving behavior with microscopic traffic simulations for the purpose of investigating scenarios that cannot be captured by the standardized behavior predetermined by general simulation models.

On that account, several attempts were made to integrate a driving simulator with commercial traffic simulation tools such as Paramics [16] and VISSIM [17], e.g. in [18–21]. Similar systems have been proposed by [22–24], who integrate the driving simulation engine SCANeR^{TM} with the microscopic simulator Aimsun [25]. Maroto et al. [26], for example, proposed a micro-simulation model with a user-driven vehicle surrounded by simulated traffic.

The possibility to control a subject vehicle externally using driving simulator input, while all other vehicles move according to their behavioral models, allows to study the effects of individual driving behavior on traffic flow dynamics and vice versa. A major limitation of such co-simulation approaches, however, is the high computational and technological complexity concomitant with the coupling of two independent, complex systems (e.g. synchronization and latency, proprietary data formats, eventually hardware setup). The reliance on driving simulator input reveals another issue, that is the inability to guarantee full reproducibility of the performed simulations, which, apparently, is inevitable in order to obtain reasonable results, especially when investigating the effects of individual driving behavior in different situations.

The behavior injection model presented in the forthcoming section addresses these particular issues. It makes use of a flexible data structure allowing for the straightforward extension and integration with microscopic traffic simulators while at the same time allowing for full reproducibility of the scenarios under investigation.

3   The Behavior Injection Model

In this section, the developed behavior injection model is elaborated in more detail. Subsequently, we present an overview of its architecture and the functional principle as well as the types of behavior which are supported by the model.

3.1   Functional Principle

As mentioned previously, the behavior injection model proposed in this paper is applicable to the class of microscopic traffic simulators, i.e. the positions and velocities of vehicles within a simulation run as well as additional parameters such as fuel consumption are modeled individually. Hereinafter, we give a brief overview of the model's layout and its interfaces required for the successful integration with such microscopic simulation frameworks. Figure 1 outlines the individual model components and their interactions with other simulator components in an abstracted manner.

The behavior injection module constitutes the integral part of the proposed model, responsible for managing the execution of behaviors throughout a simulation run. These behaviors are parametrized using external configuration data which specify, among others, the behavior's time of execution and its duration, as indicated by (1). The injection module on the other hand is directly linked to the simulation time updater, a core component of microscopic traffic simulators

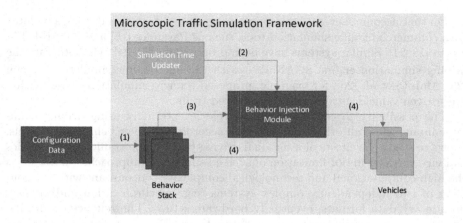

Fig. 1. Conceptional layout of the proposed behavior injection model. Interactions with model components (blue) and other simulator components (gray) are indicated by arrows, the parenthetic numbers indicate the sequence of interactions. (Color figure online)

which repeatedly updates other simulator components (e.g. crash detectors, longitudinal and lane-change models, traffic control models) in fixed time intervals in order to drive on the simulation (2). In every simulation step the injection module processes the given set of behaviors (3) and performs modifications either to this set or selected vehicles in the simulation, respectively (4). Thereby, it follows the functional principle outlined by the pseudo-code below.

```
 1: function BEHAVIORUPDATE(simRunTime)
 2:    for i = 1 :SIZEOF(behaviorStack) do
 3:       b ←GETBEHAVIOR(behaviorStack, i)
 4:       if CANEXECUTE(b,simRunTime) then
 5:          if CANFINISH(b,simRunTime) then
 6:             STOPBEHAVIOR(b)
 7:             REMOVEBEHAVIOR(behaviorStack,b)
 8:          else
 9:             EXECUTE(b,simRunTime)
10:          end if
11:       end if
12:    end for
13: end function
```

In every update step, the injection module verifies whether the execution of either one or multiple of the specified behaviors has to be started or stopped, respectively, depending on the currently elapsed simulation run time. For each behavior b the function CANEXECUTE ascertains whether the behavior is ready for execution or not, i.e. its time of execution is smaller than the simulation run time. If this condition evaluates to true, the function CANFINISH determines if the behavior has successfully finished execution, i.e. the current simulation run time exceeds the behavior's time of execution plus its specified duration. If this is the case, the behavior's execution is stopped. Furthermore, the behavior is removed from the set for performance reasons, and, thus, it is not considered in upcoming update time steps anymore. Otherwise, the behavior is executed just as desired, i.e. it is applied to the target vehicle.

This approach is not only a rather simple mechanism to alter the standardized behavior of selected vehicles in the scope of microscopic simulations, much more it also guarantees full reproducibility of the scenarios under investigation. This reproducibility is achieved by the behavior execution mechanism which ensures that behaviors with an identical time of execution and duration are injected at the same point in time and last for the very same period of time.

3.2   Behavior Types

Basically, the proposed model is capable of introducing any kind of behavior into microscopic traffic simulations. This comprises behaviors affecting a vehicle's longitudinal and lateral movements as well as such influencing its lane-change behavior, respectively. What's more, also the modeling of hazardous events such as driver distractions is conceivable. With reference to the exemplary integration of the injection model with the traffic simulator TraffSim [1], which is outlined in Sect. 4, we will delineate two specific behaviors that have been implemented for that particular reason.

Acceleration and Deceleration: The first type of behavior is related to acceleration and deceleration, respectively. It allows to force a subject vehicle to carry out an acceleration or a brake maneuver for a given period of time using a desired intensity. After behavior execution has finished, the vehicle's speed and acceleration values are either imposed by the underlying longitudinal model or remain unaffected until the end of the simulation, except for modifications caused by subsequent behaviors, depending on the behavior's parametrization. Such kind of behavior is useful e.g. when evaluating the stability of vehicle platoons in response to unexpected driving maneuvers of the leading vehicle (see e.g. in [11,27]).

Control Behavior: In contrast to the former, control behaviors allow to realize more complex driving scenarios by making use of predefined speed and acceleration traces. Such data could be obtained from real vehicular measurement campaigns or from driving simulator studies, respectively. Instead of setting the subject vehicle's acceleration to a predefined value, control behaviors continuously vary the vehicle's speed and acceleration in accordance to the provided data traces. Finally, the behavior's parametrization decides whether or not control is handed over to the vehicle's longitudinal model after the control behavior has finished. Control behaviors allows for the reconstruction of real driving scenarios in a simulation environment, which is useful not only when studying the effects of certain maneuvers under varying conditions, but also to validate car-following models under development on the basis of real data.

4 Integrating the Behavior Injection Model with the Microscopic Simulation Framework TraffSim

After having introduced the theoretical concepts related to the proposed behavior injection model, we will now demonstrate its applicability by integrating it with the microscopic simulator TraffSim [1]. TraffSim allows for the time-discrete and state-continuous simulation of vehicular traffic, supporting numerous configurable models and parameters. Throughout a simulation run a wide range of traffic-relevant data are recorded for each modeled vehicle, including but not limited to acceleration, current speed, position and fuel consumption, which guarantees full reproducibility of the performed simulations. TraffSim is implemented as Eclipse Rich Client Platform (RCP) application using the Java programming language, which reveals a number of benefits, including but not limited to platform independence, automated update mechanisms and a commonly known user interface [1].

4.1 Behavior Specification

TraffSim makes use of a number of XML files for defining all input parameters relevant for a simulation, e.g. road network, vehicles, traffic lights. We extend this data model by a separate input file which contains configuration parameters for the behavior types outlined in Sect. 3.2. Exemplary configurations of these types are shown in Fig. 2.

```
                                    <Behavior id="2">
    <Behavior id="1">                 <type>Control</type>
      <type>Acceleration</type>       <vehicle>01</vehicle>
      <vehicle>01</vehicle>           <offset>60</offset>
      <intensity>2.0</intensity>      <trace>
      <duration>4.0</duration>          <sample/>
      <offset>60.0</offset>            <sample/>
    </Behavior>                        </trace>
                                    </Behavior>
            (a)
                                            (b)
```

Fig. 2. Configuration of an acceleration (a) and a control behavior (b) to be used in a TraffSim simulation.

It can be obtained that both configurations have several parameters in common, including the behavior *type*, an *offset* to determine the time of execution measured from simulation start, and the *vehicle* field identifying the target vehicle for the respective behavior. The acceleration and deceleration behaviors additionally require an *intensity* and a *duration* to be specified. Whilst the former indicates the absolute acceleration value (either positive or negative), the latter defines how long this value is actually applied.

For the control behavior, these two settings are defined implicitly by the *trace* parameter, which is composed of a set of any number of samples. Each sample, in turn, provides several parameters such as a time stamp, a speed and an acceleration value. Such traces can either be obtained by performing vehicular measurement campaigns, from driving simulators or from data provided by open-source projects such as NGSIM (**N**ext **G**eneration **SIM**ulation, [28]), respectively.

4.2   Data Model

Hereinafter, we outline the individual components of the behavior injection model and their relations to existing components within the TraffSim infrastructure. The model is strongly decoupled from the remaining simulator components, allowing for its modification or even replacement without affecting any of the other components. Figure 3 gives an overview of the relevant simulator architecture and the integration of the behavior injection model into the very same. Afterwards, we provide a more detailed description of the particular components and their respective responsibilities.

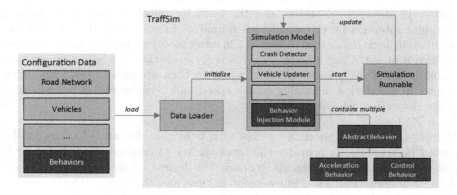

Fig. 3. Concrete implementation of the behavior injection model and its integration with the TraffSim infrastructure. Components associated to the behavior injection model are highlighted in blue. (Color figure online)

Data Loader: Before starting a simulation in TraffSim, all relevant configuration files have to be loaded into the simulation environment. The data loader provides the functionality to process the XML files containing the required input parameters (see Sect. 4.1) and to create the corresponding simulation objects from them, e.g. road segments, vehicles.

Simulation Model: Given the entities created by the data loader, a simulation model is created for every single simulation. This model provides all information required for a simulation run and manages a number of components which encapsulate particular simulation facilities, e.g. crash detection, statistics recording or, likewise, behavior injection.

Simulation Runnable: A simulation runnable constitutes the equivalent to the simulation time updater outlined in Fig. 1 and is one of the key components in TraffSim. It is responsible for continuously updating particular simulator components handled by the simulation model, e.g. crash detector, behavior injection module, in fixed time intervals in order to drive on the simulation. In every update step each of these components carries out its desired functionality. Each simulation runnable is executed in a separate thread, allowing to perform multiple simulation runs in parallel.

Vehicle Updater: One of the components controlled by the simulation runnable is the vehicle updater. This component is responsible for updating all vehicle-specific parameters such as position, speed and fuel consumption. In each simulation step it processes every individual vehicle in the simulation and updates its properties accordingly.

Behavior Injection Module: Among other components such as the vehicle updater or the crash detector, also the behavior injection module is updated in regular intervals by the simulation runnable. In every iteration the module executes the logic delineated in Sect. 3.1 in order to determine whether to execute a behavior or not. Once a behavior is ready for execution, the behavior injection module notifies the vehicle updater, which in turn updates the corresponding vehicles in simulation according to the speed and acceleration values provided by the respective behavior.

Abstract Behavior: This entity serves as a base class for all behaviors implemented in TraffSim. It provides the functionality to determine if a behavior is ready for execution and methods to obtain the desired manipulation values (e.g. speed or acceleration) for a given point in time and the target vehicle, respectively. The acceleration and control behavior represent concrete implementations of this abstract behavior. Whilst the former yields constant manipulation values at any point in time, these values vary over time for the latter, as in every update step a different sample of the associated data trace is processed. In that regard it is important to ensure that the sampling time of the underlying data trace matches the simulation interval in order to obtain reasonable results.

4.3   Simulation Results

In order to demonstrate the proposed behavior injection model's functionality we carried out a number of simulations using TraffSim. More precisely, we simulated different scenarios to outline how both the acceleration and deceleration behavior as well as the control behavior affect a target vehicle's longitudinal movement in a different manner. While in the first scenario a vehicle is being exposed to both an acceleration and a deceleration behavior, the target vehicle's behavior is imposed by a speed and acceleration trace obtained from the publicly available NGSIM project [28] in the second one. In all simulations performed in the scope of this work we used the popular Intelligent Driver Model [8] to model the vehicles' longitudinal movements.

Acceleration and Deceleration: In this scenario we outline the implications of the most simple type of behavior, namely acceleration and deceleration maneuvers. To do so, we simulated a single vehicle traveling along a straight road at a desired speed of $14 \, \text{m/s}$. After $t = 500 \, \text{s}$ we inject a deceleration behavior which causes the vehicle to brake with an intensity of $2 \, \text{m/s}^2$ until it reaches the new target speed of $10 \, \text{m/s}$. Finally, an acceleration behavior is triggered at $t = 530 \, \text{s}$, lasting for two seconds and applying a constant acceleration of $2 \, \text{m/s}^2$. Figure 4 outlines the acceleration and speed traces for the target vehicle in the relevant time interval. Figure 4a depicts the described scenario in the case where the vehicle's velocity and acceleration are affected only by subsequent behaviors after the first behavior has been executed. In contrast, Fig. 4b shows the very same scenario, however, control is handed over to the vehicle's longitudinal model after each of the behaviors has been executed. In case of the latter it can easily be seen that the longitudinal model immediately counteracts the deviated behavior introduced by the two behaviors in order to reach the desired target speed of $14 \, \text{m/s}$ by performing an according acceleration and brake maneuver, respectively.

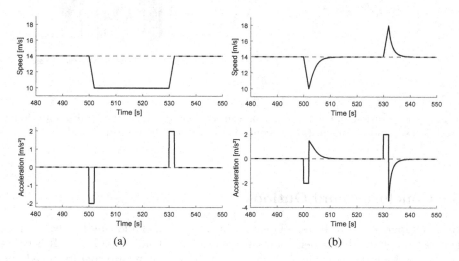

(a)   (b)

Fig. 4. Acceleration and speed traces of a target vehicle being exposed to a deceleration and an acceleration maneuver at $t = 500 \, \text{s}$ and $t = 530 \, \text{s}$, respectively. The blue traces result from applying both a deceleration and an acceleration behavior, the greyed-out, dotted line corresponds to situations where no behavior is injected. (Color figure online)

Control Behavior: In the second scenario we demonstrate the proposed model's capability to reproduce realistic driving maneuvers by integrating speed and acceleration traces obtained from vehicular measurement campaigns or driving simulator studies, respectively. Therefore, we setup a control behavior which is parametrized using a corresponding trace from the publicly available Lankershim Boulevard dataset (refer to the NGSIM project [28]). The selected speed and acceleration traces have a length of roughly 66 s and were recorded in a congested arterial road, i.e. in dense traffic. Similar to the first scenario, we simulated a single vehicle traveling along a straight road at a desired speed of approximately 7 m/s, before the behavior is finally injected at t = 500 s. Figure 5a and b show the original traces as obtained from the NGSIM dataset and the corresponding traces reproduced with an accordingly parametrized control behavior, respectively.

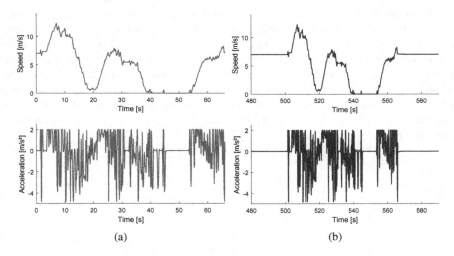

(a)   (b)

Fig. 5. Acceleration and speed traces of a selected sample from the Lankershim Boulevard dataset and its integration as control behavior on the right-hand side.

5   Conclusion and Outlook

In this paper, we introduced a behavior injection model allowing for the integration of predefined driver behaviors into microscopic traffic simulators. It is capable of manipulating a vehicle's longitudinal movement by altering its speed and acceleration in accordance to predefined acceleration and deceleration maneuvers or to real data traces obtained from vehicular measurement campaigns or driving simulator studies, respectively. In principle, also the integration of behaviors affecting the vehicles' lateral movements or lane-change behavior would be feasible. The proposed model is useful for a number of use cases, including but not limited to study the stability of vehicle platoons in response to unexpected driving maneuvers of the leading vehicle or to investigate the impacts of individual driving behavior under varying conditions. At all times, our model guarantees full reproducibility of the performed simulations by ensuring that identically parametrized behaviors are injected at the same point in time. We demonstrated the model's applicability by integrating it with the microscopic simulation framework TraffSim [1] and the aid of two exemplary simulation scenarios. However, it should be mentioned that the model is applicable to a wide range of microscopic traffic simulators.

We emphasize that, to this point, the behavior injection model is limited to modeling behaviors affecting the longitudinal movements of individual vehicles. Future work will include the extension of the model so as to allow for the integration of driving behaviors influencing both lateral movements and lane-change behavior, respectively.

Acknowledgments. The authors greatly acknowledge the support by the Austrian Research Promotion Agency (FFG) in the scope of the program "Industrienahe Dissertationen".

References

1. Backfrieder, C., Ostermayer, G., Mecklenbräuker, C.: Extended from EMS2013. TraffSim - a traffic simulator for investigations of congestion minimization through dynamic vehicle rerouting. Int. J. Simul. Syst. Sci. Technol. IJSSST **15**, 38–47 (2015)
2. Behrisch, M., Bieker, L., Erdmann, J., Krajzewicz, D.: SUMO - simulation of urban mobility - an overview. In: SIMUL 2011, The Third International Conference on Advances in System Simulation, pp. 55–60, October 2011
3. Gora, P.: Traffic simulation framework. In: 2012 UKSim 14th International Conference on Computer Modelling and Simulation, pp. 345–349, March 2012
4. Miller, J., Horowitz, E.: FreeSim - a free real-time freeway traffic simulator. In: IEEE Intelligent Transportation Systems Conference, ITSC 2007, pp. 18–23, September 2007
5. Treiber, M., Kesting, A.: An open-source microscopic traffic simulator. IEEE Intell. Transp. Syst. Mag. **2**(3), 6–13 (2010)
6. Bando, M., Hasebe, K., Nakayama, A., Shibata, A., Sugiyama, Y.: Dynamical model of traffic congestion and numerical simulation. Phys. Rev. E **51**(2), 1035–1042 (1995)
7. Gipps, P.: A behavioural car-following model for computer simulation. Transp. Res. Part B: Methodol. **15**(2), 105–111 (1981)
8. Treiber, M., Hennecke, A., Helbing, D.: Congested traffic states in empirical observations and microscopic simulations. Phys. Rev. E **62**(2), 1805–1824 (2000)
9. Bando, M., Hasebe, K., Nakanishi, K., Nakayama, A.: Analysis of optimal velocity model with explicit delay. Phys. Rev. E **58**(5429), 1035–1042 (1998)
10. Newell, G.F.: Nonlinear effects in the dynamics of car-following. Oper. Res. **9**(2), 209–229 (1961)
11. Treiber, M., Kesting, A., Helbing, D.: Delays, inaccuracies and anticipation in microscopic traffic models. Phys. A: Stat. Mech. Appl. **360**(1), 71–88 (2006)

12. Wiedemann, R.: Simulation des Strassenverkehrsflusses. In: Schriftenreihe des Instituts für Verkehrswesen der Universität Karlsruhe, Germany (1974)
13. Kesting, A., Treiber, M., Helbing, D.: General lane-changing model MOBIL for car-following models. Transp. Res. Rec.: J. Transp. Res. Board **1999**, 86–94 (2007)
14. Toledo, T., Koutsopoulos, H., Ben-Akiva, M.: Integrated driving behavior modeling. Transp. Res. Part C: Emerg. Technol. **15**(2), 96–112 (2007)
15. Gipps, P.: A model for the structure of lane-changing decisions. Transp. Res. Part B: Methodol. **20**(5), 403–414 (1986)
16. Cameron, G., Wylie, B.J.N., McArthur, D.: Paramics: moving vehicles on the connection machine. In: Proceedings of the 1994 ACM/IEEE Conference on Supercomputing, Supercomputing 1994, pp. 291–300. IEEE Computer Society Press, Los Alamitos (1994)
17. Fellendorf, M.: VISSIM: a microscopic simulation tool to evaluate actuated signal control including bus priority. In: Proceedings of the 64th ITE Annual Meeting (1994)
18. Jenkins, J., Rilett, L.: Integrating driving simulators and micro-simulation models: a conceptualization. In: Transportation Research Board 81st Annual Meeting (2002)
19. Jin, M., Lam, S.H.: A virtual-reality based integrated driving-traffic simulation system to study the impacts of intelligent transportation systems (ITS). In: Proceedings, 2003 International Conference on Cyberworlds, pp. 158–165, December 2003
20. Vladisavljevic, I., Cooper, J.M., Martin, P.T., Stray, D.L.: The importance of integrating driving and traffic simulations, illustrated through a case study that examines the impact of cell phone drivers on traffic flow. In: Proceedings of the 88th TRB Annual Meeting, Washington, D.C. (2009)
21. Hou, Y., Zhao, Y., Hulme, K.F., Huang, S., Yang, Y., Sadek, A.W., Qiao, C.: An integrated traffic-driving simulation framework: design, implementation, and validation. Transp. Res. Part C: Emerg. Technol. **45**, 138–153 (2014)
22. Punzo, V., Ciuffo, B.: Integration of driving and traffic simulation: issues and first solutions. IEEE Trans. Intell. Transp. Syst. **12**(2), 354–363 (2011)
23. That, T.N., Casas, J.: An integrated framework combining a traffic simulator and a driving simulator. Proc. Soc. Behav. Sci. **20**, 648–655 (2011)
24. Barceló, J., Casas, J.: Dynamic network simulation with AIMSUN. In: Kitamura, R., Kuwahara, M. (eds.) Simulation Approaches in Transportation Analysis, pp. 57–98. Springer, Boston (2005). doi:10.1007/0-387-24109-4_3
25. Aimsun: Microsimulator and Mesosimulator in Aimsun 6.1. User Manual. TSS - Transport Simulation Systems, Barcelona, Spain (2010)
26. Maroto, J., Delso, E., Felez, J., Cabanellas, J.: Real-time traffic simulation with a microscopic model. IEEE Trans. Intell. Transp. Syst. **7**(4), 513–527 (2007)
27. Davis, L.: Modifications of the optimal velocity traffic model to include delay due to driver reaction time. Phys. A **319**, 557–567 (2003)
28. Department of Transportation, U.S: NGSIM: Next Generation Simulation. http://ops.fhwa.dot.gov/trafficanalysistools/ngsim.htm. Accessed 05 Jan 2017

Ship Fire-Fighting Training System Based on Virtual Reality Technique

Rui Tao$^{(\boxtimes)}$, Hong-xiang Ren, and Xiu-quan Peng

Navigation College,
Dalian Maritime University, Dalian 116026, Liaoning, China
654992156@qq.com

Abstract. The purpose of this paper is to improve the efficiency and the level of the crew fire-fighting training and save training costs. The whole framework of fire-fighting training system is designed. Fixed water fire extinguishment system, fixed carbon dioxide extinguishment system, and fire-fighting garment model are developed via the three dimension modeling technology. The action of the virtual character is simulated with the method of Inverse Kinematics (IK) applied, which reflects the imagination of the system. The nebulization of the fire and carbon dioxide is realized with utilizing particle system, enhancing the immersion of the system. The collision detection technology improving the interaction of the system is made use of to determine whether an interaction exists between virtual character and equipment, equipment and equipment, carbon dioxide and fire. The prompt information in the process of training can be provided to assist a trainee to accomplish the training. According to the experimental results, the simulation system has a favorable training effect which can be applied to ship fire-fighting training.

Keywords: Virtual reality · Unity · Ship fire-fighting · Training

1 Introduction

The fire on ship owns particular characteristics because of the special function and structure of the ship [1]. It is necessary to conduct fire drills in order to examine the ability of the crew to respond to fire hazards in the various parts of the ship, familiarity with individual contingency tasks, and mutual support and coordination among the crew during the emergency [2]. At present, the ship fire drills are carried out in the real environment in most cases. Not only can it pollute the environment and cost much money, but also can have high risk. In addition, Owing to the obstructions and restrictions of certain factors such as time, money, and the environment, these kinds of fire drills has a limited impact.

In recent years, with the rapid development of computer virtual reality technology, the application of virtual reality in ship fire drills has drawn wide attention [3]. Gao et al. applied virtual reality technology to fire training and developed a remote fire training system [4]. Later, Jia and Wang built the simulation model of fire pump system operation process in combination of the training of fire engines [5]. In general, the simulation of the fire-fighting process above is limited to land-based virtual buildings.

© Springer Nature Singapore Pte Ltd. 2017
M.S. Mohamed Ali et al. (Eds.): AsiaSim 2017, Part II, CCIS 752, pp. 249–260, 2017.
DOI: 10.1007/978-981-10-6502-6_22

Domestic research on ship fire simulation training is still in its infancy, and some key technologies for ship fire training system simulation need to be further studied.

The virtual reality of ship fire protection is to build a virtual ship environment and fire scene with 3I (Immersion, Interactivity, Imagination) characteristics via the computer, which can make the firefighters conduct simulated training in a realistic environment to enhance the handling and decision-making capacity of the crew when complex fires break out on the ship [6]. Based on 3dsMax and Unity3D, a virtual ship fire-fighting training system is developed, which provides the simulation training function of ship fire-fighting equipment.

2   Overall Design

2.1   Function Analysis of Ship Fire Training System

Ship fire training involves two parts, the use of fire-fighting equipment and fire drill in respectively. Ship fire equipment includes fire detection and fire alarm systems, fixed fire extinguishment systems, fireman equipment and emergency communications equipment. Ship fire drill is a process of using a variety of fire-fighting equipment to extinguish the fire source in a certain procedure. General marine fire drills will be conducted in the following areas (fire sites), engine room, living area, deck area, cargo hold, painting room and so on., Even though there will be some differences in the exercise process due to the different characteristics of different regions, the process is basically the same. General steps are to find the fire and the police, to assemble and count the population, to detect fire, to put out the fire, and finally to end the drill (Fig. 1). If there is a special situation so that the fire cannot be controlled, the ship will be abandoned. Fire-fighting training system needs to complete two tasks which are the establishment and virtual operation of three-dimensional model of ship fire equipment, and the completion of the simulation of ship fire drills with the use of specific fire equipment.

2.2   System Design

In this paper, taking Panama bulk cargo ship "CSH" as the parent ship, we make the 3D model of the scene objects such as the fire control room, fire-fighting equipment, and carbon dioxide rooms in 3dsMax software. The virtual reality technology is applied to build the 3D virtual scene of the ship in which the fire drills are executed [7]. In training process, the trainee can be familiar with the layout of the fire-fighting equipment and related operation requirements.

Unity3D, a graphical environment, is a high performance development platform of 3D virtual reality, which owns friendly interface and powerful program compilation ability. Compared to other virtual reality development platform, it has its own huge benefits of multi-platform release, simple operation, rich functionality and various online resources, ensuring the system developed has a strong sense of reality. As for weaknesses of it such as non-open source and some expenses, it has little effect on the reality of system. Therefore, Unity3D is taken as the development tool of the system.

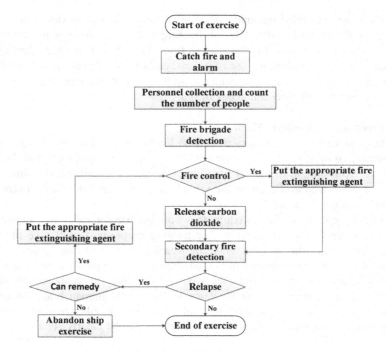

Fig. 1. Fire drill flow chart

Based on modular programming idea [8], the system is divided into different modules, including fixed water extinguishment system module, fixed carbon dioxide extinguishment system module, fireman equipment module, and so on. The functional design of each module is as follows.

2.2.1 Fixed Water Extinguishment System Module

Fixed water fire extinguishment system is the most basic and effective extinguishment systems that all ships must be equipped with. In order to increase the system immersion and be closer to the real scene, three-dimensional model of fire hose, fire hydrant and fire-fighting pipe should be realistic enough. In the use of water extinguishment system for fire-fighting training, we mainly study the familiarity of the trainees with device and the ability of collaboration. Participants as virtual identities log into the system, and the other role is replaced by the virtual robot. Students can communicate with virtual crew by clicking the command buttons on the interface to complete collaborative training. Specific training includes the use of guns, laying and recycling of the fire hose, the use of hydrants and so on.

2.2.2 Fixed Carbon Dioxide Extinguishment System Module

The ship fixed carbon dioxide extinguishment system is composed of carbon dioxide cylinder, control system, fire-fighting pipeline and injection device. Among them, the first two are placed in the carbon dioxide room. The opening of carbon dioxide cylinders can be controlled manually or automatically. Carbon dioxide is released by manipulating the control valve. The fire-fighting system needs regular maintenance, and makes blowing test to ensure the smooth flow of pipeline. During the development of simulation training system, the use of internal carbon dioxide equipment and the real effect of carbon dioxide vent are considered. In this way, it can meet the requirements of the blowing test and meet the needs of daily use.

2.2.3   Fireman Equipment Module

Firefighter equipment is a necessary protection for the personal safety of fire detectors. As a detector, he must be very familiar with the wearing of equipment and the use of precautions. According to the actual situation of the ship, the firefighter equipment will be placed in the fire control room in the virtual scene. Students should be aware of the firefighter's storage location.

After taking out the firefighter equipment from the fire control room, trainees wear them in the correct order of wearing. For training purposes, it will give the wrong operating tips to warn the students when the wearing order is obviously unreasonable. Each part of the fireman's equipment is made into a separate module, including a total of 12 parts. Trainees in a third character point of view drag the equipment through the mouse so that the equipment can be worn in the virtual human body. In order to facilitate trainees to select equipment, the equipment will be enlarged when the mouse moves to specific equipment and the specific details can be clearly seen.

3   Key Technology

3.1   Inverse Kinematics

Most of the character animations are created by rotating the joint angles of bones to a predetermined value. A joint position is determined by the rotation angle of the parent node. Thus, the node position at the end of the node chain is determined by the rotation angle and the relative displacement of each node on the chain. This method of determining the position of bone is called forward dynamics [9]. However, the inverse process of the above process is very practical in the practical application. That is to say, the location of the end node is given, and the reasonable position of all the other nodes in the node chain is deduced [10]. This demand is very common. For example, when the character's arm is to touch a fixed object or foot on an uneven surface, this method will be used. This method is called the inverse kinematics (IK). In this paper, the simulation of virtual human motion adopts the inverse kinematics.

3.2   Particle System

In the virtual environment, most of the scene elements, such as roles, objects, and collision objects and so on, belong to the grid model (mesh). These are made by 3DS Max, Maya tools and imported into the scene. However, in order to simulate the effect of smoke, flame, cloud, droplets of water in the scene, it needs to use the particle system. The particle system will transmit a large number of simple particles in a continuous and efficient manner to simulate various complex natural phenomena and special effects.

The simulation process of particles is divided into the following steps [11].

(1) Initialization. It needs to determine the simulation object, analyze the movement law of objects and set the initial value for the simulation of the number of particles, each particle value of life, location, speed, acceleration, color and other information.

(2) Drawing. It needs to select the appropriate size of texture and match the appropriate color, to draw the state of current particle.

(3) Update. The life cycle, position, velocity, acceleration, color and other information of all particles are updated for the next rendering.

3.3 Collision Detection

Objects in the scene must be given colliders if they need to sense a collision. The Unity engine provides five types of colliders for objects, the Box Collider, the Sphere Collider, the Capsule Collider, the Mesh Collider and the Wheel Collider included. According to the characteristics of the object shape to select the collider, it can reduce the amount of calculation of the computer and improve the system fluency. Collision can be divided into two categories which is the collision between objects and objects, the collision between particles and objects. Collision detection algorithm between the bounding box and the bounding box is used to detect the collision between the object and the object. The common method includes: axis-aligned bounding box (AABB) method, oriented bounding box (OBB) method and sphere bounding method. Collision detection algorithm between the point and the bounding box is used to detect the collision between the particle and the object.

4 System Implementation

4.1 Scene Development

4.1.1 Production of Three Dimensional Model

The 3D model of fire-fighting equipment is established in 3D max, which is the foundation of this paper. According to the actual proportion of fire-fighting equipment and the effect of real equipment, we product the white model and texture. After rendering the final three-dimensional model, we import them into the scene of whole ship for the interaction of equipment. Figure 2 is the effect chart of whole ship scene.

4.1.2 Development of UI

We need to meet the following needs for fire training: multiple assist in operation, the demand to observe from a different view in the process of operation, select the location of the fire. Therefore, we complete the above functions through the UI of the three modules which is the module of auxiliary view window, the module of auxiliary

Fig. 2. Entire ship

command menu, the module of environment setting in respectively in the ship platform, as is shown in Fig. 3.

The module of auxiliary view window: The window is located in the upper right corner of the main interface, and uses a different camera with the UI system. In fire training, it provides students with an optimal overlooking view. There are other small windows in this position, which are mutually exclusive in the process of using these small windows. The windows are activated by the corresponding item in the upper left corner of the main interface.

The module of auxiliary command menu: Its position is the same as the module of auxiliary view window' position. In the training of multiple persons, the action of virtual person is completed by clicking on the auxiliary command menu button. The number of auxiliary command buttons of different training subjects is different. For the fixed water extinguishment system training, it includes twelve auxiliary commands, which lined up in the left top of the screen in vertical direction.

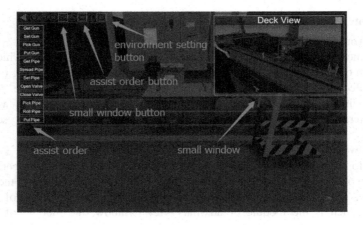

Fig. 3. UI layout

The module of environment setting: The module is set in the main menu of the interface. The module is used to set the fire position and initialize flame and smoke, the development trend of the fire, etc. The entire interface is implemented by UGUI which are redesigned by Unity.

4.2 Production of Fixed Water Extinguishment System Module

4.2.1 Implementation Process

The interaction of this part is mainly two parts, which are simulation that the trainee (first-person perspective) and the virtual crew operate the device.

Trainees operate the device in the manner of clicking on the device with a mouse in the first-person perspective. To get the click event, it needs to add a script to the object. The script is used to define the behavior of the user in the game. The prepared script is dragged on the object which needs to implement this behavior. When the program is running, the object will move according to the rules that the script edits. To the end, it achieves a variety of simulation of the operation to equipment. When the wrong operation happens, the system will give the corresponding tips.

4.2.2 Simulation of Key Action

The simulation to the action that trainees operate the fire hoses and hydrant is the core that ensures the training real and effective. In order to simulate the complex motion of virtual human in a virtual reality system, the motion model of virtual human must be established. According to the principle of inverse kinematics, the movement of virtual human is regarded as a joint motion, and the articulation model is established for the virtual human. The clavicle, shoulder, elbow and palm are regarded as interrelated and joint objects. Each joint has a father-son relationship, a parent joint has multiple sub-joints, a sub-joint has only one parent joint. The tree structure is used to express the hierarchical structure of virtual human motion model, as is shown in Fig. 4.

Fig. 4. Hierarchy of virtual human's joint

4.2.3   Case Analysis

We take the action that trainees operate the fire hydrant as an example to illustrate the case. At first, we create a "hand controller" in the scene - empty object of left hand. The position of the "hand controller" is controlled by scripts each frame so that it moves from the hand position to the optimum position of installation. Then, the computer calculates the rotation angle of the elbow and shoulder from the theory of inverse kinematics in the process of hand movement. Finally, the simulation of action is completed when the hand moves to the end point. Fixed water extinguishment system training in the actual environment is completed by two persons. When the trainee needs support of virtual crew, he can click on the command button on the interface to work with it. The enlarged effect of the upper right corner of the small window is shown in Fig. 6.

Fig. 5. Training of fixed water extinguishment system

Fig. 6. Magnifying display of small window

4.3   Production of Fixed Carbon Dioxide Extinguishment System Module

Difficulties in the training of fixed carbon dioxide fire extinguishment system are simulation to the atomization effect of carbon dioxide and flame particle, and the collision detection between them.

The flame is divided into three parts: inner flame, outer flame and smoke. We create three 'Particle Systems' in the scene to simulate the effect of these three parts respectively. In the microscopic we change the specific effects of the three parts by adjusting the number of particles, particle size and color and other characteristics firstly. Then, in the macroscopic, we display the overall effect of the flame by making texture in Photoshop. Finally, we achieve the dynamic simulation of the flame by adjusting the life cycle, speed and other information of particles. The above three steps are combined together to make the simulation effect of the flame more realistic. Similar to the simulation of flame, the carbon dioxide will not be repeated here.

The collision detection between carbon dioxide and flame is to judge whether the carbon dioxide particles are in the bounding box of flame. A collision occurs when the carbon dioxide enters the rectangular bounding box of the flame particles. With the continuous entry of carbon dioxide particles, we calculate the number of carbon dioxide particles which enter the rectangular bounding box. At this time, the particles produced by the flame particle source will gradually decrease, and then the size of the flame will be controlled. After a period of time, the flame will go out. The effect of cargo hold extinguishment is shown in Fig. 7.

Fig. 7. Cargo hold extinguishment

4.4   Production of Fire Man Equipment Module

We simulate the process of wearing actually, based on the order that fire man wear the firefighter protective clothing. And students can control the process of wearing. The concrete realization process is as follows.

In order to achieve the effect that equipment is dragged by mouse, we add collision to each equipment to detect the mouse. Then we obtain the mouse cursor position in the three-dimensional space through Unity's built-in function - ScreenToWorldPoint (). The obtained position is the position of the dragged equipment in the three-dimensional space. In the process of dragging, we assign the position to the dragged equipment each frame to achieve the dragging effect.

The technology of ray detection is used to achieve the effect of wearing. We use the technology of ray detection to determine whether the clothing has been dragged to the specific parts of virtual human body. If the clothing is dragged to a specific position, the clothing will highlight and prompt the operator. At this time, the operator can release the mouse to complete the wearing. The dragging effect is shown in Fig. 8, and the wearing effect is shown in Fig. 9.

Fig. 8. Drag the fire-fighting garments

Fig. 9. Wear the fire-fighting garments

4.5   Examples of Fire Drills

In the case of cargo fire drills, we set the initial fire location to 1 cabin, fire time, fire size (as is shown in Fig. 10) and so on in the environment setting module of the main scene.

The smoke detection panel issues an alarm. And then the duty officer issues the whole ship alarm. The relevant persons begin to conduct the fire drills according to the process of Fig. 1. During the process, the fire detector wear fire man's outfit (Fig. 9). The hose group uses the fixed water extinguishment system to cool the cargo bulkhead (Fig. 5). After finishing the wearing, the fire detector detects the fire, founding the fire uncontrollable. Then the duty officer turns off the ventilation system and power. The carbon dioxide in CO_2 room is released and the fire-fighting effect is shown in Fig. 7. In the second fire detection, the detector determines whether there is the possibility of fire relapse or not. If recovery is possible, remedial action should be taken. The detector detects the fire again, and the hose group continues to cool the cargo bulkhead. When the combustion area and intensity in the cargo compartment are relatively low, the hose group can inject water into the combustion area at the cargo hatchway firstly. Then the hose group can inject water from the hatch to the interior until the fire becomes weakened, using the fixed ladder in the cargo and the lifting bucket of the ship or dock. If the fire is large, the detector should withdraw from the hatch, continue to inject carbon dioxide and close the cargo. The process is repeated until the fire is completely extinguished. Then the exercise is over.

Fig. 10. Fire of cargo hold

5 Conclusion

The simulation training system of fire drill is realized with the virtual reality technology applied in the field of ship firefighting,which can reduce the training costs, protect the crew safety effectively and conduct the relatively-free training that is no longer limited by space and time. The development process of the system is illustrated by scene development, module implementation, and fire drill examples. From the whole and the part, we demonstrate how to develop the training system of ship fire-fighting by applying virtual reality technology, providing an important guiding significance in further research on virtual training of other equipment.

The following areas can be carried out in the follow-up research process, which are multi-computer networking for multi-person fire drill exercises, simulation of fire spreading, and intelligent evaluation procedures for each training.

Acknowledgements. This work is supported by the National High Technology Research and Development Program of China (863 Program, No. 2015AA010504), and the Science and Technology Planning Project of Ministry of Transport (No. 2015329225240).

References

1. Chang, Z.-X.: Study of VR Technology Applied in the Processing of Ship Cabin. Dalian Maritime University, Dalian (2015)
2. Dalian Maritime University: Advanced Fire-fighting. Press of Dalian Maritime University, Dalian (2008)
3. Jiang, X.-P.: Development and Design of Virtual Training System for Fire Engine. Chinese Ocean University, Qingdao (2014)
4. Gao, Y.-Z., Cao, S.-F., Liang, H.-W.: Research on the application of virtual reality technology in fire training. In: Proceedings of China Annual Fire Association Science and Technology, pp. 382–384 (2014)
5. Jia, L.-S., Wang, L.-W.: Construction of real-time simulation model of fire fighting pump system of airport fire engine. J. Syst. Simul. **27**(6), 1209–1213 (2015)
6. Tate, D.L., Sibert, L., King, T.: Virtual environments for shipboard fire-fighting training. In: Proceedings of IEEE 1997, Virtual Reality Annual International Symposium, pp. 61–68 (1997)
7. Jiang, D.-Z., Yao, W.-L., Zhang, J.-D.: Development of engine room resource management simulator based on Unity3D. J. Navig. China **38**(3), 13–17 (2015)
8. Chen, J.-B., Shi, C.-J., Chen, X.-Z., et al.: Integrated smiulator training system for ship command. J. Shanghai Marit. Univ. **28**(1), 150–155 (2007)
9. Wu, B., Huang, Z.-Z., Guo, X.-F., et al.: Unity4.x from Entry to Proficient. Press of China Railway, Beijing (2013)
10. Li, C.-X., Liu, F., Wang, Z.-Q., et al.: Applying IK solvers to realizing 3D simulation of beam pumping movements. J. Yangtze Univ. **2**(4), 89–91 (2007)
11. Li, Q.-C., Yang, G.-B., Wang, X.-J.: Particle system based fireworks modeling and its algorithm simulation. J. Syst. Simul. **21**(8), 2179–2184 (2009)

Dynamic Modelling for High Pressure CO_2 Absorption from Natural Gas

Faezah Isa, Haslinda Zabiri$^{(\boxtimes)}$, Salvinder Kaur Marik Singh, and Azmi M. Shariff

Department of Chemical Engineering,
Research Centre for CO_2 Capture (RCCO2C),
Universiti Teknologi PETRONAS, 32610 Bandar Seri Iskandar, Perak, Malaysia
haslindazabiri@utp.edu.my

Abstract. This paper reports the dynamic simulation model of high content CO_2 from natural gas at elevated pressure. The common process of CO_2 modelling are mostly reported in steady state condition at atmospheric pressure. However, disturbances such as startup, shut down, and temperature rise might occur during the absorption process. Therefore, the dynamic study has been conducted in this paper via equilibrium approach with some adjustments to observe the efficiency of CO_2 removal at the top of the column. Input data for the simulation had been acquired from the pilot plant in Universiti Teknologi PETRONAS (UTP). Aspen Dynamic simulator is not able to support the rate based approach and therefore, several adjustments such as the number of stages and Murphree efficiency need to be imposed on the equilibrium stage model to produce similar result as the pilot plant and as well as rate based approach. The error percentage of CO_2 removal observed between actual plant and simulation using equilibrium based approach is less than 5% with several adjustment implemented in the simulator. The results show that the equilibrium approach with some adjustments is able to replicate the pilot plant under dynamic conditions. In dynamic study, the lean solvent flowrate is varied to study the performance of CO_2 removal and it is observed the higher solvent lean solvent flowrate improves the efficiency of CO_2 removal.

Keywords: Dynamic model · High pressure · Natural gas

1 Introduction

Natural gas (NG) that consists primarily of methane (CH_4) is considered as the cleanest fossil fuel with high energy conversion and crucial for commodity as power of electricity, transportation, heating energy and chemical feedstock [1]. As high-quality NG reservoirs depleted due to high demand of NG, this has open up the exploration of alternatives resources including the untapped and undeveloped reservoirs. The development of such a CO_2-rich type of gas resources poses significant challenges in the sour gas treatment industry due to bulk CO_2 contaminants, aging facilities, and raw natural gas pressure is extremely high which up to 200 bar [2]. The influence of pressure on both the thermodynamics as well as the hydrodynamics and mass transfer

© Springer Nature Singapore Pte Ltd. 2017
M.S. Mohamed Ali et al. (Eds.): AsiaSim 2017, Part II, CCIS 752, pp. 261–271, 2017.
DOI: 10.1007/978-981-10-6502-6_23

aspects in absorption system for CO_2 removal is tremendous. It should be highlighted that earlier studies have shown that information obtained at atmospheric pressure could not be directly used to represent the same condition at elevated pressure [3–5].

High CO_2 content in gas fields in Malaysia is an important challenge for CO_2 capture and storage (CCS). Chemical absorption via amine solutions, e.g. MEA, is the most frequently used technologies for CO_2 removal in the natural gas industry and power plant flue gases [6]. Although pilot plant trials have provided data and demonstration for CO_2 capture, there remained critical issues that need to be resolved. First, how to control the overall of CO_2 removal operated at elevated pressure and how the performance of the absorption rate during the transient condition. Thus, a proper simulation model is required for assessing various operating condition and disturbances. Besides, the essential of simulation cannot be neglected as it provides process alternatives, assess feasibility and preliminary economic. Moreover, simulation also offers the interpretation of pilot plant data, increase yield and improve pollution control [7]. Another point to ponder, most of the simulations program are often based on low pressure experimental data and simple empirical models. Therefore, the capability of such models to higher operation pressures is questionable.

The work by Fitz et al. [8] demonstrated that distillation process at elevated pressure for packed column exhibits different separation efficiency behaviors from those under lower pressures. The experimental work has been executed in the pressure range between 2–27.6 bar and the observation has been conducted on the mass transfer zone. Another finding indicates that high pressure will also influence effective interfacial area and volumetric mass transfer coefficient but the results are sometimes contradictory [3, 4, 9]. Due to the effect of high pressure, Zhang et al. [5] has introduced high-pressure modification factor called as index f. It represents the complexity of pressure on the surface disturbance due to hydraulic and mass transfer phenomena resulting from temperature and concentration difference between the surface and the bulk liquid. This phenomenon is called Marangoni effect.

To understand the operational characteristic and identifying any operational bottlenecks at transient condition that may arise, dynamic simulation and analysis is very important. Although, there is a number of dynamic studies available in literature [10–12] but mostly they are only demonstrated for CO_2 capture for post-combustion process. Besides, the validation for those campaigns are also difficult due to lack of plant data and mostly validated only at steady state conditions. Typically, CO_2 removal via chemical absorption has been modeled and simulated using well known equilibrium stage model where the absorber is divided into a few stages based on the height equivalent to a theoretical plate (HETP) but this method is inadequate because chemical absorption is strongly non-ideal and it is a rate controlled phenomenon. Hence, a better estimation using a rate based approach is introduced by considering the influence of chemical reaction on mass transfer using enhancement factors [13].

This method is more suitable for the reactive process such as CO_2 absorption in MEA. In rate-based approach, the vapor–liquid equilibrium (VLE) is assumed to occur at the phase interface. The mass transfer between the vapor and liquid phases is modeled based on the two-film theory and the Maxwell-Stefan formulation. The rate-based approach is more rigorous, but the accuracy of the calculation is higher than equilibrium rate [14]. The liquid film thickness is one of the influencing parameters in the rate based model and generally estimated via empirical mass transfer correlations. Various factors will be considered such as type of column, hydraulics and transport properties [15, 16]. It has direct connection from the column internal and the concept is illustrated in Fig. 1. However, this approach is more complex and it is not supported by certain simulators such as Aspen Dynamic for transient analysis and control studies.

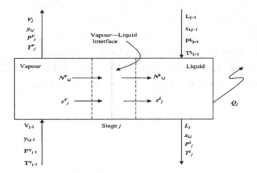

Fig. 1. Schematic diagram of mass transfer model based on the two-film theory. Adopted from Mac Dowell et al. [18].

Certainly, wide models and simulators in recent years have allowed the process performance to be simulated and predicted within a relatively short time without the necessity to define the complex mathematical equations. Nevertheless, the process is not a straightforward task since it demands a considerable amount of trial and error method. In order to investigate the transient performance of the CO_2 removal from natural gas at elevated pressure, experimental work has been conducted using synthetic natural gas at high pressure pilot plant located in Universiti Teknologi PETRONAS. In this paper, the experimental data from the pilot plant has been used as input for simulation and validated. Aspen Plus V8.0 has been employed as platform for the simulator and the transient condition had been simulated in Aspen Dynamic V8.0.

Due to inability of Aspen Dynamic to support rate based approach, equilibrium method has been employed but a few modifications have been made to ensure a similar result is achieved. To compensate for the deviations of these two modelling approaches, the present study adopted similar technique as presented in Trapp et al. and He and Ricardez-Sandoval [12, 17].

2 Methodology

2.1 Pilot Plant Setup

Figure 2 presents the experimental setup for CO_2 removal at elevated pressure. This pilot plant consists of two types of columns which are structured and random packing but in this study only structured packing is utilized. Structured packing had been selected since it provides a lower pressure drop per theoretical stage and the capacity is improved compared to trays or random type packing. Initially, CO_2 and CH_4 will be mixed in static mixer at a ratio 1:1 to imitate sour gas condition. Then, it will be compressed into packed column until it reaches 50 bar. Back pressure regulator is installed to control the pressure in the column regularly. Solvent solution is prepared in the solvent tank and sent up to the top of the column using high pressure pump. The absorption process is initiated by setting the percentage opening of high pressure pump for liquid solvent and countercurrent absorption process takes place in the absorber. The steady state absorption is usually achieved after 45 min up to 1 h. The column is operated at 50% to 75% of flooding which is typical condition for gas absorber. The reading of CO_2 percentage is observed through Infrared (IR) gas analyzer model ZRJF4Y25 (Fuji Electric Instrument) installed at the outlet line. The rich solvent that contains CO_2 is cooled down and delivered to the storage tank.

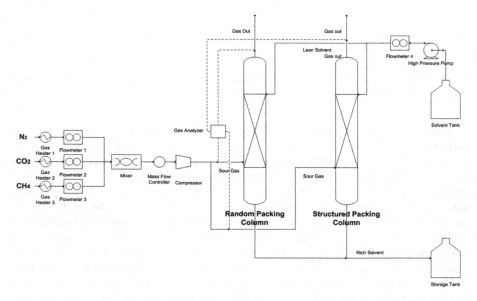

Fig. 2. The schematic diagram of UTP Carbon Hydrogen Absorption System (CHAS) high pressure pilot plant

2.2   Simulation of Steady State Absorption

Aspen Plus V8 has been selected as the platform to simulate CO_2 removal at high operating pressure of 50 bar. The selected fluid package is Electrolyte NRTL (ELECNRTL) as it is widely used to describe the liquid phase non-ideality with electrolyte. Since the simulation has been performed at elevated pressure, Poynting correction has been selected for pressure correction to the pure component liquid fugacity coefficient. In simulation environment, RadFrac column has been chosen to simulate the absorption process of packed column and both the available approaches which are equilibrium and rate based had been studied. In order to simulate the steady state condition, the present model follows the following assumptions [19]:

- Countercurrent with well mixed between vapor and liquid.
- The vaporization of solvent is negligible.
- The heat release to surrounding is very small.
- The heat and mass transfer between phases follow the two-film theory.

In rate based approach, more inputs need to be specified such as mass transfer coefficient, heat transfer correlation, effective interfacial area and flow model. Thus, correlation of Bravo has been selected due to suitability of correlation with structured packed column. The default heat transfer correlation value 1 is used while the flow model is counter current. Film non-ideality correction for liquid has been selected and effective interfacial area factor has been maintained at 1. In the convergence section, strongly non-ideal liquid has been chosen due to the use of MEA and high operating pressure. Four basic components are inserted which comprises of MEA, CO$_2$, H$_2$O and CH$_4$ and the other conventional components are extracted from the electrolyte wizard application in Component section. Eqs. 1–5 show the chemical reactions of CO$_2$ and MEA solvent [17, 20]:

Water Ionization

$$2H_2O \leftrightarrow H_3O^+ + OH^- \tag{1}$$

Dissociation of Bicarbonate

$$H_2O + HCO_3^- \leftrightarrow CO_3^{-2} + H_3O^+ \tag{2}$$

Hydrolysis and Dissolved CO$_2$ Ionization

$$2H_2O + CO_2 \leftrightarrow HCO_3^- + H_3O^+ \tag{3}$$

Carbamate Reversion to Bicarbonate

$$H_2O + MEACOO^- \leftrightarrow MEA + HCO_3^- \tag{4}$$

MEAH$^+$ Dissociation

$$H_2O + MEAH^+ \leftrightarrow MEA + H_3O^+ \tag{5}$$

Input of steady state simulations has been acquired from UTP pilot plant and the main aim is to ensure the agreement between CO$_2$ removal of actual plant and simulation. A comparative analysis based on column profile and CO$_2$ removal has been carried out before entering the dynamic simulation. Table 1 shows the nominal operating condition for steady state simulation in this study.

Table 1. Operating conditions for steady state simulation

Operating condition	Inlet data
Sour gas	
1. CO_2	0.5 mol
2. CH_4	0.5 mol
Lean solvent	
1. H_2O	0.8 mol
2. MEA	0.2 mol
Flowrate	
(1) Sour gas	50 l/min
(2) Lean solvent	4.7 l/min
Temperature	
(1) Sour gas	31.0° C
(2) Lean solvent	30.0 °C
Pressure	
(1) Sour gas	50 bar
(2) Lean solvent	50 bar

2.3   Entering Dynamic Simulation

In order to export the steady state result into the dynamic simulation, the equilibrium method has been adopted with a few modifications which comprise of the number of stages and Murphree efficiency. The Murphree tray efficiency has been used for a long time to relate the theoretical number of stages with the actual trays in an absorber. This efficiency can be based upon the liquid or the vapor composition on a particular stage at certain conditions of temperature and pressure [21]. The definition of Murphree efficiency based on gas phase mole fraction is illustrated in Fig. 3.

$$EM = \frac{(y - y^{n-1})}{(y* - y^{n-1})} \tag{6}$$

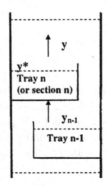

Fig. 3. Illustration of Mole Fraction for The Definition of Murphree Efficiency [16]

where
> n is stage number
> y is the mole fraction of CO_2 in the gas leaving the stage,
> y^{n-1} is the mole fraction leaving the stage below,
> y* is the mole fraction CO_2 in equilibrium with the liquid leaving the stage.

Then, additional equipment sizing need to be specified such as vessel geometry and vessel type. For dynamic analysis, two modes of simulation either pressure driven or flow driven need to be selected and in this study flow driven is selected since it more suitable for good flow controllability. This is also useful for first approach of dynamic behavior of the process. In Aspen Dynamic simulation environment, two types of controller are automatically installed which are the pressure controller and level controller.

3   Results and Discussion

The simulation results of CO_2 absorption operated at high pressure was compared with the actual data from pilot plant for steady state condition. Both equilibrium and rate based approaches have been applied in Aspen Plus V8 simulator to observe CO_2 removal percentage in sweet gas line. Table 2 shows the CO_2 removal percentage between pilot plant and the simulation result. It can be observed that the performance of rate based approach produces a better outcome even though there is a slight over estimation. The deviation of result from actual data is less than 5%. The result is expected as rate based approach has a higher accuracy in the formulation of reactive system such as CO_2 and MEA since it takes into account many aspects such as mass transfer and effective interfacial area factor.

Table 2. The removal percentage of actual pilot plant and simulation

	Removal of CO_2 (%)
Experimental	85.0
Equilibrium based	60.6
Rate based	89.75

The equilibrium approach produces a large deviation where the removal percentage observed is only 60%. The accumulated average error from the actual pilot plant is about 38% and such result is expected as equilibrium approach assume perfect mixing occurs in all stages. Nevertheless, even though equilibrium stage model is inadequate to replicate the highly non-ideal absorption system, the mathematical formulation is simpler and in this study, the equilibrium approach is used to study the transient condition at elevated pressure in the dynamic simulation model. Besides, Aspen Dynamic simulator is not able to support the rate based approach and therefore, several adjustments need to be imposed on the equilibrium stage model to produce similar result as the pilot plant and as well as rate based approach [17]. This step is also important to achieve a stable steady state condition for transient analysis in Aspen Dynamic.

3.1 Re-adjustment in Murphree Efficiencies and Number of Stages

Based on the previous result, a few parameters have been adjusted in the simulation model especially the number of stages and Murphree efficiency. In structured packed columns, mass transfer efficiency is related to the vapor and liquid mass transfer between both phases. The most common technique to estimate the height of a packed column related to separation efficiency is defined by:

$$\text{Height} = \text{number of stages} \times \text{height equivalent to theoretical plate (HETP)}$$

Unfortunately, there are only a few generalize methods available in the open literature for estimating the HETP and most of the methods are empirical and supported by the vendor's advice [22]. According to the vendor, Koch Glitsch estimated HETP for structured column of Flexipac type 1Y is about 0.21 m and dividing the height of column to HETP, the estimated number of stages is 5. It is also a rule of thumb in designing the height of packed column that 4 m in height equal to 20 stages. However, the initial setting for number of stages produced a large deviation in the equilibrium approach, hence this parameter is tuned to achieve a similar result as in the rate based approach or the pilot plant data.

It is a good practice to start the simulation with small number of stages and vary the number of stages until the desirable result is achieved. It is well acknowledged that number of stages play an important role in the stability of the numerical solution. A large number of stages associated with fast reaction such as MEA can cause difficulty in convergence [23] and this has restricted the maximum number of stages to 8. Figure 4 presents CO_2 profile against the number of stages of the packed column where stage 1 represents the top of the column while stage 7 represents the bottom. CO_2 removal is calculated by dividing the difference between the mole fraction of CO_2 in the sour gas and sweet gas stream with the mole fraction of CO_2 in the sour gas stream. Almost 82% removal of CO_2 is recorded when the number of stages is varied to 7.

Another approach to compensate the deviation between equilibrium and rate based approach is by tuning the Murphree efficiency value. For each section of the packed column in the rate based mode in Aspen Plus, RadFrac calculates the fractional approach to equilibrium using the same definition as used for Murphree efficiency. This reports the height of packing required to achieve equilibrium between the vapor and liquid phase which is similar to the Height Equivalent to a Theoretical Plate (HETP) for that section. However, the adjustment of Murphree efficiency does not have significant changes for the CO_2 removal at high pressure. Thus, with the adjustment of number of stages and slight changes in the operating parameters, the simulation is converged and exported to Aspen Dynamic simulation for transient analysis.

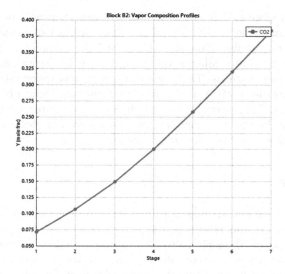

Fig. 4. CO_2 composition profile versus the column height

3.2 Dynamic Performance at the Variation of Lean Solvent Flowrate

In order to improve the removal efficiency of CO_2 at the sweetgas stream, the amount of lean solvent need to be increased. During the process simulation, after constant output of the CO_2 composition in the sweetgas stream is observed, +10% step change has been imposed in the lean solvent flowrate. Initially, at time 0 to 2 h of operation, the CO_2 composition is constant at 0.8 kmol/kmol in sweet gas stream. Once the flowrate of lean solvent is increased, CO_2 composition drops instantaneously. This

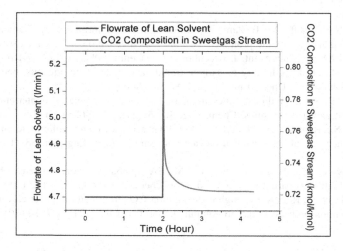

Fig. 5. CO_2 composition of +10% lean solvent flowrate

result is expected since L/G is one of the most important factors in CO_2 absorption because the present of more active site of chemical solvent will enhance the chemical reaction, thus improves the removal of CO_2. Blue line represents the lean solvent flowrate into the absorption column whereas the green line represents the CO_2 composition in the sweetgas stream. This result deduces the absorption rate will increase in absorber as the amount of MEA used is increased since the contact between the vapor and liquid phase is improved. This result shows that dynamic simulation can successfully simulate the transient condition of CO_2 removal at elevated pressure using equilibrium based approach via few re-adjustments (Fig. 5).

4   Conclusion

This project studied the modelling and dynamic of a high-pressure novel pilot scale absorption packed column processing natural gas stream with high pressure using Aspen Plus and Aspen Dynamic software. Aqueous solutions of monoethanolamine (MEA) is used to capture CO_2 from natural gas at elevated pressure by absorption. The simulation of steady state has been established and several re-adjustments have been added in steady state environment to match the equilibrium and rate based model performance before the simulation for dynamic state can be established. The results show that the equilibrium approach with some adjustments is able to replicate the pilot plant under dynamic conditions.

Acknowledgement. The authors would like to acknowledge the funding received from YUTP (0153AA-E09) grant which enabled the completion of this work. The authors are also grateful to Universiti Teknologi PETRONAS and Research Centre of CO_2 Capture for their guidance and support.

References

1. Hairul, N., Shariff, A., Bustam, M.: Mass transfer performance of 2-amino-2-methyl-1-propanol and piperazine promoted 2-amino-2-methyl-1-propanol blended solvent in high pressure CO_2 absorption. Int. J. Greenhouse Gas Control **49**, 121–127 (2016)
2. Addicks, J., et al.: Solubility of carbon dioxide and methane in aqueous methyldiethanolamine solutions. J. Chem. Eng. Data **47**(4), 855–860 (2002)
3. Benadda, B., et al.: Hydrodynamics and mass transfer phenomena in counter-current packed column at elevated pressures. Chem. Eng. Sci. **55**(24), 6251–6257 (2000)
4. Maalej, S., Benadda, B., Otterbein, M.: Interfacial area and volumetric mass transfer coefficient in a bubble reactor at elevated pressures. Chem. Eng. Sci. **58**(11), 2365–2376 (2003)
5. Zhang, X., et al.: Absorption rate into a MDEA aqueous solution blended with piperazine under a high CO_2 partial pressure. Ind. Eng. Chem. Res. **42**(1), 118–122 (2003)
6. Tan, L.S., et al.: Removal of high concentration CO_2 from natural gas at elevated pressure via absorption process in packed column. J. Nat. Gas Chem. **21**(1), 7–10 (2012)

7. Kvamsdal, H., Jakobsen, J., Hoff, K.: Dynamic modeling and simulation of a CO_2 absorber column for post-combustion CO_2 capture. Chem. Eng. Process.: Process Intensif. **48**(1), 135–144 (2009)

8. Fitz, C.W., Kunesh, J.G., Shariat, A.: Performance of structured packing in a commercial-scale column at pressures of 0.02–27.6 bar. Ind. Eng. Chem. Res. **38**(2), 512–518 (1999)

9. Kojima, H., Sawai, J., Suzuki, H.: Effect of pressure on volumetric mass transfer coefficient and gas holdup in bubble column. Chem. Eng. Sci. **52**(21), 4111–4116 (1997)

10. Chikukwa, A., et al.: Dynamic modeling of post-combustion CO_2 capture using amines–a review. Energy Procedia **23**, 82–91 (2012)

11. Lawal, A., et al.: Dynamic modeling and simulation of CO_2 chemical absorption process for coal-fired power plants. Comput. Aided Chem. Eng. **27**, 1725–1730 (2009)

12. Trapp, C., et al.: Dynamic modelling and validation of pre-combustion CO_2 absorption based on a pilot plant at the Buggenum IGCC power station. Int. J. Greenhouse Gas Control **36**, 13–26 (2015)

13. Mores, P., Scenna, N., Mussati, S.: A rate based model of a packed column for CO_2 absorption using aqueous monoethanolamine solution. Int. J. Greenhouse Gas Control **6**, 21–36 (2012)

14. Bui, M., et al.: Dynamic modelling and optimisation of flexible operation in post-combustion CO_2 capture plants—A review. Comput. Chem. Eng. **61**, 245–265 (2014)

15. Biliyok, C., et al.: Dynamic modelling, validation and analysis of post-combustion chemical absorption CO_2 capture plant. Int. J. Greenhouse Gas Control **9**, 428–445 (2012)

16. Lawal, A., et al.: Demonstrating full-scale post-combustion CO_2 capture for coal-fired power plants through dynamic modelling and simulation. Fuel **101**, 115–128 (2012)

17. He, Z., Ricardez-Sandoval, L.A.: Dynamic modelling of a commercial-scale CO_2 capture plant integrated with a natural gas combined cycle (NGCC) power plant. Int. J. Greenhouse Gas Control **55**, 23–35 (2016)

18. Mac Dowell, N., Samsatli, N.J., Shah, N.: Dynamic modelling and analysis of an amine-based post-combustion CO_2 capture absorption column. Int J. Greenhouse Gas Control **12**, 247–258 (2013)

19. Cormos, A.-M., Gaspar, J.: Assessment of mass transfer and hydraulic aspects of CO_2 absorption in packed columns. Int. J. Greenhouse Gas Control **6**, 201–209 (2012)

20. Liu, Y., Zhang, L., Watanasiri, S.: Representing vapor – liquid equilibrium for an aqueous MEA – CO_2 system using the electrolyte nonrandom-two-liquid model. Ind. Eng. Chem. Res. **38**(5), 2080–2090 (1999)

21. Queiroz, J.A., et al.: Modeling of existing cooling towers in ASPEN PLUS using an equilibrium stage method. Energy Convers. Manag. **64**, 473–481 (2012)

22. Mendes, M.F.: HETP evaluation of structured and randomic packing distillation column. INTECH Open Access Publisher (2011)

23. Fan, Z., et al.: Aspen modeling for MEA–CO_2 loop: dynamic gridding for accurate column profile. Int. J. Greenhouse Gas Control **37**, 318–324 (2015)

WESS: A Generic Combat Effectiveness Simulation System

Yonglin Lei[✉], Zhi Zhu, Qun Li, Feng Yang, and Yifan Zhu

College of Information System and Management,
National University of Defense Technology,
Changsha 410073, People's Republic of China
{yllei,zhuzhi,liqun,forestyoung,yfzhu}@nudt.edu.cn

Abstract. Combat Systems Effectiveness Simulation (CESS) is an important supportive means to combat systems analysis and conceptual design. Traditional approaches in developing CESS systems fall into two general categories. One is to apply generic simulation formalisms and platforms to build simulation applications each specific to a set of concrete application requirements. The other is to focus on a certain combat system domain for which a dedicated simulation system is developed. When confronted with non-functional issues like model reusability, simulation composability, and system evolvability, both find their limitations. Based on years experiences in CESS field and best practices found in overseas CESS systems, the model architecture is believed to be the key to develop CESS systems. In this paper, a model architecture-based generic CESS system, named WESS, is introduced. The design rationale, software architecture, application processes, and key aspects of WESS are briefed. A typical case study is given to demonstrate the functionalities of WESS. Practical applications tell WESS is able to help modelers to achieve those aims important to CESS including reusability, composability, and evolvability.

Keywords: Effectiveness Simulation · Model architecture · Cognitive behavior modeling · WESS · Air combat

1 Introduction

In recent years, Combat Systems Effectiveness Simulation (CESS) is becoming one of the most important technical means to combat systems acquisition and conceptual design. Plenty of researches have been carried out and a number of CESS systems are developed as a result. Traditional approaches in developing CESS applications generally fall into two categories. One is to adopt a generic simulation platform in which one or few generic modeling formalisms are realized, such as KD-HLA [1], CISE [2], DEVS-C++ [3], and develop CESS applications for different combat systems and mission requirements. The other is to create a dedicated simulation systems for a specific type of combat systems, such as [4, 5]. One shortcoming of the former is that it's relatively difficult to abstract and prebuild domain-level knowledge for different CESS applications. It is also uneasy to realize semantic model reusability among

M.S. Mohamed Ali et al. (Eds.): AsiaSim 2017, Part II, CCIS 752, pp. 272–283, 2017.
DOI: 10.1007/978-981-10-6502-6_24

different CESS applications even though they all share the same simulation platform. Consequently, each CESS application has to be built from scratch in most cases. Whereas the latter suffers from model architectures lacking flexibility and with relatively limited application scope. The simulation models developed for a combat system are difficult to reuse in other close-related application domains. In this regard, both approaches are unable to fulfill the diversified requirements of the whole CESS domain. Domain-oriented generic CESS simulation systems, like EADSIM [6], SEAS [7] and JointMEASURE [8, 9], are highly desired when non-functional requirements like model reusability, simulation composability [10], and evolvability are taken into consideration.

We have been conducting CESS researches and developing CESS applications along the abovementioned first approach for a few decades. The generic simulation platforms implemented include multi formalism-based Sim2000 [11], HLA-based SimKit [12], and SMP2-based Sim2000 2.0 [13, 14]. Within these simulation platforms, a lot of simulation models have been developed for a large spread of CESS applications. During this whole period, simulation model reusability remains as a non-achieved aim. For a new and related CESS application requirement, the simulation models developed for previous applications are hard to reuse in a straightforward manner. In order to reuse these simulation models, the work required to revise and debug them is not much less than implementing them from scratch. This make us to reconsider the role of those generic modeling and simulation technologies played in reusability. They are certainly necessary. However, they might not be the key to model reusability and composability. The key probably lies in an appropriate model abstraction of the CESS application domain. Such abstraction could make each simulation model semantically reusable across different CESS applications. The model abstraction here is different from traditional one which only covers one simulation application. To realize a generic CESS system, the model abstraction should theoretically cover all CESS simulation applications at the same time. To achieve this aim, one practical strategy is to make a separation between domain-level abstraction and application-level abstraction. The domain-level abstraction would represent all domain-invariant knowledge, whereas application-level abstraction only represents application-specific knowledge by ways of inheriting domain-level abstraction.

Various modeling formalisms (including object-oriented, component-based design, event-based design, design patterns, etc.) and specifications (including SMP and UML), are applied to realize this strategy. Inspired by the definition of architecture in construction engineering, software engineering, and system engineering fields, we propose the concept of simulation model architecture (model architecture in short) to refer to the implemented two-level model abstraction of CESS [15, 16]. Specifically, the concepts of domain model architecture (DMA) and application model architecture (AMA) are used to stand for domain-level abstraction and application-level abstraction respectively.

Based on the model architecture and by integrating those simulation models developed before, we developed a generic CESS system, called WESS, to support effectiveness evaluation of combat systems from fields of air force, navy, space, etc. In this paper, the design rational, software architecture, and key technologies of WESS are briefed. Then a non-trivial CESS application example is presented for illustrative purpose.

2   Design Rational of WESS

2.1   Engagement-Level Models with System of Systems (SoS) Features

Mostly, combat scenarios of one on one or few on few are enough and sufficient to evaluate the combat effectiveness of a combat system for the purpose of exploring and optimizing its design alternatives. Measures of performance (MOPs) and mission data are the input whereas measures of effectiveness (MOEs) are the output of CESS. Apparently, the model granularity of CESS (and WESS) should be at engagement level which is higher than engineering level [17]. However, almost all combat systems are combating in the context of SoS. It is necessary to incorporate SoS features in CESS. To this end, SoS related model components like air defense group and air combat group are provided in WESS simulation model architecture.

2.2   Evolving DMA with the Incorporation of Various AMAs

It is unlikely to enumerate all CESS applications and cover them in the WESS simulation model architecture, even though we have developed many CESS simulation applications for combat systems of air force, navy, space, and other fields. By dividing model architecture into one DMA and many AMAs, we could implement the DMA with certain kind of extensive mechanisms and evolve it when various AMAs are developed. One extensive mechanism here is ontological object-oriented abstraction, by which the structure and behavior of each model component are divided and implemented over a hierarchy of abstract classes at different ontological levels with one being derived from another, and one concrete class. These abstract classes and their relationships constitute DMA, whereas the concrete class subclassing the lowest abstract class of DMA and other pertinent concrete classes will constitute AMA. Such design not only facilitates model composability, but allows each model class to be extended as needed and become more and more stable as more AMAs are developed. Currently, there are more than sixty different kinds of concrete weapon and equipment model component classes in WESS, which allow simulation users to rapidly compose desired CESS applications according to the patterns and relationships defined within DMA.

2.3   Script-Based Representation of Cognitive Behavior for Flexibility and User-Friendliness

The behaviors of each combat system are divided into two parts. One is in physical and information domain, referred as physical behavior; the other is in cognitive and social domain, referred as cognitive behavior. The physical behaviors are relatively stable across different missions. Therefore we represent them with C++ and build them into different dynamic linkage libraries (DLLs). On the contrary, the cognitive behaviors are largely dependent on warfighters or commanders and specific to missions. The script language Python is used to represent cognitive behaviors so as to be dynamically integrated with the physical behaviors. The simulation users can revise or extend the cognitive behavior scripts according to the needs. WESS provide more than 250 cognitive behavior modeling application programming interface (API) functions and an integrated development environment (IDE) to simplify the cognitive behavior modeling.

3   System Structure

3.1   WESS System Architecture

From bottom up in a detail, in Infrastructure & Platform layer are third party libraries and infrastructures employed in WESS. Data & Resources layer summarizes various kinds of input and output data files used or produced by WESS. Development & Runtime layer lists the functionalities provided by WESS to support simulation model development and execution. These tools or modules are independent of various kinds of CESS applications. In fact, to extend, modify, or test CESS model architecture according to the new CESS application needs, the modelers use these functionalities. In the Modeling Services layer, there are some simulation services to be invoked by simulation models. These modeling services provide functionalities similar to software tools and modules in the Development Runtime layer; however, they are dependent on the model architecture. Stated differently, when the model architecture changes, it is very likely to cause changes to the implementations of one or more modeling services. For example, when a new entity model type is added into the model architecture, the modelers are likely to modify the entity manager service to support dynamic instantiation of this entity. The display service is probably supposed to be modified to support the visualization of the new entity type specific features. In this regard, Model Architecture layer plays a decisive role within the WESS software architecture. The Application Tools layer is also dependent on the Model Architecture. The tools in Application Tools layer are mainly used by the CESS analysts to compose various CESS applications according to their needs. The Domain Specific Decision Modeler is used to support the analysts to specify cognitive decision behaviors in a combat platform specific manner. The top layer is Application Composition where various CESS applications can be composed using tools in Application Tools layer thanks to the powerful support of the Model Architecture layer.

3.2   WESS Workflow

The workflow of applying WESS system, as shown in Fig. 2, can be intentionally divided into two sub workflows: one for application composition, the other for model architecture extension or modification. For combat system effectiveness analysts, the model architecture and physical model components are ready for customization and composition. There are three kinds of information to prepare before running a simulation. The first is the mission scenario. By synthesizing scenario, the relevant model components within the model architecture are instantiated and composed automatically. The second is the combat system data, e.g. the design or performance parameters of F15 typed by *tmAeroObject*. These data will drive and determine the physical domain behaviors of the WESS model architecture. The third is the cognitive behaviors of the combat platforms involved in the simulated mission. Model-instance separation of cognitive behavior models and corresponding diagrammatical domain-specific behavior editor allow analysts to specify cognitive behaviors in a user-friendly and evolvable manner.

When the existent WESS model architecture cannot meet the needs of new CESS applications, e.g. a new model type of weapon, or platform, or sensor, or some other is introduced, the architects can extend or modify the model architecture according to the new extra requirements following the workflow of model architecture maintaining, as shown in the left part of Fig. 2. Actually, this workflow is the very one we followed to create the WESS model architecture. The first step is to do system conceptual analysis. As stated in previous sections, UML is used to describe the conceptual model architecture while keeping modeling capabilities provided by Simulation Modeling Portability (SMP) in mind. In this step when revising the model architecture for a certain modeling requirement, the key is to select the pertinent abstract base model class from which the new model class will inherit.

In the next step, model architecture design, the new structural model architecture is formally designed (extended or modified) and represented based on SMP. The SMP Catalogue Editor is used to edit and verify the structural model architecture. After that, two tasks can be carried out concurrently. The first is simulation model development. For the structural model architecture, C++ code is automatically generated. While for the physical behavior, the mappings between UML behavior diagram and C++ can be established to support automated behavior code fill-up. The second task is to update the model architecture related application tools, like scenario editor, domain-specific cognitive behavior editors, performance data manager, display tools, analysis tool, etc., to reflect the change of the model architecture. With these modified tools and new developed simulation models, model assembly and test can be done based on the runtime support engine and tools. After that, the new simulation model components are effectively integrated into the WESS system, and the composition and application workflow can be commenced as usual to solve the application problems encountered at the beginning.

4   A Demonstrative Example: Air Combat Effectiveness Simulation

In order to demonstrate the proposed WESS principles, this section presents a scenario of air combat in which each side is a fighter aircraft. Following typical application workflow presented above, we develop the simulation progressively from problem analysis to data preparation to scenario creation, then cognitive behavior modeling to simulation running.

4.1 Problem

Assume a new fighter aircraft, named as Fighter A, is under conceptual design. Compared to the presumptive target aircraft, e.g. Fighter B, Fighter A will have powerful airborne radar and smaller RCS in the front side and larger RCS in the board side. Fighter A is also equipped with a powerful electronic support measure (ESM). The purpose of CESS simulation is to evaluate whether Fighter A can defeat Fighter B under disadvantageous conditions. To this end, there should be many scenarios to be simulated. One of them is schematized in Fig. 3. In wartime, Fighter A occasionally exposes its board side to the Fighter B and is captured by the airborne radar of Fighter B. The latter then launches a missile toward Fighter A. Thanks to its powerful ESM, Fighter A knows of the threat from Fighter B timely. It then turns to the direction of Fighter B and gets ready to strike back. Immediately, Fighter B is detected by the long range airborne radar of Fighter A. In the meantime, the airborne radar of Fighter B loses Fighter A since the RCS of Fighter A on the front side is very small. Thereafter, the in-flying missile launched by Fighter B fails to lock onto Fighter A since the guidance instructions from Fighter B are no longer available. Meanwhile, Fighter A can lock onto Fighter B and launch a missile to win the combat.

4.2 Performance Data Preparation

Following the workflow of composition and application of the WESS system, the first step would be to prepare relevant performance data for each combat system involved in the simulated scenario, including those of Fighter A and Fighter B, ESM, airborne radars, air-to-air missiles, etc. The data manager tool is supposed to assist this step. Of course, the users can edit the underneath performance database directly. When the database grows up as editing directly becomes clumsy, it is very necessary to develop a specific tool for managing these performance data as well as the complex relationships embedded. Figure 4 shows the performance data of air to air missile. Within this clear window, we can select a wanted category of device from the left tree view, and easily view or edit corresponding data on the right panel. The right panel is divided into two regions. The up one consists of several text field groups and each group represents a category of performance data. The down one has a couple of tabbed panes and each pane exhibits a curve diagram or a data table.

4.3 Scenario Creation (Model Composition) and Experiment Design

Given that the performance data is ready, the scenario can be created conveniently by instantiating the concrete models within the model architecture as partly shown in the right part (see Fig. 1). Thanks to the composability characteristic of the model architecture, all model instances are naturally semantically composable within the scenario. Actually, there is nothing magic behind this since the scenario editor is strictly aligned with the model architecture. The experiment design is also aligned with the model architecture. As a result, for each combat platform models, all their performance parameters designed in the model architecture can be chosen for experiment design.

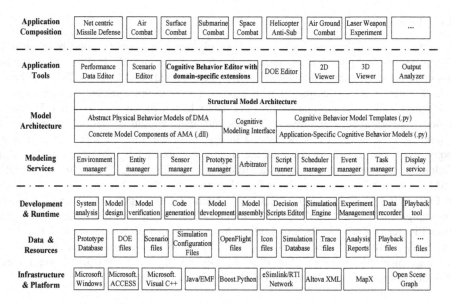

Application Composition	Net centric Missile Defense	Air Combat	Surface Combat	Submarine Combat	Space Combat	Helicopter Anti-Sub	Air Ground Combat	Laser Weapon Experiment	...

Application Tools	Performance Data Editor	Scenario Editor	Cognitive Behavior Editor with domain-specific extensions	DOE Editor	2D Viewer	3D Viewer	Output Analyzer

Model Architecture	Structural Model Architecture			
	Abstract Physical Behavior Models of DMA	Cognitive Modeling Interface	Cognitive Behavior Model Templates (.py)	
	Concrete Model Components of AMA (.dll)		Application-Specific Cognitive Behavior Models (.py)	

Modeling Services	Environment manager	Entity manager	Sensor manager	Prototype manager	Arbitrator	Script runner	Scheduler manager	Event manager	Task manager	Display service

Development & Runtime	System analysis	Model design	Model verification	Code generation	Model development	Model assembly	Decision Scripts Editor	Simulation Engine	Experiment Management	Data recorder	Playback tool

Data & Resources	Prototype Database	DOE files	Scenario files	Simulation Configuration Files	OpenFlight files	Icon files	Simulation Database	Trace files	Analysis Reports	Playback files	... files

Infrastructure & Platform	Microsoft. Windows	Microsoft. ACCESS	Microsoft. Visual C++	Java/EMF	Boost.Python	eSimlink/RTI Network	Altova XML	MapX	Open Scene Graph

Fig. 1. Layered WESS software architecture.

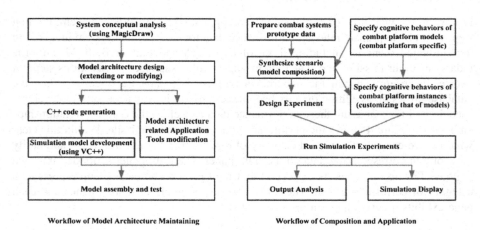

Fig. 2. Two typical application workflows of WESS system

Figure 5 shows the scenario creation of air combat example. The purpose of scenario creation is to deploy the forces belonging to two opposing sides in a combat and their initial status as well as configuring attributes of each entity. From the tree view of the left active window of Fig. 5, we select the *"Fighter2"* shadowed. Correspondingly, we can set up its prototype and tactical data, associate or create a new decision script, add various devices such as weapons, sensors, and countermeasures, and plan the waypoints for the route. Also, there are many functional icons listed in the toolbar for

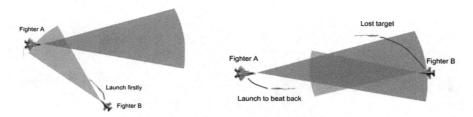

Fig. 3. A sample air combat scenario

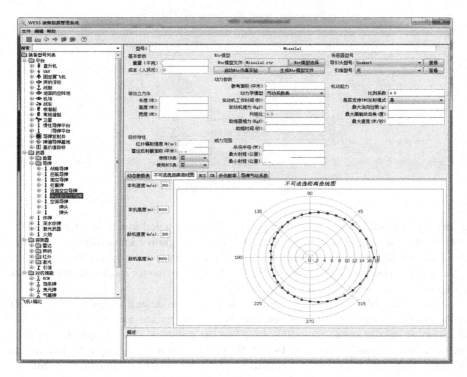

Fig. 4. Performance data preparation

linking to other tools. Orderly starting from left, they are for general project management, data management, experiment management, output analyzed module, model integrated development, and some assistant displaying tools.

4.4   Cognitive Behavior Modeling

Cognitive behavior has long been known to be flexible, especially in military domain where decision models may be different with outside changing field environment. Consequently, they should be regarded independently from simulation models which

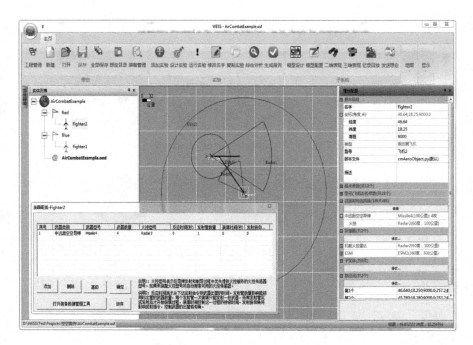

Fig. 5. Scenario creation

generally stay unchanged. A domain specific language tailed in a more understandable and modifiable way is needed to represent the rich cognitive knowledge. To simulate the scenario, the behaviors of each combat platform have to be specified. This step is greatly simplified given the domain-specific cognitive behavior modeling language and those default template behavior script files.

In this example, the analysts could directly use the default script file, i.e. tmAeroObject.py, or customize it. For instance, by modifying the air-to-air missile launch decision or missile avoidance policy based on the graphical domain-specific cognitive model editor as partly shown in Fig. 6. From the toolbar in the right figure, we can identify five kinds of nodes including *"Tactical Stage"*, *"junction"*, *"initial"*, *"choice"*, and *"FinalState"*, one transition *"Transition"*, and two events including *"InternalEvent"* and *"ExternalEvent"*. Using them most cognitive behavior models could be designed in the left region.

4.5 Simulation Running

Now everything is ready to run the simulation to produce the desired outputs. Figure 7 shows the snapshots of the running simulation experiment engine and situation display. From the right figure, it is straightforward for the analysts to see the dynamic air combating process. The simulation data outputs are also collected in the background for statistical analysis and report generation, which is realized by the output analyzer module.

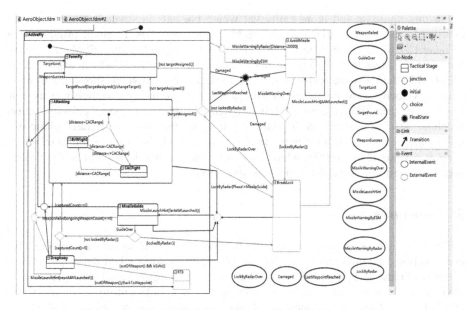

Fig. 6. Graphical domain-specific cognitive behavior modeling

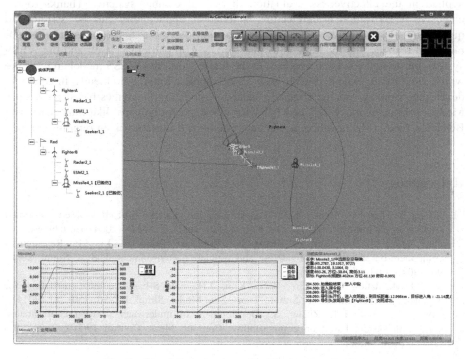

Fig. 7. Simulation running with 2D situation display

In this figure, at left is an entity list which presents the overall running entities enrolled in the combat. Illustratively the blue side *"Blue"* is a fighter, prototyped as *"FigherA"*, which is equipped with one radar *"Radar1"*, one ESM (Electronic Surveillance Measures) *"ESM1"*, and one missile *"Missile3"* which has a seeker *"Seeker1"*. Below is the real-time data of a selected entity, which shows the trend of altitude, velocity, yaw, pitch, roll by time, and some real-time status messages as well. As can be seen from the first trend diagram of *"Missile3"*, the *"velocity"* curve accelerates sharply by time at the start, which means the initial accelerated phase of a missile after launched. But when the time is to about 295, the curve becomes relatively even at a value about 10000, which indicates that the missile has got to the desired speed and will keep a relative unchangeable speed to the target.

5 Conclusions

CESS is a traditional and complex application domain of system simulation. The non-functional requirements play even more important roles when developing CESS systems. Traditional approaches, whether using a generic simulation platform or developing a dedicated simulation system, are not sufficient to meet all CESS requirements, especially model reusability, simulation composability, and system evolvability. There need generic CESS simulation systems based on extensive model architectures. WESS is such a generic CESS system we have developed for years and applied in the effectiveness evaluation of several combat systems. Thanks to the extensive WESS model architecture, simulation applications can be synthesized quickly by ways of model reuse and composition. As more applications are incorporated and realized, the model architecture (or DMA in particular) itself and the WESS system are strengthened and evolved. In the future work, the WESS model architecture would be further extended with new CESS application requirements. In addition, developing domain-specific cognitive behavior modeling languages based on Eclipse Modeling Framework (EMF) and behavior modeling formalisms, like Statecharts and Behavior Tree [18], for different combat systems and missions is an ongoing effort.

References

1. Huang, J., Hao, J.G., Huang, K.D.: The research and application of HLA-based distributed simulation environment KD-HLA. J. Syst. Simul. **16**(2), 214–221 (2004). (in Chinese)
2. Qing, D.Z., Li, B.H., Sun, L., Zhang, L., Zhou, M., Zhang, H., Li, Z.P.: Research of component-based integrated modeling and simulation environment. J. Syst. Simul. **20**(4), 900–904 (2008). (in Chinese)
3. Seo, K.M., Choi, C.B., Kim, T.G., Kim, J.H.: DEVS-based combat modeling for engagement-level simulation. Simul.: Trans. Soc. Model. Simul. Int. **90**, 759–781 (2014)
4. You, Y.J., Kang, F.J., Zhang, S.: Development of underwater weapon confrontation simulation system based on composability. Comput. Meas. Control **19**(10), 2462–2466 (2011). (in Chinese)

5. Nie, W.D., Kang, F.J., Chu, Y.J., Gu, H.: Modeling and simulation of torpedo trajectory using WISE. J. Syst. Simul. **16**(7), 1441–1449 (2004). (in Chinese)
6. Azar, M.C.: Assessing the treatment of airborne tactical high energy lasers in combat simulations. MS thesis, Air Force Institute of Technology (2003)
7. Miller, J.O., Honabarger Lt, J.B.: Modeling and measuring network centric warfare (NCW) with the system effectiveness analysis simulation (SEAS). In: 11th ICCRTS (2006)
8. Hall, S.B., Zeigler, B.P., Sarjoughian, H.S.: JointMEASURE: distributed simulation issues in a mission effectiveness analytic simulator. In: Simulator Interoperability Workshop (SIW), 99F-SIW-159 (1999)
9. Zeigler, B.P., Hall, S.B., Sarjoughian, H.S.: Exploiting HLA and DEVS to promote interoperability and reuse in lockheed's corporate environment. Simulation **73**(5), 288–295 (1999)
10. Davis, P.K., Anderson, R.H.: Improving the composability of DoD models and simulations. Appl, Methodol. Technol. **1**(1), 5–17 (2004)
11. Wang, W.P., Zhu, Y.F., Li, Q.: Sim 2000: a flexible simulation development environment. J. Syst. Simul. **12**(1), 61–64 (2000). (in Chinese)
12. Lei, Y.L., Zhao, W., Wang, W.P.: Design and implementation of a distributed model integration tool HLAWrapper. J. Syst. Simul. **17**(1), 245–248 (2005). (in Chinese)
13. Lei, Y.L., Zhang, W., Zhao, X., Liu, J., Wang, C., Li, X.B.: Research of SMP2-based missile countermine simulation system. J. Syst. Simul. **21**(14), 4312–4316 (2009). (in Chinese)
14. Li, Q., Wang, C., Wang, W.P., Zhu, Y.F.: Design and implementation on simulation engine compliant with SMP2.0. J. Syst. Simul. **24**(12), 2312–2316 (2008). (in Chinese)
15. Lei, Y.L., Li, Q., Yang, F., et al.: A composable modeling framework for weapon systems effectiveness simulation. Syst. Eng.-Theory Pract. **33**(11), 2954–2966 (2013)
16. Lei, Y.L., Zhu, Z., Sarjoughian, H.S.: Model architecture-oriented combat system effectiveness simulation. In: Proceedings of Winter Simulation Conference (2015)
17. Trevisani, D.A., Sisti, A.F.: Air force hierarchy of models: a look inside the great pyramid. In: Proceedings of SPIE 4026, Enabling Technology for Simulation Science IV, p. 150 (2000)
18. Yao, J., Zhu, N., Xu, J.Q., Chen, S., Lei, Y.L.: A domain specific language for tactic representation in engagement level simulation. In: European Simulation and Modelling Conference (2016)

A Systematic Web Mining Based Approach for Forecasting Terrorism

Tarik A. Rashid[1,3]($\boxtimes$), Didar D. Rashad[2], Hiwa M. Gaznai[2],
and Ahmed S. Shamsaldin[1]

[1] Department of Computer Science and Engineering,
University of Kurdistan Hewler, Erbil, Kurdistan, Iraq
{tarik.ahmed,ahmed.saadaldin}@ukh.edu.krd
[2] Information Technology, Khabat Technical Institute, Erbil, Kurdistan, Iraq
didar.rashad@epu.edu.krd, hiwa.gaznai@gmail.com
[3] Software Engineering Department, Salahaddin University-Erbil,
Erbil, Kurdistan, Iraq

Abstract. As the volume of accessed information on the World Wide Web is enormous, there might be various web environments of terrorist groups that might comprise various types of information like images, voice, texts which might be a danger for entire web costumers. Thus, a superior technique to detect wicked and non-wicked information is necessitated. This research study provides web sites' users a solution to prevent them from terrorist threats via developing an intelligent system to recognize the useful contents. The main aim of this study is to understand the behavior of the system, and determine the best solution for securing the susceptible users, state and society. The Naïve Bayes approach (NB) and K-Nearest Neighbor (K-NN) algorithms are investigated on various Kurdish-Sorani data sets as an alternative for replacing traditional approaches. In regards to precision, the Naïve Bayes algorithm demonstrates promising outcomes. The results of this paper will show that the Naïve Bays technique generates greater Kappa Statistics and excellent precision compared with K-Nearest Neighbors.

Keywords: Web mining · Cyber terrorism · Kurdish stemming · Classification

1 Introduction

Nowadays, people rely heavily on internet since it is the largest database in general. Internet regularly supplies people with thorough and comprehensive data in various fields to help them to realize their goals to gain material and understanding. Remarkably, internet is mainly shaped from websites which are considered as a vital element of internet. In recent times, wicked websites have been significantly distributed through the internet, accordingly, considerable amount of documentation from various wicked websites have been developed, designed and become accessible for users. For that reason, both valuable and wicked knowledge might be collected by users impulsively through some wicked sites by perhaps stealing personal information, learning penetration, etc. Therefore, the process of filtering or retrieving information has turned out to be crucial. Document or text classification process is considered as allocating

© Springer Nature Singapore Pte Ltd. 2017
M.S. Mohamed Ali et al. (Eds.): AsiaSim 2017, Part II, CCIS 752, pp. 284–295, 2017.
DOI: 10.1007/978-981-10-6502-6_25

different texts or documents to diverse classes. This process relies largely on the document's contents. Moreover, the text or document classification is valuable and can solve various issues and applications such as web mining, email message mining, indexing and organizing object articles, etc. [1–4]. While modern web pages are mostly enclosing keywords which aid to recover related documents quickly and accurately, on the other hand, still there are different earlier documents or texts which have no proper keywords. Consequently, spontaneous detecting wicked websites classification system is needed to organize the different texts or documents based on their contents.

Consequently, English, Chinese, Spanish, Portuguese and other languages in general are regarded as predominant and major verbal communications and they are extensively utilized via users to convey conversations on the net. So, several unconventional representational models have been designed for solving problems of text or document classification in the above stated languages [5, 6]. In addition, automatic work models for categorizing the Kurdish texts are not found or few, this is because the categorizing process for the Kurdish documents is completely different from the above-mentioned languages. The Kurdish language is enormously derivational and exceptionally inflectional language. The investigation and analysis of monophonic in the Kurdish language is a complicated task.

This investigation is carried out for designing an intellectual and automatic Kurdish system for classifying web pages. Sets of data are accumulated from numerous Kurdish websites for achieving the aim of this investigation. The most significant motivation behind this investigation is to accomplish a better comprehension of classification techniques for the Kurdish texts and identify wicked websites by utilizing appropriate procedures. Additionally, the people in Kurdistan region speak Kurdish Sorani dialect and now fight against a terrorist organization (ISIS) along 1010 km. Besides, ISIS uses different terror mechanisms and tools against Kurds. One of the most widely used mechanisms is websites through which they advertise for their activities and start a psychological war against Kurdistan. Likewise, there are websites which broadcast their news and subjects in Kurdish Sorani. Furthermore, ISIS has its partition in these websites regarding its size. Thus, establishing an intelligent system to distinguish Kurdish websites which publish terroristic ideas and materials from those that broadcast subjects about how to stand against terrorism is immediately needed.

This paper is outlined as follows: Related works concerning the classification of web content methods are illustrated in Sect. 2. Then, in Sect. 3, Kurdish Language is described in brief. Next, the proposed approach is explained clearly in Sect. 4, eventually, the major conclusion points are summarized.

2   Related Work

For classifying English documents, many techniques were examined and explored by numerous research projects [7]. In addition to English language, several examinations were carried out in other languages, for instance, German, French, Spanish, Chinese and Japanese [8–11]. Additionally, there are also some research works in Arabic language. Naïve Bayes algorithm was applied by El-Kourdi et al. for classifying Arabic document automatically [10]. It was expressed that the mean accuracy was around 68.78%. Sawaf et al. [12] projected a new technique via which the numerical categorization approach such as the highest entropy is utilized for classifying clustering news articles. The study stated that the optimum precision of the classification was 62.7% with accuracy of 50% which is extremely low accuracy in this study area. Moreover, the behavior of two categorization algorithms; C5.0 and Support Vector Machine upon the classification of Arabic text was estimated by Al-Harbi et al. [13] via utilizing seven Arabic text groups. The Support Vector Machine produced average accuracy 68.65%; however, the mean precision for the C5.0 was 78.42%. The dataset consisted of 17,658 text documents with more than 11,500,000 words. Harrag and El-Qawasmah in [14], applied Artificial Neural Network algorithm for classifying texts in Arabic language. The investigational test results demonstrated that Artificial Neural Network technique via Singular SVD obtained 88.33%. This is much better than the standard Neural Network which produced 85.75% on the same task. The Hadith data set was used in their work and it consisted of 453 file documents taken from several books disseminated over 14 categories. Another research about this subject was carried out by Wang Wenwen and Deng Qian for Chinese News Information Classification and Code (CNICC) [15, 16]. Qi and Davison in [17] produced another approach to select best features to classify web pages so that to enhance the speed and accuracy of their techniques. The model had to have best features taken from the websites to identify if a web page belongs or not to a category such as learners' profile, lecturing courses, and others. Since each constituent in a webpage like HTML terms and tags could be considered as a feature. Thus, the categorization space for both support vector machines and decision tree might grow extremely high. Thus, a genetic algorithm was used to identify the most excellent features for a provided webpage set to reduce feature space. The precision is improved to approximately 95% by employing KNN classifier.

With regards to Kurdish-Sorani dialect, there are no research works or any techniques to atomically recognize decent and bad Kurdish web sites via utilizing data mining techniques. This research work aims at solving this problem through an appropriate and intelligent system.

3   Kurdish Language

Kurdistan is a vast geographical zone in Turkey, Iraq, Syria and Iran. The spoken language in Kurdistan is Kurdish. It is one of the Indo-European languages. The Kurdish language comprises of two major dialects which are Kermanji and Sorani. The direction of writing in Kurdish language is from right to left, in contrast to Latin-grounded alphabets. Also, there are no gender specifications in Kurdish Sorani words. The population of Kurds is as follows: in Iraq is around five to seven million speakers, in Iran is around five to eight million speakers. This language script form is identical to Urdu, Arabic, and Persian languages. The alphabet in Kurdish language entails of the 33 characters as indicated in Fig. 1.

ا، ە، ب، پ، ت، ج، چ، ح، خ، د، ر، ڕ، ز، ژ، س، ش، ع، غ، ف، ڤ، ق، ڧ،
ک، گ، ل، ڵ، م، ن، و، ۆ، وو، ھ، ی، ئ

Fig. 1. Kurdish Sorani characters.

4   Proposed Method

The differentiation between good and bad Kurdish websites is the purpose of this research. This depends on analyzing the texts in these websites through using both K-Nearest Neighbor and Naive Bayes techniques. The main steps of the proposed approach are as follows: Data collection, preprocessing, classification and evaluation (See Fig. 2).

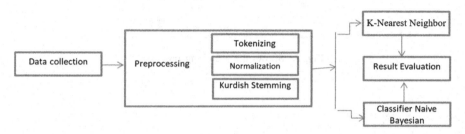

Fig. 2. The proposed system.

4.1   Data Collection

In this research work, online Kurdish newspapers such as Rudaw, NRTTV, KNN, K24, Payam, Speda, GK, Kurdsat, Xendan, and Dwaroje as well as a few other specialized websites are utilized as a source for collecting a corpus of Kurdish text documents. Since the Kurdish corpus is one of the difficult issues that encountered this investigation when assessing text classification algorithms, therefore, a small corpus that comprises of 2000 papers belonging to 2 diverse classes, is prepared and proposed. In addition, another obstacle that encounters this research work is that Kurdish text classification and morphology rely upon the components of documents, besides, vast quantity of keywords or features is existed in Kurdish text might be generated from one root (for instance, morphemes). This may have undesirable impact on performance in terms of precision and time. Thus, the keywords are not vowelized and the number of removed features is diminished to cope with such an issue. The whole documents; documents to be classified or training documents are passed through a preprocessing stage for extracting stop words, punctuation marks, non-letters and diacritics. Figures 3, 4 and 5 illustrate snapshots of the designed software for performing the searching, extracting, cleaning and saving processes.

4.2   Preprocessing

The utilized data in this paper are gathered from several Kurdish websites. The data set is consisted of 2000 Kurdish documents of various duration that fit in to two categories, which are "Good" or "Bad". Table 1, demonstrates the number of documents for every

Fig. 3. Shows the searching process.

Fig. 4. Shows the extracting process.

Table 1. The number of documents for each category

Category name	Number of documents
Good	1000
Bad	1000
Total	2000

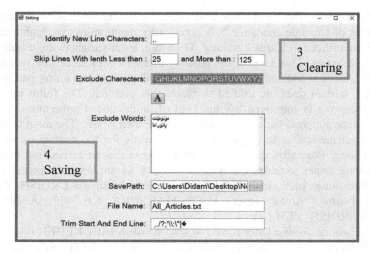

Fig. 5. Shows the cleaning and saving processes.

class. The preprocessing stage is divided into three sub stages; these are Tokenization, Normalization and Stemming, each of which is explained in detail as follows:

(a) Tokenization: The basic and substantial stage in natural language process is tokenization.

The process of tokenization is used for transforming a text stream into tokens through segmenting the texts. The tokenization process involves the decomposition of the sentences and the texts into delimited words by different line and white space. Thus, in this pre-processing phase, several useful semantic tokens are produced. Figure 6, displays an example of this tokenization stage.

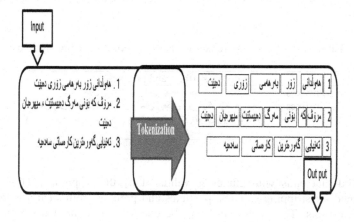

Fig. 6. Indicates an example of tokenizing process.

(b) Normalization: The most imperative base for the normalization process is the features of Unicode character. It is noteworthy mentioning that Arabic electronic texts are utilized in Kurdish writing. Therefore, letter variances are usually caused to some extent. This kind of discrepancy problem is produced by typescripts of multi-Unicode, and ultimately is adversely effected the regaining pertinent data. Hence, written texts are unified to tackle this problem. The following stage of preprocessing is improved by this kind of unification. Furthermore, this correspondence supports the removal affixes and related words. The main target of the proposed method is to prepare consistent words for the next steps in the preprocessing. Basically, the normalization process can be carried out through the following stages to tackle the issue of Kurdish Sorani language procedures:-

(1) Substitute Arabic letter YAA (ي) with Arabic format KURDISH_YEH (ی).

(2) Substitute Arabic letter ALEF MAKSURA (ى) with Arabic format KURDISH_YEH (ی).

(3) Substitute Arabic letter KAF (ك) with Kurdish letter KEHEH (ک).

(4) Substitute ("ﻪ" which is consisted of "ZWNJ + HEH (ﻪ)") with Kurdish letter AE (ه).

Where ZWNJ is demonstrated as zero width, which is a non-printing character utilized in the computerization of writing systems that makes utilize of ligatures. As it is located between two characters that would otherwise be linked into a ligature.

(c) Kurdish Stemming-Steps: It is a step grounded method on stages which are experienced through a word till the root of the word is extracted [18]. The proposed approach in this investigation is utilized for removing affixes. In Kurdish Sorani dialect, several situations have been re-accustomed on the letters that are affixes situated at the end of words. Therefore, this stemmer is specialized to the words that have numerous affixes such as a word that consists of "prefix" + "root" + "suffix1" + "suffix2" +......"suffixN"). Accordingly, to get the root of such a word, it must move through a group of simplified guidelines relying on the circumstances. The collections of potential suffixes and prefixes which are generally employed in Kurdish text document is the base for this approach. Table 2, exhibits some Kurdish Sorani suffixes and prefixes which necessitate exclusion.

Table 2. Suffixes and prefixes excluded by Kurdish stemming-steps

Kurdish suffixes and prefixes	
Prefixes	هەڵ ,دەر , سەر، بێ ,لەەرا ،به ،
Suffixes	دا ,ش , ی , هات ,یان ,تان , مان , مكان ,و , یک , مکه , یه ,
	و , وه ,هوه , تن , ین , ان , دن , ه , ن , یت , تر ,بوون , تا ,کار
	هات ,

A word that ends with affixes is validated by this approach. This module is designed for stripping suffixes, postfixes and prefixes from such a word to grasp possible roots. The given word will be checked throughout the entire steps of Kurdish Stemming-step to map the string of letters that are situated at the start or end of the root of word. It is significant to observe that the Kurdish Stemming-Steps process doesn't utilize a dictionary for checking the root. For example a word (هەڵوەشانەوەی) is decreased to its root (وەشان) directly throughout step1 which eliminates prefixes (هەڵ) and then goes through the subsequent stage for mapping it up until reaches the step 6 for removing suffix (ی), then remains (وەشانەوە) subsequently. Then after, the system associates the suffixes of such a word with suffixes in the following steps to reach to the step as it discovers a matching and removes it from the word at step 16. Consequently, suffixes (ەوە) are detached. Figure 7, indicates the overall process of Kurdish Stemming-steps for such a word. As it was utilized in other languages, this system is not only eliminating affixes from verbs and nouns, but also eliminating affixes from the stop words which are utilized widely in Kurdish Sorani dialect (See Table 3). Figure 7, displays the overall process of Kurdish Stemming step by step.

Input Word not stemmed

If word>5 and starts with " دە" and ends with " ن"or" م" then remove both " دە & م or دە & ن" else go to the next step..

If word>6 and starts with " دە " and ends with " يت then remove both "دە & يت " else go to the next step..

If word >5 and ends with "مان" or " كان "or" يان" then remove it Except"كان" in "سكان" else go the next step..

If word>5 and ends with " دن " or " ين " " كن " or "ان" then remove it Except"ان" in "ران" else go the next step..

If word>5 and starts with " را " or " لە " then remove it else go to the next step...

If word>6 and starts with " هەل " or" سەر "or" دەر " then remove it else go to the next step..

If word >4 and ends with " و " then remove it else go to the next step...

If word >4 and ends with "دا" then remove it else go to the next step...

If word >4 and ends with " ش" then remove it else go to the next step...

If word >4 and ends with " ی " then remove it else go to the next step...

If word >6 and ends with " وە " then remove it else go to the next step...

If word >5 and ends with "كە" then remove it else go to the next step...

If word >7 and ends with " كان " then remove it else go to the next step...

If word >5and ends with " يە " then remove it else go to the next step...

If word >4 and ends with " يك " then remove it else go to the next step...

If word >4 and ends with " ە " then remove it else go to the next step....

If word >4 and ends with " كار " then remove it else go to the next step...

If word >5 and ends with "گا" then remove it else go to the next step....

If word >5 and ends with "تر" then remove it else go to the next step...

If word >6 and ends with " بوون " or " بوو " then remove it else go to the next step...

If word >5 and ends with " هات " then remove it else go to the next step...

Output equal word stem

Fig. 7. Shows the stemming steps.

Table 3. The process of removing affixes from stop word.

Root of Stop word		English meaning	Stop word
خوێند	Xwend	Study	...خوێندنی،خوێندنەوە،خوێنێد،دەخوێندن هێد
کوشت	Kusht	Kill	کوشتن،کوشتی،دە کوشت ،کوشتنەوە ...هێد
فڕی	Fri	Fly	فڕین،دەفڕی ،فڕینەوە، دەفڕی ،....هێد

4.3 Classification

To tackle web mining categorization, there are two kinds of methods, these are physical and automatic methods. In the physical method, generally human comprehension is utilized. Nonetheless, in automatic method, machine learning techniques are employed [19]. Because automatic method can deal with vast quantities of data that necessitates to be categorized, thus, the automatic method is broadly utilized. Methods like Naïve Bays and K-Nearest Neighbors have performed efficiently for tackling the process of the classification of document [19]. The following subsections provide details on each classifier.

(a) Naïve Bays Classifier: They are called Independence or simply Bayes. They are a family of both machine learning and direct probabilistic classifiers which they rely on putting on theorem of Bays on features independently. These are the simplest type of Bayesian network wherein the entire features are self-determining and openly related to groups. This is known as provisional independence [20–22].

(b) K-Nearest Neighbor Classifier: It is preferable to consider that in various space, every single feature in the training set is like a separate dimension. For this trait, the value is taken to be its organizer in that dimension. Then, collection of points in space is attained. Subsequently, when the distance in this space under same acceptable metric, the likeness of two points can be considered. The technique K-Nearest Neighbor may be described as: first, K is indicated as a positive number, in conjunction with a novel example. Second, the K entries that are closest to the new example are chosen from the data set. Third, the foremost common classification of those entries will be found. And finally, this is the categorization, the study tends to provide to the novel sample [23].

5   Result Evaluation and Discussions

The results are computed and assessed based on measurement formulas used in [19]. For building a classifier, the program was trained utilizing the training set, moreover, the program was examined utilizing the testing set. Therefore, around 67% of infor-mation was employed for the training session, while the remained 33% was applied for the testing session. Table 4 indicates confusion matrices for Naïve Bays and K-Nearest Neighbors classifiers.

Table 4. Confusion matrix for both K-NN and NB

Classifier	Predicted class	Class (good)	Class (bad)
CK-NN	Class (good)	TP (67)	FP (1)
	Class (bad)	FN (3)	TN (69)
CNB	Class (good)	TP (64)	FP (4)
	Class (bad)	FN (2)	TN (68)

The results of the classification algorithms regarding correctly classified instances (CCL), incorrectly classified instances (ICI), percentage of both CCI and ICI, time to build the classifier (TB) were shown in Table 5.

Table 5. Indicates the results based on accuracy and time.

Classifier	CCI	CCI%	ICI	ICI%	TB
NB	643	94.55	37	5.45	1.84
K-NN	609	90.37	68	9.63	1.89

It was observed that NB produced the highest accuracy which was 94.55%. Based on the time and precision, NB classifiers were the optimum in classifying the detection dataset of wicked web pages. Table 6, displays the Mean Absolute Error (MAE), Root Mean Square Error (RMSE), and percentage of both Relative Absolute Error (RAE), and Root Relative Square Error (RRSE). It can be seen the Kappa statistics was very high, this indicated that the observer satisfied more than would be expected. Regarding the time, it was too little time to establish a model for both classifiers.

Table 6. Displays results based on errors

Classifier	Kappa statistics	MAE	RMSE	RAE (%)	RRSE (%)
NB	0.891	0.095	0.20	19.055	41.75
K-NN	0.885	0.023	0.19	6.075	39.81

6   Conclusions

Noticeably, internet is utilized massively all over the world and it has abundant wicked web pages. This study attempted to identify the wicked websites. The system was designed to process input documents and atomically identify wicked websites via employing the techniques of data mining. To achieve the aim of this investigation Naïve Bays and K-Nearest Neighbors approaches are utilized. The outcomes of the investigation demonstrate that Naïve Bays technique generates higher Kappa Statistics and superior precision in comparison to K-Nearest Neighbors. Ultimately, it can be stated that the designed program can be simply modified and extended to deal with other security utilization for example fraud documents.

References

1. Abouenour, L., Bouzouba, K., Rosso, P.: Improving Q/A using Arabic WordNet. In: Proceedings of Arab Conference on Information Technology, (CIT 2008). IBTIKARAT Research Group, Tunisia (2008)
2. Alkhalifa. M., Rodríguez, H.: Automatically extending NE coverage of Arabic WordNet using Wikipedia. In: Proceedings of 3rd International Conference on Arabic Language Processing, Rabat, Morocco, pp. 23–30 (2009)
3. Boudabous, M., Kammoun, C., Khedher, N., Belguith, H., Sadat, F.: Arabic WordNet semantic relations enrichment through morpholexical patterns. In: Proceedings of 1st International Conference on Communications, Signal Processing and their Applications, pp. 1–6. IEEE Xplore Press, Sharjah (2013)
4. Elberrichi, Z., Abidi, K.: Arabic text categorization: a comparative study of different representation modes. Int. Arab J. Inform. Technol. 9, 465–470 (2012)
5. El-Halees, A.: A comparative study on Arabic text classification Egypt. Comput. Sci. J. 20, 57–64 (2008)
6. Yousif, S., Samawi, W., Elkabani, I., Zantout, R.: Enhancement of Arabic text classification using semantic relations of Arabic WordNet. J. Comput. Sci. 11, 498 (2015)
7. Aas, K., Eikvil, L.: Text categorisation: a survey. Technical report, Norwegian Computing Centre (1999)
8. Ciravegna, F., Gilardoni, L., Lavelli, A., Ferraro, M., Mana, N., Mazza, S., Matiasek, J., Black, W., Rinaldi, F.: Flexible text classification for financial applications: the FACILE system. In: Proceedings of PAIS-2000, Prestigious Applications of Intelligent Systems Sub-conference of ECAI (2000)
9. Mesleh, A.: Chi square feature extraction based SVMs Arabic language text categorization system. J. Comput. Sci. 3(6), 430–435 (2007)
10. El-Kourdi. M., Bensaid, A., Rachidi, T.: Automatic Arabic document categorization based on the Naïve Bayes algorithm. In: 20th International Conference on Computational Linguistics, Geneva, August 2004
11. Peng, F., Huang, X., Schuurmans, D., Wang, S.: Text classification in Asian languages without word segmentation. In: Proceedings of 6th International Workshop on Information Retrieval with Asian Languages. Association for Computational Linguistics, Sapporo (2003)
12. Sawaf, H., Zaplo, J., Ney, H.: Statistical classification methods for Arabic news articles. Natural Language Processing in ACL, Toulouse (2001)
13. Al-Harbi, S., Al-Thubaity, A., Khorsheed, M., Al-Rajeh, A.: Automatic Arabic text classification. Presented at the GES Journes Internationals, France (2008)
14. Harrag, F., El-Qawasmah, E.: Neural network for arabic text classification. Presented at 2nd International Conference on the Applications of Digital Information and Web Technologies, ICADIWT, pp. 778–783 (2009)
15. Wang, W.: The Application of Chinese News Information Classification and Codes in the News Reference Room. Library No. 5 (2007)
16. Deng, Q., Ling, H., Conception and implementation of automatic indexing and classification for chinese news information. Science Technology for China's Mass Media, vol. 9, no. 115 (2005)

17. Qi, X., Davison B.D.: Web page classification: features and algorithms, ACM Comput. Surv. 41(2), 12 (2009)
18. Mustafa, A., Rashid, T.A.: Kurdish stemmer - preprocessing steps for improving relevant information retrieval. J. Inf. Sci. (2017). doi:10.1177/0165551516683617
19. Rashid, T.A., Mohamad, S.O.: Enhancement of detecting wicked website through intelligent methods. In: Mueller, P., Thampi, S.M., Alam Bhuiyan, M.Z., Ko, R., Doss, R., Alcaraz Calero, Jose M. (eds.) SSCC 2016. CCIS, vol. 625, pp. 358–368. Springer, Singapore (2016). doi:10.1007/978-981-10-2738-3_31
20. Hand, D.J., Yu, K.: Idiot's Bayes-not so stupid after all? Int. Stat. Rev. 69(3), 385–398 (2001)
21. Rish, I.: An empirical study of the naive Bayes classifier, T.J. Watson Research Center, (2001)
22. Zhang, H.: The optimality of Naive Bayes. Am. Assoc. Artif. Intell. 1, 3 (2004)
23. Sergios, T., Konstantinos, K.: Pattern Recognition, 2nd edn. Academic Press, Boston (2003). ISBN 10:0126858756, 13:9780126858754

Biased Robust Composite Nonlinear Feedback Control of Under Actuated Systems

Amir A. Bature[1], Salinda Buyamin[2(✉)], Mohamad N. Ahmad[2],
Auwalu M. Abdullahi[3], Mustapha Muhammad[3],
and Mohamad Shukri Zainal Abidin[2]

[1] Department of Electrical Engineering, Bayero University, Kano, Nigeria
[2] Faculty of Electrical Engineering, Universiti Teknologi Malaysia,
Johor Bahru, Johor, Malaysia
salinda@utm.my
[3] Department of Mechatronics Engineering, Bayero University Kano,
Kano, Nigeria

Abstract. This paper proposes a method of designing composite nonlinear feedback (CNF) control for under actuated systems. By biasing the output error feedback of the nonlinear part of CNF, a state that is not the reference state but also important, can be given attention not only in the linear part but in the nonlinear part of CNF as well. The proposed scheme is tested on two wheeled inverted pendulum (TWIP) mobile robot which is highly under actuated robot, and shows a better performance in balancing the robot and also in energy consumption.

Keywords: Composite nonlinear feedback · Robust control · Integral sliding mode · Two wheeled inverted pendulum

1 Introduction

In most mechanical machines, tracking a desired position, stabilization and vibration suppressions, are one of the most vital problems that researchers have been working on for a long time [1]. Stabilization is the convergence of a plant to a closed region around the origin, while still attaining a desired response from the machine, for instance tracking a distance or velocity, and at same time achieving robustness and disturbance rejection.

When tracking a set point, two factors are the most important, quick settling time and avoiding overshoot [2]. In achieving one of the goals, a compromise is made on the other. To overcome this problem, Lin et al. [2], proposed a technique called Composite Nonlinear Feedback (CNF) control scheme for single input single output (SISO) system, which consists of linear and nonlinear feedback control law. The nonlinear part increase the damping ratio as the output reaches the target reference to reduce overshoot. With these concepts, a fast response is achieved with no or little overshoot. In [3], the result of Lin was extended to multiple inputs multiple output (MIMO) systems. The concept of state feedback CNF was extended to output measurement feedback

© Springer Nature Singapore Pte Ltd. 2017
M.S. Mohamed Ali et al. (Eds.): AsiaSim 2017, Part II, CCIS 752, pp. 296–305, 2017.
DOI: 10.1007/978-981-10-6502-6_26

CNF in [4], the nonlinear part of the CNF was also modified to achieve better performances [3–5], (see details in Sect. 2).

Under actuated systems are systems that have their input to the system less than the number of outputs, these types of systems are difficult to control all output behaviors with less inputs [3]. Using CNF approach to control under actuated systems, Yu et al. [6] proposed an additional term in the nonlinear function of CNF. In this work, CNF controller is utilized to control under actuated systems by biasing not only the linear term but also the nonlinear part of the CNF. An integral sliding mode (ISM) controller is added to make the propose control structure robust to disturbance just as in [7]. With this new scheme, less energy is required to achieve better response from systems.

The rest of the paper is as follows, Sect. 2 describes the CNF design and the robust ISM integration, Sect. 3 gives example design of the propose controller, while Sect. 4 gives result and discussion. Finally, Sect. 5 concludes the work.

2 Biased CNF Design

The CNF design steps are given in this section. The basic steps in designing CNF controller are fully shown in [2, 3, 7], in summary the following steps are followed: Given a system in Eq. 1.

$$\dot{x} = Ax + Bu(sat), \quad x(0) = x_0$$
$$y = Cx. \tag{1}$$

Design a linear feedback controller

$$u_L = Kx + Nr. \tag{2}$$

Find K using any linear techniques, LQR, pole placement, etc., so that $A + BK$ is Hurwitz.

   i. Calculate $N = -\left[C(A + BK)^{-1}B\right]^{-1}$ which is the scaling input factor.
  ii. Calculate $H = \left[1 - K(A + BK)^{-1}B\right]N$
 iii. Calculate $x_e := G_e r := -(A + BK)^{-1}BNr$
 iv. H, G_e and x_e will be used later.
  v. We solve the Lyapunov Eq. 3 to find real symmetric matrix P

$$(A + BK)'P + P(A + BK) = -W. \tag{3}$$

where $P > 0$, and *given any* $W > 0$

Design the nonlinear feedback control

$$u_N = \rho(r, y)B'P(x - x_e). \tag{4}$$

The function $\rho(r,y)$ is used as the tuning parameter to enhance the transient response of a system. In order for the closed loop system to be stable, the function $\rho(r,y)$ is always negative, furthermore is a function of the tracking error. In [2], the function is given as in Eq. 5

$$\rho(r,y) = \beta e^{-\alpha|y-r|}.\tag{5}$$

In [3], the function is modified to add another parameter α as in Eq. 6

$$\rho(x,r) = \beta e^{-\alpha|y|}.\tag{6}$$

In order to make the function to be from 0 to β, it is modified to Eq. 7 in [4], and further modified to Eq. 8 in [5]

$$\rho(h,r) = -\frac{\beta}{1-e^{-1}}(e^{-|1-(h-h_0)/r-h_0)|} - e^{-1}).\tag{7}$$

$$\rho(y,r) = -\beta|e^{-\alpha_i||h(t)-r||} - e^{-\alpha_i||h(0)-r||}|.\tag{8}$$

Also, [8] suggested Eq. 9 for the function.

$$\rho(x,r) = \beta e^{-\alpha\alpha_0|y-r|} \text{ where } \alpha_0 = \left\{ \frac{1}{y_0-1}, \quad \begin{matrix} y_0 \neq r \\ y_0 = r \end{matrix} \right\}.\tag{9}$$

Where $\alpha_0 = \left\{ \frac{1}{y_0-1}, \quad \begin{matrix} y_0 \neq r \\ y_0 = r \end{matrix} \right\}$

To control under actuated systems, [6] suggested $\rho(x,r)$ as follows

$$\rho(r) = \rho_1(r_1) + \rho_2(r_2).\tag{10}$$

Where

$$\rho_1(r_1) = -\beta_1 e^{-\alpha_0\alpha_1|h_1-r|}$$
$$\rho_2(r_2) = -\beta_2 e^{-\alpha_s\alpha_2 h_2}$$

Combined linear and nonlinear feedback

The combined linear and nonlinear feedback law are combined to form

$$u = u_L + u_N = Kx + Nr + \rho(r,y)B'P(x - x_e).\tag{11}$$

The following assumptions are made as in theorem 1 of [4]: Consider the given system in Eq. 1, the linear control law of Eq. 2, and the composite nonlinear feedback control law of Eq. 11. For any $\delta \in (0,1)$, let $c_\delta > 0$ be the largest positive scalar satisfying the following condition:

$$|Kx| \leq u_{max}(1 - \delta), \forall x \in X_\delta := \{x : x'Px \leq c_\delta\}$$

Then, the linear control law of Eq. 2 is capable of driving the system controlled output $h(t)$ to track asymptotically a step command input r, provided that the initial state x_0 and r satisfy:

$$\tilde{x}_0 := (x_0 - x_e) \in X_\delta, |Hr| \leq \delta_{max}. \tag{12}$$

Furthermore, for any nonpositive function $\rho(r, y)$, locally Lipschitz in y, the composite nonlinear feedback law in Eq. 11 is capable of driving the system controlled output $h(t)$ to track asymptotically the step command input of amplitude r, provided that the initial state x_0 and r satisfy Eq. 12. The proof is given in [2, 4].

Biased CNF with ISM control
Integral sliding mode control allows to combine two independent controllers to achieve robustness. It works as disturbance observer [7]. The combined control law becomes

$$u = u_0 + u_{N1} = u_L + u_N + u_{N1}$$
$$u_{N1} = -M(x, t)sign((GB)^T s(x, t))$$

$M(x, t) > \rho_{max}$, which is maximum disturbance. $s(x, t)$ is the sliding surface and define as:

$$s(x, t) := G[x(t) - x(t_0) - \int_{t_0}^{t} (f(x, \tau) + Bu(x, \tau))d\tau]. \tag{13}$$

G is chosen so that GB is invertible. $x(t_0) + \int_{t_0}^{t} (f(x, \tau) + Bu_0(x, t))d\tau$ is the trajectory of the system due to normal control $u_0(x, t)$ in the absence of disturbance, while $x(t)$ is the actual trajectory. Then the theorem 5.3.1 in [7] can be extended to Theorem 1.

Theorem 1. *If all the assumption of 1 are met and P is the solution of the Lyapunov equation of Eq. 3, let $c_\delta > 0$, $|K\tilde{x}| \leq u_{max}(1 - \delta) \forall \tilde{x} \in X_\delta = \{\tilde{x}|\tilde{x}'P\tilde{x} \leq c_\delta\}$, $\delta \epsilon(0, 1)$, $Jx - x_e = \tilde{x}$, then the control $\bar{u} := u_0 + u_{N1}$ makes the system to track a desired constant output r, when the initial error satisfies: $\forall \tilde{x} \in X_\delta, |Hr| \leq \delta_1 u_{max}$, where $0 < \delta_1 < \delta$ and $|(\delta - \delta_1)u_{max}| = \rho(x, t)_{max}$.*

The added condition that biased the nonlinear part of the CNF is $Jx - x_e \in X_\delta$ where $J = diagonal\, matrix$, with elements $j_1, j_2 \ldots \ldots J_n > 0$ which are weighted element to bias the error of chosen unattended state variable. The chosen state variable should have a value of $x_e = 0$. If $j_1, j_2 \ldots \ldots J_n = 1$, then the theorem is same as [7]. The new control law of Eq. 11 now becomes

$$u = u_L + u_N = Kx + Nr + \rho(r, y)B'P(jx - x_e). \tag{14}$$

Therefore the unattended output will be weighted not only in the Kx term of the linear part of the controller, but also in the nonlinear part by the term j.

Prove:
Considering the error transformation $\tilde{x} = jx_0 - x_e$,

$$\dot{\tilde{x}} = (A + BK)\tilde{x} + Bw + B\rho(x, t) = (A + BK)\tilde{x} + Bg$$
$$g := w + \rho(x, t)$$
$$w := sat(K\tilde{x} + Hr + u_N + u_{N1}) - K\tilde{x} - Hr$$

We define Lyapunov function $V = \tilde{v}^T P\tilde{x}$

$$\dot{V} = -\tilde{x}^T W\tilde{x} + 2\tilde{x}^T PBg$$

Case 1: If $u = |K\tilde{x} + Hr + u_N + u_{N1}| \le u_{max} \Rightarrow sat(u) = u$
Therefore $Sat(K\tilde{x} + Hr + u_N + u_{N1}) = K\tilde{x} + Hr + u_N + u_{N1}$

$$g = K\tilde{x} + Hr + u_N + u_{N1} - K\tilde{x} - Hr + \rho(x, t)$$

Using definition of equivalent control $(u_{N1})_{eq} = u_{eq} = -\rho_d(x, t)$

$$\therefore g = u_N = \Psi(r, y)B^T P\tilde{x}$$
$$\dot{V} = -\tilde{x}^T W\tilde{x} + 2\Psi(r, y)\tilde{x}^T PBB^T P\tilde{x} \le -\tilde{x}^T W\tilde{x}$$
$$hence, \dot{V} < 0$$

Case 2: If $u = K\tilde{x} + Hr + u_N + u_{N1} > u_{max}$,
therefore $\Rightarrow at(Kx + Hr + u_N + u_{N1}) = u_{max}$

$$\text{So } g = u_{max} - K\tilde{x} - Hr - \rho(x, t)$$

By design $|K\tilde{x} + Hr + \rho(x, t)| \le u_{max}$.
Therefore $g > 0$, Using equivalent control it follow

$$u_N > u_{max} - K\tilde{x} - Hr + u_{N1} > 0$$
$$\text{This implies } \tilde{x}^T PB < 0, \text{ therefore } \tilde{x}^T PBg < 0$$
$$\dot{V} = -\tilde{x}^T W\tilde{x} + 2\tilde{x}^T PBg \le -\tilde{x}^T W\tilde{x}$$
$$hence\ again\ \dot{V} < 0$$

Case 3: From $u = K\tilde{x} + Hr + u_N + u_{N1} < -u_{max}$
Negative definiteness of $\dot{V}$ can be proved using similar argument.

$$g = -u_{max} - K\tilde{x} - Hr + \rho(x, t).$$
$$\text{By design } |K\tilde{x} + Hr + \rho(x, t)| \le u_{max}. \therefore g < 0$$

This imply that

$$u_N < -u_{max} - K\tilde{x} - Hr - u_{N1} < 0, \tilde{x}^T PB > 0,$$
$$2x^T PBg < 0, \text{ therefore } \dot{V} < 0$$

In all the three cases stability is guaranteed.

3   Example of Biased Robust CNF Design

A SIMO system will be used to test the performance of the proposed method. A two wheeled inverted pendulum (TWIP) mobile robot is an example of an under actuated, highly nonlinear robot [9]. The robot will be used to track a constant reference while maintaining tilt angle to zero degrees. Therefore the biased nonlinear state of the CNF is the tilt angle. Given the TWIP linear system equations as in [9]:

$$\dot{x} = Ax + B$$
$$y = Cx. \tag{15}$$

Where $A = \begin{bmatrix} 0 & 1 & 0 & 0 \\ 0 & 0 & -3.7706 & 0 \\ 0 & 0 & 0 & 1 \\ 0 & 0 & 68.9659 & 0 \end{bmatrix}$, $B = \begin{bmatrix} 0 \\ 0.599 \\ 0 \\ -5.776 \end{bmatrix}$, $x(t) = \begin{bmatrix} x\dot{x}\phi\dot{\phi} \end{bmatrix}^T$

The control law is given by

$$u(x,t) := u_0(x,t) + u_1(x,t) \tag{16}$$

$$u_0(x,t) = Kx + Nr + u_n.$$

Linear matrix inequalities (LMI) pole placement technique as in [10] is used to design the linear part of $u_0(x,t), K$ and N.

$$K = [\, 4.4251 \quad 8.6866 \quad 28.4699 \quad 4.4880 \,]$$
$$N = -4.4251$$

For u_n, $\rho(r,y) = \beta e^{-\alpha \alpha_0 |y-r|}$ where $\alpha_0 = \left\{ \begin{matrix} \frac{1}{y_0 - 1}, & y_0 \neq r \\ 1, & y_0 = r \end{matrix} \right\}$ is used. With $\alpha = 0.4$.

For the ISM part $u_1(x,t)$:

$$u_1(x,t) = \sigma sgn(s(x,t)). \tag{17}$$

$$s(x,t) = G[x(t) - x(t_0) - \int_{t_0}^{t} (f(x,\tau) + Bu_0(x,t))d\tau]$$

G is computed using $G = (B^T B)^{-1} B^T$ as in [11].

$$G = [\, 0 \quad 0.0166 \quad 0 \quad -0.1715 \,].$$

The disturbance of $d = \sin(0.4t)$ is used. Therefore $\sigma = 1.1$, as 1.0 is the maximum disturbance. Also tangent hyperbolic function is used instead of the signum function to avoid chattering problem. The tilt angle of the TWIP is always required to remain at zero degrees, since the horizontal position of the robot is the reference state, the tilt angle becomes the unattended state of the CNF, and is biased. The value of $j = diag[111.551]$, was computed using simple steepest decent algorithm with maximum tilt angle as the cost function to be minimized. Figure 1 shows the block diagram of the system.

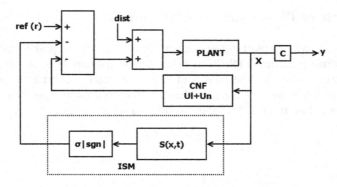

Fig. 1. Biased CNF-ISM block diagram

4 Results and Discussion

Using the proposed method of the previous section, the TWIP was set to track a step of 2 m. The results was generated using simulation in MATLAB Simulink environment. The actual nonlinear model of the TWIP was build using the nonlinear model of [9].

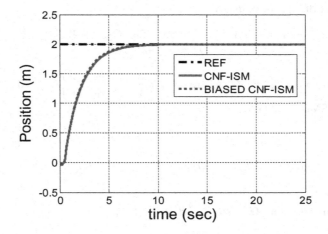

Fig. 2. Step response

Figure 2 shows the step response of both the CNF-ISM and biased CNF-ISM method. It was observed that the two almost have the same fast response and no overshoot. The effectiveness of the biased CNF-ISM concept can be seen in Fig. 3 which is the tilt response when tracking the desired 2 m position, and Fig. 4 the control signal. The maximum tilt angle swing is less using the biased CNF-ISM method and consumes less energy as seen in Fig. 4. The ISM in both biased and the common CNF was able to reach the sliding surface at almost the same time as shown in Fig. 5. Tables 1 and 2 summarizes the results.

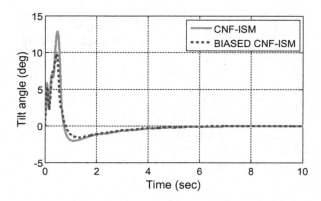

Fig. 3. Tilt response (first 10 s)

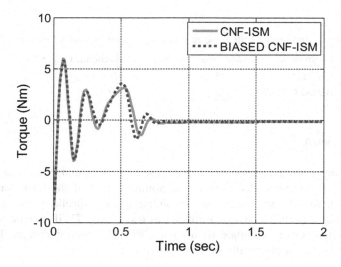

Fig. 4. Control signal under step signal

Table 1. Summary of position response under step signal

Controllers	Settling time (s)	Overshoot (%)
CNF-ISM	10	0
Biased CNF-ISM	10	0

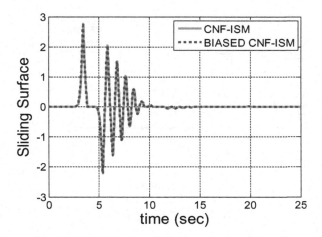

Fig. 5. Sliding surface

Table 2. Summary of tilt angle response and control signal under step signal

Controllers	Maximum angle (deg)	Maximum torque (Nm)
CNF-ISM	12.85	6.0
Biased CNF-ISM	9.75	5.76

5   Conclusion

This paper has presented a way to utilize the use of CNF in under actuated systems by biasing one of the unattended state in the nonlinear part of the CNF function. The proposed method was then integrated with sliding mode controller to make the system robust to input disturbance. The controller was tested on a TWIP mobile robot which shows an improvement compare to normal CNF-ISM control design. The control scheme will be tested practically on real system in future work.

Acknowledgments. These authors are grateful to the Ministry of Education (MOE) and Universiti Teknologi Malaysia for the financial support through the GUP research fund, Vote Q. J130000.2523.11H31and special thanks to Bayero University, Kano, Nigeria for their support.

References

1. Mobayen, S., Majd, V.J., Sojoodi, M.: An LMI-based composite nonlinear feedback terminal sliding-mode controller design for disturbed MIMO systems. Math. Comput. Simul. **85**, 1–10 (2012)
2. Lin, Z., Pachter, M., Banda, S.: Toward improvement of tracking performance nonlinear feedback for linear systems. Int. J. Control Theory Appl. **70**, 1–11 (1998)

 3. Turner, M.C., Postlethwaite, I., Walker, D.J.: Non-linear tracking control for multivariable constrained input linear systems. Int. J. Control **73**, 1160–1172 (2000)
 4. Chen, B.M., Lee, T.H., Kemao, P., Venkataramanan, V.: Composite nonlinear feedback control for linear systems with input saturation: theory and an application. IEEE Trans. Autom. Control **48**, 427–439 (2003)
 5. He, Y., Chen, B.M., Wu, C.: Composite nonlinear control with state and measurement feedback for general multivariable systems with input saturation. Syst. Control Lett. **54**, 455–469 (2005)
 6. Yu, X., Lin, X., Lan, W.: Composite nonlinear feedback controller design for an overhead crane servo system. Trans. Inst. Meas. Control **36**, 662–672 (2014)
 7. Bandyopadhyay, B., Deepak, F., Kim, K.-S.: Sliding Mode Control Using Novel Sliding Surfaces. Springer, Heidelberg (2009)
 8. Weiyao, L., Chen, B.M.: On selection of nonlinear gain in composite nonlinear feedback control for a class of linear systems. In: 46th IEEE Conference on Decision and Control, pp. 1198–1203 (2007)
 9. Bature, A.A., Buyamin, S., Ahmad, M.N., Muhammad, M.: A comparison of controllers for balancing two wheeled inverted pendulum robot. Int. J. Mech. Mechatron. Eng. **14**, 62–68 (2014)
10. Mohamed, Z., Khairudin, M., Husain, A.R., Subudhi, B.: Linear matrix inequality-based robust proportional derivative control of a two-link flexible manipulator. J. Vib. Control **22** (5), 1244–1256 (2016)
11. Castanos, F., Fridman, L.: Analysis and design of integral sliding manifolds for systems with unmatched perturbations. IEEE Trans. Autom. Control **51**, 853–858 (2006)

Realization of 3D Sound Effect System in Navigation Simulator

Qianfeng Jing, Yong Yin$^{(\boxtimes)}$, Wei You, Xiaoxi Zhang,
and Xiaochen Li

Key Laboratory of Maritime Simulation and Control,
Dalian Maritime University, Dalian, China
jqf@dlmu.edu.cn, bushyin_dmu@263.net

Abstract. Three-dimensional sound effect is a relatively weak link in the navigation simulator. The location information, distance attenuation, Doppler Effect and special environment effect cannot be reflected by the sound system at this stage. In this article, a three-dimensional sound effect system is developed based on OpenAL to solve these problems. All kinds of sound sources in simulator are reasonably categorized. Methods are proposed to handle considerable number of sound sources and synchronization problem. The PIMPL mode is applied for completely decoupling the sound module from the simulator main program. The test program of the system is developed under Microsoft Foundation Classes and the test procedure is performed in a real simulator. It can be confirmed that the established system conducted a good simulation of the various sound effects in the navigation environment with a high real-time performance.

Keywords: 3D sound effect · Navigation simulator · Microsoft Foundation Classes · Real-time simulation

1 Introduction

As a virtual reality system, the navigation simulator is required to include all the perception of people, such as visual, auditory, tactile, power, movement and other perception [1]. Furthermore, the DNV standards for maritime simulator system state that the sound system of a simulator is considered to be satisfactory if the following criterions are complied with: The simulator shall provide an own ship engine sound, reflecting the power output; The signals shall be individually controlled by the instructor, and the sound signals shall be directional and fade with range; The simulator shall be capable of providing environmental sound according to conditions simulated; An alarm shall be announced by sound in the control room [2].

There have been some studies on this problem. Lishan JIA developed a 3D sound system for flight simulator based on Direct Sound of Microsoft [3]. A similar system is applied to simulate sound effect in virtual battlefield by Huang and Zhao [4]. However, cross-platform features is not considered in the method using Direct Sound of Microsoft. Begault made it possible to improve sound direction perception and expanse feelings based on five loudspeakers [5]. The arrangement of loudspeakers is based on

© Springer Nature Singapore Pte Ltd. 2017
M.S. Mohamed Ali et al. (Eds.): AsiaSim 2017, Part II, CCIS 752, pp. 306–318, 2017.
DOI: 10.1007/978-981-10-6502-6_27

the purpose of the study, while it is expensive for a navigation simulator. Wu proposed a method to simulate the environment in a driving simulator [6]. An audio simulation system in a flight simulator is introduced in detail by Sheng et al. [7]. The sound module of other brands simulator is also relatively simple in function [8, 9]. To sum up, the 3D sound module is close to maturity in other types of simulators, but a weak link in navigation simulators. Due to the special features of ship and sea environment, special treatment shall be applied to handle considerable number of sound sources and synchronization between visual and sound.

This article realizes the three-dimensional sound system based on open-source cross-platform 3D audio programming interface OpenAL to solve the problem above. In order to achieve better sound field positioning and lifelike sound effects, real-time simulation of different types of sound effects in navigating is performed by the system through multi-layer rendering processing on mono audio resources. The results show that the established system could conduct simulation of sound effects and position information with high real-time performance which enhance the immersion of the navigation simulator.

2 OpenAL

OpenAL (Open Audio Library) is a programming interface for developing interactive 3D audio. Because of its good cross-platform features, more and more application developers use it to develop their audio systems, for the work can be reused on most

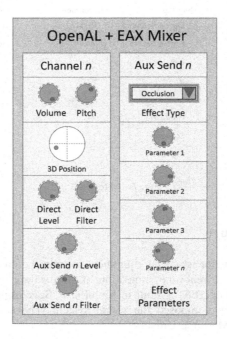

Fig. 1. Mixer of OpenAL with EAX

major platforms. The basic data types of it are similar to OpenGL, which can be seamlessly integrated with OpenGL code. Some common sound effects, such as distance-based attenuation, directionality, Doppler Effect are provided by OpenAL base library [10]. There is no implementation for some special environmental effects in the base library, such as the occlusion effect. For instance, the sound of engine room will be clearly heard under the main deck but weaker above the bridge deck due to the attenuation from decks. Therefore, Environmental Audio Extensions (EAX) of Creative Company is introduced to add process special environment sound. The special effects such as blocking, reverb and reflection can be achieved by this toolkit, the process of OpenAL with EAX is similar to a mixer, as shown in Fig. 1.

3 Sound in Simulator

The principle of the sound system is to simulate the sound source from different categories. The Exercise, Ownship, Target and Environment are the four fundamental categories. There are several sub items under each category as shown in Fig. 2. Each sub items has different attributes to indicate the status of the sound. The amount of them will not be fixed, that is, new items could be added in any category if needed in future. The implementation for new items would be simple due to the advantage of PIMPL.

Fig. 2. Categories

4 System Structure

The navigational simulator is a vital equipment to train the crew. The virtual reality technology is applied to real-time simulation of ship sailing in the real world. The integrated bridge system (IBS) is built in actual size. Several projectors as well as a 360° cylindrical screen composed the visual system. The software for training is developed by Dalian Maritime University.

A. *Hardware Configuration*

The hardware configuration of 3D sound effect system in the simulator is shown in Fig. 3. The projector is used to display real-time simulation scene on a 360° cylindrical screen, and the IBS is surrounded by the cylindrical screen. The trainees are in the middle position of the simulator as the listener in the sound system. The three speakers as the sound source in the sound system will be placed at an adjacent interval of 120°. Simplification is applied to remove the front speaker and combines the left and right rear speakers into one based on the arrangement of multichannel surround sound recommended by 5.1 format [11]. This arrangement will retain information of front and rear sound sources as much as possible as well as save resources and simplify simulator installation. The actual results show that the system has been able to achieve a very realistic sound effects under this arrangement.

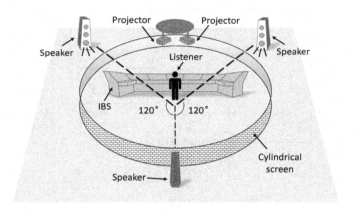

Fig. 3. Hardware configuration

B. *Software Workflow*

The sound system is implemented in the form of a simulation cycle. When the console program starts running an exercise, the initialization interface function is called to initialize the sound module and conduct some preparation work. After entering the simulation cycle, all the status information is collected by the main console program, and update information interface function is called to send the status information to the sound system. Then, the pointer resources of main console program is immediately released after the information is saved by the sound system. A child thread will be created to execute calculation and playback.

In the child thread, the position data of the targets is converted into the relative coordinates. After the distance attenuation processing and the Doppler shift calculation, the special sound effect is applied to the sources. At the end of the simulation circle, corresponding three-dimensional sound is played. If a pause command is given from the console, the sound system will pause all the sound sources and record the status of the current sound. If a resume command is transmitted after then, the system will continue to play all the sound source according to the recorded status. This could keep the continuity of the sound without re-initializing the sound module. If a stop command is transmitted, all sound source is stopped and buffers are cleared initially and then the exit interface function is called to exit the sound system. In the next simulation cycle all of above steps is repeated. The program flow chart is shown in Fig. 4.

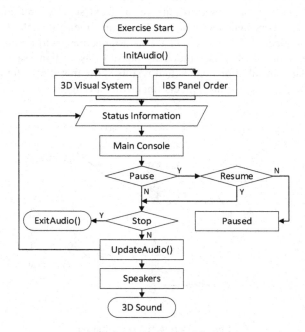

Fig. 4. Software workflow

5 Logic of Sound

The internal logic of the three-dimensional sound effect system is described clearly in this part. The overall operational logic is introduced at first, then the sub items logic is explained using whistle as a sample.

In the categories mentioned above, the main four categories is divided into lots of sub items. Each of the sub items should be processed in different logic. For example, the logic of ownship whistle is shown in Fig. 5.

The logic of the whistle is divided into manual and automatic broadcast. At the manual mode, whistle should be continuous playing if the button on the IBS panel is pressed. In the fog environment, the whistle should be auto broadcast at a specified period. Whistle type and period is determined by the command of IBS panel. If the change of type or period is needed, the system will clear current playing queue, and then queue new buffers of specified type.

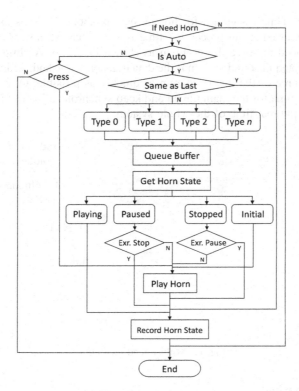

Fig. 5. Whistle logic

6 Technical Points

The three-dimensional sound system contains a lot of technical points, the six key technical points involved in the system are described in detail in this part. The point 1, 3 and 6 are the main innovation in this article. These technical points form the basic framework of the three-dimensional sound effect system.

6.1 Synchronization

Since the sound effect is calculating and playing in real time after receiving the status information. The amount of status information will directly influence the performance of the system. For the main thread, other tasks cannot be handled before the finish of data transfer between sound module and main console. This will result in blocking of main thread. Figure will not be synchronized with the sound. The sound module have to separate from main thread immediately after the data transfer to ensure synchronization.

The performance of the sound system is represented by the number of frames of the visual. If the number of frames is 40 per second, a simulation cycle will be 25 ms, which mainly includes the visual processing time, the data transfer time and the sound processing time. Time resolution for human ears is about 5–15 ms and obvious lag phenomenon occurred if the processing time is more than 15 ms. Multi-thread technique is introduced to solve the problem as shown in Fig. 6. A child thread will be immediately created in sound system if the data transfer is finished, which could release the pointer resource of the main program as quickly as possible. Obviously, this will reduce blocking time for the main thread and keep synchronization of visual and sound so as to ensure the real-time of the whole system.

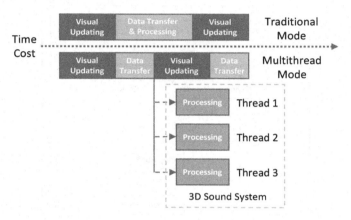

Fig. 6. Multi-thread technique

6.2 Buffer Sharing

Various types of sound sources are required due to the particularity of the navigation simulator, such as the whistle according to the International Regulations for Preventing Collisions at Sea (COLREGS) [12]. There are different signal types for whistle in different situations, each of which is made up of a different combination of short and prolonged blast. For a certain tone of whistles, preliminary work is to prepare audio source made of different combination of blasts for every type as shown in Fig. 7. It is a waste of system resources, moreover, system will become very slow at startup because of the resources loading of huge amounts of audio files.

In order to ensure physical realism of the simulator, the tones of different ship types should be distinct. If the above method is applied, the space occupied by the audio resources will multiply, which will not only influence the convenience of installation of

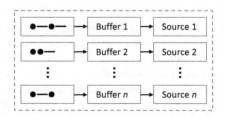

Fig. 7. Traditional mode

the system, but lead to an increase in the probability of error. In this article, the buffer queuing technology is applied for various kind of tones. Only two sources for a certain tone need to be prepared. In the sound system, different types of sound implemented by queuing buffer of the short and the prolonged blast as shown in Fig. 8. It is based on efficient mechanism of buffer sharing in OpenAL which could save plenty of pre-processing on audio resources. The number of tones is also easier to increase. The results show that the size of the installation package reduced considerably in the control of the sampling rate of the audio which ensure the overall performance of simulator.

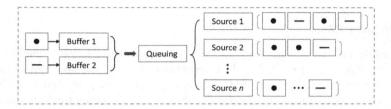

Fig. 8. Buffer sharing mode

6.3 Attenuation

The distance between the sound and the listener is generally determined by the loudness acting on ears. Since the sound will attenuate with the distance. A reasonable distance attenuation model for the three-dimensional sound system is important [13]. Linear model is not suitable for real scene owing to the rapid and stiff attenuation, the exponential model is chosen here and the sketch is shown in Fig. 9. When the distance is greater than the reference distance, the sound begins to decay and no longer increases when the distance is less than the reference distance.

The sound is almost impossible to hear when the distance increases to a certain extent for human ears. This distance is defined as the disappearance distance in this article. Likewise, the human ear is insensitive to the distance variation of the source when it is close enough which called reference distance. The reference distance is one of the

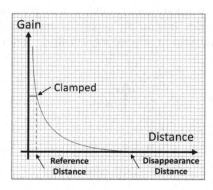

Fig. 9. Exponential distance clamped model

attributes of the sound source. The disappearance distance is not implemented in OpenAL. The distance limit function is developed on the basis of the exponential distance model above. The sound will be no longer played when the distance of the source exceeds the calculated results. As long as the original decibels of the sound source are known, the disappearance distance can be calculated easily by Eq. 1. The dL represents the amount of attenuation and r represents the distance between the source and listener [14].

$$dL = 10 \lg\left(\frac{1}{4}\pi r^2\right) \tag{1}$$

6.4 Doppler Effect

Doppler Effect occurred when the sound source moved relative to the listener as shown in Fig. 10. There are two API calls to provide control of the speed of sound and Doppler factor. AL_DOPPLER_FACTOR is a simple scaling of source and listener velocities to exaggerate or deemphasize the Doppler shift resulting from the calculation and AL_SPEED_OF_SOUND is used to set the propagation speed of the sound. The pseudo code of mathematical representation is shown in Appendix 1.

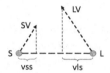

Fig. 10. Doppler shift

6.5 Special Environment Effect

For navigation simulator, there are some special environment sound effects. For instance, the noise of Engine Room is heard with a large loudness in the cabin but relatively small in the bridge. It is because of the occlusion effect by several layers of deck as shown in Fig. 11. The effect is not implemented in the OpenAL base API. The Environmental Sound Expansion (EAX) toolkit of Creative Company is introduced to simulate special sound effect. It is mainly applied in the simulation of occlusion effect of the environment sound field to achieve more realistic feeling.

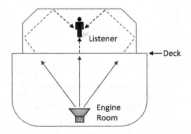

Fig. 11. Occlusion effect

6.6   Object-Oriented

Herb Sutter of Microsoft first proposed the concept of PIMPL [15]. A private pointer to the implementation class is defined in the interface class to avoid exposing the internal structure as shown in Fig. 12. Only the header file of interface class is provided to the client program so as to avoid the coupling between the function modules and the client program. The method is also known as compilation firewalls.

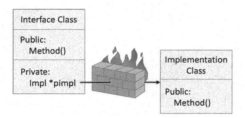

Fig. 12.   PIMPL mode

The three-dimensional sound system is encapsulated into a dynamic link library with the above-mentioned PIMPL mode. The upgrade of either the sound module or the main program is convenient which does not affect each other as well. The cost of compiling is reduced through the method. There are three public functions in the interface class and part of the code is shown below. The first function is used to initialize the sound system and load audio resources. The second function is used to update the status information of the sound in each simulation circle and the last one is used to release the buffer resources and exit the sound system.

```
BOOL InitAudio();
BOOL UpdataAudio(Exr_Status Exr_out, OS_Status OS_out,
   vector<TS_Status>&TS_Vec_out, Env_Status Env_out);
BOOL ExitAudio();
```

7   Test of System

The test program is developed based on the Microsoft Foundation Classes (MFC) with an interactive interface. The logic of the test program is in full accordance with the simulator.

A. *Test Program*
The gain of each sub items could be adjusted simply in the program. The target vector is defined to simulate different movement of the sound source. The program interface is shown in Fig. 13.

B. *Test Environment*
The test is carried out in a navigation simulator as shown in Fig. 14. The simulator is absolutely same as the configuration mentioned above in order to obtain accurate test results.

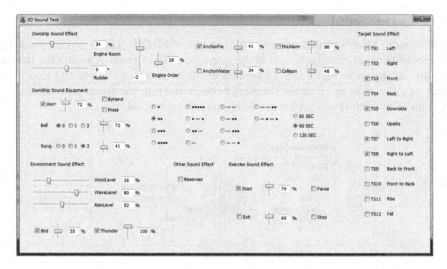

Fig. 13. Test program

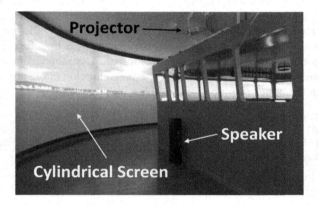

Fig. 14. Configuration of simulator

C. *Evaluation Results*

Since the three-dimensional sound is a subjective concept, there is no suitable objective indicators to evaluate the effect [16]. The test is conducted by a subjective method. Eight different positions (0 represents front direction and increase clockwise) of the sound are selected as samples and 20 people are invited as testers. The direction effect of the samples is evaluated in five levels by testers, that is, the direction is unable to distinguish if level 1 is chose and able to clearly identify if level 5 is chose. The evaluation results are shown in Table 1. It can be seen that the accuracy of the 135° and 225° direction is the lowest ones due to the arrangement of speakers, but the direction could still be roughly distinguished at these directions. Other directions are able to be a distinguished clearly which indicates the effectiveness of the system.

Table 1. Evaluation results

Direction	0°	45°	90°	135°	180°	225°	270°	325°
Average level	4.1	4.5	4.0	3.8	4.8	3.6	4.1	4.6

8 Conclusion

The three-dimensional sound effect system in the navigation simulator based on OpenAL is realized in this article. The test results show that the system can effectively reflect the position information of the sound source with a good real-time performance, which could improve the immersion of trainees. The weak link of the simulator on sound is improved as a complete virtual reality system.

Acknowledgment. The author would like to acknowledge the support from the National High Technology Research and Development Program of China ("863" Program) [No. 2015AA0 16404], Marine public welfare industry research [No. 201505017-4] and the Fundamental Research Funds for the Central Universities [No. 3132016310].

Appendix 1: Mathematical Representation of Doppler Shift

```
S: Sound source  L: listener
SV = Source velocity vector
LV = Listener velocity vector
SL = source to listener vector
SS: AL_SPEED_OF_SOUND = speed of sound
DF: AL_DOPPLER_FACTOR = Doppler factor
vls: Listener velocity scalar
vss: Source velocity scalar
f: Frequency of sound source
f': effective Doppler shifted frequency
vls = DotProduct(SL, LV) / Mag(SL)
vss = DotProduct(SL, SV) / Mag(SL)
vss = min(vss, SS/DF)
vls = min(vls, SS/DF)
f' = f * (SS - DF*vls) / (SS - DF*vss)
```

References

1. Jin, Y., Yin, Y.: Development strategy of marine simulator in light of the manila amendments to STCW convention. Navig. China **35**(3), 5–10 (2012)
2. Standard DNVGL-ST-0033:2014-08:2014. DNV GL AS and Maritime Simulator Systems
3. Sheng, X.W., Zheng, S.T., Han, J.W., et al.: Simulation and realization of 3D sound for flight simulator. J. Shenyang Univ. Technol. **34**(1), 48–55 (2012)

4. Huang, X.Y., Zhao, D.H.: Implementation of 3D sound effect based on direct sound method. J. Syst. Simul. (2006)
5. Begault, D.R.: 3-D Sound for Virtual Reality and Multimedia. Academic Press Professional Inc., Boston (1994)
6. Wu, S.: Engine sound simulation and generation in driving simulator. Missouri University of Science and Technology (2016)
7. Sheng, X.W., Han, J.W., Hao, M.H.: Sound analysis and synthesis for audio simulation system of flight simulator. Adv. Mater. Res. **748**, 708–712 (2013)
8. Kongsberg: K-Sim Navigation Ship Bridge Simulator. http://www.km.kongsberg.com
9. VStep: NAUTIS Ship Bridge Simulator. http://vstepsimulation.com
10. OpenAL User Documentation. https://www.openal.org
11. Tanno, K.: 3D sound system with horizontally arranged loudspeakers. Ph.D. dissertation, University of Aizu (2014)
12. US Coast Guard, Commandant: International regulations for prevention of collisions at sea, 1972 (72 COLREGS). US Department of Transportation, US Coast Guard, COMMANDANT INSTRUCTION M, 16672 (1999)
13. Khalilian, H., Bajić, I.V., Vaughan, R.G.: A simulation study of a three-dimensional sound field reproduction system for immersive communication. IEEE/ACM Trans. Audio Speech Lang. Process. **25**(5), 980–995 (2017)
14. Yan, S., Wang, S.: Numerical simulation of nonlinear acoustic attenuation of multi-component gas mixture. Chin. J. Acoust. **2009**(2), 97–115 (2009)
15. PIMPL. https://herbsutter.com/gotw/_101
16. Nakahara, M., Mikami, T., Omoto, A.: Evaluating acoustical features of 3D sound rendering systems by using a visualizing tool of sound intensities. J. Acoust. Soc. Am. **140**(4), 3177 (2016)

Real-Time Fluid Simulation with Complex Boundary Based on Slice Voxelization Method

Changjun Zou, Yong Yin$^{(\boxtimes)}$, and Qianfeng Jing

Key Lab of Marine Simulation and Control Lab,
Dalian Maritime University, Dalian 116021, China
bushyin@163.com

Abstract. In view of the present restriction in complex boundary interaction in real time fluid simulation. A physically based real-time fluid simulation method with complex boundary is proposed and implemented. The pressure projection algorithm is used to solve the N-S equation. The implicit scheme is employed to guarantee the stability of the nonlinear advection term. This paper presents and implements the idea of slicing and voxelization of the solid boundary in a unified way. The algorithm is independent of the specific model, which can simulate the fluid interaction with complex boundary flow field of different 3D models efficiently.

Keywords: Real time fluid simulation · Complex boundary interaction · Slicing voxelization method

1 Introduction

Physically based fluid simulation is one of the hotspots and difficulties in the re- search of realistic graphics rendering in recent years, it has a very important application in special effects, animation games, and virtual reality simulation and so on. Physically based fluid simulation is mainly based on computational fluid dynamics (CFD) theory. At present, a lot of research work has been done at home and abroad by solving the Navier-Stokes (N-S) equation. However, due to the nonlinear term in the N-S equation, the numerical solution is difficult. In addition, it is also difficult to deal with the interaction with complex obstacles in the flow field. Stam [1] put forward the concept of Stable Fluid, the non-linear advection term is calculated in implicit solution to ensure the stability as well as the large time step during the simulation in his method. Stam [1] realized fluid simulation based on physical in real-time for the first time, which is of great value in fluid simulation. Foster [2] adopted the modified Semi-Lagrange method and Level Set method to track the free surface. He realized the fluid interaction with simple geometry obstacles. Batty et al. [3] employed the potential function in representing the obstacle boundary, but the potential function is difficult to obtain and the potential function can hardly be used to represent the complex boundary. Liu et al. [4] has realized the real-time simulation with complex obstacles, but the complex obstacles are not portable, the algorithm is not obstacles independent. Zhang et al. [5] uses LBM method to simulate the fluid in real time, but it is still unable to deal with different complex boundary efficiently. Liu and Xiong [6] introduces a fast water interaction

© Springer Nature Singapore Pte Ltd. 2017
M.S. Mohamed Ali et al. (Eds.): AsiaSim 2017, Part II, CCIS 752, pp. 319–326, 2017.
DOI: 10.1007/978-981-10-6502-6_28

method, in which the continuousness of the N-S equation is secured by Perfectly Matched Layers. However there is still much room for improvement in physical reality. Li et al. [7] implements a real-time water environment interaction method, but the method is in 2 dimensions. Sandim et al. [8] Ferstl et al. [9] put forward a fluid interaction method based on particles, thought this method enhanced the interaction with complex obstacles, the method is not applicable for real-time system due to the huge computation.

In this paper, the pressure projection algorithm is utilized in solving the NS equation. In the equation, the non-linear advection term is dealt in implicit scheme for stability and large time step; the diffusion term is discrete in upwind scheme for high accuracy.

For dealing with the interaction with complex boundary, the slicing voxelization [10] method is used in discretization of the obstacles. The sliced obstacle is transferred into the GPU as an obstacle texture; the boundary of each slice is searched and identified by texture sampling in GPU. This method takes good advantages of the Graphics Card's ability in parallel computing for higher efficiency.

In the following: Sect. 2 introduces and validated the pressure projection method; Sect. 3 addresses the complex boundary process; Application and testing of the mentioned is carried in Sect. 4; Sect. 5 concluded the paper.

2 Numerical Method in Solving N-S Equation

2.1 The Difficulties in N-S Equation Calculation

Simulation of fluid is carried out in numerical calculation of N-S equation. But the nonlinear term in the N-S equation will always result in unstable for the explicit numerical scheme. Therefore, the numerical solution of the original N-S equation has the many difficulties: The velocity $\vec{u}$ and pressure P in the original variable N-S equations are decoupled, the velocity field calculated from momentum Eq. (1) can hardly satisfy the continue Eq. (2). This will always results divergence of the numerical scheme. On the other hand, how to couple the velocity and pressure in the calculation is another problem. In addition, numerical treatment of the boundary is very important. As we know that the N-S equation partial differential equation of elliptic property, which means that the boundary will influence the whole domain. Inappropriate treatment of the boundary will result in the unstable and divergence.

$$
\begin{aligned}
\frac{\partial u}{\partial t} + u\frac{\partial u}{\partial x} + v\frac{\partial u}{\partial y} &= -\frac{\partial p}{\partial x} + \frac{1}{Re}\left(\frac{\partial^2 u}{\partial x^2} + \frac{\partial^2 u}{\partial^2 y}\right) \\
\frac{\partial v}{\partial t} + u\frac{\partial v}{\partial x} + v\frac{\partial v}{\partial y} &= -\frac{\partial p}{\partial y} + \frac{1}{Re}\left(\frac{\partial^2 u}{\partial x^2} + \frac{\partial^2 u}{\partial^2 y}\right) - g
\end{aligned}
\tag{1}
$$

$$
\frac{\partial u}{\partial x} + \frac{\partial v}{\partial y} = 0
\tag{2}
$$

2.2   Pressure Projection Method

Pressure projection method was first put forward by Chorin [11] in 1967. The method has many advantages such as it is very easy to understand with simple calculation; Good adaptability for different Reynolds number with high stability and high precision. Therefore, it is widely used in incompressible viscous flow simulation.

Projection algorithm is a Multi-step algorithm. Momentum equation in vector form can be seen in Eq. (3):

$$\frac{V^{n+1} - V^*}{\Delta t} + A(V^n) + \nabla p^{n+1} - \frac{1}{Re} \nabla^2 V^n = 0 \tag{3}$$

The momentum equation is divided into two steps. The first step is to ignore the pressure effect in the momentum equation, obtain the modified momentum equation as shown in Eq. (4):

$$\frac{V^{n+1} - V^*}{\Delta t} + A(V^n) - \frac{1}{Re} \nabla^2 V^n = 0 \tag{4}$$

The term $A(V^n)$ is the advection term. The second step is the pressure effect correction:

$$\frac{V^{n+1} - V^*}{\Delta t} + \nabla p^{n+1} = 0 \tag{5}$$

Then the pressure correction equation is obtained by using the continuity equation, yield:

$$\nabla^2 p^{n+1} = \frac{1}{\Delta t} \nabla \cdot V^* \tag{6}$$

After the pressure is obtained, the velocity correction is performed according to Eq. (5). The above is a time step of the calculation process, and then repeats the above steps until the convergence of the calculation.

2.3   Pressure Projection Realization and Validation

For the nonlinear convection term in the N-S equation, the implicit method is used to ensure the stability of the calculation. The viscous term is in upwind difference scheme, and the pressure projection is calculated by iteration. In order to verify the accuracy of the pressure projection algorithm, the pressure projection algorithm is used to calculate the CFD benchmark problem, and the results are compared with those in the literature. The results are shown in Fig. 1.

The solid line represents the U component of the velocity at the center line, and the dash line represents the V component of the velocity in the horizontal midline. It can be seen from the results that the calculated results are in good agreement with the literature, and the reliability of the projection algorithm is verified.

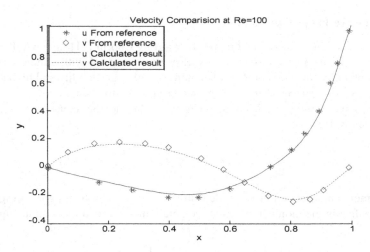

Fig. 1. Result comparison of cavity flow with Ref. [12]

3 Complex Obstacle Boundary Treatment

3.1 Boundary Treatment Method

Another difficulties in fluid simulation is the interaction with obstacles. In this paper, the solid obstacles were discrete by the slice voxel method [10], and the GPU was utilized to accelerate the voxel process.

In slicing voxel method, the obstacle is sliced first, then the slices are rasterized in the GPU in the raster hardware as texture. In this process it makes full use of the hardware device in GPU for geometry rasterization. It is easy to identify the location of obstacles and the obstacle boundaries by texture sampling in the next. The method is obstacle independent, any obstacle of mesh model can be treated with the same pipeline. As shown in Figs. 5, 6 and 7, the computational results of the flow field for different complex obstacles are presented (Fig. 2).

3.2 Boundary Searching Strategy and Implementation

In order to find out the boundary quickly, the proximity search strategy is used to identify whether the gird is the boundary or not. In the search process, the property of the four neighbor grids are searched as shown in Fig. 3 on the left. If all the grids are of the same type, the node will be an internal grid, otherwise it is a boundary node as shown in Fig. 3 on the right side.

As can be seen from Fig. 4, on the left is the Armadillo obstacle model, on the right side is the slice result from our method. The slice number in Z direction is 50, on the right of Fig. 4 shows the results from different view direction.

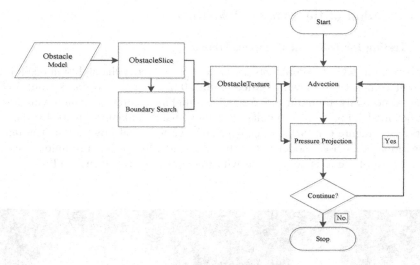

Fig. 2. Chart flow of obstacle process

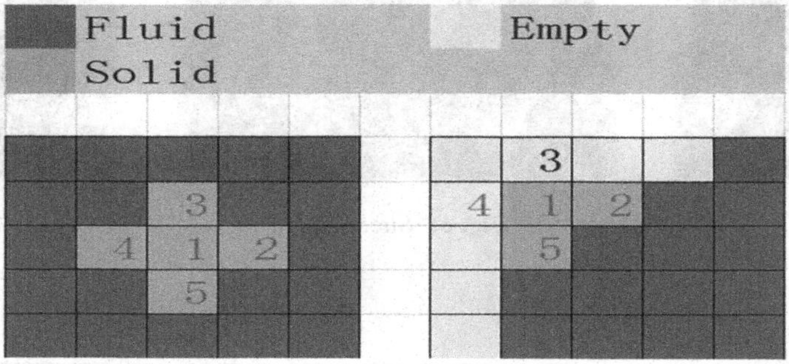

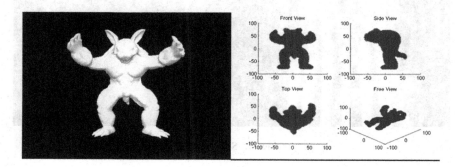

Fig. 3. Boundary searching strategy

Fig. 4. Obstacle and slice results

4   Validation of the Proposed Method

4.1   Testing for Different Complex Model

In this section, sets of experiments are carried out to verify the ability in dealing with different complex model with vertices from 2022 to 8176, and faces from 3692 to 11566 respectively. From Figs. 5, 6 and 7 are fluid interaction simulation with different complex model, Fig. 5 is the simulation result with a street lamp with 4044 vertices and 8836 faces. Figure 6 is Skyscraper with 2022 vertices and 3692 faces. The detailed information of the used model and the frame rate at different grid resolution is listed in Table 1. All of the tests are running with frame rate not less than 24 FPS.

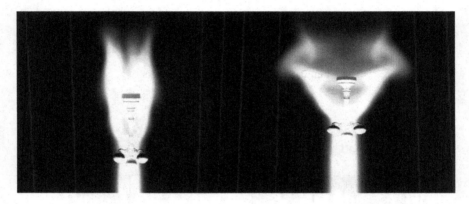

Fig. 5.   Street lamp

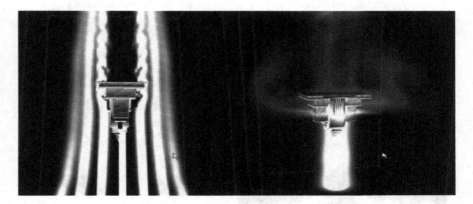

Fig. 6.   Skyscraper

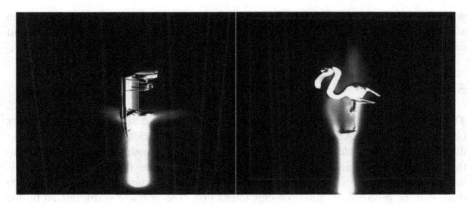

Fig. 7. Airboat and flamingo

Table 1. Model information and frame rate at different grid resolution

	Vertexes	Faces	32^3	64^3	128^3
Skyscraper	2022	3692	60	51	26
Lamp	4044	8836	58	49	26
Flamingo	6902	12862	58	48	25
Airboat	8176	11566	53	41	24

4.2 Testing for Different Grid Dimensions

In this section, different set of experiments with different grid dimension from 32^3 to 128^3 are carried out. The results are shown in Fig. 8. The frame rate is around 60 FPS, 50 FPS and 25 FPS from the above said grid dimension. As can be seen that the frame rate does not differ much even with huge difference in vertexes and faces numbers, the

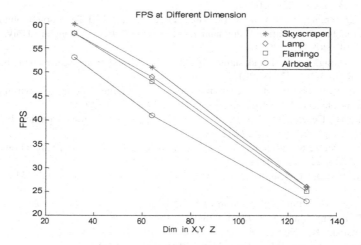

Fig. 8. Running test with different gird dimension

possible reason for this is the parallel implementation of the pressure projection algorithm. In this way the calculation is carried in the GPU at the same time instead of calculate vertex by vertex in serial in CPU.

5 Conclusion

This paper presents a real time simulation method for fluid simulation and complex obstacle interaction. Aiming at the problem that the numerical simulation is easy to diverge and the time step cannot be too large, the implicit method is used to deal with the nonlinear convection term in the NS equation. Since the implicit method is unconditionally stable, large time steps can be adopted. A unified method is used to deal with the problem of fluid obstacles interaction. The obstacle is discretized by the slice voxelization method. This method makes full use of the hardware of the rendering pipeline to in geometry rasterization. The test results meet the requirements for real-time system with a number of different complex obstacles.

Acknowledgment. The authors would like to acknowledge the support from the National High Technology Research and Development Program of China ("863" Program) [No. 2015A A016404], Marine public welfare industry research [No. 201505017-4].

References

1. Stam, J.: Stable fluids. In: Conference on Computer Graphics & Interactive Techniques (1999)
2. Foster, N.: Practical animation of liquids. In: Proceedings of 28th Annual Conference on Computer Graphics and Interactive Techniques (2001)
3. Batty, C., Bertails, F., Bridson, R.: A fast variational framework for accurate solid-fluid coupling. ACM Trans. Graph. **26**(3), 100–107 (2007)
4. Liu, Y., Liu, X., Wu, E.: Real-time 3D fluid simulation on GPU with complex obstacles. J. Softw. **3**(3), 247–256 (2006)
5. Zhang, Q., Zhang, Z.P., Wang, C.B., Xia, Z.D., Cui, J.Y.: Real-Time flow around obstacles simulation based on lattice Boltzmann method on GPGPU. J. Donghua Univ. (Nat. Sci. Edn.) 37(4): 408–411 (2012)
6. Liu, S., Xiong, Y.: Fast and stable simulation of virtual water scenes with interactions. Virtual Real. **1**(17), 77–88 (2013)
7. Li, Y., Peng, J., Fan, F., et al.: Real-time simulation of large-scale water environments with interacting objects. J. Comput. Inf. Syst. **9**(11), 3257–3264 (2015)
8. Sandim, M., Cedrim, D., Nonato, L., et al.: Boundary detection in particle-based fluids. Comput. Graph. **2**(35), 215–224 (2016)
9. Ferstl, F., Ando, R., Wojtan, C., et al.: Narrow band flip for liquid simulations. Comput. Graph. **3**(35), 225–232 (2016)
10. Fang, S., Chen, H.: Hardware accelerated voxelization. Comput. Graph. **24**(3), 433–442 (2000)
11. Chorin, A.: The numerical solution of the Navier-Stokes equations for an incompressible fluid. Bull. Am. Math. Soc. **73**(6), 928–931 (1967)
12. Poochinapan, K.: Numerical implementations for 2D lid-driven cavity flow in stream function formulation. ISRN Appl. Math. **2012**(4), 1–18 (2012)

Simulation of CO$_2$ Rich Natural Gas Pilot Plant Carbon Dioxide Absorption Column at Elevated Pressure Using Equilibrium and Rate Based Method

Salvinder Kaur Marik Singh, Haslinda Zabiri$^{(\boxtimes)}$, Faezah Isa, and Azmi M. Shariff

Research Centre for CO2 Capture (RCCO2), Universiti Teknologi PETRONAS, 32610 Bandar Seri Iskandar, Perak, Malaysia
haslindazabiri@utp.edu.my

Abstract. This paper reports a steady state model for CO$_2$ removal using MEA solvent that operates at elevated pressure and the behaviour that affects the performance of CO$_2$ absorption process. All the input for the simulation has been acquired from the experimental work using pilot plant which is located at Universiti Teknologi PETRONAS (UTP). Steady state simulation has been demonstrated using Aspen Plus utilizing both equilibrium and rate based approaches. Modifications for the equilibrium based method has been done to ensure similarity between rate based and equilibrium based simulation. Since Aspen Dynamic does not support rate based model, adjustment made to the equilibrium model will enable the model to be used for future studies which involves dynamic and control study. The most relevant input parameters of the equilibrium model are methodically varied and the influence of that variation on the simulation results based on CO$_2$ removal percentage was monitored. The evaluation has been conducted to observe the percentage of CO$_2$ removal by setting the Murphree efficiency and varying number of stages of absorber unit.

Keywords: Natural gas · CO$_2$ removal · High pressure · Steady state

1 Introduction

Natural gas (NG) is formed in the underground and can usually be found in areas where both coal and oil are situated. When cleaning natural gas, the content of water, carbon dioxide (CO$_2$) and hydrogen sulphide (H$_2$S) have to be removed to secure a high-quality product for the end user. The process for removing H$_2$S and CO$_2$ from a natural gas stream is referred to as gas sweetening [1]. There are different methods for gas sweetening and the commonly used are adsorption and absorption. For gas sweetening for offshore absorption columns, liquid solutions of an amine mixed with water are the commonly used as sweetening agent [2]. With the increasingly strict environmental regulations on emissions from natural gas treatment plants and the market demand for high quality natural gas, the gas sweetening process has become mandatory [3].

© Springer Nature Singapore Pte Ltd. 2017
M.S. Mohamed Ali et al. (Eds.): AsiaSim 2017, Part II, CCIS 752, pp. 327–336, 2017.
DOI: 10.1007/978-981-10-6502-6_29

Natural gas reserves usually have high flowing pressure at the wellhead which is reduced to about 70–100 bar operation pressure at the offshore platform. A rate-based steady-state model for CO_2 capture by chemical absorption at an atmospheric condition was developed in literatures and validated for low CO_2 partial pressure in the range of 1–20 kPa. However, the validation of the model for CO_2 absorption at a high CO_2 partial pressure has yet to be reported due to the unavailability/limitations of the performance data at high pressure conditions [4]. MEA, DEA, and MDEA are conventional chemical absorbents [5]. Industrially, the monoethanolamine (MEA) process is the most effective among different technologies for CO_2 capture from flue gas [6].

CO_2 absorption technology has been extensively applied to many industrial processes including nature gas, synthesis gas and hydrogen production with high CO_2 contents [7]. Potential absorbents for CO_2 removal in the range of 1 to 15% from flue gases are being explored by researchers and also the CO_2 removal at atmospheric conditions. However, the CO_2 concentration in some natural gas reservoirs can be very high. For example, it could be as high as 71% in the Natuna gas field, Indonesia [8]. The advantage of a chemical absorption technology is that it is the most matured technology for CO_2 capture and it has been commercialized for many decades.

The simulation software plays a key role in studying process alternatives, interpreting pilot plant data, conducting technical and economic feasibility studies [9]. Natural gas industry relies heavily on theoretical approaches to design, improve and optimize production and processing units. Testing at large scale is so expensive and it is common to use process simulation to evaluate such processes. The computer-aided process simulation tools are also helpful in determining the optimum operating conditions with a minimum of time, effort, and cost [10].

CO_2 removal by amine scrubbing has been extensively studied which describes the process behavior using steady state models to optimize the MEA-based CO_2 capture process operating conditions [11–13]. It should be noted that many researchers are using rate-based model for the modelling of CO_2 capture by aqueous solutions of MEA [13–16]. Extensive research has been conducted for CO_2 removal for post combustion process where the CO_2 content is in the range of 1–15%. However, the CO_2 concentration in some natural gas sweetening can be very high. In addition, the main differences between CO_2 absorption from flue gas and natural gas is the operating pressure in terms of process condition and CO_2 compositions.

There are two basic stage models in order to develop dynamic simulation model of CO_2 removal in simulation software which are the equilibrium-based and rate based. Aspen Plus [17] supports two main separation models for the modelling of absorber and stripper, including equilibrium stage and non-equilibrium stage (rate-based) models for steady state condition but dynamic model; they only support the equilibrium approach.

A clear purpose why equilibrium based method is preferred compared to rate based method had been demonstrated [18]. The packed column is modelled following the equilibrium based approach and the column is divided in theoretical stages. Equilibrium between the vapour and liquid phase of the working fluid within each volume is assumed. In order to match the steady state performances, the number of equilibrium stages is tuned by comparison with the simulation results of a full rate based model.

This paper focuses on CO$_2$ capture from natural gas at elevated pressure by absorption with an aqueous solution of monoethanolamine (MEA). This amine is the most frequently used solvent for this process, due to its relatively high loading, i.e. the ratio of moles of absorbed acid gas per mole of amine. Aspen Plus simulator was found suitable for user customization and it has been chosen as framework for the model proposed in this work. The modelling procedure has to take into account both thermodynamics and mass transfer. Kinetics and mass transfer can be described using two different approaches: the equilibrium based stage efficiency model or the rate based model [19]. The equilibrium based stage efficiency approach corrects the performance of a theoretical stage by a factor called stage efficiency. It takes into account mass transfer and non-equilibrium chemical reactions for all species [20] or only mass transfer for non-reactive species, when kinetics is considered. The rate based model avoids the approximation of efficiency, by analysing the mass transfer based on the two film theory as in Fig. 1 and heat transfer phenomena that occur on a real tray or actual packing height. Thus, in this study, both the models are tested and compared and the equilibrium based is adjusted to be similar with rate based results. The result of the model developed is validated with the pilot plant data.

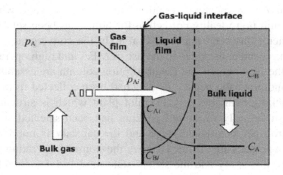

Fig. 1. A schematic diagram of mass transfer model based on the two film theory [21]

The chemistry description for CO$_2$ removal via chemical absorption are considered by the following equilibrium reactions [22]:

$$2H_2O \leftrightarrow H_3O^+ + OH^- \tag{1}$$

$$H_2O + HCO_3^- \leftrightarrow CO_3^{-2} + H_3O^+ \tag{2}$$

$$2H_2O + CO_2 \leftrightarrow HCO_3^- + H_3O^+ \tag{3}$$

$$H_2O + MEACOO^- \leftrightarrow MEA + HCO_3^- \tag{4}$$

$$H_2O + MEAH^+ \leftrightarrow MEA + H_3O^+ \tag{5}$$

2 Simulation Models

Aspen Plus V8 has been utilized to simulate CO_2 removal at high operating pressure of 10 bar. In the Aspen simulator, the Electrolyte NRTL thermal property package is employed to describe the liquid phase non-ideality and Poynting correction has been selected due to high pressure for pure component liquid fugacity coefficient estimation. Once all the properties have been checked, the process flow can be setup in simulation environment. Radfrac column is the best feature available in this simulator to simulate the process once either equilibrium or rate based has been selected. In order to simulate the steady state condition, the present model follows the following assumptions [23];

- Counter current with well mixed between vapour and liquid.
- The vaporization of solvent is negligible.
- The heat release to surrounding is very small.
- The heat and mass transfer between phases follow the two-film theory.

In the rate-based approach, more inputs need to be specified such as mass transfer coefficient, heat transfer correlation, effective interfacial area and flow model. In this study, correlation of Bravo has been selected due to suitability of correlation with structured pack column. A heat transfer correlation had used default value while flow model is counter current. Film non-ideality correction for liquid has been selected and effective interfacial area factor has been maintained at 1. In the convergence section, strongly non-ideal liquid has been chosen due to the use of MEA and high operating pressure.

The data for the feed stream and the absorption column are essential for simulation of steady state conditions and hence, the data had been collected from UTP pilot plant. Two types of packing available in UTP pilot plant which is structured and random packing. In this study, only structured packing had been selected since it provides a lower pressure drop per theoretical stage and the capacity is improved compared to trays or random type packing. Table 1 shows the nominal operating condition steady state simulation in this study and the steady state model is developed as in Fig. 2.

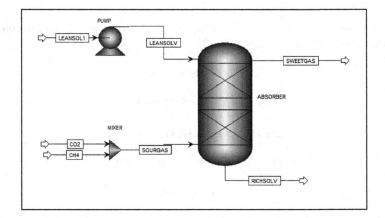

Fig. 2. Steady state model in Aspen Plus environment simulation

Table 1. Operating condition for steady state simulation

Operating condition	Inlet data
Sour gas	
1. CO$_2$	0.5 mol
2. CH$_4$	0.5 mol
Lean solvent	
1. H$_2$O	0.8 mol
2. MEA	0.2 mol
Flowrate	
(1) Sour gas	50 l/min
(2) Lean solvent	1.06 l/min
Temperature	
(1) Sour gas	35.0 °C
(2) Lean solvent	25.0 °C
Pressure	
(1) Sour gas	10.5 bar
(2) Lean Solvent	10.6 bar
Absorption column data	
(1) Diameter of column	0.145 m
(2) Height of column	1.5 m
(3) Structured packing type	FLEXIPAC 1Y
(4) Material	Metal
(5) No. of stage	5

3 Simulation and Discussion

3.1 Simulation of Steady State Absorption

The results of CO$_2$ removal from the Aspen Plus has been compared with the actual data from UTP pilot plant absorption column. In steady state simulation, a reduction of CO$_2$ content in sweet gas had been observed and this shows that chemical absorption had taking place successfully at elevated pressure with the usage of aqueous MEA solvent. From the experimental work data obtained from the pilot plant, the percentage of CO$_2$ removal conducted at 10 bar is about 85%. The CO$_2$ content has been collected at the top of the column through infrared gas analyzer and compared with the inlet CO$_2$ content in sour gas stream. Both of equilibrium and rate based approaches have been applied in Aspen simulator to observe CO$_2$ removal percentage.

Table 2 shows the CO$_2$ removal percentage between the pilot plant and the simulation result. It can be observed that performance of rate based approach produce a better outcome where minimal deviation is observed. Meanwhile, in the equilibrium approach, a significant deviation of 35.29% is observed. A predictable result is obtained since rate based approach is more efficient in describing separation model.

However, since Aspen Plus only support the equilibrium approach for dynamic simulation, various adjustment has been introduced to produce similar result as rate based approach [22]. This step is also important to achieve a stable steady state condition for

Table 2. The CO_2 removal of pilot plant and simulation steady state

	Removal of CO_2 (%)
Experimental	85.0
Equilibrium based	55.0
Rate based	84.3

Aspen Dynamic model. In the simulation, the steady-state based model is developed by involving the Murphree efficiency and number of stages effects. Murphree efficiency is varied by trial and error in order to observe the effectiveness of this factor in rectifying activities in stages and yields out the best process performance [22]. The operating pressure is maintained at 10 bar and the efficiency values are tuned from 0.1 to 0.3. The results obtained are then compared with the pilot plant experimental data.

Figure 3 shows the percentage of CO_2 removal of equilibrium based and rate based approaches before adjustment is made. The result shows clearly the gap between these two approaches, where rate based has a closer agreement to the experimental data whereas equilibrium model has higher deviation from experimental data before Murphree efficiency is applied. The graph shows the CO_2 capture efficiencies against the number of stages from 2 to 10. In the Rate Sep study by [24], rate based modelling approach offers the model exactness compared to equilibrium based modelling which is the traditional way in stage modelling. The complexity of mathematical computation embedded in rate based has provided a surplus value in accuracy and longer computational time needed for vast number of differential equations accommodated in [25, 26]. In real situation, vapour and liquid phases are never in phase equilibrium with each other as commonly assumed in equilibrium model [24]. Therefore, actual operations conventionally incorporate efficiencies such as local efficiency, Murphree efficiency and overall efficiency in the model simulation [25]. In this work, Murphree efficiency

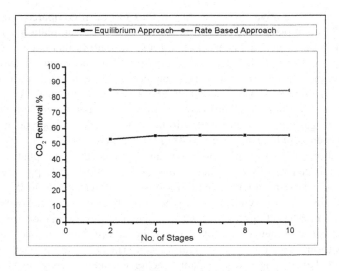

Fig. 3. Percentage of CO_2 removal before adjustments

of 0.15 is selected based on the trial and error technique to improve the performance of the equilibrium based approach which will be presented in the steady state result.

3.1.1 Variation of Number of Stages by Maintaining the Murphree Efficiency at 0.15

The number of stages are varied with a constant Murphree efficiency of 0.15 (Equilibrium * M). Murphree efficiency has been used for decades in relating the theoretical with actual number of stages in a distillation column or absorber. This efficiency can be based upon the liquid or the vapour composition on a particular stage at the specified conditions of temperature and pressure [28]. The enhanced performance in CO$_2$ capture is anticipated by the increasing of the number of stages similar to the work by [18]. It is well known that number of stages play an important role in the stability of the numerical solution.

Since, the absorption is taking place in structured packing column, height equivalent to theoretical plate (HETP) has been applied and number of stages is determined by dividing the height over HETP. However, since the value of HETP is uncertain except the estimation given by vendor, thus number of stages is varied with a constant Murphree efficiency of 0.15 until the output match the actual pilot plant data.

In Fig. 4, CO$_2$ removal using equilibrium based approach with and without Murphree efficiency is compared to the CO$_2$ removal using rate based approach. Initially, equilibrium based approach at 10 bar is simulated without Murphree efficiency and the trend observed does not have the significant changes as the number of stages increases. When the equilibrium based approach with Murphree efficiency of 0.15 is simulated, increasing percentage of CO$_2$ removal is exhibited.

According Koch Glitsch, estimated HETP for structured column of Flexipac 1Y is about 0.21 m and this lead to number of stages is about 5 since the height of packing is about 1 m. It can also be observed from Fig. 4 that with a Murphree efficiency value of 0.15 and 5 stages, the percentage of CO$_2$ removal is around 85% which matches the experimental data. As the number of stages increases, the percentage of CO$_2$ removal also increases. In rate based approach, the simulation model is successfully converged with less than 0.07% of error percentage for different number of stages. Rate based is well known of its accuracy as it demands reliable predictions of diffusion coefficients, interfacial areas and mass transfer coefficients [25].

A comparative observation between equilibrium approach with Murphree efficiency of 0.15 and rate based approach appears to validate the experimental data. Murphree efficiency acts as an intermediate of equitable agreement between rate based and equilibrium based where the value is tuned until the rational results of both approaches are achieved [22]. Murphree efficiency has acted effectively upon the equilibrium of vapour with the liquid that is leaving every number of stages [29]. Murphree efficiency has the ability in improving the thermodynamic, hydrodynamic and mass transfer of liquid and vapour [27]. Hence, it usually gains the utmost potential of the process besides, more realistic assessment is performed [30].

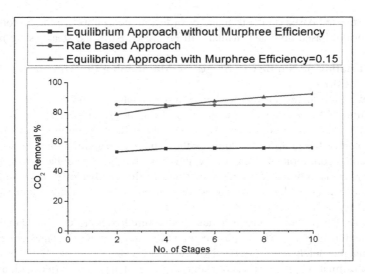

Fig. 4. The percentage of CO_2 removal versus number of stages for rate based and equilibrium approach

4   Conclusions and Future Work

This project studied the simulation of steady state with several re-adjustments including the application of Murphree efficiency and variation of number of stages to match the equilibrium and rate based model performance before the simulation for dynamic state can be established. The application of standard absorption models (e.g. either rate based or equilibrium based) for CO_2 removal can be exploited to imitate the treatment of CO_2 removal at any conditions with various type of situation or disturbance. Certain studies had started to evoke the importance of dynamic model but the task is not simple as the mathematical formulation might be very complex and challenging. This, equilibrium based approach is employed to ensure the model converges and the next stage in this study is to perform the dynamic analysis and control study. Then, the overall process will be developed by incorporating the stripper section, thus energy usage can be thoroughly studied.

References

1. Abkhiz, V., Heydari, I., Taheri, M.: Operational investigation of multi feed amine process performance in comparison with conventional process. Int. J. Oil Gas Coal Eng. **2**, 7 (2014)
2. Tan, L., Shariff, A., Lau, K., Bustam, M.: Impact of high pressure on high concentration carbon dioxide capture from natural gas by monoethanolamine/N-methyl-2-pyrrolidone solvent in absorption packed column. Int. J. Greenhouse Gas Control **34**, 25–30 (2015)
3. Rezakazemi, M., Niazi, Z., Mirfendereski, M., Shirazian, S., Mohammadi, T., Pak, A.: CFD simulation of natural gas sweetening in a gas–liquid hollow-fiber membrane contactor. Chem. Eng. J. **168**, 1217–1226 (2011)

4. Hairul, N., Shariff, A., Tay, W., Mortel, A., Lau, K., Tan, L.: Modelling of high pressure CO_2 absorption using PZ+ AMP blended solution in a packed absorption column. Sep. Purif. Technol. **165**, 179–189 (2016)

5. Seo, J.-B., Jeon, S.-B., Kim, J.-Y., Lee, G.-W., Jung, J.-H., Oh, K.-J.: Vaporization reduction characteristics of aqueous ammonia solutions by the addition of ethylene glycol, glycerol and glycine to the CO_2 absorption process. J. Environ. Sci. **24**, 494–498 (2012)

6. Kittel, J., Idem, R., Gelowitz, D., Tontiwachwuthikul, P., Parrain, G., Bonneau, A.: Corrosion in MEA units for CO_2 capture: pilot plant studies. Energy Procedia **1**, 791–797 (2009)

7. Olajire, A.A.: CO_2 capture and separation technologies for end-of-pipe applications–a review. Energy **35**, 2610–2628 (2010)

8. Suhartanto, T., York, A.P., Hanif, A., Al-Megren, H., Green, M.L.: Potential utilisation of Indonesia's Natuna natural gas field via methane dry reforming to synthesis gas. Catal. Lett. **71**, 49–54 (2001)

9. Solbraa, E.: Equilibrium and non-equilibrium thermodynamics of natural gas processing. Fakultet for ingeniørvitenskap og teknologi (2002)

10. Sehgal, V.: Technical and economic comparison of natural gas sweetening process. ProQuest (2009)

11. Abu-Zahra, M.R., Schneiders, L.H., Niederer, J.P., Feron, P.H., Versteeg, G.F.: CO_2 capture from power plants: Part I. A parametric study of the technical performance based on monoethanolamine. Int. J. Greenhouse Gas Control **1**, 37–46 (2007)

12. Alie, C., Backham, L., Croiset, E., Douglas, P.L.: Simulation of CO_2 capture using MEA scrubbing: a flowsheet decomposition method. Energy Convers. Manag. **46**, 475–487 (2005)

13. Freguia, S., Rochelle, G.T.: Modeling of CO_2 capture by aqueous monoethanolamine. AIChE J. **49**, 1676–1686 (2003)

14. Kvamsdal, H.M., Rochelle, G.T.: Effects of the temperature bulge in CO_2 absorption from flue gas by aqueous monoethanolamine. Ind. Eng. Chem. Res. **47**, 867–875 (2008)

15. Zhang, Y., Zhang, S., Lu, X., Zhou, Q., Fan, W., Zhang, X.: Dual amino-functionalised phosphonium ionic liquids for CO_2 capture. Chem.–Eur. J. **15**, 3003–3011 (2009)

16. Dugas, R., Alix, P., Lemaire, E., Broutin, P., Rochelle, G.: Absorber model for CO_2 capture by monoethanolamine—application to CASTOR pilot results. Energy Procedia **1**, 103–107 (2009)

17. AspenTech (2016). http://www.aspentech.com

18. Trapp, C., de Servi, C., Casella, F., Bardow, A., Colonna, P.: Dynamic modelling and validation of pre-combustion CO_2 absorption based on a pilot plant at the Buggenum IGCC power station. Int. J. Greenhouse Gas Control **36**, 13–26 (2015)

19. Pellegrini, L.A., Moioli, S., Picutti, B., Vergani, P., Gamba, S.: Design of an acidic natural gas purification plant by means of a process simulator. Chem. Eng. Trans. **24**, 271–276 (2011)

20. AspenTech: ASPEN HYSYS V7.2 (2010)

21. Chikukwa, A., Enaasen, N., Kvamsdal, H.M., Hillestad, M.: Dynamic modeling of post-combustion CO_2 capture using amines–a review. Energy Procedia **23**, 82–91 (2012)

22. He, Z., Ricardez-Sandoval, L.A.: Dynamic modelling of a commercial-scale CO_2 capture plant integrated with a natural gas combined cycle (NGCC) power plant. Int. J. Greenhouse Gas Control **55**, 23–35 (2016)

23. Gáspár, J., Cormoş, A.-M.: Dynamic modeling and validation of absorber and desorber columns for post-combustion CO_2 capture. Comput. Chem. Eng. **35**, 2044–2052 (2011)

24. Zhang, Y., Chen, H., Chen, C.-C., Plaza, J.M., Dugas, R., Rochelle, G.T.: Rate-based process modeling study of CO_2 capture with aqueous monoethanolamine solution. Ind. Eng. Chem. Res. **48**, 9233–9246 (2009)

25. Ramesh, K., Aziz, N., Shukor, S.A., Ramasamy, M.: Dynamic rate-based and equilibrium model approaches for continuous tray distillation column. J. Appl. Sci. Res. **3**, 2030–2041 (2007)
26. Dutta, R., Nord, L.O., Bolland, O.: Prospects of using equilibrium-based column models in dynamic process simulation of post-combustion CO_2 capture for coal-fired power plant. Fuel **202**, 85–97 (2017)
27. Queiroz, J.A., Rodrigues, V.M., Matos, H.A., Martins, F.: Modeling of existing cooling towers in ASPEN PLUS using an equilibrium stage method. Energy Convers. Manag. **64**, 473–481 (2012)
28. Vazquez-Esparragoza, J., Polasek, J., Hernandez-Valencia, V., Hlavinka, M., Bullin, J.: A simple application of Murphree tray efficiency to separation processes. Chem. Eng. Commun. **160**, 91–101 (1997)
29. Taylor, R., Kooijman, H.: ChemSep Tutorial: Efficiencies (2012)
30. Darde, V., Maribo-Mogensen, B., van Well, W.J., Stenby, E.H., Thomsen, K.: Process simulation of CO_2 capture with aqueous ammonia using the extended UNIQUAC model. Int. J. Greenhouse Gas Control **10**, 74–87 (2012)

Acceleration of Particle Based Fluid Simulation with Adhesion Boundary Conditions Using GPU

Yasutomo Kanetsuki[1](✉) and Susumu Nakata[2]

[1] Graduate School of Information Science and Engineering,
Ritsumeikan University, Kusatsu, Japan
is0061ee@ed.ritsumei.ac.jp
[2] College of Information Science and Engineering,
Ritsumeikan University, Kusatsu, Japan
snakata@is.ritsumei.ac.jp

Abstract. We present adhesion boundary conditions for smoothed particle hydrodynamics (SPH) with implicit surfaces. An existing method called ghost SPH addresses adhesion boundary conditions and produces plausible liquid animations using ghost particles. The generation of ghost particles, however, takes considerable computation time when it is implemented on graphics processing units (GPUs). The purpose of this paper is to accelerate ghost SPH using GPUs. In order to accelerate the processing of adhesion boundary conditions, we propose a new boundary model that can skip the ghost particle generation process in air and solid objects. The proposed technique is not just efficient but also inherits other advantages of implicit surfaces such as smoothness. Our test results show that the proposed method efficiently produces natural fluid adhesion motion without air or solid particles and achieves more than a hundredfold speed up compared to ghost SPH.

Keywords: Smoothed particle hydrodynamics · Implicit surfaces · Boundary condition · Graphics processing unit

1 Introduction

We propose adhesion boundary conditions for smoothed particle hydrodynamics (SPH) with implicit surfaces. Figure 1 shows an example of the effect of adhesion around an implicitly defined spherical obstacle. The boundary condition produces adhesive forces on the fluid particles, giving natural fluid flows around the obstacles. In particle based fluid simulations typified by SPH [1], handling boundary conditions is a challenging problem. In ghost SPH [2], adhesion boundary conditions between liquids and solids are achieved by generating ghost air and solid particles. Although ghost SPH successfully produces plausible adhesion fluid effects, the process of handling ghost particles can be time-consuming depending on the situation and is not suitable for interactive simulation. Our aim is to develop a model of particle based fluids with adhesion effects that can be executed on graphics processing units (GPUs) in interactive speed.

© Springer Nature Singapore Pte Ltd. 2017
M.S. Mohamed Ali et al. (Eds.): AsiaSim 2017, Part II, CCIS 752, pp. 337–348, 2017.
DOI: 10.1007/978-981-10-6502-6_30

Fig. 1. An example scene generated by our method. The solid sphere is represented as an implicit surface. The adhesion boundary conditions are appropriately affected to the fluids.

Particle based fluid simulation has several benefits over other simulation methods, such as simple handling of complex flow motion, mass conservation, and its Lagrangian characteristics. In an SPH context, interactive fluid simulation has been achieved by [3], and incompressible properties of fluids have been captured using explicit [4,5] and implicit [6–8] methods. Another method called the moving particle semi-implicit method [9] has also been developed for industrial purposes.

A recently-proposed method called position based fluids [10] is one of the fastest particle based methods and is suitable for multiphysics applications. In addition, a modified algorithm [11] provides further acceleration. The formulation of these methods is based not on the Navier-Stokes equations but on particle positions and in this sense, the direction of this approach is different from that of traditional SPH based methods. In order to achieve fluid simulation that is both physically based and interactive, we employ the standard SPH formulation developed by [3].

Ghost SPH is a method that gives adhesion effects, as mentioned previously, using ghost particles in the air and solid objects around the fluids. The ghost particles are generated using Poisson disk sampling (PDS) [12], which generates randomly-distributed points satisfying certain statistical properties and which has been applied to many problems in image processing and computer graphics. For the interactive simulation of ghost SPH, over ten million particles need to be generated per second in our rough estimation. This speed requirement is, however, difficult to satisfy even using the latest fast PDS techniques [13–15], and consequently, interactive fluid simulation with ghost SPH is not practical.

After ghost SPH [2], a variety of methods have been proposed to simulate adhesion and cohesion effects with SPH [16,17]. In [17], an approach to reproduce large surface tension and adhesion effects is developed without using ghost particles. The method proposed by [16] addressed the robustness and stability issues in small-scale thin fluid simulation. Although these methods simulate plausible fluid motion, additional artificial forces or assumptions must be introduced in stead of ghost particles. Our method produces almost the same adhesion effects by following the same solid boundary handling policy without any additional artificial forces.

In computer graphics, implicit surfaces are used to model three-dimensional shapes [18]. Representing objects using implicit surfaces allows simple interactive modeling [19,20] and surface reconstruction of real-world objects from surface points [21,22]. These features of implicit surfaces are particularly convenient when simulating fluid motion. In this paper, we adopt implicit surfaces to model solid boundaries with SPH and to speed up our fluid simulation.

In order to perform ghost SPH like fluid motion with interactive speed, we address the following problems.

1. Slip, no-separation, and no-penetration boundary conditions are imposed for the implicit surfaces, following the same policy as ghost SPH but without solid particles. Implicit surfaces avoid unnecessary solid boundary treatment where far from the fluid particles.
2. Hybrid pressure calculation provides a model of pressure that satisfies two requirements: preventing unnatural particle clustering at free surfaces and enforcing the no-separation fluid-solid boundary conditions. Our hybrid pressure calculation prevents negative pressure for fluid-fluid interaction but allows it for fluid-solid interaction. This relaxes clustering at the fluid surfaces and enforces the no-separation fluid-solid boundary conditions at the same time without air particle generation.

Since our proposed technique can be simply implemented on GPUs, the total speed up outperforms ghost SPH by more than two orders of magnitude while still generating sufficiently plausible fluid motion.

2   Ghost SPH Boundary Conditions for Implicit Surfaces

In this section, we present a way to apply the fluid-solid boundary conditions for adhesion [2] to SPH with implicitly defined obstacles. This solid representation with implicit surfaces allows us to avoid the generation of solid particles and contributes to computational efficiency.

2.1 Discretization with SPH

In order to achieve interactive fluid simulation, we employ a fast SPH formulation developed by [3]. Assuming that the fluid is represented by particles, and the i-th fluid position and velocity are represented by $\boldsymbol{x}_i$ and $\boldsymbol{v}_i$, respectively, with $i = 1, 2, \cdots, N$ in three-dimensional space, the positions and velocities are updated using the Navier-Stokes equations as follows:

$$\boldsymbol{v}_i^{t+\Delta t} = \boldsymbol{v}_i^t + \Delta t (\boldsymbol{f}_i^{\mathrm{press}} + \boldsymbol{f}_i^{\mathrm{visc}} + \boldsymbol{g}),$$
$$\boldsymbol{x}_i^{t+\Delta t} = \boldsymbol{x}_i^t + \Delta t \boldsymbol{v}_i^{t+\Delta t},$$

where t indicates time, Δt is the time step, and $\boldsymbol{f}_i^{\mathrm{press}}$, $\boldsymbol{f}_i^{\mathrm{visc}}$, and $\boldsymbol{g}$ denote the pressure term, viscosity term, and acceleration due to gravity, respectively.

The pressure and viscosity terms are discretized with SPH as

$$\boldsymbol{f}_i^{\mathrm{press}} = -\frac{1}{\rho_i} \sum_j m_j \frac{p_i + p_j}{2\rho_j} \nabla W(\boldsymbol{x}_i^t - \boldsymbol{x}_j^t, h), \tag{1}$$

$$\boldsymbol{f}_i^{\mathrm{visc}} = \frac{\mu}{\rho_i} \sum_j m_j \frac{\boldsymbol{v}_j^t - \boldsymbol{v}_i^t}{\rho_j} \nabla^2 W(\boldsymbol{x}_i^t - \boldsymbol{x}_j^t, h) \tag{2}$$

where μ is the viscosity and, m_i, p_i, and ρ_i are the mass, pressure, and density of the i-th fluid particle, respectively. The function $W(\boldsymbol{x}, h)$ is called the smoothing kernel with kernel support radius h. In this paper, we use the same kernel functions as [3], namely

$$W(\boldsymbol{x}, h) \equiv \frac{315}{64\pi h^9} \begin{cases} (h^2 - \|\boldsymbol{x}\|^2)^3 & (0 \le \|\boldsymbol{x}\| \le h) \\ 0 & (\text{otherwise}) \end{cases},$$

$$\nabla W(\boldsymbol{x}, h) \equiv -\frac{45}{\pi h^6} \begin{cases} (h - \|\boldsymbol{x}\|)^2 \frac{\boldsymbol{x}}{\|\boldsymbol{x}\|} & (0 \le \|\boldsymbol{x}\| \le h) \\ 0 & (\text{otherwise}) \end{cases},$$

$$\nabla^2 W(\boldsymbol{x}, h) \equiv \frac{45}{\pi h^6} \begin{cases} (h - \|\boldsymbol{x}\|) & (0 \le \|\boldsymbol{x}\| \le h) \\ 0 & (\text{otherwise}) \end{cases}.$$

Using the abovementioned kernel functions, the density of the i-th fluid particle is evaluated as

$$\rho_i = \sum_j m_j W(\boldsymbol{x}_i^t - \boldsymbol{x}_j^t, h). \tag{3}$$

For the computation of pressure, we use two different definitions:

$$\tilde{p}_i = \max\left(k(\rho_i - \rho_0), 0\right), \tag{4}$$
$$\hat{p}_i = k(\rho_i - \rho_0) \tag{5}$$

where the rest density $\rho_0 = 1000$ and the coefficient $k = 7500$. The first definition, (4), has the effect of preventing fluid particles from gathering at free surfaces too much and is used in many SPH-based methods. The second definition, (5), has the effect of giving adhesion forces to fluid particles around solid objects. In our formulation, the appropriate definition is selected depending on the situation; see Sect. 3 for further discussion.

2.2 Evaluation of Physical Quantities at Implicit Surfaces

The above mentioned formulation of SPH can be applied when all objects in the computational area are represented by particles. Throughout this paper, we assume that all solid objects in the computational area are modeled by implicit surfaces, i.e., each solid boundary is given by a zero level set of a C^1 scalar function, $\{x|f(x) = 0\}$. Let us assume that the value of $f(x)$ is positive inside the surface and negative outside it. In this case, since there are no particles at the solid surfaces, the summations in (1), (2), and (3) have to be modified.

Therefore, we employ an idea from [23]. If solid particles exist inside the solid objects, the summations appearing in (1), (2), and (3) can be divided into the contributions of the fluid particles and the solid particles as

$$f_i^{\text{press}} = -\frac{1}{\rho_i} \sum_{j \in N^{\text{fluid}}} m_j \frac{\tilde{p}_i + \tilde{p}_j}{2\rho_j} \nabla W_{ij} - \frac{1}{\rho_i} \sum_{j \in N^{\text{solid}}} m_j \frac{\hat{p}_i + \hat{p}_j}{2\rho_j} \nabla W_{ij}, \quad (6)$$

$$f_i^{\text{visc}} = \frac{\mu}{\rho_i} \sum_{j \in N^{\text{fluid}}} m_j \frac{v_j^t - v_i^t}{\rho_j} \nabla^2 W_{ij} + \frac{\mu}{\rho_i} \sum_{j \in N^{\text{solid}}} m_j \frac{v_j^t - v_i^t}{\rho_j} \nabla^2 W_{ij},$$

$$\rho_i = \sum_{j \in N^{\text{fluid}}} m_j W_{ij} + \sum_{j \in N^{\text{solid}}} m_j W_{ij}$$

where N^{fluid} and N^{solid} represent the index sets of the fluid and solid particles, respectively, and $W_{ij} \equiv W(x_i^t - x_j^t, h)$. In (6), the two different pressure definitions (4) and (5) are both adopted. Furthermore, if we assume that the mass, pressure, density, and velocity of the solid particles are determined not by the positions of the solid particles but by the positions of the fluid particles and the solid surfaces, the quantities m_j, $\hat{p}_j$, ρ_j, and v_j^t (for $j \in N^{\text{solid}}$) in the abovementioned equations can be replaced by $\bar{m}_i$, $\bar{p}_i$, $\bar{\rho}_i$, and $\bar{v}_i^t$, which are determined independently of the solid particles. We discuss how these quantities are determined later. This assumption leads to the following equations.

$$f_i^{\text{press}} = -\frac{1}{\rho_i} \sum_{j \in N^{\text{fluid}}} m_j \frac{\tilde{p}_i + \tilde{p}_j}{2\rho_j} \nabla W_{ij} + \frac{1}{\rho_i \bar{\rho}_i}(\hat{p}_i + \bar{p}_i) \frac{\nabla f(x_i^t)}{\|\nabla f(x_i^t)\|} \alpha, \quad (7)$$

$$f_i^{\text{visc}} = \frac{\mu}{\rho_i} \sum_{j \in N^{\text{fluid}}} m_j \frac{v_j^t - v_i^t}{\rho_j} \nabla^2 W_{ij} + \frac{1}{\rho_i \bar{\rho}_i}(\bar{v}_i^t - v_i^t)\beta, \quad (8)$$

$$\rho_i = \sum_{j \in N^{\text{fluid}}} m_j W_{ij} + \gamma,$$

where the quantities $\alpha \equiv \frac{\bar{m}_i}{2} \left\| \sum_{j \in N^{\text{solid}}} \nabla W_{ij} \right\|$, $\beta \equiv \mu \bar{m}_i \sum_{j \in N^{\text{solid}}} \nabla^2 W_{ij}$ and $\gamma \equiv \bar{m}_i \sum_{j \in N^{\text{solid}}} W_{ij}$. These quantities, α, β, and γ, can be precomputed as functions of the distance from a fluid particle to the closest solid and can be evaluated by storing the precomputed values in lookup tables, as described in [8,23]. As a result, $\boldsymbol{f}_i^{\mathrm{press}}$, $\boldsymbol{f}_i^{\mathrm{visc}}$, and ρ_i can be evaluated without introducing solid particles and the process of generating ghost solid particles can be avoided.

The unknown solid quantities $\bar{\rho}_i$, $\bar{p}_i$, and $\bar{\boldsymbol{v}}_i^t$ have to be carefully set so that they satisfy the fluid-solid boundary conditions of ghost SPH. Note that the mass $\bar{m}_i$ is a user-defined parameter and we have chosen to set $\bar{m}_i = m^{\mathrm{solid}}$. In the rest of this section, we discuss how to appropriately set these solid quantities.

2.3 Slip Boundary Condition

Throughout this study, we assume that solid boundary conditions apply in the area wherein the distance to the nearest solid is smaller than the kernel support radius h. In this section, we describe a way to determine velocity $\bar{\boldsymbol{v}}_i^t$ in (8) so that the fluid particles satisfy the slip boundary condition. This condition implies that the normal components of the velocities of pairs of neighboring fluid and solid particles are the same, while their tangential components are decoupled. This indicates that the fluid particles can move freely in the tangential direction but not in the normal direction under this slip condition. In our method, this is achieved by applying sufficient solid velocity $\bar{\boldsymbol{v}}_i^t$ for each fluid particle.

In ghost SPH, this slip condition is satisfied by applying the sum of the tangential component of the fluid velocity nearest to the ghost solid particle and the normal component of the solid velocity to each ghost particle. This process simply cannot be applied to implicit surface solids because no solid particles are defined at the boundary.

We avoid this situation by focusing on features of implicit surfaces and by appropriately evaluating solid velocities at the boundary. Unlike solids modeled by particles, the solid velocity $\bar{\boldsymbol{v}}_i^t$ is only required for the fluid particles near the solids in our implicit surface model but not for all solid particles in the computational domain. Therefore, we only evaluate the velocity $\bar{\boldsymbol{v}}_i^t$ for the fluid particles whose distance to the solids is less than h.

To evaluate $\bar{\boldsymbol{v}}_i^t$, we first find the point on the solid nearest to the fluid particle, $\boldsymbol{x}_i^{\mathrm{solid}}$, via

$$\boldsymbol{x}_i^{\mathrm{solid}} = \boldsymbol{x}_i^t - d\frac{\nabla f(\boldsymbol{x}_i^t)}{\|\nabla f(\boldsymbol{x}_i^t)\|}, \tag{9}$$

where the distance d between the fluid particle and the closest point on the solid is approximated as

$$d = \frac{|f(\boldsymbol{x}_i^t)|}{\|\nabla f(\boldsymbol{x}_i^t)\|}.$$

As shown in Fig. 2, (9) means that the nearest solid position from the fluid particle can be found at the point to the solids with the distance d. We define the solid velocity $\bar{\boldsymbol{v}}_i^t$ in the same way as in ghost SPH:

$$\bar{\boldsymbol{v}}_i^t = \boldsymbol{v}_{\|}^{\mathrm{fluid}} + \boldsymbol{v}_{\perp}^{\mathrm{solid}},$$

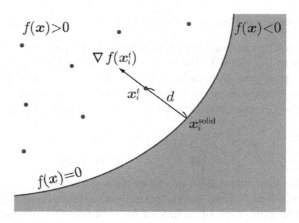

Fig. 2. The distance between a fluid particle and a solid boundary is displayed. The blue points indicate fluid particles and the brown line is the solid boundary. (Color figure online)

where $v_\parallel^{\text{fluid}}$ indicates the tangential component of the velocity of the fluid particle nearest to x_i^{solid} and $v_\perp^{\text{solid}}$ denotes the normal component of the velocity of the closest solid.

2.4   No-Separation Boundary Condition

In ghost SPH, an adhesion force is produced when a fluid particle close to a solid moves a way from the solid because the empty space between fluid and solid creates a gradient in the pressure field and as a result, the pressure force oriented toward the solid increases. In this section, we show how to determine the solid-related quantities $\bar{\rho}_i$ and $\bar{p}_i$ in (7) and (8) so that the method of producing adhesion force used in ghost SPH is applied appropriately to our formulation.

Since we already know that the nearest point on a solid to a fluid particle is given by (9), we can copy the density and pressure of the fluid particle nearest to x_i^{solid} to $\bar{\rho}_i$ and $\bar{p}_i$, in accordance with the idea introduced in ghost SPH. Applying these values, $\bar{\rho}_i$ and $\bar{p}_i$, to (7) yields a natural no-separation boundary condition without any other external artificial forces. According to the assumption stated at the beginning of Sect. 2.3, $\bar{\rho}_i$ and $\bar{p}_i$ are required only when the distance from the i-th particle to its closest solid is smaller than h. In practical computation, $\bar{\rho}_i$ and $\bar{p}_i$ values for each fluid particle satisfying the above are determined by searching for the fluid particle x_k^t that is closest to x_i^{solid} and copying the relevant quantities, i.e., $\bar{\rho}_i = \rho_k$ and $\bar{p}_i = \hat{p}_k$. Note that the quantities $\bar{\rho}_i$ and $\bar{p}_i$ are determined at the same time as the velocity $\bar{v}_i^t$ is computed and no additional search is required. In our implementation, the density $\bar{\rho}_i$ is also used in (8) for consistency.

2.5   No-Penetration Boundary Condition

In order to enforce the no-penetration condition, an extra force, which we denote as $\hat{f}_i^{\text{press}}$, needs to be added to the pressure force (7). A method for preventing particle penetration into implicitly defined solids is proposed in [23]. In this method, the fluid particles are pushed out when they approach the zero level set of $f(\boldsymbol{x})$. This correction to the pressure force can be written in the following form:

$$\hat{f}_i^{\text{press}} = \begin{cases} \frac{l-d}{\Delta t^2} \frac{\nabla f(\boldsymbol{x}_i^t)}{\|\nabla f(\boldsymbol{x}_i^t)\|} & (d \leq l) \\ \mathbf{0} & (\text{otherwise}) \end{cases}, \tag{10}$$

where l indicates the initial spacing of the fluid particles. We add the pressure force correction (10) to (7) and use the combined pressure force as $\boldsymbol{f}_i^{\text{press}}$ for position updates. The same type of technique for avoiding fluid particle penetration is also used in the original ghost SPH.

Note that the quantities $f(\boldsymbol{x}_i^t)$ and $\nabla f(\boldsymbol{x}_i^t)$ in (7), (9), and (10) need to be evaluated only once for each fluid particle per time step. All we have to do for the fluid-solid boundary condition is to estimate d for each fluid particle and, if $d \leq h$, estimate solid quantities as discussed above.

3   Hybrid Pressure for Free Surfaces

In our formulation, one of two pressure definitions, (4) or (5), is selected depending on the situation, as described in Sect. 2.1. In this section, we discuss the idea behind the hybrid pressure definition and the reason for its computational efficiency.

In ghost SPH, the pressure is defined using the Tait equation, and (5) is a special case of this definition. Although the pressure given by this definition can be negative depending on the particle density, the value is expected not to be too small because each fluid particle is always surrounded by fluid, solid, and/or air particles, which prevents the particle density from being much smaller than the rest density ρ_0. One important property of this approach is that particles that are moving away from solid surfaces feel an adhesion force toward the solid. The pressure definition (5) contributes to producing this adhesion force around solid surfaces because the pressure reduces as the distance between fluid and solid increases, resulting in larger pressure field gradients at the fluid particles. In order to inherit this property, we divide the computation of the pressure gradient into two parts, namely, the contributions of N^{fluid} and N^{solid}, and adopt (5) for the latter part of the pressure gradient given by (6).

Ghost SPH uses air particles for free surfaces, which gives a plausible pressure field. In order to compute the pressure without air particles, we adopt (4) to cut negative pressure. In other words, we adopt (4) for the contribution of the fluid particles to the pressure gradient given by (6).

Fig. 3. The comparison of the previous method (top) and our method (bottom). The equivalent frames produced by the same simulation paramaters are displayed.

Finally, from (7) and (10), we obtain the following equation for the pressure force:

$$
\boldsymbol{f}_i^{\text{press}} =
\begin{cases}
-\frac{1}{\rho_i} \sum_{j \in N^{\text{fluid}}} m_j \frac{\tilde{p}_i + \tilde{p}_j}{2\rho_j} \nabla W_{ij} \\
\qquad + \left\{ \frac{\alpha}{\rho_i \bar{\rho}_i}(\hat{p}_i + \bar{p}_i) + \frac{l-d}{\Delta t^2} \right\} \frac{\nabla f(\boldsymbol{x}_i^t)}{\|\nabla f(\boldsymbol{x}_i^t)\|} & (d \le l) \\
-\frac{1}{\rho_i} \sum_{j \in N^{\text{fluid}}} m_j \frac{\tilde{p}_i + \tilde{p}_j}{2\rho_j} \nabla W_{ij} + \frac{\alpha}{\rho_i \bar{\rho}_i}(\hat{p}_i + \bar{p}_i) \frac{\nabla f(\boldsymbol{x}_i^t)}{\|\nabla f(\boldsymbol{x}_i^t)\|} & (\text{otherwise})
\end{cases}
.
$$

4   Results

We tested the proposed method with a tomato example, as presented for ghost SPH. In the tomato test case, fluid particles are continuously emitted onto a sphere-shaped solid object defined as an implicit surface $f(\boldsymbol{x}) = 0$. Although the fluid particles are generated using PDS in ghost SPH, we simplified this process to avoid the non-negligible computational costs of PDS by sampling fluid particles at a fixed grid of positions (a total of 8217 grid points were used). Using these grid points, we generated fluid particles at each grid point if there were no other fluid particles within a radius of l, and this sampling was performed after every 30 time steps, as for ghost SPH.

Figure 3 shows a comparison of our method and the previous method [23] for the tomato case, with an acceleration due to gravity of $\boldsymbol{g} = (0, -9.8, 0)$. For both the methods, we used a counting sort neighbor search algorithm [24] and a zeroth-order kernel correction [25]. The test results show that the proposed method appropriately produces slip and adhesion effects at the fluid-solid boundary, while the previous method sticks fluid particles to the solid sphere and makes them fall freely down from the side of the sphere. These results also show that our fluid surfaces do not suffer from too much surface tension-like force caused by negative pressure from the lack of air particles.

In our method, the computation time per step is only 8.6 ms, including rendering using point sprites with 59k particles on an NVIDIA GTX970M, while ghost SPH takes 1.92 s with the same number of particles for the same test case on a quad-core Intel i7-2600. Clearly, our method outperforms ghost SPH by more than two orders of magnitude in speed for almost the same animation quality. Note that our method achieves not only a speed up, but also a memory reduction because it does not need to store any ghost particles.

5   Conclusion

We developed adhesion boundary conditions for SPH with implicit surfaces. These boundary conditions for the implicit surface model allow for efficient fluid simulation with interactive speed while satisfying slip, no-separation, and no-penetration conditions. We also introduced a hybrid pressure estimation method. This technique simply relaxes surface tension-like effects at the free fluid surfaces.

The test results showed that our proposed method produces plausible fluid animation very efficiently. The method also reduces memory consumption by avoiding the need to store ghost particles around the fluid.

Acknowledgement. This work was supported by JSPS KAKENHI Grant Number JP00351320.

References

1. Monaghan, J.J.: Smoothed particle hydrodynamics. Rep. Prog. Phys. **68**(8), 1703–1759 (2005)
2. Schechter, H., Bridson, R.: Ghost SPH for animating water. ACM Trans. Graph. **31**(4), 61:1–61:8 (2012)

3. Müller, M., Charypar, D., Gross, M.: Particle-based fluid simulation for interactive applications. In: Proceedings of the 2003 ACM SIGGRAPH/Eurographics Symposium on Computer Animation, pp. 154–159 (2003)
4. Monaghan, J.J.: Simulating free surface flows with SPH. J. Comput. Phys. **110**(2), 399–406 (1994)
5. Becker, M., Teschner, M.: Weakly compressible SPH for free surface flows. In: Proceedings of the 2007 ACM SIGGRAPH/Eurographics Symposium on Computer Animation, pp. 209–217 (2007)
6. Solenthaler, B., Pajarola, R.: Predictive-corrective incompressible SPH. ACM Trans. Graph. **28**(3), 40:1–40:6 (2009)
7. Ihmsen, M., Cornelis, J., Solenthaler, B., Horvath, C., Teschner, M.: Implicit incompressible SPH. IEEE Trans. Vis. Comput. Graph. **20**(3), 426–435 (2014)
8. Bender, J., Koschier, D.: Divergence-free smoothed particle hydrodynamics. In: Proceedings of the 14th ACM SIGGRAPH/Eurographics Symposium on Computer Animation, pp. 147–155 (2015)
9. Koshizuka, S., Oka, Y.: Moving-particle semi-implicit method for fragmentation of incompressible fluid. Nucl. Sci. Eng. **123**(3), 421–434 (1996)
10. Macklin, M., Müller, M.: Position based fluids. ACM Trans. Graph. **32**(4), 104:1–104:12 (2013)
11. Köster, M., Krüger, A.: Adaptive position-based fluids: improving performance of fluid simulations for real-time applications. Int. J. Comput. Graph. Animation **6**(3) (2016)
12. Cook, R.L.: Stochastic sampling in computer graphics. ACM Trans. Graph. **5**(1), 51–72 (1986)
13. Bridson, R.: Fast Poisson disk sampling in arbitrary dimensions. In: ACM SIGGRAPH 2007 Sketches, vol. 22, p. 1 (2007)
14. Ebeida, M.S., Mitchell, S.A., Patney, A., Davidson, A.A., Owens, J.D.: A simple algorithm for maximal Poisson-disk sampling in high dimensions. Comput. Graph. Forum **31**(2pt4), 785–794 (2012)
15. Ip, C.Y., Yalçin, M.A., Luebke, D., Varshney, A.: PixelPie: maximal Poisson-disk sampling with rasterization. In: Proceedings of the 5th High-Performance Graphics Conference, pp. 17–26 (2013)
16. He, X., Wang, H., Zhang, F., Wang, H., Wang, G., Zhou, K.: Robust simulation of sparsely sampled thin features in SPH-based free surface flows. ACM Trans. Graph. **34**(1), 7:1–7:9 (2014)
17. Akinci, N., Akinci, G., Teschner, M.: Versatile surface tension and adhesion for SPH fluids. ACM Trans. Graph. **32**(6), 182:1–182:8 (2013)
18. Berger, M., Levine, J.A., Nonato, L.G., Taubin, G., Silva, C.T.: A benchmark for surface reconstruction. ACM Trans. Graph. **32**(2), 20:1–20:17 (2013)
19. Reiner, T., Mückl, G., Dachsbacher, C.: Interactive modeling of implicit surfaces using a direct visualization approach with signed distance functions. Comput. Graph. **35**(3), 596–603 (2011)
20. Schmidt, R., Wyvill, B., Sousa, M.C., Jorge, J.A.: ShapeShop: sketch-based solid modeling with BlobTrees. In: ACM SIGGRAPH 2006 Courses, pp. 14:1–14:10 (2006)
21. Kazhdan, M., Hoppe, H.: Screened Poisson surface reconstruction. ACM Trans. Graph. **32**(3), 29:1–29:13 (2013)
22. Zagorchev, L.G., Goshtasby, A.A.: A curvature-adaptive implicit surface reconstruction for irregularly spaced points. IEEE Trans. Vis. Comput. Graph. **18**(9), 1460–1473 (2012)

23. Nakata, S., Sakamoto, Y.: Particle-based parallel fluid simulation in three-dimensional scene with implicit surfaces. J. Supercomput. **71**(5), 1766–1775 (2015)
24. Hoetzlein, R.C.: Fast fixed-radius nearest neighbors: interactive million-particle fluids. In: GPU Technology Conference (GTC) 2014 (2014)
25. Shepard, D.: A two-dimensional interpolation function for irregularly-spaced data. In: Proceedings of the 1968 23rd ACM National Conference, pp. 517–524 (1968)

Introduction of OpenStudio® for Work Integrated Learning: Case Study on Building Energy Modelling

Vincent Chieng-Chen Lee[(⊠)] and Ke San Yam

Curtin University Malaysia, CDT 250, 98009 Miri, Sarawak, Malaysia
vincent@curtin.edu.my

Abstract. Work integrated learning (WIL) is an innovative teaching pedagogy integrating industrial practical experience with academic learning experience. This paper presents an introduction of OpenStudio® as tool for modelling and simulating building energy. OpenStudio® is an open source building energy software for conducting thermal and energy balance simulation on buildings, with inclusion of weather effects, wind speeds and directions. Hence, a good approximate model on the interactions of the actual environment can be modelled. An industrial collaborative educational case study is presented in this work for the learners' WIL experience. Preliminary results showed promising use of OpenStudio® for modelling and simulating building energy performance.

Keywords: OpenStudio® · Work integrated learning · Building energy · Modelling

1 Introduction

Work integrated learning (WIL) is an innovative teaching pedagogy integrating industrial practical experience with academic learning experience. WIL is widely used in the Australasian context, and increasingly gaining international recognition as a form of teaching pedagogy in ensuring students' exposure to authentic learning experiences with opportunity to apply theoretical knowledge gained in classroom, to industrial practical tasks [1, 2].

WIL is particularly useful in ensuring successful attainment of engineering graduate attributes. The International Engineering Alliance (IEA) defines engineering as an activity that "involves the purposeful application of mathematical and natural sciences and a body of engineering knowledge, technology, and technique [3]." Hence, an engineering graduate is expected to possess the ability of "applying knowledge of mathematics, science, engineering fundamentals and an engineering specialization as specified in their knowledge profiles respectively to solution of complex engineering problems [3]." Knowledge profiles expected from an engineering graduate is as presented in Table 1.

WIL describes experiences that are (1) authentically engaged with the practices and experiences of the workplace [4], (2) located within an intentional discipline-centered curriculum [5], and (3) a focus towards graduate learning outcomes and career

M.S. Mohamed Ali et al. (Eds.): AsiaSim 2017, Part II, CCIS 752, pp. 349–358, 2017.
DOI: 10.1007/978-981-10-6502-6_31

Table 1. Knowledge profile for a washington accord engineering program [3]

WK1	A systematic, theory-based understanding of the natural sciences applicable to the discipline
WK2	Conceptually-based mathematics, numerical analysis, statistics and formal aspects of computer and information science to support analysis and modelling applicable to the discipline
WK3	A systematic, theory-based formulation of engineering fundamentals required in the engineering discipline
WK4	Engineering specialist knowledge that provides theoretical frameworks and bodies of knowledge for the accepted practice areas in the engineering discipline; much is at the forefront of the discipline
WK5	Knowledge that supports engineering design in a practice area
WK6	Knowledge of engineering practice (technology) in the practice areas in the engineering discipline
WK7	Comprehension of the role of engineering in society and identified issues in engineering practice in the discipline: ethics and the professional responsibility of an engineer to public safety; the impacts of engineering activity: economic, social, cultural, environmental and sustainability
WK8	Engagement with selected knowledge in the research literature of the discipline

pathways. WIL is also a valuable mechanism for demonstrating authentic learning and providing evidence of graduate attributes. Hence, it is strongly believed that WIL is one of the best teaching pedagogy for achieving engineering graduate attributes, as highlighted by the IEA.

In order to execute a successful WIL addressing the IEA graduate attributes, a delicate case study is required. The case study should be industrial-based, preferably an actual or close-to-actual scenario. The case study should also be open-ended with significant level of complexities, reflecting test of competencies on the IEA knowledge profile.

In this work, an industrial collaborative educational project is used for the WIL case study. The case study will require some literature reviews of existing methods, and use of modern tool for development of solutions. Solutions are to be evaluated, where the best solution is proposed to address the case study objective(s). Multiple constraints will be included in the case study as well to increase the complexity of the case study. Level of thinking for the case study is Level 5 and 6 of Bloom's revised taxonomy, Evaluating, and Creating [6].

2   An Educational Example: Building Energy Modelling

An educational example on building energy modelling is proposed in this WIL case study. The case study is planned to be an open-ended problem. For that purpose, an industrial collaborative educational project was initiated. This case study is an actual scenario where a sport complex in Miri is experiencing high room temperature within the building.

The complex has a gross area of 25000×45000 mm^2. Within the complex are nine squash courts, one administrative office, one activity room, two washrooms, and one sports equipment room. Each squash court includes a wall partition with dimension of 10000×6600 mm^2. The roof consists of corrugated sheets made of galvanized steel. The complex wall is concrete.

Multiple complaints were lodged on the unusually high room temperature in the afternoon. Several possible factors were anticipated, for example,

1. Miri experiences hot and humid weather all year long, especially during the dry season, typically in the months of March to September.
2. The high sunlight intensity during dry season increases the radiation heat on the surface of complex. Coupled with the conduction and convection of heat into the building environment, this could cause an increase in temperature.
3. The complex lacks of proper and efficient ventilation system, which result in heat being concentrated within the complex.

The objectives of this case study are to produce a proposal of a passive cooling mechanism (i.e. no air-conditioning system) to effectively reduce the room temperature within the complex, and to increase the thermal comfort of the complex users. Cost is an important constraint in the case study, where a budget for the proposed work is already given.

Numerical tool will be used in this case study for the building energy modelling, analysis, and evaluation. The tool used in this case study is OpenStudio® [7], which is elaborately described in the next section.

Based on the project scope of work, the learner is expected to achieve the IEA graduate attributes as tabulated in Table 2.

Table 2. Graduate Attribute Profiles [3]

WA1	Apply knowledge of mathematics, natural science, engineering fundamentals and an engineering specialization as specified in WK1 to WK4 respectively to the solution of complex engineering problems	√
WA2	Identify, formulate, research literature and analyze complex engineering problems reaching substantiated conclusions using first principles of mathematics, natural sciences and engineering sciences. (WK1 to WK4)	√
WA3	Design solutions for complex engineering problems and design systems, components or processes that meet specified needs with appropriate consideration for public health and safety, cultural, societal, and environmental considerations. (WK5)	√
WA4	Conduct investigations of complex problems using research-based knowledge (WK8) and research methods including design of experiments, analysis and interpretation of data, and synthesis of information to provide valid conclusions	√
WA5	Create, select and apply appropriate techniques, resources, and modern engineering and IT tools, including prediction and modelling, to complex engineering problems, with an understanding of the limitations. (WK6)	√

(continued)

Table 2. (*continued*)

WA6	Apply reasoning informed by contextual knowledge to assess societal, health, safety, legal and cultural issues and the consequent responsibilities relevant to professional engineering practice and solutions to complex engineering problems. (WK7)	
WA7	Understand and evaluate the sustainability and impact of professional engineering work in the solution of complex engineering problems in societal and environmental contexts. (WK7)	√
WA8	Apply ethical principles and commit to professional ethics and responsibilities and norms of engineering practice. (WK7)	
WA9	Function effectively as an individual, and as a member or leader in diverse teams and in multi-disciplinary settings	
WA10	Communicate effectively on complex engineering activities with the engineering community and with society at large, such as being able to comprehend and write effective reports and design documentation, make effective presentations, and give and receive clear instructions	√
WA11	Demonstrate knowledge and understanding of engineering management principles and economic decision-making and apply these to one's own work, as a member and leader in a team, to manage projects and in multidisciplinary environments	√
WA12	Recognize the need for, and have the preparation and ability to engage in independent and life-long learning in the broadest context of technological change	

3   Tool for the Case Study: OpenStudio®

The main objective of WIL is to allow learner to gain practical experience, and relevance of practical tasks to knowledge gained in classroom. Therefore, a less complicated tool is employed for the case study.

The tool used in this WIL case study is OpenStudio®. OpenStudio® is an open source building energy software, using EnergyPlus and advanced daylight analysis using Radiance, for conducting thermal and energy balance simulation on buildings. OpenStudio® also includes graphical interfaces, hence making the software more user friendly, as compared to other modelling software, where programming skills may be required.

Similar to other modelling software, OpenStudio® includes governing equations such as the heat balance-based solution of conduction, convection, and radiation effects to determine building temperature and thermal comfort. In addition, the solutions also take into account the weather effects, which include the solar radiation, daylight illuminance, and precipitation, the standard parameters of temperature, humidity, pressure, wind speed and direction. Hence, a good approximate model on the interactions of the actual environment can be modelled.

While the learner works on the problem using the software, they can then related the theoretical knowledge gained in classroom to actual situations, such as the effects of conduction, convection, and radiation on a certain materials, and how the materials will affect the overall room temperature and thermal comfort. The additional features of the software further enhance the practicability of the simulation where external effects such as weather, and wind speeds can be included as well. Hence, this software makes an excellent tool for this case study. The tool allows the learner to have opportunity to relate and apply theoretical knowledge gained in classroom, to industrial practical tasks.

Using EnergyPlus to perform the whole building energy modelling, the software contains surface and air heat balance modules and acts as an interface between the heat balance and the building systems simulation manager as shown in Fig. 1. The Surface Heat Balance Module incorporates the simulation of the inside and outside surface heat balance, interconnections between heat balances and boundary conditions, conduction, convection, radiation, and mass transfer (water vapor) effects. The Air Mass Balance Module ensures mass conversation in various mass streams such as ventilation and exhaust air, and infiltration. It accounts for thermal mass of zone air and evaluates direct convective, heat gains. The temperature in the zone is determining by resolving the following energy balance equation:

$$C_z \frac{dT_z}{dt} = \sum \dot{Q} + \sum hA(T_s - T_z) + \sum \dot{m} C_p (T_{zi} - T_z) + \dot{m}_{inf} C_p (T_\infty - T_z) + \dot{Q}_{sys} \tag{1}$$

where $\sum \dot{Q}$ is the sum of the convective internal loads, $\sum hA(T_s - T_z)$ is convective heat transfer from the zone surfaces, $\sum \dot{m} C_p (T_{zi} - T_Z)$ is heat transfer due to interzone air mixing, $\dot{m}_{inf} C_p (T_\infty - T_z)$ is the heat transfer due to infiltration of outside air, $\dot{Q}_{sys}$ is systems output.

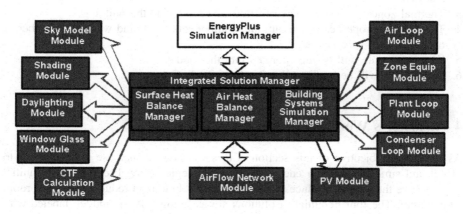

Fig. 1. Integrated simulation manager [8].

3.1 Modelling Procedure

The modelling follows set of simple procedure as follows. A summarized step on the modelling procedure is as presented in Fig. 2.

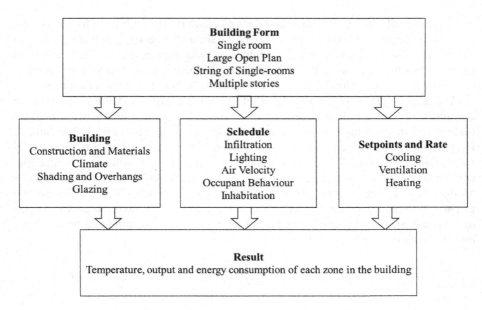

Fig. 2. Modelling process in OpenStudio®

1. 3D computer model will be created using any available Computer Aided Design (CAD) software.
2. The model is then imported into the OpenStudio® for the thermal energy balance analysis.
3. Thermal zone(s) will be created for the airspace inside the building.
4. The thermal properties of the building components (roof, and wall) and number of occupants will be assigned.
5. Weather profile will be incorporated into the model.
6. Simulations will be performed using OpenStudio®.

4 Learner's Work and Outcome

As stated, the objective of this section is to show how learner use OpenStudio® to model and simulate building energy. Cooling strategies were discussed at the initial stage, where the learner produces four potential resolutions in reducing the high room temperature. The four potential resolutions are as follows. A 3D model, labeled with potential resolutions to the problem is shown in Fig. 3.

1. **Resolution A** considers a layer of thermal conductive resistance material (glass wool with thermal conductivity of 0.04 W/mK) overlain with a thin layer of aluminium foil to be installed underneath the roof of the complex, to reduce the heat transfer from the roof into the building. Three thicknesses in the range of 0.1 to 0.3 m will be considered to evaluate the effects of the thickness.

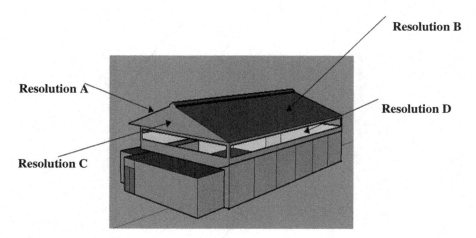

Fig. 3. Cooling strategies for the complex.

2. **Resolution B** considers a white paint (solar absorptance of 0.1) to be included on the roof as the solar radiation reflector, in addition to the installation of the insulation material in Resolution A.
3. **Resolution C** considers the roof to be partitioned using a layer of wooden platform in order to create a closed 'room' between the roof and the inner section of the building. The 'room' is expected to function as a thermal insulation in addition to a layer of glass wool on top of the wooden platform.
4. **Resolution D** considers the size of the openings that exists in the original building to be increased by 25%. This resolution is to investigate whether the room temperature will decrease by enhancing the air circulation of the building.

Based on the resolutions proposed, the learner then proceed with the individual simulation to obtain the results. Simulations were performed to predict the hourly temperature profile inside the complex. The results as shown in Fig. 4 were presented and evaluated for most efficient passive cooling mechanism.

Resolution A shows the overall room temperature can be reduced with installation of thermal insulation under the roof. Peak temperature at noon is observed to reduce by approximately 1.5 °C. Unfortunately, the installation of insulation also allows the building to retain the heat and therefore reduce the rate of temperature drop after 2 pm. As a result, no significant temperature reduction is observed from 2 pm to 8 pm. Increasing thickness twice or three times shows no improvement in heat reduction, suggesting that insulation of 0.1 m is sufficient for maximum conductive insulation.

Resolution B shows that the overall room temperature can be reduced through coating of white pain on the roof. The temperature is significantly reduced in the period of 12 pm to 4 pm, where the peak temperature is reduced by approximately 3 °C. Similar to Resolution A, temperature reduction is lesser after 4 pm due to the heat retention by the roof insulation.

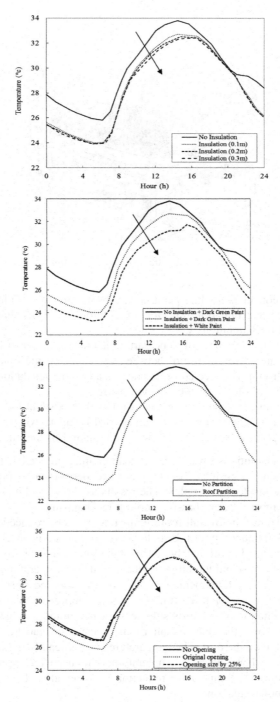

Fig. 4. Prediction on the temperature profile of the complex with proposed cooling strategies for the complex using OpenStudio® (top to bottom): Resolution A, Resolution B, Resolution C, and Resolution D.

Resolution C predicts the peak temperature was reduced by approximately 2 °C. The effect of partitioning the roof into closed airspace insulation produces similar effect as the installation of insulation underneath the roof. The temperature reduction become lesser after 4 pm due to heat retention in the roof partition. Since installing roof partition incurs greater cost but does not yield any significant improvement, Resolution B is more favorable.

Resolution D shows that the opening is essential for cooling the building. Significant temperature rise is predicted with no opening exist in the building. However, the existing opening size is sufficient as increasing the opening size by 25% does not yield much difference to the temperature.

Based on the behavior shown, the learner would then be able to evaluate each case and propose for an optimized solution to the complex owner. Furthermore, the learner would also be able to perform parametric study in relating the parameters for optimizing the building energy performance.

5 Conclusion

WIL is an innovative teaching pedagogy integrating industrial practical experience with academic learning experience to enhance student learning. An industrial collaborative educational project was presented to the learner for proposal of solution. Using the OpenStudio® software, the learner was able to easily simulate four conditions where possible reduction in room temperature could happen. In addition, the learner was able to relate and apply the knowledge learned in classroom onto practical engineering problem. The software architecture is highly versatile with powerful graphical user interface. Hence, OpenStudio® is indeed powerful and potential software to be used as a tool in WIL for building energy modelling. Implementation of OpenStudio® in WIL can provide a significant learning experience to the learners. In addition, the software can be used at home where learners can develop, model, and simulate his own case studies. With the advantage of the software's generality, OpenStudio® can also be used by engineers in the solution of building energy problems.

Acknowledgement. The authors would like to thank the Office of Learning and Teaching, Curtin University Malaysia for supporting this study.

References

1. Knight, P., Yorke, M.: Learning, Curriculum and Employability in Higher Education. Psychology Press, Abingdon (2004)
2. Peach, D., Matthews, J.H.: Work integrated learning for life: encouraging agentic engagement (2011)
3. International Engineering Alliance. Graduate attributes and professional competencies (2013)
4. Cooper, L., Orrell, J., Bowden, M.: Work Integrated Learning: A Guide to Effective Practice. Routledge, Abingdon (2010)

5. Patrick, C.-J., et al.: The WIL (Work integrated learning) report: a national scoping study [final report]. Queensland University of Technology (2008)
6. Airasian, P.W., Anderson, L.W., Krathwohl, D.R. (eds.) et al.: A taxonomy for learning, teaching, and assessing: a revision of Bloom's taxonomy of educational objectives (2000)
7. OpenStudio®. https://www.openstudio.net/
8. United States Department of Energy: EnergyPlus engineering reference. The reference to EnergyPlus calculations (2012)

VCG Auction Based Idle Instance Bidding to Increase IaaS Provider's Profit in Hybrid Clouds

Hongnan Xie[1], Xiao Song[1(✉)], Jing Bi[2], and Haitao Yuan[3]

[1] School of Automation Science, Beihang University (BUAA), Beijing, China
xiehn007@sina.com, songxiao@buaa.edu.cn
[2] Beijing University of Technology, Beijing, China
[3] Beijing Jiaotong University, Beijing, China

Abstract. In cloud computing, it is desirable for an infrastructure as a service (IaaS) provider to gain more profit by executing more tasks with hybrid clouds scheduling strategy. Most existing methods suggest IaaS provider to execute tasks within its limit processing capacity. This means the excessive tasks are abandoned and revenue is lost. In this paper, the low cost idle instances in public cloud are bided and rented to execute these tasks. Meanwhile, the bidding process is modeled as a VCG auction which can guarantee social welfare maximization. Simulation experiments are carried out with Google task data of 370 min. The profit of our proposed method is compared with the method rejecting excessive tasks and the approach scheduling excessive tasks to on-demand instances, and it shows that our method that using bided instances averagely increase the profit 69.39% and 33.96% respectively.

Keywords: Hybrid clouds · VCG auction · Bidding · Profit

1 Introduction

Cloud computing has become one of the most important schemes to provide Infrastructure as a Service (IaaS) via internet to worldwide consumers [1]. Typical IaaS providers such as Amazon EC2 provide services to consumers based on a pay-per-use model in the form of instances [2]. From the perspective of an IaaS provider, the private cloud provider in this paper denotes an IaaS provider that aims to increase its profit by intelligently scheduling tasks while guaranteeing the corresponding service delay bound.

Normally, the processing capacity of private cloud is not infinite because its computing resource is limited. Luo et al. [3] refuse to execute these excessive tasks, which will cause profit loss for private cloud provider. To avoid this loss, Zuo et al. [4] propose a task scheduling framework in which the private cloud provider can outsource its tasks to external public clouds when its own resources are not sufficient to meet the demand. Yuan et al. [5] present a hybrid clouds framework including private cloud and public clouds to schedule tasks while guaranteeing service delay bound. Similar to the work [4] and work [5], private cloud provider in this paper can schedule the tasks

© Springer Nature Singapore Pte Ltd. 2017
M.S. Mohamed Ali et al. (Eds.): AsiaSim 2017, Part II, CCIS 752, pp. 359–368, 2017.
DOI: 10.1007/978-981-10-6502-6_32

exceeded its processing capacity to public clouds to increase the obtained profit. This hybrid clouds mechanism enables a private cloud provider to make use of public clouds where resources are delivered in the form of virtual machines (VMs) when the resource of a private cloud is fully occupied [6].

However, the instance of public cloud used in work [4] and work [5] is on-demand instance, whose renting price is relatively high among the various types of instances. As such, this renting strategy cannot reduce the renting cost of instances in public cloud due to the fact that they do not take into account the purchasing model diversity of instances in public cloud. Currently, public cloud computing vendors, such as Amazon EC2, Google, etc., let customers bid on their idle instances to take advantage of the unused computing capacity. Launched eight years ago by Amazon Web Services, spot instances benefit the customers from potentially huge discounts—possibly up to 90% compared to its pricier on-demand instances [7]. Similarly, Google launched what it called "preemptible VMs" as in virtual machines can be had for up to 70% discount off of Google's standard compute pricing [8]. Although the above idle instances are relatively cheap, there is existing market risk of service interruption. For example, Amazon EC2 cloud updates its spot price every 5 min and shut down the customer's instances when customer's bidding price is lower than the spot price [9]. Therefore, customers may need to restart bidding idle instances during the period of service delay bound and the bidding process can be considered as an auction.

Auction is usually carried out by a third party, called the market-maker, which collects the bids, selects the winners and computes the payments [10]. We propose to use Vickrey–Clarke–Groves (VCG) [11] mechanism to calculate the transaction price of idle instance in this paper. VCG auction is a type of sealed-bid auction of multiple items. Bidders submit bids that report their valuations for the items, without knowing the bids of the other people in the auction. The core concept of VCG auction is that each bidder needs to compensate for the economic losses he brings to other bidders. This bidding manner can not only increase the total socially welfare, but also encourage bidders to bid their true valuations. Gui et al. [12] utilize VCG to optimize social welfare in bandwidth reservation allocation. In this paper, we describe the staged bidding for idle instances with VCG mechanism, and the bidding price of each bidder is generated by triangular distribution of idle instance's historical price.

2 Modeling and Formulation

In this section, we establish the cloud system model and present the formulation of task scheduling that increase the profit obtained by private cloud provider within the service delay bound.

2.1 Framework of Task Scheduling in Hybrid Clouds

In this paper, cloud system is modeled as a discrete time system [13] that evolves in a sequence of equal length time slots. All arrival tasks have a service delay bound B, i.e., tasks arrived in time slot t must be scheduled from time slot $t+1$ to $t+B$ and be executed with instances in private cloud and idle instances in public cloud. Meanwhile, the arrival tasks which cannot be executed during the period of service delay bound have to be abandoned, which means we strictly guarantee the service delay bound to all tasks. The process of task scheduling in hybrid clouds is shown in Fig. 1. In addition, the problem parameters and decision variables used in this section are summarized in Tables 1 and 2, respectively.

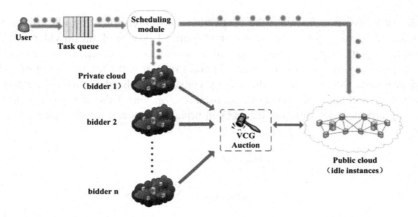

Fig. 1. Process of task scheduling in hybrid clouds

Table 1. Problem parameters

Notation	Definition
B	Service delay bound of arrival task
r_t	Runtime of each task in time slot t
δ_t	Amount of power consumed to execute task in private cloud in time slot t
n	Idle instance n
N_t	Renting number of idle instances in time slot t
w_t^n	Renting time of idle instance n in time slot t
$power_t$	Power price in private cloud in time slot t
$private_t$	Charging price of unit instance of private cloud in time slot t
$idle_t^n$	Transaction price of idle instance n in time slot t
CPU_t	Number of CPU required by each task executed in private cloud in time slot t
Mem_t	Size of memory required by each task executed in private cloud in time slot t
CPU_{max}	CPU capacity of private cloud
Mem_{max}	Memory capacity of private cloud

Table 2. Decision variables

Notation	Definition
λ_t	Number of arrival tasks in time slot t
μ_t^p	Number of arrival tasks executed in private cloud in time slot t
μ_t^n	Number of arrival tasks executed in idle instance n in time slot t
a_t	Number of abandoned tasks in time slot t

Our objective is to increase the profit via reasonably utilize the idle instances in public cloud. Let *profit* denote the obtained profit of private cloud provider, which is determined by its gained revenue and corresponding cost symbolized as *revenue* and *cost*, respectively. As is shown in Eqs. (2) and (3), *cost* is the total expense of private cloud provider, which includes the energy consumed utilized for executing tasks in private cloud and the renting cost of idle instances. *revenue* is the earning brought from executing arrival tasks with the instances in private cloud and idle instances in public cloud.

$$profit = revenue - cost \tag{1}$$

$$cost = power_t \delta_t \mu_t^p + \sum_{n=1}^{N_t} idle_t^n w_t^n \tag{2}$$

$$revenue = private_t \left(\mu_t^p r_t + \sum_{n=1}^{N_t} \mu_t^n r_t \right) \tag{3}$$

Consumers pay money for the execution of their tasks to the private cloud on the basis of the *private_t*, which denotes the charging price of unit instance of private cloud in time slot t. However, the computing resource including CPU and memory [14] in private cloud are limited, and therefore it may take advantage of the instances provided by public cloud to execute the excessive tasks. To reduce the renting cost of private cloud provider, we utilize idle instances instead of the standard on-demand instances. Let $idle_t^n (1 \leq n \leq N)$ denote the transaction price of idle instance n in time slot t which is calculated with VCG mechanism (The computing process of $idle_t^n$ will be specifically described in the following part 2.2), *private_t* should be set greater than $idle_t^n$ so that private cloud provider would obtain profit by scheduling tasks to execute in public cloud. Meanwhile, based on (1)–(3), some constraints to the whole task scheduling process are shown as (4)–(7).

$$\mu_t^p CPU_t \leq CPU_{max} \tag{4}$$

$$\mu_t^p Mem_t \leq Mem_{max} \tag{5}$$

$$\sum_{n=1}^{N_t} \mu_t^n r_t \leq \sum_{n=1}^{N_t} w_t^n \tag{6}$$

$$\sum_{j=0}^{t+B} \left(\mu_j^p + \sum_{n=1}^{N_t} \mu_j^n + a_j \right) = \sum_{i=0}^{t} \lambda_i \tag{7}$$

Constraints (4) and (5) show that the total CPU and memory demand of tasks executed in private cloud cannot exceed the processing capacity of private cloud in each time slot. Let $w_t^n (1 \leq n \leq N)$ denote the renting time of idle instance n in time slot t. Constraint (6) means the total runtime of tasks execution should not beyond the total renting time of idle instances. Constraint (7) establishes the relation between arrival tasks and scheduled tasks. By time slot $t + B$, all tasks that arrive in time slot t or earlier must have been scheduled to execute in private cloud and public cloud or be abandoned.

2.2 Staged Bidding Process Modeled with VCG Auction

As mentioned, the price of idle instance, such as spot instance of Amazon EC2, is updated per 5 min when consumers may need to bid for idle instances again. If we set our time slot to be 5 min, private cloud provider has chance to bid for idle instances in each time slot. This process of bidding for idle instances is staged because we cannot guarantee the bidding is always successful, and the tasks failed to be executed in this time slot will be transferred to the next time slot.

Among the various auction mechanisms, VCG mechanism is proven to be the only type of auctions that can simultaneously guarantee truthfulness and economy efficiency (social welfare maximization) [10]. VCG auction requires each bidder to compensate for the economic losses he brings to other bidders, which can encourage bidders to bid their true valuations. This auction mechanism can effectively prevent the malignant competition, and the final expense of each bidder can be greatly cut down. In this paper, to further reduce the renting cost of instances in public cloud, the staged bidding process is modeled with VCG auction and the transaction price of idle instance can be calculated as follows.

Assume that there are M bidders denoted as $\{b^1, b^2, \ldots, b^M\}$ bidding for N_t idle instances denoted as $\{I^1, I^2, \ldots, I^{N_t}\}$ in time slot t. The information of bidders except our private cloud provider cannot be obtained because bidding is carried out by the vendor and sealed for bidders. However, some public cloud computing vendor, such as Amazon, provides the historical price of spot instances to the registered consumers. Therefore, we can utilize this price list to establish a simple but practical statistic model, i.e., a triangular distribution [15] shown in Fig. 2 to generate the bidding price of each bidder.

$$f(x) = \begin{cases} \frac{2(x-a)}{(b-a)(c-a)}, & (a \leq x \leq c) \\ \frac{2(b-x)}{(b-a)(b-c)}, & (c \leq x \leq b) \end{cases} \tag{8}$$

The probability density of triangular distribution is calculated as Eq. (8). In the probability distribution curve of instance's historical price, a is lower limit, b is the

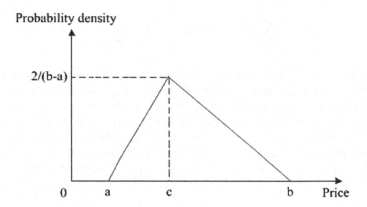

Fig. 2. Triangular distribution of instance's historical price

upper limit, and c is the mode which indicates the most likely bidding price. For example, the historical price information [16] in Amazon EC2 cloud (m3.medium, from 2017, Jan 25 to 2017, Feb 25) is shown in Fig. 3. The parameters of price triangular distribution can be acquired as a = 0.010($/H), b = 0.020($/H), c = 0.014($/H). Thus, the generated bidding price of the M bidders mostly concentrated in 0.014($/H).

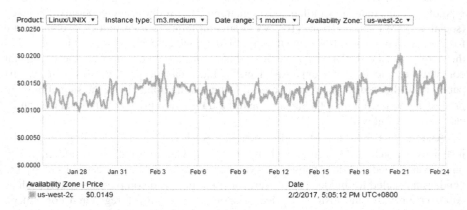

Fig. 3. Snapshot of historical price of spot instance in Amazon EC2 cloud (m3.medium, from 2017, Jan 25 to 2017, Feb 25)

Since the bidding price of each bidder can obtained, we can calculate the transaction price of idle instance computed with VCG mechanism. Firstly, we order these bidding prices from high to low and the bidder who provides higher bidding price has priority to obtain the idle instances. The auction cannot finish until all idle instances provided by public cloud have been chosen. Then we use VCG mechanism to optimize this pricing process.

$$idle_t^n = \begin{cases} 0, & \textit{if bidder } j \textit{ does not obtain idle instance} \\ V_{M\setminus\{b_j\}}^{I^n} - V_{M\setminus\{b_j\}}^{N_t\setminus\{I^n\}}, & \textit{if bidder } j \textit{ obtains idle instance item } I^n \end{cases} \quad (9)$$

The bidder j denoted as b_j represents the private cloud provider. Let $V_{M\setminus\{b_j\}}^{I^n}$ denote the total payment obtained by public cloud vendor when bidder j does not participate in this bidding, and $V_{M\setminus\{b_j\}}^{N_t\setminus\{I^n\}}$ denote the total payment obtained by public cloud vendor except the payment of bidder j. The final transaction price of idle instance $idle_t^n$ is calculated as Eq. (9). If private cloud provider does not obtain any idle instance, the tasks cannot be executed in this time slot and will be transferred to the next time slot.

3 Case Study

In this section, we adopt public real-world workload traces in Google compute systems [17] to evaluate the efficiency of our task scheduling method. The dataset in Fig. 4 shows the number of arrival tasks in each time slot, which derives from the Google production cluster for 370 min in Nov 2014. Figure 4 illustrates four types of tasks, i.e., task type 1, 2, 3, and 4. In this experiment, we use tasks of type 1 to evaluate the performance of the proposed task scheduling method and the other three types of task can be simulated as the bidders except the private cloud provider in the VCG auction. In addition, the historical price data of spot instance used in this paper refers to the information in Amazon EC2 cloud shown as Fig. 3. The parameter setting is shown as follows.

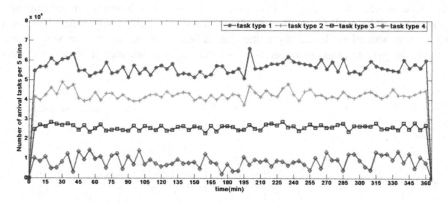

Fig. 4. Arrival tasks in each time slot

Cloud system: $CPU_{max} = 512$(cores), $Mem_{max} = 1024$(GB), $private_t = 0.48(\$/H)$, $power_t = 0.02(\$/KWH)$, $\delta_t = 0.05$(kWH). Besides, r_t(H) is sampled from the uniform distribution over intervals (0, 5/60).
Triangular distribution: a = 0.010($/H), b = 0.020($/H), c = 0.014($/H).

Figure 5 illustrates the task scheduling situation in each time slot. It is obviously observed that private cloud provider schedule the tasks exceeding its processing capacity to the public cloud to execute. In addition, most arrival tasks can be executed during the period of service delay bound which is set as three time slots, because the number of abandoned tasks in most time slots tends to be a minute value as shown in Fig. 5.

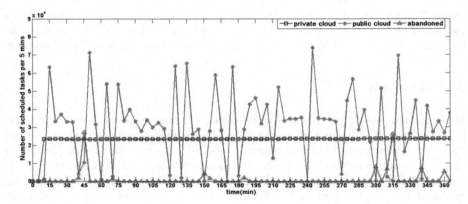

Fig. 5. Scheduled tasks in each time slot

Figure 6 illustrates the comparison between bidding price and transaction price of idle price in each time slot. Transaction price is always lower than bidding price because the VCG mechanism increase the total socially welfare and make each bidder bid its true valuation. In addition, the transaction price in some time slots is zero because the private cloud provider does not bid any idle instance in these time slots.

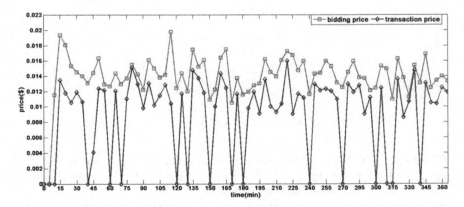

Fig. 6. Bidding price and transaction price in each time slot

Figure 7 illustrates the profit comparison with the task scheduling method in paper [3] and paper [5]. The tasks refused by private cloud in paper [3] bring a mass of profit loss. However, in our task scheduling method, these refused tasks can be scheduled to execute in public cloud. As is shown in Fig. 7, compared to scheduling method in paper [3], the profit calculated by our method can be increased by 69.39% on average. The instance in public cloud used in paper [5] is on-demand instance whose price is higher than idle instance. However, in our cloud system, idle instances in public cloud are used to execute tasks and their charging price can be greatly reduced via VCG auction. As is shown in Fig. 7, compared to scheduling method in paper [5], the profit calculated by our method can be increased by 33.96% on average.

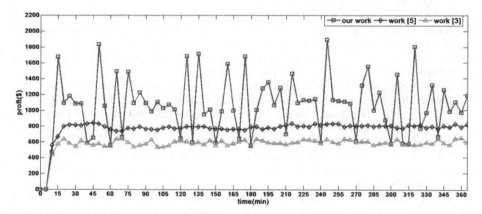

Fig. 7. Compared with the method rejecting excessive tasks [3] and the method scheduling excessive tasks to on-demand instances [5], the proposed approach averagely increases the profit 69.39% and 33.96% respectively.

4 Conclusion and Future Works

In this paper we implemented a hybrid clouds framework that IaaS Provider can schedule the tasks exceeding its processing capacity to public cloud to execute. The instance in public cloud we used is idle instance whose transaction price is calculated with VCG mechanism. Experiment results show that the proposed task scheduling method can greatly increase the profit obtained by IaaS provider. In the future, we would like to investigate the pricing mode of combinatorial heterogeneous Virtual Machine instances.

References

1. Bruneo, D.: A stochastic model to investigate data center performance and QoS in Iaas cloud computing systems. J. IEEE Trans. Parallel Distrib. Syst. **25**(3), 560–569 (2014)

2. Ou, Z., Zhuang, H., Lukyanenko, A., et al.: Is the same instance type created equal? Exploiting heterogeneity of public clouds. J. IEEE Trans. Cloud Comput. **1**(2), 201–214 (2013)
3. Luo, J., Rao, L., Liu, X.: Temporal load balancing with service delay guarantees for data center energy cost optimization. J. IEEE Trans. Parallel Distrib. Syst. **25**(3), 775–784 (2014)
4. Zuo, X., Zhang, G., Tan, W.: Self-adaptive learning PSO-based deadline constrained task scheduling for hybrid IaaS cloud. J. IEEE Trans. Autom. Sci. Eng. **11**(2), 564–573 (2014)
5. Yuan, H., Bi, J., Tan, W., et al.: Temporal task scheduling with constrained service delay for profit maximization in hybrid clouds. J. IEEE Trans. Autom. Sci. Eng. **14**(1), 337–348 (2017)
6. Menzel, M., Ranjan, R., Wang, L., et al.: CloudGenius: a hybrid decision support method for automating the migration of web application clusters to public clouds. J. IEEE Trans. Comput. **64**(5), 1336–1348 (2015)
7. Bhise, V.K., Mali, A.S.: EC2 instance provisioning for cost optimization. In: 2013 International Conference on Advances in Computing, Communications and Informatics (ICACCI), pp. 1891–1895. IEEE (2013)
8. Gu, Y., Tao, J., Li, G., et al.: A preemptive truthful VMs allocation online mechanism in private cloud. J. Comput. Sci. **17**, 647–653 (2016)
9. Singh, V.K., Dutta, K.: Dynamic price prediction for amazon spot instances. In: 2015 48th Hawaii International Conference on System Sciences (HICSS), pp. 1513–1520. IEEE (2015)
10. Mihailescu, M., Teo, Y.M.: Dynamic resource pricing on federated clouds. In: Proceedings of the 2010 10th IEEE/ACM International Conference on Cluster, Cloud and Grid Computing, pp. 513–517. IEEE Computer Society (2010)
11. Elkind, E.: True costs of cheap labor are hard to measure: edge deletion and VCG payments in graphs. In: Proceedings of the 6th ACM conference on Electronic commerce, pp. 108–116. ACM (2005)
12. Gui, Y., Zheng, Z., Wu, F., et al.: SOAR: strategy-proof auction mechanism for distributed cloud bandwidth reservation. In: 2014 IEEE International Conference on Communication Systems (ICCS), pp. 162–166. IEEE (2014)
13. Yulin, W., Xiao, S.: Guanghong G: Real-time load balancing scheduling algorithm for periodic simulation models. Simula. Model. Pract. Theory **52**(1), 123–134 (2016)
14. Xiao, S., Shaoyun, Z., Xuecheng, S.: Measurement of network complexity and capability in command and control system. J. Stat. Comput. Simul. **84**(6), 1232–1248 (2013)
15. Triangular Distribution. http://mathworld.wolfram.com/TriangularDistribution.html
16. Historical price of m3.medium instance in Amazon EC2 cloud from 25 January 2017 to 25 February 2017. https://us-west-2.console.aws.amazon.com/console/home?region=us-west-2
17. Public real-world workload traces in Google compute systems. https://code.google.com/p/googleclusterdata

Optimal Forwarding Probability for Vehicular Location Prediction Handover Algorithm

Arfah A. Hasbollah[1(✉)], Sharifah H.S. Ariffin[2], and Nurzal E. Ghazali[2]

[1] Politeknik Ibrahim Sultan, Pasir Gudang, Malaysia
arfah.hasb@fkegraduate.utm.my
[2] Universiti Teknologi Malaysia, Johor Bahru, Malaysia
{sharifah,effiyana}@fke.utm.my

Abstract. Existing wireless networks aim to provide communication service between vehicle by enabling the vehicular networks to support wide range applications for enhancing the efficiency of road transportation. As the vehicle moves between the different cell with higher speed than the regular mobile node, a handover process is needed to change its point of attachment to the predicted next cell. When a vehicle moves, the path loss and shadow fading contribute to the large scale variation of reference symbols received quality (RSRQ), especially in an urban area where small cells are located. Since traditional handover decision based on RSRQ induce the ping-pong effect, it is a pressing need to develop an intelligent approach to predict the handover decision process, thus yielding seamless handovers. This paper proposes a Vehicular Location Prediction Handover Algorithm (VLPHA) approach to predict the handover decision and utilize the optimization method by using optimal forwarding probability. The vehicle location and target cell RSRQ are considered as inputs to the handover algorithm to predict the handover decision, hence switching to the best preferable access point. The VLPHA approach has implemented in NS-3 to find the best optimal forwarding probability value. The result shows that the proposed method able to reduce the number of unnecessary handovers as well as ping-pong effect from 35% to 0%.

Keywords: Vehicular network · Handover · Prediction · Ping-pong effect

1 Introduction

Recent advances in the integration of communication and sensor technologies have triggered the deployment of numerous attractive applications for road transportation systems. In this regard, the network of connected vehicles contributes the main building block of intelligent transportation system (ITS) and the basis for a diversity of applications that can enhance the safety and comfort of road transportation such as accident prevention, road traffic condition, and others. [2,9]. In order to have a reliable system and good real-time performance, underlying technologies such as handover performance must be reliable and real-time

© Springer Nature Singapore Pte Ltd. 2017
M.S. Mohamed Ali et al. (Eds.): AsiaSim 2017, Part II, CCIS 752, pp. 369–380, 2017.
DOI: 10.1007/978-981-10-6502-6_33

in the first place. On one hand, handover is a fundamental element in wireless networks in order to provide Quality of Service (QoS) for mobile users. However, due to the nature of mobility, ping-pong effect may happen in the vehicular networks, which cause increase signaling resources, increase traffic delay caused by buffering data on the incoming traffic at the target cell and degrading network performance, thus posing a challenge for resource allocation in handover algorithm. The ping-pong effect caused by the frequent movement of the user between serving and target cell and vice-versa or signal fluctuation at the edge of these cells [14,19]. The main targets are reducing the number of unnecessary handovers, ping-pong effect and dropped calls.

To date, various handover algorithms have been proposed to improve handover performance and lessen the ping-pong effect in wireless networks. For instance, in [15], mobile location and velocity are figured based on the fading environment without using GPS is proposed. The authors in [4] study an algorithm to detects the ping-pong handover or normal handover. Further, a handover procedure based on frequency separation in a twin state network provide stable handover without ping-pong effect even though the interference may cause to some user's radio link failure presented in [12]. In [5], the authors propose a mobility prediction using Markov Chains as a technique to assist handover procedure in LTE femtocell. The self-optimization handover algorithm is proposed in [13] tunes the handover control parameters individually for each cell. The work in [10] proposes ping-pong handover filter to filtering ping-pong handover phenomenon in user's trajectories. The objective of the work in [17] is to implement the handover mechanism with suitable handover parameters to avoid ping-pong effect in self-optimization features of self-organizing network (SON). In addition, the work in [8] proposes a SON features to eliminate overlapped femtocells from neighbor femtocell list. Further, the use of Semi-Markov decision process model to calculate the handoff decision policy is studied in [21] for proactive vehicle safety monitoring.

Most of the existing work in handover algorithm have focused on handover decision process and tunes the handover parameters to get the appropriate handover decision time to reduce ping-pong effect as well as ping-pong handover detector and filter. Nonetheless, one challenging aspect of handover algorithm for vehicular networks that remains unexplored is the design of handover algorithm to assign available resources efficiently to satisfy different requirements for different scenarios. A keen handover resource allocation algorithm efficient and optimal characteristic which can allocate handover resource within a short time as well as allocate an appropriate amount of time to each user [20]. If the two techniques are combined, the network performance can be improved and this, in turn, diminishes the handover algorithm that typically exists in conventional techniques. For example, instead of tunes the handover parameters such as threshold level, hysteresis margin and time-to-trigger that might be different depending on each scenarios, user can predict next target cell to reduce resource allocation time and optimize the resource by calculate the appropriate resource needed by each user depending on priorities, QoS and system resource constraints. Therefore, by using an efficient handover algorithm, all the vehicles moving between APs will acquire appropriate resources and handoff to target cell within the short time. By doing so, the network can provide better user QoS and optimize the network overloads. Further, from the vehicle's perspective, due to the short duration that vehicle spends at an AP, it is common that a vehicle merely has time to handoff to the target cell. By enabling prediction algorithm, the vehicles will obtain more time to handoff because they do not need to scan for the target cell. To the best of our knowledge, no existing work has studied this cooperation of prediction and optimization for handover algorithm, notably from a vehicular network perspective.

The main contribution of this paper is an optimal forwarding probability for VLP handover algorithm. The optimal forwarding probability is applied to select the optimal forwarding choice based on next predicted cell and ratio of RSRQ for serving cell and target cell. There are several existing works has already explored various aspects of optimal forwarding. For instance, [3] proposed optimal forwarding probability for real-time routing protocol with load distribution (RTLD). The authors in [18] applied an optimal forwarding for a trade-off between delivery delay and energy consumption in a delay tolerant network (DTN). Further, the optimal forwarding used to maximizes the expected delivery rate while satisfying some number of forwarding per message for DTN in [16]. In [7], the authors model the different class on nodes in heterogeneous DTN and optimizes forwarding control to deliver messages from source to destination under a given energy budget. The objective of this research is to find the optimal point for triggered handover while choosing between the predicted cell and RSRQ. In order to select the best probability value for the parameters that mention earlier, the handover performance will be evaluated using NS-3 simulator.

The remainder of this paper are organized as follows: Sect. 2 presents the proposed system model. In Sect. 3, the model of the optimal forwarding probability will be explained, and Sect. 4 will describe the simulation study. Finally, Sect. 5 will conclude the paper.

2   Handover Procedure and Parameters

The main procedure to provide mobility management in wireless communication systems is the handover procedure. In the case of LTE networks, the procedure starts with the measurement report (MR) sent by the user equipment (UE) to the serving eNB (SeNB). The UE periodically performs downlink radio channel measurements of the reference symbols received quality (RSRQ) on the pilot channel. UE will send the corresponding MR if certain network conditions to indicate the triggered event. The proposed handover algorithm is developed based on standard handover algorithm with event triggered reports of Event A2 and Event A4 which is also known as A2A4 handover algorithm [1]. UE may consider for handover if Event A2 as in Eq. 1 is true, while the decision to handoff UE from serving cell to target cell is taken if the condition of Event A4 in Eq. 2 is true. Based on MR, the cell indicates which cell should be the target eNB (TeNB).

$$RSRQ_S < t_h \qquad\qquad (1)$$

$$RSRQ_T - RSRQ_S \geq O_C \qquad\qquad (2)$$

Equations 1 and 2 shown the condition of event A2A4 handover algorithm. $RSRQ$ is the signal strength values for the serving cell, S, whereas T is denoted as the target cell. t_h is the handover threshold value while O_C is a cell offset value. Figure 1 shows a timeline of RSRQ values of two cells with additional cell offset and where a measurement trigger and timeline of connection. The handover threshold value, t_h, allows UE to select stronger cell when current signal strength is less than the threshold value. The cell offset, O_C, is a cell pair specific value, which shifts the actual cell border. This value can act as a handover margin where it can delay the handover for a while based on the offset value.

The SeNB will subsequently communicate with the target cell, and UE will be controlled to close the radio link to its serving cell and start a new radio connection in the target cell. Since the handover in LTE is hard handover where UE can only connect to one cell at a time, the LTE performance is affected (high number of handover, reduce system throughput, increase system delay). The significant number of handover may cause ping-pong effect where the UE is handover between the two cell, to and forth. Normally, the ping-pong effect occurs if the decision factors which is RSRQ level changes fast. Thus, it is necessary to have efficient decision algorithm which can minimize the number of handover and system delays.

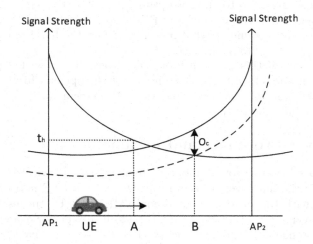

Fig. 1. Handover design

3   Optimal Forwarding Probability

The optimal forwarding probability for VLPHA starts by determining predicted cell and ratio of RSRQ for serving cell and target cell. Then, the proposed mechanism gives weighting value (between 0.1 to 0.9) for each parameter to achieve the best performance in terms the number of ping-pong handover and delivery ratio. This procedure continues until the optimal weighting value is determined.

3.1   VLPHA Overview

VLP handover algorithm consists several features that include location prediction, handover threshold, and neighbor cell offset. The handover threshold value will determine where the handover consider being triggered if the serving cell RSRQ is less to the handover threshold value. Then, the best neighbor cell with the higher RSRQ is verified. Theoretically, the handover triggered when the serving AP provides less signal strength than the neighbor AP. As the user moves far away from the serving AP towards the neighbor AP, the signal strength receives from the neighbor AP is increased. An intersection point between signal strength from the serving AP and neighbor AP is called as an optimal point for handover. In order to achieve the optimal handover point, the fast handover is required. The flow of VLPHA is shown in Fig. 2.

Additional steps of verifying the best neighbor cell with the prediction results are introduced. The location prediction for each access point (AP) is based on vehicle's trajectory history and can be calculated using Markov Chain as shown in Eq. 3.

$$p_n = p_t \times [P]^n \tag{3}$$

where p_n is a position of the vehicle which is the predicted cell after n movement, p_t is initial distribution and P is transition probability matrix. The prediction cell is acquired by the real time data traces and using data mining, the next location of predicted cells are stored in the transaction database. The database will be updated from time to time if there are any changes in vehicle's trajectory. The procedure to determine the vehicle's location prediction is explained in [11].

On the other hand, UE also will select target cell based on RSRQ mention in Sect. 2. In LTE, the handover is design based on UE-assisted network-controlled. It means the handover is decided by the source AP based on measurement reports provided by the UE. The UE required to measure the RSRP and RSRQ periodically and report to the source AP. RSRP is defined as an average power of the resource elements that carry cell-specific reference signal. The RSRQ provides a cell-specific quality metric where it takes the interference level into account in addition to the signal strength. Mathematically, the RSRQ is defined as in Eq. 4.

$$RSRQ = \frac{N * RSRP}{(E - UTRA \, carrier \, RSSI)} \tag{4}$$

where N is the number of Resource Block (RB) of the E-UTRA carrier RSSI measurement BW, and $RSSI$ is Received Signal Strength Indicator. The RSRQ measurement is chosen because it can measure the quality of the cell signal including the interference level. An offset value, O_C are applied during the verification steps. The handover will be triggered within a certain time to ensure

RSRQ for target AP is stable and achieve optimal point before the handover is performed. As the handover is closer to the optimal point, the handover performance is much better This is because the user will connect to the AP with better signal much earlier. Thus the packet delivery ratio (PDR) can be increased.

The handover will be triggered to target cell that has optimal forwarding probability. If the best neighbor cell is same as the predicted cell, it is assumed that the target cell is the location that user will go. Thus, the handover is necessary. On the other hand, if the best neighbor cell is not same as the predicted cell, it is assumed that the target cell might not represent the location that the user will go. Therefore, the handover will only be triggered if target cell RSRQ is higher than serving cell RSRQ at least by the offset value. This action is necessary to reduce the number of unnecessary handovers. The optimal forwarding probability is computed as follows:

$$OF = (\lambda_1 \times Predicted\,cell) + (\lambda_2 \times RSRQ) \tag{5}$$

where $\lambda_1 + \lambda_2 = 1$. The values of λ_1 and λ_2 are estimated from the simulation as explained in next section. The main parameter considered for the equation is predicted cell and RSRQ value. These parameters are chosen because they are the main parameters that triggered and verified the handover in VLPHA. As mention before, the handover will be triggered if the best neighbor cell is same with the predicted cell. At the same, RSRQ value also must evaluate before triggered the handover. In that case, the probability of choosing these two parameter value must done carefully in order to get accurate and optimal handover point.

4   Simulation Study

This section discusses the detail of the handover parameters values. The network simulation scenarios are set as shown in Table 1. For the of creating a realistic simulation environment, the optimal forwarding probability of VLPHA was simulated based on Google Maps Places API using RoutesMobilityModel [6]. NS3 simulator was used to simulate vehicular network which reflects real access

Table 1. Simulation parameters

Parameter	Value
Propagation model	Hybrid building propagation model
Transmission power	20 dBm
Simulation time	263 s
Number of UE	1
Number of APs	19
Critical ping-pong handover time	5 s
Source handover threshold	−5 dB

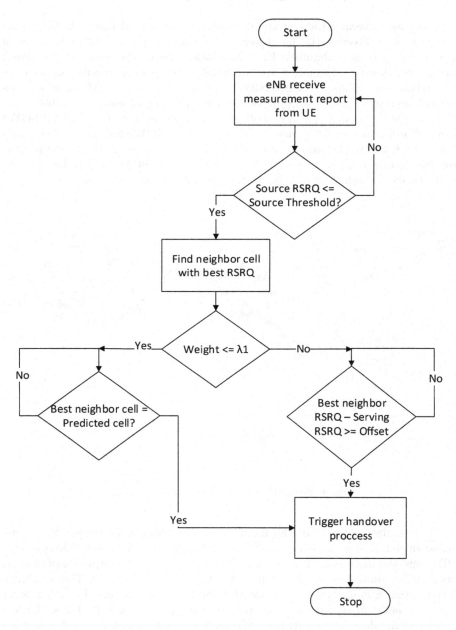

Fig. 2. Vehicular Location Prediction Handover Algorithm (VLPHA)

mechanism in the wireless network. The vehicles are equipped with a wireless communication that is On-Board-Unit (OBUs). All APs have the same characteristics which transmit 20 dBm powers. The scenario considers open access mode for all APs. Hence, the UE can connect to the APs without any restriction.

There are several handover simulations was performed using the NS3 simulation tool to observe the handover performance with the different value of optimal forwarding probability. Each simulation result was recorded, tabulated and the handover performance was analyzed. The network simulation scenario is based on real topology in University Teknologi Malaysia (UTM) campus. This network scenario consists a group of wireless APs organized for 1 mobile user. It also consists mobility management entity and service gateway (MME/ SGW) nodes affording to the AP region and core network. SGW shall forward the data that come from the AP and packet data network gateway. MME is used to control the high-level operation such as choosing the right SGW for the UE and authenticating them. Figure 3 illustrated the simulation scenario.

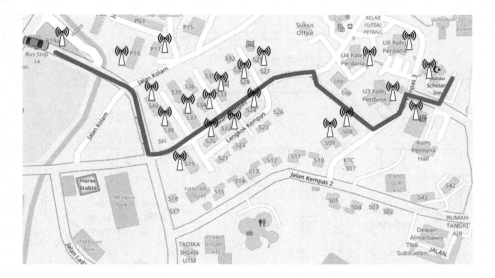

Fig. 3. Simulation scenario on UTM topology

The simulation result of the handover performance was analyzed and discussed in detail. The number of ping-pong handover and packet delivery ratio (PDR) are the metrics that use to analyze all probability performance of the two forwarding parameters employed in VLPHA as mention in Eq. 5. The reliability of the network is analyzed based on the number of handovers. Each handover consumes network resources to reroute the call to the new cell. Thus, the less number of handover is better. If a call handed over to a new cell and is handed back to the source cell in less than the critical time, this handover becomes unnecessary handover and can cause ping-pong effect that is resulting degrading QoS and system capacity. PDR is the ratio of packets received at the destination to the total number of packets sent from the source. PDR will give direct effect to the user's QoS. Therefore, if PDR is higher, the handover performance is much better. In Eq. 5, λ_1 and λ_2 are between 0.9 and 0.1. For example, if λ_1 is

0.1, λ_2 should be not exceeding 0.9 for the summation of λ_1 and λ_2 to become 1. Table 2 shows all the probability of λ_1 and λ_2. In this table, the total outcomes are equal to 9 trails.

Table 2. Probability of all trails

Trail	λ_1	λ_2
1	0.1	0.9
2	0.2	0.8
3	0.3	0.7
4	0.4	0.6
5	0.5	0.5
6	0.6	0.4
7	0.7	0.3
8	0.8	0.2
9	0.9	0.1

The performance of VLPHA with optimal forwarding is evaluated based on the prior probability for λ_1 and λ_2. Figure 4 shows the number of ping-pong handover and delivery ratio for each probability of λ_1 and λ_2. In addition, the offset in Fig. 4b and a were varied as the default value (0), 1 and 2 respectively. The simulation results in Fig. 4a show that VLPHA provides the lesser number of ping-pong handover at three trails (2, 8, 9) for offset 0. However, for offset 1 reveals that VLPHA provides the fewer number of ping-pong handover at trails (1, 8, 9) and for offset 2 the less number of ping-pong handover at four trails (1, 7, 8, 9). In order to decide which trails are best, the optimal delivery ratio is compared. Figure 4b show that the trails (2, 8, 9) for offset 0 have optimal delivery ratio than the trails (1, 8, 9) for offset 1 and trails (1, 7, 8, 9) for offset 2. Hence, VLPHA has the best performance when the trails (2, 8, 9) are applied as summarized in Table 3. From this analysis, Eq. 6 can be written as:

$$OF = (0.2 \times Predicted\ cell) + (0.9 \times RSRQ)$$
$$OF = (0.8 \times Predicted\ cell) + (0.2 \times RSRQ) \qquad (6)$$
$$OF = (0.9 \times Predicted\ cell) + (0.1 \times RSRQ)$$

Table 3. Summary of handover best performance

Trails	λ_1	λ_2	Unnecessary handover	PDR
2	0.2	0.8	4	98%
8	0.8	0.2	4	94%
9	0.9	0.1	0	87%

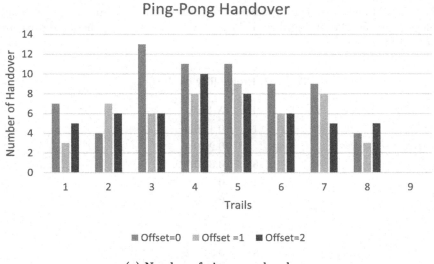

(a) Number of ping-pong handover

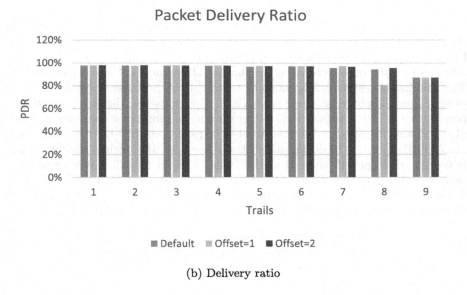

(b) Delivery ratio

Fig. 4. Handover performance of optimal forwarding probability

5   Conclusion

This paper presents the optimal forwarding probability for VLPHA which is designated for LTE. In general, the finding concludes that VLPHA provides high delivery ratio and spend less number of ping-pong handover if the probability is used for the two parameters of VLPHA (predicted cell and RSRQ). In addition, the finding shows that they are three trails out of nine that have good performance in term of delivery ratio and ping-pong handover. In future, the optimal forwarding probability will be evaluated in real experimental test bed network on the vehicular network.

Acknowledgment. The authors would like to thank all who contributed toward making this research successful. The authors wish to express their gratitude to Ministry of Higher Education (MOHE), Research Management Center (RMC) for the sponsorship, and Advanced Telecommunication Technology (ATT), Universiti Teknologi Malaysia for the financial support and advice for this project. (Vot number Q.J130000.2723.02K47).

References

1. 3GPP TS 36.331: 3rd Generation Partnership Project; Technical Specification Group Radio Access Network; Evolved Universal Terrestrial Radio Access (E-UTRA) Radio Resource Control (RRC); Protocol Specification (Release 8) (2007)
2. Al-Sultan, S., Al-Doori, M.M., Al-Bayatti, A.H., Zedan, H.: A comprehensive survey on vehicular ad hoc network. J. Netw. Comput. Appl. **37**, 380–392 (2014)
3. Ali, A., Rashid, R.A., Arriffian, S.H.F., Fisal, N.: Optimal forwarding probability for real-time routing in wireless sensor network. In: 2007 IEEE International Conference on Telecommunications and Malaysia International Conference on Communications. ICT-MICC 2007, pp. 419–424. IEEE, Penang (2007)
4. Alradwan, H., Motermawy, A., Ghanem, K.: Reducing ping-pong handover effect in LTE mobile networks using TRIAS. Tishreen Univ. J. Res. Sci. Stud. **4**(33), 237–250 (2011)
5. Amirrudin, N.A., Sharifah, H.S., Malik, N.N.N.A., Ghazali, N.E.: Mobility prediction in Long Term Evolution (LTE) femtocell network. In: Handbook of Research on Progressive Trends in Wireless Communications and Networking, pp. 99–121. IGI Global, Pennsylvania (2014)
6. Cerqueira, T., Albano, M.: RoutesMobilityModel: easy realistic mobility simulation using external information services (2015)
7. Chahin, W., El-Azouzi, R., De Pellegrini, F., Azad, A.P.: Blind online optimal forwarding in heterogeneous delay tolerant networks. In: Wireless Days (WD), 2011 IFIP, pp. 1–6 (2011)
8. Chowdhury, M.Z., Jang, Y.M.: Handover management in high-dense femtocellular networks. EURASIP J. Wirel. Commun. Netw. **2013**(1), 1–21 (2013)
9. Faezipour, M., Nourani, M., Saeed, A., Addepalli, S.: Progress and challenges in intelligent vehicle area networks. Commun. ACM **55**(2), 90 (2012)
10. Hadachi, A., Batrashev, O., Lind, A., Singer, G., Vainikko, E.: Cell phone subscribers mobility prediction using enhanced Markov chain algorithm. In: IEEE Intelligent Vehicles Symposium (IV), pp. 1049–1054. IEEE, Michigan (2014)
11. Hasbollah, A., Ariffin, S.H.S., Fisal, N., Prediction, M., For, M., Network, V., Markov, U.: Mobility prediction method for vehicular network using Markov chain. Jurnal Teknologi (Sci. Eng.) **2**(6), 7–13 (2015)
12. Hunukumbure, M., Agarwal, R., Vadgama, S.: Handover mechanisms for planned cell outage in twin state green wireless networks. In: 2011 IEEE 73rd Vehicular Technology Conference (VTC Spring), pp. 1–5. IEEE (2011)

13. Jansen, T., Balan, I., Turk, J., Moerman, I.: Handover parameter optimization in LTE self-organizing networks. In: 2010 IEEE 72nd Vehicular Technology Conference Fall (VTC 2010-Fall). IEEE (2010)
14. Lin, C.C., Sandrasegaran, K., Zhu, X., Xu, Z.: Limited CoMP handover algorithm For LTE-advanced. J. Eng. **2013**, 1–9 (2013)
15. Lin, H.P., Juang, R.T., Lin, D.B.: Validation of an improved location-based handover algorithm using GSM measurement data. IEEE Trans. Mob. Comput. **4**(5), 530–536 (2005)
16. Liu, C., Wu, J.: Proceedings of the Tenth ACM International Symposium on Mobile Ad Hoc Networking and Computing, pp. 105–114 (2009)
17. Md Isa, I.N., Baba, M.D., Ab Rahman, R., Yusof, A.L.: Self-organizing network based handover mechanism for LTE networks. In: I4CT 2015–2015 2nd International Conference on Computer, Communications, and Control Technology, Art Proceeding, pp. 11–15. IEEE, Kuching (2015)
18. Singh, C., Altman, E., Kumar, A., Sundaresan, R.: Optimal forwarding in delay-tolerant networks with multiple destinations. IEEE/ACM Trans. Netw. (TON) **21**(6), 1812–1826 (2013)
19. Zeng, Q.A., Agrawal, D.P.: Handoff in Wireless Mobile Networks. In: Stojmenovic, I. (ed.) Handbook of Wireless Networks and Mobile Computing, chap. 1, p. 662. Wiley (2002)
20. Zhou, Y., Ai, B.: Handover schemes and algorithms of high-speed mobile environment: a survey. Comput. Commun. **47**, 1–15 (2014)
21. Zhu, L., Yu, F., Ning, B., Tang, T.: Design and performance enhancements in communication-based train control systems with coordinated multipoint transmission and reception. IEEE Trans. Intell. Transp. Syst. **15**(3), 1258–1272 (2014)

Big Data Skills Required for Successful Application Implementation in the Banking Sector

Abeer Ahmed Abdullah AL-Hakimi$^{(\boxtimes)}$

Asia Pacific University of Technology and Innovation, Kuala Lumpur, Malaysia
abeerahmed1213@gmail.com

Abstract. The fundamental significance of Big Data is in the possibility to enhance effectiveness and advancement for employees with regards to utilize a big volume of data, of various type. If Big Data is defined clearly and strongly characterized, banks can improve in their business, thence prompting to efficiency in various fields. The aim of this study is to identify what are factors that effect on Big Data Analytics skills and further propose a long-term development, self-efficacy and level of analytics as framework for a successful career in Big Data analytics in banking sector. This is because banking sector is one of the most services sector which are having big flow of data. Using quantitative approach to emphasize objective measurements and the statistical, numerical analysis survey in this research, 161 bankers were randomly selected from ten banks in Malaysia. The result of the study revealed that two independent variables significantly affect the successful of Big Data in banking sector which were long-term development and self-efficacy. On the other hand, the third variable (level of analytics) has fairly affect the success of Big Data through the skills indirectly.

Keywords: Big data analytics · Long-term development · Self-efficacy · Level of analytics · Big data required skills · Big data success in banking sector

1 Introduction

1.1 Background of Research

Banking sectors generate huge amount of data through its various practices on information technology applications. With each financial transaction process, there is digital data generated calls Big Data. Banks are increasingly interested to form methods and tools to handle this type of data which should essentially assist them to improve their performance. Big Data create a new evolution opportunities for existing banking sector and entirely new categories [1]. The generated data is analyzed in a way to provide understandings into either the customer or the decision makers or both. There are many sources of banks data like customer conduct, emails, internet banking, voice call, social media, websites etc. the good analyze of the big data provides banks' ability to get all possible information to analyses products, markets and customer's data. Analyzed data may indicate to the main client, and how do the customers spending money and so on.

© Springer Nature Singapore Pte Ltd. 2017
M.S. Mohamed Ali et al. (Eds.): AsiaSim 2017, Part II, CCIS 752, pp. 381–392, 2017.
DOI: 10.1007/978-981-10-6502-6_34

All these and many other factors and variables should eventually help to achieve better decision making in the bank. Banking sector can create worth from Big Data by working on different levers [2]: first, creating a more transparent holistic approach of taking decisions; second, enabling experimentation to discover requirements, expose variability, and improve performance for data analyzers based on actual data.

Many approaches and algorithms are introduced to manage, analyze, visualize and store these data. All these practices and others are important to identify the requirements to improve the organization performance and competences. Big Data is "the buzz word" that captures the attention of many managers.

1.2   Research Problem

1.2.1   Factors Impacting on Skills Required for Successful Implementation

Many of the presented studies discussed the available applications and the usefulness of Big Data in various fields, these studies argue that Big Data and Analytics faces professional skills gap that is felt over all of banks sectors.

To date, filling this ability gab has represented a significant challenge in wide parts since the banks commonly have been looking for unicorns. As employers challenging to employ, retain, and train enough of the data analyzer to collect, organize, analyses, interpret, and communicate today's unprecedented volumes of data [3].

Although there is wide growing in big data analytics, there is critical challenge in banking sector with the hugely exploiting "Big Data" and world class technology is lack of adequate skills and pressing need to know what are the factors impacting on skills in BDA [4].

1.2.2   Lack of Talent Skills Studies in Big Data

Since beginning of Big Data generation, researchers and computer scientists focused on technical part and system development for processing, storing and managing and systems developments [5]. Now, there is necessity to extend the research on Big Data in terms of its acceptance by banking users. There is a lack of an in-depth analysis of the factors that may influence of implementation of Big Data analytics in banking sector.

In recent years, many academicians and practitioners showed big interest in "Big Data Analytics" (BDA) due its immense potential [6]. The importance of Big Data has also found huge application in the Banking and financial Services [7]. But the senior professional practitioners don't have the capability or proper understanding for gearing up and analyzing Big Data. Scrutinized the firms' investment policies expecting significant returns on investment in Big Data, but this cannot have satisfied without proper preparing for user's skills [8, 9]. Also confirmed a positive relationship amongst BDA and professional's performance [10].

1.3   Research Questions

Due to the need of conducting a research to study the impacts of skills on Big Data in banking sector for the administrators and practitioner of Big Data prospective, it is crucial to form this problem into number of questions so it can be easily analysis and investigated. In this study, I addressed the following questions:

1. What are factors affecting successful Big Data implementation in banking sector?
2. How these factors effect on the skillset in banking sector?

1.4   Integration Previous Models

To answer the first question, (**Model of Big Data Success Indicators**) model has been chosen to identify the factors that are affecting the successful Big Data implementation in banking sector [11].

1.4.1   Model of Big Data Success Indicators
The model consists of six main indicators. The indicators could be considered as success factors that contribute towards Big Data successful implementation with proper planning. Figure 1 represents the Model of Big Data Success Indicators [11].

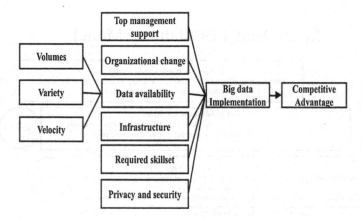

Fig. 1. Model of big data success indicators [11]

To answer the second question, we will identify the factors that effect on the (required skillset) from the previous model.

The process of gathering data across different sectors and from various stakeholders and integrating it through an adaptable processing infrastructure needs high proficiency [12].

Besides, the notion of self-efficacy may represent the key personal resource that is able to promote both work engagement and a positive work environment. Furthermore, based on the Social Cognitive Theory, the most pervasive mechanism of human agency is perceived self-efficacy, which reflects the perceived control individuals have over certain situations, as well as themselves [13]. In fact, bankers with high self-efficacy are likely to attain success and further attempt this behavior [14]. In addition, talents in the light of being analytical have increased tremendously for better decision-making. Moreover, data analysis has advanced from just being descriptive to a more predictive and prescriptive analysis. This is because; descriptive analysis has been noted as the most fundamental form in providing hindsight view of an event, thus functions as the platform in transforming raw data to meaningful information [15]. Similarly, Craig and McCarthy claimed, "via predictive analytics, banks can generate the insight necessary to help build more profitable customer relationships, manage and mitigate risks more effectively, as well as transform business strategies" [16].

The second model used to evaluate the level of data analytics through statistical analyses and examine the key levels for advancing their efforts skills.

1.4.2   Talent Analytics Maturity Model

Talent Analytics Maturity Model Fig. (2) indicate to specific areas that can boost an organization's capabilities. Leaders can use these outcomes to assess their position in business and their performance, helping decision makers solve their talent challenges using statistical analyses and inspect the main levers for increasing their efforts [17]. Talent analytics' field is still in its very early stages, with a limited number of companies' way ahead of the curve and the rest underdeveloped.

Talent Analytics Maturity Model

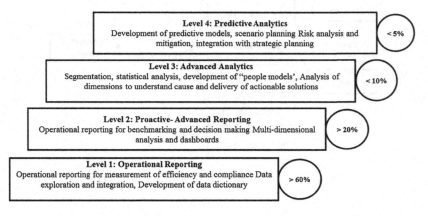

Fig. 2. Talent analytics maturity model [17]

According to Bersin the organizations go through four stages of reports as they build Big Data in organizations strategies by Talent Analytics Maturity Model [17]:

Level 1: Operational Reporting, using data primarily for ad-hoc.
Level 2: Advanced Reporting, using data to keep a pulse trends and goals.

Level 3: Advanced Analytics, this is data is finally used to solve problems and make decisions.

Level 4: Predictive Analytics, organizations at the highest level of maturity are able to use data to predict future talent outcome.

These three skills have been taking in this study to measure their impact on the success of Big Data implementation. The population for the study is all practitioners that working with Big Data in banking sector. Merging between Model of indicators of Big Data and Talent Analytics Maturity Model is the evaluation tool to study the talent analytics skills [11, 17].

2 Hypothesis Developing and Methodology

H1: Long term development has strongly positively affect success of Big Data through the skills indirectly.

H2: Self-efficacy has strongly positively affect success of Big Data through the skills indirectly.

H3: Level of analytics has strongly positively affect success of Big Data through the skills indirectly.

2.1 Method of Sampling and Population

The target of population for the study are the practitioners of Big Data analytics in Malaysian banks. This study looks into the prerequisite skills that are possessed by Big Data analysis employed in banks around Malaysia. Hence, the simple random sampling was adopted in this study. Random sampling describes the method of selecting information with similar possibility of selecting any surveillance. In fact, Zaial and Rjdeh asserted that the method of random sampling is indeed the best option available to obtain better participants [18]. Therefore, the random sampling approach is employed to acquire information from practitioners of Big Data within the banking industry in Malaysia. In fact, structured questionnaire had been used to determine the influence of several variables upon the identified required skills [19].

2.1.1 Data Collection

The method of purposive sampling had been adopted in this study. Thus, a number of analytics were contacted via e-mail to invite them to participate in the e-survey. In total, 149 participants had agreed to get involved in this study. Moreover, based on the Raosoft Sample software programme (a technique for calculating public service offered by creative research Systems), the confidence level was 95%, the confidence interval was 8%, and the population, as suggested by Tanburn, the size of sample did not deviate very far for a population exceeding 20,000, in which had been selected as the size of population [20]. Upon confirmation that 149 participants were indeed adequate, e-mails were sent to all participants, accompanied with a note that elaborates the intent of the study, as well as the questionnaire. In the end of collecting data, the total respondents were 161. The responses, which were gathered from e-survey (Google form) after couple of weeks, had been recorded and constantly updated. The questionnaire was employed to look into the behaviour displayed by participants towards the influential factors upon skills related to Big Data. In addition, the Likert scale was adopted to gather the responses provided by participants.

2.1.2 Success of Big Data Analytics in Banking Sector

Out of 12 questions of success of Big Data in banking sector 161 respondent's answers. They have been questioned about the indicators that affect successful implementation of Big Data in banks. Based on five point Likert scale in this study minimum value = 1 and maximum = 5. According to Marcus [21], five-points Likert-type scale are:

1–1.79 = Strongly Disagree, 1.80–2.59 = Disagree, 2.60–3.39 = uncertain, 3.40–4.19 = agree and 4.20–5 = Strongly Agree.

The Average standard deviation is 0. 46237, and the average for success of Big Data analytic is 3.9283 which shows that the answer is agree. Which is mean the banks agreement that the successful implementation of Big Data in banks and the skills are one of important indicator to successful of Big Data.

2.2   Affected Factors on Big Data Skills

2.2.1   Long-Term Development

Based on the long-term development variable result shows that out of 6 questions the descriptive statistic of long-term development have average standard deviation 0.56973 and average value of mean is 3.7215 which shows that the answer is agree. The result shows that the agreement of long term development is affecting on skills of Big Data positively.

2.2.2   Self-efficacy

Based on the Self-efficacy variable result shows that out of 6 questions the descriptive statistic of Self-efficacy have average standard deviation .49215 and average value of mean is 3.5694 which shows that the answer is agree. It means that the self-efficacy has acceptable and affect skills of employees who works in Big Data in banking sector.

2.2.3   Level of Analytics

Based on the level of analytics variable result shows that out of 6 questions the descriptive statistic of level of analytics average standard deviation 0.45814 and average value of mean is 3.8344 which shows that the answer is agree. It means that the percentage of answers are positive and this variable affect skills of employees who works in Big Data in banking sector.

The following chart Fig. (3), shows that the responses are agree with long term development, self-efficacy and level of analytics on the required skills on Big Data analytics regarding to Marcus [21] result from 3.40 to 4.19 = agree.

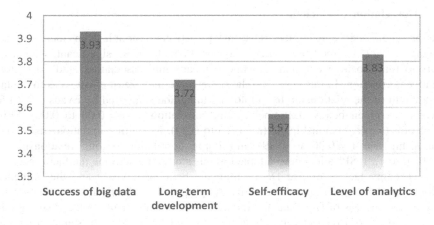

Fig. 3. Responses rate

2.3 Reports Used in Banking Sector

The question number 28 in the survey was about the reports are used in banking sector, the answer was multi choice and the answer was as following:

The level of reports can indicate that can accelerate bank's capabilities high. From finding result Fig. (4) we can say that the banking sector used level No. three, which is advanced analytics, this is data is finally used to solve problems and make decisions by 42%. While the predictive reports were obtained 33%. Those percentage are high Index for reporting.

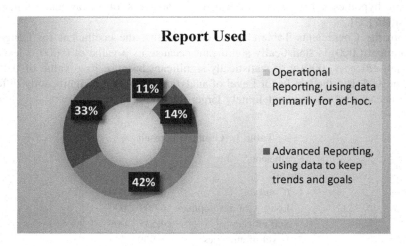

Fig. 4. Report used responses rate

2.4 Correlation Coefficient

Pearson coefficient depicts the relationship between variables. In fact, Ott and Longnecker [22] claimed that values between +1 and −1 are significant, whereby 1 refers to total positive correlation, while 0 means null association, and −1 is total negative correlation. In this case, correlation refers to the size of effect so as to explain the strength of the relationship by employing the guide suggested by Evans (1996) for r- value, as given below: Extremely weak correlation is (r = 0.00 to 0.09), Small correlation (weak relationship) is (r = 0.10 to 0.29), Medium correlation (reasonable relationship) is (r = 0.30 to 0.49) and Large correlation (strong relationship) is (r = 0.50 to 1.0). SPSS had been adopted in this study to determine the factor between the succeeding factors of Big Data within the banking industry and the influential factors (variables) upon the related skills. As projected by the results, the relationship between the success of Big Data and the long-term development is indeed strong with (0.525) and (0.463) respectively, along with self-efficacy. As such, statistical significance is also observed. However, a weak relationship (0.247) was noted on the analytical level, thus reflecting insignificant relationship and thus, statistically unimportant.

2.5 Multiple Regression

Part of the statistical approach is estimating the correlations between the variables. Hence, some techniques were used in determining the correlations between the successful implementation of Big Data analytics within the banking industry, which refers to the variable of influential factors upon required skills for banking and the independent variables (self-efficacy, level of analytics, and long-term development).

Such determination exhibits the effect of modification between independent and dependent variables, especially after maintaining other independent variables. Moreover, all hypotheses had been confirmed via analyses of linear and multi-linear regressions [23].

From the Coefficients Table (1), we can find that the coefficient for Long-term development (.000) is statistically significant because its p-value of 0.000 is less than 0.05. Self-efficacy (.000) also statistically significant because its p-value of 0.000 is less than 0.05. But the last factor Level of analytics (.354) is not significantly different from 0 because its p-value is definitely larger than 0.05.

Table 1. Coefficients result

Coefficients[a]			
Model		t	Sig.
1	(Constant)	6.262	.000
	Long-term development	6.009	.000
	Self-efficacy	4.535	.000
	Level of analytics	−.930	.354

[a] Dependent Variable: Success of Big Data in banking sector

2.6   Results of Hypotheses Testing

The hypotheses testing results in null or alternative hypotheses. Null hypothesis or H0 depicts that did not happen. While that alternative hypothesis or H1 refers to meaningful or true assumption [24]. *P-value method* determines a condition that is "likely" or "unlikely" by determining that a null hypothesis is true by employing a more test statistics from the position of alternative hypothesis. Hence, when *P-value* is less, for instance, below or equivalent to α, the result is "unlikely" or in other words, the null hypothesis is rejected and the alternative hypothesis is supported.

On the contrary, when *P-value* is more, for example, exceeding α, the result is "likely" or simply put, the null hypothesis is accepted [25].

Furthermore, all the hypotheses had been verified via analyses of linear and multi-linear regressions [26].

After testing hypothesis by *P* value, the final hypothesis test results, acknowledge that:

1. Long term development strongly positively affect success of Big Data through the skills indirectly.
2. Self-efficacy has strongly positively affect success of Big Data through the skills indirectly.
3. Level of analytics has fairly affect success of Big Data through the skills indirectly.

From the analyses that had been performed, one can determine if the important factors had indeed affected the skills required for Big Data analytics in the banking sector.

The first factor, which is long-term development with skills related to high performance work practices, displayed a significantly positive correlation $r = .525$, $p < .05$ with the success of Big Data in the banking industry. Hence, it is suggested that banks should opt for frameworks and methods of training and development that could accurately fit within the bank culture. Furthermore, several essential business skills and training approaches are yet to be examined. This is because; appropriate managerial methods, as well as an all-inclusive framework must be realized to organise operational training and development events for staff with Big Data motivation, thus lowering gap in work performance, as well as achieving goals and aims outlined by these banks [27]. Similarly, Khawaja and Nadeem [28] asserted that the notion 'development' points to the fact that the staff enjoy and are committed towards their work, thus, have no impediment in developing their skills for optimal performance. Moreover, a job in a bank that deals with Big Data pushes a bank staff to comprehend their customers, besides understanding essential elements like attitudinal, analytical, and behavioural attributes. Nonetheless, frustrating conflicts can occur if the said qualities lack among the bank staff, hence their commitment too can be affected negatively.

Additionally, this study further demonstrates a significant relationship between the second factor, which is self-efficacy, and success of Big Data in the banking sector with $r = 0.463$, $p < .05$. Therefore, the aspect of self-efficacious among bank staff ensures more productivity, result-oriented attribute, and committed towards their job. In fact, this notion supports the assertion made by Virginie [29], in which self-efficacy is indeed very essential; thus, emerging as the primary predictor for commitment in organization. In addition, perceived efficacy highly contributes to the function of human as it influences one's behaviour not only in a direct manner, but also through its impact upon other vital aspects, for instance, objectives and aims, prospects and awareness of hurdles, as well as prospects within the social setting. Besides, self-efficacy affects the actions opted by individuals in their pursuit of personal challenges, ambitions, and commitment, inclusive of their effort in achieving a goal or a task, their expectations based on their efforts to succeed, as well as their perseverance in facing glitches related to career development. For example, Masood et al. [30] revealed that self-efficacy is indeed the basic element to positive organizational approaches, such as career satisfaction and unfailing commitment. Similarly, Dixit and Bhati [31] believe that staff that display commitment towards their job generate sustenance in the aspect of productivity. likewise, Salami [32] opined that committed employees must be sought by banks in facing the global economic struggle.

3 Proposed Model

The model is the Big Data Success Indicators Model which is extended by adding two factors that are affecting on required of skill set, it shows the strongly positively affect success of Big Data through the skills indirectly.

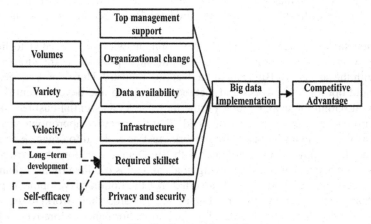

Fig. 5. Proposed model

4 Conclusions

Big Data is the new essence in the banking sector that has been developing at a rather rapid rate. Every financial institution must look into the policy to determine if it suits the setting of the organisation. In fact, the indicators of Big Data outlined in this study have been confirmed in the literature review as the indicators of a successful banking sector.

This paper is an extended to the model of Halaweh and Massry [11] that focus on required skills as an important indicator to attain higher achievement of Big Data in the banking sector. The results portray that long-term development and self-efficacy have strong and positive effects upon the success of Big Data through the skills in an indirect manner.

The results retrieved from this research advocate that both development and training do influence the job performances exerted by workers. Correspondingly, self-efficacy plays a positive role in productivity of banking works through the discovery of risk from the analyses of Big Data, which generated fast solutions and quick decisions.

References

1. Schermann, M., Hemsen, H., Buchmuller, C., Bitter, T., Krcmar, H., Markl, V., Hoeren, T.: Big data - an interdisciplinary opportunity for information systems research. Bus. Inf. Syst. Eng. **6**(5), 261–266 (2014)
2. Wamba, S.F., Akter, S., Edwards, A., Chopin, G., Gnanzou, D.: How 'big data' can make big impact: findings from a systematic review and a longitudinal case study. Int. J. Prod. Econ. **165**, 234–246 (2015)
3. Nikam, A.V., Bhoite, S.D.: Leverage of big data analytics for banking sector. Indian J. Appl. Res. 5(8) (2016)
4. Sivarajah, U., Kamal, M.M., Irani, Z., Weerakkody, V.: Critical analysis of big data challenges and analytical methods. J. Bus. Res. **70**, 263–286 (2016)
5. Kwon, O., Lee, N., Shin, B.: Data quality management, data usage experience and acquisition intention of big data analytics. Int. J. Inf. Manag. **34**, 387–394 (2014)
6. Waller, M.A., Fawcett, S.E.: Data science, predictive analytics, and big data: a revolution that will transform supply chain design and management. J. Bus. Logistics **34**(2), 77–84 (2015)
7. LaValle, S., Lesser, E., Shockley, R., Hopkins, M.S., Kruschwitz, N.: Big data, analytics: and the path from insights to value. MIT Sloan Manag. Rev. **52**(2), 21–31 (2014)
8. Shah, S., Horne, A., Capellá, J.: Good data won't guarantee good decisions. Harvard Bus. Rev. **90**(4), 23–25 (2014)
9. Provost, F., Fawcett, T.: Data science and its relationship to big data and data-driven decision making. Big Data **1**(1), 51–59 (2013)
10. Wixom, B., Yen, B., Relich, M.: Maximizing value from business analytics. MIS Q. Executive **12**(2), 37–49 (2013)
11. Halaweh, M., Massry, A.E.: Conceptual model for successful implementation of big data in organizations. J. Int. Technol. Inf. Manag. **24**(2), 2 (2015)
12. Martindale, R.J.J., Collins, D., Wang, J.C.K., McNeill, M., Lee, K.S., Sproule, J., Westbury, T.: Development of the talent development environment questionnaire for sport. J. Sports Sci. **28**(11), 1209–1221 (2010)
13. Bandura, A.: On the functional properties of perceived self-efficacy revisited. J. Manag. **38** (1), 9–44 (2012)
14. Onyishi, I.E., Ogbodo, E.: The contributions of self-efficacy and perceived organizational support when taking charge at work. SA J. Ind. Psychol. **38**(1), 1–11 (2012)

15. Grillo, M., Hackett, A.: What types of predictive analytics are being used in talent management organizations? Cornell University (2015). http://digitalcommons.ilr.cornell.edu/student/74. Accessed 8 Feb 2017
16. Craig, E., Hou, C., McCarthy, B.F.: The looming global analytics talent mismatch in banking (2013)
17. Bersin, J., O'Leonard, K., Wang-Audia, W.: High-impact talent analytics: Building a world-class HR measurement and analytics function. Bersin by Deloitte (2013)
18. Zaial, A., Rjdeh, S.M.: Information seeking behaviour among post graduate students. Tourism research and innovations (2012)
19. Becker, R., Doyle, D.: Sampling in SAS ® using PROC SURVEYSELECT. SAS Institute Inc., New york (2016)
20. Tanburn, R.: Practical Advice for Selecting Sample Sizes, The Donor Committee for Enterprise Development, May 2015. http://www.enterprise-development.org/wp-content/uploads/Practical_advice_for_selecting_sample_sizes_May2015.pdf. Accessed 27 Dec 2016
21. Marcus, A. (ed.): DUXU 2015. LNCS, vol. 9188. Springer, Cham (2015). doi:10.1007/978-3-319-20889-3
22. Ott, R.L., Longnecker, M.T.: An Introduction to Statistical Methods and Data Analysis. Nelson Education, Scarborough (2015)
23. Mercy, J.L.: Analytical report on, Luxembourge: Luxembourg: Publications Office of the European Union (2016)
24. Masson, M.E.: A tutorial on a practical Bayesian alternative to null-hypothesis significance testing. Behav. Res. Methods 43(3), 679–690 (2011)
25. Levine, T.R., Weber, R., Hullett, C., Park, H.S., Lindsey, L.L.M.: A critical assessment of null hypothesis significance testing in quantitative communication research. Hum. Commun. Res. 34(2), 171–187 (2008)
26. Knapp, C.W., McCluskey, S.M., Singh, B.K., Campbell, C.D., Hudson, G., Graham, D.W.: Antibiotic resistance gene abundances correlate with metal and geochemical conditions in archived Scottish soils. PLoS ONE 6(11), e27300 (2011)
27. Roshan, S., Madhumita, M.: Impact of training practices on employee productivity. Intersci. Manag. Rev. 2, 87–92 (2012)
28. Khawaja, J., Nadeem, B.A.: Training and development program and its benefits to employee and organization: a conceptual study. Eur. J. Bus. Manag. 5(2) (2013)
29. Virginie, M.: A study of the effect of national culture value and self-efficacy on organizational commitment in Haiti. Graduate Institute Human Resource Development (2010)
30. Masood, U.H., Rabia, K., Kashif, N.: The effects of personal characteristics on organizational commitment. through job satisfaction: an empirical study of Pakistan's financial sector. Middle-east. J. Sci. Res. 16(7), 942–951 (2013)
31. Dixit, V., Bhati, M.: A study about employee commitment and its impact on sustained productivity in Indian auto-component Industry. Eur. J. Bus. Soc. Sci. 1(6), 34–51 (2012)
32. Salami, S.O.: Demographic and psychological factors predicting organizational commitment among industrial workers. Anthropologist 10(1), 31–38 (2008)

Physically-Based Facial Modeling and Animation with Unity3D Game Engine

Bo Li$^{(\boxtimes)}$, Guang-hong Gong, and Yao-pu Zhao

School of Automation Science and Electrical Engineering,
Beihang University, Beijing, China
ribo_email@126.com

Abstract. Facial expression plays a fundamental role in conveying emotions to a 3D virtual character. This paper presents an automatic and effective approach for 3D face segmentation, feature extraction, rigging and animation. The 3D model we used is a triangular mesh model in OBJ file format. Combining the position information and neighbor coordinates of the points, the facial segmentation and feature extraction can be finished based on Gaussian curvature, shape indexes and face geometry. Furthermore, face rigging mainly includes two sub-models: skeleton and muscle model. Our rigging method is general that people can define their own rig and then quickly apply it to different model. Finally, the rigging model can be driven by emotion data in BVH file format. Also, to validate our approach, we have achieved in running experimentations on 3D facial in Unity3D engine. The result illustrates that our approach is usable and effective.

Keywords: 3D facial segmentation · Feature extraction · Rig · Facial animation

1 Introduction

In recent years, a tremendous interest in CG (Computer Graphics) and VR (Virtual Reality) animation has been increased. Facial expression simulation, as a way to promote the exchange nonverbal message between people, obtains more and more attentions from researchers. Indeed, thanks to the technological growth in hardware development, it is easy to show a virtual character and animation in the eyes of users. But the task is still difficult in respect of the real facial expression for an avatar. This difficulty arises from the lack of a standard definition of what is a rig and multitude approaches on how to setup a face. Today, facial animation is done manually by skilled artists, who spends so much time to manipulate the animation controls for creating the desired motion. If it is automatic and portable to rig and drive a virtual facial expression, the facial expression simulation will be directly more dramatic in facial animation.

There are a large variety of different modeling methods for facial animation. These methods are divided in three groups: blendshape, geometric deformation and physically-based facial rigging. Blendshape is one of the most common methods for rigging facial model. However, it is necessary to create a large number of shapes to

© Springer Nature Singapore Pte Ltd. 2017
M.S. Mohamed Ali et al. (Eds.): AsiaSim 2017, Part II, CCIS 752, pp. 393–404, 2017.
DOI: 10.1007/978-981-10-6502-6_35

provide control over every region of the face and take a much long time to adjust the blendshape. Costigan [1] improves blendshape performance with GPU and GPGPU techniques, but the quality impact is still minimized by the subset they selected. Geometric deformation rigging is used to deform 2D and 3D shapes to manipulate them and animate complex shapes, which provide a higher level and simpler Interface to the deformations. The commonly used operators include the Free-Form Deformer (FFD) and its improvement methods, such Rational Free-Form Deformer (RFFD), Generalize Free-Form Deformation (GFFD), Multilevel Free-Form Deformation (MFFD) and so on. And geometric deformation rigging also requires lots of training sample data. Cui and Feng [2] designed various time consuming evaluations and achieved by method of highly parallel processing on GPGPU to gain acceleration for FFD. However, this method has several limitations in terms of modeling and controlling, one of the prime influence of which is the distortion of the facial expression. Physically-based rigging [3] simulates the viscoelastic properties of soft-tissues, skin and muscles, achieving more biologic behavior and realistic animation of these tissues. Chen [4] proposes a hybrid model for facial expression simulation, including three sub-models: elastic skin model, muscle model and skeleton model. Albeit the improvement, the simulation is a problem when dealing with the distortion of motion. In this paper, we propose a dynamic rigging method to solve this problem. And we use the MoCap (Motion Capture) data to drive the model directly, which can reduce the loss caused by data conversion.

2   Research Methodology

Data-driven facial animation requires solving two main technical challenges: one is the segmentation of the mesh and feature extraction, which is important to our work and constitutes its first step; another is rigging models to suitable animation controls, which drives the virtual character. Moreover, we use the engine of Unity3D to verify our method.

2.1   Facial Segmentation and Feature Extraction

Facial segmentation and feature extraction from 3D facial model is a typical problem that attracts many researchers. Before, researchers focused on 2D face. Nowadays, many researches focus more on the 3D faces. The facial segmentation can output a set of 3D points which provide the topology of the object. The topological structure is always a triangulated, and it is ready for any follow-up processing. Features give more consideration on messages for 3D object. Feature extraction is following work of segmentation, and a beforehand processing for rigging and animation.

2.1.1   Principal Curvature and Shape Analysis

The physical surface curvature is independent of the coordinate system, and is not affected by the motion of the rigid body. For each sampling point $p(x, y, z)$ on the MLS (Moving Least Squares) surface $S(p)$, the curved surface $S(p)$ is described in the form of $z = f(x, y)$. The parameters of the surface $S(p)$ is $(u, v) = (x(u, v), y(u, v),$ $z(u, v)) = (u, v, f(u, v))$. Here, two vectors (X_u, X_v) are defined as parameters of the surfaces, whose subscript indicates the different local direction. Thus, a basic parameter $\{X_u, X_v\}$ is formed on the tangent plane $T(u, v)$ at $X(u, v)$. The intersection of the surface $S(p)$ and the plane P contain a tangent vector $t(u, v) \in T(u, v)$. The surface normal $n(p)$ is the normal of the surface $S(p)$ at $X(u, v)$ along the normal direction $t(u, v)$, and the curvature of the normal segment is called the normal curvature.

At point $p(x, y, z)$, the Gaussian curvature $K_G(p)$ and Mean Curvature $K_H(p)$ are describe by the main curvature $(k_1(p), k_2(p))$ as:

$$K_G(p) = k_1(p)k_2(p). \tag{1}$$

$$K_H = \frac{k_1(p) + k_2(p)}{2}. \tag{2}$$

$$k_1(p), k_2(p) = K_H(p) \pm \sqrt{K_H^2(p) - K_G(p)}. \tag{3}$$

To describe the shape of the model, we adapt the conclusion proposed by [5], which directly and clearly describes the shape of the 3D face based on $K_G(p)$ and $K_H(p)$. The face can be divided into four kinds of shapes:

- When $K_G(p) > 0, K_H(p) > 0$, the shape of surface is convex.
- When $K_G(p) > 0, K_H(p) < 0$, the shape of surface is concave.
- When $K_G(p) < 0$, the shape of surface is saddle.
- When $K_G = 0$, the shape of surface is plane or paraboloid.

In this paper, the 3D model is made by 3dsMax which contains 2636 vertices. For the shape type of face, Fig. 2(a) shows the result which is judged by K_G and K_H. Defining the largest and smallest value of K_H as boundaries, Fig. 2(b) obviously shows main parts of face which consistent with ellipsoid characteristics (Max $(K_G(p)) = -0.1621$), Min$(K_G(p)) = 0.7664$), and the forehead, cheek and chin can be found easily.

2.1.2   Shape Index and Shape Analysis

The shape index can be used to measure the shape of the 3D face at each point accurately. The shape index $S(p)$ is the estimation of the curvature determined by maximum principal curvature $k_1(p)$ and minimum principal curvature $k_2(p)$ at $p(x, y, z)$. The range of $S(p)$ is from 0 to 1 (see Fig. 1).

The function of the shape index is:

$$S(\mathrm{p}) = \frac{1}{2} - \frac{1}{\pi} arctan \frac{k_1(p) + k_2(p)}{k_1(p) - k_2(p)}. \tag{4}$$

According to the method of [6], $S(p)$ can make more use of the information of curvature, which can describe the shape of the 3D face more precisely (See Fig. 2). In this paper, the value of $S(p)$ is in the range of 0.0186 to 0.9923. Here we get the

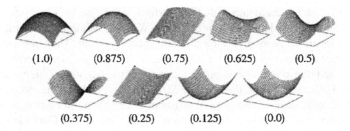

(1.0)   (0.875)   (0.75)   (0.625)   (0.5)

(0.375)   (0.25)   (0.125)   (0.0)

Fig. 1. Nine representative shapes on the shape index scale.

complete contour line of mandibular and forehead (see Fig. 2(c)), which helps to determine the range of mouth in the next step.

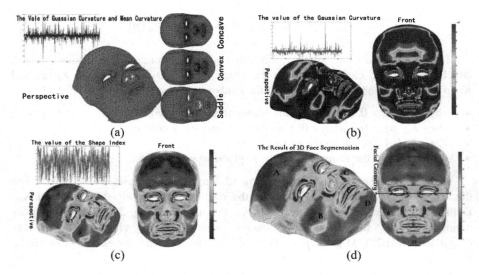

Fig. 2. (a) Shows the concave, convex and saddle face in red, green and yellow which judged by Gaussian curvature and Mean Curvature; (b) Shows the value of Gaussian curvature in different color; (c) Shows the value of face indexes in different color; (d) Shows the result of 3D face segmentation (Area_A\B\C\D\E). (Color figure online)

2.1.3   Facial Geometry and Major Segmentation

According to the distribution rules of facial organs, the experimental results of human facial measurement are summarized. Facial geometric characteristics can be used as the basis of the secondary local correction, and provide a priori knowledge for the feature extraction.

- **Three Width Theory**. Human face is generally divided into three equal regions: from the hair to the eyebrows, from the eyebrows to the mouth and from the mouth to the jaw (see Fig. 2(d)).

- **Five Eyes Width Theory**. Human face's width is about "five eyes width". There is "one eye's width" between our eyes (see Fig. 2(d)).
- **The Rule of Bisection**. The distance from the head to the eye is equal to the distance from the eye to the bottom of the jaw. Along the longitudinal axis of the tip of the nose, vertically divide the face into two parts, which are roughly symmetrical.
- **The Rule of Distance**. The distance from the mouth to the lower jaw is greater than half of the distance from the nose to the lower jaw. Meanwhile the distance between the nose and lower jaw is greater than half of the width of human face. And the distance between the eye and the nose is greater than 1/4 of the width of human face.

According to the facial geometry, we make local corrections to the result of segmentation. Figure 2(d) shows the five major divisions (Area_A\B\C\D\E) on the surface of the 3D face. The Area_A and the Area_E will help to determine the range of the tip of the nose.

2.1.4   Feature Extraction

The determination of the feature points is important for the subsequent work. Based on the information of the curvature, the segmentation can be obtained, and will provide a spatial constraint for feature extraction. Using the facial geometry to constrain and exclude the inappropriate points, we can find the extreme point or the extreme point set with the Gaussian Curvature and Mean Curvature. Table 1 gives the details of the feature points in this paper, where the position of the nose can be determined by the information of the depth and curvature.

Table 1. Details of the feature points.

Name	Index	Coordinate	Judgement
BrowL	1086	(−2.7391, 9.9132, 9.2307)	Area_A
BrowR	2427	(2.7391, 9.9132, 9.2307)	Area_A
NoseTip	919	(−0.3947, 12.5203, 2.0166)	No area belonged, but judged by the depth information
CheekL	641	(−7.106, 7.0122, 3.0283)	Area_B
CheekR	2005	(7.106, 7.0122, 3.0283)	Area_C
LipL	418	(−3.2791, 8.7855, −2.4637)	Area_E
LipR	1794	(3.2791, 8.7855, −2.4637)	Area_E
UpperLipL	439	(−1.2347, 10.6516, −1.3552)	Area_E
UpperLipR	1816	(1.2347, 10.6516, −1.3552)	Area_E
LowerLipL	383	(−1.2589, 10.4142, −3.2635)	Area_E
LowerLipR	1764	(1.2589, 10.4142, −3.2635)	Area_E
Chin	519	(0, 9.6584, −6.7298)	Area_D
JawLowerL	64	(−7.595, 1.1127, −3.1363)	Area_B
JawLowerR	1450	(7.595, 1.1127, −3.1363)	Area_C

2.2   Physically-Based Rigging and Facial Animation

As a motion data converter of geometric deformation, rigging plays a fundamental role in the animation process as it eases the manipulation and editing of expression. However, rigging is usually time-consuming and cumbersome for artists. As for this difficult, a method of dynamic rigging will be presented in this paper. There is one skeleton model and three muscle models to set up a face as below. And we use the engine of Unity3D and the emotion data in BVH file format to animating the 3D face model.

Combing with the knowledge of the human anatomy and biomechanics, we simplify the structure of the bone and muscle in the face (see Fig. 3(a)). The skeleton rig can not only simplify the calculation for the movement of the chin, but also play an important role in the deformation of the skin. And the muscle rig is independent form the underlying skeleton, offering portability, and can drive the skin deformations. Based on the feature extraction in Sect. 2.1, 16 key points are set in the face to accept the control of the rigging model (see Fig. 3(b)). And these will be the interface of the motion data later.

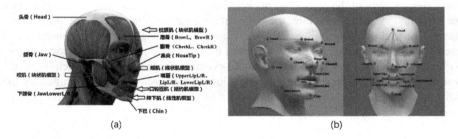

(a)   (b)

Fig. 3. (a) The distribution and name for part of the muscle and skeleton in human face; (b) The spatial distribution of the control-points as we expected.

V_k represents the kth segmentation of the facial point set, and denote $Area\_A\backslash B\backslash C\backslash D \backslash E$ with $\{V_1, V_2, V_3, V_4, V_5\}$. $F_l^{V_k}(t_i)$ represents the position of the feature point F_l of the segmentation V_k at the ith frame, where the value of l is $\{1,2,\ldots,14\}$. $P^{V_k}(t_i)$ represents the position of the point P of the segmentation V_k at the ith frame. The rigging models of the mandibular, sphincter and linear muscle are described below.

2.2.1   Mandibular Model and Its Adjacent Area

The skeleton model of the mandible can be abstracted as a model that rotates around a fixed axis, with two DOF: from up to down and from left to right (see Fig. 4).

For easier description, put the key point *Jaw* at the center of the axis. In the 3D coordinate, the function of mandibular model can be written as follow:

$$P^{V_k}(t_j) = P^{V_k}(t_i) + w_\theta(\alpha)\left(w_d^{F_1}\overrightarrow{F_1(\Delta t)}\right) + w_\theta(\beta)\left(w_d^{F_2}\overrightarrow{F_2(\Delta t)}\right) . \tag{5}$$

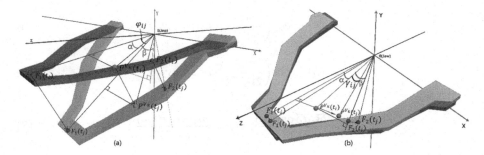

Fig. 4. The model of mandibular.

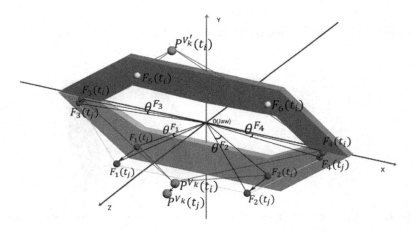

Fig. 5. The model of sphincter.

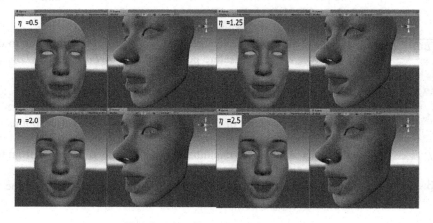

Fig. 6. The effect of muscle factor η.

$$w_\theta(\alpha) = \cos\left(\frac{\pi\alpha}{2\Omega^{F_1 F_2}}\right)\cos\varphi_{ij}\cos\gamma_{ij}. \tag{6}$$

$$w_\theta(\beta) = \cos\left(\frac{\pi\beta}{2\Omega^{F_1 F_2}}\right)\cos\varphi_{ij}\cos\gamma_{ij}. \tag{7}$$

$$w_d^{F_1} = \frac{\overline{OF_1(t_i)} \cdot \overline{OP^{V}k(t_i)}}{|\overline{OF_1(t_i)}|^2}, \ w_d^{F_1} = \frac{\overline{OF_1(t_i)} \cdot \overline{OP^{V}k(t_i)}}{|\overline{OF_1(t_i)}|^2}. \tag{8}$$

$$\overline{F_1(\Delta t)} = \overline{OF_1(t_j)} - \overline{OF_1(t_i)}, \ \overline{F_2(\Delta t)} = \overline{OF_2(t_j)} - \overline{OF_2(t_i)}. \tag{9}$$

In the model above, the parameters are defined as below:

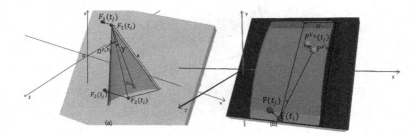

Fig. 7. (a) The model of narrow linear muscle; (b) The model of wide linear muscle.

$P^{V_k}(t_i)/P^{V_k}(t_j)$:	the position of points of the segmentation V_k at the ith and j^{th} frame, where k is 4 (i.e., Area_D).
O:	the position of the feature point *Jaw*.
$\overline{F_1(\Delta t)}/\overline{F_2(\Delta t)}$:	the offset vector of the feature point F_1/F_2 from the ith frame to the jth frame, where the feature points include *JawLowerL, JawLowerR* and *Chin*.
$w_\theta(\alpha)/w_\theta(\beta)$:	the influencing factor of the angle of the feature point F_1/F_2.
$w_d^{F_1}/w_d^{F_2}$:	the influencing factor of the distance of the feature point F_1/F_2.
$\Omega^{F_1 F_2}$:	the maximum range of the angle affected by the feature points F_1 and F_2.
φ_{ij}/γ_{ij}:	the offset angle of the mandibular rotating around X/Y axis from the ith frame to the jth frame.
α/β:	the angle between the vector $\overline{OF_1}/\overline{OF_2}$ and vector $\overline{OP^{V}k}$ at the ith frame.

2.2.2 Sphincter Model

The sphincter is composed of muscle fibers surrounding the mouth and eyes, which mainly the orbicularis muscle. It can be modeled with an elliptical shape, and with six key points to control the contraction and relaxation. The Fig. 5 shows the sphincter model of the mouth. The key points of F_1–F_4 and F_3–F_6 control the points of the upper and lower regions of the plane XOY respectively.

In the sphincter model, the point $P_i^{V_k}$ can be computed as below:

$$P^{V_k}(t_j) = P^{V_k}(t_i) + \sum_l^4 w_\theta^{F_l}(\Delta t) \left(w_d^{F_l}\overrightarrow{F_l(\Delta t)}\right) . \tag{10}$$

$$w_\theta^{F_l}(\Delta t) = \sin(\theta^{F_l}(\Delta t)) = \sin\theta^{F_l}\left(t_j - t_i\right). \tag{11}$$

$$w_d^{F_l} = \frac{\left|P^{V_k}(t_i)F_l(t_i)\right|^{-\eta}}{\sum_{m=1}^4 \left|P^{V_k}(t_i)F_m(t_i)\right|^{-\eta}} . \tag{12}$$

$$\overrightarrow{F_l(\Delta t)} = \overrightarrow{OF_l(t_j)} - \overrightarrow{OF_i(t_i)} . \tag{13}$$

In the model above, the parameters are defined as below:

$P^{V_k}(t_i)/P^{V_k}(t_j)$: the position of points of the segmentation V_k at the ith frame and the jth frame, where k is 5 (i.e., *Area_E*).

O: the center of the six feature points of the mouth area.

$\overrightarrow{F_l(\Delta t)}$: the offset vector of the feature point $\overrightarrow{OF_l}$ from the ith frame to the jth frame, where the feature points include *LipL, LipR, LowerLipL, LowerLipR, UpperLipL and UpperLipR*.

$w_\theta^{F_l}(\Delta t)$: the influencing factor of the angle of the feature point F_l.

$w_d^{F_l}$: the influencing factor of the distance of the feature point F_l.

η: the muscle factor of the feature point F_l, whose value we used is 1.25 based on several experiments (see Fig. 6)

$\theta^{F_l}(\Delta t)$: the rotation angle of the vector $\overrightarrow{OF_l}$ from the ith frame to the jth frame.

2.2.3 Linear Muscle Model

The linear muscle mainly distributes in the cheek and the forehead, like a bunch of rope. For the narrow linear muscle, the points are centered on and stretched by the key point *CheekL(CheekR)* whose controlling range is cone (Fig. 7(a)). For the wide linear muscle, the controlling range of the key point *BrowL(BrowR)* is rectangular, and the points are only affected by the length factor (Fig. 7(b)).

For the narrow linear muscle model, the point $P_i^{V_k}$ can be computed as below:

$$P^{V_k}(t_j) = P^{V_k}(t_i) + w_\theta(\gamma)w_d^F(\overrightarrow{F_1(\Delta t)} + \overrightarrow{F_2(\Delta t)}) \ . \tag{14}$$

$$w_\theta(\gamma) = \cos\left(\frac{\pi\gamma}{2\Omega^{F_1 F_2}}\right)\cos\gamma. \tag{15}$$

$$w_d^F = \cos\{\frac{\pi}{2}\left(1 - \frac{\left|\overrightarrow{P^{V_k}(t_i)F_1(t_i)}\right|}{\left|\overrightarrow{F_1(\Delta t)}\right|}\right)\} \ . \tag{16}$$

In the model above, the parameters are defined as below:

$P^{V_k}(t_i)/P^{V_k}(t_j)$:   the position of points of the segmentation V_k at the ith frame and the jth frame, where k is 2 and 3 (i.e., *Area_B* and *Area_C*).

$\overrightarrow{F_1(\Delta t)}/\overrightarrow{F_2(\Delta t)}$:   the offset vector of the feature point F_1/F_2 from the ith frame to the jth frame, where the feature point F_1/F_2 can be CheekL/LipL or CheekR/LipR.

$w_\theta(\gamma)$:   the influencing factor of the angle of the feature point F_1.

w_d^F: the influencing factor of the distance of the feature point F_1.

γ: the angle between the vector $\overrightarrow{F_1 P^{V_k}}$ and the vector $\overrightarrow{F_1 F_2}$ at the ith frame.

$\Omega^{F_1 F_2}$:   the maximum controlling angle of the feature point F_1 from the ith frame to the jth frame (i.e., the top angle of the cone).

And the point $P_i^{V_k}$ of the wide linear muscle model is defined as below:

$$P^{V_k}(t_j) = P^{V_k}(t_i) + w_d^F \overrightarrow{F(\Delta t)} \ . \tag{17}$$

$$w_d^F = \cos(\frac{\pi \overrightarrow{P^{V_k}(t_i)} \cdot \overrightarrow{tangent^F}}{2H}) \ . \tag{18}$$

In the model above, the parameters are defined as below:

$P^{V_k}(t_i)/P^{V_k}(t_j)$:   the position of points of the segmentation V_k at the ith frame and the jth frame, where k is 1 (i.e., *Area_A*).

$\overrightarrow{F(\Delta t)}$:   the offset vector of the feature point F from the ith frame to the jth frame, where the feature point F can be *BrowL* or *BrowR*.

w_d^F: the influencing factor of the distance of the feature point F.

$\overrightarrow{tangent^F}$:   the tangent vector of the feature point F at the ith frame.

H: the maximum controlling distance of the feature point F (i.e., the width of the arch).

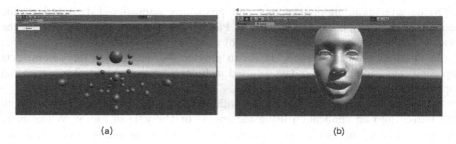

(a)   (b)

Fig. 8. (a) The motion data in one frame; (b) The facial expression by inputting the data of (a) in Unity3D.

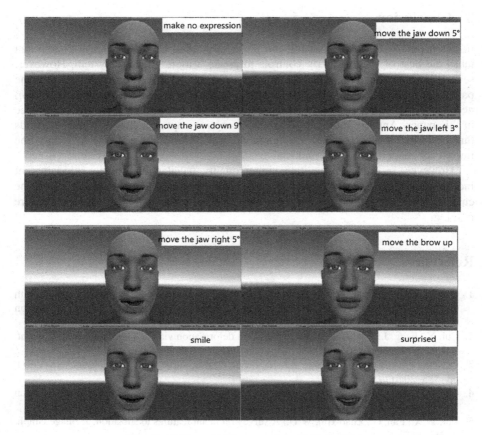

Fig. 9. Various facial expressions in Unity3D.

2.2.4 Results and Discussion

Finished the rig above, we can input the motion data to animate the facial model. Three inputs of motion to the skinning system that depending on the rig, can be mixed:

keyframe animation, motion capture and procedural animation [3]. Based on the support of the motion capture system of Phase Space Impulse System, we get the motion data tracking from facial markers of an actor.

In this paper, 14 key points are set to provide the interface to the motion data inputting. The capture motion data we used includes 24 makers in the face, which can support the animation sufficiently (see Fig. 8).

Finally, we imported the face model with 3637 vertices and the motion data with 780 frames into an application using the engine of Unity3D in Fig. 9. While many professional facial animation systems need hundred controls of details, our method may be impractical. Our method to rig and animate is flexible for usage with typical articulation and facial expression systems.

3 Conclusion

In this paper, we present a flexible and physically-based facial rig control system that takes the best of traditional rig controls to create a more effective system. However, several limitations remain with this approach. One of the limitation of this setup is the parameter of the muscle models. While in complex movement, the parameters (like η) need to be trained by a large of motion data in reality, rather than using the experience in this paper. Another limitation is from the motion capture method, which demands that performer's face resembles as close as possible the target's face to reduce the impact for mapping the data and rig.

However, in order to facilitate higher quality facial animation in entertainment industry and gaming, techniques and hardware should be developed to extend the current practice. And our system could benefit from additional attention in the future training.

References

1. Costigan, T., Gerdelan, A., Carrigan, E.: Improving blendshape performance for crowds with GPU and GPGPU techniques. In: Proceedings of the 9th International Conference on Motion in Games, pp. 73–78. ACM (2016)
2. Cui, Y., Feng, J.: Real-time B-spline free-form deformation via GPU acceleration. J. Comput. Graph. **37**(1), 1–11 (2013)
3. Orvalho, V., Bastos, P., Parke, F.I.: A facial rigging survey. In: Eurographics (STARs), pp. 183–204 (2012)
4. Chen, Q.: Research of Facial Expression Simulation Based on Hybrid Model. Xiamen University (2008)
5. Lin, W.X., Pan, G., Zhao-Hui, W.U.: A survey on facial features localization. J. Image Graph. **8**, 850–857 (2003)
6. Guo, Z., Zhang, Y., Lin, Z.: 3D faical feature extraction based on curvature information. J. Comput. Eng. Appl. **43**(24), 239–241 (2007)

A Study on the Behavior Modeling Method of Helicopter Force

Ni Li, Yan-cheng Hou$^{(\boxtimes)}$, and Guang-hong Gong

School of Automation Science and Electrical Engineering,
Beihang University, Beijing, China
butterfly2sea@gmail.com

Abstract. The behavior modeling is an important part of CGF (Computer Generated Forces) and the helicopter CGF is an indispensable character in the simulation battlefield. In this article, a hierarchical behavior modeling method is raised for the helicopter force. Eleven kinds of atomic behavior models are established on the foundation of the interfaces of our helicopter physical model. Based on the atomic behavior, three types of doctrines for the helicopter force are implemented with the finite state machine. In the case study, the behavior model is proved to be effective with our test scenario and is capable to support the development of a helicopter training system.

Keywords: Behavior modeling · Helicopter force · Finite state machine · Atomic behavior

1 Introduction

As an important means of national defense construction, modeling and simulation provide a better way to learn battle skills, tactics, new equipment with lower cost. Having the advantages of efficient, controllable, repeatable, free from time, space and environment, battlefield simulation is getting people's attention and developing rapidly. In the military training system, Computer Generated Forces (CGF) plays the roles such as allies, opponents or neutral side. It's a worthy study to generate a reliable behavior model of the CGF since it allows them to have similar behavior in the real world. The helicopter CGF is an important part in the simulation battlefield. But the research on behavior modeling for helicopter is much less than that for the fixed wing vehicle.

There are many ways to build a behavior model. The different models made by different ways have the certain advantages and disadvantages. Hao makes a research on CGF fixed wing aircraft behavior modeling technology based on rule, which uses the production rule method to describe method for the decision-making knowledge, and implements a rule-based decision-making method for behavior modeling [1]. This modeling method has a clear logic structure and easy to understand, but the workload for development is great. Agent-based and multi-agent-based modeling methods enable entities to make autonomous decisions and achieve different levels of reasoning, responsiveness, and autonomy. In the US WARSIM 2000 system, many behavior models adopt this method, but the standard concept and definition of agent is still unclear. Based on that, Hu proposed a CGF agent decision-making modeling based on

© Springer Nature Singapore Pte Ltd. 2017
M.S. Mohamed Ali et al. (Eds.): AsiaSim 2017, Part II, CCIS 752, pp. 405–416, 2017.
DOI: 10.1007/978-981-10-6502-6_36

prospect theory [2]. The CGF Agent modeling framework has been verified to prove that the proposed method has improved the authenticity of decision-making behavior to a certain extent. Lu takes the influencing factor of human into the simulation process and verifies the feasibility of the framework [3] by using behavior modeling based on context-based reasoning. Sun proposed a command and control behavior modeling method which is based on task. It simplifies the modeling, betters the scalability and flexibility to some extent, by means of the composite task module of the hierarchical task network [4]. As a common modeling method, the finite state machine has great advantages such as considerable scalability and flexibility. Finite state machine is applied to the Royal Air Force in the beyond sight battle simulation training successfully [5]. The modeling method of finite state machine also has its own advantages in the military field. For the behavior modeling, it is necessary to use the military knowledge. Describing the behavior modeling in the form of graphic language can build a bridge between the developers and the military expert [6].

A large part of current researches on the aircraft in the CGF system are aimed at the fixed-wing aircraft. The different characters and applications between fixed-wing aircraft and rotate-wing aircraft determine that the behavior modeling of helicopter has a big difference. Building a proper behavior modeling is the first step to make usage of helicopter CGF in the simulation system. This article focuses on the modeling methods of the behavior model of helicopter.

A simplified physical model of helicopter is used for our behavior modeling. It offers the interfaces to the behavior modeling for manipulating purpose. The hierarchical behavior modeling of helicopter is divided into two categories. The low-level one is modeled with the code-based behavior modeling method, the other uses the finite state machine to establish the behavior decision model in air combat and the attack behavior model. This behavior model is applied to the actual simulation scenario for testing the feasibility and reliability of the modeling method.

This article has 4 sections. The Sect. 1 is about the structure of our helicopter force and its physical model interfaces. The physical model interface gives the behavior model the method to manipulate the helicopter. In the Sect. 2 11 atom behaviors are built based on the physical interfaces. The Sect. 3 is about building the three types of doctrine based on the atom behaviors with finite state machine. The Sect. 4 gives the case study of the helicopter force model. The behavior model is tested in a scenario and can provide support for a helicopter training system.

2   Structure of the Helicopter Model

The structure of the helicopter force model is shown in the Fig. 1. It includes the physical model and the behavior model. The physical modeling of helicopters is divided into eight parts, including kinematics model, missiles model, radar model, interference model, communication model, fire controlling model, protection model and damage model.

The physical model has 4 types of interfaces for the behavior model, shown in Fig. 2.

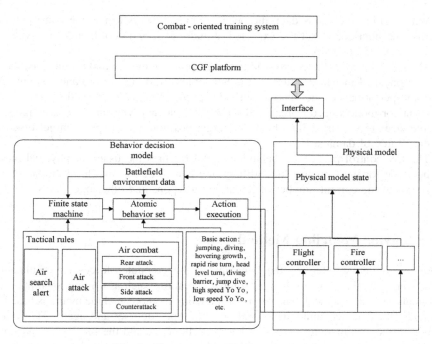

Fig. 1. The structure of helicopter model.

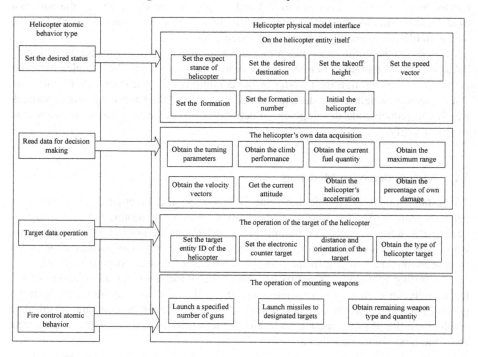

Fig. 2. Connection between helicopter physical interface and behavior.

1. When setting the status data, the behavior model needs to use the corresponding physical interface to set the expected attitude, expected coordinates, and velocity vectors of the helicopter.
2. The behavior model needs to read the corresponding data to make decisions, which uses physical interfaces, such as the helicopter's turning performance parameters, climb performance, fuel margin, attitude speed, damage degree and so on.
3. Behavior models need to read and write data relevant with target. It uses physical interfaces to set target ID, obtain the target position, target speed, target type and the degree of damage.
4. The fire control part of the behavior model requires the usage of physical model interface for the launch of the artillery, the launch of the missile to the target and access to the current number of remaining weapons and other operations.

3 Behavior Modeling Method

Behavior modeling refers to the behavior of the computer forces to simulate the maneuvering of the pilots in the real combat operations such as driving, manipulating, reconnaissance and tactical. The behavior modeling methods include methods based on the code, the rule set, finite state machines, the operation set and agent. This article mainly introduces modeling methods based on the code and the finite state machine.

The basic action of the helicopter is established as an atomic behavior, which is a connection between the behavior model and the physical model. It makes the behavior model established by the finite state machine based on atomic behavior is so flexible and portable that does not depend on a specific model.

Based on the finite state machine, the behavior modeling method take atomic behavior or the assembly of atomic behavior as a state, modeling the complex behavior of the helicopter through the transfer of the conditions between states. Using the finite state machine modeling, the description and the code of the CGF entity are separated, which can reduce code development effectively. CGF behavior patterns are clear and easy to modify.

3.1 Atomic Behavior Modeling

The establishment of atomic behavior is based on the kinematic model. Atomic behavior state is divided into seven categories, which are motor, sensor strategies, target selections, weapons, communications, selections of interest points, electronic warfare tactics. The maneuvering state is necessary while other categories can be added as appropriate. This article focuses on the modeling of motorized parts (Fig. 3).

According to the flow chart of the atomic behavior, after the initialization of the force entity, in each step to promote loop, the entity read the required data from the general data area, call the callback function, calculate the simulation time length data results with the physical model, and write the new data back to the general data area, enter the next simulation step at last.

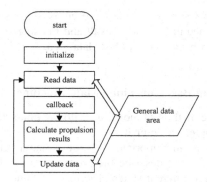

Fig. 3. The flow chart of the atomic behavior.

There are 11 atomic behaviors, including jump maneuver, dive maneuver, reverse jump maneuver, obstacle diving maneuver, sharp up maneuver, horizon turn, jump back maneuver, high-speed Yoyo maneuver, low-speed Yoyo maneuver and chase maneuver.

The code proses of high speed yoyo is used as an example to explain the modeling (Figs. 4 and 5).

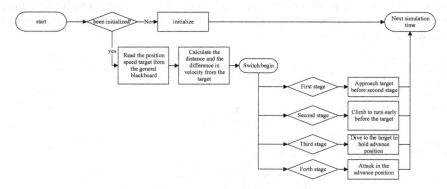

Fig. 4. The code proses of high speed yoyo.

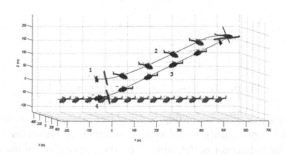

Fig. 5. The stages of high speed yoyo maneuver.

After initialization of CGF entity, the CGF entity starts simulating. It reads data from public data area to acquire the new result and the stage of action. After that, the entity sends the new data back to the public data area.

3.2   Behavior Modeling Based on Finite State Machine

This article introduces the method of modeling with the finite state machine to build up the process of the helicopter air combat.

Finite state machine is an important tool for dynamic modeling in object programming. It is mainly used to describe the process and mechanism of the transformation of objects between different states. The core of finite state machine is that an object can only be in one state of a level in a certain moment. The conversion between objects needs certain conditions to be activated. There are three elements in the finite state machine: the state, the condition and the secondary state.

1. Refers to the state of entity in present, which can be a single atomic behavior or a combination of atomic behavior through a finite state machine.
2. When a condition is satisfied in the finite state machine, a state transition will be performed.
3. The state where the entity moving to after the condition is met is named the secondary state. The secondary state is a concept that is comparative to the current state. When the secondary state is activated by the condition, it will convert into a new state (Fig. 6).

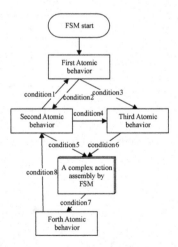

Fig. 6. The finite state machine example chart.

In the finite state machine, according to the current state and the transition condition of the state, the helicopter entity transforms in different maneuvering and attack states. The behavior of the helicopter is determined by the conversion of the atomic behavior under different conditions, and builds up more complicated decision-makings. The conditions are divided into five types: time conditions, the strength of the entity's own state, the state of force entity state, geographical environment, incoming weapons, which includes the distance from enemy and height difference, relative speed, quantity of ammunition, remaining fuel and other conditions. In the helicopter forces, the behavior is divided into three types, the aerial search alert, the aerial attack and aerial combat.

1. The aerial search alert includes the aerial reconnaissance, the aerial alert and the aerial cover.
2. The air attack includes the maximum damage attack, the stage attack and the continuous attack.
3. The air combat includes the airborne ambushes, the air interdiction, the air fight and the air avoidance.

3.3   Doctrines Based on Three Types of Rules

Take the air combat for example to show the steps of modeling with a flow chart (Figs. 7 and 8):

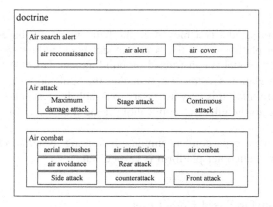

Fig. 7. Three types of doctrines.

The first step is reaching the action site to counter the enemy. The second step is determining whether to avoid. the CGF entity choose the attack mode on the basis of the relative position of the enemy. After finishing the attack, the entity will decide whether to complete the task. If not completing, the entity will determine whether to avoid again. The part of the air combat is an inerratic module that is composed of another finite state machine.

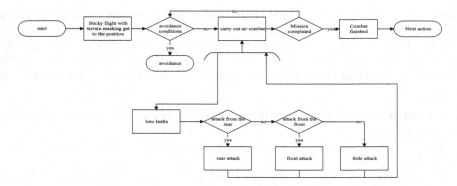

Fig. 8. The step of modeling air combat.

3.4   The Relationship Between Atomic Behavior and Finite State Machine

In the helicopter CGF, the atomic behavior which acts as the basis of a finite state machine, is composed of three complex types of helicopter behavior (Fig. 9).

4   Case Study

The atomic behavior model is achieved by the helicopter CGF based on the physical and the simulation platform, and the whole model is assembled with the finite state machine. Helicopter model is constructed by building simulation testing and scenarios in the platform simulation systems. In particular, the application of behavior model is related to combat training. It is very necessary to establish a test and verify model in the platform according to the effective application of the model and the realization of the model.

In the Army Air Corps combat simulation training system, behavior- modeling based on MAXSim helicopter platform is carried out.

4.1   Atomic Behavior-Based Code-Level

The atomic behavior is composed of the snake-shaped maneuver, hovering speed, dive, climb, horizontal turn, sharp down turn, sharp up turn, vertical maneuver, jump back, diving obstacle, zigzag forward, low speed Yoyo, anti-low speed Yoyo, tail chase maneuver, anti-tail chase maneuver, high-speed Yoyo, anti-high speed Yoyo, steady flight, hover, fixed-point fixed speed flight, climbing trapezoidal reconnaissance maneuver and so on (Fig. 10).

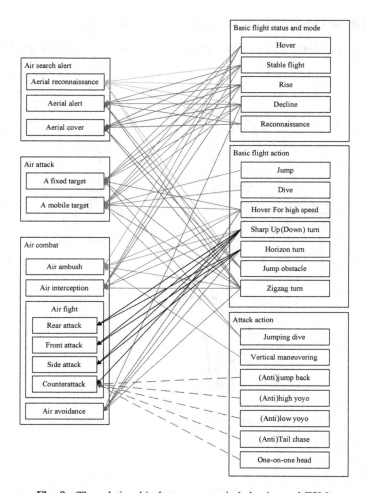

Fig. 9. The relationship between atomic behavior and FSM.

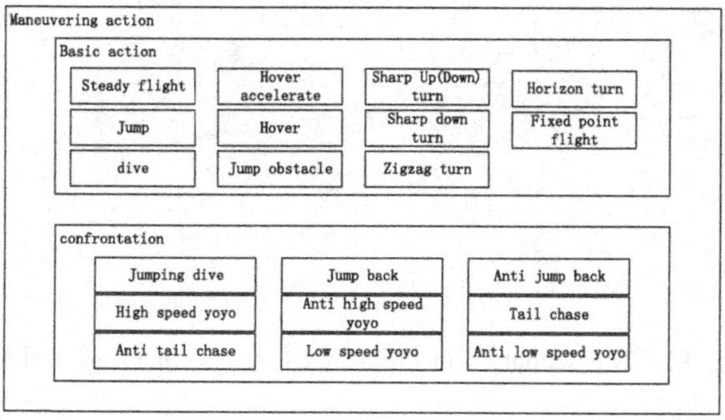

Fig. 10. The atomic behaviors.

4.2   Based on Three Types of Rules Finite State Machine

Here following the finite state machine made in the MAXSim platform (Figs. 11 and 12).

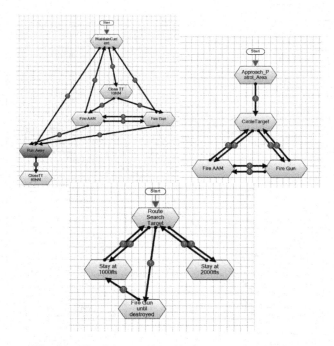

Fig. 11. The finite state machine in MAXSim platform.

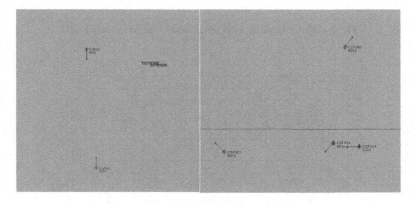

Fig. 12. The scenarios in the MAXSim. (Color figure online)

We conducted a test based on a group of scenarios. The helicopter of the blue side took the flight patrol along the waypoint while the red helicopter took the patrol. After the discovery of the blue helicopter, it jumped to the height that could attack the enemy and launched missiles when satisfied the missile launch conditions. It would launch the missile until the helicopter of the blue side was destroyed, or missile had been used up. In this test, the result turned out to be that the helicopter of the blue side was destroyed by a missile. We built another scenario to test group work. There are four helicopters in two group and every helicopter chases one enemy helicopter and is chased by the other enemy helicopter. The whole process of the attitude curve of both sides is depicted by MATLAB as is shown below (Fig. 13).

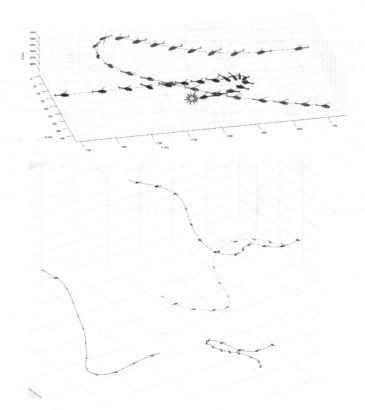

Fig. 13. The attitude curve of the both side. (Color figure online)

5   Summary

In this paper, the behavior model completes helicopter force model which provides full support troops for the simulation platform, reaching the target of using helicopters digitized troops against combat training, and implemented on MAXSim platform.

Applying to a land Training Simulation in this paper, a two-level behavior model is established by studying the helicopter force modeling and simulation technology. Based on the physical model, the atomic behavior is established. Based on the atomic behavior, the complex behavior model is established by the assembly of finite state machine, including three types of helicopter behavior This article has made some research results, but some behavior models are not enough, need further study, as a more comprehensive simulation of helicopter training tasks, but also should provide more behavior model, the establishment should be more complete and comprehensive.

References

1. Hao, L.-S., Xia, H.-B., Tian, S.-C.: Research on CGF entity behavior modeling technology based on rule. J. Fire Control Command Control **40**(1), 96–99 (2015)
2. Hu, J.-W., Yin, Q.-J., Feng, L.: Research of CGF agent decision-making modeling based on prospect theory. J. Natl. Univ. Defense Technol. **32**(4), 131–136 (2010)
3. Lu, Y.-T., Han, L., Song, X.: Behavior modeling of air to ship fighter based on context-based reasoning. In: Zhang, L., Song, X., Wu, Y. (eds.) AsiaSim 2016, SCS AutumnSim 2016. Communications in Computer and Information Science, vol. 644, pp. 450–457. Springer, Heidelberg (2016). doi:10.1007/978-981-10-2666-9_45
4. Sun, L., Zha, Y., Jiao, P., et al.: Mission-based command and control behavior model. In: 2016 IEEE International Conference on Mechatronics and Automation (ICMA) (2016)
5. Toubman, A., Roessingh, J.J., Spronck, P., et al.: Rapid adaptation of air combat behavior (2016)
6. Xiu-Luo, L., Huang, K.-D., Xiao-Jun, Z.: The application of finite state machine in the CGF's behavior modeling. J. Acta Simulata Systematica Sinica (2001)

A Particle Swarm Optimization Based Predictive Controller for Delay Compensation in Networked Control Systems

Abdin Yousif Elamin, Nurul Adilla Mohd Subha$^{(\boxtimes)}$,
Norikhwan Hamzah, and Anita Ahmad

Faculty of Electrical Engineering, Universiti Teknologi Malaysia, 81310 Skudai,
Johor, Malaysia
nuruladilla@utm.my

Abstract. This paper addresses transmission delays problem in network control systems. Network-induced delay is an inherent constraint in NCS implementation that could lead to system degradation and destabilization. A particle swarm optimization (PSO) tuning algorithm was adopted to optimally tune the parameters of Generalized Predictive Controller (GPC) to solve networked-induced delay problem. Furthermore, a modified PSO-GPC was designed by replacing the standard GPC objective function with an Integral Time Squared Error (ITSE) performance index in the GPC controller design. A particle swarm optimization based PI controller in the Smith predictor structure is designed to compare the performances of the original PSO-GPC and the modified PSO-GPC. The results show that the modified PSO-GPC performed better than the PSO-GPC in terms of transient response and enhanced NCS performance in the occurrence of network delays.

Keywords: Network control systems · Delay compensation · Particle swarm optimization · Generalized predictive control · Smith predictor

1 Introduction

NCS are started to be utilized in various industrial applications such as automotive [1], human surveillance [2], and process control [3] due to several clear advantages. When control system is designed using communication network, it is known as a networked control system (NCS). In NCS, the control signals are shared among the system's elements in form of information packets through wireless or hard wired connections. Utilization of networks communication allow for efficient centralized control systems with minimal wiring across the system, hence reducing initial cost of a system [4]. Furthermore, NCS is a flexible structure that allows the addition or reduction of system components without any significant change to the hardware of the system [5].

In general, there are two common problems with NCS application. NCS prone to problem of network delay and data dropout. These problems may lead to system performance degradation or even system destabilization. Current progress in data dropout management can be review in [5–7]. Network-induced delay occurred due to

© Springer Nature Singapore Pte Ltd. 2017
M.S. Mohamed Ali et al. (Eds.): AsiaSim 2017, Part II, CCIS 752, pp. 417–431, 2017.
DOI: 10.1007/978-981-10-6502-6_37

number of factor, such as limited bandwidth, network congestion, and network transmission protocols. Short time delays delay effect on the NCS is studied using Markov model shows that network-induced delays can lead to uncontrollable or unobservable system [8, 9]. In case of network-induced delay, system stability depends on the upper and lower bounds of the time delay [10]. Several control methodologies have been formulated to compensate the negative effects of network delays in NCS based on different network configurations, constraints, and behaviors.

The event-based control methodology is introduced to control robotic manipulators over the Internet. For example, in [11, 12] the optimal stochastic control methodology is used, which treat the network delays as a Linear–Quadratic–Gaussian (LQG) problem. There is time-based methodology such as Model Predictive Control (MPC) which predict future plant output to compensate network delay problem. The main difference between event-based and time-based control methodology is that the event-based control treats a system motion as a system reference [8]. Other than that, robust control theory which doesn't need any prior knowledge about the network delays have been studied in [13]. Combination of these methodology has also been explored by other researchers [14–16].

There is a growing interest in MPC-based approach due to its ability to predict future plant outputs, hence effectively compensate the network induced constraints such has network delay and packets dropouts [17, 18] even within system with state and input constraints [19, 20]. In model predictive control, there is no unique method to determine the control algorithm, but rather a wide variety of methods to predict future plant outputs from current plant outputs along a specific prediction horizon at each sampling interval [21]. In a study conducted in [17], a novel generalized predictive control (GPC) algorithm is proposed to design the control signals which include the employment of buffer in order to compensate both the control-to-actuator (C-A) and sensor-to-controller (S-C) delays. In [18], to solve for random time delays and packet dropouts, the delays are modeled using Markov chains, a modified GPC algorithm is proposed and the stability analysis is established.

The study of MPC for nonlinear NCSs is more practical than linear NCSs. However nonlinear NCS is more technically challenging due to increased computational complexities. In literature, several promising results of networked nonlinear MPC have been proposed such as Lyapunov based MPC (LMPC) strategy which able to control a nonlinear system subjected to constraints [22] and LMPC strategy for nonlinear NCSs with time-varying network-induced delays [23].

Many studies have been conducted in MPC tuning, both heuristic and deterministic [24–26]. However, most previous research focused on improving performance for systems without consideration of communication networks-induced problems. A summary of tuning methods for GPC and Dynamical matrix control (DMC) based on the Integral Square Error (ISE) as a performance criterion is illustrated in [27]. Some methods suggest heuristics while others are based on stability criteria, closed loop analysis, analysis of variance [28], optimization-based algorithms [29]. Most studies agree on the influence of these parameters in improving the system performance but which parameter has the highest influence is still debatable. While some suggest that the weighting factor is the most significant parameter, others suggest the prediction horizon having the most effect on system performance [30]. In this paper, a particle swarm optimization (PSO) is adopted to optimally tune the parameters of the generalized predictive control (GPC) algorithm. PSO effects on NCS performance is investigated with focus on constant network-induced delay. The main aim of the algorithm is to compensate the network-induced delays through the generated output and control input prediction sequences.

This paper is structured as follows: Sect. 2 introduces the generalized predictive control algorithm and its parameters; Sect. 3 introduces the particle swarm optimization algorithm and its formulation to solve the GPC cost function; Sect. 4 presents results from MATLAB simulation; the conclusion is presented in Sect. 5.

2 Generalized Predictive Control in Delay Compensation

Characteristic of network delay depends on the network and transmission protocol which can be constant or time variant [31]. In this paper, Fig. 1 represents the basic structure of the considered NCS consisting of a sensor that sends information through a network to a controller, which then produced control signals to an actuator.

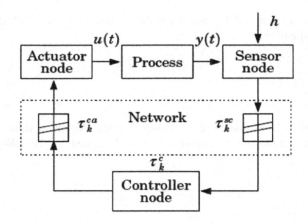

Fig. 1. A NCS with time delays

2.1 NCS with Network-Induced Delays

Network-induced delay exist in the controller to actuator channel (feed forward delay) and the sensor to controller channel (feedback delay), denoted by τ^{ca} and τ^{sc} respectively.

From Fig. 1, τ^{sc} is the first delay which represents the time taken to generate a control signal from the sensor. The controller to actuator delay τ^{ca} indicates the time taken for a control signal to reach the actuator. Another delay called the computation delay τ^{c} also exists in the system and is defined as the time taken to generate a control signal from the sensor feedback signal. However, for simplification the computation delay τ^{c} is considered to be embedded within the overall network-induced delays τ [7].

Assumption 1. The clock-driven sensor samples the plant outputs periodically at specific sampling instant T_S.

Assumption 2. The event-driven controller and actuator act as soon as the sensor data and control data become available.

Assumption 3. The network-induced delays in the system are time varying but bounded. Moreover, let $\overline{a_k^{max}}$, $\overline{b_k^{max}}$, $\overline{a_k^{min}}$ and $\overline{b_k^{min}}$ symbolize the maximum and minimum delays in the feedforward channel and in the feedback channel. Number of sampling periods is a positive integer.

Remark 1. The delay considered in the feed forward and feedback channels have maximum and minimum value, therefore we can treat the network delays as dead time denoted by d.

Since the delays present in the system are time varying but bounded by maximum and minimum values,

$$d_m \le d \le d_M. \tag{1}$$

Where d_m is the minimum delay and d_M is the maximum delay which determined by the following equations,

$$d_m = \overline{a_k^{min}} + \overline{b_k^{min}}. \tag{2}$$

$$d_M = \overline{a_k^{max}} + \overline{b_k^{max}}. \tag{3}$$

Based on (2) and (3), the delay d is calculated using the mean value of the delays present in the communication network which is described by the following relation [23],

$$d = \frac{d_m + d_M}{2}. \tag{4}$$

2.2 Generalized Predictive Control Algorithm

Generalized predictive control uses the following CARIMA model to describe the controlled object

$$A(z^{-1})y(t) = z^{-d}B(z^{-1})u(t-1) + \frac{e(t)C(z^{-1})}{D(z^{-1})}. \tag{5}$$

Where (t), $u(t-1)$ and $e(t)$ are the plant output, control signal, and white noise with zero mean value. It is assumed that there is no disturbance acting on the system, therefore $e(t)$ will be zero. $A(z^{-1})$ and $B(z^{-1})$ are the plant polynomials while $C(z^{-1})$ and $D(z^{-1})$ are the disturbance polynomials having the following expressions,

$$A(z^{-1}) = 1 + a_1 z^{-1} + \cdots + a_{n_A} z^{-n_A}. \tag{6}$$

$$B(z^{-1}) = b_0 + b_1 z^{-1} + \cdots + b_{n_A} z^{-n_B}. \tag{7}$$

$$C(z^{-1}) = 1. \tag{8}$$

$$D(z^{-1}) = 1 - z^{-1}. \tag{9}$$

Where n_A and n_A represent the polynomial degrees.

The control algorithm for a generalized predictive controller (GPC) consists of two steps, first is the prediction model which predicts the future plant outputs, based on past and current input values. The prediction model has the form below

$$\hat{y}(t + N|T_S) = G(z^{-1})D(z^{-1})z^{-d-1}u(t + N|T_S) +$$
$$\frac{H(z^{-1})D(z^{-1})}{C(z^{-1})}u(t - 1|T_S) + \frac{F(z^{-1})}{C(z^{-1})}y(t|T_S). \tag{10}$$

Where N is the prediction horizon, $\hat{y}(t + N|T_S)$ are the predicted plant outputs a computed at time k and $u(t + N|T_S)$ are the future control signals computed at every sampling time T_S. To determine the polynomial $G(z^{-1})$, $H(z^{-1})$ and $F(z^{-1})$ two Diophantine equations are used,

$$\frac{C(z^{-1})}{A(z^{-1})D(z^{-1})} = E(z^{-1}) + z^{-(N-d)}\frac{F(z^{-1})}{A(z^{-1})D(z^{-1})}. \tag{11}$$

$$E(z^{-1})B(z^{-1}) = C(z^{-1})G(z^{-1}) + z^{-(N-d)}H(z^{-1}). \tag{12}$$

Where

$$E(z^{-1}) = 1 + e_1 z^{-1} + \cdots + a_{n_E} z^{-n_E}. \tag{13}$$

$$F(z^{-1}) = f_0 + f_1 z^{-1} + \cdots + f_{n_F} z^{-n_F}. \tag{14}$$

$$G(z^{-1}) = g_0 + g_1 z^{-1} + \cdots + g_{n_G} z^{-n_G}. \tag{15}$$

$$H(z^{-1}) = h_0 + h_1 z^{-1} + \cdots + h_{n_H} z^{-n_H}. \tag{16}$$

With

$$n_E = N - d - 1. \tag{17}$$

$$n_F = \max(n_A + n_D - 1, n_c - (N - d)). \tag{18}$$

$$n_G = N - d - 1. \tag{19}$$

$$n_H = \max(n_C, n_B + d) - 1. \tag{20}$$

After determining the values of the previous polynomials and collecting the N step predictions, the prediction model can be written in a matrix notation as,

$$\hat{y} = Gu_d + \hat{y}_0. \tag{21}$$

Where $\hat{y}$ is predicted plant output vector, u_d is the vector of future control sequences, G is the system dynamic matrix and $\hat{y}_0$ represents the predicted free response vector.

$$\hat{y} = [\hat{y}(t+d+1|T_S) \quad \hat{y}(t+d+2|T_S) \ldots \hat{y}(t+d+N|T_S)]^T. \tag{22}$$

$$u_d = [\Delta u(t|T_S) \quad \Delta u(t+1|T_S) \ldots \Delta u(k+N-1|T_S)]^T. \tag{23}$$

$$\hat{y}_0 = [\hat{y}_0(t+d+1|T_S) \quad \hat{y}_0(t+d+1|T_S) \ldots \hat{y}_0(t+d+1|T_S)]^T. \tag{24}$$

$$G = \begin{bmatrix} g_0 & 0 & \cdots & 0 \\ g_1 & g_0 & \cdots & 0 \\ \vdots & \vdots & \ddots & \vdots \\ g_{N-1} & g_{N-2} & \cdots & g_0 \end{bmatrix}. \tag{25}$$

The second step in the GPC controller design consists on determining the optimal control sequence. The optimizer calculates these signals by taking into consideration the objective function J. The objective function is based on the minimization of both the controller output and tracking error, the control weighting factor λ is introduced to make a trade-off between these objectives.

$$J = (Gu_d + \hat{y}_0 - w)^T (Gu_d + \hat{y}_0 - w) + \lambda u_d^T u_d. \tag{26}$$

Where w is the reference trajectory vector, by minimizing the above objective function $\left(\frac{\partial J}{\partial u_d} = 0\right)$ the optimal control signal is expressed as,

$$u_d^* = (G^T G + \lambda I)^{-1} G^T [w - \hat{y}_0]. \tag{27}$$

The control algorithm is calculated in a recursive (off-line) manner, which has the advantage of very fast computation.

2.3   GPC Parameter Tuning

The objective function from (26) can be rewritten as

$$j = \sum_{k=1}^{N} (\hat{y}(t+k) - w(t+k)) + \lambda \sum_{k=1}^{N_u} \Delta u(t+k-1). \qquad (28)$$

Equation (28) shows there are three parameters that affect the control signal generated in (27); N, N_U, and λ. Prediction horizon N and control horizon N_U are related to each other. Prediction horizon is selected early in the controller design and then holds it constant while tuning other controller settings. The control horizon is used to reduce computational processes by minimizing computational variables at each control interval. The value of the control horizon is in between 1 and the value of the prediction horizon. To deal with network-induced delays, its recommended that the difference between the prediction horizon and the control horizon must be larger than delay introduced by the communication network at each sampling instant, which is denoted by d [32]. The control weighting factor λ is present in (26) to restrict the control signal. The aggressiveness of the control signal is inversely proportional to λ. If λ has a small value, the controller will minimize the error between the reference and the output, forgetting about the control effort. Thus, the response of the system will tend to be faster but this might also result in an increase in overshoot and response oscillation.

3 Particle Swarm Optimization Based Approach for GPC Tuning

In this section, an overview on particle swarm optimization will be presented. The particle swarm optimization algorithm will then be implemented to tune the parameters of the GPC controller based on two objective functions. Finally, the PSO-GPC controller performance will be compared with the performance of a Smith predictor-PI controller in which the PSO will be applied to tune K_p and K_i.

3.1 Particle Swarm Optimization

The term optimization refers to the process of selecting the best element from a group of alternative elements based on a defined goal called the objective function. Mathematically, this is achieved by finding the values of the parameters that will maximize or minimize the objective function. Solving optimization problems analytically is quite tedious because the objective function might be non-linear, multidimensional, constrained or have many local optimums. Heuristic optimization method is an efficient alternative to solve the problem [29–31].

Particle swarm optimization is meta-heuristic optimization method developed by Kennedy and Eberhart to imitate the seeking behavior in bird flocks or fish schools [33]. In PSO, the solution for the optimization problem is represented by a vector called a particle which contains a set of parameters and every particle has the same number of parameters. Initially, a population containing a number of particles is initialized with random parameters and then enters an iterative process to search for the optimum solution. After each iteration, particles are compared and evaluated by substituting the values of their parameters in the objective function. In one iteration it might occur that one of the particles comes out with the best solution, called the globally best solution. In the succeeding iteration, another particle might be the globally best solution. Hence, at the end of each iteration, a velocity estimate for each particle is calculated based on its best solution called the personal best and the globally best. Furthermore, the velocity is used to update the particle following these equations,

$$v_i^{K+1} = Wv_i^k + C_1R_1\left(P_i - x_i^k\right) + C_2R_2\left(P_g - x_i^k\right). \tag{29}$$

$$x_i^{k+1} = x_i^k + v_i^{K+1}. \tag{30}$$

Where v_i^k represents the current velocity for particle i at iteration k while v_i^{K+1} is the velocity at iteration $K+1$. x_i^k represents the current position for particle i at iteration k while x_i^{k+1} is the updated position at iteration $K+1$. C_1 and C_2 are the cognitive coefficient and social coefficient which help modulate the steps taken by a particle in the direction of its personal best and global best. R_1 and R_2 are random values between 0 and 1. P_i represents the personal best of the particle i, P_g is the global best and W is the inertia weighting coefficient. As iterations continue, the particles are updated and they all move from different directions towards the global best which results in the best solution.

3.2   PSO Based Generalized Predictive Control Design

As mentioned in the previous section, the main parts of the GPC are (10) and (26). Other equations are used to get the optimal control input in (27) to minimize the objective function found in (26). However, the objective function relies on three GPC parameters which are the prediction horizon N, the control horizon N_U and the weighting factor λ. Hence, a particle swarm optimization method can be implemented to tune these parameters and minimize the objective function as shown in Fig. 2. The particles are represented by $P = [N, N_u, \lambda]^T$ and formulated as follows:

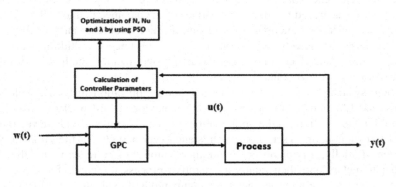

Fig. 2. PSO-GPC block diagram

(1) Identify the number of particles, the upper and the lower boundary of each tunable parameter, number of iterations and search parameters: cognitive coefficient (C_1), social coefficient (C_2) and inertia weighting coefficient (W).
(2) The particle position and velocity are initialized randomly.
(3) Simulate the GPC with the tuning parameters (N, N_U and λ) for each particle.
(4) Evaluate the objective function for each particle.
(5) Update, if any, the personal best Pi and global best Pg.
(6) Update the particle positions and velocities with values of step 5.
(7) Repeat step 3 to 6 until the last iteration count or the desired precision is achieved. The particle that produces the latest global best is the optimal value.

Equation 26 reveals the objective function as a summation of two terms. The first term is $\sum_{k=1}^{N} (\hat{y}(t+k) - w(t+k))$ which ensures fast transient response, settling time, and minimizes overshoot. The other term is $\lambda \sum_{k=1}^{N_u} \Delta u(t+k-1)$ that prevents the control signal from increasing indefinitely as it can lead to actuator saturation. Furthermore, to achieve better performance and tracking accuracy, the objective function in (28) will be replaced by one of the time domain integral performance indices called the Integral Time Square Error (ITSE) which will be solved by the particle swarm optimization.

$$e(t) = w(t) - y(t). \tag{31}$$

$$ISE = \int_{0}^{t_{ss}} e(t)^2 dt. \tag{32}$$

$$IAE = \int_{0}^{t_{ss}} |e(t)| dt. \tag{33}$$

$$ITSE = \int_{0}^{t_{ss}} te(t)^2 dt. \tag{34}$$

Where $e(t)$ is the error signal and t_{ss} is the time it takes to reach steady state. The goal behind this replacement is to formulate the tuning selection to account for the time domain performance goals such as settling time, rise time, and overshoot. The control systems based on these indices has fast response speed, large oscillation, relatively weak stability. In addition, control system based on ITSE force the error to be small at future instants with minimal oscillation compared to other performance indices such as Integral Absolute Error (IAE) and Integral Squared Error (ISE) [34].

3.3   PSO Implemented on a Smith Predictor Controller

The Smith predictor is one of the most used control strategies for time delay compensation. Smith predictor introduces an internal feedback into a controller to counterbalance the effects of delays on the main controller. Figure 3 illustrates the basic structure of a smith predictor controller in NCS [35].

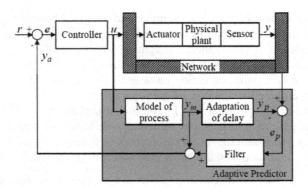

Fig. 3. Smith predictor structure in NCS

In Fig. 2, u, y, y_m, y_p and e_p are the control signal, actual output, predicted output, estimated output and output error, respectively. The controller shown above is selected to be a PI controller, which is described by the discrete form,

$$G_{PI}(z) = \frac{K_p T_s z}{K_i z - K_i}. \tag{35}$$

K_p and K_i represent the proportional gain and the integral gain respectively and are the controller parameters that will be tuned offline with the particle swarm optimization algorithm. The Integral Square Error (ISE) is used as the objective function to ensure the error signal approach zero while achieving faster transient response and minimum overshoot.

4   Results and Discussion

Simulation is carried out using MATLAB/Simulink 2016a, and it is assumed that both feedback and feedforward channel exhibit constant network-induced delays of 2 s ($\tau^{ca} = \tau^{sc} = 2$). The controlled plant is a liquid level tank with the following discrete transfer function,

$$G(z^{-1}) = \frac{0.001703z^{-1} + 0.005419z^{-2}}{1 - 0.9718z^{-1} - 0.025z^{-2}} = \frac{A(z^{-1})}{B(z^{-1})}$$

The particle swarm optimization method is then used to tune the parameters of the GPC over a predefined search region such that the objective functions in (28) is minimized. The upper and lower value of the search regions are specified as listed in Table 1. The lower values of the prediction horizon and control horizon are selected based on the works in [24] to address the network-induced delays. The upper bound of the prediction horizon and control horizon are set at 40 and 10 respectively to minimize computational time. The lower search region for the Smith Predictor parameters are

Table 1. Search region of the tunable parameters

Parameters	Lower values	Upper values
Prediction horizon (N)	30	40
Control horizon (N_U)	5	10
Weighting factor (λ)	0.001	1
Proportional gain (K_P)	0.0001	200
Integral gain (K_I)	0.0001	200

chosen to be 0.0001 for both, while the upper values have a value of 200 to prevent destabilizing the plant by introducing high value gains. In PSO, the number of particles crucial in ensuring accurate results. The number of particles is set to 20 based on the work in [33] which illustrate that a suitable number of particles is in between 20 to 50. The number of iterations and the PSO search parameters used in the simulation is presented in Table 2.

Table 2. Parameters of the PSO algorithm

Parameters	Values
Particle dimensions	3
Number of particles	20
Number of iterations	30
Cognitive coefficient (C_1)	1.5
Social coefficient (C_2)	1.5
Inertia weighting coefficient (w)	.4–.9

To compare with GPC, the PSO procedure is repeated on a Smith predictor to obtain the optimal parameter values as tabulated in Table 3. In Table 4, the control performance in terms of transient response of each controller is presented. It is clear that the PSO-Smith predictor outperformed the PSO-GPC in terms of transient response.

Table 3. Tuning parameters obtained through PSO

Controllers	Prediction horizon (N)	Control horizon (N_U)	Weighting factor (λ)	Proportional gain (K_P)	Integral gain (K_I)
PSO-GPC	40	6	0.1329	–	–
Modified PSO-GPC	40	9	0.0094	–	–
PSO-Smith predictor	–	–	–	93.75	3.906

Table 4. Transient response analysis for step input signal

Controllers	Rise time(s)	Settling time (s)	Overshoot (%)
PSO-GPC	2.038	11.171	2.6%
Modified PSO-GPC	0.458	4.9	–
PSO-Smith predictor	0.251	4.56	–

In Fig. 4, it is obvious that the PSO-Smith predictor produces larger undershoot compared to the PSO-GPC when the water level is reduced. This indicates that the PSO-GPC is more efficient in dealing with non-minimum phase systems compared to PSO-Smith Predictor. However, the PSO-GPC resulted with a small overshoot and slower transient response toward the set point. Thus, a modified PSO-GPC is proposed through the replacement of the cost function in (28) by the ITSE objective function shown in (34). With a modified PSO-GPC, faster settling time and rise time can be achieved. Plus, GPC algorithm also allows for incorporation of output constraint in the optimization to tackle the overshoot problem. This is a clear advantage of GPC compared to the other control algorithm.

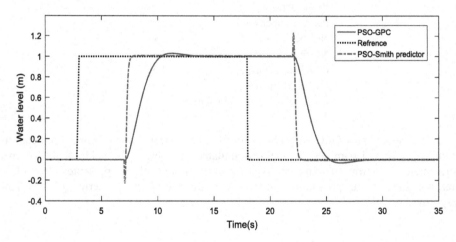

Fig. 4. Comparison of closed-loop step response

From Fig. 5, it can be seen that the modified PSO-GPC produced a better transient response than the original PSO-GPC. When compared with PSO-Smith predictor, the modified controller was slightly outperformed in terms of settling time and rise time as illustrated in Table 4, but produced a smaller undershoot. Thus, it can be concluded that GPC is a preferable controller in NCS applications because it is capable to deal with non-minimum systems, ability to handle constraints and its clear potential for other types of network-induced delays such as random time delay.

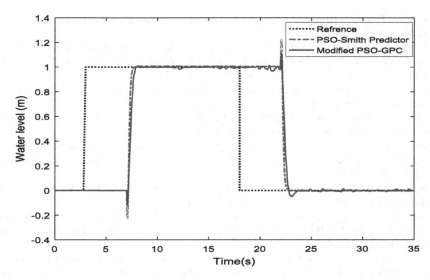

Fig. 5. Modified PSO-GPC closed-loop step response

5 Conclusion

In this paper, a standard GPC objective function and an ITSE performance index were applied in the generalized predictive controller design by using a particle swarm optimization to compensate the network-induced delays occurring between the components of a networked control system. The aim of the particle swarm optimization is to optimally tune the GPC parameters based on the above objective functions. The simulations result in MATLAB/SIMULINK show significant improvement of the controllers using the proposed techniques compared to PSO-Smith predictor. Although both predictive controllers can compensate the effects of network delays, the modified PSO-GPC, which is based on the ITSE performance index, achieved better transient response when compared with the original PSO-GPC.

References

1. Zhang, L., Gao, H., Kaynak, O.: Network-induced constraints in networked control systems-a survey. IEEE Trans. Ind. Informat. **9**(1), 403–416 (2013)
2. Kaneko, S.-I., Capi, G.: Human-robot communication for surveillance of elderly people in remote distance. IERI Procedia **10**, 92–97 (2014)
3. Dasgupta, S., Halder, K., Banerjee, S., Gupta, A.: Stability of Networked Control System (NCS) with discrete time-driven PID controllers. Control Eng. Practice **42**, 41–49 (2015)
4. Yang, S.-H.: Internet-Based Control Systems. Springer, Heidelberg (2011)
5. Saif, A.W.A., AL-Shihri, A.: Robust design of dynamic controller for nonlinear networked control systems with packet dropout. In: 2015 IEEE International Conference on Control System, Computing and Engineering (ICCSCE), Penang, pp. 557–562 (2015)

6. Elia, N., Eisenbeis, J.: Limitations of linear control over packet drop networks. IEEE Trans. Autom. Control **56**(4), 826–841 (2011)
7. Dong, X., Zhang, D.: H» Fault detection observer design for networked control systems with packet dropout using delta operator. In: 2016 12th World Congress on Intelligent Control and Automation (WCICA), Guilin, pp. 2547–2551 (2016)
8. Zhu, Q.X.: Controllability of multi-rate networked control systems with short time delay. In: Advanced Materials Research, pp. 219–220 (2011)
9. Zhu, Q.X.: Observability of multi-rate networked control systems with short time delay. Commun. Comput. Inf. Sci. **144**, 396–401 (2011)
10. Zhang, H., Zhang, Z., Wang, Z., Shan, Q.: New results on stability and stabilization of networked control systems with short time-varying delay. IEEE Trans. Cybern. **46**(12), 2772–2781 (2016)
11. Mahmoud, M.S., Sabih, M., Elshafei, M.: Event-triggered output feedback control for distributed networked systems. ISA Trans. **60**, 294–302 (2016)
12. Wu, J., Zhou, Z.-J., Zhan, X.-S., Yan, H.-C., Ge, M.-F.: Optimal modified tracking performance for MIMO networked control systems with communication constraints. ISA Trans. **68**, 14–21 (2017)
13. Feng, Y., Luo, J.: Robust H8 control for networked switched singular control systems with time-delays and uncertainties. In: Seventh International Symposium on Computational Intelligence and Design, Hangzhou, pp. 457–460 (2014)
14. Niu, Y., Liang, Y., Yang, H.: Event-triggered robust control and dynamic scheduling co-design for networked control system. In: 2017 14th International Bhurban Conference on Applied Sciences and Technology (IBCAST), Islamabad, pp. 237–243 (2017)
15. Zhang, Z., Zhang, H., Wang, Z., Feng, J.: Optimal robust non-fragile H∞ control for networked control systems with uncertain time-delays. In: Proceeding of the 11th World Congress on Intelligent Control and Automation, Shenyang, pp. 4076–4081 (2014)
16. Zhang, L., Wang, J., Ge, Y., Wang, B.: Robust distributed model predictive control for uncertain networked control systems. IET Control Theory Appl. **8**(17), 1843–1851 (2014)
17. Tang, P.L., de Silva, C.W.: Compensation for transmission delays in an ethernet- based control network using variable-horizon predictive control. IEEE Trans. Control Syst. Technol. **14**(4), 707–718 (2006)
18. Yu, B., Shi, Y., Huang, J.: Modified generalized predictive control of networked systems with application to a hydraulic position control system. J. Dyn. Syst. Meas. Control **133**(3) (2011)
19. Song, H., Yu, L., Zhang, W.A.: Stabilisation of networked control systems with communication constraints and multiple distributed transmission delays. IET Control Theory Appl. **3**(10), 1307–1316 (2009)
20. Li, H., Shi, Y.: Network-based predictive control for constrained nonlinear systems with two-channel packet dropouts. IEEE Trans. Ind. Electron. **61**(3), 1574–1582 (2014)
21. Yang, L., Yang, S.H.: Multi-rate control in internet-based control systems. IEEE Trans. Syst. Man Cybern. **37**(2), 185–192 (2007)
22. Das, B., Mhaskar, P.: Lyapunov-based offset-free model predictive control of nonlinear systems. In: 2014 American Control Conference, Portland, pp. 2839–2844 (2014)
23. Liu, J., Muñoz de la Peña, D., Christofides, P.D., Davis, J.F.: Lyapunov-based model predictive control of nonlinear systems subject to time-varying measurement delays. Int. J. Adaptive Control Sig. Process. **23**(8), 788–807 (2009)
24. Bunin, G.A., Fraire, F., François, G., Bonvin, D.: Run-to-Run MPC tuning via gradient descent. Comput. Aided Chem. Eng. **30**, 927–931 (2012)

25. Zermani, M.A., Feki, E., Mami, A.: Application of genetic algorithms in identification and control of a new system humidification inside a newborn incubator. In: 2011 International Conference on Communications, Computing and Control Applications (CCCA), Hammamet, pp. 1–6 (2011)

26. van der Lee, J.H., Svrcek, W.Y., Young, B.R.: A tuning algorithm for model predictive controllers based on genetic algorithms and fuzzy decision making. ISA Trans. **47**(1), 53–59 (2008)

27. Yamuna Rani, K., Unbehauen, H.: Study of predictive control tuning methods. Automatica **33**, 2243–2248 (1997)

28. Neshasteriz, R., Khaki-Sedigh, A., Sadjadian, H.: An analysis of variance approach to tuning of generalized predictive controllers for second order plus dead time models. In: IEEE ICCA 2010, Xiamen, pp. 1059–1064 (2010)

29. Aicha, F.B., Bouani, F., Ksouri, M.: Automatic tuning of GPC synthesis parameters based on multi-objective optimization. In: 2010 XIth International Workshop on Symbolic and Numerical Methods, Modeling and Applications to Circuit Design (SM2ACD), Gammath, pp. 1–5 (2010)

30. Rossiter, J.A.: Model-Based Predictive Control: A Practical Approach. CRC Press, Boca Raton (2003)

31. Zhang, X.M., Han, Q.L., Wang, Y.L.: A brief survey of recent results on control and filtering for networked systems. In: 2016 12th World Congress on Intelligent Control and Automation (WCICA), Guilin, pp. 64–69 (2016)

32. Camacho, E., Bordons, C.: Model Predictive Control Book. Springer, Heidelberg (2007)

33. Poli, R., Kennedy, J., Blackwell, T.: Particle swarm optimization an overview. Swarm Intell. **1**, 33–57 (2007). Springer

34. Pan, F., Liu, L.: Research on different integral performance indices applied on fractional-order systems. In: 2016 Chinese Control and Decision Conference (CCDC), Yinchuan, pp. 324–328 (2016)

35. Witrant, E., Georges, D., Canudas-de-Wit, C., Alamir, M.: On the use of state predictors in networked control systems. In: Chiasson, J., Loiseau, J.J. (eds.) Applications of Time Delay Systems. LNCIS, vol. 352, pp. 17–35. Springer, Heidelberg (2007). doi:10.1007/978-3-540-49556-7_2

A Generic Architecture for a Model-Management-System (MMS)

Facilitating Quality Assurance and Long-Term Usability Along the Whole Model Lifecycle

Günter Herrmann[1], Axel Lehmann[2](✉), and Robert Siegfried[3]

[1] Institut für Technik Intelligenter Systeme (ITIS) GmbH, Neubiberg, Germany
[2] Institut für Technische Informatik, Universität der Bundeswehr München, Neubiberg, Germany
axel.lehmann@unibw.de
[3] aditerna GmbH, Hohenbrunn, Germany

Abstract. The demand for rapid system and product innovations pushes the need for the availability of a wide spectrum of computational models, simulations and data (M&S). Efficient and credible M&S applications require model modularity, flexibility, scalability, and reusability, large and diverse model development teams, and above all M&S management tools. Such tools should facilitate and automate not only the coordination of those teams but also the easy, reliable and traceable reuse of model components, in particular regarding model repository search functions and developer team guidance, with emphasis on quality assurance and comprehensive lifecycle documentation. After justifying the needs for availability of a collaborative platform combining all team and M&S management tasks as well as for documenting every phase of the lifecycle of a model in a standardized manner, a generic conceptual architecture of a Model Management Architecture (MMS) meeting these requirements is introduced, along with a demonstrator compatible with current institutional quality assurance approaches for modeling and simulation, such as verification, validation and accreditation (VV&A).

1 Introduction

In the digital age, modeling and simulation is a major technical enabling technology for rapid innovations and knowledge generation.

In the past, most models, simulations and data have been developed for a specific purpose, and have been subsequently used only within this well-defined context. In regard of permanently decreasing time frames for increasingly complex product innovations, rapidly changing educational needs, or for decision making processes impose new requirements on M&S development processes and products. In order to cope with these new requirements, a variety of models, simulations and data (M&S)

- may be applied for various purposes, like for training, analysis, decision support, or procurement,

© Springer Nature Singapore Pte Ltd. 2017
M.S. Mohamed Ali et al. (Eds.): AsiaSim 2017, Part II, CCIS 752, pp. 432–446, 2017.
DOI: 10.1007/978-981-10-6502-6_38

- may have to be adapted to new requirements or used in a changing context,
- may be coupled with other models as well as with real systems forming distributed simulations,
- may be used or adapted by different types of users and
- have to be designed in a flexible and extensible way.

In order to match these requirements, development as well as documentation of M&S has to satisfy the following criteria:

- M&S have to be developed according to well-defined, standardized development and lifetime process including detailed guidelines on the required design, development, quality assurance and usage documentation.
- A standardized set of M&S documentation templates enables the evaluation of M&S features like model quality, adaptability, or coupling restrictions with other models,
- The variety of potential users requires the provisioning of different views on the documentation of simulation models.
- Usability of M&S products and documentation over lifetime requires availability of standardized M&S technical services and management functions

These requirements may be met by applying organizational and technical measures. A sound and solid conceptual framework is of crucial importance for the success of such an integrated approach.

At first sight, a technical solution would be the provision of a documentation and management system for M&S and their applications. Regarding the new paradigm of network-centricity, such a technical solution has to be put into the proper organizational and institutional context. New and continuously evolving requirements of an institution directly influence this genuine technical solution. Each approach to an integrated, solid conceptual foundation has to bear these evolving requirements and conditions in mind.

Therefore, the challenges of future M&S are in particular:

- Problem-suited and efficient representation of systems, processes and interrelations to be simulated;
- Flexible, modular, component-oriented model design, development and maintenance promoting reusability and upgradeability;
- Efficient and effective collaboration of the parties in charge over lifetime of the models, simulations, data or their components, including sufficient knowledge transfer;
- Traceable compliance with predefined quality requirements;
- Design and documentation processes promoting longer lifecycles of individual models and components;
- Support of ongoing model adjustments and adaptations throughout its lifecycle.

This multiplicity of these requirements, along with an increasing longevity of the M&S, leads to the conclusion that a comprehensive assistance of all participants of model-development and -usage over the entire M&S lifecycle is necessary.

We refer to such a holistic collaborative platform as a *Model-Management-System* (MMS) [6]. Such an MMS must not only integrate the domain-specific concepts for model design, development, documentation and VV&A but also has to offer project organization assistance for carrying out domain-specific concepts.

2   MMS Requirements and Design Principles

An MMS must satisfy three fundamental requirement groups which are complementary to one another:

- The MMS must integrate domain-specific concepts for M&S application specification, design, development, documentation and quality assurance (VV&A).
- The MMS must offer project organization support for performing domain-specific concepts.
- The MMS must support ever increasing complexity requirements. Its fundamental concepts must therefore intrinsically support high flexibility and upgradeability of the architecture and its use.

On the basis of experience in other technical fields, we therefore decided to consider *Model Engineering* as an engineering discipline like any other, and to manage M&S specification, development, usage, maintenance and quality control as an engineering process.

2.1   Domain-Specific Concepts

The main MMS design motivation of domain-specific concepts for model development and VV&A consists in structuring M&S development and lifetime process as a multi-phase process. Each phase of this process results in an intermediate product that has to be systematically documented and qualified according to predefined templates and rules.

Figure 1 shows the 7 phases of an M&S development process as proposed in [2] as well as the 7 corresponding intermediate phase products and documentations (see also [4,5]). The process is starting with the *Preliminary Phase* and ending with the *Interpretation* phase, possibly after iterations caused by error detections, required adjustments or new versions. Each of those modeling phases, as well as each of the intermediate products of each phase must be documented according to predefined, standardized but tailorable templates [7]. As an example: in Fig. 1, the phase product *Structured Problem Definition* and its documentation represent a precise specification of M&S objectives, restrictions and acceptance criteria as an *intermediate product* resulting from the *Problem Definition* phase. All phase products of phase i form basically the specification or prerequisite for work and activities to be performed in phase $i + 1$. In [5], we have also specified precisely the roles of team members within each phase of an M&S-project. This proposed concept of M&S-roles guarantees that responsibilities as well as contributors of the project are known and visible for all project members.

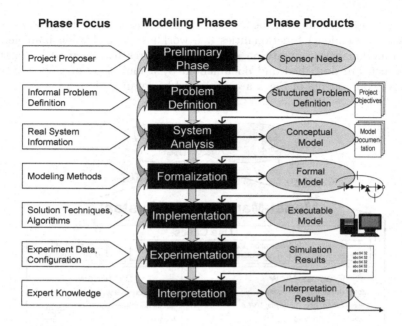

Fig. 1. Model development process [2].

The specialized aspects and functions of the MMS are however not only restricted to model development: they are really intended to cover the entire lifecycle of an M&S development and application. In particular, aspects of model usage, reuse, adaptation and replacement must be supported. Additional documentation and quality assurance concepts have been developed for these further model lifecycle phases as well. As starting points for these documentation and quality assurance measures, the family of products developed during the M&S development phases was enlarged to include products relevant to further phases of the model lifecycle. Examples for these additional products include experiment descriptions and scenario definitions.

The use cases in these further phases of the model lifecycle include for instance support for integrating existing data bases, for taking over documentation from existing repositories, as well as for designing and conducting experiments. For instance they offer component search and coupling support, the follow-up documentation of models, as well as extended search and output possibilities (queries, reports, documentation).

Figure 2 illustrates an overview of the architecture of the proposed MMS, including the use cases which are to be supported. Especially, Fig. 2 highlights that the various user groups (like end user, developer, etc.) have very different demands and therefore will use the MMS within very different use cases. Each use case in turn combines processes and data in a coherent way, thereby providing the exact right amount of information needed by the user within the actual use case. Technically, the use cases and processes are built on top of basic (domain-independent) functionalities like workflows and version management. These functionalities operate on so-called structures (e. g. a model is a structure) which are described and documented by a multitude of associated data fields. All components of Fig. 2 are explained in detail in Sect. 3.

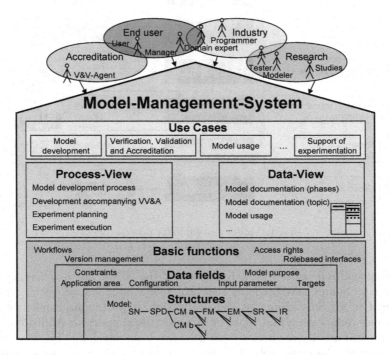

Fig. 2. High-level overview of the architecture of the proposed Model-Management-System (MMS).

2.2   Project Organization Support

Clearly, functional demands of the MMS are closely related with project organization demands. In fact, project support functions (e. g. search functions, coupling assessment) are fundamental for usability of the MMS and are certainly applicable within various use cases. The basis for the project support functions is *constituted of low level and technical functionalities*, which are either context independent or which only become useful through being linked to a specialized context. The MMS supports interactive and collaborative functions (e. g. know-how exchange, Wiki, Blog) as well as general administrative functions such as workflow and role management, version management, history management, problem management, change management, document management and configuration management.

2.3 Flexibility

Figure 3 provides an overview of use cases resulting from the requirements analysis and of the supporting functions on which these use cases are built. Expectations include, for instance, the use of the MMS as a central model catalogue within an organization, its integration in existing experimental and simulation environments as well as enabling the establishment of competence networks. Heterogeneity of user communities as well as future requirements and developments have to be continually integrated into the MMS concept. Therefore, the MMS concept was developed in such a way that additional use cases can be flexibly and adaptively designed and MMS extensions can be tolerated.

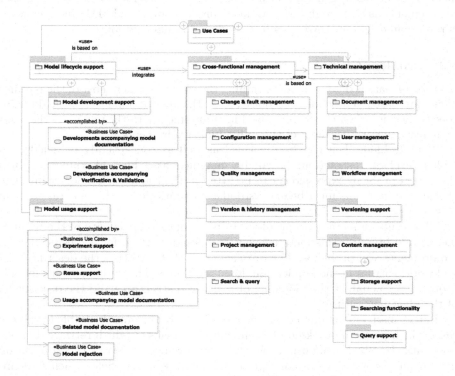

Fig. 3. Overview of the MMS use cases and of the supporting functions on which these use cases depend.

3   MMS Concept

3.1 MMS Meta Concept as Design Pattern

The general approach to develop a partial solution for each management requirement, independent from the other requirements, is neither desired nor implementable for a future-proof MMS concept and MMS development. Such an ad hoc approach would contradict the basic premise of the coordinating and centralizing function of an MMS in which the fundamental core is a unitary and consistent domain model.

Our approach is the development of a *structurally abstract* MMS meta concept. The result of this abstraction is a design pattern for requirements and problems of a specific problem class. The advantage of this abstract design pattern is that it permits in principle a unitary representation of all present and future, known and yet unknown requirements and problems. In summary, the intention of this MMS meta concept is to provide a design pattern within which the presently known documentation requirements for an M&S can be implemented, while being general and flexible enough to seamlessly integrate further requirements as they might arise in the future. The proposed MMS meta concept is represented here in UML (Unified Modeling Language) [3].

3.2 Problem Class

A problem class is defined by determining the ideas on which most of the requirements are based. These ideas do not exist on the abstraction level of the domain-specific problems which are very specific requirements. Rather they are the commonalities underlying most of the individual requirements.

This problem class can be identified as well as conceptually modeled on a higher level of abstraction. It can be imagined as a kind of frame in which the actual problem expressions can be fitted in their appropriate locations. The specific requirements must be understood as instantiation of this general problem class.

The resulting meta concept allows to represent the specificity of the requirements, and in a way this meta concept is a design pattern for a specific class of requirements and problems. The problem class of the MMS is the description of real world entities in the application domain of M&S. The design pattern for this problem class enables the modeling of real world structures and the description of the identified entities.

In this manner, the meta concept of the MMS is in principle usable for all use cases which perform any kind of documentation tasks or which retrieve description data. However, semantic consistency requirements restrict the application domain of the MMS meta concept to a limited semantic field which is definable without contradiction. This is due to the fact that for all core elements (i.e. the Structures, Data Fields and Roles as described in the following) of the specific domain model first clarity and unicity of meaning must be guaranteed; and second disjoint meanings between these elements must be ensured. Since the meaning of a term is dependent on the context of its use, this context must be restricted according to specialized fields in order to exclude the possibility of multiple meanings. In the case of the MMS, this context is the application domain of M&S.

Requirements which go beyond the mere description of modeled entities and beyond the mere providing of information about these entities (for instance, actual coupling of components) must therefore be excluded from the concept.

These functionalities have to be considered separately and added using a different structural concept.

3.3   Benefits of the MMS Meta Concept

Introducing a design pattern to describe the use cases may seem to be lots of effort for unclear reasons. We believe that the strict use of the proposed design patterns helps to meet the various (and continuously evolving) requirements, thus leading to considerable benefits:

- Most notably, following the design pattern ensures that all use cases are modeled (and subsequently implemented) in the same way. This eases the comparability of use cases and allows to define globally valid quality requirements. Specific requirements may be defined once in the meta concept, and are in turn applied to all use cases. As an example, the meta concept states that all activities are executed by specific roles. Assigning an activity to a single person or a whole organization is therefore prohibited.
- A direct consequence of this is that the MMS is based on a consistent domain model. Especially, this implies that all parts (roles, data fields, structures, views) may be reused. In fact, they are modelled just once and have to be reused. When creating a new use case, already existing parts have to be reused and only parts, which are not yet included in the domain model have to be added. The meta concept forces the modeller/developer to reuse existing parts and secures the consistency of the domain model. As an example, a data field for the description of the "Problem statement" may be referenced in several use cases.
- The MMS domain model is limited to the domain of modelling and simulation. This limitation is necessary to ensure the unambiguousness of the concepts defined within the domain model.

3.4   The MMS Meta Concept in Detail

The basis of the MMS meta concept as design pattern is the strict separation of static elements (domain model) and dynamic elements (model management), as depicted in Fig. 4. The strength of the MMS meta concept as design pattern resides in its ability to define unlimited interaction possibilities with the modeled entities. These interaction possibilities represent user specific views in the application domain of M&S, and are modeled as USE CASES. The design pattern covers these use cases in their dynamic and static aspects. (Note: Terms in SMALL CAPITALS explicitly denote classes which are part of the MMS meta concept.)

Each modeled USE CASE may and will in general extend the domain model of the MMS. This can occur because additional real world entities must be documented or because additional description data fields must be assigned to existing or newly modeled entities. The first priority when introducing these extensions is to use the existing STRUCTURES and DATA FIELDS. If new aspects

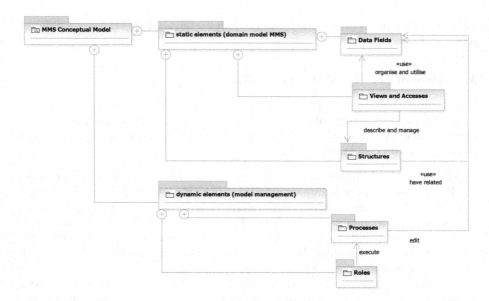

Fig. 4. The very fundamental idea of the MMS meta concept is to separate the static and dynamic elements.

must be introduced at all, these must be integrated as conservatively and as generically as possible in the structure model and data model, taking care of integrating them as seamlessly as possible with the existing ones.

The goal is to saturate the domain model with STRUCTURE and DATA FIELD definitions by integrating a sufficiently large number of USE CASES, so that the resulting MMS ends up being based on a consistent, comprehensive and self-consolidated domain model for the problem class.

Static Elements: MMS Domain Model

Structures. The domain model of the MMS consists of a representation of the entities relevant for the problem class. These entities are modeled in their inner and outer relations as STRUCTURES. This modeling of STRUCTURES makes it possible to explicitly work with the modeled entities like MODEL, PHASE MODEL and SUBMODEL in the MMS. Especially, every instance of such a STRUCTURES can be described by data fields.

Data Fields. Since the problem class of the MMS is the description of real world entities (which are represented in the MMS meta concept as STRUCTURES) in the application domain M&S and since a central requirement is to maintain the consistency of the data model, the STRUCTURES have been conceptually separated from their description. For this reason, the MMS structure model is supplemented by a separate data model, in which all possible description aspects in the application domain are modeled in the form of DATA FIELDS.

In principle it would be sufficient to model the DATA FIELDS as an unstructured set of classes. But to ensure a clear overview and understanding, an aspect-oriented description hierarchy was modeled internally to the MMS, the leaves of this hierarchy being the DATA FIELD classes.

The main benefit of using separate DATA FIELD classes is the possibility to reuse data fields for describing various structures. For example, a data field "Classification/Copyright" might be used for models as well as experiments.

Views and Accesses. Only the actual instantiation of a STRUCTURE is associated with specific description data (instantiated DATA FIELDS). This association is determined by a predefined and prespecified USE CASE.

The link between the DATA FIELDS on the one hand and the STRUCTURES on the other hand are the VIEWS AND ACCESSES, which define how structures are described by the DATA FIELDS. For every USE CASE, there are one or more association possibilities of DATA FIELDS to STRUCTURES. It is possible to specify several views as, for instance, several combinations of DATA FIELDS might be desired for describing a STRUCTURE (e. g. a MODEL). The totality of these associations constitutes the third pillar of the MMS domain model: the VIEWS AND ACCESSES.

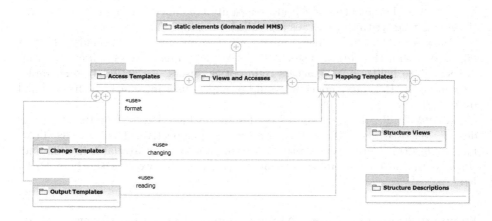

Fig. 5. MMS meta concept: VIEWS AND ACCESSES are the linking element between the DATA FIELDS on the one hand and the STRUCTURES on the other hand.

As shown in Fig. 5 the description of a STRUCTURE has two aspects: Firstly, it must be clear which data fields will be used at all in order to describe the entity, out of the large pool of available DATA FIELDS. Often the chosen DATA FIELDS are grouped according to their content, respectively are part of a thematic hierarchy. The DATA FIELDS are then associated to STRUCTURES as specific description templates. These content description templates are called

MAPPING TEMPLATES. They are further subdivided into use case specific mappings (STRUCTURE VIEWS) and into general mappings (STRUCTURE DESCRIPTIONS) internally defined within the MMS.

A small example may clarify this. If we consider a STRUCTURE (like a "model"), the structure description of this structure contains all DATA FIELDS which are currently defined (e. g. "Problem statement", "Input parameters", or "Simulation results"). A single structure view refers only to a subset of these data fields. A structure view for the use case "Model documentation" might only refer to the "Problem statement" and "Input parameters". Another structure view, related to the use case of model usage, might refer to the "Simulation results".

To summarize, the structure description contains all DATA FIELDS related to a specific STRUCTURE. The structure views in turn, refer to the specific subset of DATA FIELDS which is required within the current use case.

Secondly, the DATA FIELDS must be accessible, either to read them or for data management. The simple content description is not sufficient as the user of the MMS must actually be able to read or write data. For this reason the content patterns must be cast in a specific form and the access rights and access methods of the user must be defined. The ACCESS TEMPLATES are the interfacing templates which perform these tasks of formatting the content description and controlling user access. For this purpose, each ACCESS TEMPLATE uses specific MAPPING TEMPLATES, according to the user specific view and use case. The ACCESS TEMPLATES which are read-only are called OUTPUT TEMPLATES, those granting writing privileges are called CHANGE TEMPLATES.

While the structure views define only the subset of data fields which is required within the current use case, the ACCESS TEMPLATES define the order of these data fields and the access rights of the users. An actual system implementing this MMS meta concept, would provide a user interface which is defined by the CHANGE TEMPLATES.

MAPPING TEMPLATES therefore describe which DATA FIELDS serve the description of which STRUCTURE from which perspective. The ACCESS TEMPLATES use this content description structure and make it available in a manner suitable to the current user, so that he can actually work with these DATA FIELDS.

Dynamic Elements: Model Management. The selection of views that are used and therefore actually receive data is determined individually by each USE CASE. A USE CASE is defined by the association of the process description and the participating ROLES (dynamic aspect), as well as by the used views with their related STRUCTURES and the DATA FIELDS (static aspect) describing them.

Processes. The dynamic aspects are modeled by processes which carry out the USE CASES. Such a process defines the sequencing order, the relations to generated products (in the form of MAPPING TEMPLATES and ACCESS TEMPLATES) as well as the participating ROLES.

Roles. ROLES define task fields and responsibilities within a process (see also Fig. 6). Instantiated processes (WORKFLOWS) associate ROLES to actual people. These ROLES are similarly defined in the ACCESS TEMPLATES, which are also USE CASE specific. The ACCESS TEMPLATES statically define the access rights of ROLES to DATA FIELDS, i. e. the access rights are not defined in the processes themselves. The actual execution of a process thus clearly defines which people take which ROLES (via the WORKFLOW) and which ROLES can access which DATA FIELD instances, and how they access them (via the instantiated ACCESS TEMPLATES).

Figure 6 represents the overall architecture of the MMS meta concept and clarifies how ROLES are integrated in it.

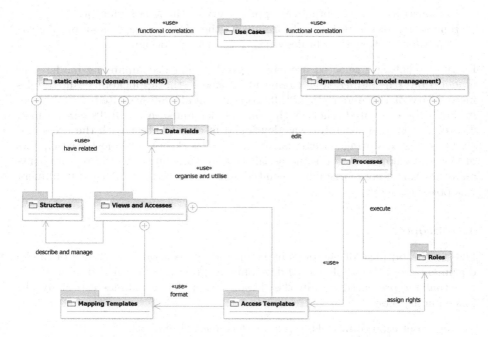

Fig. 6. Overview of the overall architecture of the MMS meta concept.

Execution of a Use Case. The execution of a USE CASE in the MMS is carried out along the following steps:

- Triggering and execution of a WORKFLOW.
- Instantiation of the ROLES and corresponding allocation of actual persons.
- Selection and instantiation of views, respectively ACCESS TEMPLATES.
- Instantiation (and versioning) of STRUCTURES.
- Instantiation of DATA FIELDS and allocation of these DATA FIELD instances to the STRUCTURE instances (according to the view).
- Content processing of the DATA FIELDS during the WORKFLOW execution.

The USE CASE execution results in additional STRUCTURE instances and associated description data (DATA FIELD instances) stored in the MMS dataset.

4 MMS Demonstrator

4.1 Purpose

In order to show the potential and flexibility of the devised MMS concept, several well selected parts were exemplary implemented within an existing software framework and made available for experimental usage. This MMS demonstrator mainly serves three purposes:

- Demonstration of the practical applicability of the MMS concept.
- Illustration of the benefits of formalising the MMS concept as an ontology.
- Confirmation that the ontology has a *well-chosen* design.

By implementing a selected use case ("development accompanying model documentation") including all its relevant concepts, the applicability and implementability of the underlying MMS concept should be evaluated. In addition, it should be evaluated whether the various demands on an MMS can be met. Therefore, the demonstrator was developed in close contact with the users and could be tested during an extensive one-week workshop. As most participants of this workshop were the same as those who contributed to the requirements analysis a direct comparison between the user's expectations and their fulfillment was possible.

4.2 Scope

Due to the purpose of the demonstrator and the central importance of model documentation, the whole model development process (as described in Sect. 2.1) is actually represented within the demonstrator. This includes especially the following aspects:

- Representation of models, phase models and sub-models.
- Representation of model documentation along all phases of the model development process.
- Definition of workflows and roles, as well as access rights associated with specific steps and roles within these workflows.
- In addition to the phase-oriented documentation, an aspect-oriented view on the model documentation was also modeled and implemented. In contrast to the default view which is oriented along the phases of the model development process, the aspect-oriented view combines the data fields according to a few well-defined topics.

In order to provide these desired aspects all necessary structures (Model, Phase Model, Sub-Model as well as the respective versions of these structures) along with the required data fields were modeled. Besides the central domain-specific functionalities (i. e. supporting the model development and documentation process), the demonstrator provides additional technical functionalities required for executing this use case:

- Version management for selected concepts (Models, Documentation)
- Role- and task-specific user interface
- User friendly templates for data input as well as several output possibilities for selected data
- Searching and browsing within the model catalog
- Management of further model-associated data (responsible person, model status, annotations)

As indicated, two different access templates to the model documentation have been implemented: phase-oriented and aspect-oriented.

4.3   Technical Realization

The MMS demonstrator is based on the framework WebGenesis [1]. Basically, WebGenesis is a three-tier system consisting of a database backend, an application server and a client (typically a browser). In this context, a notable feature of WebGenesis is its capability of directly importing an OWL ontology for the use as internal data model.

At this point, the chosen approach via a formalisation of the MMS concept as ontology shows its benefits: The development of the ontology can be done with powerful external tools and is (in the best case) completely independent from the actual software environment used for the demonstrator.

4.4   Evaluation of the MMS Demonstrator

The MMS demonstrator implements a selected subset of the MMS concept and shows practically how the realized functionality was build from the MMS meta-concept in a component-oriented way. Furthermore, by using the underlying technical and ontological structures, the demonstrator illustrates in a very straightforward way the extensive conceptual and technical flexibility and extensibility of the MMS with regard to future use cases. Last but not least, technical constraints of the system used for the current implementation could be identified.

5   Summary

This paper describes a Model-Management-System (MMS) which is both a concept as well as an exemplary implementation of a management system along the whole model lifecycle, thereby also integrating all further relevant products of the domain M&S.

The MMS meta concept as central aspect of the overall MMS concept serves as design pattern for arbitrary documentation processes within the designated application domain of M&S (using a more general term, this application domain is the actual problem class which is addressed by the MMS). Within this design pattern specific use cases need to be modeled which are finally executed by a specific group of users (which are organized in roles).

A user evaluation of the exemplary MMS implementation revealed that the MMS meta concept is not just very powerful, but at the same time very comfortable to work with. This is due to the fact that the user does not experience the complexity of the meta concept but instead can work very efficiently with the predefined use cases defined within the framework of the MMS meta concept.

Acknowledgements. The authors would like to thank the former Bundeswehr Transformation Centre (ZTransfBw, Division 322, Ottobrunn) and the Federal Office of Defense Technology and Procurement (BWB, now BAAINBw, P2.3, Koblenz) for supporting this research over several years.

References

1. IITB, F.: Framework für Generierung und Support Web-basierter Informationssysteme. Internet. http://www.iitb.fraunhofer.de/servlet/is/2223/
2. Lehmann, A.: Quality assurance of models and simulations - demands and solutions for verification and validation. In: International Top forum on Engineering Science and Technology Development Strategy (2013)
3. Object Management Group: UML 2.2, February 2009. http://www.omg.org/spec/UML/2.2/
4. Rabe, M., Spieckermann, S., Wenzel, S.: Verifikation und Validierung für die Simulation in Produktion und Logistik. Springer, Heidelberg (2008)
5. Wang, Z., Lehmann, A.: Quality assurance of models and simulation applications. Int. J. Model. Simul. Sci. Comput. **1**(1), 27–45 (2010)
6. Wang, Z., Lehmann, A.: Mastering quality, credibility and utility of complex M&S applications. In: Breitenecker, F. (ed.) Proceedings of AsiaSim 2015. CCIS, vol. 19, no. 2, pp. 12–20. Springer, Heidelberg (2015). doi:10.11128/sne.19.2.0993
7. Wang, Z., Lehmann, A., Karagkasidis, A.: A multistage approach for quality- and efficiency-related tailoring of modelling and simulation processes. In: Simulation News Europe (SNE), Special Issue "Quality Aspects in Modeling and Simulation" (2009)

EEG Analysis for Pre-learning Stress in the Brain

Omar AlShorman[1], Tariq Ali[2(✉)], and Muhammad Irfan[1]

[1] Najran University, Najran, Kingdom of Saudi Arabia
Omar2007_ahu@yahoo.com, irfan16.uetian@gmail.com
[2] COMSATS Institute of Technology, Sahiwal, Pakistan
tariqhsp@gmail.com

Abstract. This paper deals with the relationship between pre-learning stress, long term memory, and EEG signals in the brain. Studying the effect of stress is very important especially in academic life for the students. Nowadays; there have been many recent methods evaluating the relationship between stress, learning and memory performance based on different techniques. The most common methods are conducted based on the biological response. Some of these methods have assessed the impact of stress based on biochemical effects by measuring specific hormones such as cortisol, adrenalin and glucocorticoids, or based on physiological effects such as blood pressure, heart rate, skin temperature. However, in all these methods, there are inconsistent findings due to the instability of hormones and a large number of related factors. The aim of this research is to discover the impact of pre-learning stress on long-term memory retrieval using EEG signals. The results indicate that there is a relationship between theta rhythm in the temporal lobe and long-term memory retrieval.

Keywords: EEG · Stress · Long-term memory · Pre-learning · Theta rhythm

1 Introduction

Nowadays, Stress is considered as a real problem in our life [1]. Importantly, the impacts of stress could be physical (i.e. a headache, increasing of blood pressure, increasing heart rate), emotional (i.e. anxiety and depression), behavioral (i.e. lacking or increasing of eating and sleeping), and cognitive (i.e. learning and memory problems) [2]. When the brain detects stress, biochemical reactions will be secreted as a response to a stressor, which includes increasing of several hormones' levels such as adrenalin and cortisol. Consequently, stress influences the human daily activities such as managing life's matters, working and educational performance depending on the kind of potential threats (stressors) [3].

Chronic stress (or in other words) a life-time stress results from a social or environmental circumstances that directly affect the human life. Moreover, chronic stress is a cumulative threat experience and traumatic event that initiates from a specific sadness or bad situation such as social difficulties or family abuse; unfortunately, it is capable to hurt a hippocampus region on the brain [4]. This stressor could be a psychosocial stressor, psychological stressor, physical stressor, or natural stressor.

© Springer Nature Singapore Pte Ltd. 2017
M.S. Mohamed Ali et al. (Eds.): AsiaSim 2017, Part II, CCIS 752, pp. 447–455, 2017.
DOI: 10.1007/978-981-10-6502-6_39

Stress cognitively affects learning and memory processes by influencing the cognitive areas (i.e. amygdala, pre-frontal cortex and hippocampus in the brain) [5]. However, stress can influence short-term memory (STM) and long–term memory (LTM) and can also influence all memory stages: encoding, consolidation, and retrieval [6]. Furthermore, studying the effects of stress on learning and memory is a complex process, because it is dependent on many factors such as: age, gender, nature of stressor, stressor duration, stressor intensity, time and source of the stressor, individual differences, and learning type [7]. On the other hand; the effect of stress on memory may be varied during the learning or during the time of stressor (post-learning stress, pre-learning stress or pre-retrieval stress) [8] as shown in Fig. 1.

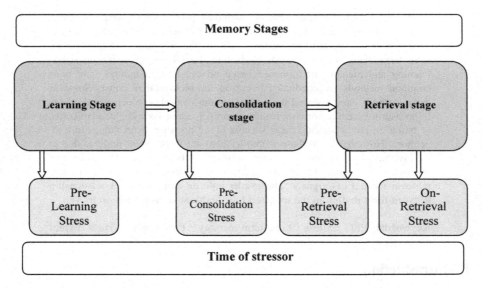

Fig. 1. The relationship between time of stressor and memory stages (stress may affect all memory stages).

However, stress enhances memory retrieval if it comes immediately or shortly follows learning because it is considered as a part of learning and memory context (stress itself will be considered as a learning experience). In contrast, stress impairs memory retrieval if it comes separately with the learning since it is considered to be outside the learning and memory context [9]. The effect of stress on long-term memory retrieval when stress comes before learning will be discussed in this research.

Recently, the electroencephalogram (EEG) has become a very important measure of brain activities and it has a vital potential to diagnose the mental disorders, abnormalities, and the state of the brain [10]. The desired features could be extracted from the signals which are recorded from the scalp of the brain. Nowadays, EEG has been used extensively to detect and study human stress [11, 12].

Before discussing stress and memory based on EEG, it's important to explore the literature from a psychological view. Recently, the impact of psychobiological response of stress on cognitive functions has been studied extensively [13–16], specifically the effect of stress on learning and memory areas in the brain, which includes Pre-frontal cortex (which has a crucial role in short–term memory) [17, 18], the hippocampus which is responsible for long- term declarative memory [19].

Many psychological and psychobiological researches have focused on studying the impact of different factors of stress on the learning and memory processes, which include, timing of stressor [20], intensity of stressor [21], source of stressor [22], gender [23], individual differences [24] and learning types [25].

In [26]; the authors have investigated that the stress and level of cortisol lead to enhance memory encoding and, on the other hand, impairs memory retrieval especially on a negative situation. In addition to cortisol and alpha- amylase; the authors in [27] have assessed the effect of stress on memory retrieval using sympathetic nervous system stress responses. Moreover, the memory retrieval is impaired after psychosocial stress [28].

As shown in the psychological and physical view; all studies have focused on assessing stress based on biological response and hormones analysis. Recently, there have been a few contributes of assessing stress using brain signals EEG.

Nowadays; there are some research conducted in this domain using different signal and image processing techniques such as FMRI, MRI, and EEG. In EEG technique; alpha, theta and gamma rhythms are analyzed and measured to extract the features, since these rhythms play an important role in human cognitive function. Theta rhythm is associated with memory and learning processes [29]. It is related to encoding and retrieval phases in working and episodic memory as well as in long-term memory. In [30], the authors found that theta power increases at parietal lobe during memory retrieval. In more details, in [31], the authors have argued that memory encoding is reflected with increasing in theta and gamma bands activities. Moreover, increasing of theta bands activity at right frontal lobe and increasing of gamma bands activity in parietal and occipital lobes influences memory encoding activity, whereas successful encoding is related to decreasing alpha band activity at pre-frontal and occipital lobes. In contrast, the increasing of alpha bands, theta band, and gamma band activity is related to long-term memory retrieval.

Nineteen (this number is calculated using sample size calculation formula) non-smoking, undergraduate university male students between 18 and 23 of age participated in the experiment. According to exclusion criteria; all subjects must be healthy and none of them has an illness history, acute disorders, chronic disorders, or took medication or drugs. All subjects will sign written informed consent.

The experiment conducted afternoon where the cortisol level was stable. As known, cortisol level is high in the morning and low at the night. The experiment consists of two sessions. The participants divided into 2 groups control group and pre-stressed group. For the control group; all subjects in this group learned some neutral content or list of neutral words without facing the stress. In the pre-stressed group, before the encoding phase in 5 min, the subjects were laid under stressor, after that, they are learned some neutral content or list of neutral words. After 2 months, the subjects in both groups asked verbally to free recall the neutral content that was learned previously in the encoding phase for 5 min. 128 channels EEG were used in both groups to record the EEG activities.

The main contribution of this paper is to discover the impact of pre-learning stress on long-term memory retrieval using EEG signals.

2 Methodology

Stress influences learning and all memory stages in the brain depending on the time of the stressor. Moreover, stress interferes with encoding stage, consolidation stage, and retrieval stage.

However, all the latest studies have investigated the relationships between biological factors with memory performance to determine the effect of stress. According to these studies, it's noticeable that there is an inconsistency in the results. This inconsistency comes from the instability of human hormones, since these hormones depend on different factors such as, time, gender, age, mood, health status, drugs, smoking and so forth. Importantly, all these factors play an important role of inconsistency in the findings. So,

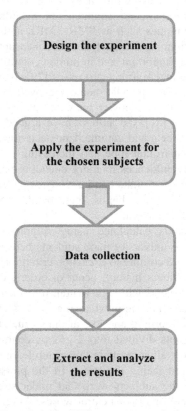

Fig. 2. Flow chart for EEG pre-stress analysis algorithm.

it's important and useful to study stress from different point of view and using different techniques. On the other hand, retrieval phase of long term memory is very important.

Impairment/enhancement of memory retrieval leads to impairment/enhancement human performance such as academic performance for students. The flowchart of this research study is shown in Fig. 2.

To extract the feature; firstly, the objective data is collected using 128 EEG channels system from all subjects in the pre-stressed group and control group. After that; the data is extracted and analyzed to discover the effect of pre-stress using EEGLab MATLAB toolbox.

3 Results and Discussion

The EEG data used in this study has been recorded from tee subjects using 128 EEG channels system after two months from the learning session in order to assess long-term memory retrieval. Firstly, the data has been filtered using a notch filter to remove AC power noise, and then passed through band pass filter with cut-off frequency 0.1– 30 Hz. As the EEG data is sensitive to other artifacts such as EOG and EMG, Independent component analysis (ICA) is applied to remove these artifacts.

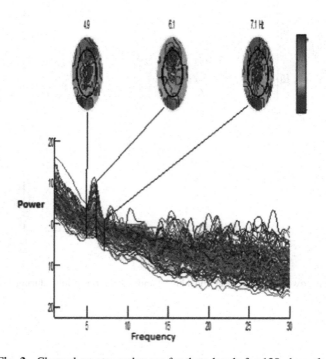

Fig. 3. Channel spectra and maps for theta bands for 128 channels.

EEGLab MATLAB toolbox for EEG processing is used to process the EEG data. Mean power spectrum for EEG bands theta (4–8 Hz) for 128 channels were extracted. The main power for theta rhythm is high as shown in Fig. 3.

For instance memory process involves temporal lobe interchangeably. Consequently, the changes in EEG rhythm (theta) temporal lobes were shown. In addition, paired sample t-test is used to investigate the significance of the difference in theta band during long-term memory retrieval and eyes open (EO, control) temporal lobes, as shown in Figs. 4 and 5.

Figure 4 shows that the Mean power of theta band in temporal lope is high compared with beta and alpha bands during LTM retrieval and compared also with EO as shown in Fig. 5.

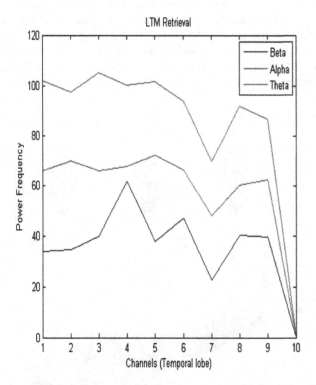

Fig. 4. Mean power of theta, beta and alpha bands at temporal lobe during LTM retrieval.

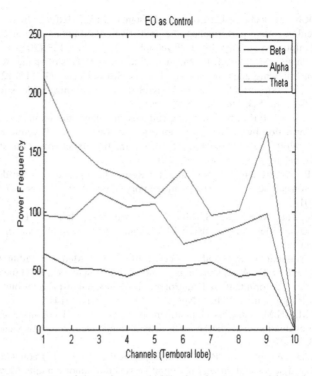

Fig. 5. Mean power of theta, beta and alpha bands at temporal lobe during EO.

4 Conclusion

It has been concluded that the theta (4–8 Hz) means power increased at temporal lobe during long term memory retrieval for the pre-stressed group. The results suggest that theta may consider as a long term memory retrieval performance index. Furthermore, statistically, paired sample t-test showed that the P value for theta band between LTM retrieval and EO at temporal lobe was equaled to 0.0439.

References

1. Raio, C.M., Phelps, E.A.: The influence of acute stress on the regulation of conditioned fear. Neurobiol. Stress **1**, 134–146 (2015)
2. Bob, P.: Stress, Conflict and the Brain. In: Bob, P. (ed.) The Brain and Conscious Unity. Freud's Omega, pp. 57–68. Springer, New York (2015). doi:10.1007/978-1-4939-2700-5_4
3. Lewis, R.S., Nikolova, A., Chang, D.J., Weekes, N.Y.: Examination stress and components of working memory. Stress **11**, 108–114 (2008)

4. Goodman, R.N., Rietschel, J.C., Lo, L.C., Costanzo, M.E., Hatfield, B.D.: Stress, emotion regulation and cognitive performance: the predictive contributions of trait and state relative frontal EEG alpha asymmetry. Int. J. Psychophysiol. **87**, 115–123 (2013)
5. Olver, J.S., Pinney, M., Maruff, P., Norman, T.R.: Impairments of spatial working memory and attention following acute psychosocial stress. Stress Health **31**, 115–123 (2015)
6. Joels, M., Pu, Z., Wiegert, O., Oitzl, M.S., Krugers, H.J.: Learning under stress: how does it work? Trends Cogn. Sci. **10**, 152–158 (2006)
7. Cadle, C.E., Zoladz, P.R.: Stress time-dependently influences the acquisition and retrieval of unrelated information by producing a memory of its own. Front. Psychol. **6**, 910 (2015)
8. Schwabe, L., Wolf, O.T., Oitzl, M.S.: Memory formation under stress: quantity and quality. Neurosci. Biobehav. Rev. **34**, 584–591 (2010)
9. Schonfeld, P., Ackermann, K., Schwabe, L.: Remembering under stress: different roles of autonomic arousal and glucocorticoids in memory retrieval. Psychoneuroendocrinology **39**, 249–256 (2014)
10. Sulaiman, N., Taib, M.N., Lias, S., Murat, Z.H., Aris, S.A., Hamid, N.H.A.: Novel methods for stress features identification using EEG signals. Int. J. Simul. Syst. Sci. Technol. **12**, 27–33 (2011)
11. Jena, S.K.: Examination stress and its effect on EEG. Int. J. Med. Sci. Public Health **4** (2015)
12. Putman, P., Verkuil, B., Arias-Garcia, E., Pantazi, I., van Schie, C.: EEG theta/beta ratio as a potential biomarker for attentional control and resilience against deleterious effects of stress on attention. Cogn. Affect. Behav. Neurosci. **14**, 782–791 (2014)
13. Van Hoef, M.E.H.M.: Successful treatment of stress-induced cognitive impairment with haloperidol; evaluation also warranted in hematopoietic stem cell transplantation. Hematol. Leukemia **3**, 1 (2015)
14. Aggarwal, N.T., Wilson, R.S., Beck, T.L., Rajan, K.B., Mendes de Leon, C.F., Evans, D.A., et al.: Perceived stress and change in cognitive function among adults 65 years and older. Psychosom. Med. **76**, 80–85 (2014)
15. Ozbeyli, D., Gokalp, A.G., Koral, T., Ocal, O.Y., Dogan, B., Akakin, D., et al.: Protective effect of exercise and sildenafil on acute stress and cognitive function. Physiol. Behav. **151**, 230–237 (2015)
16. Berg, R.J., Inaba, K., Sullivan, M., Okoye, O., Siboni, S., Minneti, M., et al.: The impact of heat stress on operative performance and cognitive function during simulated laparoscopic operative tasks. Surgery **157**, 87–95 (2015)
17. Muller, N.G., Knight, R.T.: The functional neuroanatomy of working memory: contributions of human brain lesion studies. Neuroscience **139**, 51–58 (2006)
18. Nebel, K., Wiese, H., Stude, P., de Greiff, A., Diener, H.C., Keidel, M.: On the neural basis of focused and divided attention. Cogn. Brain Res. **25**, 760–776 (2005)
19. Czeh, B., Varga, Z.K., Henningsen, K., Kovacs, G.L., Miseta, A., Wiborg, O.: Chronic stress reduces the number of GABAergic interneurons in the adult rat hippocampus, dorsal-ventral and region-specific differences. Hippocampus **25**, 393–405 (2015)
20. Pinnock, S.B., Herbert, J.: Corticosterone differentially modulates expression of corticotropin releasing factor and arginine vasopressin mRNA in the hypothalamic paraventricular nucleus following either acute or repeated restraint stress. Eur. J. Neurosci. **13** (2001)
21. Joels, M.: Corticosteroid effects in the brain: U-shape it. Trends Pharmacol. Sci. **27**, 244–250 (2006)
22. Luine, V.: Sex differences in chronic stress effects on memory in rats. Stress **5**, 205–216 (2002)
23. Davila, J., Cobb, R.J.: Predicting change in self-reported and interviewer-assessed adult attachment: tests of the individual difference and life stress models of attachment change. Personal. Soc. Psychol. Bull. **29**, 859–870 (2003)

24. Moscovitch, M., Nadel, L., Winocur, G., Gilboa, A., Rosenbaum, R.S.: The cognitive neuroscience of remote episodic, semantic and spatial memory. Curr. Opin. Neurobiol. **16**, 179–190 (2006)
25. Preuss, D., Wolf, O.T.: Post-learning psychosocial stress enhances consolidation of neutral stimuli. Neurobiol. Learn. Mem. **92**, 318–326 (2009)
26. Rimmele, U., Besedovsky, L., Lange, T., Born, J.: Emotional memory can be persistently weakened by suppressing cortisol during retrieval. Neurobiol. Learn. Mem. **119**, 102–107 (2015)
27. Buchanan, T.W., Tranel, D., Adolphs, R.: Impaired memory retrieval correlates with individual differences in cortisol response but not autonomic response. Learn. Mem. **13**, 382–387 (2006)
28. Kuhlmann, S., Piel, M., Wolf, O.T.: Impaired memory retrieval after psychosocial stress in healthy young men. J. Neurosci. **25**, 2977–2982 (2005)
29. Hsieh, L.-T., Ranganath, C.: Frontal midline theta oscillations during working memory maintenance and episodic encoding and retrieval. Neuroimage **85**, 721–729 (2014)
30. Jacobs, J., Hwang, G., Curran, T., Kahana, M.J.: EEG oscillations and recognition memory: theta correlates of memory retrieval and decision making. Neuroimage **32**, 978–987 (2006)
31. Friese, U., Köster, M., Hassler, U., Martens, U., Trujillo-Barreto, N., Gruber, T.: Successful memory encoding is associated with increased cross-frequency coupling between frontal theta and posterior gamma oscillations in human scalp-recorded EEG. Neuroimage **66**, 642–647 (2013)

Elucidation on the Effect of Operating Temperature to the Transport Properties of Polymeric Membrane Using Molecular Simulation Tool

Serene Sow Mun Lock[1], Kok Keong Lau[1(✉)],
Al-Ameerah Binti Mash'al[1], Azmi Muhammad Shariff[1],
Yin Fong Yeong[1], Irene Lock Sow Mei[2], and Faizan Ahmad[3]

[1] Department of Chemical Engineering, Research Center for CO2 Capture,
Universiti Teknologi PETRONAS, 32610 Seri Iskandar, Perak, Malaysia
serenelock168@gmail.com, alameerah.mashal@gmail.com,
{laukokkeong,azmish,yinfong.yeong}@utp.edu.my
[2] Process Department, Group Technical Solutions,
Project Delivery and Technology Division,
PETRONAS, Kuala Lumpur, Malaysia
irene.lock@petronas.com.my
[3] School of Science and Engineering, Teesside University, Middlesbrough, UK
f.ahmad@tees.ac.uk

Abstract. Existing reports of gas transport properties within polymeric membrane as a direct consequence of operating temperature are in a small number and have arrived in diverging conclusion. The scarcity has been associated to challenges in fabricating defect free membranes and empirical investigations of gas permeation performance at the laboratory scale that are often time consuming and costly. Molecular simulation has been proposed as a feasible alternative of experimentally studied materials to provide insights into gas transport characteristic. Hence, a sequence of molecular modelling procedures has been proposed to simulate polymeric membranes at varying operating temperatures in order to elucidate its effect to gas transport behaviour. The simulation model has been validated with experimental data through satisfactory agreement. Solubility has shown a decrement in value when increased in temperature (an average factor of 1.78), while the opposite has been observed for gas diffusivity (an average factor of 1.32) when the temperature is increased from 298.15 K to 323.15 K. In addition, it is found that permeability decreases by 1.36 times as the temperature is increased.

Keywords: Molecular simulation · Polymeric membranes · Transport properties · Operating temperatures

1 Introduction

Natural gas is defined as the gaseous fossil fuel that is rich with hydrocarbon occurring naturally underground as is utilized as fuels for petrochemical plants [1]. It is a source of energy for heating, cooking in homes, generating electricity and also vehicles' fuels

© Springer Nature Singapore Pte Ltd. 2017
M.S. Mohamed Ali et al. (Eds.): AsiaSim 2017, Part II, CCIS 752, pp. 456–471, 2017.
DOI: 10.1007/978-981-10-6502-6_40

[2]. Before supplying to users all over the world, the natural gas has to be treated by removing all unwanted residual gases, e.g. acid gases (CO_2), inert gases (N_2) and oxidizers (O_2), prior to entering the pipeline to obtain highly concentrated methane (CH_4) that constitutes to its actual heating value [3, 4]. Polymeric membranes play a pivotal role in gas separation applied in industrial application attributed to their various advantages, such as occupying a relatively smaller footprint, chemical free, cost effective, high process flexibility, simplicity and high energy efficiency [5]. In typical natural gas processing, the entering natural gas are in the range of 30 °C to 50 °C in order to suit the temperature for membrane separation [6].

A number of existing reports shows that a mere minor changes or fluctuations in operating temperature has affected the transport performance and selectivity of the membrane [7]. Although there have been a lot of studies related to membrane technology, the issue of temperature dependent phenomena onto membrane remains an unclear cut and unexplored. Majority of the experimental data have been confined to gas transport in polymer films at temperatures near 25 or 35 °C, which is devoted to measurement at ambient operating condition, attributed to challenges and cost to control the operating temperatures at different ranges [7].

Rising effort has emerged to elucidate the temperature dependent gas transport behavior of penetrants through membrane. Koros and Paul reported the CO_2 sorption in poly (ethylene terephthalate) (PET) from 25 to 115 °C, while fitting the values to dual mode sorption model [8]. The gas permeabilities and solubilities of five different gases are reported for bisphenol-A polycarbonate (PC), tetramethyl polycarbonate (TMPC), and tetramethyl hexafluoro polycarbonate (TMHFPC) at temperatures up to 200 °C [7]. Costello and Koros studied the same transport properties in meta/para-isomers of hexafluoroisopropylidene-containing polyimides at ambient and higher temperatures [9]. Merkel et al. studied the solubility and permeability of light gases, 2 hydrocarbons, and fluorocarbons in a glassy random copolymer of polytetrafluoroethylene and poly (2, 2-bis (trifluoromethyl)-4, 5-difluoro-1, 3-dioxole) (AF2400®) from 25 to 45 °C [10]. Gameda et al. elucidated the mixed gas sorption of CO_2/CH_4 in polymer of intrinsic microporosity (PIM-1) in between 25 and 50 °C [11]. Stevens et al. reported the decrement in gas solubilities with increment in temperature at varying thermally rearranged (TR) polymeric membranes [12].

Based on review of published literature, it is found that many transport property studies include only permeability measurements near ambient conditions. Complementary information on the individual contributions of the sorption and diffusion coefficients to the overall performance at non-ambient and elevated temperatures is rarely reported. The condition thereby limits the availability of data necessary to understand, at a fundamental level, membrane performance at temperatures away from ambient operating conditions. In addition, the systematic studies on temperature dependency of gas transport properties are often obscure, whereby the effect of temperature to different gas penetrants has arrived in contrary and diverging values. In this context, molecular simulation has been proposed as a feasible and complementary alternative of experimentally studied materials to provide insights into gas transport characteristic from an atomistic point of view, usually achieved via a coupling of molecular dynamics (MD) and Monte Carlo (MC) technique. In this context, adaptation of molecular simulation tool overcomes the barrier, cost and time in preparation and testing of gas permeation membrane at the laboratory scale since it appears to be relatively convenient to control operating conditions of the simulation [13].

Nevertheless, although molecular simulation work has been demonstrated to be rather successful to model transport properties in membrane, the study has been confined to sorption and trajectory of gas molecules at ambient operating temperature. The study on the impact of different operating temperature onto the efficiency of polymer membrane via MD simulation has received less scrutiny. Therefore, this work aims for assembling a sequence of molecular modeling procedure to simulate experimentally validated membrane structures at different operating temperatures. Subsequently, they can be employed to elucidate the effect of operating temperatures to transport properties of membrane structures, which encompass that of gas solubilities, diffusivities, and permeabilities.

2   Methodology

The methodology is subdivided into three subsections, whereby the first is molecular simulation to construct PSF polymeric membrane at various operating temperatures, the second is procedure for determination of glass transition temperature in the polymeric membranes, and the third is sequence for evaluation of varying transport properties of gas penetrants within the polymeric structures.

2.1   Atomistic Packing Models

This section commences the basis and methodology for simulation of glassy polymeric membrane at different operating temperatures. The simulations are performed using Materials Studio (MS) 8.0 software developed by Accelrys Software Inc. [14]. For this work, Polysulfone (PSF) is chosen due to its commercial use and also suitability for separation of gas mixtures [15]. The repeating unit of the PSF polymeric membrane is provided in Fig. 1.

Head ———▶   ◀——— Tail

Fig. 1. The chemical structure for polysulfone repeated single chain, purple: hydrogen, grey: carbon, yellow: sulphur, red: oxygen atom. (Color figure online)

The Condensed-phase Optimized Molecular Potentials for Atomistic Simulation Studies (COMPASS) force field has been adopted consistently. In addition, the Ewald method with an accuracy of 0.001 kcal/mol has been adopted to describe the electrostatic interactions, while the van der Waals interaction has been characterized via the Lennard-Jones-6-12 function with a cut-off-distance of ~ 11 Å (spline width of 1 Å and buffer width of 0.5 Å), whereby this value is selected since it is less than half of the expected cell length.

A single polymer chain with 20 repeat units is constructed. The initial polymeric chain has been located in the Forcite module of Materials Studio 8.0 and has been subjected to energy minimization and geometry optimization. The COMPASS force field has been adopted alongside the smart algorithm, which is a combination of the steepest descent; adjusted basis set Newton-Raphson (ABNR) and quasi-Newton algorithms in a cascading manner, in order to refine geometry of the initial polymeric chain. Later, the polymeric membrane chain has been folded into Amorphous Cell module adopting Construction task. The polymer chains have been embedded in the hypothetical cell under the periodic condition at initial density corresponding to 70% of the targeted experimental density (1.24 g/cm^3) [16]. Similarly, the COMPASS force field has been adopted to pack the polymeric chains.

Subsequently, the PSF structure has been treated adopting the molecular treatment procedure as highlighted in our previous work [17]. The NPT-NVT protocol has been repeated until changes in the successive density values are within predefined tolerance. Thereafter, in order to simulate the effect of operating temperatures to the molecular structure of PSF polymeric membrane, the procedures are repeated at temperature of 308.15 K, 313.15 K and 323.15 K instead of 298.15 K.

2.2 Glass Transition Temperature

In this study Tg s of PSF samples have been determined by mimicking the heating and cooling protocols in laboratory scale adapting a series of thermodynamic treatment in Forcite Module. Firstly, the optimized and equilibrated configuration has been subjected to an additional Canonical (NVT) ensemble at designated operating temperature with a time step of 1 fs and total simulation time of 10 ps by framing the output every 1000 steps. This procedure is aimed to obtain the trajectory files of PSF polymeric films with 10 frames for each operating temperature, such that an average Tg can be deduced to increase accuracy of the computed value when the series of thermodynamic treatment is iterated while calculating an independent Tg for each frame. Then, the individual frame located within the PSF trajectory has been exposed to gentle heating from 353.15 K to 553.15 K, which surpasses that of the bulk glass transition temperature of PSF polymer, with an interval of 1 K. Subsequently, a 100 ps NPT dynamic ensemble has been conducted at the designated heating temperature and operating pressure. Thereafter, the system is cooled down from 553.15 K to 353.15 K with the temperature interval of 1 K while computing density of the structure at each temperature. This protocol is looped over all frames contained in the trajectory file and eventually the values are averaged at the end.

2.3 Gas Transport Properties

In order to elucidate transport properties of penetrants within the simulated PSF polymer films, gas molecules of O_2, N_2, CH_4 and CO_2 have been generated. Analogously, they have been treated with energy minimization and geometry optimization prior to incorporation within the simulated polymeric matrix. Later, the transport properties of gases, which are of paramount interest to determine separation performance of polymeric membranes, comprising of diffusivity, solubility, and permeability characteristics have been studied. The procedure and underlying theory supporting the evaluation of transport behavior are elaborated in this subsection.

2.3.1 Gas Diffusivity

In current work, the diffusivity of gas penetrants has been determined adopting the means of molecular positioning theory, or more commonly known as the Einstein relationship [18–24]. In Einstein correlation, he related the self-diffusion coefficient of gas particles i, D_i to the mean square displacement (MSD) as a function of observation time, such as that presented in (1), through the assumption of particle random walk [25].

$$D_i = \frac{1}{6N} \lim_{t \to \infty} \frac{d}{dt} \sum_{t=1}^{N} \left\langle \left| r_i(t)^2 - r_i(0)^2 \right| \right\rangle \tag{1}$$

N is resemblance of the total number of diffusing atoms i within the hypothetical cell under consideration, r_i is the position vector of atom i, $\left| r_i(t)^2 - r_i(0)^2 \right|$ represents ensemble averages of the gas particles MSD, while $r_i(t)$ and $r_i(0)$ depicts the final and initial position vector of the centre of mass of gas molecule over the time span of interest, t. Based on (1), the gas diffusivity coefficient can be analysed from the slope of mean-squared displacement against simulation time, divided by 6.

Subsequently, in order to simulate diffusivities, 10 molecules of each gas species are incorporated within the optimized and equilibrated PSF films, as prepared in Sect. 2.1 of present study. 10 gas molecules have been simulated to collect sufficient trajectory in order to validate a reasonable and accurate pathway of penetrants within the polymeric matrix. Each of the gas molecules has been assigned with a centroid of centre of mass before being embedded inside the hypothetical cell of interest in order to track its respective pathway. Initially, the gas molecules together with the final optimized membrane structure have been subjected to an additional 1000 ps isothermal-isobaric ensemble (NPT) molecular dynamics run to obtain the equilibrated configuration of the gas/polymer system at 2 atm and designated operating temperatures. When approaching the end of dynamic run, an additional Canonical (NVT) simulation has been performed for 2 ns to elucidate the detailed trajectory of the gas molecules. A time step of 1 fs has been employed consistently throughout the simulation process to increase the frequency of consecutive motion of diffusing gas. Ultimately, the MSD computed as a function of time was analyzed using conventional and log–log plots.

2.3.2 Gas Solubility

Solubility of the mentioned gases dedicated to O_2, N_2, CO_2 and CH_4 in PSF polymeric films have been investigated employing the adsorption isotherm task located in Sorption module of Materials Studio 8.0. The embedded adsorption isotherm simulation allows end users to perform a series of grand canonical Monte Carlo ensemble (GCME), in which fugacities of all related components and temperature of the hypothetical system are remained constant. In this simulation work, the gas penetrants have been incorporated within the equilibrated cell adopting the Metropolis methodology since it has been demonstrated in previous published molecular simulation works to be an adequate characterization for system with relatively small sorbates as compared to pore size of the polymeric matrix and inherits low degree of torsion flexibility, which are highly applicable to gas molecules such as O_2, N_2, CO_2 and CH_4 [23, 26]. The GCME in sorption module has been executed for 100 fugacity steps between 0.00001 to 101.325 kPa in equidistant steps. At each pressure, 100000 steps of GCMC calculation are carried out with an initial equilibration period of 10000 steps.

Most simulation techniques are inclined towards determining the condition at infinite dilution and relating it to the solubility coefficient, such as that depicted in (2) [23, 27–29].

$$S_i = \lim_{f_i \to 0} \left(\frac{c_i}{f_i} \right) = k_{Di} + c'_{Hi} b_i \tag{2}$$

Hence, in this work, the solubility coefficient, S_i, has been found through slope of the straight line connecting a point on the solubility isotherm to the origin. In (2), C_i is the total concentration of gas in the polymer, b_i and C'_{Hi} is the Langmuir hole affinity parameter and the capacity parameter respectively, while f_i is fugacity.

2.3.3 Gas Permeability

Permeability is one of the gas transport properties behaviors, which is related to diffusivity and solubility. Permeability is obtained from the product of diffusion coefficient, D_i and solubility constant, S_i, as shown below in (3) [15, 30–32].

$$P_i = S_i D_i \tag{3}$$

3 Results and Discussion

In this section, the molecular simulation results related to PSF polymeric membranes at different operating temperatures have been presented, whereby it has been subdivided into two major subcategories, such as (1) molecular structure and physical property and (2) gas transport properties.

3.1 Molecular Structure and Physical Property

As described in Sect. 2.1, molecular dynamics simulation has been executed for all PSF polymeric films by keeping the operating parameters at the designated operating temperature condition, while the other configurations are constantly updated in quest of determining the most probable polymeric membrane film. Since the structure has been initialized from a lower targeted experimental density, without setting any confinements throughout the molecular dynamics treatment, the evolution of density towards a constant value provide phenomenological interpretation that the constructed molecular cells have converged to a metastable state. Example of the finalized and optimized PSF membrane, as well as progression of density during the MD process is provided in Fig. 2 (a) and (b) respectively.

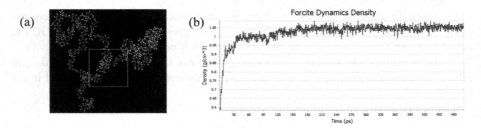

Fig. 2. The schematic diagram of (a) equilibrated and optimized PSF polymeric membrane cell and (b) alteration in molecular density.

In this work, the simulated densities at varying operating temperatures have been compared to the Tait equation [33] and Zoller's correlation [34, 35], such as that depicted in (4), which has been demonstrated to be particularly successful to provide a convenient mathematical characterization of pressure-volume-temperature (PVT) behavior for PSF membranes over a wide range of operating conditions.

$$V(P, T) = 0.8051 + 1.756$$
$$\times 10^{-4} T \left\{ 1 - 0.089 \ln \left[1 + \frac{P}{4408 \exp\left(-1.543 \times 10^{-3} T\right)} \right] \right\} \quad (4)$$

Whereby $V(P, T)$ represents the specific volume of the polymer at a particular temperature, T, and pressure, P, of interest.

Table 1 shows the comparison between densities by using Tait-Zoller's calculation and this work simulation calculation.

Table 1. Comparison of calculated density by using Tait-Zoller formula and simulation.

Temperature (K)	Density (g/cm³) [Experimental correlation]	Density (g/cm³) [This work]	Percentage error (%)
298.15	1.235	1.220	1.21
308.15	1.233	1.211	1.78
313.15	1.231	1.205	2.11
323.15	1.229	1.198	2.52

From the comparison of density between the experimental values, formula calculation and simulated values, it is observed that the deviations are consistently less than 3%. Tentatively, it is found that the molecular simulation tool is of sufficient capability to capture the trend characterizing effect of operating temperature to the density of molecular structure, such that the density decreases with increment in temperature. The observation can be rationalized through expansion of the simulation cell when operating temperature is raised attributed to higher activation energy for relaxation [34, 35]. Deviation between simulated and experimentally observed PSF density can be explained through the assumption in molecular simulation, whence cut off distance has been applied that deemed long range molecular interaction to be negligible.

In this study, the optimized configuration of the built PSF was heated from temperature of 353.15 K to 553.15 K to obtain the glass transition temperature, whereby the trend of density versus temperature has been plotted in Fig. 3.

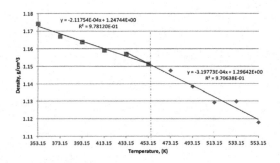

Fig. 3. Graph of density against temperature to obtain glass transition temperature.

As it can be seen from Fig. 3, initially the density decreases linearly with increment in temperature, and then shows an abrupt alteration in the value before continuing to embark in another linear region. Change in linear relationship is demonstrated through the difference in slope between the two curves, whereby the first at lower temperature is representative of the glassy state region, while the latter describes the rubbery state. The point at which the glassy and rubbery linear correlation meets to form an intercept provides graphical representation of Tg The intersected point at 454.94 K is Tg obtained from current simulated work. When comparing the obtained T_g through this simulation, to literature record of 460.15 K [23], the error is at -1.13%. Thus, it can be said that the proposed methodology is reliable to obtain molecule structures of high accuracy, before applying in subsequent section to study the gas transport properties at varying operating temperatures.

3.2 Gas Transport Properties

In this section, the results pertaining to molecular simulation of PSF polymeric membranes at different operating temperature is presented from the aspect of transport behaviour evolution associated to the temperature, followed by integration of existing correlations to quantify the effect.

3.2.1 Gas Diffusivities

The example of mean square displacements (MSDs) for gas penetrants, O_2, N_2, CO_2 and CH_4 within PSF polymeric matrix at 308.15 K are summarized in Fig. 4. The mean square displacement is found to increase in a relatively linear manner with time, suggesting that the collected data are of sufficient reliability to constitute the diffusivity data, which would be determined from slope of the graph.

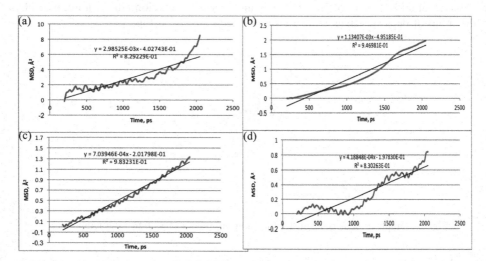

Fig. 4. Graph of mean squared displacement (MSD) against time at 308.15 K for (a) O_2 (b) N_2 (c) CO_2 and (d) CH_4.

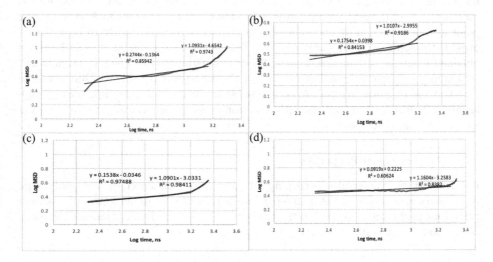

Fig. 5. Graph of logarithmic MSD against time for (a) O_2 (b) N_2 (c) CO_2 and (d) CH_4.

In order to demonstrate that the selected time regime is of sufficient accuracy to characterize the consecutive motion of gas molecules, the logarithmic plot of MSD versus time has been provided in Fig. 5.

When approaching approximately 1500 ps (Log time $\approx$ 3.2), an apparent change in slope of the curve has been observed for all gas penetrants and approaching unity at the end of the simulation (e.g. 1.0931 from 0.2744 for O_2; 1.0107 from 0.1754 for N_2; 1.0901 from 0.1538 for CO_2 and 1.1604 from 0.09199 for CH_4). Similar observation has been reported in previous simulation work by Cuthbert *et al.* who observed a slope of 1 when the gas penetrants reached the diffusive regime [36]. Therefore, it is concluded that the allocated simulation time of 2000 ps is appropriate and sufficiently long to capture the diffusive behavior of all gas penetrants in the studied membranes.

The computed diffusivity data at varying operating temperatures for the gas penetrants are tabulated in Table 2.

Table 2. Simulated diffusivity for O_2, N_2, CO_2 and CH_4 at 298.15 K, 308.15 K, 313.15 K and 323.15 K.

Temperature (K)	Diffusivity ($\times 10^{-8}$ cm^2/s)			
	O_2	N_2	CO_2	CH_4
298.15	4.064	1.542	1.013	0.541
308.15	4.590 (4.2)[a]	1.741 (1.2)[a]	1.112 (1.19)[a]	0.616 (0.27)[a]
313.15	4.975	1.890	1.173	0.698
323.15	5.319	2.039	1.218	0.775

[a]The number in bracket is the experimental value by Ahn *et al.* [16]

Accuracy of the simulated diffusivity data has been verified through comparison between simulation and experimental measured results by Ahn *et al.* [16] at 308.15 K, whereby a small deviation between the two conditions has been observed consistently for all gas penetrants. As it can be seen in Table 2, as the temperature increases, the diffusion coefficient is also increasing. The contributing factor is free volume within the structure of the polymer has increased as the temperature is further increased [37]. Once the free volume of a polymer increases, it allows higher diffusivity of bigger molecules to have a bigger energy to pass through.

It is found that slope of the linear correlation and subsequently diffusion coefficients are similarly in the order of $O_2 > N_2 > CO_2 > CH_4$. Such results have been rationalized through the ability of gas molecules to enhance their energy through collision with membrane polymeric chains to jump to neighboring pathway with an appropriate size in order to accommodate their new trajectory. The findings are consistent with various published reports on the diffusivity of gas molecules through polysulfone membranes [16, 38–40]. It has been reported that oxygen is the species that gain most energy and have the energy to execute longest diffusional jump among all penetrants [23].

The impact of operating temperature to gas diffusivity has been quantified through an Arrhenius correlation, as shown in (5), whereby a good fit has been obtained with sufficiently good R^2 for all gas penetrants.

$$D_i = D_{0,i} e^{-\frac{E_{d,i}}{RT}} \tag{5}$$

In (5), $E_{d,i}$ is the diffusion activation energy, $D_{0,i}$ is the temperature independent pre-exponential factor and R is the universal gas constant. The plot of diffusivity as a function of Arrhenius relationship has been provided in Fig. 6.

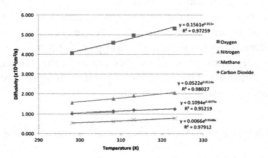

Fig. 6. Graph of diffusivity against temperature for O_2, N_2, CO_2, and CH_4 as an exponential function characterizing the Arrhenius correlation (Expression 5).

3.2.2 Gas Solubilities

The solubility coefficients can be determined from slope of the concentration curve versus pressure when approaching the zero pressure limits. The example at temperature of 308.15 K for all gas molecules has been provided in Fig. 7, while all the simulated data at varying operating temperatures are summarized in Table 3.

It can be seen that the solubility decreases with increment in temperature attributed to the nature of gas molecules to sustain in its gas state rather than being sorbed within

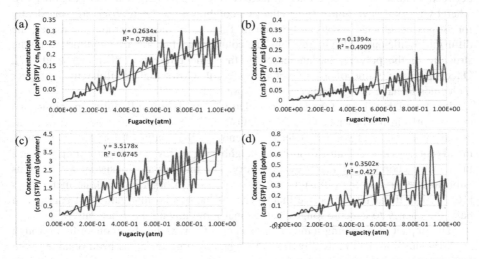

Fig. 7. Graph of concentration against fugacity at 308.15 K for (a) O_2 (b) N_2 (c) CO_2 and (d) CH_4.

Table 3. Simulated solubility for O_2, N_2, CO_2 and CH_4 at 298.15 K, 308.15 K, 313.15 K and 323.15 K.

Temperature (K)	Solubility (cm^3 (STP)/cm^3 atm)			
	O_2	N_2	CO_2	CH_4
298.15	0.313	0.177	3.951	0.403
308.15	0.263 (0.25)[a]	0.139 (0.15)[a]	3.518 (4.02)[a]	0.350 (0.27)[a]
313.15	0.239	0.130	2.996	0.281
323.15	0.185	0.099	2.339	0.204

[a]The number in bracket is the experimental value by Ahn *et al.* [16]

the polymeric matrix at higher operating temperature. In a similar manner, the simulated solubility values are found to demonstrate good accordance with experimentally reported data by Ahn *et al.* [16].

The solubility coefficients, are in the order of $CO_2 > CH_4 > O_2 > N_2$. Similarly, the trend in gas solubilities in PSF membranes is in good conformity with previous published literatures [16, 38–40]. The good accordance is found to be related to the critical temperature of the gas penetrants, whereby CO_2 with a critical temperature of 304.15 K is highly condensable within the polymeric matrix in comparison to CH_4 (190.56 K), followed by oxygen (154.55 K) and subsequently nitrogen (126.2 K) [41, 42]. Solubility always favors those of higher critical temperature since it indicates ease of gas penetrants to liquefy within the polymer.

In addition, solubility is reported to tally with the Arrhenius calculation with respect to operating temperature based on previous published literatures [12, 23], such as that demonstrated (6).

$$S_i = S_{0,i}e^{-\frac{\Delta H_{S,i}}{RT}} \tag{6}$$

In which $S_{0,i}$ and $H_{S,i}$ characterize the temperature independent pre-exponential constant and enthalpy of dissolution respectively. The characterization of gas solubility based on expression (6) is provided in Fig. 8.

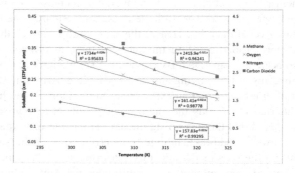

Fig. 8. Graph of solubility against temperature for O_2, N_2, CO_2, and CH_4 as an exponential function characterizing the Arrhenius correlation (Expression 6).

3.2.3   Gas Permeabilities

The gas permeabilities as a product of diffusivities and solubilities have been calculated and provided in Table 4, while validated with published experimental results by Ahn *et al.* [16].

Table 4. Simulated permeability for O_2, N_2, CO_2 and CH_4 at 298.15 K, 308.15 K, 313.15 K and 323.15 K.

Temperature (K)	Permeability (Barrer, $\times$ 10^{-10} cm^3/cm^{2}s.cmHg)			
	O_2	N_2	CO_2	CH_4
298.15	1.271	0.273	4.002	0.218
308.15	1.209 (1.4)[a]	0.243 (0.24)[a]	3.912 (6.3)[a]	0.216 (0.22)[a]
313.15	1.190	0.246	3.515	0.196
323.15	0.986	0.202	2.849	0.158

[a]The number in bracket is the experimental value by Ahn *et al.* [16]

Theoretically, it is found that gas permeability decreases with temperature, which has been rationalized through the rapid decrement in gas solubility as reported in previous section that surpasses the effect of increment in diffusivity. Similar behavior has been observed in previous published work [43].

4   Conclusion

This simulation work has shown how affected the membrane polymer are as the operating temperature varies from one to another. It is observable from the modeling structure that the configurations are rather affected. Thus, the first objective of this work, which is the assembling of a sequence of molecular modeling procedure to simulate experimentally validated membrane structures at different operating temperatures, has been successfully achieved. Other than that, it can be concluded that the transport properties are hugely affected by the changing in operating temperature. The diffusivity has shown a positive change in increased temperatures but solubility has shown a decrement in its coefficient as the temperature increases. Permeability is also affected by this whereby it decreases as the temperature increases due to the solubility gaining dominance over diffusivity. Hence, the second objective of this work of elucidating the transport properties of membrane structures at different operating temperatures has also been accomplished. By conducting simulation onto this case study, it has contributed in terms of time saving and cost saving in determining the effects rather than having a lot of time to conduct an experiment. Simulation studies has proven to be another reliable alternative to study the microscopic details of a polymer and its effects as it has been compared that there is no significant variance to the experimental values from literature records. In addition, individual contributions of the sorption and diffusion coefficients to the overall permeability performance at varying operating conditions can be obtained conveniently since it provides phenomenological information towards the correlation between membrane morphology and gas transport properties.

Therefore, it is hopeful to apply this methodology in further studies so that temperature dependent gas transport properties can be further elucidated and quantified to assist in design of separative performance within existing and next-generation polymeric membranes.

Acknowledgement. This work is done with the financial support from Universiti Teknologi PETRONAS.

References

1. Solarin, S.A., Shahbaz, M.: Natural gas consumption and economic growth: the role of foreign direct investment, capital formation and trade openness in Malaysia. Renew. Sustain. Energy Rev. **42**, 835–845 (2015)
2. Liang, F.Y., Ryvak, M., Sayeed, S., Zhao, N.: The role of natural gas as a primary fuel in the near future, including comparisons of acquisition, transmission and waste handling costs of as with competitive alternatives. Chem. Cent. J. **6**, 1–24 (2012)
3. Baker, R.W., Lokhandwala, K.: Natural gas processing with membranes: an overview. Ind. Eng. Chem. Res. **47**, 2109–2121 (2008)
4. U.G. Limited: Chemical Composition of Natural Gas (2017)
5. Lock, S.S.M., Lau, K.K., Ahmad, F., Shariff, A.M.: Modeling, simulation and economic analysis of CO2 capture from natural gas using cocurrent, countercurrent and radial crossflow hollow fiber membrane. Int. J. Greenh. Gas Control **36**, 114–134 (2015)
6. Safari, M., Ghanizadeh, A., Montazer-Rahmati, M.M.: Optimization of membrane-based CO2-removal from natural gas using simple models considering both pressure and temperature effects. Int. J. Greenh. Gas Control **3**, 3–10 (2009)
7. Costello, L.M., Koros, W.J.: Temperature dependence of gas sorption and transport properties in polymers: measurement and applications. Ind. Eng. Chem. Res. **31**, 2708–2714 (1992)
8. Koros, W.J., Paul, D.R.: CO2 sorption in poly(ethylene terephthalate) above and below the glass transition. J. Polym. Sci., Part B: Polym. Phys. **16**, 1947–1963 (1978)
9. Costello, L.M., Koros, W.J.: Thermally stable polyimide isomers for membrane-based gas separations at elevated temperatures. J. Polym. Sci., Part B: Polym. Phys. **33**, 135–146 (1995)
10. Merkel, T.C., He, Z., Pinnau, I., Freeman, B.D., Meakin, P., Hill, A.J.: Sorption and transport in Poly(2,2-bis(trifluoromethyl)-4,5-difluoro-1,3-dioxole-co-tetrafluoroethylene) containing nanoscale fumed silica. Macromolecules **36**, 8406–8414 (2003)
11. Gemeda, A.E., De Angelis, M.G., Du, N., Li, N., Guiver, M.D., Sarti, G.C.: Mixed gas sorption in glassy polymeric membranes. III. CO2/CH4 mixtures in a polymer of intrinsic microporosity (PIM-1): effect of temperature. J. Membr. Sci. **524**, 746–757 (2017)
12. Stevens, K.A., Smith, Z.P., Gleason, K.L., Galizia, M., Paul, D.R., Freeman, B.D.: Influence of temperature on gas solubility in thermally rearranged (TR) polymers. J. Membr. Sci. **533**, 75–83 (2017)
13. Barnard, A., Li, C.M., Zhou, R., Zhao, Y.: Modelling of the nanoscale. Nanoscale **4**, 1042–1043 (2012)
14. Accelrys Software Inc. (2015)
15. Freeman, B.D., Pinnau, I.: Polymeric materials for gas separations. In: Polymer Membranes for Gas and Vapor Separation, pp. 1–27. American Chemical Society (1999)

16. Ahn, J., Chung, W.-J., Pinnau, I., Guiver, M.D.: Polysulfone/silica nanoparticle mixed-matrix membranes for gas separation. J. Membr. Sci. **314**, 123–133 (2008)
17. Lock, S.S.M., Lau, K.K., Mei, I.L.S., Shariff, A.M., Yeong, Y.F.: Cavity energetic sizing algorithm applied in polymeric membranes for gas separation. Proc. Eng. **148**, 855–861 (2016)
18. Hu, N., Fried, J.R.: The atomistic simulation of the gas permeability of poly(organophosphazenes). Part 2. Poly[bis(2,2,2-trifluoroethoxy)phosphazene]. Polymer **46**, 4330–4343 (2005)
19. Liu, Q.L., Huang, Y.: Transport behavior of oxygen and nitrogen through organasilicon-containing polystyrenes by molecular simulation. J. Phys. Chem. B **110**, 17375–17382 (2006)
20. Wang, X.-Y., Raharjo, R.D., Lee, H.J., Lu, Y., Freeman, B.D., Sanchez, I.C.: Molecular simulation and experimental study of substituted polyacetylenes: fractional free volume, cavity size distributions and diffusion coefficients. J. Phys. Chem. B **110**, 12666–12672 (2006)
21. Follain, N., Valleton, J.-M., Lebrun, L., Alexandre, B., Schaetzel, P., Metayer, M., Marais, S.: Simulation of kinetic curves in mass transfer phenomena for a concentration-dependent diffusion coefficient in polymer membranes. J. Membr. Sci. **349**, 195–207 (2010)
22. Hertäg, L., Bux, H., Caro, J., Chmelik, C., Remsungnen, T., Knauth, M., Fritzsche, S.: Diffusion of CH4 and H2 in ZIF-8. J. Membr. Sci. **377**, 36–41 (2011)
23. Golzar, K., Amjad-Iranagh, S., Amani, M., Modarress, H.: Molecular simulation study of penetrant gas transport properties into the pure and nano sized silica particles filled polysulfone membranes. J. Membr. Sci. **451**, 117–134 (2014)
24. Budhathoki, S., Shah, J.K., Maginn, E.J.: Molecular simulation study of the solubility, diffusivity and permselectivity of pure and binary mixtures of CO2 and CH4 in the ionic liquid 1-n-Butyl-3-methylimidazolium bis(trifluoromethylsulfonyl)imide. Ind. Eng. Chem. Res. **54**, 8821–8828 (2015)
25. Nagar, H., Vadthya, P., Prasad, N., Sridhar, S.: Air separation by facilitated transport of oxygen through a Pebax membrane incorporated with a cobalt complex. RSC Adv. **5**, 76190–76201 (2015)
26. Siepmann, J.I., Frenkel, D.: Configurational bias Monte Carlo: a new sampling scheme for flexible chains. Mol. Phys. **75**, 59–70 (1992)
27. Anderson, K.E., Siepmann, J.I.: Molecular simulation approaches to solubility. In: Letcher, T.M. (ed.) Developments and Applications in Solubility, pp. 171–177. R. Soc. Chem., Cambridge (2007)
28. Jiang, Y., Willmore, F.T., Sanders, D., Smith, Z.P., Ribeiro, C.P., Doherty, C.M., Thorton, A., Hill, A.J., Freeman, B.D., Sanchez, I.C.: Cavity size, sorption and transport characteristics of thermally rearranged polymers. Polym. **52**, 2244–2254 (2011)
29. De Angelis, M.G.: Solubility coefficient (S). In: Drioli, E., Giorno, L. (eds.) Encyclopedia of Membranes, pp. 1–5. Springer, Berlin (2015). doi:10.1007/978-3-642-40872-4_631-1
30. Alexander, S.S.: Polymers for gas separations: the next decade. J. Membr. Sci. **94**, 1–65 (1994)
31. Ghosal, K., Freeman, B.D.: Gas separation using polymer membranes: an overview. Polym. Adv. Technol. **5**, 673–697 (1994)
32. Freeman, B.D., Pinnau, I.: Polymer Membranes for Gas and Vapor Separation. American Chemical Society, Washington, D.C. (1999)
33. Tait, P.G.: Report on some of the physical properties of fresh water and sea, Report on the scientific results of the voyage of the H.M.S. Challenger during the years 1873–1876. Phys. Chem. **2**, 1–76 (1988)

34. Zoller, P.: Specific volume of polysulfone as a function of temperature and pressure. J. Polym. Sci., Part B: Polym. Phys. **16**, 1261–1275 (1978)
35. Zoller, P.: A study of the pressure-volume-temperature relationships of four related amorphous polymers: polycarbonate, polyarylate, phenoxy, and polysulfone. J. Polym. Sci., Part B: Polym. Phys. **20**, 1453–1464 (1982)
36. Cuthbert, T.R., Wagner, N.J., Paulaitis, M.E., Murgia, G., D'Aguanno, B.: Molecular dynamics simulation of penetrant diffusion in amorphous polypropylene: diffusion mechanisms and simulation size effects. Macromolecules **32**, 5017–5028 (1999)
37. Robeson, L.M.: Polymer membranes for gas separation. Curr. Opin. Solid State Mater. Sci. **4**, 549–552 (1999)
38. McHattie, J.S., Koros, W.J., Paul, D.R.: Gas transport properties of polysulphones: 1. role of symmetry of methyl group placement on bisphenol rings. Polymer **32**, 840–850 (1991)
39. Aitken, C.L., Koros, W.J., Paul, D.R.: Effect of structural symmetry on gas transport properties of polysulfones. Macromolecules **25**, 3424–3434 (1992)
40. Ghosal, K., Chern, R.T., Freeman, B.D., Daly, W.H., Negulescu, I.I.: Effect of basic substituents on gas sorption and permeation in polysulfone. Macromolecules **29**, 4360–4369 (1996)
41. Timmerhaus, K.D.: Advances in Cryogenic Engineering. Springer, US (1995). doi:10.1007/978-1-4613-9847-9
42. de Oliveira, M.J.: Equilibrium Thermodynamics. Springer, Heidelberg (2013). doi:10.1007/978-3-642-36549-2
43. Ohlrogge, K., Stürken, K.: Membranes: separation of organic vapors from gas streams. In: Ullmann's Encyclopedia of Industrial Chemistry. Wiley-VCH Verlag GmbH & Co. KGaA (2000)

The Effect of Matrix C in Sliding Mode Control with Composite Nonlinear Feedback Control Strategy in MacPherson Active Suspension System

Muhamad Fahezal Ismail[1](✉), Yahaya Md. Sam[2], Shahdan Sudin[2], Kemao Peng[3], and Muhamad Khairi Aripin[4]

[1] Industrial Automation Section, Universiti Kuala Lumpur Malaysia France Institute, Section 14 Jalan Teras Jernang, 43650 Bandar Baru Bangi, Selangor, Malaysia
fahezal@unikl.edu.my
[2] Faculty of Electrical Engineering, Universiti Teknologi Malaysia (UTM), 81310 Skudai, Johor, Malaysia
{yahaya, shahdan}@fke.utm.my
[3] Temasek Laboratories, National University of Singapore, 5A, Engineering Drive 1, Singapore 117411, Singapore
kmpeng@nus.edu.sg
[4] Faculty of Electrical Engineering, Universiti Teknikal Malaysia Melaka, Hang Tuah Jaya, 76100 Durian Tunggal, Melaka, Malaysia
khairiaripin@utem.edu.my

Abstract. The C matrix in Sliding Mode Control (SMC) is significant to the control performance in MacPherson active suspension system. The SMC was combined with Composite Nonlinear Feedback (CNF) controller due to its characteristics on the transient response and fast settling time. The Neural Network is used to determine the matrix of C based on the road profiles used in this research work. The Proportional Integral (PI) was combined with SMC to overcome the uncertainties, unmatched condition and steady state error occurred in the MacPherson active suspension system. The three road profiles have been applied to this research work. The multi-body dynamics system software called CarSim is used for validation. The numerical experiment results are shown the effect of the C matrix in SMC with CNF controller performance in acceleration of sprung mass.

Keywords: Transient response · Sliding mode control · Composite nonlinear feedback · Uncertainties · Unmatched condition · Steady state error

1 Introduction

A MacPherson active suspension system is the common suspension design in the modern automotive suspension system. Hong *et al.* [1] has formulated the mathematical modeling for MacPherson active suspension system based Lagrange equation. Fallah *et al.* [2] studied on the variation of control arm subject to active and semi active

© Springer Nature Singapore Pte Ltd. 2017
M.S. Mohamed Ali et al. (Eds.): AsiaSim 2017, Part II, CCIS 752, pp. 472–484, 2017.
DOI: 10.1007/978-981-10-6502-6_41

forces in the kinematic parameter behaviour; however the analysis did not focus on the control strategy performance and discuss self-steer.

In active suspension system, the nonlinear control plays an important role to achieve a good ride quality and handling quality. Alleyene and Hedrick [3] proposed a nonlinear adaptive control applied to an electro-hydraulic active suspension system. The authors used a nonlinear quarter car model for validation purposes. The authors claimed that the system under the nonlinear sliding controller performed better than the passive system when the road input frequency was near the body mode of the vehicle. However, the proposed controller can be used to test more than one road profile to observe the robustness control performance. Hsiao *et al.* [4] proposed Sliding Mode Control (SMC) with filtered feedback scheme for improving a ride comfort and road handling. The Kalman filter is designed to estimate the state responses as required for active force calculation. The authors claimed that the proposed controller improved the ride quality and handling quality. Ashari [5] proposed SMC with a unit vector approach for an active suspension system. The robust eigenstructure assignment technique is implemented in the sliding surface design. The authors claimed that the proposed controller gives a good robustness of the SMC. The results on the vertical sprung mass give a better control performance for the half-car model. However, the authors did not make any comparison with the passive system and others control strategies.

Composite Nonlinear Feedback (CNF) tracking control law based on a nominal linear controller has been proposed by Lin *et al.* [6, 7]. The design is based on nonlinear feedback laws that capable to increase the speed of the closed-loop system response to the command input and reduce the overshoot simultaneously. Guowei *et al.* [8] investigated the Composite Nonlinear Feedback (CNF) control technique for linear singular systems with input saturation. A linear feedback gain is designed to make the closed-loop system stable and impulse free. Guowei *et al.* [8] discussed on the modeling and flight control system design for the yaw channel of an unmanned aerial-vehicle (UAV) helicopter using CNF control technique. The authors claim that the CNF is utilized to design an efficient control law and given excellent overall control performance. Cheng *et al.* [9] developed Composite Nonlinear Feedback (CNF) control method to track general target references for systems with input saturation. The simulation and experimental results on an XY-table showed that the proposed technique gives a very satisfactory performance. Cheng *et al.* [10] discussed on the Matlab toolkit with a user friendly graphical interface for Composite Nonlinear Feedback control system design. The CNF toolkit is used for general SISO systems with actuator and other nonlinearities, external disturbances, and high-frequency resonance.

This paper presents the effect of Matrix C of PISMC-CNF in a MacPherson active suspension system based on three different road profiles. The significant of this testing is to evaluate the control performance based on the sets of Matrix C in the system.

This paper is organized as follows: Sect. 2: mathematical modeling of a nonlinear quarter car active suspension system, Sect. 3 – the controller design PISMC-CNF based on a MacPherson active suspensions and determination of Matrix C using Neural Network, Sect. 4: results and analysis based on the performance comparison between sets of Matrix C applied to a MacPherson active suspension system, and conclusions will be drawn in Sect. 5.

2 Mathematical Modelling

The quarter car model for MacPherson active suspension system also used the Lagrange equation of the motion method. The free body diagram as a MacPherson strut model is shown in Fig. 1. As shown in Fig. 1, let (Y_A, Z_A), (Y_B, Z_B), and (Y_C, Z_C) denote the coordinates of point A, B and C, respectively, when the suspension system is at an equilibrium point. Then, the equation become;

$$Y_A = 0 \tag{1}$$

$$Z_A = Z_s \tag{2}$$

$$Y_B = l_B(\cos(\theta - \theta_0) - \cos(-\theta_0)) \tag{3}$$

$$Y_B = Z_s + l_B(\sin(\theta - \theta_0) - \sin(-\theta_0)) \tag{4}$$

$$Y_C = l_C(\cos(\theta - \theta_0) - \cos(-\theta_0)) \tag{5}$$

$$Y_C = Z_s + l_C(\sin(\theta - \theta_0) - \sin(-\theta_0)) \tag{6}$$

where θ_0 is the initial angular displacement of the control arm at an equilibrium point.

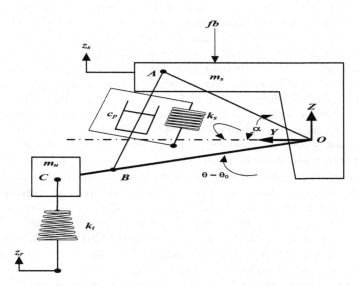

Fig. 1. A free body diagram of a quarter car model of the MacPherson passive suspension system in Hong *et al.* [1].

Let $\alpha' = \alpha + \theta_0$. Then, the following relations are obtained from the triangle OAB.

$$l = \left(l_A^2 + l_B^2 - 2l_A l_B \cos \alpha'\right)^{1/2} \tag{7}$$

$$l' = \left(l_A^2 + l_B^2 - 2l_A l_B \cos \alpha' - \theta\right)^{1/2} \tag{8}$$

where l is the initial distance from A to B at an equilibrium state, and l' is the changed distance from A to B with the rotation of the control arm by θ. Therefore, the deflection of the spring, relative velocity of the damper and deflection of the tyre are, respectively

$$(\Delta l)^2 = (l - l')^2 = 2a_l - b_l(\cos \alpha' + \cos(\alpha' - \theta))$$
$$- 2\{a_l^2 - a_l b_l(\cos \alpha' + \cos(\alpha' - \theta) + b_l^2 \cos \alpha' \cos(\alpha' - \theta))\}^{\frac{1}{2}} \tag{9}$$

$$\Delta \dot{l} = \dot{l} - \dot{l'} = \frac{b_l \sin(\alpha' - \theta)\dot{\theta}}{2(a_l - b_l \cos(\alpha' - \theta))^{1/2}} \tag{10}$$

$$Z_C - Z_r = l_C(\sin(\theta - \theta_0) - \sin(-\theta_0)) - Z_r \tag{11}$$

where $a_l = l_A^2 + l_B^2$ $b_l = 2l_A l_B$.

The equations of motion of the new model are now derived by the Lagrangian mechanics. Let T, V, and D denote the kinetic, potential and the damping energies of the system, respectively. Then the equations are:

$$T = \frac{1}{2}m_s \dot{Z}_s^2 + \frac{1}{2}m_u \left(\dot{Y}_C^2 + \dot{Z}_C^2\right) \tag{12}$$

$$V = \frac{1}{2}k_s(\Delta l)^2 + \frac{1}{2}k_t(Z_C - Z_r)^2 \tag{13}$$

$$D = \frac{1}{2}c_p\left(\Delta \dot{l}\right)^2 \tag{14}$$

Substituting the derivatives of Eqs. (5), (6), (9), (10), and (11) into Eqs. (12), (13) and (14) yields

$$T = \frac{1}{2}(m_s + m_u)\dot{Z}_s^2 + \frac{1}{2}m_u l_C^2 \dot{\theta}^2 + m_u l_C \cos \theta \dot{\theta} \dot{Z}_s \tag{15}$$

$$V = \frac{1}{2}k_s[2a_l - b_l(\cos \alpha' + \cos(\alpha' - \theta))$$
$$- 2\{a_l^2 - a_l b_l(\cos \alpha' + \cos(\alpha' - \theta) + b_l^2 \cos \alpha' \cos(\alpha' - \theta))\}^{\frac{1}{2}}]^2$$
$$+ \frac{1}{2}k_t[Z_s + l_C(\sin(\theta - \theta_0) - \sin(-\theta_0)) - Z_r]^2 \tag{16}$$

$$D = \frac{c_p b_l^2 sin^2(\alpha' - \theta)\dot{\theta}}{8(a_l - b_l \cos(\alpha' - \theta))} \qquad (17)$$

Finally, for the two generalized coordinates, $q_1 = Z_s$ and $q_2 = \theta$ the motion equation for a quarter car model of the MacPherson passive suspension system in Fig. 2 can be represented as follows, Hong *et al.* [1]:

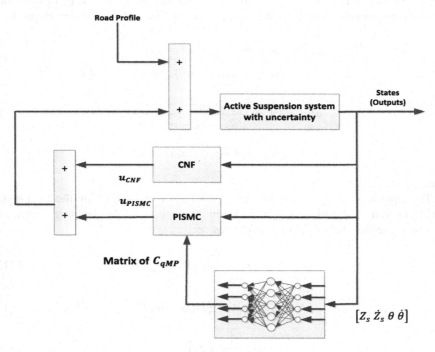

Fig. 2. A block diagram of MacPherson active suspension system using Neural Network to determine the matrix of C_{qMP}.

The first Lagrange equation of motion yields

$$(m_s + m_u)\ddot{Z}_s + m_u l_C \cos(\theta - \theta_0)\ddot{\theta} - m_u l_C \sin(\theta - \theta_0)\dot{\theta}^2 + k_t(z_s + l_C(\sin(\theta - \theta_0)) - \sin(\theta_0) - Z_r) = -f_b \qquad (18)$$

The second Lagrange equation of motion gives

$$m_u l_C^2 \ddot{\theta} + m_u l_C \cos(\theta - \theta_0) \ddot{Z}_s + \frac{c_p b_l^2 \sin(\alpha' - \theta_0)\dot{\theta}}{4(a_l - b_l \cos(\alpha' - \theta))} + k_t l_C \cos(\theta - \theta_0)(Z_s +$$

$$l_C(\sin(\theta - \theta_0) - \sin(-\theta_0)) - Z_r) - \frac{1}{2}k_s \sin(\alpha' - \theta)\left[b_l + \frac{d_l}{\left(c_l - d_l \cos(\alpha' - \theta)^{1/2}\right)}\right]\dot{Z}_s =$$

$$- l_B$$

(19)

where $c_l = a_l^2 - a_l b_l \cos(\alpha + \theta_0)$ $d_l = a_l b_l - b_l^2 \cos(\alpha + \theta_0)$.

The nomenclatures are m_s = mass of the car body (kg), m_u = mass of the car wheel (kg), k_s = stiffness of the car body spring (N/m), k_t = stiffness of car tyre (N/m), c_p = damper coefficient (Ns/m), l_A = distance from point 0 to A, l_B = distance from point 0 to B, l_C = distance from point 0 to C, f_b = weight of human body, f_a = actuator force, Z_s = displacement of sprung mass, $\dot{Z}_s$ = velocity of sprung mass $\ddot{Z}_s$ = acceleration of sprung mass, θ_0 = initial angular displacement of control arm, θ = angular displacement of control arm, $\dot{\theta}$ = angular velocity of control arm, $\ddot{\theta}$ = angular acceleration of control arm, Z_r = displacement of road profile, c_{p1} = the linear damping coefficient, c_{p2} = the nonlinearity damping coefficient, k_{s1} = the linear stiffness of car body spring, and k_{s2} = the nonlinearity stiffness of car body spring. Table 1 shows the detail parameters used in the mathematical modeling of a MacPherson model based on (Hong et al. [1], Falah et al. [2]), as follows:

Table 1. Physical parameters used by Hong et al. [1].

Parameter	Value
Sprung mass, m_s	455 kg
Unsprung mass, m_u	71 kg
Stiffness of spring, k_s	17,659 N/m
Stiffness of car tire, k_t	183,888 N/m
Damper coefficient, c_p	1950 Ns/m
Distance from point 0 to A	0.37 m
Distance from point 0 to B	0.64 m
Distance from point 0 to C	0.66 m

3 Proportional Integral Sliding Mode Control with Composite Nonlinear Feedback (PISMC-CNF) Controller Design

3.1 The Controller Design

The MacPherson active suspension system is transform into the following equation;

$$\dot{x}_{qMP}(t) = \left(A_{qMP} + \Delta A_{qMP}(t)\right)x_{qMP}(t) + \left(B_{qMP} + \Delta B_{qMP}(t)\right)sat\left(u_{qMP}(t)\right) + \\ f_{qMP}(x(t)) + R(d(t)) \tag{20}$$

where $x_{qMP} \in \mathfrak{R}^n$, is the state vector, $u_{qMP}(t) \in \mathfrak{R}^m$, is the control input vector, $A_{qMP} \in \mathfrak{R}^{m*n}$ is the system matrix, and $B_{qMP} \in \mathfrak{R}^{n*m}$ is the input matrix with full rank m, Meanwhile, $\Delta A_{qMP}(t)$, $\Delta B_{qMP}(t)$, $f_{qMP}(x(t))$, and $R(d(t))$, represent the system matrix uncertainty, the input matrix uncertainty, the nonlinearity of the system and the external disturbance, respectively. However the Eq. (20) can be rewritten as follows;

$$\dot{x}_{qMP}(t) = A_{qMP}x_{qMP}(t) + B_{qMP}u_{qMP}(t) + f_{qMP}(x,\delta,t) + f_{qMP}(x(t)) + R(d(t)) \tag{21}$$

where $f(x,\delta,t)$ is state bounded unmatched uncertainties. The unmatched condition is,

$$rank\left[B_{qMP}, f_{qMP}(x,\delta,t)\right] \neq rank\left[B_{qMP}\right] \tag{22}$$

$$f_{qMP}(x,\delta,t) = \Delta A_{qMP}(t) + \Delta B_{qMP}(t) \tag{23}$$

where $\delta \in \Delta \subseteq \mathfrak{R}^l$ is uncertainty parameter vector and its norm satisfies

$$\left\|f_{qMP}(x,\delta,t)\right\| \leq \gamma_{qMP}\|x\| \tag{24}$$

where γ_{qMP} is known as positive constants. The $\|\cdot\|$ indicates a norm vectors that is similar to the standard Euclidean norm.

$$sat\left(u_{qMP}(t)\right) = \begin{cases} u_{qMP}(t), & \left|u_{qMP}(t)\right| \leq u_{qMP}(t)_{max} \\ u_{qMP}(t)_{max}, & u_{qMP}(t) > u_{qMP}(t)_{max}, \\ -u_{qMP}(t)_{max}, & u_{qMP}(t) \leq -u_{qMP}(t)_{max}, \end{cases} \tag{25}$$

where $u_{qMP}(t)_{max} > 0$ denotes the ceiling of $u_{qMP}(t)$ and the following are the condition satisfied:

(i) (A, B) is stabilizable,
(ii) (A, C) is detectable (The system is detectable if all states that cannot be observed decay to zero asymptotically.), and
(iii) (A, B, C) is invertible and has no zero at $s = 0$.

The proportional integral sliding surface has the capability to overcome the uncertainties and the steady state error in the MacPherson active suspension system. The PI sliding surface is designed as follows:

$$\sigma_{qMP}(t) = C_{qMP}x(t) - \int_0^t \left[C_{qMP}A_{qMP} + C_{qMP}B_{qMP}u_{CNF}\right]x(\tau)d\tau \tag{26}$$

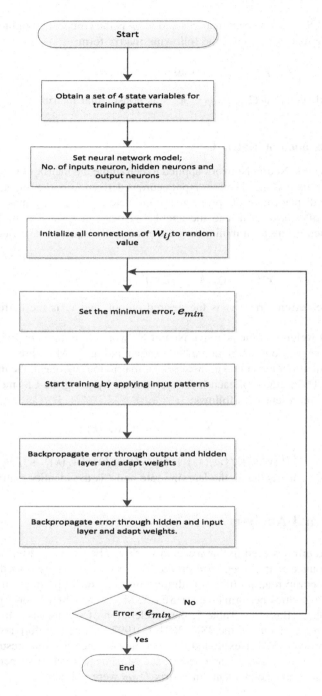

Fig. 3. A backpropagation algorithm to search the set of matrix C_{qMP}.

where $C_{qMP} \in \Re^{m*n}$ is constant matrices and u_{CNF} is the composite nonlinear feedback controller. The matrix C_{qMP} has the following matrix form:

$$C_{qMP} = [\, C_{qMP1} \quad C_{qMP2} \quad \ldots\ldots\ldots\ldots \quad C_{qMPn} \,] \tag{27}$$

and is selected such that $C_{qMP}B_{qMP} \in \Re^{m*m}$ is nonsingular matrix.

3.2   Determination of Matrix C

Figure 2 shown the Neural Network applied to determine the matrix of C_{qMP} which had a dimension of four by one. The four input neurons derived from the four state variables which are the displacement of sprung mass, the velocity of sprung mass, the angular displacement of control arm, and the angular velocity of control arm. The learning algorithm which is based on minimizing the error (mean square error) can be given as follows:

$$e^2(k) = (y_d(k) - y_a(k))^T (y_d(k) - y_a(k)) \tag{28}$$

where e is the current error, y_d is the desired output, and y_a is the current output at iteration-k.

The initial weights of the adaptive Neural Network were tuned by off-line training by using a set of previous simulation data as shown in Fig. 3. After three iterative trials, the matrix C_{qMP} is demonstrated in three sets of matrix four by one in the three different road profiles. The weights of each layer are updated by using the LM method in time $t > 0$ which is represented as follows:

$$w_{ij}(k+1) = w_{ij}(k) + \Delta w_{ij}(k) \tag{29}$$

where $\Delta w_{ij}(k) = \left[J^T\left(w_{ij}(k)\right)J\left(w_{ij}(k)\right) + \mu_1\right]^{-1} J\left(w_{ij}(k)\right)e\left(w_{ij}(k)\right)$ $w_{i,j}$ is the weight, J is the Jacobian matrix, μ_1 is the learning rate and I is the identity matrix.

4   Results and Analysis

The three road profiles used in this research work can be shown in Fig. 4 until Fig. 6. Figure 4 is Bounce Sine Sweep road profile, Fig. 5 Chassis Twisted road profile, and Large smooth bump road profile. In addition Figs. 7(a) to (c) portrays an acceleration of sprung mass control performance for SET 1, SET 2, and SET3 correspondingly as shown in Table 2. Based on Table 3, the acceleration of sprung mass for those three sets met the requirement of the ISO 2631-1, 1997 as ride comfort level less than 0.35 m/s^2. However, SET 1 exhibited the best performance from the results obtained. Since all states in the quarter car model of the MacPherson active suspension system were independent, all the elements in matrix C_{qMP} were not zero.

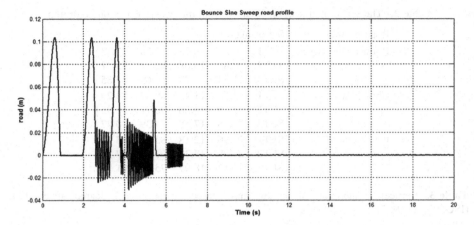

Fig. 4. Bounce sine sweep road profile.

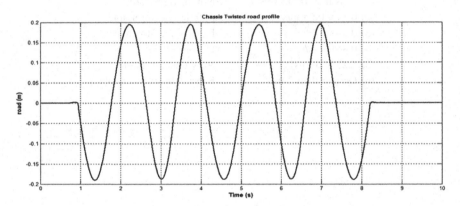

Fig. 5. Chassis twisted road profile.

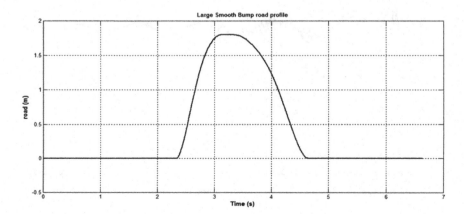

Fig. 6. Large smooth bump road profile.

Table 2. The set of matrix C_{qMP} obtained from the backpropagation algorithm.

Road profiles	Set of matrices
Bounce sine sweep	SET1: $[20.56 \quad 10.75 \quad 75.54 \quad 80.33]$
	SET2: $[20.88 \quad 12.68 \quad 89.87 \quad 85.47]$
	SET3: $[21.54 \quad 16.72 \quad 73.69 \quad 89.85]$
Chassis twisted	SET1: $[22.64 \quad 11.43 \quad 80.84 \quad 83.29]$
	SET2: $[23.55 \quad 13.26 \quad 90.72 \quad 86.95]$
	SET3: $[23.86 \quad 17.58 \quad 74.39 \quad 90.77]$
Large smooth bump	SET1: $[22.96 \quad 12.18 \quad 82.96 \quad 83.93]$
	SET2: $[24.08 \quad 14.33 \quad 91.74 \quad 87.15]$
	SET3: $[24.82 \quad 18.97 \quad 75.09 \quad 91.38]$

Table 3. Vertical acceleration of sprung mass based on level and degree of comfort. (ISO2631-1, 1997).

RMS vertical acceleration level	Degree of comfort
(1) Less than 0.315 m/s^2	Not uncomfortable
(2) 0.315–0.63 m/s^2	A little uncomfortable
(3) 0.5–1 m/s^2	Fairly uncomfortable
(4) 0.8–1.6 m/s^2	Uncomfortable
(5) 1.25–2.5 m/s^2	Very uncomfortable
(6) Greater than 2 m/s^2	Extremely uncomfortable

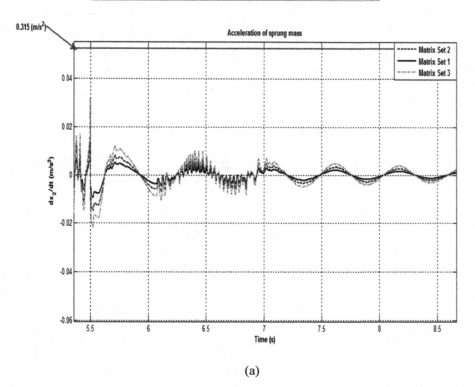

(a)

Fig. 7. Acceleration of sprung mass the effects for: (a) Bounce sine sweep. (b) Chassis twisted. (c) Large smooth bump.

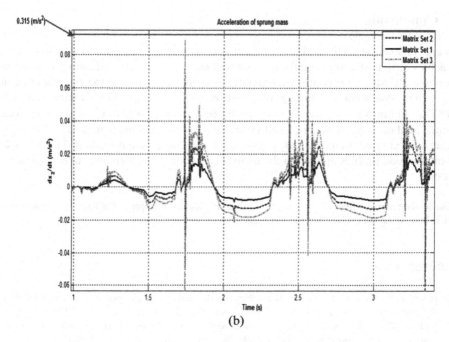

(b)

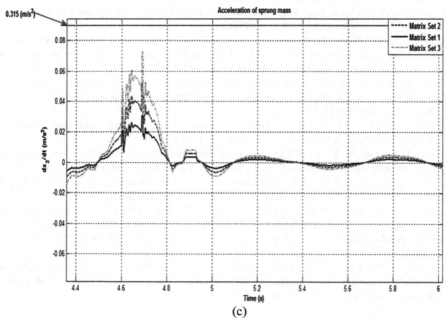

(c)

Fig. 7. (continued)

5 Conclusion

As conclusion, the set 1 of Matrix C was the best selection compare to others in order to achieve the best control performance based on an acceleration of spring mass. The proposed PISMC-CNF controller proved the ability to minimize the uncertainties in unmatched condition by tuning the best matrix of C_{qMP}. The Neural Network (NN) algorithm was employed to ensure the best value of matrix C_{qMP}. The previous testing method applied the trial and error method (conventional method). This technique offered more accurate value compared to the conventional method. The NN also learnt the road profiles applied in the quarter car model MacPherson active suspension system.

Acknowledgement. Special thanks to Universiti Kuala Lumpur (UniKL) and Universiti Teknologi Malaysia (UTM) for their support of this research works.

References

1. Hong, K.S., Jeon, D.-S., Yoo, S.K.A.: New model and an optimal pole-placement control of the macpherson suspension system. SAE Tech. Pap. Ser. **1331**(01), 1–10 (1999)
2. Fallah, M.S., Bhat, R., Xie, W.F.: New model and simulation of Macpherson suspension system for ride control applications. Veh. Syst. Dyn. **47**(2), 195–220 (2008)
3. Alleyne, A., Hedrick, J.K.: Nonlinear adaptive-control of active suspensions. IEEE Trans. Control Syst. Technol. **3**(1), 94–101 (1995)
4. Hsiao, W.Y., Chiang, H.H., Lee, T.T.: Sliding-mode-based filtered feedback control design for active suspension system. In: IEEE International Conference on Systems, Man, and Cybernetics (SMC), Anchorage, AK, USA, pp. 2021-2026 (2011)
5. Ashari, A.E.: Sliding-mode control of active suspension systems: unit vector approach. In: IEEE Proceedings of International Conference on Control Applications, Taipei, Taiwan, vol. 1, pp. 370–375 (2004)
6. Lin, Z., Pachter, M., Banda, S.: Toward improvement of tracking performance nonlinear feedback for linear systems. Int. J. Control **70**, 1–11 (1998)
7. Lin, D.Y., Lan, W.Y., Li, M.Q.: Composite nonlinear feedback control for linear singular systems with input saturation. Syst. Control Lett. **60**, 825–831 (2011)
8. Guowei, C., Chen, B.M., Peng, K., Miaobo, D., Lee, T.H.: Modeling and control of the yaw channel of a UAV helicopter. IEEE Trans. Ind. Electron. **55**, 3426–3434 (2008)
9. Cheng, G.Y., Peng, K.M., Chen, B.M., Lee, T.H.: Improving transient performance in tracking general references using composite nonlinear feedback control and its application to high-speed XY-table positioning mechanism. IEEE Trans. Ind. Electron. **54**, 1039–1051 (2007)
10. Cheng, G.Y., Chen, B.M., Peng, K.M., Lee, T.H.: A MATLAB toolkit for composite nonlinear feedback control. In: 8th International Conference on Control, Automation, Robotics and Vision, vol. 1–3, pp. 878–883 (2004)

Modeling of Membrane Bioreactor of Wastewater Treatment Using Support Vector Machine

Nur Sakinah Ahmad Yasmin, Norhaliza Abdul Wahab[✉],
and Zakariah Yusuf

Control and Mechatronics Engineering, Faculty of Electrical Engineering,
Universiti Teknologi Malaysia, 81310 Skudai, Johor Bahru, Malaysia
nursakinahyasmin@gmail.com, aliza@fke.utm.my,
zakariah2@live.utm.my

Abstract. Membrane bioreactor (MBR) is one of the advanced and new efficient reliable technology that replace the conventional activated sludge process in wastewater treatment plant. Therefore, understanding of dynamic behaviour of membrane filtration process is crucial to ensure good estimation of the filtration process. This paper presents the support vector machines (SVM) and artificial neural network to model and predict the membrane fouling. The predicted models are validated using an experimental data from a pilot scale palm oil mill effluent MBR located at Process Control Laboratory, Universiti Teknologi Malaysia. Simulation results showed that SVM able to produce good prediction as neural network model.

Keywords: MBR · SVM · Neural network · Filtration process

1 Introduction

Wastewater basically produce a variety of waste such as liquid and solid effluent that contain inorganic pollutants which can be easily decomposable but gives significant impact load on the ecosystem. The wastewater contain significant quantities of chemical oxygen demand (COD) or Biochemical Oxygen Demand (BOD_5), Total Suspended Solids (TSS) including grease and oils, harmful nutrients that require treatment before they are conveyed into water bodies [1]. The treatment is usually done using conventional activated sludge (CAS) process. However the process of CAS have become increasingly expensive in order to comply with more stringent permissible discharge standard. Therefore, the increased cost associated with CAS have led to interest in alternative technology that can enable the effluent water to be treated. Membrane bioreactor (MBR) has been one of the promising technology to replace conventional activated sludge process plant [2, 3]. MBR technology has proven to be very effective in terms of producing high quality effluent of wastewater either from industrial or domestic waste. Unlike CAS, the configuration of MBR does not have fixed stages of the process. The treatment process varies depend on the configuration they have set. Some MBR plant is made from the combination of CAS process with membrane filtration that

© Springer Nature Singapore Pte Ltd. 2017
M.S. Mohamed Ali et al. (Eds.): AsiaSim 2017, Part II, CCIS 752, pp. 485–495, 2017.
DOI: 10.1007/978-981-10-6502-6_42

replace two stages of CAS which are clarification and settlement [4]. There are even more simplified MBR plants, where it includes the process of nitrification and denitrification process. The most crucial part is the membrane filtration process because this process is the last stage of wastewater filtration where the treated water is released. The filtration membrane system use either hollow-fibre types or flat-sheet technology for ultrafiltration (UF) system or microfiltration (MF) system [5]. The membranes filtration can be submerged direct into the bioreactor as shown in the Fig. 1.

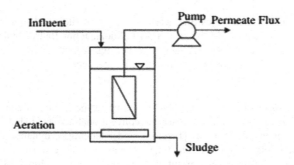

Fig. 1. Submerged membrane filtration system [5]

MBR possessing advantages such as small footprint demand due to the compactness of treatment process, excellent effluent quality, better process reliability, a low sludge production rate and disinfection odour control [3, 6]. Notwithstanding these advantages, the treatment process of the MBR is constrained by membrane fouling. Membrane fouling is one of the major problems in membrane filtration as it reduces productivity permeate water through the membrane, abridge membrane life due to aggressive cleaning agents, blocking membrane pores and damages the fractionation capability of filtration's membrane [3, 7]. Membrane fouling are found out occurred due to the following mechanisms which are adsorption of solutes on the membrane surface, deposition of sludge flocs on the membrane surface, formation of cake layer on membrane surface, the detachment of foulant attributed mainly to shear forces and foulant composition during long-term process [8]. In a simple word, fouling can be expressed as the undesirable accumulation of colloids, microorganism, and cell debris on/within membranes. If not carefully handle, the maintenance of membrane filtration replacement can lead to high capital equipment and high operating cost [9].

There is a few technique cleaning mechanism has been done in preventing fouling development such as aeration air flow, backwashing, relaxation and chemical cleaning process mechanism [5]. The technique does not fully resolved a fouling problem but it helps to enhance the performance of membrane filtration [10]. Membrane fouling also can be reduced by developing a reliable prediction model for membrane filtration system. It gives a better understanding to plant operator of the fouling formation and helps to predict the filtration performance more accurately. A development of reliable model is very important to represent the real system as this model will determine the true dynamic of the membrane filtration system and improvement will be made based on this model.

Several case study using neural network modeling for wastewater treatment have been developed. For example Wu et al. [11] used Artificial Neural Network (ANN) technique to predict the performance characteristic of a reversibly used cooling tower for heating system in winter. The result of this study reveals that ANN model are capable to obtain a high degree of accuracy and reliability for predicting the performance characteristic. ANN model also demonstrated high accuracy prediction model in a work done by Gissler et al. [12]. The authors developed two permeate flux models for membrane filtration process. The first model comprises model parameters which were calibrated using data from pilot scale submerged hollow fiber MBR, while the second model is more empirical build by using ANN.

Support Vector Machine (SVM) is one of the highly effective techniques used for limited sets of training data. SVM has been widely applied in many fields for classification [13, 14], prediction [15], and regression. The SVM method relies on statistical learning theory, which enables learning machine theory to generalize the unseen data. SVM known as a technique which uses the minimum possible of the data [16, 17]. In general, there are at least three reasons for the success of SVM which are its ability to learn with a small number of data set, their robustness against error of the model and computational efficiency compared with several other methods such as ANN and fuzzy network [16, 18].

1.1 Support Vector Machine

The underlying principle of SVM is explained in this section. According to Vapnik [16], the principle of SVM is based on structural risk management (SRM). SVM was initially developed to solve classification problem but it has been extends to estimation and regression problems. SVM is a relatively machine learning method constructed based on statistical learning theory classifier. The aimed of SVM is to find an optimal separating hyperlane between the two classes of a data set as shown in Fig. 2. For example in mapping some unknown and nonlinear dependency of a function $y = f(x)$ between high-dimensional input vector, x and scalar output, y.

In order to solve a SVM regression problem, it is required to understand how significantly misclassifications should be treated and how large the insensitive loss

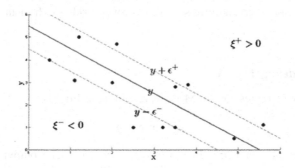

Fig. 2. Separating hyperlane between two classes of data sets

function region by selecting suitable values for parameters cost, C and gamma, γ. The set of training data $D = \{(x_i, y_i)|X, Y\}, i = 1$ where i is training data pair of the same size data D and D and y_i is the predicted target value. Hence, SVM is basically a type of supervised learning method.

1.2   Kernel Function

Kernel function plays crucial role in determine the performance of SVM. The right selection of kernel function will result in the best accuracy and prediction model. The idea of kenel function is to enable the operations to be performed in the input space rather than the potentially high dimensional future space. There are three types of kernel available in SVM which is linear, polynomial and radial basis function as illustrated in Table 1.

Table 1. Performance evaluation

Kernel type	Kernel function
Linear	$K(x_i, x) = \langle x, x_i \rangle$
Polynomial	$K(\langle x_i, x) = (x, x_i) + 1)^d$
Radial basis function (RBF)	$K(x_i, x) = \exp\langle -|x, x_i|^2 / 2\alpha^2 \rangle$

Generally, RBF is the most popular kernel function used by researcher for regression problem. However, the choices of kernel function itself are differ based on types of problems, scaling method and parameters.

1.3   C and Gamma Parameter

In developing regression SVM model of RBF kernel function, two parameters are needed to be considered which are regularization cost C and gamma γ value parameter. The C parameter is to control the trade-off between slack variable size and margin while gamma parameter influences the predicted outcome in feature space. There are several steps in determining C and γ parameter which is trial and error implementation, feature selection approach and grid search. However, grid search method is more time consuming.

1.4   SVM Modeling Theory

The basic theory of regression SVM is expressed as in Eq. (1)

$$y_i = w.x_i + b \tag{1}$$

where w is a weight vector, b is bias, x is input and y is scalar output.

The new predicted SVM for each x' is determined by evaluating Eq. (2)

$$y' = \sum_{i=1}^{L} (\alpha_i^+ - \alpha_i^=)x_i.x' + b \tag{2}$$

1.5 Validation of Prediction Model

After the best prediction models have been developed, then we need to validate the model. In this work, the performance of prediction for all methods was based on two criteria which are correlation coefficient (R^2) and root mean square error (RMSE). The best prediction model will yield highest correlation value and lowest RMSE value. The aim for this criteria is to justify the prediction model will gives the best prediction value as expected output. The equation R^2 and RMSE are given in Eqs. (3) and (4) respectively.

$$R^2 = 1 - \frac{\sum_{i=0}^{n-1} (y_i - \hat{y}_i)^2}{\sum_{i=0}^{n-1} (y_i - \bar{y}_i)^2} \tag{3}$$

$$RMSE = \sqrt{\frac{\sum_{i=0}^{n-1} (y_i - \hat{y}_i)^2}{n}} \tag{4}$$

where $\hat{y}_i$ is the predicted value, $\bar{y}_i$ denotes the mean of the measured value and y_i is the actual value from the measurement data and N is the number of data point.

1.6 RBF Neural Network Model

Figure 3 present the structure of Radial Basis Function Neural Network (RBFNN). The RBFNN structure can be represented by Eq. (5)

$$y(t) = \sum_{i}^{i} w_i \theta_i(t) \tag{5}$$

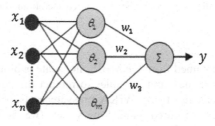

Fig. 3. RBF neural network structure

Output hidden layer can be denoted by Eq. (5)

$$\theta_i(t) = e^{\frac{\|(x(t)-c_i(t)^2\|}{\psi_i^2}} \tag{6}$$

where $i = 1,2,3...k$. w is the weight number of output layer, k is the number of hidden nodes, x is the input vector, c is the center of the hidden node and ψ is the width of output layer and y indicates the output of the RBF neural network.

2   Experimental Setup

The experimental setup involved with 20 l of Palm oil mill effluent (POME) which is supplied by Sedenak Palm Oil Mill Sdn. Bhd, Johor, Malaysia. The experiment was conducted with three double-walled cylindrical column bioreactor. The POME effluent is fed into the supply tank and will go through the membrane bioreactor for filtration process. The working temperature for bioreactor is at 27 ± 1 °C. The operation time is 90 s for permeate and 30 s for relation period. For the first half of the experiment, the airflow is maintained around 8 SLPM and was reduced to 5 SLPM at the second half of the experiment. The data plant was monitored and controlled using LabVIEW 2009 software with NI USB 6009 interfacing hardware. Figure 4 shows the schematic diagram of pilot plant setup for the experiment.

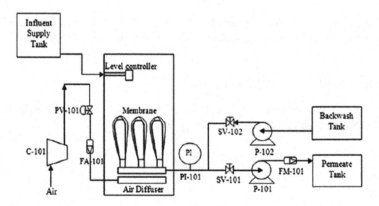

Fig. 4. Schematic diagram of the submerged membrane bioreactor. [19]

2.1   Data Collection

The experimental data obtained from the MBR pilot scale is plotted as shown in Fig. 5. Airflow rate and TMP are the input variables to predict the performance of permeate flux. The TMP was measured using WIKA pressure transducer from −1 to 1.5 bar while permeate flux was measured using flow sensor (RS 508-2704) range between 0.05 to 10 litre per minute (LPM).

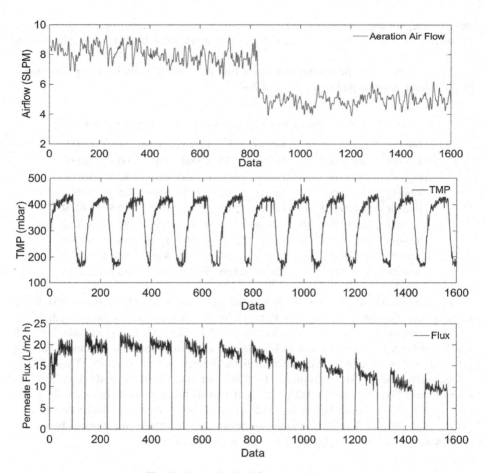

Fig. 5. Data obtained from experiment

The data obtained from the experiment are separated into two blocks which M1 and M2. The M1 and M2 block data are taken from high air flow rate. For M1 block, comparison between the kernels is tested while the M2 block comparison between SVM and neural network is performed for verification. A detailed grid search method with 10 folds cross validation is used to derive the optimal parameter of SVM.

3   Result and Discussion

In SVM, there are three types of kernel which are linear, polynomial and radial basis function. The parameter cost, C is tuned between the value of 10 and 1000 while gamma, y is set from 0.1 to 100. The model is then tested for each type of kernel in order to determine the best result of prediction values. The value of epsilon ε determine the level of accuracy of the approximated function. If ε is larger than the range of the target value, not a good result will be produced. If epsilon is zero, overfitting should be expected. After the grid search method is performed, the largest score obtained is $\varepsilon = 0.001$.

Table 2 shows the performance metrics for each type of kernels. The performance of the model is evaluated using R^2 and RMSE.

Table 2. Comparison in term of performance for each type of kernels

Data	C	ε	y	Kernel	$\%R^2$	RMSE	Kernel	$\%R^2$	RMSE
Dataset1	10	0.001	0.1	Linear	53.05	6.1860	RBF	60.95	5.6962
Dataset2	10	0.001	10	Linear	53.05	6.1860	RBF	83.77	3.7239
Dataset3	10	0.001	100	Linear	53.05	6.7137	RBF	85.33	3.4068
Dataset4	100	0.001	0.1	Linear	53.05	6.7137	RBF	62.57	5.6109
Dataset5	100	0.001	10	Linear	53.05	6.7137	RBF	85.33	3.4068
Dataset6	1000	0.001	0.1	Linear	53.05	9.0505	RBF	66.86	5.2768
Dataset7	1000	0.001	10	Linear	53.05	9.0505	RBF	85.33	3.4608
Dataset8	1000	0.001	100	Linear	53.05	9.0505	RBF	85.33	3.4045

For the first dataset, C value is set with 10 and γ varies from 0.1, 10 and 100. It can be seen that the third data set for RBF yields the highest performance with R^2 of 85.33% compared to linear kernel which is 53.05%. The RMSE performance for RBF and linear kernel is 3.4068 and 6.7137, respectively. For C value of 100 and γ value is 10, RBF yields better performance than linear kernel, with %R of 85.33 and 53.05, respectively. The RMSE performance for RBF and linear kernel is 3.4068 and 6.7137, respectively. For C value of 1000, $\%R^2$ and RMSE for RBF is of respectively 85.35 and 3.4045, while linear kernel is 53.05 for RBF and 9.0505 for linear kernel. The polynomial showed less performance of result and therefore not discuss here. The comparison between three types of kernels is shown in Fig. 6.

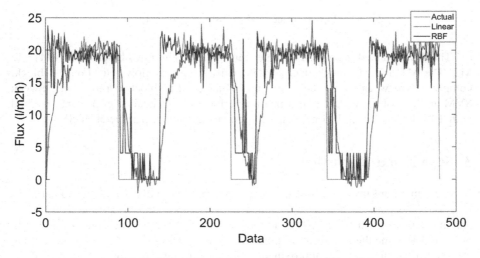

Fig. 6. Comparison between three types of kernels

The third block M3 data is for high airflow rate data. Figure 7 shows the comparison between SVM method and neural network method using M3 block data. The data shows fast declined of permeate flux at every cycle. The RBFSVM gives more accurate and reliable prediction compared to RBFNN. This can be seen from the result of %R^2 and RMSE performance obtained. RBFSVM gives 81.37% with 2.4667 value of RMSE, while RBFNN gives only 79.5% with 4.0943.

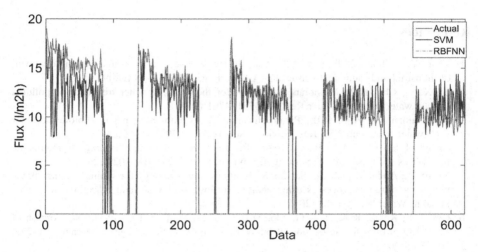

Fig. 7. Validate RBF SVM data with RBF neural network

Table 3 presents the performance evaluation of RBFSVM and RBFNN for M3 data set.

Table 3. Performance evaluation

Data/method	%R^2	RMSE
M3/RBFSVM	81.37	2.4667
M3/RBFNN	79.50	4.0943

4 Conclusion

This paper presented model prediction using two different models of permeate flux in submerged membrane bioreactor filtration. In this work, the data set was divided into three set of data blocks which are M1, M2 and M3. For M1 block, the data is compared between the SVM types of kernels which are linear, polynomial and RBF. From the simulation, RBF kernel yields better performance compared to linear and polynomial kernels. In order to obtain good performance, the value of C and gamma, γ parameters need to undergo grid search to find out the best parameters. Then, the model is tested using the best parameter to obtain the best model of permeate flux. For model validation, the proposed model prediction was compared with neural network. From the experiment, both methods, RBFSVM and RBVNN are suitable for prediction of MBR wastewater treatment.

Acknowledgments. The authors would like to thank the Research University Grant (GUP) vote 13H70, Universiti Teknologi Malaysia and the MOHE for the financial support.

References

1. Chan, Y.J., Chong, M.F., Law, C.L., Hassell, D.: A review on anaerobic–aerobic treatment of industrial and municipal wastewater. Chem. Eng. J. **155**, 1–18 (2009)
2. Li, X.-Y., Chu, H.P.: Membrane bioreactor for the drinking water treatment of polluted surface water supplies. Water Res. **37**, 4781–4791 (2003)
3. Visvanathan, C., Aim, R.B., Parameshwaran, K.: Membrane separation bioreactors for wastewater treatment. Crit. Rev. Environ. Sci. Technol. **30**, 1–48 (2000)
4. Chang, I.-S., Le Clech, P., Jefferson, B., Judd, S.: Membrane fouling in membrane bioreactors for wastewater treatment. J. Environ. Eng. **128**, 1018–1029 (2002)
5. Yusuf, Z., Abdul Wahab, N., Sahlan, S.: Fouling control strategy for submerged membrane bioreactor filtration processes using aeration airflow, backwash, and relaxation: a review. Desalin. Water Treat. 1–13 (2015)
6. Qin, J.-J., Kekre, K.A., Tao, G., Oo, M.H., Wai, M.N., Lee, T.C., et al.: New option of MBR-RO process for production of NEWater from domestic sewage. J. Membr. Sci. **272**, 70–77 (2006)
7. Judd, S.: The status of membrane bioreactor technology. Trends Biotechnol. **26**, 109–116 (2008)
8. Meng, F., Chae, S.-R., Drews, A., Kraume, M., Shin, H.-S., Yang, F.: Recent advances in membrane bioreactors (MBRs): membrane fouling and membrane material. Water Res. **43**, 1489–1512 (2009)
9. Le-Clech, P., Chen, V., Fane, T.A.: Fouling in membrane bioreactors used in wastewater treatment. J. Membr. Sci. **284**, 17–53 (2006)
10. Judd, S.: Fouling control in submerged membrane bioreactors. Water Sci. Technol. **51**, 27–34 (2005)
11. Wu, J., Zhang, G., Zhang, Q., Zhou, J., Wang, Y.: Artificial neural network analysis of the performance characteristics of a reversibly used cooling tower under cross flow conditions for heat pump heating system in winter. Energy Build. **43**, 1685–1693 (2011)
12. Geissler, S., Wintgens, T., Melin, T., Vossenkaul, K., Kullmann, C.: Modelling approaches for filtration processes with novel submerged capillary modules in membrane bioreactors for wastewater treatment. Desalination **178**, 125–134 (2005)
13. Schölkopf, B., Sung, K.-K., Burges, C.J., Girosi, F., Niyogi, P., Poggio, T., et al.: Comparing support vector machines with Gaussian kernels to radial basis function classifiers. IEEE Trans. Signal Process. **45**, 2758–2765 (1997)
14. Vapnik, V.: Pattern recognition using generalized portrait method. Autom. Remote Control **24**, 774–780 (1963)
15. Vapnik, V.: The Nature of Statistical Learning Theory. Springer, New York (1999)

16. Martínez-Ramón, M., Christodoulou, C.: Support vector machines for antenna array processing and electromagnetics. Synth. Lect. Comput. Electromagnet. **1**, 1–120 (2005)
17. Anzai, Y.: Pattern Recognition and Machine Learning. Elsevier, Amsterdam (2012)
18. Wang, W., Xu, Z., Lu, W., Zhang, X.: Determination of the spread parameter in the Gaussian kernel for classification and regression. Neurocomputing **55**, 643–663 (2003)
19. Yusuf, Z., Wahab, N.A., Sahlan, S.: Modeling of submerged membrane bioreactor filtration process using NARX-ANFIS model. In: 2015 10th Asian Control Conference (ASCC), pp. 1–6 (2015)

Relayout Planning to Reduce Waste in Food Industry Through Simulation Approach

Muhammad Faishal[1(✉)], Adi Saptari[2], and Hayati Mukti Asih[3]

[1] Fakultas Teknologi Industri Universitas Ahmad Dahlan, Jl Prof Dr Soepomo,
Janturan Yogyakarta 66421, Indonesia
muhammad.faishal@ie.uad.ac.id
[2] Faculty of Technology Management and Technopreurship,
UTeM, Melaka, Malaysia
adi@utem.edu.my
[3] Faculty of Manufacturing Engineering, UTeM, Melaka, Malaysia

Abstract. A good layout can streamline transportation within the factory, it contributes to lower cost and delivery time. This research is based on the case in a food company in Indonesia. This company produces snack. The characteristic of this production process is made to stock system with 24-working hours. From the observation of the production process, it indicates that layout planning is ineffective. This showed on long distance to move design items, a high number of worker and low throughput as well. The aim of this research is to re-layout in order to improve throughput and also reduce the number of workers and the distance. A conceptual model was developed to determine factors and responses of the system. Three scenario layouts were developed by using MULTIPLE methods. These scenario layouts were then translated and analyzed into operational models using the ProModel 6.0 Simulation Software. The results indicate an improvement of throughput by 15% for scenario 1, 28% for scenario 2, 21% for scenario 3. And for the number of workers reduce 13% for scenario 1, 2, and 3. For the over distance reduce 83% for scenario 1, 87% for scenario 2, 86% for scenario 3. Generally, scenario 2 give the largest improvement than other although need more expensive cost investment.

Keywords: Relayout planning · Food industry · Simulation

1 Introduction

Competition among industries is getting intense nowadays. Globalization not only makes the industry compete locally but also globally. Each industry is looking for its strength to be able more competitive. All industries compete not only on cost, time, quality, but also environmental impact and sustainability. Industry, in general is an integrated system of people, equipment, material, information, and energy makes the manufacturing process becomes more complex. There is a growing concern to improve the productivity, safety, and quality in the manufacturing system, however many industries neglect layout planning [8].

Layout planning is one of the most important factors should be considered if a company wants to more competitive particularly in cost, delivery, and quality. A good

© Springer Nature Singapore Pte Ltd. 2017
M.S. Mohamed Ali et al. (Eds.): AsiaSim 2017, Part II, CCIS 752, pp. 496–508, 2017.
DOI: 10.1007/978-981-10-6502-6_43

layout that can streamline transportation directly influence the cost and delivery time. Layout planning deals with the physical arrangement of various resources that are available in the system with increasing the operating system performances as the objectives [7]. About 20% to 50% of total production time are spent on non-added value material handling activities [10]. Material handling is to do with movement within the layout. Poor facility layout may result in high distance moved by items and time consumed, high work-in-process and hence high throughput time. Therefore, providing efficient and safe movement is important in planning the layout.

According to Wild [11], there are some reasons why the company needs redesign the layout, i.e. enlarging or reducing existing departments, movement of a department, adding or removing a department, and also replacing equipment and adding new equipment. Hence, good facility layout contributes some advantages to the manufacturing system. There is a reduction in material handling and transportation, work-in-process, movement made by workers, and also waiting time. Other advantages improve the utilization of space, facilities, and labor, increase the work method and hence reduce the production cycle time [3].

This research is based on the case in a food company in Indonesia. From the observation of the production process, it indicates that layout planning is ineffective. This showed on the long distance moved of items, a high number of worker and low throughput as well. The objective of this research is to re-design layout in order to improve throughput and also reduce the number of workers and the distance. To achieve that objective, this research developed scenarios – based re-layout planning model and then simulation was employed to evaluate those scenarios.

2 Background of Research

According to Amit et al. [1], Layout is a design for the floor plan of the plant which illustrates the arrangement of facilities or working activities whereby these facilities are located within a particular area according to its functions. The development of the modern industry has posed new challenges for facility layout design. To meet the fast-changing production targets, enterprises nowadays need to reconfigure the existing shop floor layouts constantly to update their operations. Facility layout design for existing shop floors have the following characteristics: (1) the presence of existing facilities poses critical constraints; (2) the facility layout design task normally tends to be small-scaled, e.g. removing and adding number of machines; and (3) the criteria used are often ad-hoc, and specific to different tasks. Hence, enterprises often settle with a less optimal layout plan [5]. Those problems lead to some effects to the company, such as high product cost, lead time and waste [9].

In developing the layout, factor consideration is one of the early data that determine in order to achieve the objective of the company. Hosseini et al. [4] stated that when comparing and evaluating scenario layouts, the decision may be related to various factors in different ways. The main cause of imprecision in layout planning is that seldom aware of specific weights and function-forms employs with respect to the various factors. Thus, by determining the factors consideration in layout planning, unwanted outcomes can be avoided and controlled by the company.

One of the elements which can be considered during conducting layout planning is the volume of products to be produced. Drira et al. [2] expressed that volume of product is also a big view when implementing the facilities design. Production volume could definitely influence the facilities load, which indicates the potential risk of designing the layout that devoted to a narrow range of product configurations. Also, this will test the designer since there will be changes in cycle time which production volume is one of the elements that will incident it.

Disregarding that, a cost of building to place the process is also a thing that must be considered as well. This is because processes or activities to be conducted occur inside the building of the organization and it is crucial to put a good decision on locating the building, or else, it will turn out to be very costly. According to Liggett [6], problems regarding facility layout would have many different scales from small to big in an example from as small as location of equipment and personnel to as big as layout of a cities or campuses. Layout problem can arise due to either planning a new layout or altering an existing layout.

This research is based on case company in a food industry in Indonesia. The characteristic of this production process is made to stock system with 24-working hours. In this line, there are two types of product, i.e. Product A and Product B. These product types have same process flows and processing time, but different shape, production volumes and seasoning.

Figure 1 shows process flow of Production. It consists of mixing, blending, grading, frying, seasoning, and packaging, then distributing process to customer. This research to use on mixing and blending processes.

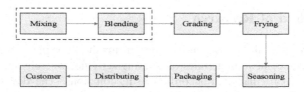

Fig. 1. Process flow of XXX food company

From the observation of the production process and discussions with the managers, plant supervisors and production line associates found that many problems occurred in "Cracker" line. Mixing and blending processes are an initial step in producing the products. The performances of both processes are the critical one for the next processes as these processes have the longest processing time and the most influence on the quality of the product. However, it was found that the layout planning was ineffective. The results showed has high distance moved by items, a high number of workers, and low throughput as well.

To overcome those problems, some models were developed. First of all, the causes of waste were identified. Then, the future condition was developed by analyzing the waste and the added value of related processes. Some scenarios were developed and MULTIPLE (Multi-floor Plan Layout Evaluation) method were employed to provide the better layout. Finally, those scenario models were developed computer model using ProModel® 6.0 simulation software. Then, the results of computer modeling evaluated by identifying the distance, lead time, cycle time, takt time, the number of workers, etc.

3   Proposed Model

3.1   Re-design Layout Planning Model

a. Base Model
There are two product families that have same base products, process flow, and raw material but different shapes. Figure 2 shows a layout for the mixing and blending processes.

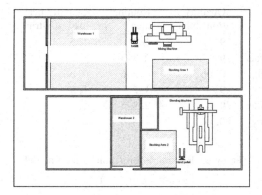

Fig. 2. Layout of mixing and blending processes

There are some steps to understand the current condition through from-to-chart analysis and also non-added-value and added-value analysis of all processes.

Step 1: Analyze the process flow from a layout of mixing and blending machine (please refer to Fig. 2) to the routing below as presented in Fig. 3.
Step 2: Collect the data related to the routing as shown in Table 1 below.
Step 3: Develop from-to-chart table of routing, loading and distance according to information above as presented in Table 2.
Step 4: Analyze all processes which is categorized as added value and non-added value categories (refer to Table 3). Area 3 and Area 5 are proposed to be removed in order to reduce the number of WIP stock. Then, Table 4 presents the proposed area and process categorization after removing the non-added value. It shows the reduction in number of worker and size area as well.

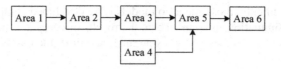

*Note
Area 1: Warehouse 1
Area 2: Mixing machine
Area 3: Stocking area 1
Area 4: Warehouse 2
Area 5: Stocking area 2
Area 6: Blending machine

Fig. 3. Routing area process

Table 1. Routing information of base model

Product	Material	Quantity (ton/shift)	Routing area	Quantity per load (ton/trip)	Number of trip (trip/shift)
Product A	Powder	9	1–2	1, 5	6
	Mixpowder	9	2–3–5–6	1	9
	Seasoning	0, 06	4–5–6	0, 06	1
Product B	Powder	9	1–2	1, 5	6
	Mixpowder	9	2–3–5–6	1	9
	Seasoning	0, 06	4–5–6	0, 06	1

Table 2. Routing information of base model

From-to-chart	Total
Routing	20
Loading	9.12
Distance (m/trip)	290
Distance (m/trip)	4160

Table 3. Area and process categorization

Area	Processes	Size area (sqm)	Worker/day	Category	Suggestion
1	As a storage	2304	12	AV	Keep
2	Mixing powder material	576	24	AV	Keep
3	As a temporary stock	576	9	NAV	Removed
4	As a storage	216	6	AV	Keep
5	As a temporary stock	48	3	NAV	Removed
6	Blending material	126	15	AV	Keep
	Total	**3846**	**69**		

Table 4. Proposed area and process categorization

Area	Processes	Size area (sqm)	Worker/day	Category
1	Storage	2304	12	AV
2	Mix powder material	576	24	AV
4	Storage	216	6	AV
6	Blending material	126	15	AV
Total		**3222**	**57**	

b. Scenario-Based Re-design Layout Planning Model

First of all, design scenario improvement that relevant to the real condition by using MULTIPLE methods. Then, this is followed by analyzing to select the best scenario.

1. Scenario 1

Step 1: MULTIPLE method is conducted by doing some exchange iteration then it leads to layout cost reduction. The largest one among three scenarios is selected. Before developing some iteration as scenario improvement, some limitations must be considered as follow:

1. Warehouse 1 cannot be moved totally.
2. Blending Machine is in fix place.

After removing stocking area 1, mixing machine is moved to that place. Therefore, the mixing machine and blending machine are closer. But, the track must be built to connect between them. Thus, the new layout of scenario 1 is shown in Fig. 4.

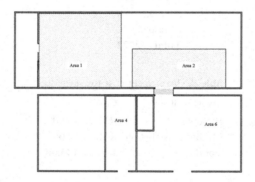

Fig. 4. Layout of scenario 1

Step 2: Constructing from-to-chart analysis from scenario 1 layout. Adjusted information for new routing is shown in Table 5 below. Based on this information, some calculations of from-to-chart can be constructed. Tables 6, 7, 8, 9 and 10 present the from-to-chart of travel flow, loading, distance per trip, distance per shift for scenario 1, respectively.

Table 5. Routing information of scenario 1

Product	Material	Quantity (ton/shift)	New routing area	Quantity per load (ton/trip)	Number of trip (trip/shift)
A	Powder	9	1–2	1, 5	6
	Mixpowder	9	2–6	1	9
	Seasoning	0, 06	4–6	0, 06	1
B	Powder	9	1–2	1, 5	6
	Mixpowder	9	2–6	1	9
	Seasoning	0, 06	4–6	0, 06	1

Table 6. Routing information of base model

From-to-chart	Total
Routing	6
Loading	5.12
Distance (m/trip)	100
Distance (m/trip)	690

Table 7. Total distance of scenario 1

Area	Space (m^2)
Area 1	2304
Area 2	576
Area 3	0
Area 4	216
Area 5	0
Area 6	126
Total	**3222**

Table 8. Investment cost for scenario 1

Investment	Cost
Building	RM 11,429.00
Machine installation	RM 3,714.00
Total	**RM 15,143.00**

Table 9. Benefits of scenario 1

Benefit	Cost
Reduction of diesel fuel consumption	RM 804.00
Reduction of number of worker	RM 3,343.00
Total	**RM 4,147.00**

Table 10. Routing information of base model

From-to-chart	Total
Routing	6
Loading	5.12
Distance (m/trip)	52
Distance (m/trip)	560

By removing some non-added value areas, then proposing new routing area and re-layout the shop floor, the new space is computed. Hence, the total space of scenario 1 is 3222 m² (refer to Table 7).

Step 3: Analyze cost and benefit. To apply scenario models, the company needs to invest some cost. It includes building cost and machine installation cost. For scenario 1, building cost is used to pay track construction to connect the mixing machine and blending machine. On the other hand, the machine installation cost is used to pay the movement of mixing machine to stocking area 1 (see Fig. 3). The investment cost for scenario 1 is presented in Table 8.

Some benefits will be gained by company. The reduction of diesel fuel consumption and number of worker. Table 9 presents the benefits for Scenario 1 as much as RM 4,147.00. And, this investment will have break-even point within four months (as shown in Eq. 1).

$$\frac{\text{Investment}}{\text{Benefit}} = \frac{\text{RM } 15,143.00}{\text{RM } 4,147.00} = 4\,\text{months} \tag{1}$$

ii. Scenario 2

Step 1: In scenario 2, the re-layout planning is conducted by moving area 2 in same building with area 6 and making area 4 become lengthwise and the track must be built to connect between area 2 and area 1. Figure 5 shows the layout of scenario 2.

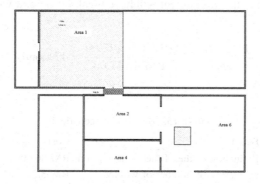

Fig. 5. Layout of scenario 2

Step 2: Constructing from-to-chart analysis from scenario 2 layout. Table 10 presents the from-to-chart of travel flow, loading, distance per trip, distance per shift for scenario 2, respectively.

By removing some non-added value areas, then proposing new routing area and re-layout the shop floor, the new space is computed. Therefore, the total space of scenario 2 is 3006 m^2 (refer to Table 11).

Table 11. Total space of scenario 2

Area	Space (m^2)
Area 1	2304
Area 2	360
Area 3	0
Area 4	216
Area 5	0
Area 6	126
Total	**3006**

Step 3: Analyze cost and benefit. To apply scenario models, the company needs to invest some cost. It includes building cost and machine installation cost. For scenario 2, building cost is used to pay the modification of wall building and track construction to connect the mixing machine and warehouse 1. On the other hand, the machine installation cost is used to pay the movement of mixing machine to other building (see Fig. 4). The investment cost for scenario 2 is presented in Table 12.

Table 12. Investment cost for scenario 2

Investment	Cost
Building	RM 191,429.00
Machine installation	RM 3,714.00
Total	**RM 195,143.00**

Some benefits will be achieved by company. the reduction of diesel fuel consumption and number of worker. Table 13 presents the benefits for Scenario 2 as much as RM 4,147.00. And, this investment will have break-even point within 46 months (as shown in Eq. 2).

$$\frac{\text{Investment}}{\text{Benefit}} = \frac{\text{RM } 195,143.00}{\text{RM } 4,147.00} = 47\,\text{months} \tag{2}$$

Table 13. Benefits of scenario 2

Benefit	Cost
Reduction of diesel fuel consumption	RM 804.00
Reduction of number of worker	RM 3,343.00
Total	**RM 4,147.00**

iii. Scenario 3

Step 1: Scenario 3 proposes re-layout that almost the same with scenario 1. In this scenario, area 2 is moved to area 3 so that it is closer to area 6. Then, as area 5 is removed, area 4 is moved to area 5 and add some spaces around that area. Figure 6 shows layout of scenario 3.

Step 2: Constructing from-to-chart analysis from scenario 3 layout. Based on same information in Table 14, some calculations in from to chart from scenario layout 3 can be constructed below:

Step 3: Analyze cost and benefit. To apply scenario models, the company needs to invest some cost. It includes building cost and machine installation cost. For scenario 3, building cost is used to pay modify building of the wall and track construction to connect the mixing machine and blending machine. On the other hand, the machine installation cost is used to pay the movement of mixing machine to stocking area 1 (see Fig. 6). The investment cost for scenario 3 is presented in Table 15.

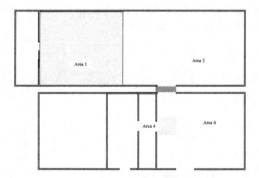

Fig. 6. Layout of scenario 3

Table 14. Routing information of base model

From-to-chart	Total
Routing	6
Loading	5.12
Distance (m/trip)	48
Distance (m/trip)	586

Some benefits will be gained by company. the reduction of diesel fuel consumption and number of worker. Table 16 presents the benefits for Scenario 3 as much as RM 4,147.00. And, this investment will have break-even point within 21 months (as shown in Eq. 3).

$$\frac{\text{Investment}}{\text{Benefit}} = \frac{\text{RM } 87,143.00}{\text{RM } 4,147.00} = 21 \text{ months} \tag{3}$$

Table 15. Investment cost for scenario 2

Investment	Cost
Building	RM 83,429.00
Machine installation	RM 3,714.00
Total	**RM 87,143.00**

Table 16. Benefits of scenario 3

Benefit	Cost
Reduction of diesel fuel consumption	RM 804.00
Reduction of number of worker	RM 3,343.00
Total	**RM 4,147.00**

3.2 Simulation Model

From the result of MULTIPLE methods above, three scenario models were modeled and analyzed using the ProModel® 6.0 Simulation Software. Figure 7 presents the model translation for three scenario models.

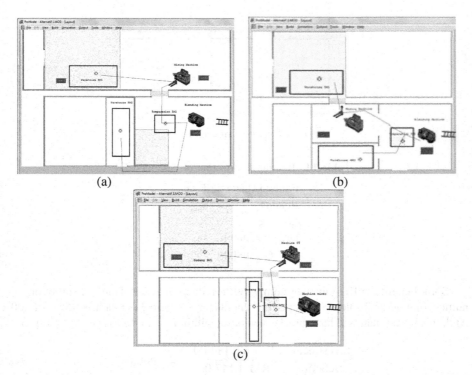

Fig. 7. Model translation of three scenario models using promodel 6.0 (a) scenario 1; (b) scenario 2; and (c) scenario 3

The simulation models are developed to evaluate the effect of all scenarios on throughput response. Those three scenarios are executed independently for six replication runs.

4 Experimental Result

The objective of model development is to reduce the non-added value processes. Then developing layout scenario conducted. Table 17 shows the improvement of throughput, number of workers, total distance, and total space between the current system and proposed scenarios. Generally, the proposed scenario has better throughput, a number of worker, total distance, and total space compared to the current system. Currently, the throughput of base model is about 75 batchs/week. On the other hand, the throughput of the proposed scenario is 86 batchs/week for scenario 1, 96 batchs/week for scenario 2, 91 batchs/week for scenario 3. Interestingly, this indicates an improvement by 15% for scenario 1, 28% for scenario 2, 21% for scenario 3. And for the number of worker of base model is needed 69 worker. for the proposed scenario is needed only 60 worker for scenario 1, scenario 2, scenario 3. This indicates an improvement by reduce worker 13% for scenario 1, 2, and 3. For the distance of base model is 4160 m/shift. On the other hand, the distance of the proposed scenario is 690 m/shift for scenario 1, 560 m/shift for scenario 2, 586 m/shift for scenario 3. This condition indicates an improvement by reducing distance 83% for scenario 1, 87% for scenario 2, 86% for scenario 3. For the space requirement of base model is 3846 m^2. On the other hand, the space of the proposed scenario is 3222 m^2 for scenario 1, 3006 m^2 for scenario 2, 3150 m^2 for scenario 3. This condition indicates an improvement by reducing space 16% for scenario 1, 22% for scenario 2, 18% for scenario 3. Generally, scenario 2 give the largest improvement than other although need more expensive cost investment.

Table 17. Summary of improvement result

Parameter	Base model	Scenario 1	Scenario 2	Scenario 3
Throughput (batch)	75	86	96	91
Δthroughput	–	15%	28%	21%
Worker	69	60	60	60
Δworker	–	−13%	−13%	−13%
Distance (m/shift)	4160	690	560	586
Δdistance	–	−83%	−87%	−86%
Space (m^2)	3846	3222	3006	3150
Δspace	–	−16%	−22%	−18%
Investment cost	–	RM 15,143	RM 195,143	RM 87,143
BEP	–	4 months	47 months	21 months

5 Conclusions

Mixing and blending processes are the initial step in producing the products. The performances of both processes are critical for the next processes since it has the longest processing time and the most influence on the quality of the product. However, it was found that the layout planning was ineffective. Three scenario layouts were developed by using MULTIPLE methods. Then, these scenario layouts were then translated and analyzed into operational models using the ProModel 6.0 Simulation Software. The simulation model was then verified and validated through statistical testing. Then the result was evaluated to identify the effect of each scenario on throughput, distance and number of workers. It shows that all scenario has higher throughput, lower distance, and lower number of worker than current system. Whereas in the selection of three scenarios some analyzes was considered i.e. space requirement and analysis cost benefit investment. From the three scenario, the scenario 2 shows the higher result than others of all parameters except investment cost. The cost to implement scenario 2 more expensive than others.

References

1. Amit, N., Suhadak, N., Johari, N., Kassim, I.: Using simulation to solve facility layout for food industry at XYZ company. In: 2012 IEEE Symposium on Humanities, Science and Engineering Research (SHUSER 2012), pp. 647–652 (2012)
2. Drira, A., Pierreval, H., Hajri-Gabouj, S.: Facility layout problems: a survey. Annu. Rev. Control 31(2), 255–267 (2007)
3. Hiregoudar, C., Raghavendra, B.: Facility Planning and Layout Design (2007)
4. Hosseini, S.S., Mirzapour, S.A., Wong, K.Y.: Improving multi-floor facility layout problems using systematic layout planning and simulation. In: Papasratorn, B., Charoenkitkarn, N., Vanijja, V., Chongsuphajaisiddhi, V. (eds.) IAIT 2013. CCIS, vol. 409, pp. 58–69. Springer, Cham (2013). doi:10.1007/978-3-319-03783-7_6
5. Jiang, S., Nee, A.Y.C.: A novel facility layout planning and optimization methodology. CIRP Ann. – Manuf. Technol. 62(1), 483–486 (2013)
6. Liggett, R.S.: Automated facilities layout: past, present and future. Autom. Constr. 9(2), 197–215 (2000)
7. Mahadevan, B.: Operation Management Theory and Practice. Pearson, London (2007)
8. Moatari-Kazerouni, A., Chinniah, Y., Agard, B.: Integration of occupational health and safety in the facility layout planning, part II: design of the kitchen of a hospital. Int. J. Prod. Res. 53(11), 3228–3242 (2014)
9. Nahmias, S.: Production and Operation Analysis, 6th edn. The McGraw-Hill Companies Inc., New York (2009)
10. Tompkins, J.A., White, J.A., Bozer, Y.A., Tanchoco, J.M.A.: Facilities Planning, 4th edn. Wiley, Hoboken (2010)
11. Wild, R.: Operation Management (2003)

Multi-stage Feature Selection for On-Line Flow Peer-to-Peer Traffic Identification

Bushra Mohammed Ali Abdalla[✉], Haitham A. Jamil, Mosab Hamdan,
Joseph Stephen Bassi, Ismahani Ismail, and Muhammad Nadzir Marsono

Department of Electronic and Computer Engineering,
Faculty of Electronic Engineering, Universiti Teknologi Malaysia,
81310 Johor Bahru, Malaysia
bushra0912115@gmail.com

Abstract. Classification of bandwidth-heavy Internet traffic is important for network administrators to throttle network of heavy-bandwidth applications traffic. Statistical methods have been previously proposed as promising method to identify Internet traffic based on packet statistical features. The selection of statistical features still plays an important role for accurate and timely classification. In this work, we propose an approach based on feature selection methods and analytic methods (scatter, one-way analysis of variance) in order to provide optimal features for on-line P2P traffic detection. Feature selection algorithms and machine learning algorithms were implemented using WEKA tool for available traces from University of Brescia, University of Aalborg and University of Cambridge. Experimental results show that the proposed method is able to achieve up to 99.5% accuracy with just six on-line statistical features. These results perform better than other existing approaches in term of accuracy and the number of features.

1 Introduction

Improvements in computing and communication nowadays bring to society tremendous benefits. Today, peer-to-peer (P2P) is considered as a standard architecture for sharing a wide range of various media throughout the Internet. The high volume of P2P traffic is due to file sharing, video streaming, on-line gaming and other activities that client-server architecture cannot accomplish as fast or as efficient as the P2P architecture. P2P traffic represents 27% to 55% of the aggregate Internet traffic, depending on geographic location [6]. The tremendous amount of P2P traffic and its rapid progression throughout the years have resulted in deteriorated network performance and congestion due to the high bandwidth consumption of P2P applications [22]. Therefore, traffic identification is required to improve the network performance.

First generation P2P applications traffic were relatively easy to be identified due to the use of fixed ports. However, current P2P applications are able to circumvent port-based identification by using dynamic port numbers or port masquerading. Besides, methods that rely on inspecting application payload

© Springer Nature Singapore Pte Ltd. 2017
M.S. Mohamed Ali et al. (Eds.): AsiaSim 2017, Part II, CCIS 752, pp. 509–523, 2017.
DOI: 10.1007/978-981-10-6502-6_44

signatures have also been proposed [15]. For privacy and impractical reasons, this method is ineffective. The diminished effectiveness of the port-based and payload-based techniques motivates the use of flow statistics as features for traffic identification. These techniques offer flexibility to detect P2P traffic compared to using port-based and signature-based methods.

There are extensive researches have been proposed over the last two decades that focused on the achievable accuracy of different machine learning (ML) algorithms. However, the impact of using different sets of statistical features has not been researched in-depth. Work in [23] found that feature selection has a positive impact to improve the performance than the selection of the classification algorithm. Presently, several feature selection algorithms have been introduced, eg. [5,27,28]. However, not all of the selected features can be extracted on-line since some features cannot be calculated before the flow is completed [28].

This paper proposes an approach based on feature selection methods and analytic methods (scatter, one-way analysis of variance (ANOVA)) in order to provide optimal features for on-line P2P traffic detection. The main aim of this work is to select on-line flow features for the identification of P2P traffic. In specific terms, the objectives include:

- To characterize on-line flow features for P2P traffic classification.
- To investigate the impact of features based inter-arrival time in on-line P2P classification accuracy.
- To propose optimal on-line features for on-line P2P traffic classification.
- To evaluate the effectiveness of the proposed features practically in terms of accuracy and recall.

The remainder of this paper is organized as follows. Section 2 introduces related works including ML concepts, traffic classification and feature selection. Section 3 discusses the methodology to select optimal on-line features. The experimental setup, result and discussion are discussed in Sect. 4. We conclude the work in Sect. 5.

2   Related Works

Machine learning (ML) is a powerful technique that has been used for data mining and knowledge discovery [18]. Recently, ML shows a good impact in the field of traffic classification. It can be categorized into two main learning methods, unsupervised and supervised learning methods. Unsupervised learning essentially clusters flows with similar characteristics. Supervised learning requires training data to be labeled in advance and produces a model that fits the training data [18].

Machine learning algorithms can be applied to learn patterns from known files in order to classify unknown files. A classifier is a rule-set that learns from known examples set. The first work using this technique was by [20]. Generally, classification can be performed in three steps, extracting the features, selection of feature and generating classifier [21].

Work in [14] suggested 249 flow statistical features that can be potentially used in ML traffic classification. However most of them can only be extracted off-line. Off-line features such as maximum bytes in packet, minimum bytes in packet, and median bytes in packet only can be extracted after receiving complete flows. Work in [1] used all 249 features suggested in [14] derived from packet streams consisting of one or more packet headers. Most of these features cannot be extracted on-line from live traffic for online traffic classification.

Feature selection is used to select subset features from the input which can efficiently describe the input data while reducing effects from noise or irrelevant features yet still provide good prediction of its class [5]. Traffic classification can be improved in terms of accuracy and computational performance by using the most relevant features [4].

Work in [12] selected online features without features related time and depending on the first quarter of packet. Works in [13] extracted first five packet in real-time and used fifteen features. This work classifies P2P traffic at line-rate.

Moore in [16] applied Fast Correlation Based Filter (FCBF) feature selection method for feature reduction and Naive Bayes algorithm to assess effects of the feature reduction. The result of the overall classification accuracy based on the features sub sets is 84.06%, which is the best than using all features. Work in [7] applied two features subsets to provide a classified traffic. This work uses flow features subsets on Support Vector Machine (SVM). The classifier accuracy is 70% while the training time is reported at 40 s. Work in [26] identified P2P traffic by using SVM and applied random search algorithm for features reduction. However, this work did not include UDP traffic although P2P traffic consists of both TCP and UDP packets.

On-line features techniques were proposed in [5,27]. These works used ten Cambridge datasets and Naive Bayes to evaluate two feature selection algorithms named Bias Coefficient Results (BFS) and selected online feature (SOF). These works achieved accuracy of 90.92% and 93.20%, respectively. Besides, the work in [5] considered inter-arrival time (IAT) as one of the proposed on-line features. These methods consider first quarter of flow as online features although first quarter features are difficult to extract online [13].

Most researches focus on the effect of features selection method applied on 249 flow statistical features as suggested in [16], meanwhile the other works focused on online features with IAT as suggested in [5,13,28]. However, the selection of statistical features for on-line P2P traffic classification still plays an important role for accurate and timely classification.

3   Overview of the Methods

Our proposed multi-stage feature selection consists of four main stages: feature extraction, features selection, features analysis and features measure. In the first stage, we extract first five packets of each flow as on-line features based on work in [13], and we categorize on-line features as shown in Table 1. In the second stage, a feature pool is formed from the inputs of few feature selection methods are filter

Table 1. Extracted features

ID	Name	ID	Name	ID	Name
1	port_a	12	ply_size_ab	23	pck_per_s
2	Port_b	13	ply_size_ba	24	byte_per_pck_ab
3	tcp_flg_ab	14	ply_size	25	byte_per_pck_ba
4	tcp_flg_ba	15	iat_ab	26	byte_per_pck
5	tcp_flg	16	iat_ba	27	ply_per_pck_ab
6	pck_num_ab	17	iat	28	ply_per_pck_ba
7	pck_num_ba	18	byte_per_s_ab	29	ply_per_pck
8	pck_num	19	byte_per_s_ba	30	time_interval_ab
9	pck_size_ab	20	byte_per_s	31	time_interval_ba
10	pck_size_ba	21	pck_per_s_ab	32	time_interval
11	pck_size	22	pck_per_s_ba	33	class

method (Chi-squared, Information gain (IG), and GainRatio (GR)) using first-twenty cut point in ranking. Also we used Principal Component Analysis (PCA) rubber method. These feature selection methods are first applied to the data and their outputs (i.e. the feature subsets selected). These features are fed into the feature pool filter from uninformative features depending on weight of each feature. All features that have sum of weight greater or equal one are selected as inputs to the third process. Scatter analytics is used to characterize all selected features and reduced the overlapping features and features that contribute less in separating the classes of traffic. In the fourth stage, we using One-way ANOVA as the mean difference measure to differentiate major significance of the selected features. All stages will be discussed in details in Sects. 3.3 and 3.4. Figure 1 shows the overview of the proposed method.

3.1 Features

Features are statistical characteristics calculated from object information. Traffic classification uses these features to allocate an object to the class. In classification procedure, the features may contain false correlation which delays the process of classification. Additional, some features may be redundant since the information they supplement is provided in other features. Extra features can increase computational time and can impact the accuracy.

3.2 Machine Learning Algorithms

The algorithms are considered in such a way that can help to choose a proper model for an on-line P2P Internet traffic classification. The classifiers used in this work are the J48, and Naive Bayes (NB). These algorithms are implemented in WEKA open-source platform [25].

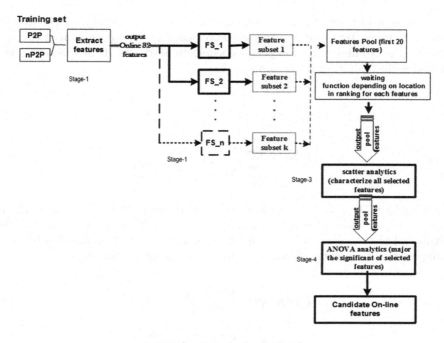

Fig. 1. Proposed method

3.3   Existing Feature Selection Methods

A good selection method for feature subsets for sample classification is needed in order to improve prediction accuracy, and to avoid complexity due to the large number of features investigated. The feature selection methods used in this work are Chi-squared [11], IG [17], GR [4] and PCA algorithms [24].

Chi-Squared. Chi-Squared is a feature selection algorithm that is based on χ^2 statistics [11]. It is built on the top of the entropy method and evaluates features individually by measuring their chi-squared statistics with respect to their classes. The χ^2 value of an attribution as shown in Eq. (1)

$$\chi^2 = \frac{(\mathcal{F}_0 - \mathcal{F}_1)^2}{\mathcal{F}_e} \tag{1}$$

where F_0 is the observed frequency, F_e is expected frequency. After calculating the χ^2 value of all considered features, the features can be ranked based on these values. The features that have higher ranks are more important than the others.

Information Gain (IG). The IG evaluates the feature according to the measurement of its information gain with respect to the class. Given entropy $E(S)$ as a measure of the impurity in a collection of items, Eq. (3) presents the equation of the entropy of a set of items S, based on c subsets of S (classes of the items), presented by Sc. Information Gain measures the expected reduction of entropy caused by portioning the examples according to attribute A, in which v is the set of possible values of A, as shown in Eq. (2) [17].

$$IG(S, A) = E(S) - \sum_{v \in V(A)} \frac{|S_v|}{|S|} . E(S_v) \tag{2}$$

$$E(S) = \sum_{c \in C} \frac{|S_c|}{S} . \log_2 \frac{|S_c|}{S} \tag{3}$$

GainRatio (GR). GR was introduced by Quinlan in the context of Decision Trees [4] which was designed to overcome bias in the IG by considering how the feature splits the data, as shown in Eqs. (4) and (5) [17]. Si are d subsets of examples resulting from portioning S by the d valued feature A.

$$GR(S, A) = \frac{IG(S, A)}{SI(S, A)} \tag{4}$$

$$SI(S, A) = \sum_{i=1}^{d} \frac{|S_i|}{S} . \log_2 \frac{|S_i|}{S} \tag{5}$$

Principal Component Analysis (PCA). The Principal Component Analysis (PCA) is one of the most widely used dimension reduction techniques for compression and data analysis. It is effective for real-time detection, high speed and masquerade due to its capacity for dimensionality reduction [24]. The idea of the PCA is described in detail in [24]. Given a set of observations (sequences) $X = X_1, X_2, X_n$. Suppose each observation is represented by a row vector of length m. The data set is thus represented by a matrix $X_{(nm)}$ as shown in Eq. (6).

$$X_{n \times m} = \begin{bmatrix} X_{11} & \dots & X_{1m} \\ \vdots & \ddots & \vdots \\ X_{n1} & \dots & X_{nm} \end{bmatrix} = \begin{bmatrix} X_1 & X_2 & X_m \end{bmatrix} \tag{6}$$

The average observation is shown in Eq. (7)

$$\mu = \frac{1}{n} \sum_{i=1}^{n} X_i \tag{7}$$

Observation deviation from the average is shown in Eq. (8).

$$\beta = X_i - \mu \tag{8}$$

3.4 Techniques for Analyzing Features

KNIME (Konstanz Information Miner) [8] is a modern, flexible and intuitive open-source data analytics platform that allows performing sophisticated statistics and data mining analysis. Scatter analytics and one-way ANOVA are implemented in KNIME benchmark. Other tools also exist such as the WEKA workspace [8].

The scatter diagram graphs pairs numerical data, with one variable on each axis, to look for a relationship between them. If the variables are correlated, the points will fall along a line. One-way ANOVA is the most effective method available for analyzing the more complex data sets [10]. In ANOVA the Sum of square (SS) is computed using Eqs. (9) and (15). Sum of Squares for Treatment (SST) is given by Eq. (13), Sum of Squares for Error (SSE) is computed using the Eq. (14), Variance Between Treatments (MST) is given by Eq. (16), Variance Within Treatments (MSE) is given by Eq. (17), and F-statistic is given by Eq. (18).

Using 95% confidence interval for mean difference, ANOVA is calculated as:

$$\text{Sum of square } (SS) = \sum_{j=1}^{k} \sum_{i=1}^{nj} (y_{ij} - \bar{y})^2 \tag{9}$$

$$= \sum_{j=1}^{k} \sum_{i=1}^{nj} (y_{ij} - \bar{y}_j + \bar{y}_j - \bar{y})^2 \tag{10}$$

$$= \sum_{j=1}^{k} \sum_{i=1}^{nj} (y_{ij} - \bar{y}_j)^2 + \sum_{j=1}^{k} \sum_{i=1}^{nj} (\bar{y}_j - \bar{y})^2 + 0 \tag{11}$$

$$SS = SST + SSE \tag{12}$$

$$SST = \sum_{j=1}^{k} \sum_{i=1}^{nj} (\bar{y}_j - \bar{y})^2 \tag{13}$$

$$SSE = \sum_{j=1}^{k} \sum_{i=1}^{nj} (\bar{y}_{ij} - \bar{y}_j)^2 \tag{14}$$

$$SS = SST + SSE \tag{15}$$

$$MST = \frac{SST}{(k-1)} \tag{16}$$

$$MSE = \frac{SSE}{(n-k)} \tag{17}$$

$$F = \frac{MST}{(MSE)} \tag{18}$$

Test $H_0 : \mu_1 = \mu_2 = \cdots = \mu_k$ and $H_1 : \mu_1 \neq \mu_2 \neq \cdots \neq \mu_k$, where $\bar{y}$ bar is the samples mean, n is the sample size, $\overline{(y_j)}$ is the specified population mean.

4   Experimental Setup, Result and Discussion

In this section, we explain the traffic traces and the evaluation method to evaluate the proposed approach for the selection of on-line features for P2P Internet traffic classification.

4.1   Dataset

Three datasets are used in this work for simulating the proposed technique, are UNIBS [3], Cambridge [14] and PAM [2]. Table 2 summarizes the used datasets, which the description of each dataset is as follows:

1. UNIBS traces [3] include packets generated by a series of workstations, located at the University of Brescia (UNIBS) in Italy in September and October 2009. These include classes, such as Web, Mail, P2P, SKYBE, and others.
2. PAM datasets was captured in Aalborg University from 25th February 2013 to 1st May and report in [2]. These include classes such as WEB, FTP, P2P, and Other.
3. Cambridge datasets are based on the traces captured on the Genome Campus network in August 2003. They are published by the computer laboratory in the University of Cambridge [14]. There are ten different datasets each from a different period of the 24-h day. These datasets consist of TCP flow. Moreover, each flow example is high dimensional since it consists of 248 features. The data with minimal class, games and interactive are not used as it is insufficient for training and testing. These include classes such as FTP-Pasv, Attack, P2P, Database, Multimedia, WEB, Mail, FTP-Control, and Services.

For the UNIBS and PAM dataset, the features are extracted based on the first-five- packets statistic of each flow. However, for the Cambridge dataset, the first-five-packet statistic are not available without access to the all raw packets. Thus, for this dataset, the complete flow statistic are used.

Table 2. Dataset used for experimental

	UNIBS	PAM	Cambridge
# Flow instances	77,303	339,061	397,030
# Classes	5	4	10
# Flow features extracted	33	33	33

4.2 Evaluation Metric and Validation

Performance and accuracy of the proposed method are validated by using accuracy and recall. These depend on true positive (a), false positive (b), true negative (c) and false negative (d).

4.3 Feature Selection Methods (FSM) Results

This subsection explains the feature selection method results. Firstly, we apply four algorithms of features selection to generate candidate subset of features from on-line extracted feature in Table 1. The features are selected for training dataset using Chi-squared, IG and GR ranking methods with cutting point equal first twenty features in ranking and also PC algorithm is used as searching method. Secondly, we evaluate the selected features is presented in Table 3 using weight function. Each feature that has weight greater than or equal one is selected. The weight result and selected features appear in Tables 4 and 5, respectively. After that the output send to the scatter. Table 3 describes position of selected features, weight of position (WP) and selected subset of features by using four feature selection algorithms.

Table 3. Selected features using FSM with cutting point equal first twenty

Position and weight of positions																			
Position	1	2	3	4	5	6	7	8	9	10	11	12	13	14	15	16	17	18	19	20
WP	0.95	0.9	0.85	0.8	0.75	0.7	0.65	0.6	0.55	0.5	0.45	0.4	0.35	0.3	0.25	0.2	0.15	0.1	0.05	0.0
FSM	ID of selected features																			
GR	5	6	2	13	18	20	28	21	23	17	32	15	30	31	26	16	14	11	10	27
IG	13	2	14	12	10	11	26	31	19	29	20	18	21	23	32	15	30	17	1	28
Chi	13	2	14	16	10	11	24	7	25	27	17	23	15	30	6	21	1	18	20	3
PC	9	8	1	2	3	4														

4.4 Scatter Results

The result of the Scatter plots in Fig. 2(a–e), indicates features (20, 18, 6, 21 and 23), are less significant in separating all classes. Furthermore, the result in Fig. 2(f and g), indicate features (16 and 17), are effective in separating class number four (other). While, the result in Fig. 2(h, i, j and k), indicate features (11, 10, 13 and 14), are effective in separating classes number (1, 3 and 4) (WEB, P2P and Other). Figure 2(l and m), indicate features numbers [1 and 2], are effective in separating most classes. The output of this method is used to select features in Table 6.

Table 4. Sum of weight

ID	Wait	ID	Wait	ID	Wait	ID	Wait
1	1.05	10	1.55	19	0.55	28	0.65
2	3.45	11	1.5	20	1.2	29	0.5
3	0.75	12	0.8	21	1.15	30	0.8
4	0.7	13	2.7	22	0.0	31	0.9
5	0.95	14	1.85	23	1.25	32	0.7
6	1.15	15	0.95	24	0.65	33	class
7	0.6	16	1.0	25	0.55		
8	0.9	17	1.05	26	0.9		
9	0.95	18	1.25	27	0.5		

Table 5. Selected features

ID	Name	Weight	ID	Name	Weight
1	port_a	1.05	16	iat_ba	1.0
2	Port_b	3.45	17	iat	1.05
6	pck_num_ab	1.15	18	byte_per_s_ab	1.25
10	pck_size_ba	1.55	20	byte_per_s	1.2
11	pck_size	1.5	21	pck_per_s_ab	1.15
13	ply_size_ba	2.7	23	pck_per_s	1.25
14	ply_size	1.85	33	class	class

Table 6. Pool features

ID	Name	Description	Subfigure
1	port_a	Source port number	(l)
2	Port_b	Destination port number	(m)
10	pck_size_ba	Total byte in Ethernet packet(Downlink)	(i)
11	pck_size	Total byte in Ethernet packet	(h)
13	ply_size_ba	Total byte in IP packet(Downlink)	(j)
14	ply_size	Total byte in IP packet	(k)
16	iat_ba	Total packet inter-arrival time(downlink)	(g)
17	iat	Total packet inter-arrival time	(f)
33	class		class

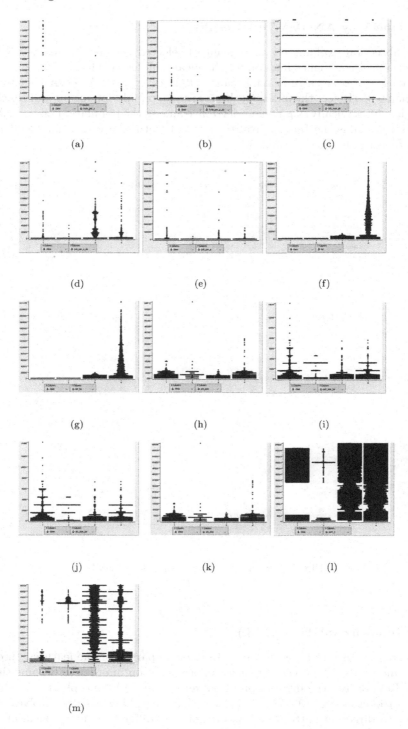

Fig. 2. Scatter result

4.5   One-Way ANOVA Test Results

This subsection explains the significant of selected features by using ANOVA test with 95% confidence interval for the mean difference. The result explains all selected features are significant because after tested with ANOVA the P-value less than 0.05 (Reject the null hypothesis of equal population means and conclude there is a (statistically) significant deference among the population means). Also, this test explains the Inter-arrival time (IAT) features are less significant than other features as shown in Fig. 3.

	Source	Sum of Squares	df	Mean Square	F	p-value
portA	Between Groups	9.26E12	3	3.09E12	5,668.7436	0.0
portA	Within Groups	1.85E14	339057	5.45E8		
portA	Total	1.94E14	339060			
portB	Between Groups	5.47E13	3	1.82E13	173,355.8736	0.0
portB	Within Groups	3.57E13	339057	1.05E8		
portB	Total	9.04E13	339060			
pck_size_ab	Between Groups	1.71E10	3	5.70E9	16,520.2872	0.0
pck_size_ab	Within Groups	1.17E11	339057	344,824.5912		
pck_size_ab	Total	1.34E11	339060			
pck_size_ba	Between Groups	1.84E9	3	6.15E8	10,702.6639	0.0
pck_size_ba	Within Groups	1.95E10	339057	57,435.3865		
pck_size_ba	Total	2.13E10	339060			
pck_size	Between Groups	1.99E10	3	6.64E9	17,676.6049	0.0
pck_size	Within Groups	1.27E11	339057	375,371.5113		
pck_size	Total	1.47E11	339060			
ply_size_ab	Between Groups	1.43E10	3	4.76E9	14,290.5108	0.0
ply_size_ab	Within Groups	1.13E11	339057	332,930.9074		
ply_size_ab	Total	1.27E11	339060			
ply_size_ba	Between Groups	1.95E9	3	6.49E8	11,378.5301	0.0
ply_size_ba	Within Groups	1.94E10	339057	57,073.045		
ply_size_ba	Total	2.13E10	339060			
ply_size	Between Groups	1.90E10	3	6.33E9	16,776.5031	0.0
ply_size	Within Groups	1.28E11	339057	377,416.4049		
ply_size	Total	1.47E11	339060			
iat_ab	Between Groups	2.00E11	3	6.68E10	554.798	0.0
iat_ab	Within Groups	4.08E13	339057	1.20E8		
iat_ab	Total	4.10E13	339060			
iat_ba	Between Groups	4.38E10	3	1.46E10	353.3253	0.0
iat_ba	Within Groups	1.40E13	339057	41,346,505.3144		
iat_ba	Total	1.41E13	339060			
iat	Between Groups	4.25E11	3	1.42E11	502.2179	0.0
iat	Within Groups	9.57E13	339057	2.82E8		
iat	Total	9.62E13	339060			

Fig. 3. Screen shot of test statistic ANOVA

4.6   Inter-arrival Time (IAT)

Inter-arrival time (IAT) as shown in Table 6 is a part of online features. Interarrival time needs pre-processing such as normalization in order to become significant. In addition, the integration of packet size and IAT morphing can heavily thwart the classifier [19]. This is because IAT morphing usually involves alternation on direction pattern [19] and depend on different network locations [9].

Therefore IAT online features are excluded in this work. Scatter result, ANOVA result and this Section are explained that IAT features are ineffective in classification P2P traffic, so we exclude the IAT features. The proposed on-line feature subset for P2P Internet traffic detection as can be shown in Table 7.

- Time-related features do not help to distinguish among applications [29].
- Creating a statistical signature of an application solely on the inter-packet time is a challenging task due to the time required by an application to generate and transfer packets to the transport layer is masked by the fact that additional time is added due to the network conditions and the TCP layer [19].
- One-way-Delay (OWD) measurement, timestamps of the same packet at different network locations is challenging task due to packet similarities [9].

Table 7. Proposed features

ID	Name	Description
1	port_a	Source port number
2	Port_b	Destination port number
10	pck_size_ba	Total byte in Ethernet packet(Downlink)
11	pck_size	Total byte in Ethernet packet
13	ply_size_ba	Total byte in IP packet(Downlink)
14	ply_size	Total byte in IP packet

4.7 Classification Results

Table 8 shows the results comparison between the proposed approach and work proposed in [5,12,29]. The works in [5,29] used ten Cambridge datasets and Naive Bayes to evaluate the feature selection algorithms named (BFS) and SOF in order.

Loo and Marsono in [12] used Cambridge datasets and classification process performs online classification on network traffic by using online flow features, while the learning process performs incremental learning to update the classification model for fair comparison. We test the features used in this work and validate on the same parameter that used to test the proposed features.

Our proposed method improves accuracy up to 1.99% for Naive Bayes, whilst, shows the smallest number of features compared with others. This smallest number of features results in improvement of reducing the testing time for our system. Also we selected features that can be extracted and applied on-line.

Table 8. Effectiveness of the proposed approach

	Naive Bayes testing				J48 testing		
	BFS [29]	SOF [5]	[12]	Proposed	SOF [5]	[12]	Proposed
Accuracy (%)	90.92	93.20	94.30	96.29	99.23	99.46	99.78
Recall	0.6	0.64	0.725	0.869	0.985	0.987	0.998
# of features	10	7	11	6	7	11	6

5   Conclusion

Classification of bandwidth heavy Internet traffic is important for network administrators to throttle the network from heavy bandwidth traffic applications. Statistical methods have been proposed as promising method to identify Internet traffic based on their statistical features. The selection of statistical features plays an important role in the classification results. In this paper, we proposed a subset of features for on-line P2P traffic classification. The experimental results indicate that our proposed on-line features result in an improved accuracy and uses smaller number of features (less classification time) and also can be extracted on-line.

References

1. Auld, T., Moore, A.W., Gull, S.F.: Bayesian neural networks for internet traffic classification. IEEE Trans. Neural Netw. **18**(1), 223–239 (2007)
2. Carela-Español, V., Bujlow, T., Barlet-Ros, P.: Is our ground-truth for traffic classification reliable? In: Faloutsos, M., Kuzmanovic, A. (eds.) PAM 2014. LNCS, vol. 8362, pp. 98–108. Springer, Cham (2014). doi:10.1007/978-3-319-04918-2_10
3. Gringoli, F., Salgarelli, L., Dusi, M., Cascarano, N., Risso, F., et al.: GT: picking up the truth from the ground for internet traffic. ACM SIGCOMM Comput. Commun. Rev. **39**(5), 12–18 (2009)
4. Henchiri, O., Japkowicz, N.: A feature selection and evaluation scheme for computer virus detection. In: 2006 Sixth International Conference on Data Mining, ICDM 2006, pp. 891–895. IEEE (2006)
5. Jamil, H.A., Mohammed, A., Hamza, A., Nor, S.M., Marsono, M.N.: Selection of on-line features for peer-to-peer network traffic classification. In: Thampi, S., Abraham, A., Pal, S., Rodriguez, J. (eds.) Recent Advances in Intelligent Informatics. AISC, vol. 235, pp. 379–390. Springer, Cham (2014). doi:10.1007/978-3-319-01778-5_39
6. Johnson, D.L., Belding, E.M., Van Stam, G.: Network traffic locality in a rural african village. In: Proceedings of the Fifth International Conference on Information and Communication Technologies and Development, pp. 268–277. ACM (2012)
7. Jun, L., Shunyi, Z., Shidong, L., Ye, X.: P2P traffic identification technique. In: 2007 International Conference on Computational Intelligence and Security, pp. 37–41. IEEE (2007)
8. KNIME. https://tech.knime.org/forum/bioinformatics/. Acceced 22 Dec 2016

9. Kögel, J.: One-way delay measurement based on flow data in large enterprise networks. University of Stuttgart, Institut für Kommunikationsnetze und Rechnersysteme (2013)
10. Kupper, L.L.: Applied Regression Analysis and Other Multivariate Methods. Duxbury Press, Pacific Grove (1978)
11. Liu, H., Setiono, R.: Chi2: feature selection and discretization of numeric attributes. In: 1995 Proceedings of the Seventh International Conference on Tools with Artificial Intelligence, pp. 388–391. IEEE (1995)
12. Loo, H.R., Marsono, M.N.: Online network traffic classification with incremental learning. Evol. Syst. **7**(2), 129–143 (2016)
13. Monemi, A., Zarei, R., Marsono, M.N.: Online NetFPGA decision tree statistical traffic classifier. Comput. Commun. **36**(12), 1329–1340 (2013)
14. Moore, A., Zuev, D., Crogan, M.: Discriminators for use in flow-based classification. Queen Mary and Westfield College, Department of Computer Science (2005)
15. Moore, A.W., Papagiannaki, K.: Toward the accurate identification of network applications. In: Dovrolis, C. (ed.) PAM 2005. LNCS, vol. 3431, pp. 41–54. Springer, Heidelberg (2005). doi:10.1007/978-3-540-31966-5_4
16. Moore, A.W., Zuev, D.: Internet traffic classification using Bayesian analysis techniques. In: ACM SIGMETRICS Performance Evaluation Review, vol. 33, pp. 50–60. ACM (2005)
17. Moskovitch, R., Stopel, D., Feher, C., Nissim, N., Japkowicz, N., Elovici, Y.: Unknown malcode detection and the imbalance problem. J. Comput. Virol. **5**(4), 295–308 (2009)
18. Nguyen, T.T., Armitage, G.: A survey of techniques for internet traffic classification using machine learning. IEEE Commun. Surv. Tutor. **10**(4), 56–76 (2008)
19. Qu, B., Zhang, Z., Zhu, X., Meng, D.: An empirical study of morphing on behavior-based network traffic classification. Secur. Commun. Netw. **8**(1), 68–79 (2015)
20. Schultz, M.G., Eskin, E., Zadok, F., Stolfo, S.J.: Data mining methods for detection of new malicious executables. In: Proceedings of the 2001 IEEE Symposium on Security and Privacy, S&P 2001, pp. 38–49. IEEE (2001)
21. Tahan, G., Rokach, L., Shahar, Y.: Mal-id: automatic malware detection using common segment analysis and meta-features. J. Mach. Learn. Res. **13**(Apr), 949–979 (2012)
22. Torres, R.D., Hajjat, M.Y., Rao, S.G., Mellia, M., Munafò, M.M.: Inferring undesirable behavior from P2P traffic analysis. In: ACM SIGMETRICS Performance Evaluation Review, vol. 37, pp. 25–36. ACM (2009)
23. Van Der Putten, P., Van Someren, M.: A bias-variance analysis of a real world learning problem: the coil challenge 2000. Mach. Learn. **57**(1–2), 177–195 (2004)
24. Wang, W., Zhang, X., Gombault, S.: Constructing attribute weights from computer audit data for effective intrusion detection. J. Syst. Softw. **82**(12), 1974–1981 (2009)
25. WEKA. http://www.cs.waikato.ac.nz/ml/weka/. Acceced 01 Dec 2016
26. Yang, Y.X., Wang, R., Liu, Y., Zhou, X.Y.: Solving P2P traffic identification problems via optimized support vector machines. In: 2007 IEEE/ACS International Conference on Computer Systems and Applications, AICCSA 2007, pp. 165–171. IEEE (2007)
27. Zhang, H., Lu, G., Qassrawi, M.T., Zhang, Y., Yu, X.: Feature selection for optimizing traffic classification. Comput. Commun. **35**(12), 1457–1471 (2012)
28. Zhao, J.J., Huang, X.H., Qiong, S., Yan, M.: Real-time feature selection in traffic classification. J. China Univ. Posts Telecommun. **15**, 68–72 (2008)
29. Zhen, L., Qiong, L.: A new feature selection method for internet traffic classification using ML. Phys. Procedia **33**, 1338–1345 (2012)

On MrR (Mister R) Method for Solving Linear Equations with Symmetric Matrices

Kuniyoshi Abe[1(✉)] and Seiji Fujino[2]

[1] Faculty of Economics and Information, Gifu Shotoku University,
Nakauzura, Gifu 5008288, Japan
abe@gifu.shotoku.ac.jp
[2] Professor Emeritus, Kyushu University, Fukuoka 8128581, Japan
seiji.fujino@gmail.com

Abstract. Krylov subspace methods, such as the Conjugate Gradient (CG) and Conjugate Residual (CR) methods, are treated for efficiently solving a linear system of equations with symmetric matrices. AZMJ variant of ORTHOMIN(2) (abbreviated as AZMJ) [1] has recently been proposed for solving the linear equations. In this paper, an alternative AZMJ variant is redesigned, i.e., an alternative minimum residual method for symmetric matrices is proposed by using the coupled two-term recurrences formulated by Rutishauser. The recurrence coefficients are determined by imposing the A-orthogonality on the residuals as well as CR. Our proposed variant is referred to as MrR. It is mathematically equivalent to CR and AZMJ, but the implementations are different; the recurrence formulae contain alternative expressions for the auxiliary vectors and the recurrence coefficients. Through numerical experiments on the linear equations with real symmetric matrices, it is demonstrated that the residual norms of MrR converge faster than those of CG and AZMJ.

Keywords: Linear equations · Krylov subspace methods · Conjugate residual method · Symmetric matrices · Rutishauser

1 Introduction

Krylov subspace methods are treated for solving a linear system of equations

$$Ax = b \tag{1}$$

for a solution vector x, where $A \in \mathbf{R}^{n \times n}$ is a given coefficient matrix and $b \in \mathbf{R}^n$ is a given vector. The Krylov subspace methods for solving the linear equations with nonsymmetric matrices, such as the Generalized Conjugate Residual (GCR) [3] and Generalized Minimum RESidual (GMRES) [8] methods, use the Arnoldi orthogonalization algorithm [2] to generate basis vectors of the Krylov subspace. The iteration proceeds by using long recurrence formulae, in which all previous vectors and constants obtained at each iteration are stored. GCR and GMRES

© Springer Nature Singapore Pte Ltd. 2017
M.S. Mohamed Ali et al. (Eds.): AsiaSim 2017, Part II, CCIS 752, pp. 524–533, 2017.
DOI: 10.1007/978-981-10-6502-6_45

are derived by minimizing the residual norms. The restarted and truncated versions of GCR are known as GCR(m) and ORTHOMIN(m) [12], respectively. The Krylov subspace methods for solving the linear equations with symmetric matrices, such as the Conjugate Gradient (CG) [5] and Conjugate Residual (CR) [10] methods, use the Lanczos orthogonalization algorithm [11]. The residual vectors and approximate solutions are updated by using the short recurrence, in which the preceding two vectors and constants are stored. The recurrence coefficients of CG and CR are obtained by imposing the orthogonality and the A-orthogonality on the residual vectors, respectively.

AZMJ variant of ORTHOMIN(2) (abbreviated as AZMJ) [1] has recently been proposed for nonsymmetric matrices. It is mathematically equivalent to CR and ORTHOMIN(2), but their implementations are different each other. AZMJ uses the different recurrence formulae from those of CR and ORTHOMIN(2) for updating the residual vectors; they contain alternative expressions for the auxiliary vectors and the recurrence coefficients, while it updates the approximate solutions by using the same recurrence formulae as CR. Thus the recurrence formulae for the approximate solutions do not correspond with those for the residual vectors in AZMJ. The recurrence coefficients of AZMJ are determined by minimizing the residual norms as done in ORTHOMIN(2), while those of CR are done by imposing the A-orthogonality on the residual vectors. It results from the decision of the recurrence coefficients that AZMJ is called not an alternative CR variant but an ORTHOMIN(2) variant.

Therefore an alternative AZMJ variant is redesigned, i.e., an alternative minimum residual method is proposed by using the coupled two-term recurrences formulated by Rutishauser [7], who suggested it for stabilizing the ORTHODIR method [13], and imposing the A-orthogonality on the residual vectors for symmetric matrices. Our variant, i.e., the Minimum residual method using the coupled two-term recurrences formulated by Rutishauser, is referred as MrR (it is called "Mister R"). It is mathematically equivalent to CR and AZMJ, but the implementations are different; the recurrence formulae contain alternative expressions for the auxiliary vectors and the recurrence coefficients. Numerical experiments show that the residual norms of our proposed MrR converge fairly faster than those of CG and AZMJ.

In the following Sect. 2, we outline CR and CG. In Sect. 3, an alternative AZMJ variant is redesigned, i.e., MrR is derived by using the coupled two-term recurrences formulated by Rutishauser and imposing the A-orthogonality. The difference between AZMJ and MrR, and the computational costs are summarized. In Sect. 4, the results of numerical experiments are presented: the convergence behavior among CG, AZMJ and MrR is compared. Finally, in Sect. 5 concluding remarks are described.

2   CR and CG Methods

In this section, we outline CR and CG for solving the problem (1) with symmetric matrices.

The residual vectors r_k^{cr} of CR are expressed by

$$r_k^{\mathrm{cr}} \equiv R_k(A)r_0$$

with the so-called Lanczos polynomial $R_k(\lambda)$ [11], which satisfies the recurrence relation

$$\begin{cases} R_0(\lambda) & = 1, \\ R_1(\lambda) & = 1 - \alpha_0\lambda, \\ R_{k+1}(\lambda) = \left(1 + \alpha_k\frac{\beta_{k-1}}{\alpha_{k-1}} - \alpha_k\lambda\right) R_k(\lambda) - \alpha_k\frac{\beta_{k-1}}{\alpha_{k-1}} R_{k-1}(\lambda), \\ \qquad\qquad\qquad\qquad\qquad k = 1, 2, \ldots, \end{cases}$$

for certain coefficients α_k and β_{k-1}. Here r_0 denotes an initial residual, which is defined by $r_0 \equiv b - Ax_0$, where x_0 is an arbitrary vector.

To update the residual vectors r_k^{cr}, a new auxiliary vector p_k^{cr} is introduced. For some polynomial $\bar{G}_k(\lambda)$, the vectors p_k^{cr} can be expressed as

$$p_k^{\mathrm{cr}} \equiv \bar{G}_k(A)r_0.$$

Then, the two sequences of polynomials $R_k(\lambda)$ and $\bar{G}_k(\lambda)$ are satisfied with the coupled two-term recurrences

$$\begin{aligned} \bar{G}_k(\lambda) &= R_k(\lambda) + \beta_{k-1}\bar{G}_{k-1}(\lambda), \\ R_{k+1}(\lambda) &= R_k(\lambda) - \alpha_k\lambda\bar{G}_k(\lambda). \end{aligned} \qquad (2)$$

The computations for the recurrence coefficients α_k and β_k of CR are described. The vectors p_k^{cr} are basis vectors of $K_k(A, r_0)$, and are obtained by using the AA-Lanczos orthogonalization algorithm [6] for CR, where $K_k(A, r_0)$ denotes the kth Krylov subspace. From this approach, we learn that the vectors p_k^{cr} satisfy

$$(Ap_i^{\mathrm{cr}}, Ap_j^{\mathrm{cr}}) = 0 \quad (i \neq j). \qquad (3)$$

Using the property (3) and induction, the orthogonality for the vectors r_k^{cr} and p_k^{cr} is obtained.

$$(r_k^{\mathrm{cr}}, Ap_i^{\mathrm{cr}}) = 0 \quad (i < k). \qquad (4)$$

The condition (4) yields

$$(r_k^{\mathrm{cr}}, Ar_i^{\mathrm{cr}}) = 0 \ (i < k). \qquad (5)$$

From the properties (3)–(5), the recurrence coefficients α_k and β_k are computed by

$$\alpha_k = \frac{(Ar_k^{\mathrm{cr}}, r_k^{\mathrm{cr}})}{(Ap_k^{\mathrm{cr}}, Ap_k^{\mathrm{cr}})}, \qquad \beta_k = \frac{(Ar_{k+1}^{\mathrm{cr}}, r_{k+1}^{\mathrm{cr}})}{(Ar_k^{\mathrm{cr}}, r_k^{\mathrm{cr}})}.$$

The CR algorithm is expressed as follows.

CR Algorithm

Let x_0 be an initial guess, and put $r_0 = b - Ax_0$

Set $\beta_{-1} = 0$

For $k = 0, 1, \ldots$

$$p_k = r_k + \beta_{k-1}p_{k-1}, \quad q_k = Ar_k + \beta_{k-1}q_{k-1}$$

$$\alpha_k = \frac{(Ar_k, r_k)}{(q_k, q_k)}$$

$$x_{k+1} = x_k + \alpha_k p_k, \quad r_{k+1} = r_k - \alpha_k q_k$$

$$\beta_k = \frac{(Ar_{k+1}, r_{k+1})}{(Ar_k, r_k)}$$

end

Note that the vectors r_k^{cg} and p_k^{cg} generated by CG use (2) for updating the residual vectors and approximate solutions. Since CG is derived from the Lanczos orthogonalization algorithm [11], the vectors r_k^{cg} satisfy the condition

$$(r_i^{\mathrm{cg}}, r_j^{\mathrm{cg}}) = 0 \quad (i \neq j). \tag{6}$$

Using (6) and induction, we obtain the orthogonalities for the vectors r_k^{cg} and p_k^{cg}.

$$(r_k^{\mathrm{cg}}, p_i^{\mathrm{cg}}) = 0 \ (i \neq k), \quad (p_i^{\mathrm{cg}}, Ap_j^{\mathrm{cg}}) = 0 \ (i \neq j).$$

Thus the recurrence coefficients α_k and β_k are computed by

$$\alpha_k = \frac{(r_k^{\mathrm{cg}}, r_k^{\mathrm{cg}})}{(p_k^{\mathrm{cg}}, Ap_k^{\mathrm{cg}})}, \qquad \beta_k = \frac{(r_{k+1}^{\mathrm{cg}}, r_{k+1}^{\mathrm{cg}})}{(r_k^{\mathrm{cg}}, r_k^{\mathrm{cg}})}.$$

3   MrR Method

In this section, MrR, i.e., an alternative minimum residual method, is designed by using the coupled two-term recurrences formulated by Rutishauser [7] and imposing the A-orthogonality.

3.1   Algorithm of MrR

With $\zeta_k \equiv \alpha_k$ and $\eta_k \equiv \beta_{k-1}\frac{\alpha_k}{\alpha_{k-1}}$, the coupled two-term recurrences (2) for CR/CG can be rewritten into a three-term recurrence for the CR/CG residuals:

$$r_{k+1}^{\mathrm{cr/cg}} = (1 + \eta_k - \zeta_k A)r_k^{\mathrm{cr/cg}} - \eta_k r_{k-1}^{\mathrm{cr/cg}},$$

or, in terms of the CR/CG residual polynomials $P_k(\lambda)$ [4,11,14],

$$P_{k+1}(\lambda) = (1 + \eta_k - \zeta_k \lambda)P_k(\lambda) - \eta_k P_{k-1}(\lambda). \tag{7}$$

The residual vectors $\boldsymbol{r}_k$ of MrR are expressed by

$$\boldsymbol{r}_k \equiv P_k(A)\boldsymbol{r}_0.$$

This scaled version of the three-term recurrence for the Lanczos polynomials has been exploited in the ORTHODIR algorithm [13] for symmetric systems: CG can be viewed as a coupled two-term variant of ORTHODIR. To stabilize ORTHODIR, Rutishauser [7] suggested an alternative coupled two-term variant. Applying Rutishauser's suggestion to (7) gives the coupled two-term recurrences

$$\begin{aligned} G_{k+1}(\lambda) &= \zeta_k \lambda P_k(\lambda) + \eta_k G_k(\lambda), \\ P_{k+1}(\lambda) &= P_k(\lambda) - G_{k+1}(\lambda), \end{aligned} \tag{8}$$

where the CR/CG formulations correspond to

$$\begin{aligned} \tilde{G}_k(\lambda) &= P_k(\lambda) + \eta_k \frac{\zeta_{k-1}}{\zeta_k} \tilde{G}_{k-1}(\lambda), \\ P_{k+1}(\lambda) &= P_k(\lambda) - \zeta_k \lambda \tilde{G}_k(\lambda). \end{aligned} \tag{9}$$

The residual vectors and approximate solutions for MrR are updated by (8). The stabilizing polynomial [9] used in the Generalized Product-type method based on Bi-Conjugate Gradient (GPBiCG) [14] is satisfied the coupled two-term recurrences

$$\begin{aligned} \hat{G}_k(\lambda) &= \zeta_k P_k(\lambda) + \eta_k \hat{G}_{k-1}(\lambda), \\ P_{k+1}(\lambda) &= P_k(\lambda) - \lambda \hat{G}_k(\lambda). \end{aligned} \tag{10}$$

The residual vectors and approximate solutions for AZMJ are updated by (10) and (9), respectively.

The G_k of (8), $\tilde{G}_k(\lambda)$ of (9) and $\hat{G}_k$ of (10) are related as $G_{k+1}(\lambda) = \lambda \hat{G}_k(\lambda)$, and $\hat{G}_k(\lambda) = \zeta_k \tilde{G}_k(\lambda)$.

Introducing an auxiliary vector

$$\boldsymbol{y}_k \equiv G_k(A)\boldsymbol{r}_0 \tag{11}$$

transforms (8) to

$$\boldsymbol{y}_{k+1} = \zeta_k A \boldsymbol{r}_k + \eta_k \boldsymbol{y}_k, \quad \boldsymbol{r}_{k+1} = \boldsymbol{r}_k - \boldsymbol{y}_{k+1}. \tag{12}$$

The update formulae for the approximate solutions

$$\boldsymbol{z}_{k+1} = -\zeta_k \boldsymbol{r}_k + \eta_k \boldsymbol{z}_k, \quad \boldsymbol{x}_{k+1} = \boldsymbol{x}_k - \boldsymbol{z}_{k+1} \tag{13}$$

are obtained from (12) for the residual by using $\boldsymbol{r}_k \equiv \boldsymbol{b} - A\boldsymbol{x}_k$ and $\boldsymbol{y}_k = -A\boldsymbol{z}_k$.

The recurrence coefficients ζ_k and η_k are computed so as to minimize the residual norm, i.e.,

$$\arg\min_{\zeta,\eta} \| \boldsymbol{r}_k - \zeta_k A \boldsymbol{r}_k - \eta_k \boldsymbol{y}_k \|_2 . \tag{14}$$

The following equivalence is applied.

$$(\alpha, \beta) = \arg\min_{\alpha,\beta} \| \boldsymbol{x} - \alpha \boldsymbol{a} - \beta \boldsymbol{b} \|_2 \quad \Longleftrightarrow \quad \boldsymbol{x} - \alpha \boldsymbol{a} - \beta \boldsymbol{b} \perp \boldsymbol{a}, \boldsymbol{b}.$$

By replacing x, a and b with r_k, Ar_k and y_k, respectively, (14) is rewritten to

$$r_k - \zeta_k Ar_k - \eta_k y_k \perp Ar_k, y_k. \tag{15}$$

When introducing two vectors $\tilde{r}$ and $\tilde{s}$:

$$\tilde{r} \equiv r_k - \gamma_1 y_k, \quad \tilde{s} \equiv Ar_k - \gamma_2 y_k,$$

the residual vector r_{k+1} is expressed by

$$r_{k+1} = \tilde{r} - \zeta_k \tilde{s},$$

where the coefficient η_k is computed by $\eta_k = \gamma_1 - \zeta_k \gamma_2$.

To facilitate computation and selection, we first orthogonalize against y_k since this is required for both vectors $\tilde{r}$ and $\tilde{s}$.

$$\tilde{r} \perp y_k, \quad \tilde{s} \perp y_k.$$

Then the computations of γ_1 and γ_2 can be obtained as

$$\gamma_1 \equiv \frac{(y_k, r_k)}{(y_k, y_k)}, \quad \gamma_2 \equiv \frac{(y_k, Ar_k)}{(y_k, y_k)}.$$

Next from (15) when imposing the orthogonality $\tilde{r} - \zeta_k \tilde{s} \perp \tilde{s}$, we obtain

$$\zeta_k = \frac{(\tilde{s}, \tilde{r})}{(\tilde{s}, \tilde{s})}.$$

The vectors r_k and y_k generated by MrR satisfy the orthogonalities

$$(r_{k+1}, Ar_k) = (r_{k+1}, y_k) = 0. \tag{16}$$

By (16), we have the property

$$(r_k, y_k) = (y_{k+1}, y_k) = 0. \tag{17}$$

The orthogonalities (16) and (17) in MrR are the same as those in AZMJ [1].

MrR and CR can be viewed as the methods for the symmetric matrices because of imposing the condition such that the next residual r_{k+1} is orthogonal to Ar_k. On the other hand, MrR as well as CR can also be applied to the linear equations with nonsymmetric matrices since imposing the A-orthogonality on the residual vectors is mathematically equivalent to the minimum residual approach. Thus MrR is mathematically equivalent to CR and AZMJ, but the implementations are different each other.

The algorithm of MrR is summarized as follows:

MrR Algorithm

> Let x_0 be an initial guess, and put $r_0 = b - Ax_0$
> Set $y_0 = -r_0 \quad z_0 = 0$

For $k = 0, 1, \ldots$

$$\mu = (\boldsymbol{y}_k, \boldsymbol{y}_k), \ \nu = (\boldsymbol{y}_k, A\boldsymbol{r}_k), \ \omega = (\boldsymbol{y}_k, \boldsymbol{r}_k)$$

$$\gamma_1 = \frac{\omega}{\mu}, \quad \gamma_2 = \frac{\nu}{\mu}$$

$$(\gamma_1 = 0, \ \gamma_2 = 0 \ \text{if } k = 0)$$

$$\boldsymbol{r}' = \boldsymbol{r}_k - \gamma_1 \boldsymbol{y}_k, \quad \boldsymbol{s}' = A\boldsymbol{r}_k - \gamma_2 \boldsymbol{y}_k$$

$$\zeta_k = \frac{(\boldsymbol{r}', \boldsymbol{s}')}{(\boldsymbol{s}', \boldsymbol{s}')}, \quad \eta_k = \gamma_1 - \zeta_k \gamma_2$$

$$\boldsymbol{y}_{k+1} = \eta_k \boldsymbol{y}_k + \zeta_k A\boldsymbol{r}_k, \quad \boldsymbol{z}_{k+1} = \eta_k \boldsymbol{z}_k - \zeta_k \boldsymbol{r}_k$$

$$\boldsymbol{r}_{k+1} = \boldsymbol{r}_k - \boldsymbol{y}_{k+1}, \quad \boldsymbol{x}_{k+1} = \boldsymbol{x}_k - \boldsymbol{z}_{k+1}$$

end

3.2   Difference between MrR and AZMJ

The difference between MrR and AZMJ can be described as follows:

1. Since the vectors $\boldsymbol{y}_k$ updated in AZMJ are introduced with $\zeta_{k-1}\hat{G}_{k-1}(A)\boldsymbol{r}_0$, it is different from (11) updated in MrR. However, the resulting recurrence formulae for the residual vectors in AZMJ coincide with those in MrR.
2. The recurrences for updating the approximate solutions in MrR and AZMJ are obtained from (8) and (9), respectively. Thus the recurrences for the approximate solutions are different each other.
3. The computations of the coefficients ζ_k and η_k in AZMJ are obtained by minimizing the residual norms. The explicit expressions of ζ_k and η_k are given by

$$\zeta_k = \frac{\zeta_{k-1}(\boldsymbol{r}_{k-1}, A\boldsymbol{r}_{k-1})(A\boldsymbol{r}_k, \boldsymbol{r}_k)}{\zeta_{k-1}(A\boldsymbol{r}_k, A\boldsymbol{r}_k)(\boldsymbol{r}_{k-1}, A\boldsymbol{r}_{k-1}) - (\boldsymbol{y}_k, A\boldsymbol{r}_k)(A\boldsymbol{r}_k, \boldsymbol{y}_k)},$$
$$\eta_k = \frac{-(\boldsymbol{y}_k, A\boldsymbol{r}_k)(A\boldsymbol{r}_k, \boldsymbol{r}_k)}{\zeta_{k-1}(A\boldsymbol{r}_k, A\boldsymbol{r}_k)(\boldsymbol{r}_{k-1}, A\boldsymbol{r}_{k-1}) - (\boldsymbol{y}_k, A\boldsymbol{r}_k)(A\boldsymbol{r}_k, \boldsymbol{y}_k)}. \tag{18}$$

The expressions of the coefficients ζ_k and η_k in MrR are obtained by imposing the A-orthogonality on the residual vectors for symmetric matrices. Thus the computations of the coefficients ζ_k and η_k are different each other. We expect that the convergence behavior of MrR is different from that of AZMJ.

Note that we obtain the MrR variant for nonsymmetric matrices, i.e., the modified AZMJ, when replacing the recurrence formulae for the approximate solutions in AZMJ with (13); the MrR variant for nonsymmetric matrices uses the recurrences (12) and (13), and the expressions (18) of the recurrence coefficients.

Table 1 summarizes the computational costs, i.e., the number of matrix vector products (indicated as MVs), inner products (indicated as Dots) and vector updates (indicated as AXPYs), for CG, AZMJ and MrR. Updates of the form $\alpha\boldsymbol{x}$ and $\boldsymbol{x} + \boldsymbol{y}$ are counted as 0.5 AXPY. The computation of $\|\boldsymbol{r}_k\|_2$ for the termination criterion requires 1 Dot per iteration. The number of Dots and AXPYs for MrR is more than that for CG and AZMJ per iteration.

Table 1. Computational costs for CG, AZMJ and MrR per iteration

	MVs	Dots	AXPYs
CG	1	3	3
AZMJ	1	4	4
MrR	1	6	6

4 Numerical Experiments

In this section, the convergence behavior among CG, AZMJ and MrR is compared on the problem (1) with real symmetric matrices, and then it is shown that MrR is effective.

Numerical experiments were carried out in double-precision floating-point arithmetic on CX400 (CPU: Intel Xeon E5-2690, clock: 2.7 GHz, main memory: 128 GB, OS: Red Hat Linux Enterprise) equipped with a Fujitsu compiler. The code was implemented using Fortran90. Optimized option of the compiler "-O3" was used. The iteration is started with $x_0 = 0$.

CG, AZMJ and MrR are applied to the linear equations with real symmetric matrices, and compare the convergence behavior. The real symmetric matrices bcsstk17, ela-pla-9-1000, msc10848, pwtk and s3dkt3m2, and the given right-hand side vectors are treated. The matrices bcsstk17, msc10848, pwtk and s3dkt3m2, and the other (i.e., ela-pla-9-1000) are offered from Matrix collection by T. Davis of Florida university and our joint work, respectively. Table 2 shows the characteristics of coefficient matrices, i.e., the dimension (indicated as N), the total number of nonzero entries (indicated as NNZ), and the average NNZ per row. The iteration is stopped when the relative residual norms $||r_k||_2/||r_0||_2$ become less than 10^{-12}.

Table 2. Characteristics of coefficient matrices

Matrix	N	NNZ	Ave. NNZ
bcsstk17	10,974	219,812	20.03
ela-pla-9-1000	28,291	3,315,555	117.19
msc10848	10,848	620,313	57.18
pwtk	217,918	5,926,171	27.19
s3dkt3m2	90,449	1,921,955	21.25

Table 3 shows the number of iterations (indicated as Iterations), the computation time (indicated as Time (in seconds)) required to obtain successful convergence, and the explicitly computed relative residual norms ($\log_{10}(||b - Ax_k||_2/||b - Ax_0||_2)$, abbreviated as True res.) at the final iteration.

Table 3. Number of iterations, computation time (in seconds) and explicitly computed relative residual norms (indicated as True res.) (displayed in order of bcsstk17, ela-pla-9-1000, msc10848, pwtk and s3dkt3m2)

	bcsstk17				ela-pla-9-1000		
	Iterations	Time[s]	True res.		Iterations	Time[s]	True res.
CG	3154	1.819	-12.0	CG	12297	106.27	-11.7
AZMJ	3067	1.739	-12.0	AZMJ	13002	105.60	-11.6
MrR	3067	1.727	-12.0	MrR	11118	90.46	-11.3

	msc10848				pwtk		
	Iterations	Time[s]	True res.		Iterations	Time[s]	True res.
CG	5640	8.674	-12.0	CG	52852	808.51	-12.0
AZMJ	5474	7.524	-12.0	AZMJ	40322	608.11	-12.0
MrR	5475	7.635	-12.0	MrR	38001	579.74	-12.0

	s3dkt3m2		
	Iterations	Time[s]	True res.
CG	50331	253.21	-11.9
AZMJ	52748	268.46	-11.9
MrR	49415	251.65	-11.9

From Table 3, we can observe the following: the number of iterations and the computation time required to obtain the successful convergence for MrR are at most 72% and 85% of those for CG and AZMJ, respectively. The residual norms of MrR converge faster than those of CG and AZMJ on the problems ela-pla-9-1000 and pwtk. The convergence speed of MrR is almost the same as that of AZMJ and faster than that of CG on the problems bcsstk17 and msc10848, and it is faster than that of AZMJ and almost the same as that of CG on the problem s3dkt3m2. MrR is more effective than CG and AZMJ. The approximate solutions solved by CG, AZMJ and MrR become almost the same accurate each other. The true residual norms attain to around 10^{-12} for the problems bcsstk17, ela-pla-9-1000, msc10848, pwtk and s3dkt3m2.

Note that the convergence of MrR is almost the same as that of CR since the recurrence coefficients are determined by the same mathematical conditions.

5   Concluding Remarks

An alternative AZMJ variant has been redesigned, i.e., an alternative minimum residual method (referred to as MrR) has been proposed, for symmetric matrices. MrR has been designed by imposing the A-orthogonality and using the coupled two-term recurrences formulated by Rutishauser. MrR is mathematically equivalent to CR and AZMJ, but the implementations are different; the recurrence formulae contain alternative expressions for the auxiliary vectors and the recurrence coefficients. Numerical experiments show that the residual norms of MrR converge fairly faster than those of CG and AZMJ.

We are to give the preconditioned algorithm and the numerical results in our future work.

Acknowledgment. We appreciate Mr. K. Iwasato of Kyushu University for executing numerical experiments. We would like to appreciate Professor G.L.G. Sleijpen and the reviewers for their insightful and helpful suggestions. This research was partly supported by JSPS KAKENHI Grant Number 26390136, 2016.

References

1. Abe, K., Zhang, S.L., Mitsui, T., Jin, C.H.: A variant of the Orthomin(2) method for singular linear systems. Numer. Algorithms **36**, 189–202 (2004)
2. Arnoldi, W.E.: The principle of minimized iteration in the solution of the matrix eigenvalue problem. Quart. Appl. Math. **9**, 17–29 (1951)
3. Eisenstat, S.C., Elman, H.C., Schultz, M.H.: Variational iterative methods for non-symmetric systems of linear equations. SIAM J. Numer. Anal. **20**, 345–357 (1983)
4. Gutknecht, M.H.: Variants of BiCGStab for matrices with complex spectrum. SIAM J. Sci. Comput. **14**, 1020–1033 (1993)
5. Hestenes, M.R., Stiefel, E.L.: Methods of conjugate gradients for solving linear systems. J. Res. Nat. Bur. Stand. **49**, 409–435 (1952)
6. Lanczos, C.: Solution of systems of linear equations by minimized iterations. J. Res. Nat. Bur. Stand. **49**, 33–53 (1952)
7. Rutishauser, H.: Theory of gradient method. In: Refined Iterative Methods for Computation of the Solution and the Eigenvalues of Self-Adjoint Value Problems, pp. 24–49. Mitt. Inst. angew. Math. ETH Zürich, Birkhäuser, Basel (1959)
8. Saad, Y., Schultz, M.H.: GMRES: A generalized minimal residual algorithm for solving nonsymmetric linear systems. SIAM J. Sci. Stat. Comput. **7**, 856–869 (1986)
9. Sleijpen, G.L.G., Sonneveld, P., van Gijzen, M.B.: Bi-CGSTAB as induced dimension reduction method. Appl. Numer. Math. **60**, 1100–1114 (2010)
10. Stiefel, E.L.: Relaxationsmethoden bester strategie zur losung linearer gleichungssysteme. Commentarii Mathematici Helvetici **29**, 157–179 (1955)
11. Stiefel, E.L.: Kernel polynomial in linear algebra and their numerical applications, In: Further contributions to the determination of eigenvalues. NBS Appl. Math. Ser. **49**, 1–22 (1958)
12. Vinsom, P.K.W.: Orthomin, an iterative method for solving sparse sets of simultaneous linear equations. In: Proceedings of the Fourth Symposium on Reservoir Simulation, pp. 149–159. Society of Petroleum Engineers of AIME (1976)
13. Young, D.M., Jea, K.C.: Generalized conjugate gradient acceleration of nonsymmetrizable iterative methods. Linear Algebra Appl. **34**, 159–194 (1980)
14. Zhang, S.L.: GPBi-CG: Generalized product-type methods based on Bi-CG for solving nonsymmetric linear systems. SIAM J. Sci. Comput. **18**, 537–551 (1997)

Racer: A Simulated Environment Driving Simulator to Investigate Human Driving Skill

Amirah 'Aisha Badrul Hisham[1], Marwan Nafea[1],
Ahmad Bukhari Aujih[2], Mohamad Hafis Izran Ishak[1(✉)],
and Mohamad Shukri Zainal Abidin[1]

[1] Department of Control and Mechatronics (CMED),
Faculty of Electrical Engineering, Universiti Teknologi Malaysia,
81310 Skudai, Johor, Malaysia
{aaisha2,nmmarwan3}@live.utm.my,
{hafis,shukri}@fke.utm.my
[2] Centre for Intelligent Signal and Imaging Research (CISIR),
Universiti Teknologi PETRONAS,
32610 Seri Iskandar, Tronoh, Perak, Malaysia
ahmad.bukhari_g03649@utp.edu.my

Abstract. The identification and the quantification of human skill is one of the major characteristics to be considered in designing an algorithm for Human Adaptive Mechatronics (HAM) application. This paper focuses on studying the Racer software, as well as the relationship of data gained and the simulated environment. The fact that Racer is chosen as the tool is described. This paper discusses the details about the software used; Racer as the driving simulator environment during the experiment. The experimental setup, data extraction process and data conversion are explained further in this paper. The experimental results meet the purpose of data collection which provides variety set of data, including many options for cars and tracks. As a conclusion, Racer is a suitable software to be used. The utmost important, the further study of this research will help during the development of car assistance system.

Keywords: Driving simulator · Racer software · Human skill · Human performance

1 Introduction

Accidents in Malaysia are reportedly increasing in number. The total number of casualties due to road accidents involving motor vehicles was 326,817 in 2004. According to the Ministry of Transport Malaysia, this number has increased to 477,204 accidents (146%) in 2013 [1]. Every day, almost two percent (or half a million) Malaysian citizens are at risk of road accidents.

Factors that cause of car road accidents can be grouped based on several factors, namely, human, vehicle, and road environment factors [2]. In general, the human factors are described as actions and behaviour of human driver throughout the time of the accident. Examples of driver characteristics include: speed is not appropriate for the situation, carelessness, driving skill, and driver impairment. Vehicle factors refer to mechanical faults or poor design of the vehicle also include lack of maintenance. Road environment factors include road design and road environment for example slippery road due to weather condition. The human factor is the greatest contributor, which contributes to 46.9% of all accidents [3]. Thus, this requires measures that can help the driver to drive in safe and practically efficient manner.

1.1 Relationship Between Drivers and Car

Generally, a human requires time and high determination in order to operate a machine. The same thing applies to a car driver; a human must get to know the car first before he/she can drive the car. This human should learn and know how to operate and manage the car in various circumstances. Hence, humans require supervision and training to increase their knowledge and understand more about the car handling.

Driving a car is considered a manual control of complicated processes [4]. It involves dynamic interleaving and implementation of numerous critical subtasks [5]. From these situations, it is portrayed that the only human has the capacity to discover and understand the car, but unfortunately, the car is unable to take part to improve the skill, accomplishment, and performance of the car driver. Finally, it shows that human (car driver) plays an important role as the main controller and the machine (car) does not have the capability to identify and to adapt the changes of human features.

1.2 Driver Support System

Due to a high number of car crashes caused by the weaknesses of human drivers. It is wise action to avoid the occurrence of an accident rather than to minimize the seriousness of injuries.

There are two types of car support system which are passive and active support systems. The passive support system is functioning to minimalize the seriousness of injuries in case of accidents take place. For instance, airbags [6–8], seat belts [9] and shatter-resistant windshields [10] are support provided from passive systems.

On the other hand, active support system is to avoid vehicular accidents. Some examples of active support systems are lane keeping [11], anti-locking brakes active safety systems [12], vehicle distance warning [8] and electronic stability control (ESC) [6, 7]. Significant necessities during the development of an active safety system are the potential on its reliability, accurately and efficiency on recognizing the necessities which would lead to an accident and to force counteractive movements. Hence, the accident could be avoided. The active system will be helpful if it comes as a Human Adaptive Mechatronics (HAM) system. As for highlight, HAM system is defined as a novel intelligent mechanism which employing high-performance mechanism by improving the human skill by designing a machine function that able to adapt human skill [13]. The concept of HAM system is to design a mechanical system that is more intelligent in a way that it has the ability to adapt human skill as well as the capability to provide the human with driving support [14, 15].

1.3 Investigation on Human Dexterity in Using Driving Simulator

The present research has come out with a great idea of improvement of driver performance. However, in order to improvise the driver's performance, there is a necessity to recognize and identify the driver's competency level of controlling the car before an appropriate car's support system could be designed. By studying the driver's competency level, it will provide a method for the driver to expand his/her driving dexterity.

Hence, this study shows the correlation between the studied variables and the driving simulator. Then, the selected variables will be utilized on quantification of driving skill for driver assistance system. It is to be highlighted that, the generic facts about the concept, understanding of driver behaviour, and modelling the behaviour are a wide range of topics either together or separately. However, this research only concentrates on car handling skill based on path tracking task.

2 Choice of Software

As a part of the research development, Racer software used during the data acquisition process. Besides Racer, there is other software namely Robot Auto Racing Simulation (RARS) [16] and The Open Racing Car Simulator (TORCS) [17] and Subsim [18]. However, the main reason for choosing Racer software besides the rest is because this software comes with a great car physics and the aim is not to study or modify the environment setting of the software.

2.1 Features of Racer Software

Racer is a free driving software that is utilizing an advanced physics model. This software also has the ability to extract the vehicle telemetry data while driving the car. The essential part is that this software able to provide various telemetric data such car position, orientation, velocity and time taken for a complete single lap. The objective is to use the car and track available in Racer software.

The log data is recorded in every 100 ms which will provide a high accuracy that up to 0.1. However, this is relatively high in term of data computing and some laptop may not have the capability to work with this software. In fact, this software requires a laptop or computer that integrated with a graphic card.

Besides that, this software is utilizing high-end car physics to accomplish a realistic feeling and an outstanding render engine for graphical realism. The car and tracks are created relatively easy for the user. The editors and support programs are also accessible to get a very customizable and expandable simulator. Since there are lot benefits that can be obtained from this software, many researchers are using this software for their studies [19–24].

It can be simplified as listed (a) Racer is easy to use during the data collection process, (b) Racer comes with various options of cars and tracks, (c) It involved simple methods to setup the car simulator with the Logitech steering wheel, gas and brake pedals, (d) It consists of comprehensive environment. It inherited many features and attributes which are useful for the data analyzation process and (e) This software provides an extensive data based on the log file that consists of data gathered during the experiment for the whole track and can easily be used using MATLAB.

2.2   Files Provided by Racer Software

This Racer software comes with an executable file that consists of numerous data gained based on the driving experiment. Figure 1 below shows the directory for each file. There are files for the car, track and 'dump'. The dump file is where all the data recorded from driving experiment is kept.

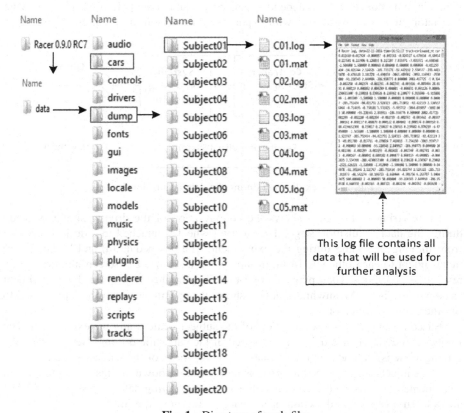

This log file contains all data that will be used for further analysis

Fig. 1. Directory of each file

3   Choice of Hardware

There are two options of working on the experimental works which are real driving and simulated driving environments. This part explained about the data acquisition system including the hardware utilized in this study. Besides that, this research also has been registered under National Medical Research Register (NMRR).

3.1 Setup of Driving Simulator

In this study, for data acquisition process, the experimental process was done by using a driving simulator based on a simulated environment. Based on research done by Wang *et al.*, it is found out that medium-fidelity simulator is able to provide an effective and safe environment which means it is acceptable to evaluate the subjects task performance using driving simulator [25].

Figure 2 illustrates the block diagram during the data acquisition process. Based on Fig. 2, it illustrates the configurations of the system as a closed loop system with a feedback that considers the driver as a part of the system. The driving simulator is controlled by a set of Momo Racing Force Feedback Steering Wheel by Logitech which included of steering, independent gas pedals and brake [21, 26–28]. The driving simulator provides the subjects with experience like driving in a real environment.

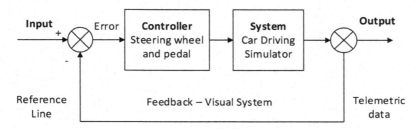

Fig. 2. Block diagram during the data acquisition process

By referring to Fig. 3, it shows the configuration of the driving simulator setup during the data acquisition stage. The steering wheel is attached to a desk to avoid it from moving or sliding during the experiment. The gas pedals (a) and brake (b) are independent to each other. A 14 in. of laptop and a 24 in. LED screen monitor with a resolution of 1920 × 1080 pixels and 64-bit colour quality is used for this experiment as shown in Fig. 3. Meanwhile, Table 1 shows the specifications of the laptop used to run the driving simulator.

Based on Fig. 4, it shows the view of the subject while doing the experiment. The subject could clearly see the gear and speed of the car while driving. Besides that, the driving view is included in a mini map on the top-right of the subject's view.

The subjects are requested to drive using the tracks shown in Figs. 5 and 6. Only at a segmented area where the driving skill is evaluated during data analysis process. The arrows demonstrate the direction of the path during the experiment.

3.2 Car Parameter

There is variety type of cars available in Racer software. However, Ford Focus is used during the whole driving experiment. It is believed to be suitable for all subjects. Table 2 shows the characteristics of the car used during the data acquisition process. The car used during the experiment was Ford Focus with an automatic transmission for all subjects [19, 20].

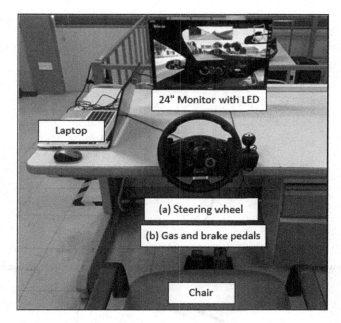

Fig. 3. Experimental setup for this research

Table 1. Specifications of the computer system

Specifications	Details
Windows edition	Windows 8.1 Pro
Processor	Intel ® Core (TM) i7-3537U CPU @ 2.00 GHz 2.50 GHz
Installed memory (RAM)	8.0 GB
System type	64-bit Operating System
Graphic card	GeForce GT 740 M

Fig. 4. The view for subject during driving experiment

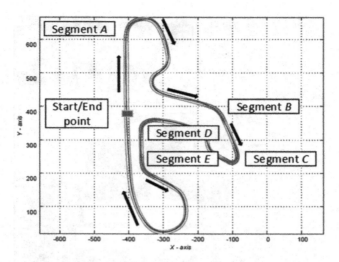

Fig. 5. Carlswood track with segmented area (*A, B, C, D* and *E*) used for data analysis process.

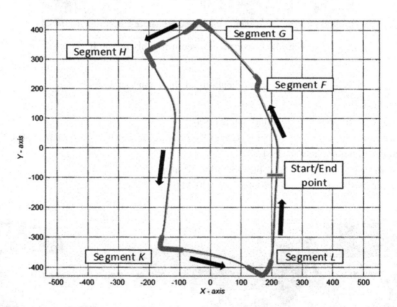

Fig. 6. Roggel track with segmented area (*F, G, H, K* and *L*) used for data analysis process.

3.3   Track Parameter

Basically, for this research, two tracks are utilized for the whole process of data acquisition which are Carlswood [23] and Roggel tracks. The tracks courses which have been selected are tracks that come with combinations of straight path and cornering course without any traffic signal.

Table 2. Important parameters for the car

Parameters	Details
Power	123 Horsepower
Type of wheel drive	All - Wheel - Drive
Mass	1270 kg
Top speed	193 km per hour
Other	0–100 km per hour in 11.7 s

For this experiment, Carlswood track resembles as highway track course while Roggel track resembles as urban track course. Carlswood track comes with low and high-speed corners that are to the right-hand and left-hand side. Meanwhile, Roggel track comes with smoothed and sharp corners and all corners are to the left-hand side.

Further details about the tracks specifications and tracks' environment setting are shown in Tables 3 and 4.

Table 3. Specifications for Carlswood track

Parameters	Details
Length	2088 m
Width	10.13–12.30 m
Time	10:00 am
Environment	Clear; No fog and rain
Track surface	Asphalt and dry

Table 4. Specifications for Roggel track

Parameters	Details
Length	2195 m
Width	3.35–7.42 m
Time	10:00 am
Environment	Clear; No fog and rain
Track surface	Asphalt and dry

3.4   Data Extraction

As mentioned earlier, the experiment data comes in a log file format. Thus, it is required to convert the log file type (x.log) to MATLAB type (x.mat) for further analysis process. Figure 7 below shows the data extraction process.

3.5   Data Conversion

The original data from the driving simulator experiment were attained in time-sampled data. The amount of data collected for each lap is very impressive since the data is recorded in every 100 ms. However, since the aim of this study is to evaluate and analyse on the specific area (segments) of the track courses as shown in Fig. 8, the data have to be converted into distance-sampled data.

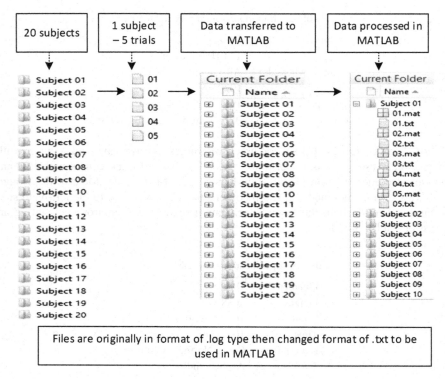

Fig. 7. Data extraction process in MATLAB

Figure 8 below shows an instance of data before and after the data conversion. This instance is based on data attained from the experiment from Carlswood track. Referring to Fig. 8 (left figure), this subject completed a single lap in 102.3 s. As for Fig. 8 (right figure), Carlswood track comes with 339 index points, which is equivalent to 6.178 m of distance between two index points.

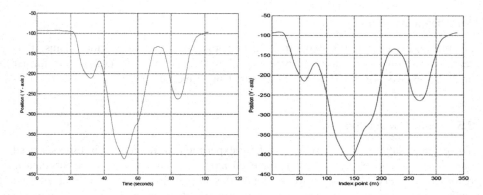

Fig. 8. Data conversion. The left figure shows time-sampled data while the right figure shows index point-sampled data

4 Methods

4.1 General Instructions for the Subjects

The proposed driving skill index is designed to measure subject's competency in maintaining the car orientation and position consistently besides maneuvering the car as careful as possible. In other terms, it is essential for the subjects to preserve the car stability in any way.

4.2 Subject Demographic

All the subjects were recruited from students and researchers from Faculty of Electrical Engineering, Universiti Teknologi Malaysia. The range of age of the subjects is 20 to 36 years old which consists of male and female subjects. The average age of the subject was 25.2 years with an average of 7.6 years of driving experiences. These experiments involved 20 subjects which have a valid Malaysian driving license with a minimum of five years of driving experiences.

5 Results and Discussion

The driving experiment is designed to measure the correlation between selected variables which represents human skill (subject) and machine (driving simulator).

5.1 Reliability Test

Since human subjects are involved in these experiments, it is important to check the reliability. Cronbach's alpha (α) is used and measured to check the reliability of the results. The coefficient alpha (α) is commonly used as a measure of the reliability of a trial score for a sample of subjects [29]. The results for all variables is shown as in Table 5. The variables were analysed using repeated measurement within subjects. The testing was based on a significance level of 0.05.

Table 5. The result of coefficient alpha (α) for all segments

Segment	Car-to-path distance, d	Car-to-path deviation angle, θ_p	Car's position correction speed, $\dot{d}$	Car's velocity along the path, $\dot{s}$
B	0.698	0.829	0.878	0.871
C	0.821	0.841	0.910	0.934
F	0.806	0.854	0.899	0.937
K	0.926	0.844	0.905	0.956
L	0.839	0.799	0.858	0.938

Based on Table 5 above, only Segment I has an excellent reliability ($\alpha > 0.9$) with variable d. While only Segment C, F, and L have a good internal consistency ($\alpha > 0.8$) with variable d. Segment F has acceptable reliability ($\alpha > 0.7$) with variable d, respectively.

In term of car-to-path deviation angle, θ_p none of the segment achieves an excellent reliability. Four segments; Segment B, C, F and K have a good internal consistency ($\alpha > 0.8$) with θ_p. Segment K has an acceptable consistency ($\alpha > 0.7$) with the θ_p.

As for the car's position correction speed, $\dot{d}$ the results from the table above show that two segments; C and K have an excellent reliability ($\alpha > 0.9$) with a variable d. While Segment B, F, and L have a good internal consistency ($\alpha > 0.8$) with d.

For the last variable, car's velocity along the path, $\dot{s}$ all segments proved to have at least good internal consistency with $\dot{s}$. Five segments; Segment C, F, G, K and L have an excellent reliability ($\alpha > 0.9$) with $\dot{s}$. Segment B has a good internal consistency ($\alpha > 0.8$) with $\dot{s}$, respectively. These results show that time attained from the experiments are reliable in all tracks.

The results show that the subjects were having familiarization problems in manoeuvring the car precisely. Whereas, it could be summarized that the subjects were not having problem concerning car's speed handling while driving at all the segments.

5.2   Correlation and Statistical Errors

The result of correlation, r and its significant level for accuracy and quickness principles for all segments are presented in Table 6 below. The closer the result of correlation, r to +1, the stronger the positive correlation. Whereas, the closer the result of correlation, r to −1, the stronger the negative correlation.

Table 6. The result of correlation, r and its significant level for all segments

Segment	Correlation	Significant level
B	−0.5963	5.904E−11
C	−0.6808	6.557E−15
F	−0.7935	7.324E−23
K	−0.6347	1.333E−12
L	−0.8339	4.814E−27

From the Table 6 above, it indicates that there are strong negative correlations for Segment F and L, respectively. Segment B, C and K have a moderate negative correlation. Based on these results, it shows that results for all segments are inversely proportional since the correlation coefficient is negative.

By choosing significant level $\alpha = 0.01$ (1.00E−02), the above table also shows the significant level for all segments. It obviously shows that Segment B, C, F, K and L are avoiding the Type I error since the value of significant levels is less than 0.01 (significant level $> \alpha$). For future works, it is more practical to minimize it by using a greater sample size (subjects more than 20) which is large enough to detect if there is a difference when one truly exists.

5.3 Discussion

Driving skill is a very objective condition to be measured. However, this Racer software is able to provide variety data which can be used and relate to car path tracking model. Based on the results attained, it shows that there is a high correlation between the subjects and studied variables. Besides that, the low cost offered and easy accessibility of Racer software inspired the researchers to use it instead of other tools. Hence, it proved that Racer software is reliable to be used as a data acquisition tool.

6 Conclusion

The presented results showed that Racer software can effectively provide useful data for the future to quantify the driving skill. This paper concludes that the useful data can be attained based on the experiment done using the simulated driving environment provides by Racer software. Furthermore, it can be further summarized that this Racer software is suitable to be used by any researchers based on its low-cost setup, data richness, high compatibility MATLAB software and can be easily used with Logitech steering wheel, gas and brake pedal.

Acknowledgments. We are grateful for the UTM Zamalah scholarship for Author 1, Malaysian Technical Cooperation Programme (MTCP) for Author 2. The authors would like to acknowledge the Ministry of Higher Education (MOHE) Malaysia and Universiti Teknologi Malaysia, Research University Grant Scheme GUP (Vote No. 08J52) and PAS (Vote No. 00K04).

References

1. Ministry of Transport Malaysia: Statistik Pengangkutan Malaysia 2013. Putrajaya, Ministry of Transport Malaysia (2013)
2. Abidin, A.N.S.Z., Faudzi, S.A.M., Lamin, F., Manap, A.R.A.: MIROS crash investigation and reconstruction. In: Annual Statistical Report 2007–2010, Kuala Lumpur, Malaysia (2012)
3. Kichun, J., Junsoo, K., Dongchul, K., Chulhoon, J., Myoungho, S.: Development of autonomous car, 2014, part II - a case study on the implementation of an autonomous driving system based on distributed architecture. IEEE Trans. Industr. Electron. **62**, 5119–5132 (2015)
4. Delice, I.I., Ertugrul, S.: Intelligent modeling of human driver: a survey. In: IEEE Intelligent Vehicles Symposium 2007, Istanbul, Turkey, pp. 648–651. IEEE (2007)
5. Salvucci, D.D.: Modeling driver behavior in a cognitive architecture. Hum. Factors: J. Hum. Factors Ergon. Soc. **48**, 362–380 (2006)

6. Ertlmeier, R., Spannaus, P.: Expanding design process of the Airbag Control Unit ACU - connection of active and passive safety by using vehicles dynamics for rollover and side crash detection. In: 6th International Workshop on Intelligent Solutions in Embedded Systems (WISES) 2008, Regensburg, Germany, pp. 1–9. IEEE (2008)

7. Raith, A., Sattler, K., Ertlmeier, R., Brandmeier, T.: Networking and integration of active and passive safety systems. In: Proceedings of the 9th Workshop on Intelligent Solutions in Embedded Systems (WISES) 2011, Regensburg, Germany, pp. 75–80. IEEE (2011)

8. Watanabe, H., Kondo, S., Hirano, K.: Introduction to Suzuki ASV technologies. In: Proceedings of the IEEE Intelligent Vehicles Symposium 1996, Seikei University, Tokyo, Japan, pp. 219–223. IEEE (1996)

9. Luo, X., Du, W., Zhang, J.: Safety benefits of belt pretensioning in conjunction with precrash braking in a frontal crash. In: IEEE Intelligent Vehicles Symposium (IV) 2015, Seoul, Korea, pp. 871–876. IEEE (2015)

10. Parsons, G.G.: An evaluation of the effects of glass-plastic windshield glazing in passenger cars. In: NHTSA Technical Report, vol. DOT HS 808 062, p. 105, Washington (1993)

11. Hermannstadter, P., Yang, B.: Identification and validation of lateral driver models on experimentally induced driving behavior. In: IEEE International Conference on Systems, Man and Cybernetics (SMC) 2012, Seoul, Korea, pp. 1165–1170. IEEE (2012)

12. Miller, R.L., Harper, T.P.: Anti-lock Braking System. United States Patent (1994)

13. Suzuki, S., Tomomatsu, N., Harashima, F., Furuta, K.: Skill evaluation based on state-transition model for human adaptive mechatronics (HAM). In: 30th Annual Conference of IEEE Industrial Electronics Society (IECON) 2004, Busan, Korea, pp. 641–646. IEEE (2004)

14. Furuta, K.: Control of pendulum: from super mechano-system to human adaptive mechatronics. In: Proceedings of the 42nd IEEE Conference on Decision and Control 2003, Maui, Hawaii, USA, pp. 1498–1507. IEEE (2003)

15. Harashima, F.: Human adaptive mechatronics - interaction and intelligence. In: 10th IEEE Conference on Emerging Technologies and Factory Automation (ETFA) 2005, Catania, Italy, p. 3. IEEE (2005)

16. Robot Auto Racing Simulation (RARS) (2003). http://rars.sourceforge.net/

17. Wymann, B., Espié, E., Guionneau, C.: The Open Racing Car Simulator (TORCS) (2001). http://torcs.sourceforge.net/

18. Boeing, A., Bräunl, T.: SubSim: an autonomous underwater vehicle simulation package. In: Murase, K., Sekiyama, K., Naniwa, T., Kubota, N., Sitte, J. (eds.) Proceedings of the 3rd International Symposium on Autonomous Minirobots for Research and Edutainment (AMiRE 2005), pp. 33–38. Springer, Heidelberg (2006). doi:10.1007/3-540-29344-2_5

19. Kujala, T.: Browsing the information highway while driving: three in-vehicle touch screen scrolling methods and driver distraction. Pers. Ubiquit. Comput. 17, 815–823 (2013)

20. Lasch, A., Kujala, T.: Can you ignore it? – effects of album artwork on driver distraction. In: Proceedings of the 3rd International Conference on Driver Distraction and Inattention 2013, Gothenburg, Sweden, pp. 1–16. Ashgate Publishing (2013)

21. García-Díaz, J.M., García-Ruiz, M.A., Aquino-Santos, R., Edwards-Block, A.: Evaluation of a driving simulator with a visual and auditory interface. In: Collazos, C., Liborio, A., Rusu, C. (eds.) CLIHC 2013. LNCS, vol. 8278, pp. 131–139. Springer, Cham (2013). doi:10.1007/978-3-319-03068-5_22

22. Andrén, P.: Identification of Road Roughness using A Fullcar Model. Swedish National Road and Transport Research Institute (VTI), Sweden (2012)

23. Quintero M.C.G., López, J.O., Pinilla, A.C.C.: Intelligent driving diagnosis system applied to drivers modeling and high risk areas identification: an approach toward a real environment implementation. In: IEEE International Conference on Vehicular Electronics and Safety (ICVES) 2012, Istanbul, Turkey, pp. 111–116. IEEE (2012)

24. Kujala, T., Saariluoma, P.: Measuring distraction at the levels of tactical and strategic control: the limits of capacity-based measures for revealing unsafe visual sampling models. J. Adv. Hum.-Comput. Interact. **2011**, 1–13 (2011)

25. Wang, Y., Mehler, B., Reimer, B., Lammers, V., D'Ambrosio, L.A., Coughlin, J.F.: The validity of driving simulation for assessing differences between in-vehicle informational interfaces: a comparison with field testing. Ergonomics **53**, 404–420 (2010)

26. Sodnik, J., Dicke, C., Tomažič, S., Billinghurst, M.: A user study of auditory versus visual interfaces for use while driving. Int. J. Hum Comput Stud. **66**, 318–332 (2008)

27. Correa, Á., Molina, E., Sanabria, D.: Effects of chronotype and time of day on the vigilance decrement during simulated driving. Accid. Anal. Prev. **67**, 113–118 (2014)

28. González, N., Kalyakin, I., Lyytinen, H.: RACER: a Non-commercial driving game which became a serious tool in the research of driver fatigue. In: Kankaanranta, M., Neittaanmäki, P. (eds.) Design and Use of Serious Games. ISCA, vol. 37, pp. 171–184. Springer, Dordrecht (2009). doi:10.1007/978-1-4020-9496-5_12

29. Cronbach, L.J.: Coefficient alpha and the internal structure of tests. Psychometrika **16**, 297–334 (1951)

Exploring the Parallelism of One Entity on Multi-core Environments

Jiawei Fei[(⊠)], Yiping Yao, and Feng Yao

College of Information System and Management, National University of Defense Technology, 137 Yanwachi, Changsha, Hunan, China
{feijiaweill,ypyao,fyao2015}@nudt.edu.cn

Abstract. Optimizing parallel discrete event simulation (PDES) on multi-core environments can bring great performance improvement and has become a research hotspot so far. Most of the optimization methods accelerate the simulators by reducing the cost of communication and synchronization with the advantages of shared memory for multi cores. However, both optimistic and conservative simulation algorithms can only support processing events of different entities in parallel, the parallelism of events belonging to one entity is ignored. Focusing on this demand, a deep parallel simulation approach based on conservative simulation algorithm is proposed to explore the parallelism of events belonging to one entity. Besides, a greedy aggregation algorithm is also designed to deal with load balancing problem by reorganizing events into blocks with similar sizes. Phold results show that the parallel simulation approach proposed in this paper gains 15% performance increase comparing to the approach without considering the parallelism of one entity.

Keywords: Events parallelization · Multi-core · PDES · Load balance

1 Introduction

Up to now, many excellent algorithms have been designed for parallel discrete event simulation. These algorithms are all aimed at how to improve the parallelism of event processing. According to whether there are rollback operations in algorithms, they can be divided into two categories, conservative and optimistic. However, both conservative and optimistic algorithms have some factors limiting parallel performance due to the limitations of their parallel mechanisms.

One factor limiting parallel performance is that current algorithms cannot explore the parallelism of events belonging to the same simulation entity. As we all know, logical process (LP) is the smallest parallel unit in PDES algorithms what means events in one LP are executed serially. However in many simulation applications, events of one logical process are able to be processed in parallel without errors. To explore the parallelism of one logical process, some researches have been carried out. The simulator Flame can process the detection function of one entity in parallel and Zhu et al. [1] introduced the method to utilize the parallelism of multi input component models. These methods achieve parallelism by developing the parallel version of models used by entity. However, they can just support some specific models and are not universal.

© Springer Nature Singapore Pte Ltd. 2017
M.S. Mohamed Ali et al. (Eds.): AsiaSim 2017, Part II, CCIS 752, pp. 548–559, 2017.
DOI: 10.1007/978-981-10-6502-6_47

Another factor is load balancing problem which has been caused great concern since the parallel discrete event simulation algorithms were proposed. Actually, how to assign tasks evenly to each core is a great problem for all the parallel algorithms. Many researches have been conducted focusing on the load balancing of PDES algorithm like Glazer and Tropper [2] and Peschlow et al. [3]. Most load balancing methods are based on performance metrics which monitor the historical interval, evaluate the performance and generate load distribution schemes for next execution period by prediction. However, these methods assume that the load situations of different execution periods are similar without considering the changes of load situation in next execution period. Some other researchers like Ahn et al. [4] choose to perform task migration during execution period to achieve load balancing. This type of algorithms has the problem that cost of task migration is always great.

Focusing on these two problems, this research chooses to expend the current SUPE [5] discrete event simulation engine to take full advantage of multi-core architecture. A new deep parallel algorithm for discrete event simulation on multi core platform is proposed. And we choose to optimize the conservative simulation algorithm in this paper, because it is usually hard or costly to save the whole state of models for rollbacks that are common in optimistic algorithm. In traditional simulation algorithms, each process performs extraction and execution of events individually. Different from them, the optimized algorithm divides the process into three steps, parallel event extraction, parallel event execution and parallel event insertion. In each step, the operation is parallel while synchronous operation is required between steps. The optimized algorithm focuses on multi-core and shared-memory environments and applies master-slave mode. Entity and event queues are centrally managed by the master thread. The algorithm proposed in this paper assigns tasks before every execution period according to actual event distribution of this period without analyzing the performance in historical interval. Besides, the optimized algorithm can also explore the parallelism of events belonging to one LP without logical errors and timing errors which cannot be realized by current parallel simulation engines.

The paper is organized as follows: Sect. 2 reviews related work and existing problems. Section 3 introduces the framework of the deep parallel simulation algorithm proposed in this paper. Section 4 describes the method to detect the parallel events of one logical process. Section 5 introduces a greedy aggregation algorithm to deal with load balancing problem. Section 6 presents the experiment result. Finally, Sect. 7 gives the conclusion.

2 Related Work

Many researches focusing on the optimization of parallel discrete event simulation on multi-core platforms have been carried out and these achievements have been applied by many high performance simulators. In early 2010, Miller [6] had optimized the simulator Warped focusing on multi-core platform and designed the ThreadedWarped. It adopted a master-slave working mode and the time management algorithm it optimized is an optimistic algorithm Time Warp (TW). Also targeted TW algorithm, Chen et al. [7] proposed a global scheduling mechanism to control event processing in parallel. Focusing on clusters with multi-core machines, Tang et al. [8] proposed a hierarchical parallel architecture which consists of the operating system process level and thread level to exploit the performance of multi-core machines in clusters. Wang et al. [9] optimized the message passing mechanism of ROSS. And based on ROSS, they designed a thread-based simulation engine ROSS-MT without modification to the event management algorithm. Besides, some recent researches started to pay attention to the optimization of some specific types of simulation. Yang et al. [10] concentrated on the simulation of the variable structures system which exhibits exchanges both at structural and behavior levels. They proposed a parallel simulators Ivy under multi-core environment for this type of system. Yang et al. [11] continued to optimize the simulator Ivy by exploring both inherent and dynamic parallelism among models and adopting a dynamic load-balancing method which can migrate models among cores with very low cost and support dynamic core allocation on demand. Lin et al. [12] proposed a multi-threaded simulator NTW-MT for the simulations of reaction diffusion. Bauer et al. [13] proposed an efficient inter-process synchronization on multi-core platform which uses time estimates from its neighbors as bounds for its time advance. The above researches are mainly focused on the parallel processing of different LPs. Different from them, some researchers apply multi-thread to accelerate calculation of some specific models invoked by events. For example the simulator Flame supports the multi-thread execution of the detect function. In the research of Zhu et al. [1], a vectorized component model (VCM) framework was proposed to better utilize the parallelism of multi-input component models.

Another factor having great influence on the performance of PDES is load balancing. For multi-core applications, load balancing is an eternal topic. And the load balancing problem is especially difficult for PDES because the events to process are generated during the running process. Many researchers have discussed this problem and proposed some methods. Glazer and Tropper [2] proposed a metric for detecting load imbalances called simulation advance rate and Peschlow et al. [3] proposed a metric of computation load depended on the number of events processed and the effective time advance. In the research of Ahn et al. [4], four different dynamic load balancing strategies were introduced and evaluated. The first is Most-Dividing (MD) algorithm based on the central redistribution work of Powley et al. [14] and Hillis [15], in which the most overloaded processor needs to send out half of its remaining jobs to other idle processors. The second is All-Redistribution (AR) algorithm which is similar to MD algorithm but the load distribution work is carried out by the master. The third is Random-Polling (RP) algorithm [16] which is a receiver-initiated decentralized load balancing algorithm. That means the idle worker processors can randomly poll half of remaining jobs from other busy processors. The last is Neighbor-Redistribution (NR) algorithm which only supports the load migration between neighbors. All these four algorithms realize load balancing by migrating load during the event processing cycle. In addition, Yang et al. [11] also proposed a new metric based on simulation advance rate by considering the processing time of events and they designed a model migration method with references to little cost.

These optimization methods offer much performance gain for PDES on multi-core platforms, but they still have some shortcomings. Most of these simulators can only support the parallelism of different LPs, the parallelism of events belonging to one logical process is not considered in their implementation. Although parallelization of model calculation can solve this problem to some degree, the number of parallel models supported by simulators is limited. Besides developing new parallel models is costly and difficult for common model developers who have not learned parallel computing. So parallelization of model calculation has problems of universality and extensibility. Thus a simulator not only supporting parallel processing of events belonging to different logical processes but also supporting parallel processing of events belonging to one LP is preferred in order to gain good performance. Another problem is about load balancing. Most of current load balancing methods based on performance metrics do not consider the changes of load situation during the execution process and the algorithms performing task migration during execution period also bring the cost of task migration. So it is meaningful to design a simple and efficient load balancing algorithm for parallel simulation on multi-core platform.

3   A Deep Parallel Simulation Algorithm Framework

In traditional PDES conservative algorithm framework, LPs are assigned to each processor in the form of LP groups at the beginning. And then every processor calculates the Lower Bound Time Stamp (LBTS) by adding Local Virtual Time (LVT) and lookahead. We define an execution cycle as the interval between LVT and LBTS. Every processor selects the event with the earliest timestamp in the LP group, and then determines whether this event is safe event (safe events represent the events with timestamp before LBTS). If this event is safe, it will be processed. The operation will stop when there is no safe event. Figure 1 describes the traditional algorithm framework.

This traditional framework achieves parallel execution between LP groups. However, this framework also has some defects. Firstly, parallel performance is very sensitive to the quality of LP allocation. Current LP allocation scheme is always obtained by prediction because the number of events of each LP to process cannot be known before the events are processed. As a result, the allocation scheme is not always good. Secondly, this framework cannot support the parallel processing of events of one LP because events belonging to the same LP must be assigned to a LP group to ensure correctness in this framework.

The new framework introduced in this section can make up for the limitations of the original framework. The core method applied in our framework to solve the above problem is separating event extraction and event execution operations. At first all the processors will select the safe events but not process them, and then these safe events will be reorganized into parallel blocks of similar size by master processor. Finally, all the processors will be scheduled to parallel process these blocks consisting of safe events. The new framework is shown in Fig. 2. As described in the figure, events that can be processed in parallel in one LP are also explored in the safe event extraction phase and the greedy event reorganization algorithm brings great benefit to load balancing. So our new framework can make up the defects existing in the traditional PDES algorithm framework properly.

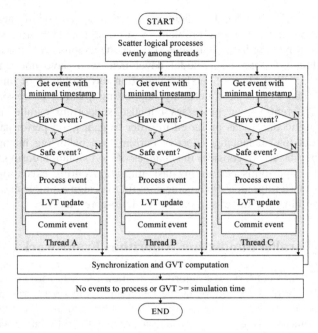

Fig. 1. The framework of traditional conservative simulation algorithm

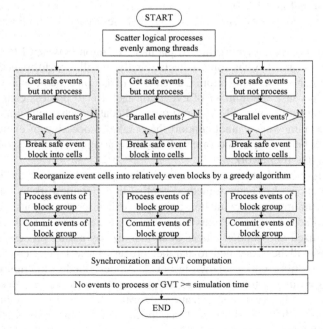

Fig. 2. The framework of deep parallel simulation algorithm proposed in this paper

4 Parallel Events in One Logical Process

As we all know, conservative time management algorithm can parallel execute events of different LPs. It calculates LBTS value in each execution cycle. And then the safe events are detected and processed in parallel. Finally, synchronization will be conducted at the end of cycle. The optimized algorithm proposed in this paper is still based on this conservative algorithm to select safe events among LPs in every execution cycle. The difference is that the selected events will not be processed immediately but stored in current event queues of LPs.

After that, we will explore the parallelism of events in one LP. The method is to check whether the events stored in current event queues of each LP can be parallel processed. In this section, we develop a specification for the detection of parallel events of one LP.

The events of one LP which can be parallel processed must meet one of the following two requirements,

1. All the events have no data write operation: events have no data access operation or only have data read operations.
2. If the events have a data write operation, the objects of all read and write operations do not intersect.

PROOF. If all the events meet one of above requirements, no data conflicts will be generated during the processing of all events. At the same time, the new events scheduled by these events will be inserted into the future event queues with the correct timing and will be processed in next cycle. So it is obvious that parallel processing of these events is equivalent to serial processing them.

In accordance with the above rules, we design the procedure shown in Fig. 3 to determine whether the events of one LP can be parallel processed.

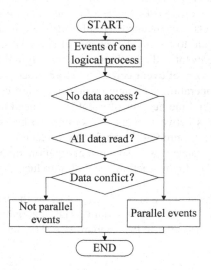

Fig. 3. The flow chart of detecting the events of one LP which can be processed in parallel

After detecting events that can be processed in parallel of every LP, we further split event blocks of different LPs into parallel cells according to the detection results. Figure 4 shows the process of splitting event blocks into cells. Events of different cells can be processed in parallel. That means events of one LP can be detected and parallel processed correctly.

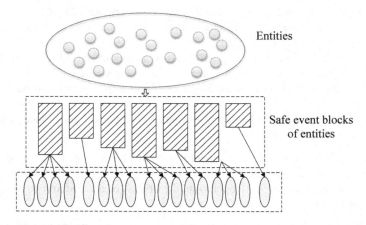

Fig. 4. The diagram of the process of splitting event blocks into cells

5   A Greedy Aggregation Algorithm for Load Balancing

In Sect. 4, we introduce the method to explore the parallelism of events between LPs and events belonging to one LP. Many event cells which are allowed to process in parallel are generated after this step. We define the size of an event cell as the number of events it contains. It is obvious that sizes of event cells are very different from each other, because some cells are obtained by splitting the parallel events of some LPs while some cells are equal to the parallel events of some LPs. If we directly schedule threads to process these event cells, load will be seriously unbalanced due to the great difference between the sizes of event cells. So before processing these event cells, we apply the aggregation operation. The aggregation operation combines event cells into multiple event blocks. And the number of event blocks need to be as large as possible while the size differences between event blocks need to be as small as possible. The aggregation operation is required at the beginning of each event processing cycle and will cause extra performance costs, so the aggregation operation should have low computational complexity. In this section, we will introduce a greedy event aggregation algorithm.

At first, we define the standard size of every block as the largest cell size due to the events of each cell must be processed serially. The aggregation algorithm will try to generate blocks with sizes similar to the standard size. The detailed process is described by the pseudo code,

```
program Aggregation Algorithm (cell container)
  Block_Container ← Empty container for saving Blocks
  CurB ← Empty Block
  CurC ← Empty Cell
  StdBS ← Maximum Size of all the cells
  CurBS ← Zero
  CurCS ← Zero
  while cell container is not empty do
    CurC ← the next cell of cell container
    CurBS ← Size of CurB
    CurCS ← Size of CurC
    if Sum of CurBS and CurCS is smaller than StdBS
      add CurC into CurB
    elseif CurBS is smaller than CurCS
      add CurC into Block_Container as a block
    else
      add CurB into Block_Container
      CurB ← CurC
  return Block_Container
end.
```

The algorithm will traverse all the event cells and choose which cells to combine. Each time a new event cell is accessed, the sum of the sizes of current event block and this cell will be compared with the standard size of block. If the sum is smaller, this cell will added into the block. Otherwise, the size of current block will be compared with the size of cell. And then, if the cell size is smaller, current block will be stored in event block set and the cell will be the new current block. And if the current block size is smaller, the cell will be stored as a block in event block set and current block remains unchanged. After that, the algorithm will access the next new event. It is clear that the computational complexity of this greedy algorithm is not high with only O (n) and a relatively good aggregation result will be obtained. The size difference between every block will not exceed half the standard block size.

Within above aggregation algorithm, many parallel event blocks of similar size will be generated. The next step is to schedule threads to process them in parallel. Focusing on the thread scheduling problem, we use three mechanisms inspired by OpenMP for comparison: static scheduling, dynamic scheduling and guided scheduling. Static scheduling mechanism will divide the event blocks into N equal-sized groups and N is the number of threads at the beginning, and each thread processes one group. Dynamic scheduling mechanism allows threads to pick up an unprocessed block by themselves when they finish the current block they processing. Finally, the guided scheduling mechanism is similar to dynamic scheduling, but the number of blocks every thread pick up starts off large and decreases to better handle load imbalance. Load balancing can be achieved by combining block aggregation algorithm and appropriate scheduling mechanism.

6 Experiments

In order to test the validity of the new PDES algorithm framework and the performance of optimized time management algorithms and load balancing methods proposed in this paper, this section demonstrates experiments based on Pholds which are usually used to test performance of simulators and analyzes the experiment results. The hardware environment of all these experiments is a high performance multi-core machine with one way 2.93 GHz Intel Xeon CPU X5670 and 24 G RAM memory. The CPU contains 6 cores and each core contains 2 physical threads. The parallel discrete event simulation engine we choose to modify is SUPE which cannot take fully advantage of multi-core environments.

At First, we compare the optimized conservative simulation algorithm described in Sect. 4 with the traditional conservative simulation algorithm. 100 entities are initialized and every entity has 5 events at the beginning. The value of lookahead in this experiment is set to 3 s and the maximum simulation time is set to 20 s. We also set the processing time of each event to simulate real application. Besides, in this experiment, we do not process events of one LP in parallel. The comparison of simulation time between original simulation algorithm and optimized algorithm is shown in Table 1. From the table we can find that the running time of the simulation shows a decreasing trend with the increase of the number of threads. However, the performance decreases when the thread number is larger than 10. This is mainly due to the cost of the synchronization of too many threads and the constraints that the machine just has 6 cores.

Table 1. Comparison of simulation running time with different numbers of threads between traditional algorithm and optimized algorithm.

Number of threads	Traditional algorithm/ms	Optimized algorithm/ms
2	17687.6	17220.75
4	9181.6	8822
6	6520	5862
8	4962	4352
10	4184.3	3526
12	7942.3	5282

In addition, as shown in Fig. 5, the speedup ratio of the algorithm is different under different threads by comparing the original conservative simulation algorithm with the optimized algorithm. The optimization effect is not obvious when thread number is too small because too few threads will lead to inefficiency of load balancing operation. When the thread number increases, the speedup rate shows an upward trend and the speedup ratio is over fifteen percent when the thread number is over 10. The results prove that the algorithm proposed in this paper is highly scalable and is suitable for multi-core environments.

We also test the performance of load balancing method based on the greedy event aggregation algorithm which is introduced in Sect. 5. When the number of threads is

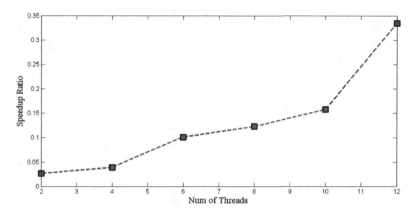

Fig. 5. The changes of speedup ratio with the increasing of number of threads

different, the effect of load balancing is different and the scheduling mechanism also affects the performance. Results are shown in Fig. 6. The results show that the static scheduling scheme is slightly worse than the other two schemes in this paper. And the dynamic scheduling scheme shows better performance than others no matter how many number of threads.

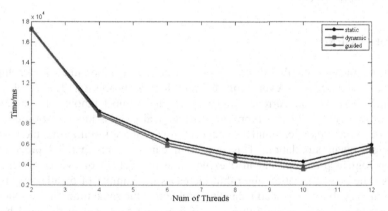

Fig. 6. The running time changes of three different thread scheduling mechanisms: static, dynamic and guided with the increasing of number of threads

Finally, the performance of parallel processing events belonging to one LP is tested in this section. We compare the algorithm performance described in Sect. 4 of different proportion of parallel events. The parallel events here are introduced in Sect. 4 and represent the events which belong to the same LP and can be processed in parallel. The results are shown in Fig. 7. The different curves in this figure represent the different proportion of parallel events. It is obvious to find that the running time of simulation

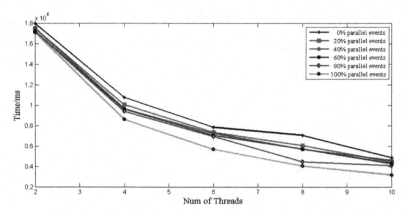

Fig. 7. The performance comparison of cases of different parallel event proportion

decreases when the proportion of parallel events increases. And the acceleration effect is better with more threads. We take the case when the number of threads is 8 as an example, the performance is improved by nearly 14% with 20% parallel events among all the events comparing to none parallel events. When the percentage of parallel events reaches up to 80%, the performance is improved by about 40%. It is proved that the exploring parallelism of events belonging to one logical process can bring great performance improvement.

7 Conclusion

At present, most of parallel discrete event simulation engines mainly gain high performance by processing events of different logical processes. The results of our investigation show that current simulation engines almost ignore the parallelism of events of one entity which is represented by logical process in simulation engines. In this paper, a deep parallel simulation algorithm is proposed to improve the parallelism of discrete event simulation. This algorithm can not only parallel process events between logical processes but also explore the parallelism of events of one logical process. The new simulation algorithm increases the number of parallel events in one execution cycle but brings load balancing problem at the same time. So a method based on a greedy aggregation algorithm is also proposed focusing on the load balancing problem. We apply these algorithms in the discrete event simulation engine SUPE and expend it to take full advantage of multi-core architectures. Experiments show that our algorithms can improve the performance greatly comparing to the original conservative simulation algorithm.

References

1. Zhu, F., Yao, Y., Tang, W., et al.: A high performance framework for modeling and simulation of large-scale complex systems. Future Gener. Comput. Syst. **51**(C), 132–141 (2015)
2. Glazer, D.W., Tropper, C.: On process migration and load balancing in time warp. IEEE Trans. Parallel Distrib. Syst. **4**(3), 318–327 (1993)
3. Peschlow, P., Honecker, T., Martini, P.: A flexible dynamic partitioning algorithm for optimistic distributed simulation. In: International Workshop on Principles of Advanced and Distributed Simulation, pp. 219–228. IEEE (2007)
4. Ahn, T.H., Sandu, A., Watson, L.T., Shaffer, C.A., Cao, Y., Baumann, W.T.: A framework to analyze the performance of load balancing schemes for ensembles of stochastic simulations. Int. J. Parallel Program. **43**(4), 597–630 (2015)
5. Yao, Y.P., Zhang, Y.X.: Solution for analytic simulation based on parallel processing. J. Syst. Simul. **20**(24), 6617–6621 (2008)
6. Miller, R.J.: Optimistic parallel discrete event simulation on a beowulf cluster of multi-core machines (2010)
7. Chen, L., Lu, Y., Yao, Y., Peng, S., Wu, L.: A well-balanced time warp system on multi-core environments. In: Principles of Advanced and Distributed Simulation, pp. 1–9. IEEE (2011)
8. Tang, W., Yao, Y., Feng, Z.: A hierarchical parallel discrete event simulation kernel for multicore platform. Cluster Comput. **16**(3), 379–387 (2013)
9. Wang, J., Jagtap, D., Abu-Ghazaleh, N., Ponomarev, D.: Parallel discrete event simulation for multi-core systems: analysis and optimization. IEEE Trans. Parallel Distrib. Syst. **25**(6), 1574–1584 (2014)
10. Yang, C., Li, B.H., Chai, X., Chi, P.: Ivy: a parallel simulator for variable structure systems under multi-core environments. Int. J. Serv. Comput. Oriented Manufact. **1**(2), 103–123 (2013)
11. Yang, C., Chi, P., Song, X., Lin, T.Y., Li, B.H., Chai, X.: An efficient approach to collaborative simulation of variable structure systems on multi-core machines. Cluster Comput. **19**(1), 29–46 (2016)
12. Lin, Z., Tropper, C., Ishlam Patoary, M.N., Mcdougal, R.A., Lytton, W.W., Hines, M.L.: NTW-MT: a multi-threaded simulator for reaction diffusion simulations in neuron. In: SIGSIM-PADS, pp. 157–167 (2015)
13. Bauer, P., Engblom, S., Jonsson, B.: Efficient inter-process synchronization for parallel discrete event simulation on multicores. In: SIGSIM PADS, pp. 183–194 (2015)
14. Powley, C., Ferguson, C., Korf, R.E.: Depth-first heuristic search on a SIMD machine. Artif. Intell. **60**(2), 199–242 (1993)
15. Hillis, W.D.: The connection machine. Sci. Am. **267**, 84–85 (1985)
16. Mermillod-Blondin, A., Stoian, R., Boyle, M.L., Rosenfeld, A., Burakov, I.M., Audouard, E., et al.: Parallel programming: techniques and applications using networked workstations and parallel computers. J. Landslides **8**(1–2), 391–401 (2000)

Numerical Simulations of Mixed-Mode II+III Delamination in Carbon/Epoxy Composite Laminate

Haris Ahmad Israr, King Jye Wong[✉], and Mohd Nasir Tamin

Centre for Composites, Faculty of Mechanical Engineering,
Universiti Teknologi Malaysia, 81310 Johor Bahru, Malaysia
{haris,kjwong}@mail.fkm.utm.my, nasirtamin@utm.my

Abstract. The objective of this study is to develop a reliable finite element model to simulate the mixed-mode II+III delamination behavior using six-point bending plate (6PBP) test. Two different cases were studied, which were 6PBP specimens with 60% (6PBP(60)) and 85% (6PBP(85)) of mode III component, respectively. The delamination behavior was simulated using cohesive zone modeling. Results showed good fits between the experimental and numerical force-displacement curves for both cases. In addition, it was found that there were three and one cohesive elements in the fracture process zone of 6PBP(60) and 6PBP(85) models, respectively. Furthermore, for both cases, the first damaged node in both cases was highly mode III dominated. Not only that, the mode III and mode II components in the first two damaged nodes were different. The numerical results from this study signified that the mode ratio of the 6PBP specimens was not constant.

Keywords: Mixed-mode II+III · Six-point bending plate · Delamination · Cohesive zone modeling

1 Introduction

Delamination is generally recognized as one of the earliest damage in composite laminates. Up to date, extensive works have been done to characterize mode I, mode II and mixed-mode I+II delamination behavior. These include the research works reported in references [1–4]. However, studies on mixed-mode delamination that involve mode III component are still very limited. Yet, mode III component is necessary to be studied due to its contribution to edge delamination [5, 6].

The available methods to characterize pure mode III delamination include split cantilever beam (SCB), simplified SCB (SSCB), modified SCB (MSCB), crack rail shear (CRS), anticlastic plate bending (ACPB), edge crack torsion (ECT), six ECT (6ECT), four point bending plate (4PBP), shear torsion bending (STB) and split-shear torsion (SST) tests [7]. As for mixed-mode delamination II+III, the available test setup include pre-stressed end notched flexure (PENF) [8], six-point bending plate (6PBP) [9, 10] and double-notched split cantilever beam (DNSCB) [11] tests. Each of these methods has its advantages and drawbacks. Firstly, all tests allow testing within a wide

© Springer Nature Singapore Pte Ltd. 2017
M.S. Mohamed Ali et al. (Eds.): AsiaSim 2017, Part II, CCIS 752, pp. 560–568, 2017.
DOI: 10.1007/978-981-10-6502-6_48

range of mixed-mode ratios. Secondly, PENF and DNSCB tests use traditional beam-like specimen geometry. Other advantages include no large displacements and geometrical non-linearity in PENF test, visual inspection of damage mode along the delamination edges for 6PBP test and stable crack propagation in DNSCB test. However, PENF test has the drawbacks of varying mode ratio with crack length and applied load, and mode ratio cannot be predetermined [8]. 6PBP has problems of geometric non-linearity, that finite element analysis is needed for experimental data reduction [9]. In addition, non-uniform mode II and III fracture energy distribution was observed in 6PBP test [9, 10]. Nevertheless, 6PBP test could be viewed as the modification from ECT test, which is currently under evaluation by American Society for Testing and Materials (ASTM) for pure mode III characterization [12]. Hence, it is worth to further explore 6PBP test for the better understanding of the test and any possible improvements.

Finite element modeling (FEM) has the advantage of minimizing the experimental works, which in turn reduces the time and cost of the research works. In addition, it provides an insight view of the delamination behavior in a progressive manner. In experiments, progressive delamination behavior could only be monitored with advanced technology equipment such as high speed camera. And yet, the crack front is difficult to be captured throughout the crack propagation period. The common modeling approaches using FEM include virtual rack closure technique (VCCT) and cohesive zone model (CZM) [13]. CZM has the advantages over VCCT such that it could predict both the onset and non-self-similar propagation of delamination without needing a pre-crack [14]. However, in the previous works on mixed-mode II+III delamination using 6PBP test, only VCCT has been adopted [9, 10]. It is thus believed that there is a potential to use CZM in simulating the delamination behavior in 6PBP specimens.

In this paper, the numerical simulations of 6PBP test were carried out based on the experimental results reported by de Morais and Pereira [9]. Two different mixed-mode ratios were considered, which were 60% and 85% of mode III component, respectively. The delamination behavior at the mid-interface was simulated using cohesive elements. Comparison was first carried out on the experimental and numerical force-displacement curves. Subsequently, the cohesive zone lengths of both cases were analyzed. Finally, the traction separation responses of both mode III and mode II components of the first two damaged nodes were compared.

2   Finite Element Modeling

The finite element models of the 6PBP specimens were developed based on the information from the literature [9]. The material was a Texipreg T300/HS 160 REM carbon/epoxy composite with the lamina properties listed in Table 1 below. The pure-mode fracture toughness were taken as $G_{IC} = 0.25$ N/mm, $G_{IIC} = 0.8$ N/mm and $G_{IIIC} = 0.9$ N/mm [15]. The stacking sequence was $[(90/0)_{3S}/0]_S$ for both models. Figure 1 shows the geometry of the finite element models along with loading and boundary conditions for the 6PBP specimens. Only half specimen was modeled due to symmetry in stacking sequence, loading and boundary conditions with respect to

Table 1. Lamina properties used in all finite element models [9].

E_1 (GPa)	E_2 (GPa)	G_{12} (GPa)	G_{13} (GPa)	G_{23} (GPa)	v_{12}
130.0	8.2	4.1	4.1	4.1	0.27

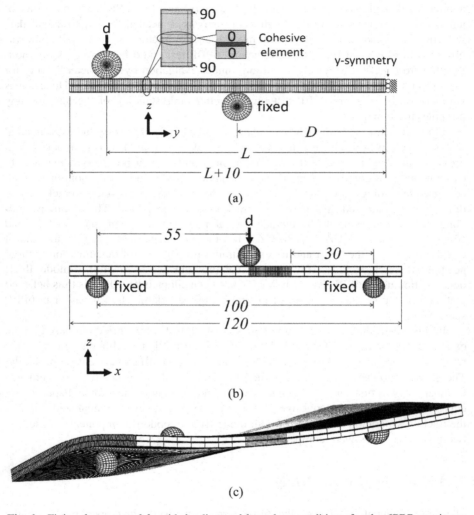

Fig. 1. Finite element models with loading and boundary conditions for the 6PBP specimens displayed in: (a) y-z plane, (b) x-z plane and (c) three-dimensional view.

y-plane [9]. The rigid spheres were tied to the specimen instead of contact surfaces used in reference [9] due to its ease of applying it while still obtaining accurate results. To take into account the local stress state effects, the adjacent upper and lower plies to the mid-plane were explicitly modeled with one element across the thickness. In addition, the two outer most plies that were subjected to loading and boundary conditions were also modeled as one element. For the remaining plies of each arm, they were modeled as equivalent composite layer with one element in thickness direction. This was to reduce the computational time while still maintaining the accuracy of the numerical results. The composite layers were modeled using 8-node continuum shell elements (SC8R). As for the mid-plane interface, 8-node cohesive elements (COH3D8) were prescribed to simulate the delamination behavior. Cohesive elements were modeled with 1 μm thickness to avoid interpenetration [16]. Elements in the fracture process zone were discretized with refined mesh of equal edge size of 0.5 mm. This mesh size has led to converged response through mesh dependence studies conducted previously on edge crack torsion (ECT) specimen [17]. Other region was modeled using element size of 5 mm. In total, there were 51000 SC8R elements and 8330 COH3D8 elements discretized for each model. With Intel(R) Core(TM) i7-4790 CPU at 3.60 GHz and 32.0 GB RAM, the computation time was approximately 6 h for each model. Table 2 lists the dimensions of the finite element models for both specimens.

Table 2. Specimen configurations and nomenclatures of 6PBP specimens [9].

Nomenclature	Mode III ratio G_{III}/G (%)	L	D
6PBP(60)	60	150	80
6PBP(85)	85	150	40

3   Results and Discussion

3.1   Force-Displacement Curves

Figure 2 compares the experimental and numerical force-displacement curves of 6PBP (60) and 6PBP(85) specimens. Close agreement was found in both specimens. The simulated initial slopes were within 5% difference as compared to the experimental slopes. Experimental results exhibited deviation from linearity after force of approximately 1000 N. Similar observation was reported using the numerical results obtained from VCCT [9]. However, larger difference in the peak loads (maximum of 18%) was noticed in both cases. This could be attributed to non-self-similar propagation or R-curve effect in mode III delamination [9].

3.2   Cohesive Zone Length

The length of the first fully developed cohesive zone is defined as cohesive zone length, $L_{cz,f}$. In other words, the numerical $L_{cz,f}$ refers to the distance between the first element at the crack tip which experiences total damage and the element which damage initiation is just attained. It is important to have sufficient number of cohesive elements in the cohesive zone to ensure accurate simulation results. Hence, the minimum number of cohesive elements, N_e, is another important parameter that is expressed as:

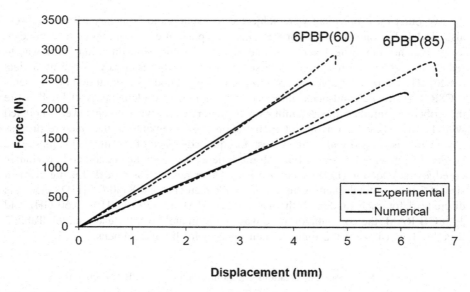

Fig. 2. Experimental and numerical force-displacement curves of 6PBP(60) and 6PBP(85) specimens.

$$N_e = L_{cz,f}/l_e. \tag{1}$$

In the above equation, l_e indicates the element size, which was fixed at 0.5 mm for the finite element models in this study.

Figure 3 plots the stress distribution of the first fully developed cohesive zone of both studied cases. The mixed-mode stress, t_{mix} on the y-axis was the resultant mode II and mode III stresses, which was calculated by:

$$t_{mix} = \sqrt{(t_{13}^2 + t_{23}^2)}. \tag{2}$$

In Eq. (2), t_{13} and t_{23} indicate the shear stresses in 1–3 and 2–3 planes, respectively. In all plots, the stress was extrapolated to a maximum value of 80 MPa before any stress drop occurred. It was because the same interface strength value was used for all modes. It was observed that $L_{cz,f}$ was 1.5 mm ($N_e = 3$) for 6PBP(60) case. As for 6PBP (85) case, $L_{cz,f}$ was 0.5 mm, which means that there was only 1 cohesive element within the cohesive zone.

3.3   Traction-Separation Responses

The plots in Fig. 4 provided the information at the location where damage was first initiated and propagated. The traction-separation responses in Fig. 4(a)–(d) illustrate the numerical mode III and mode II components of the first two damaged nodes in both

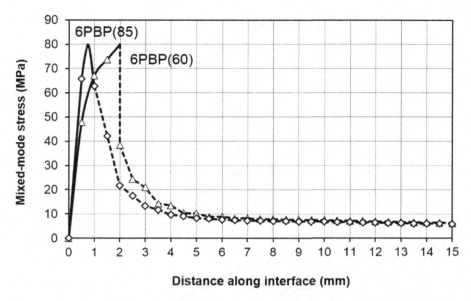

Fig. 3. Stress distribution of the first fully developed cohesive zone of 6PBP(60) and 6PBP(85) cases.

cases. Those were the only two nodes that have experienced total damage when the numerical peak load was attained. The traction-separation responses of pure- and fixed-mode ratio were also plotted for comparison. For mode III component, both mode ratios (Fig. 4(a) and (b)) showed that node 1 was highly mode III dominated. 6PBP(85) was found to be closer to pure mode III compared to 6PBP(60). This was reasonable because it has larger mode III component (85% as compared to 60%). As for the second node, both cases showed lower mode III component compared to the node 1. This implied that the mode ratio was not constant along the crack propagation path. When compared along with the fixed mixed-mode ratio as well, it was obvious that both nodes were deviated from the theoretical traction-separation response. Similar observations were found when comparing the theoretical and numerical traction-separation responses for mode II components. In addition, Fig. 4(c) and (d) show that the mode II component in node 2 was larger compared to node 1. This observation was opposite to mode III component as depicted in Fig. 4(a) and (b). This was reasonable as the mode III and mode II components at each node must complement each other. When one component was high, another one must be low. Both cases indicated that the mode ratio was actually changing when damage accumulated. This highlighted the importance of numerical simulations to provide the predicted mode ratio at different instants and locations.

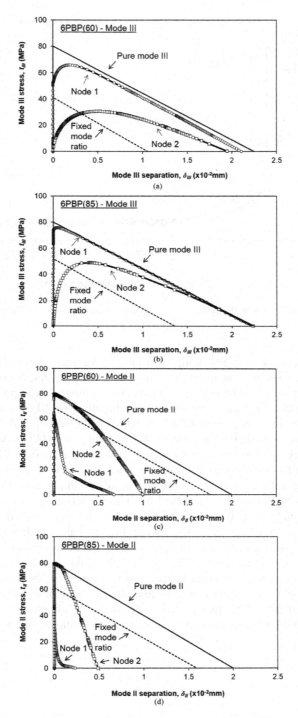

Fig. 4. Pure- and mixed-mode traction-separation responses of (a) 6PBP(60) – mode III, (b) 6PBP(85) – mode III, (c) 6PBP(60) – mode II and (d) 6PBP(85) – mode II components.

4 Concluding Remarks

This paper employed cohesive elements in modeling the delamination behavior of mixed-mode II+III using six-point bending plate (6PBP) test. Numerical simulations were carried out on 6PBP specimens with mode III component of 60% (6PBP(60)) and 85% (6PBP(85)). From the results, it was found that the experimental and numerical force-displacement curves were well compared. In addition, it was found that there were three elements in the cohesive zone for 6PBP(60) case. As for the 6PBP(85) case, there was only one element in the cohesive zone. Through the traction-separation plots, it was found that the first damaged node for both cases were mode III dominated. Besides, there was a significant variation in the traction-separation responses between the first and second damage nodes. This highlighted that the mode ratio was actually not a fixed value in both cases. The results from this research provided the insight details of the delamination behavior in the composites under mixed-mode II+III loading using 6PBP test, which the information could not be easily obtained from experiments.

Acknowledgments. This work is supported by Universiti Teknologi Malaysia under Research University Grant (RUG) No. 13H75.

References

1. Zhao, Y., Liu, W., Seah, L.K., Chai, G.B.: Delamination growth behavior of a woven E-glass/bismaleimide composite in seawater environment. Compos. Part B-Eng. **106**, 332–343 (2016)
2. LeBlanc, L.R., LaPlante, G.: Experimental investigation and finite element modeling of mixed-mode delamination in a moisture-exposed carbon/epoxy composite. Compos. Part A: Appl. Sci. **81**, 202–213 (2016)
3. Liu, Y., Zhang, C., Xiang, Y.: A critical plane-based fracture criterion for mixed-mode delamination in composite materials. Compos. Part B-Eng. **82**, 212–220 (2015)
4. Zhao, L., Gong, Y., Zhang, J., Chen, Y., Fei, B.: Simulation of delamination growth in multidirectional laminates under mode I and mixed mode I/II loadings using cohesive elements. Compos. Struct. **116**, 509–522 (2014)
5. O'Brien, T.K., Raju, I.S.: Strain energy release rate analysis of delamination around an open hole in composite materials. In: 25th AIAA/ASME/ASCE/AHS Structures, Structural Dynamics and Materials Conference, pp. 526–536, Palm Springs, New York (1984)
6. Wang, S.S.: Fracture mechanics for delamination problems in composite materials. J. Compos. Mater. **17**(3), 210–223 (1983)
7. López-Menéndez, A., Viña, J., Argüelles, A., Rubiera, S., Mollón, V.: A new method for testing composite materials under mode III fracture. J. Compos. Mater. **50**(28), 3973–3980 (2016)
8. Szekrényes, A.: Delamination fracture analysis in the GII–GIII plane using prestressed transparent composite beams. Int. J. Solids Struct. **44**(10), 3359–3378 (2007)
9. de Morais, A.B., Pereira, A.B.: Mixed mode II+III interlaminar fracture of carbon/epoxy laminates. Compos. Sci. Technol. **68**(9), 2022–2027 (2008)
10. Mehrabadi, F.A.: Analysis of pure mode III and mixed mode (III+II) interlaminar crack growth in polymeric woven fabrics. Mater. Des. **44**, 429–437 (2013)

11. Suemasu, H., Kondo, A., Gozu, K., Aoki, Y.: Novel test method for mixed mode II and III interlaminar fracture toughness. Adv. Compos. Mater **19**(4), 349–361 (2010)
12. Reeder, J.R.: 3D mixed mode delamination fracture criteria – an experimentalist's perspective. In: 21st Annual Technical Conference, pp. 1—19, Dearbon, Michigan (2006)
13. Turon, A., Dávila, C.G., Camanho, P.P., Costa, J.: An engineering solution for mesh size effects in the simulation of delamination using cohesive zone models. Eng. Fract. Mech. **74**(10), 1665–1682 (2007)
14. Xie, D., Waas, A.M.: Discrete cohesive zone model for mixed-mode fracture using finite element analysis. Eng. Fract. Mech. **73**(13), 1783–1796 (2006)
15. de Morais, A.B., Pereira, A.B., de Moura, M.F.S.F., Magalhães, A.G.: Mode III interlaminar fracture of carbon/epoxy laminates using the edge crack torsion (ECT) test. Compos. Sci. Technol. **69**(5), 670–676 (2009)
16. Sørensen, B.F., Goutianos, S., Jacobsen, T.K.: Strength scaling of adhesive joints in polymer-matrix composites. Int. J. Solids Struct. **46**(3–4), 741–761 (2009)
17. Wong, K.J., Israr, H.A., Tamin, M.N.: Cohesive zone modeling of mode III delamination using edge crack torsion test. In: Symposium on Damage Mechanisms in Materials and Structures, Bangi, Malaysia (2016)

A New Simulation Framework for Intermittent Demand Forecasting Applying Classification Models

Gisun Jung[1], Seunglak Choi[1], HyunJin Jung[1], Young Kim[1],
Yohan Kim[2], Yun Bae Kim[2(✉)], Nokhaiz Tariq Khan[1],
and Jinsoo Park[3]

[1] Department of Industrial Engineering, Sungkyunkwan University, 2066
Seobu-ro, Jangan-gu, Suwon, Korea
{gsjung09, choi-lak, hjjung217}@naver.com,
lmjlguard@gmail.com, nokhaiz.tariq@hotmail.com
[2] Department of Systems Management Engineering, Sungkyunkwan University,
2066 Seobu-ro, Jangan-gu, Suwon, South Korea
{yohan.kim, kimyb}@skku.edu
[3] Department of Management Information Systems, Yongin University, 134,
Yongindaehak-ro, Cheoin-gu, Yongin-si, South Korea
jsf001@yongin.ac.kr

Abstract. Demand Forecasting is a key to effective inventory management. In forecasting fields, intermittent demand forecasting remains to be a very important but challenging problem. Intermittent demand is characterized by many empty demands, stochastic periods between them, and high variance of non-zero values. These characteristics make intermittent demand forecasting a difficult task, for both parametric and non-parametric approaches. The parametric methods have shown many limitations to provide accurate information. Though non-parametric methods provide better information for decision making than parametric case, they cannot forecast any exact information of point values. This paper proposes a new simulation framework that takes into consideration the correlation structure between demand of assembly and demand of parts, leading to more precise information of point values. In particular, we demonstrate how sub-parts for classification can affect to prediction performance of the overall model via an experiment using artificial data.

Keywords: Intermittent demand · Demand forecasting · Classification · Simulation framework · Inventory management

1 Introduction

Demand forecasting is key to an effective and agile inventory management of spares, where its accuracy can minimize tradeoffs between out of stock costs and inventory costs. Many good parametric methodologies have been developed to forecast highly efficient point values based on historical demand patterns. But these methodologies fail when it comes to forecasting demand for stagnant or slow moving items. The reason,

© Springer Nature Singapore Pte Ltd. 2017
M.S. Mohamed Ali et al. (Eds.): AsiaSim 2017, Part II, CCIS 752, pp. 569–578, 2017.
DOI: 10.1007/978-981-10-6502-6_49

hidden behind this fact, is that stagnant items generate quite different patterns of demand, having many periods of zero demand. Time periods for these empty demand values are added in parametric methods making forecast results less precise. This type of demand is known as intermittent demand. To make matters more complex, such intermittent demand often show large variance in size of its empty demand periods. Uncertainty lies in both the time and the size of demand [1]. Additionally, conventional performance measures like mean absolute percentage error (MAPE) also cannot be used for intermittent demand because when the true value is zero, it may not be defined because it will be infinite value. Intermittent demand forecasting is usual problem in heavy machine industries such as aircraft, military, and auto industries. For such industries, out of stock costs and inventory costs are comparatively larger, making it a tangible concern.

On the contrary to the parametric methods, many non-parametric methods are well known to handle intermittent demand. Such non-parametric methods make it possible to predict the empirical distribution for a particular time frame, but still it does not answer to the question of industrial level managers or decision makers whether there will be demand in the next time period. Additionally, non-parametric approaches are usually complex while parametric methods are simple [2]. This calls for a new methodology that can address the issues of accurate forecasting for intermittent demand.

In this work, we propose a new way of forecasting that uses historical data to predict point values for intermittent demand, as well as, predict if next value will be a non-zero value. The proposed model uses conventional time series methods to predict point values and basic classification models to predict between zero and non-zero values.

The detailed analysis of the proposed methodology is presented in the following sections. Section 2 consists of the review of latest related research work done regarding intermittent demand forecasting. Sections 3 and 4 contain framework of suggested model and the experiment done using simulated data, respectively. The classification model used in experiment is elaborated in Sect. 3. Finally, last section conjectures our study, limitations, and future aspects of our proposed model.

2 Literature Review

Forecasting intermittent demand is not a new issue, where many researchers have undergone through different parametric and non-parametric studies for intermittent demand. Conventional parametric methods like exponential smoothing, moving average, and autoregressive integrated moving average (ARIMA) are ineffective in forecasting intermittent demand due to the presence of empty demand for various time periods and the clustered nature of intermittent demand forecasting. A widely used methodology for intermittent demand forecasting is Croston's method originally developed in 1972, essentially an extension of exponential smoothing. This method requires to take exponential smoothing of time period and size of demand, separately, then the size over time period ratio is used for estimation [3]. Many researchers have modified and revised Croston's method to improve accuracy for demand forecasting [4, 5]. For example, one modification is to first implementing logarithmic function to the demand data and then applying the Croston's method.

Willemain et al. suggested a non-parametric approach using binary Markov model and bootstrap method [6]. Mixed non-parametric bootstrapping with jittering technique resulting in good solution. The solution of this approach is a form of distribution of lead time demand. Inventory managers can utilize the results of this approach to make decisions related to inventory control. Syntetos et al. compared bootstrapping technique with some simple parametric methods like simple exponential smoothing and Croston's method [2]. Syntetos et al. inferred that bootstrapping yields better information but adds complexity as well while parametric approach is simple and SES is one of those parametric approaches that performs well [2]. Kourentzes presented a neural network approach to forecast intermittent time series [1]. In his proposed model neural networks did not achieve superior forecasting accuracy but his study exhibited that neural network variants achieved better service levels when compared to Croston's method variants.

Kocer proposed a non-parametric approach for intermittent demand forecasting based on Markov chain model [7]. With the modification of Markov chain model, suggested to consider each state in proportion to their probabilities while forecasting next state rather considering only the state with the highest probability.

Jung et al. proposed a modified Markov bootstrap method to predict the distribution pattern for a particular time frame [8]. Previous Markov bootstrap model assumed first-order autocorrelation of each point demand and independent lead time demands. Using the methods proposed by [6], the case that lead time demands have correlations cannot be treated. Thus, modified Markov bootstrap would be used when lead time demands have autocorrelations.

As shown in the literature review, many parametric and non-parametric methods have been studied for intermittent demand forecasting. In case of parametric methods, they can provide some information for point values of demand, but its accuracy is quite inferior. On the other hand, non-parametric methods can provide more useful information for decision making, but they cannot suggest any information of point values. Thus, a new approach which can utilize these two approach at once is needed for intermittent demand forecasting. Using proposed simulation framework, analysts can obtain information of not only the distribution but each point value. Also, they can utilize the information to inventory management strategies.

3   Simulation Framework for Intermittent Demand Forecasting

3.1   Proposed Simulation Framework

Figure 1 shows the structure of suggested framework. The new framework for intermittent demand forecasting consists of conventional time series method and classification model which predicts whether the next demand would be zero or not. For classification model based on historical data, any method can be used that is capable to predict binary class. In this work, three classical methods are used for simple experiment and they are introduced in Sect. 3.2. In order to forecast the non-intermittent demands of parts and non-zero values in intermittent demand, we can use any of the

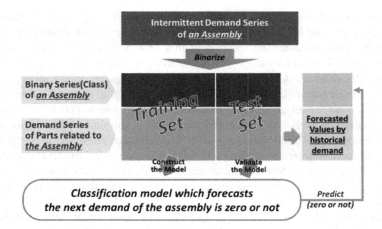

Fig. 1. Simulation framework for intermittent demand forecasting based on classification

conventional forecasting methods such as moving average, exponential smoothing and regression models.

The prediction performance depends upon the performance of three forecasting models, model for classification, non-intermittent demand, and non-zero values in intermittent demand. In general, forecasting models for demand of parts perform quite well. As such, the performance of the classification model has bigger influence on the performance of the overall model. As such, the classification model is critically important in our suggested framework.

As a solution to the problem of selecting appropriate performance measure for intermittent demand, measures like absolute deviation (AD), mean absolute deviation (MAD), and fulfillment rate can be used for overall model. Therefore, this proposed model emphasizes on classification model only so we use accuracy and misclassification as performance measures.

As our framework uses the correlation structure among related demands by using classification model, the assumption for data structure should be similar to Table 1. Simulated data has intermittent demand series of an assembly (ASSB 1 in Table 1), such as engine, transmission, and demand series of the parts (Part_A, Part_B,... in Table 1) which are related to the assembly (ASSB 1 in Table 1) such as cylinder cover, spark plug, and so on. In this paper, we assume that the demand series of parts is non-intermittent since it is hard to forecast the intermittent demand. If demands of parts are intermittent, the forecasting accuracy may be considerably poorer.

3.2 General Classification Models

For binary classification, the three methods - decision tree, linear discriminant analysis, and K-nearing neighbor - are used for our experiment. We selected these three methods because of their simplicity and ease of use to avoid complexity.

Table 1. Example of data structure for suggested framework

Period	Week 1	Week 2	Week 3	Week 4	⋯
ASSB 1	Y_1	0	0	Y_2	⋯
Part_A	X_{11}	X_{12}	X_{13}	X_{14}	⋯
Part_B	X_{21}	X_{22}	X_{23}	X_{24}	⋯
⋮	⋮	⋮	⋮	⋮	⋱

Decision tree is a very powerful tool for classification and decision making [9]. Basically decision tree is a graphical way of interpreting the possible outcomes of some events, these possible outcomes are based on some predefined decision rules. When these all possible outcomes are drawn graphically, a tree like structure is observed. This tree like structure consists of different nodes; those can be categorized in three different types. Decision nodes: represented by squares, Chance/Event nodes: represented by circles and End nodes: represented by triangles.

Originally introduced by R.A Fisher in 1936, idea behind the classic method of LDA is to carry out classification for two or more classes of events. LDA uses categorical dependent variables and continuous independent variables unlike to other techniques like ANOVA and regression analysis. Fundamental assumption of LDA is that independent variables are normally distributed. As a methodology, first, a linear transformation is found to discriminate classes excellently and then classification is carried out in transformed space based on some metric. Scatter Matrix analysis bases the mathematical interpretation to perform LDA [10].

Nearest neighboring technique is a very simple but efficient non-parametric methodology for regression and classification. In particular, it is known as the simplest of all machine learning algorithms. Its simplicity and versatility makes it easy for many applications like text classification, pattern recognition and object recognition. This technique uses data in which data points lie in various classes and helps predicting the class of new sample point [11]. The method uses weight of neighboring contributions to make sure that nearing neighbor has higher participation to the average than those having relatively larger distance.

3.3 Flow Chart for Applying the Framework

Figure 2 shows the flow chart explaining the flow of applying the procedure of the proposed framework. In order to apply the framework, as a first step, we transform the intermittent demand series into binary series for the usage in classes; set the value 1 if the value of demand is not zero, otherwise set to 0. Then, partition the historical data into two parts, training set and test set. This is the general way to apply classification model. After partitioning the data, we construct classification model from the training

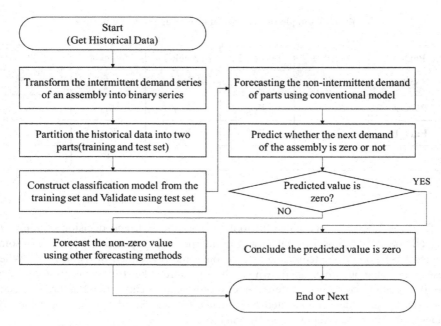

Fig. 2. Flow chart of the suggested framework

set and validate it using the test set. From this classification model, we can predict whether the next value of intermittent demand is zero or not if we have the predicted values of demand of parts which are related to assembly. Accordingly, we should have the forecasting model for the non-intermittent demand of parts. Finally, if the prediction result is zero, then we conclude that the next value is zero. If the prediction result is non-zero, we have to predict one more value from historical data.

4   Experiment Using Data Simulation

In this section, a simple experiment which applies suggested framework is introduced. The presence of the appropriate forecasting models which predict the demand values of parts and non-zero demand values in the intermittent demand is assumed. As this paper focuses on introduction of classification model for intermittent demand forecasting, we only check the possibilities of using classification model for intermittent demand by using artificial data sets. It is difficult to obtain the real data set of the intermittent demand and demand of parts because most companies are not willing to share their data for security reasons.

As mentioned previously, three classical classification methods – decision tree, k-nearest neighbor, and discriminant analysis – are used in this experiment. These are widely used in the construction and prediction of binary class. Some information of each method is introduced in Sect. 3.2.

For this experiment, we made artificial data sets using Markov model and random numbers. The compositions of artificial data sets are shown as Fig. 3. The intermittent

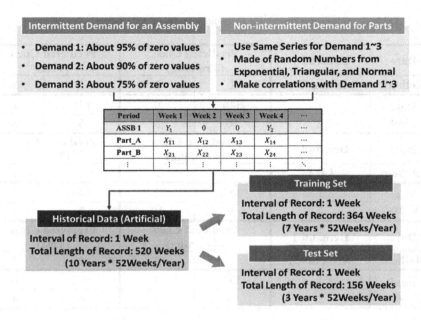

Fig. 3. Construction of artificial data for an experiment

demands are generated by Markov model and simple bootstrap and demands of parts are generated from triangular, exponential, and normal distribution. There are correlations between demand of the assembly and demand of parts by adding the demand of assembly to demand of parts since assuming that demands of some parts are surely occurred when the demand of assembly occurs.

In this experiment, we apply three methods to forecast whether the demand of assembly is zero or not. Thus, the results of application are shown as confusion matrices which are widely used to show the results of classification. Tables 2, 3 and 4 show the results of experiments.

From the results, decision tree shows more appropriate performance when the ratio of zero values is relatively low and k-nearest neighbor performs worse than other two methods for all cases. Linear discriminant analysis shows weak performance for classification of class 2 which indicates non-zero values. Because this type of intermittent data is an imbalanced classification problem, it is reasonable that linear discriminant analysis has weakness for class 2.

Table 5 shows the values of accuracy and misclassification rate from our experiments. The two performance measures, accuracy and misclassification rate, are widely used in classification fields. The other measures for classification such as area under ROC curve (AUC) can be used for classification in suggested framework. Since this experiment uses artificial data, the results of experiment may not be able to show complete nature of real cases. However, we can identify the possibilities for forecasting using our framework.

Table 2. Confusion matrix for Demand 1 (ratio of zero values = about 95%)

Data	Demand 1	Predicted Class (Training)		Predicted Class (Test)	
Methods	**Decision Tree**	1	2	1	2
Real Class	1	346	0	145	1
	2	10	8	5	5
Data	**Demand 1**	Predicted Class (Training)		Predicted Class (Test)	
Methods	**LDA**	1	2	1	2
Real Class	1	344	2	146	1
	2	8	10	3	7
Data	**Demand 1**	Predicted Class (Training)		Predicted Class (Test)	
Methods	**KNN (k=3)**	1	2	1	2
Real Class	1	337	9	141	6
	2	14	4	6	4

Table 3. Confusion matrix for Demand 2 (ratio of zero values = about 90%)

Data	Demand 2	Predicted Class (Training)		Predicted Class (Test)	
Methods	**Decision Tree**	1	2	1	2
Real Class	1	318	6	140	5
	2	10	30	7	5
Data	**Demand 2**	Predicted Class (Training)		Predicted Class (Test)	
Methods	**LDA**	1	2	1	2
Real Class	1	323	1	143	2
	2	15	25	8	4
Data	**Demand 2**	Predicted Class (Training)		Predicted Class (Test)	
Methods	**KNN (k=3)**	1	2	1	2
Real Class	1	309	15	138	7
	2	20	20	7	5

Table 4. Confusion matrix for Demand 3 (ratio of zero values = about 75%)

Data	Demand 3	Predicted Class (Training)		Predicted Class (Test)	
Methods	**Decision Tree**	1	2	1	2
Real	1	262	16	105	8
Class	2	10	76	11	33
Data	**Demand 3**	Predicted Class (Training)		Predicted Class (Test)	
Methods	**LDA**	1	2	1	2
Real	1	278	0	113	0
Class	2	41	45	24	20
Data	**Demand 3**	Predicted Class (Training)		Predicted Class (Test)	
Methods	**KNN (k=3)**	1	2	1	2
Real	1	249	29	105	8
Class	2	39	47	19	25

Table 5. Accuracy of the experiments

Training	Demand 1	Demand 2	Demand 3
Decision Tree	97.25%	95.60%	92.86%
LDA	97.25%	95.60%	88.74%
KNN	93.68%	90.38%	81.32%
Test	**Demand 1**	**Demand 2**	**Demand 3**
Decision Tree	95.54%	92.36%	87.90%
LDA	97.45%	93.63%	84.71%
KNN	92.36%	91.08%	82.80%

5 Concluding Remarks

In this paper, we proposed a new simulation framework for intermittent demand forecasting with classification concept. The framework considers zero and non-zero value of demand as a binary class. Based on the forecasting for parts related to an assembly which has intermittent demand, whether the value of demand of the assembly is zero or not is predicted by some classifier. Then, if the value is non-zero, then forecast the non-zero values from the historical data.

In suggested framework, prediction is divided into three parts; parts demands, non-zero values, and class (zero or not) of intermittent demand. Generally, the performance of forecasting for normal numerical value is relatively superior. So, for our framework, the classification part is most important than other two prediction parts. Accordingly, a simple experiment using artificial data is introduced in Sect. 4. From the result, we can identify possibility of application of our framework and test our framework with three classical classification models. Also, we can be sure that the selection of classifier can lead to different results of our overall model.

Though suggested framework has potential for solving the difficulty of intermittent demand, this study has some limitations. First, there must be correlation structure between demand of assembly and demand of parts. If there is no correlation, the framework cannot be applied. Second, in this study, we use only artificial data. It is hard to obtain the real data set since most companies do not share their data. Third, the classification problem of intermittent demand can be imbalance classification problem. Then, we have to consider the classifier for imbalanced classification. This problem has many issues which are hard to solve.

After this study, the authors will perform additional experiments for applying other classification methods and applying conventional forecasting models for non-intermittent values. The authors are also working on obtaining real world data related to military industries. Should this be successful, experiments for our framework can be more accurate and precise than before. We hope that this study will set a precedence for further investigation into solving the industry and academic difficulties in intermittent demand forecasting.

References

1. Kourentzes, N.: Intermittent demand forecasts with neural networks. Int. J. Prod. Econ. **143**, 198–206 (2013)
2. Syntetos, A., Babai, M.Z., Everette, S.G.: Forecasting intermittent inventory demands: simple parametric methods vs. bootstrapping. J. Bus. Res. **68**(8), 1746–1752 (2014)
3. Xu, Q., Na, W., Heping, S.: Review of Croston's method for intermittent demand forecasting. In: 2012 9th International Conference on Fuzzy Systems and Knowledge Discovery (FSKD). IEEE (2012)
4. Johnston, F.R., Boylan, J.E.: Forecasting intermittent demand: a comparative evaluation of Croston's method. Int. J. Forecast. **12**(2), 297–298 (1996)
5. Syntetos, A., Boylan, J.E.: On the bias of intermittent demand estimates. Int. J. Prod. Econ. **71**(1), 457–466 (2001)
6. Willemain, T.R., Charles, N.S., Henry, F.S.: A new approach to forecasting intermittent demand for service parts inventories. Int. J. Forecast. **20**(3), 375–387 (2004)
7. Kocer, U.: Forecasting intermittent demand by Markov chain model. Int. J. Innov. Comput. Inf. Control **9**(8), 3307–3318 (2013)
8. Jung, G., Park. J., Kim, Y.B.: A new bootstrap method for intermittent demand forecasting for spare parts. In: Proceedings of the 2015 Asia Simulation Conference (2015)
9. Breiman, L., FriedMan, J., Stone, C.J., Olshen, R.A.: Classification and Regression Trees. CRC Press, Boca Raton (1984)
10. Fukunaga, K.: Introduction to Statistical Pattern Recognition. Academic Press, Cambridge (1990). pp. 401–405
11. Bhatia, N.: Survey of nearest neighbor techniques (2010)

Visualizing Overlapping Space-Time Regions of Time-Series 2D Experimental Data and 3D Simulation Data: Application to Plasma-Plume Collisions

Kyoko Hasegawa[1], Liang Li[1], Yushi Uenoyama[2], Shuhei Kawata[2],
Taku Kusanagi[2], Toshinori Yabuuchi[3], Kazuo Tanaka[4], and Satoshi Tanaka[1(✉)]

[1] College of Information Science and Engineering, Ritsumeikan University,
1-1-1 Noji-higashi, Kusatsu, Shiga, Japan
{hasegawa,stanaka}@media.ritsumei.ac.jp, liliang@fc.ritsumei.ac.jp
[2] Graduate School of Information Science and Engineering, Ritsumeikan University,
1-1-1 Noji-higashi, Kusatsu, Shiga, Japan
[3] RIKEN SPring-8 Center, Sayo-cho, Hyogo 679-5148, Japan
tyabuuchi@spring8.or.jp
[4] IFIN-HH ELI-NP, Magurele, Ilfov, Romania
kazuo.tanaka@eli-np.ro

Abstract. It is of critical importance in many physics fields to compare results both from simulation and experiments. In order to make this comparison efficient, visualization of experimental and simulation data is rather essential. In this paper, we focus on the colliding plasma plumes using laser produced plasmas to understand the basic physics in a nuclear laser fusion reactor. To visually compare dynamical data acquired through experiments and simulations, we propose a visualization method to highlight overlapping space-time regions of XYT-space volumes. The visualization of the XYT-space volumes is conducted based on particle-based techniques. First, input data for an experiment and a simulation are both converted into the XYT-space volumes and then further converted into particle data. Second, we perform the particle-based volume fusion. Third, we conduct the particle-based evaluation of the degrees of overlapping and highlight highly overlapping regions using colors with large whiteness. We demonstrate the effectiveness of our method by applying it to the plasma plume collision of tungsten. Our method has visually proven that the univalent ionized plasma is the most dominant plasma in the experiment.

Keywords: Comparative visualization · Simulation · Experiment · Overlapping space-time regions · Plasma physics · XYT-space volume

1 Introduction

As known well in physics research, theoretical prediction may lead and call for a new experiment. Alternatively, the experiment may come up with a result that

© Springer Nature Singapore Pte Ltd. 2017
M.S. Mohamed Ali et al. (Eds.): AsiaSim 2017, Part II, CCIS 752, pp. 579–592, 2017.
DOI: 10.1007/978-981-10-6502-6_50

requires a theoretical analysis. However, the theory involves often complicated mathematical models and equations resulting in relying heavily on computer simulations these days. Visualization of data can function to assist this comparison between the simulation and the experiment. In this paper, we deal with plasma physics and propose a visualization method to support the comparison between the simulation and the experiment.

Plasma is a state of matter that is often considered to be a very hot ionized gas. The characteristics of plasma are quite different from those of ordinary neutral gases, and studies on plasma are still actively conducted by physicists. In particular, further studies are required to develop reliable nuclear fusion reactors, where plasma very frequently appears [3]. Generating power via nuclear fusion is recognized as one of the important future energy sources. In the nuclear fusion reaction, many high-energy particles, such as photons and alpha particles, are created. The created particles collide with the reactor walls. Then, high-speed *plasma plumes*, which are localized clouds of plasma particles, of the wall material are generated via ablation and fly through the reactor. The generated plasma plumes collide with each other, and heat (thermal energy) is released. The heated plasma plumes become obstacles for the chain reaction of nuclear fusion. It is also expected that plasma plumes are available for protecting the reactor walls [4,8,9]. Irrespective of whether the plasma-plume collisions lead to obstacles or benefits, understand their physics is of importance.

Based on the above consideration, in this paper, we study the process of two plasma plumes colliding with each other (see Fig. 1). We visually compare data obtained from a 3D particle simulation with a set of time-series 2D photographic images that record a real collision process in the experiment.

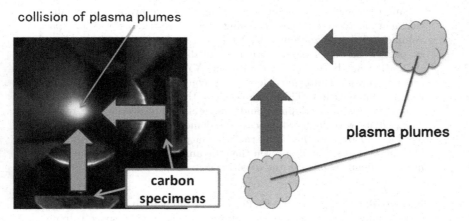

Fig. 1. The plasma-plume collision experiment. The plasma plumes are generated from irradiated specimens that imitate reactor walls. The left figure shows a snapshot photographic image of the experiment using carbon specimens. The collision occurs at the cylindrical center of the experimental equipment.

2   Visualized Data and Their Preprocessing

In this section, we describe the data visualized in this paper. In Sect. 2.1, we explain the 2D time-series data, which are the photographic images acquired from real experiments. In Sect. 2.2, we explain the 3D time-series data, which are a set of 3D point clouds generated through computer simulations. The purpose of this paper is to visually compare these two types of data.

2.1   Experimental Data

Our first target for visualization is time-series photographic images recorded during the experiment, as shown in Fig. 1 (left). During the experiment, specimens of a selected material, which imitate parts of the cylindrical reactor walls, are irradiated by high-energy laser beams. The specimens are placed at two positions on the hypothetical cylinder such that the laser beams to each specimen run at right angles to one another. Then, the plasma plumes generated from each specimen also run at right angles to one another, and the two plasma plumes collide at the cylindrical center, which is 1.4 cm away from the specimens on the wall (see Fig. 1 (right)).

In the above experiment, a time series of photographic images are collected using a fast frame intensified ICCD camera (see Fig. 2 (left)). The observation frame is shifted in time with 50 ns time steps at the camera trigger. Thus, we obtain a time series of photographic images that show the plasma plume collision process. The standard approach to visualize these photographic images is through an animation, which displays each image in order with small time intervals. However, such an animation is not always convenient for observing the entire collision process. Therefore, to observe the entire process at one glance, we stack the time series of the 2D images, each of which is recognized as defined in the XY-coordinate space (see the illustrations in Fig. 2 (middle and right)). In other words, we stack the XY-plane images in the time (T) direction. This creates a 3D volume in the XYT-coordinate space.

The resolution of the photographic images (raw data) is 1024^2. For convenience in visualization, we smooth the images to a resolution of 100^2. Since we stack images for 100 time steps to create a XYT-space volume, the above-mentioned procedure creates a 100^3 cubic volume. The voxel values, each of which originates from the pixel intensity of a photographic image, are normalized to sizes between 0 and 255.

Figure 3 shows a volume rendering of the created XYT-space volume. In this rendering, space-time regions of the three temperatures, that is, the innermost hot region, the outermost cool region, and the in-between medium-temperature region, are selectively visualized by properly tuning the opacity transfer function with three peaks. The visualization is performed using the particle-based volume rendering (PBVR) [5, 10] (see Sect. 3.1). In Fig. 3, we can easily observe the entire plasma plume collision process at one glance. We can chronologically observe that two medium-temperature plasma plumes collide at the early stage. Then, they merge into one and become hotter. Finally, the merged plasma plume diffuses

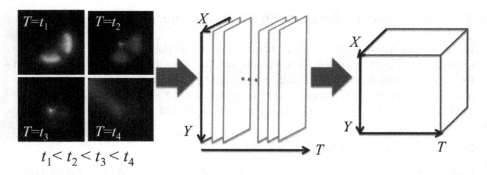

Fig. 2. Construction of the XYT-space volume data to show the entire collision process. We stack the time series of the XY-plane photographic images in the time (T) direction.

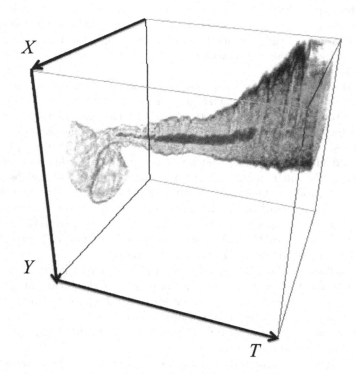

Fig. 3. Volume rendering of the carbon plasma plume collision using the constructed XYT-space volume data. Space-time regions of the focused three temperatures are visualized.

and cools down. In this paper, we apply such an XYT-space volume rendering for a comparative visualization of the experiment and the simulation.

2.2   Simulation Data

We conducted computer simulations to reproduce the experiment shown in Fig. 1. We adopted the direct simulation Monte Carlo (DSMC) method [1,2]. The DSMC method is a powerful tool for studying gas flows that involve low densities. In this method, we assume that a simulated physical system is composed of small 3D points with proper physical properties. (In this paper, we use the term "points" for the simulation primitives of the DSMC method. We use the term "particles" for the rendering primitives of PBVR (see Sect. 3.1).) Therefore, the method generates a time series of 3D point clouds. Details on the DSMC simulation for the plasma plume collision shown in Fig. 1 are reported in [6]. In this paper, we focus on utilizing the simulation results to demonstrate our proposed visualization.

When conducting the DSMC simulation, we assume that each plasma plume consists of localized 2.5×10^5 points in a $3\,\text{cm}^3$ cubic space. Collisions of the plasma plumes are evaluated by considering elastic two-body collisions of the constituent points. The point collision is affected by the coulomb force. We consider two types of plasma plumes: the charged (ionized) plume and the neutral (non-ionized) plume. The behavior of the both types of plumes are very different in the collisions.

The above-mentioned simulation outputs a time series of point clouds in the ordinary 3D space, that is, the XYZ space (see Fig. 4). To compare the simulation with the experiment shown in Fig. 1, we convert the output data to the XYT-space volume as follows: For each point cloud, we project the constituent

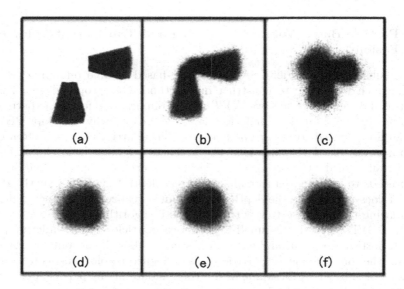

Fig. 4. Time series of 3D point clouds obtained by the simulation of the plasma-plume collision. Time develops in alphabetical order.

3D points to the XY space, which is divided into 100^2 uniform square cells. For each cell, we count the number of projected points and calculate the point-image density at the location. Then, regarding the cells as pixels, we create an image, where the pixel intensities are proportional to the point-image densities. The created images are comparable to the photographic images taken in the experiment shown in Fig. 1. This result occurs because the point densities in the simulation correspond to the real plasma densities in the experiment. The higher the local plasma density is, the larger the local energy density becomes in plasma physics. Therefore, the 2D local point-image density corresponds to the local energy density integrated along the Z direction. This local energy density should determine the local brightness of the experimental photographic images in the XY space. Thus, by stacking the obtained images in the same way as in Fig. 2, we obtain the XYT-volume that describes the entire collision process generated by the simulation.

3   Method of Comparative Visualization of the Experiment and the Simulation

In this section, we propose our method for defining proper colors that can highlight the *degrees of overlapping* of two given volumes. Comparative visualization generally focuses on differences in two given datasets, particularly, in scientific visualization [7]. Conversely, we aim at highlighting overlapping or affinity. This policy is suitable for investigating the degrees of coincidence between a simulation and an experiment.

3.1   Particle-Based Volume Rendering and Transparent Volume Fusion

In this subsection, we briefly review particle-based volume rendering (PBVR) [5,10], which we utilize to construct our method. Our proposed visualization performs data fusion of the two XYT-space volumes: one for the experimental data and the other for the simulation data. The reason why we adopt PBVR is that we do not need to worry about the rendering artifacts, which often occur in transparent fused visualization. The artifacts originate from the ambiguity in the results of depth sorting of rendering primitives along the line of sight, which needs to be executed to realize a correct depth feel. Note that the PBVR method does not include the depth sorting, but it realizes the correct depth feel by replacing the depth sorting with a stochastic algorithm.

The PBVR method uses small hypothetical particles as its rendering primitives. A particle is opaque and has a cross section whose image only overlaps one pixel on the image plane. A particle is also assigned a color that is determined corresponding to the scalar value of the volume data at the particle position. In the case that the shading effect should be incorporated in the visualization, we also assign normal vectors to the particles. The normal vectors are calculated from gradients of the scalar field of the volume data at the particle position.

The following three steps realize transparent volume visualization. The origin of the transparency is the probabilistic determination of pixel colors.

- **STEP 1. Particle generation:** The first step is to convert the target volume into particle data, in which the particle density distribution is made to be proportional to the opacity distribution. The opacity distribution is determined by the user-defined opacity transfer function applied to the volume. The local particle densities are determined in units of cubic cells, each of which is formed by eight voxels. The eight voxel values are averaged, and the result is used to determine the local particle density of a cell. We repeat the particle generation until L_R statistically independent particle sets are prepared. We call L_R the repetition level.
- **STEP 2. Particle projection with occlusion:** The second step is to project the generated particles to the image plane. Since the opaque property is assigned to the particles, we perform particle occlusion during the projection. Namely, at each pixel, we save the color of the one projected particle closest to the camera position. This particle projection with the occlusion effect is executed for each particle set prepared in STEP 1. Consequently, L_R similar images are created.
- **STEP 3. Averaging images:** The final step is to generate an average image of the L_R images created in STEP 2. At each pixel on the image plane, the pixel colors of the L_R images are averaged to determine the final pixel color.
  - Thus, L_R can function as a parameter to tune the statistical quality of the created images. In this paper, we set $L_R = 200$.

By executing the above three steps, we can realize the transparent volume rendering, which creates images identical to the conventional ray casting method [11]. Each cell contains particles of a number, N, which is related to the opacity α as follows:

$$N = -\frac{\log(1 - \alpha)}{d^2 \Delta t} . \tag{1}$$

Here, d is the 3D particle diameter that corresponds to the pixel width in the image plane. Δt is a parameter that corresponds to sampling step width of the conventional ray-casting volume rendering. This means that we should set a value of the order of 1 in units of the cell width. In the current work, we set $\Delta t = 0.5$.

Note that PBVR is suitable for fused visualization of multiple volumes. We merge multiple particle sets, each of which is created from a constituent volume dataset, according to the operations of STEP 1. Then, by executing STEP 2 and STEP 3 for the unified larger particle set, we can realize the transparent fused volume visualization.

3.2   Particle-Based Definition of the Degree of Overlapping

Our purpose is to establish a visualization method to highlight overlapping regions of two given XYT-space volumes: one for the experimental data and the other for the simulation data. The PBVR method explained in Sect. 3.1 provides a simple and effective method for this purpose. Here, in a more general manner, we consider investigating the overlapping of volume A and volume B.

First, we execute STEP 1 of PBVR for each of volumes A and B. Then, we obtain two particle sets, one for volume A and the other for volume B. Next, we divide the 3D XYT space into small cubic cells. In the current work, we create 100^3 cells, whose resolution is identical to that of the XYT-space volume data created in Sect. 2 (see Fig. 5). In each cell, we evaluate the degree of overlapping of the two volumes by comparing the numbers of particles.

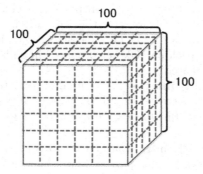

Fig. 5. Division of the XYT space into cubic cells. We evaluate the degree of overlapping of two given volumes in each cell. The resolution of the division is 100^3, which is identical to the resolution of our XYT-space volume data.

In a cell, let the number of particles of volume A be n_a and the number of particles of volume B be n_b. We consider that the cell has the maximum degree of overlapping if $n_a = n_b$. In general, we define the degree of overlapping, $D(n_a, n_b)$, by the following formula:

$$D(n_a, n_b) = \frac{2\min(n_a, n_b)}{n_a + n_b} .$$ (2)

According to formula (2), $D(n_a, n_b)$ takes the maximum value of 1 if $n_a = n_b$ and vanishes if $n_a = 0$ or $n_b = 0$.

3.3   Highlighting Colors for Overlapping Volume Regions

In this subsection, we propose a method to define proper *highlighting colors* to visually emphasize highly overlapping volume regions, that is, regions with large $D(n_a, n_b)$. After the highlighting color is determined in each cell, we visualize the fused volume, which is created according to the operations explained at the end of Sect. 3.1, by assigning the highlighting color to all the particles in the cell.

As is well known, a color has three attributes: hue, saturation, and brightness. In each cell, we define the highlighting color by properly tuning the saturation S according to the value of $D(n_a, n_b)$:

$$S(n_a, n_b) = 255(1 - D(n_a, n_b)) \, , \tag{3}$$

assuming that we use 256-color volumes for visualization. For the brightness attribute, we use the maximum value of 255. For the hue attribute, we adopt the color of volume A if $n_a > n_b$ and the color of volume B if $n_a < n_b$. The colors of volumes A and B are given through user-defined color transfer functions in the same way as the conventional volume rendering. In the case that $n_a = n_b$, the saturation $S(n_a, n_b)$ vanishes, and the highlighting color becomes white. This means that white color visually exhibits the maximum degree of overlapping. We can also state that the degree of overlapping is expressed with the degree of whiteness.

Figure 6 presents a schematic illustration of how to define the highlighting colors. The hexagon shows a simplified base plane of the HSV cone, where the brightness is 255. On this plane, our highlighting color is defined at a point along the path that connects the colors of volume A and volume B by way of the center (see the path with the black outline):

- If $n_a = n_b$, that is, in the case of the maximum degree of overlapping, the highlighting color is at the hexagonal center that corresponds to the white color.
- If $n_a \neq 0$ and $n_b = 0$, that is, in one case of the minimum degree of overlapping, the highlighting color coincides with the color of volume A that is on a edge of the hexagon.
- If $n_a = 0$ and $n_b \neq 0$, that is, in the other case of the minimum degree of overlapping, the highlighting color coincides with the color of volume B that is on another edge of the hexagon.
- If $n_a > n_b$, the highlighting color is in the half path between the color of volume A and the hexagonal center.
- If $n_a < n_b$, the highlighting color is in the other half path between the color of volume B and the hexagonal center.

The policy of the above-mentioned highlighting colors is to focus on the saturation attribute and to not modify the hue attribute. This policy is convenient because we do not need to introduce different hues in addition to the ones for the user-defined colors of volumes A and B.

4   Visualization Results

In this section, we demonstrate our visualization method proposed in Sect. 3 by applying it to real experimental and simulation data. We take the collision of

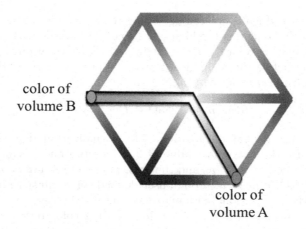

color of
volume B

color of
volume A

Fig. 6. A schematic illustration of defining the highlighting colors. The hexagon shows the simplified base plane of the HSV cone, where the brightness is 255. The highlighting color is defined at a point along the path outlined with black color. The path connects the colors of volume A and volume B by way of the center (white) (Color figure online).

plasma plumes, whose material is tungsten. Tungsten is a promising material for the walls of nuclear fusion reactors.

Figure 7 summarizes the XYT-space volumes to be fused and used for our visualization. The volume of Fig. 7(a) is created based on the experimental data, that is, the time-series photographic images. The volumes of Figs. 7(b), (c), and (d) are created based on the simulation results. Figure 7(b) is for univalent ionized plasma, Fig. 7(c) is for bivalent ionized plasma, and Fig. 7(d) is for non-ionized (neutral) plasma. We execute fused visualizations of Fig. 7(a) with Figs. 7(b), (c), and (d).

Figure 8 shows the fused visualization of the experimental data (Fig. 7(a)) and the simulation result for the univalent ionized plasma (Fig. 7(b)). Their highly overlapping regions are highlighted with white color. The existence of the large white regions proves that the simulation for the univalent ionized plasma is in good agreement with the experiment.

Figure 9 shows the fused visualization of the experimental data (Fig. 7(a)) and the simulation result for the bivalent ionized plasma (Fig. 7(c)). Similarly, Fig. 10 shows the fused visualization of the experimental data (Fig. 7(a)) and the simulation result for the non-ionized neutral plasma (Fig. 7(d)). In Figs. 9 and 10, we observe only small white regions, which are clearly different from Fig. 8. The small sizes of the white regions in Figs. 9 and 10 indicate that the simulations for the bivalent and neutral plasmas cannot explain the experimental results.

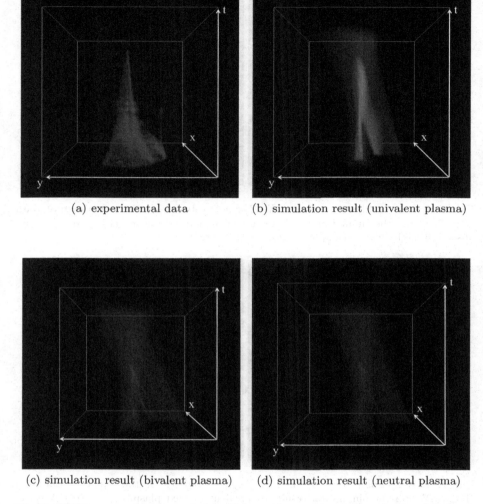

(a) experimental data   (b) simulation result (univalent plasma)

(c) simulation result (bivalent plasma)   (d) simulation result (neutral plasma)

Fig. 7. XYT-space volumes to show collisions of tungsten plasma plumes: (a) exper-imental data, (b) simulation result for univalent ionized plasma, (c) simulation result for bivalent ionized plasma, and (d) simulation result for non-ionized neutral plasma.

Thus, from Figs. 8, 9, and 10, we can conclude that the univalent plasma is dominant in the experiment and that the bivalent and neutral plasmas are not. Our visualization has successfully derived a clear-cut conclusion in plasma physics.

In this work, the computations were executed on our laptop PC with an Intel Core i7 processor (1.7 GHz, 8 GB of memory) CPU and an Intel HD Graphics 5000 1536 M GPU. The calculation speed for creating the above images were

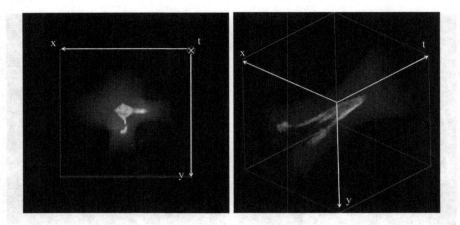

Fig. 8. Fused visualization of the XYT-space volumes of the experimental data (Fig. 7(a)) and the simulation result for univalent ionized plasma (Fig. 7(b)). We can observe large highly overlapping regions with white color.

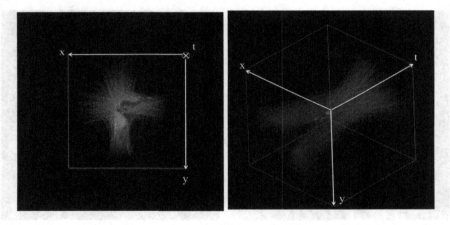

Fig. 9. Fused visualization of the XYT-space volumes of the experimental data (Fig. 7(a)) and the simulation result for bivalent ionized plasma (Fig. 7(c)). We can observe only small highly overlapping regions (white regions).

quick enough for interactive analyses in a laboratory. For each image with $L_R = 200$ and image resolution 512^2, the particle generation and the particle fusion took about 30 or 40 s, and the rendering took 1 or 2 s.

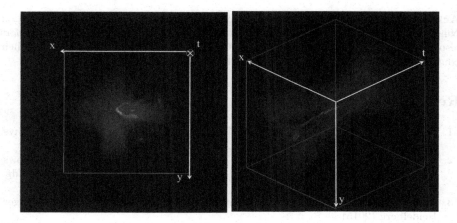

Fig. 10. Fused visualization of the XYT-space volumes of the experimental data (Fig. 7(a)) and the simulation result for non-ionized neutral plasma (Fig. 7(d)). We can observe only small highly overlapping regions (white regions).

5   Conclusions

In this paper, we have proposed a visualization method to highlight overlapping regions of experimental data and simulation results. The experimental data are time-series photographic images. The simulation is conducted using the direct simulation Monte Carlo (DSMC) method, whose results are acquired by time-series point clouds. Directly comparing these different two types of time-series datasets becomes possible by creating the XYT-space volume for each dataset and by performing their fused visualization. In general, the fused visualization of volumes with spatially overlapping portions is not easy because rendering artifacts often appear. This problem is, however, avoidable if we use particle-based volume rendering (PBVR). In the fused visualization of the XYT-space volume, we define proper highlighting colors. According to the degrees of overlapping, which are calculated based on the numbers of PBVR particles. Then, we can visually highlight common features of the experiment and the simulation if any such features are present.

We have demonstrated our visualization method by applying it to the plasma collision experiment of tungsten. Our method can visually prove that the univalent ionized plasma is the most dominant plasma in the experiment. This demonstration clearly shows that our policy, which is to visualize common features rather than different features, is effective when comparing experiments and simulations. Of course, visualizing the different features is also important. We are planning to construct a new method to highlight the common and different features simultaneously.

Acknowledgments. This work was supported in part by JSPS KAKENHI Grant Number 16H02826. The authors thank Prof. R. Xu for his valuable advice. The authors also thank Y. Hatanaka, N. Kawamoto, H. Oda, M. Osada, and T. Yamamoto for their contributions in the early stage of this work.

References

1. Bird, G.A.: Approach to translational equilibrium in a rigid sphere gas. Phys. Fluids **6**(10), 1518–1519 (1963)
2. Bird, G.A.: Molecular Gas Dynamics and the Direct Simulation of Gas Flows. Oxford Engineering Science Series, 2nd edn. Clarendon Press, Wotton-under-Edge (1994)
3. Chen, F.F. (ed.): Introduction to Plasma Physics and Controlled Fusion. Springer, Heidelberg (2015)
4. Hirooka, Y., Tanaka, K.A., Sato, H., Ishihara, K., Sunahara, A.: Laboratory experiments on cluster/aerosol formation by colliding ablation plumes. J. Phys. **244**, 32–37 (2010)
5. Koyamada, K., Sakamoto, N., Tanaka, S.: A particle modeling for rendering irregular volumes. In: proceedings of International Conference on Computer Modeling and Simulation (UKSIM 2008), pp. 372–377 (2008)
6. Misaki, S., Yabuuchi, T., Kono, T., Oishi, T., Tanaka, K.A., Sunahara, A.: Particle simulations for plasma-plasma intersecting experiments. In: proceedings of American Physical Society, 53rd Annual Meeting of the APS Division of Plasma Physics, 14–18 November 2011, pp. 372–377 (2011)
7. Schmidt, J., Grölle, E., Bruckner, S.: VAICo: visual analysis for image comparison. IEEE Trans. Vis. Comput. Graph. **19**(12), 2090–2099 (2013)
8. Sunahara, A., Tanaka, K.A.: Atomic number Z dependence of dynamics of laser-ablated materials. Fusion Eng. Des. **85**(1), 935–939 (2010)
9. Tanaka, K.A., Hassanein, A., Hirooka, Y., Kono, T., Misaki, S., Ohishi, T., Sunahara, A., Tanaka, S.: Carbon plume stagnation: platform for vapor shield study. Fusion Sci. Technol. **60**(1), 329–333 (2011)
10. Tanaka, S., Hasegawa, K., Shimokubo, Y., Kaneko, T., Kawamura, T., Nakata, S., Ojima, S., Sakamoto, N., Tanaka, H.T., Koyamada, K.: Particle-based transparent rendering of implicit surfaces and its application to fused visualization. In: proceedings EuroVis 2012 (Short Paper), pp. 25–29 (2012)
11. Watt, A., Watt, M.: Advanced Animation and Rendering Techniques: Theory and Practice. Addison-Wesley, Reading (1992)

Data Visualization for Human Capital and Halal Training in Halal Industry Using Tableau Desktop

Fatin Zulaikha Fezarudin[1(✉)], Mohd Iskandar Illyas Tan[1],
and Faisal Abdulkarem Qasem Saeed[2]

[1] Halal Informatics (HOLISTICS) Research Lab, Block S45,
Universiti Teknologi Malaysia, 81310 Johor Bahru, Johor, Malaysia
fatinfeza@gmail.com
[2] Department of Information System, Faculty of Computing, Universiti
Teknologi Malaysia, 81310 Johor Bahru, Johor, Malaysia

Abstract. Data visualization describes any effort to help people understand the raw data by changing it into an interactive way of data presentation. In this study, researchers applied the data visualization concept to identify the trends or patterns of the human capital and Halal training in the Halal industry. The visualization tool used in this study is known as Tableau, which is a good visualization tool with a variety of interactive graphs. The human capital dataset used in this study was gathered from Jobstreet portal. This study has analyzed the growth of human capital in the Halal industry and the relationship between the human capital and Halal training in Malaysia. The graph analysis shown in this study will enable people such as halal training providers and job seekers to make a wise decision.

Keywords: Halal · Human capital · Jobstreet · Tableau

1 Introduction

Data is a raw fact that can exist in any form such as text and number. It does not represent any meaning by itself. Nowadays, people can find data everywhere, for instances social media, website, and server. This situation led to the huge amount of data with varying types of data in a dataset. The dataset will become large dataset from small dataset. With the large dataset, people will confront with difficulties to understand the data and unable to make a better decision in a short period of time.

Over the past few years, data visualization has become a famous topic to talk about. Data visualization can helps people to understand and discover the patterns of the dataset. Moreover, the goal of data visualization is to present users with data where trends can be detected and relationships can be established. Good visualization tools allow users to understand data in order to make hypotheses, look for patterns, and notice exceptions [1]. There are many visualization tools that have been introduced through online platforms such as Tableau, D3.js, Fusion-Charts, and Leaflet. As describes by the previous research, visualization tools allow users to filter, sort, and

M.S. Mohamed Ali et al. (Eds.): AsiaSim 2017, Part II, CCIS 752, pp. 593–604, 2017.
DOI: 10.1007/978-981-10-6502-6_51

visualize large datasets and then derive new data from the input data [2]. In this article, authors has used Tableau as visualization tools in order to visualize the data to make it more understandable for the users. As defined by Kale and Balan [3], Tableau provides valuable insights on the data at a rapid rate making it an excellent data visualization tool. Moreover, Tableau offers a wide variety of graph options such as pie, bar, bubble chart, maps, and scatter plots that can be created instantly from diverse datasets.

The principles of data visualization can be applied in the Halal industry in order to generate a trend of the human capital and Halal training. Halal industry is a wide industry, which can be classified into many categories such as food, premises, finance, logistics, tourism, pharmaceuticals, and others. The demand for the Halal industry increase due to the attention of Muslims and non-Muslims as they believe in the characteristics of the Halal products and services which are simplicity, purity, and humanity [4]. Due to the increasing demand of the Halal products and services, it leads to the need of human capital in the halal industry. The human capital that are involved in the Halal oriented business must be equipped with the skills and knowledge about the Syariah law and 'Halalan Thoyyiban'. According to the Ministry of International Trade and Industry (MITI), there will be a huge number of employment chances which makes the growth of the Halal industry [5]. In order for the companies to obtain the Halal certificate, companies must appoint a Halal executive position or establishing a Halal committee inside the company. This statement is clearly explained by the Department of Malaysian Standard in the Malaysian Standard (MS) for the Halal related matter clause 3.1.1 [6]. Therefore, the increasing number of Halal certified companies in Malaysia will also increase the needs or demand of the human capital in the Halal industry.

However, to cater human capital in this industry, it requires trainings that are specifically for Halal. This kind of trainings is to improve the skills and knowledge of the employees related to the Syariah law and 'Halalan Thoyyiban' matters. In Malaysia, there are numerous Halal training programs that have been held to cater the human capital. The training providers for these Halal programs came from universities, government, and non-government organizations. Unfortunately, the Halal training being setup did not match with the job scope demand from the companies. The Halal training providers do not exactly know the types of Halal training needed by the companies and job seekers based on the specific job position. Furthermore, job seekers also faced difficulties to identify the appropriate Halal training required to fulfill the companies' requirements. It happened due to the large dataset with variety of data inside it that people can get it through online job portal such as Jobstreet, Monster, and Indeeed. It makes the Halal training providers and job seekers have difficulties to decide the types of Halal training needed to fulfill the companies' requirements.

The main purpose of this study is to identify the human capital trends in the Halal industry. By using Tableau, we can identify the growth of the human capital in the Halal industry by yearly and also monthly. Researchers also can discover the highest job demand and Halal training. Finally, this study will show the relationships between human capital and Halal training. Therefore, researchers can identify the types of the Halal training needed for the human capital based on the company's requirements.

1.1 Human Capital Development in the Halal Industry

Human capital refers to the knowledge, ideas, and skills of individuals gained through activities, such as formal education and off-the-job and on-the-job training, crucial for increasing the business growth opportunities [7]. By expanding the Halal markets it requires competent human capital to ensure the Halal status of the products and services in the industry. In Malaysia, there are a lot of companies starting to involve in the Halal oriented business and eager to get the Halal certificate in order to get the consumer's trust. Therefore, the needing of the human capital is very crucial in order to help companies getting a Halal certificate. Recently, Malaysia government has proposed a Halal ecosystem in order to boost up the economics of the Halal industry. The Halal ecosystem consists of five sectors and one of the important sectors is called "Human Capital" [8]. Through this human capital sector, Malaysia government will provide more job opportunities in this Halal industry especially for the fresh graduates. Figure 1 shows the Halal ecosystem proposed by the Malaysia government during the World Halal Summit (WHC) 2015.

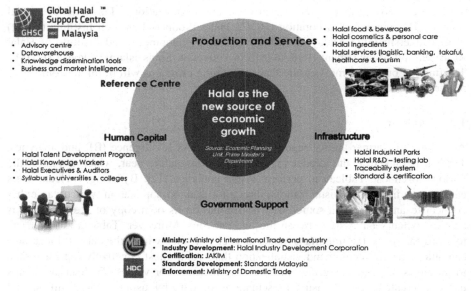

Fig. 1. Halal ecosystem [8]

Unfortunately, Halal industry had faced many problems regarding the human capital development. The biggest problem is the shortage of the human capital competent in this Halal industry [9]. This happened because job seekers did not know the basic requirements to get that job in the Halal certified companies. At the same time, job seekers also lack of awareness or inadequate education about Syariah law and 'Halalan Thoyyiban' concept [10]. All of these problems need to be solved by providing the appropriate Halal trainings to the job seekers or the current employees.

1.2 Halal Training

According to [11], the employees must pursue more training to improve the current skills or develop new ones with assumption that training lead to higher standard of living and better job. The numbers of training related to the Syariah and 'Halalan Thoyyiban' concept have increased as there is high demand for the human capital in the Halal industry. The need for the Halal training in the Halal industry is really important to make sure the products and services delivered to the consumers are totally Halal according to the Syariah law. Ministry of International Trade and Industry Malaysia stated that the inputs and objectives for the Halal trainings programs serve to:

   (i)   Provide knowledge and understanding about "Halalan Thoyyiban" as defined by the Halal Industry Development Corporation (HDC) Malaysia.
 (ii)   Provide knowledge on the process of obtaining Malaysian Halal certification.
(iii)   Products are not just Halal but also Thoyyib (hygiene and nutritious).
(iv)   Identify the benefits of the Halal certification.

    Many training providers have evolved in providing numerous Halal training programs to cater the human capital for the Halal industry. The training providers are from universities, government, and non-government organizations. For example Halal Industry Development Corporation (HDC), Halal Products Research Institute (HPRI) from Universiti Putra Malaysia (UPM), ElZhar Development, and Institute of Halal Research and Management (IHRAM) from Universiti Sains Islam Malaysia (USIM). The training providers must ensure that the training programs will fulfill the company's requirement of the job.

1.3 Tableau

According to Gartner annual report 2016 on Business Intelligence (BI) and analytics, Tableau is ranked as the Leader for the fourth consecutive year, which is one of the reasons to choose Tableau to perform visual analytics [12]. By using Tableau, users can prepare interactive visualizations through a desktop application, which can either connect to an online data source or work offline on its own copy of the data, and is able to switch seamlessly between the two versions. Moreover, Tableau allows users to more easily see the important trends and relationships within the data. Tableau also can automatically recommend visualization that would most effectively represent data to the users after selecting the attributes and measures or values. Tableau also helps users to create effective visual presentations of data by using color, form, spatial position, and motion [13]. The advantage of using Tableau is that it can provide valuable insights on the data at a rapid rate making it an excellent data visualization tool. Figure 2 shows the interface of Tableau software that is easy to use and understand for the users.

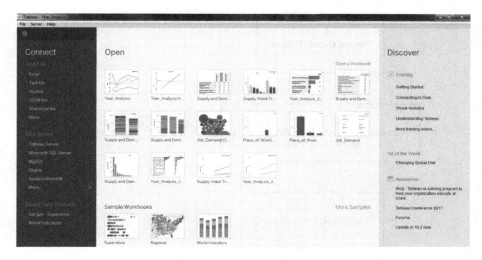

Fig. 2. Tableau interface (Color figure online)

2 Methodology

In this study, the human capital dataset was generated from Jobstreet website. Jobstreet is known as the most preferable online job portal access by job seekers. The attributes of the dataset consist of the advertisement_id, position_title, company_requirement, qualification_skill, denormalized_work_location, years_of_experience, company_-name, and posting_date. This dataset displays the information of the jobs from the Jobstreet website in three consecutive years from year 2013 until 2015. The dataset was displayed in excel format (.XLs). When the users search "Halal" as a keyword through the Jobstreet search engine, it will display lists of job that have a "Halal" keyword. The lists of job related to Halal will be recorded in the human capital dataset. The needed Halal training for each job can be seen through the company's requirements or candidate qualifications and skills. Therefore, different job position requires different types of Halal training. Figure 3 shows the research methodology for this study.

Before visualization part, the dataset needs to undergo a data cleaning process. The data cleaning process is to ensure that the human capital dataset were totally clean by removing a noise data, inconsistent data, and missing data. At first, the human capital dataset consists of 2300 items but after the data cleaning process it consists of only 1437 items. In the human capital dataset, it contains irrelevant data due to the keyword that researchers used which is "Halal". Some of the job positions listed in the human capital dataset is not specifically for the Halal industry because it is written as non-Halal after the position name. The example of job listed in the Jobstreet that are not related to Halal industry such as a chef (non-Halal). Unfortunately, these kinds of job position have been listed together in the human capital dataset because of the "Halal" keyword. Therefore, it is important for the researchers to remove all the unnecessary data before visualize the data. The values inside the human capital dataset also contain a HyperText MarkUp Language (HTML) format such as <div> , <strong> , and <li> .

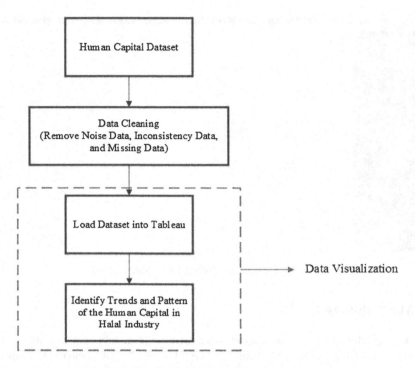

Fig. 3. Research methodology

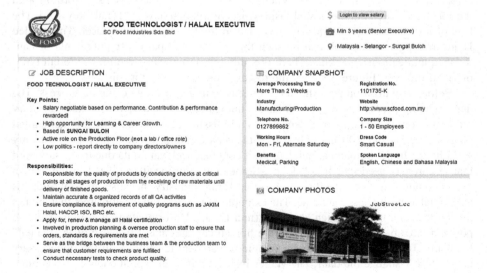

Fig. 4. Example of jobstreet advertisement

These HTML formats also need to be removed before uploaded into Tableau. With the inconsistent data, it can cause the user to misinterpret the data and have poor recall and interpretation of the information [14]. The cleaning process is very important to ensure the accuracy of the results after visualization process. Figure 4 shows the example of job advertisement on the Jobstreet website.

After the data cleaning process, the human capital dataset in excel format (.XLs) was then loaded into Tableau. The raw data of the human capital were converted into valuable information through the data visualization process. Tableau software can represent the data in interactive graphs such as a pie chart, bar chart, bubble chart, map, and scatter plots. By using Tableau, researchers can directly identify the trends and patterns of the human capital and Halal training in the Halal industry. The trends and patterns of the human capital and Halal training will be discussed in the results and discussion section.

3   Results and Discussion

This section describes the result of this study. The trend of the human capital in the Halal industry can be seen by yearly and monthly in Figs. 5 and 6. Figure 5 shows the growth of job offered in the Halal industry based on the Jobstreet website from year

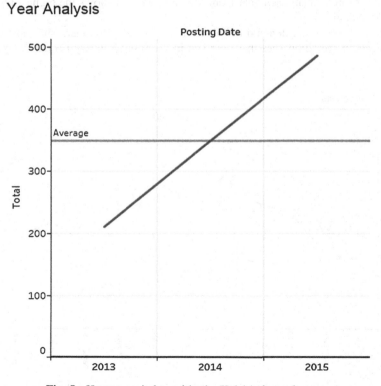

Fig. 5. Human capital trend in the Halal industry by year

2013 to 2015. The graph shows that the jobs offered by the companies have continually increased from one year to another year. For year 2013, there are 211 jobs related to Halal been advertised in the Jobstreet. The number of jobs increases from 211 to 349 for the year 2014. In the year 2015, it shows the increment number of jobs from 349 to 486. This result proves the statement defined by MITI that there will be a huge number of employment chances in the Halal industry. Moreover, it shows that human capital development is needed in order to boost up the economics of the Halal industry. Besides that, the increasing numbers of job also due to the rules that was stated in the Malaysian Standard (MS) regarding the Halal committee. The companies must appoint one or more person to handle the Halal matters in order to get the Halal certificate. Therefore, it is important to cater human capital that has knowledge and expertise in the Halal procedure and guidelines to fulfill the companys' requirements.

The job trends in the Halal industry by monthly were found depicted in Fig. 6. This monthly analysis was based on the 3 years from year 2013 to 2015. The line colors in the graph represent the year. Each year has a different color. Red color is for the year 2015; yellow color is for the year 2014, and followed by blue color is for the year 2013. By looking at this monthly analysis of the human capital dataset, it can be concluded that the jobs that related to Halal offered by the companies are not really consistent from one month to another month in each year. However, the numbers of jobs are keeping on increasing in the year 2015 from February to July compare to the year 2014 and 2013. Moreover, in each year from March to May, it shows the highest job offered by the companies.

Figure 7 shows the demand of job from the industry by year. The most common job offered by the companies that involved in the Halal industry is quality control and

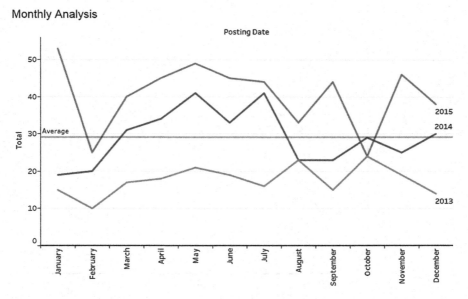

Fig. 6. Human capital trend in the Halal industry by month (Color figure online)

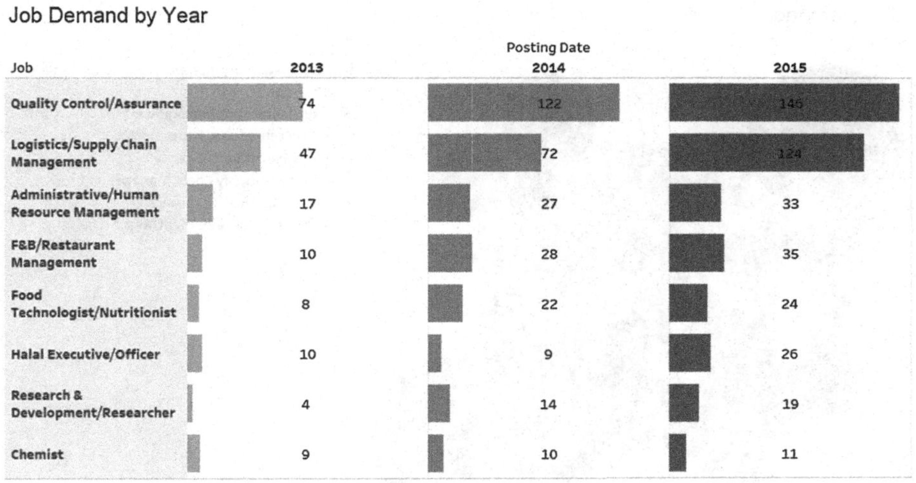

Job Demand by Year

Job	Posting Date 2013	2014	2015
Quality Control/Assurance	74	122	146
Logistics/Supply Chain Management	47	72	124
Administrative/Human Resource Management	17	27	33
F&B/Restaurant Management	10	28	35
Food Technologist/Nutritionist	8	22	24
Halal Executive/Officer	10	9	26
Research & Development/Researcher	4	14	19
Chemist	9	10	11

Fig. 7. Job demand by year

quality assurance. Followed by quality control and quality assurance, there is position for logistics and supply chain management. In this graph, researchers only list the top eight jobs that are commonly offered by the companies involved in the Halal industry. Each position can help companies to comply with the Halal standards and guidelines and also maintain the 'Halalness' of the products and services. By increasing the numbers of job in the Halal industry, it can also fulfill the gap of the growth in the Halal industry economics. Figure 7 graph can helps job seekers to identify the types of job required by the companies.

Figure 8 present the distribution of the jobs located at each states in Malaysia. The circles in the bubble graph represent the location of the jobs. Further, the color of the circles represents the name of the jobs. Based on the graph produce by Tableau, it shows the highest jobs offered in Malaysia are located at Selangor follow by Johor, Kuala Lumpur, Penang, and Melaka. This statement can be verified by looking at the annual statistic of the Halal certified companies produce by HDC [15]. According to the statistic, Selangor and Johor have the highest Halal certified companies. The total Halal certified companies in Selangor are 556 companies and 287 companies in Johor. Therefore, the bubble graph here shows that a lot of jobs offered in Selangor and Johor area are due to the number of Halal certified companies. The more Halal certified companies in one state will required more human capital in order to get Halal certificate and to maintain the integrity of Halal.

Figure 9 describes the Halal training analysis by year. In this graph, researchers take the top five highest Halal training that has been held during the three consecutive years. In the graph, it shows the increment of Halal training from one year to another year. Every year training, focusing on the Hazard Analysis and Critical Control Points (HACCP), Good Manufacturing Practice (GMP), and International Organization for Standardization (ISO) is the most needed for each type of positions involved in this Halal industry. Followed by Malaysian Standard (MS), Halal Certification, Internal

Job Demand

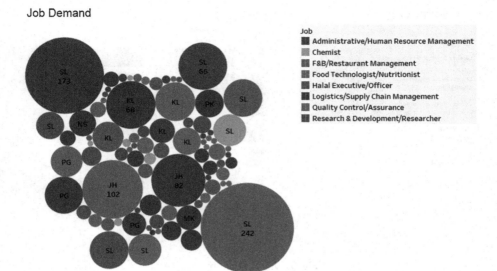

Fig. 8. Job demand by year (Color figure online)

Auditing, and Halal Awareness. This Halal training is needed to fulfill the demand of the company's requirement. The job seekers must attend this Halal training in order for the job seekers to have knowledge and expertise in Halal related matters.

Halal Training

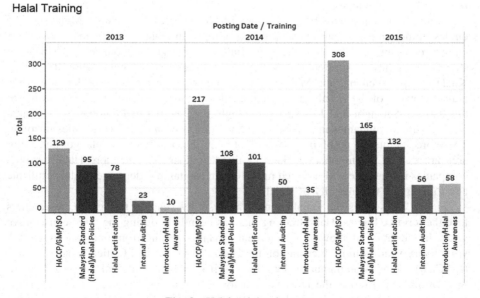

Fig. 9. Halal training by year

Figure 10 describes the analysis of Halal training and human capital in the Halal industry. By using Tableau, it helps training providers and job seekers to know the types of training based on the specific job position. When the cursor is pointed to a particular part of the bar chart, the important information for the user will appear. The information displays for user are job position, types of training, and the amount of job. By looking at this graph, job seekers can identify which types of training they required to get a job that related to Halal matters. Training providers also can identify the most Halal training prefers by the companies, so that the training providers can hold a Halal training based on the companies demand. Therefore, both job seekers and training providers can make a wise decision in a shorter time and efficient way.

Supply and Demand Analysis (Job)

Job	HACCP/GMP/ISO	Malaysian Standard (Halal)/Halal Policies	Halal Certification	Internal Auditing	Introduction/Halal Awareness	Food Safety Awareness	Halal Serving/ Management	Professional Halal Executive	Halal Assurance Management	Halal Logistics	Lab Safety and Chemical Handling	Practical in Microbiology	Halal Analysis (DNA/Alcohol)	Cleaning and Sanitation
Quality Control/Assurance	363	172	155	79	50	34	15	7	12		4	4		1
Logistics/Supply Chain Management	242	134	70	20	49	25	5	2	8	21				1
Halal Executive/Officer	24	44	47	36	2	1	1	35	17					
Food Technologist/Nutritionist	45	25	19	7	9	13	7					1		
Administrative/Human Resource Management	42	13	39	15	10		1		1					
F&B/Restaurant Management	18	17	16		4	8	25		1					
Research & Development/Researcher	31	10	18	3	13	1	1	1	1		2	2		
Chemist	27	20	3		9	1			1		10		3	

Fig. 10. Halal training and human capital analysis

4   Conclusions

This study demonstrates the trends of human capital and Halal training in the Halal industry. Data visualization principles have been applied throughout this study to identify the trends and patterns of the human capital dataset. Data visualization helps users to interpret data into a knowledgeable data in a faster way, easier way, and interactive way. The visualization tool used in this study is Tableau. Tableau can produce a variety of graphs by applying drag and drop concept. Users can differentiate the value of each attributes inside the graph by the color or shape chosen.

The data analysis produced in this study will be useful for the job seekers and Halal training providers. Job seekers can identify beforehand the types of Halal training needed before they applied the job. Job seekers also can prepare themselves by attending the specific Halal training based on the company's requirements. This visualization also helps Halal training providers to identify the most needed Halal training based on the company perspective. The Halal training providers can make a decision on what types of Halal training they should offer to the customers. Therefore, data visualization can help users to make a wiser decision in an efficient way.

In the future, researchers will identify the best prediction models for this human capital dataset by using RapidMiner software. The prediction models included will be Naïve Bayes, k-Nearest Neighbors (k-NN), Decision Tree, and Neural Network. The best prediction models will be determined by looking at the accuracy, precision, and recall in each models. The whole process will follow the data mining concept.

Acknowledgements. Our thanks to the Jobstreet team (Dr. Sandra Hanchard, Mr. Fabian Chan, and Nuhaa Bakry) for their kindness and support by helping us to get the human capital dataset in the halal industry.

References

1. Rosling, H.: Visual technology unveils the beauty of statistics and swaps policy from dissemination to access. Stat. J. IAOS: J. Int. Assoc. Off. Stat. **24**(1), 103–104 (2007)
2. Heer, J., Shneiderman, B.: Interactive dynamics for visual analysis. Queue **10**(2), 30 (2012)
3. Kale, P., Balan, S.: Big data application in job trend analysis. In: 2016 IEEE International Conference on Big Data, USA, pp. 4001–4003. IEEE Press, (2016)
4. Yunus, N.S.N.M., Rashid, W.E.W., Ariffin, N.M., Rashid, N.M.: Muslim's purchase intention towards non-muslim's halal packaged food manufacturer. Procedia Soc. Behav. Sci. **130**, 145–154 (2014)
5. Ministry of International Trade and Industry. http://www.slideshare.net/Adrienna/status-of-the-halal-industry-2016
6. Standards Malaysia: Halal Food - Production, Preparation, Handling, and Storage: General Guidelines (Second Revision) (2009)
7. Becker, G.S.: Human Capital Revisited in Human Capital: A Theoretical and Empirical Analysis with Special Reference to Education, 3rd edn, pp. 15–28. The University of Chicago Press, Chicago (1994)
8. Halal Industry Development Corporation. http://www.lscm.hk/sites/summit2016/files/file/Presentation/08%20%20Jamie%20Haniff%20RAMLEE_Halal%20Malaysia%20-%20Hong%20Kong%20(23%20Sep).pdf
9. Hashim, H.I.C., Shariff, S.M., Mohamad, S.: Halal supply chain trainings in Malaysia: a review paper. **28**(2), 1775–1779 (2016)
10. Khan, M.: Transformasi Industri Halal. Dewan Ekonomi, pp. 3–5 (2011)
11. Karmel, T., Cully, M.: The demand for training: paper presented at the national centre for vocational education research (NCVER), Adelaide: National Centre for Vocational Education Research (2009)
12. Nair, L.R., Shetty, S.D., Shetty, S.D.: Interactive visual analytics on Big Data: Tableau vs D3. js. J. e-Learn. Knowl. Soc. **12**(4), 139–450 (2016)
13. Few, S.: Now You See it: Simple Visualization Techniques for Quantitative Analysis. Analyticals Press, Berkeley (2009)
14. O'Hare, D., Stenhouse, N.: Redesigning a graphic weather display for pilots. Ergon. Des. **16**(4), 11–15 (2008)
15. Halal Industry Development Corporation. http://www.hdcglobal.com/publisher/gwm_industry_statistics

Application of Simulation Model of Traffic Operations on Single Carriageway Roads

Zamri Bujang[1(✉)] and Othman Che Puan[2]

[1] Department of Civil Engineering, Faculty of Engineering,
Universiti Malaysia Sarawak, Kota Samarahan, Sarawak, Malaysia
bzamri@unimas.my
[2] Department of Geotechnics and Transportation, Faculty of Civil Engineering,
Universiti Teknologi Malaysia, Johor Bahru, Johor, Malaysia

Abstract. The application of the simulation model in examining a road section's potential capacity. The varying degree to overtake provision and diverse traffic features on capacity and speed/flow relationships effects were evaluated. The application of the model was to evaluate the potential effects of different number of junctions and different turning volumes level of on the traffic operation effectiveness. Generally, the model applied shows the need for more experiential studies as the simulation outcomes proposed that higher capacity is achievable.

Keywords: Simulation model · Capacity · Traffic operations · Speed/flow · Traffic characteristics · Journey speed

1 Introduction

The development of this simulation was carried out in this study aspect of traffic operations of single carriageway road at or near the road's capacity. The speed/flow/geometry relationships played a significant role in the single carriageway roads assessment procedures which are founded on an important operation survey for uncongested situations. The capacity formulae took into consideration how the width of the carriageway and HGV contents are affected and how it seemed to be founded on certain congested flow observations.

HCM 2010 [1] believed that several factors influence capacity such as road layout, carriageway's width, and traffic configuration. In U.K, the carriageway's width and the HGVs percentage determined a single carriageway road's capacity (DTp [2]). Taking into consideration the variances between the above two capacity assessment approaches, the application of the model is to evaluate the road layout's potential effects, directional split, and HGV capacity content.

In an overtaking section, the expectation is that the opposing lane flow will lessen overtaking chances. Therefore, it would affect the chances to travel at preferred speeds. Nevertheless, this effect was deemed as insignificant in single carriageway roads' COBA speed/flow/geometry relationships (Lee and Brocklebank [3]). Journey speed and its link to the opposing flow will be scrutinised. U.K. single carriageway roads' speed/flow/geometry relationships (Lee and Brocklebank [3]) included the how

© Springer Nature Singapore Pte Ltd. 2017
M.S. Mohamed Ali et al. (Eds.): AsiaSim 2017, Part II, CCIS 752, pp. 605–619, 2017.
DOI: 10.1007/978-981-10-6502-6_52

junctions affect speed. The relationships, on the other hand, were not included on how turning flow clearly affects individual junctions. Instinctively, it is expected that the through vehicles delays at a single-approach junction rises with the number of turning movements. The application of this model studies this aspect. The developed model adequately represents the behaviour of traffic on single carriageway roads, with and without considering turning movements at priority T-junctions. Therefore, the results of the simulation model can be used with confidence to draw conclusions corresponding to the objectives of the analysis [4].

1.1   Simulated Systems Overview

In the process of simulation, different sets of road layout and traffic conditions were taken into consideration. The each road section's length (namely the evaluation section) was 4 km and the carriageway and verge's width were 7.3 m and 3 m. The description of the conditions are below.

(a) Capacity evaluation simulated system
     To assess capacity, three road layouts of diverse hilliness and bendiness were made. The choice of these layouts' was meant to cover the potential road geometry that may affect traffic operations in various ways. Each of these road layouts specifications together with the traffic parameters utilized in the simulation model are shown in Table 1. All road sections were presumed (i.e. no access was permitted inside the simulated section). Figure 1(a) and (b) displays two of the road layouts utilized in the model.

Table 1. Road and traffic characteristics used in the model for capacity evaluation

Layout no.	Road characteristics	Overtaking provision (%)	Traffic directional split	HGV content (%)	Motorcycle content (%)
1	Flat and straight: Hilliness = 0 m/km Bendiness = 0 deg/km Visibility = 550 m	100 100 0	50/50 100/0 50/50	15 15 15	5, 15, 30
2	Flat and moderately bendy: Hilliness = 0 m/km Bendiness = 90.6 deg/km Visibility = 440 m	54	50/50	15	5
3	Hilly and straight: Hilliness = 30.4 m/km Bendiness = 0 deg/km Visibility = 380 m	50	50/50	5 15 15 20 30	5

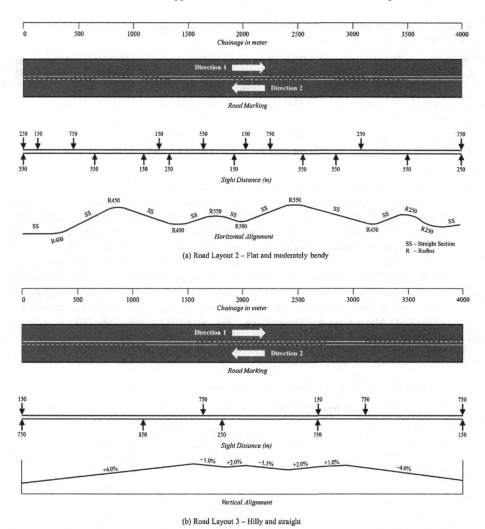

Fig. 1. Geometry layouts for two of the sections used in the model

(b) Simulated system to evaluate opposing flow effects on journey speed
The usage of a flat and straight road section was used to evaluate the directional split or opposing flows potential effects on vehicle speeds, a flat and straight road section (i.e. Layout no. 1 in Table 1). In the process of simplifying simulation results' interpretation, road layouts with diverse gradients and horizontal curves, and road features for example junctions were not taken into consideration. Table 2 lists the conditions of road and traffic that was utilized in the model.

Table 2. The usage of road and traffic characteristics in the model to investigate opposing flow effect on speed

Road characteristics	Overtaking provision (%)	Flow in the assessed direction (veh/h)	Opposing flow (veh/h)	HGV content (%)	Motorcycle content (%)
Flat and straight (i.e. Layout 1 from Table 1)	100	400	0–1200	15	5
		600	0–1200	15	5
		800	0–1200	15	5
		1000	0–1200	15	5

(c) Simulated system to investigate junctions' effect on speed
   To investigate junctions' effect on speed, a 4 km length of flat and straight road section (i.e. Layout no. 1 in Table 1) was presumed in containing numerous priority T-junctions. Three levels of traffic flow, four levels of turning flow and three levels of number of junctions were taken into consideration. The Table 3 showed the combinations of traffic operations' range that are being focused on. Traffic with low volumes would produce few stops and minimum delay in traffic. On the other hand, traffic with high volumes would give rise to congested flows and considerable delays for the reason that the section's capacity would be exceeded. All turning movements were permitted at all junctions. The junctions' layouts are shown in Fig. 2.

Table 3. Conditions simulated for investigating the effect of junction on speed

Major road flow (veh/h/dir)	Junctions		Percentage turning flow			
	No/km	Total	0%	5%	10%	15%
400	0.5	2	x	x	x	x
	0.75	3	x	x	x	x
	1	4	x	x	x	x
600	0.5	2	x	x	x	x
	0.75	3	x	x	x	x
	1	4	x	x	x	x
800	0.5	2	x	x	x	x
	0.75	3	x	x	x	x
	1	4	x	x	x	x

The junctions were similarly spaced along the evaluated road section's alternate sides. Instinctively, the junctions considered were located within the road section which could affect the whole traffic operations' efficacy. A sample of the junctions' arrangement along the assessment section is shown in Fig. 3.

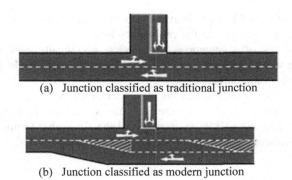

(a) Junction classified as traditional junction

(b) Junction classified as modern junction

Fig. 2. Types of junctions considered in the model

Fig. 3. Example of the arrangement of 2 junctions along the evaluation section

1.2 Simulation Constraints and Assumptions

6 km length of a road that contained the evaluation section's 4 km length of covered area was used in the whole simulation rounds. The road was separated into 3 sections, warm up (1 km), evaluation (4 km), and cool-off (1 km). Figure 4 expresses the organisation used by the simulated road system in the simulation rounds. Both the warm up and cool-off sections were believed to be flat and straight. The evaluation section characteristics are based on road layouts given in Tables 1, 2 and 3

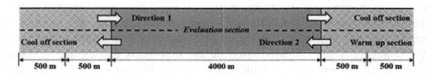

Fig. 4. Arrangement of the simulated road system used in the model

The traffic parameters' capacities are made when a vehicle enters, moves, and leaves the assessment section. The expectations given below were made concerning traffic flow, vehicles, and drivers' characteristics.

- The distribution of vehicle headways at all entry points into the system were based on a shifted negative exponential probability function.
- Traffic constitutes of 3 categories of vehicles, specifically cars, motorcycle and HGVs. There were 3 categories of cars, 1 category of motorcycle and 4 categories of HGVs in the traffic streams.
- The drivers' basic desired speed are dependent on road geometry. The cars and HGVs mean values calculation were from the speed/flow/geometry relationships (Lee and Brocklebank [3]) by comprising all the applicable terms.
- The speed limit does not constrain the desired speed.

1.3   Simulation Processes

The following subsections give the description for simulation processes adopted to run the model for the analysis' diverse objectives

- Capacity assessment
  When evaluating the designated road and traffic conditions possible capacity, the input flows were amplified slowly and the real traffic flows in the system (specifically inside the evaluation section) and the consistent average speeds were tested at an intermission of 15 min simulated time. The procedure was sustained until both directions reached maximum flows. Throughout the authentication procedure and the model, trial runs, one direction reached the maximum flow when the input flow was in the range of 1600 to 1800 veh/h/dir. Each of the designated road and traffic conditions had to go through four runs.
- Opposing flow effect on journey speed
  In evaluating the opposing flow effect on journey speed, each flow in the evaluated direction (as given in Table 2), and the opposing flow was different from 0 veh/h to 1200 veh/h with 200 veh/h increase. For each flows' combination, the model was simulated for 1 h without the warm up period. The average journey speed was attained based on averaging 10 runs simulation results.
- Junctions effect on journey speed
  To simulate traffic, a sequence of runs was operated on the selected section while changing the traffic flow, turning percentages, and the junctions involved. In the process of interpreting simulation output, all simulation runs involved only cars. The average speed utilized in the conforming section defining this aspect denotes solely the cars' average journey speed. All simulation runs had the assumption of 50/50directional split. This is based on the hypothesis that the delay maximum possible effects will happen with a 50/50 split (McCoy et al. [5]; Ballard and McCoy [6, 7]).

2 Result and Discussion

2.1 Capacity Evaluation

A road section's capacity is usually an inference from speed/flow/density relationships. The relationships seen classically as parabolic, however, due to the difficulty in obtaining the form from the site data, numerous potential shapes have been examined and recommended by many researchers (Lane [8]; Wright an Hyde [9]; Duncan [10–12]; Lee and Brocklebank [3]). Duncan [11] speculation for instance was that being parabolic or in shapes with curved shaped' (as utilized in describing speed/flow relationship) is founded on insufficient knowledge of the basic statistical effects. Nevertheless, the linear speed/flow relationship for example those suggested by Duncan [12] and Lee and Brocklebank [3] indicated no flow rate at road capacity. Therefore, the selected flow where the designated road section capacity is attained may be different in accordance with how different researchers interpret them. The relationships' application was Lee and Brocklebank [3] derivation in the COBA software (DTp [2]).The Department of the Environment, Transport and the Regions (DETR) [13], yet stipulates single carriageway trunk and principal roads constant capacities in the modelling traffic forecasts procedure for Great Britain. These roads' capacity setting was 1300 veh/h/dir. The vehicles' average speed at the capacity was selected at 57 km/h. The values where the basis is unclear and inconsistent COBA's suggestion might differ based on to the road's width and traffic composition. Fascinatingly, the capacity's speed set by DETR is near to the capacity's average speed of 35 mile/h, set by HCM TRB, [14] for single carriageway roads with mountainous terrain layouts.

There is a possibility in using a simulation model representing the flow rates just beyond the estimated capacity and therefore the speed/flow relationship imaginable pattern if several kilometers of a length road section is taken into consideration. This simulation model, for example, used a 4 km road section together with 1 km warm up and 1 km cool-off sections and it was enough to allow flow breakdown being characterized over a period of time.

With discussion in focus, the flat and straight road section with an uninterrupted provision to overtake simulation outcomes and a 50/50 directional split were utilized. HGV percentage was 15% and Fig. 5 showed the speed/flow relationships scatter plot for the designated road and traffic conditions. Generally, the plot is an indicator of a curved speed/flow relationship. The expectation from the relationship's traditional interpretations (HRM TRB [14]), the Figure reveals a decrease in speed as the flow is increased until a region is reached where the flow stops cumulating. Figure 5 also showed the speed/flow curves for identical road and traffic conditions that were plotted using the methods recommended by HCM 1994 and HCM 2010.

For precise speed/flow relationship and capacity assessment that uses the HCM method, the road section speed's design was presumed ≥ 60 mile/h (i.e. ≥ 96.5 km/h) for the reason that the desired speed for cars calculated is greater than 90 km/h. The speed/flow curve was attained when expected capacity was calculated for the designated road and traffic conditions. Hence, for the designated road and traffic conditions, the HCM 1994 speed/flow curve is openly equivalent to the simulation outcomes. The HCM 1994 speed/flow curve breaks at a flow 1072 veh/h/dir where the travel

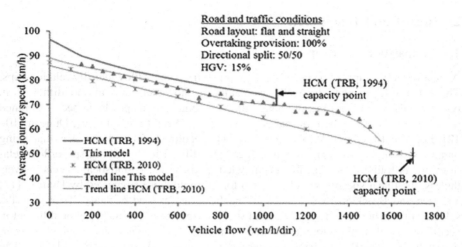

Fig. 5. Speed/flow relationships based on simulation results and Highway Capacity Manual

speed is approximately 72.4 km/h. For the designated road and traffic conditions, the simulation results propose a maximum flow of 1580 veh/h for single direction. The simulation outcomes also established that traffic operating at acceptable journey speeds for flows in the range of 900 to 1300 veh/h/dir. It can be concluded from the simulated speed/flow curve trend that a road section maximum flow is also affected by drivers' car following behaviour.

The current version of HCM 2010 appear to suggest that a single carriageway based on a modern design standard is expected to be able to accommodate a capacity of 1700 veh/h/direction, which is much higher than the value derived from HCM 1994. For the particular road segment used in the analysis, the HCM 2010 estimated that the capacity would be reached when the average journey speed dropped around 50 km/h. In general, HCM 2010 gives estimates of the average journey speed for each traffic volume, lower than the estimates value by HCM 1994.

2.2 Road Layout Effects on Capacity

The speed and flow data's two road layouts simulation results are a flat with moderate bends, hilly and straight roads, are shown in Fig. 6 and its reveals the description for road layouts speed/flow relationships for a flat and straight road in the earlier section. The simulation outcomes showed that the chosen road layouts have the capability to carry an identical maximum flow, specifically ranging between 1550 and 1580 veh/h/dir with 15% HGVs. This shows that the road section capacity is founded on the description accepted in this study, is not significantly influenced by the road layouts.

In similar traffic situations, the average journey speed's variations for three diverse road layouts congested flow conditions are significantly minor. This is in support of the recommendation that the region's flow is individualised by the drivers' car following behaviour. Generally the expectation is that road layout is being influenced by journey

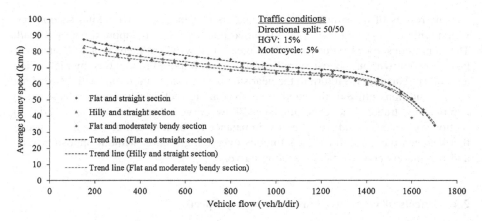

Fig. 6. Simulation results for speed/flow relationships for different road layouts

speed. The flat and straight road's average speed is higher than the other two layouts. The hilly and straight road's average speed is somewhat higher than flat road with moderate bend. This is due to the simulation where it only affects an uphill grade specific type of HGVs, while it affects all vehicles in a curve section.

2.3   Effects of Overtaking Provision on Capacity

In demonstrating overtaking provision and opposing flow potential influence on capacity, for the flat and straight road section simulation results with diverse overtaking provision and opposing flow in Fig. 7. Based on the study's capacity definition, the demonstration of simulation results reveals that flat and straight road with incessant overtaking section without opposing traffic has the capability to carry a maximum flow of approximately 1650 veh/h/dir. In a situation where flow has balance in both directions, or in a non-overtaking section, the maximum flow is 1580 veh/h/dir.

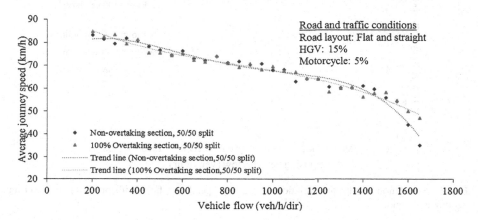

Fig. 7. Simulation results for speed/flow relationships for different road layouts

The results of the simulation are indicators that incessant overtaking section provision without opposing traffic has increased journey speed by approximately 8 km/h. The continuous speed reduction with increased flow where there is a constant overtaking section without opposing traffic results from imposed limitations, by higher flow and linked density, on a return to the near side lane. In simulation runs and the road and traffic conditions utilized, the continuous overtaking section advantage is lessened by approaching traffic. The condition speed/flow curve where there is an overtaking section continuously and with the flow in balance for both directions lies, it is expected that between the curve for the continuous overtaking section without opposing traffic and continuous non-overtaking section curve.

2.4   Effects of Opposing Flow on Journey Speed

To show the opposing flow potential effect on speed, the flat and straight road with an overtaking section and an assortment of opposing flow's simulation outcomes were shown in Fig. 8. The simulation results showed that speed was reduced with the increase of the opposing flow. The decrease in speed continues till it reaches a situation where the opposing flow is in a congested condition.

Instinctively, the expectation is that the chance to overtake is associated to the opposing flow. Overtaking sections gives the driver's the chance to travel at the desired speed as overtaking is allowed to happen at the roadway's specific sections. In reality, overtaking opportunities would be minimal when traffic volume or the opposing flow is considerably high. In a non-overtaking section, there is no expectation that the vehicle speed is significantly influenced by the level travelling vehicles flow in the opposing direction.

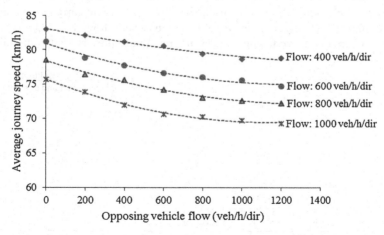

Fig. 8. Simulation results for variation of journey speed and flow with opposing flow on an overtaking section

As mentioned earlier that single carriageway speed/flow relationships saw the insignificance of the opposing flow. The results from the simulation showed that this may be the issue when there is a balance in the flow of both directions.

2.5 Effect of Motorcycle on Journey Speed

From the car following behaviour characteristic, motorcycle is considered and assumed as the simulation model that have the same behaviour to cars and the percentage of motorcycle at single carriageway roads are considered small in numbers. But still the model takes into consideration motorcycle based on its category and how it performs. This consideration allows the examination of motorcycle effect on the entire traffic operations. To demonstrate the possible effect of motorcycle's percentage on speed, the simulation results for the flat and straight road with a continuous overtaking section and at a non-overtaking section were plotted in Figs. 9 and 10. The outcomes of the simulation showed that the speed decreases as the motorcycle percentage increases. The simulation results also indicate that the presence of motorcycle appeared to have no or little effect on the journey speed as shown in Figs. 9 and 10.

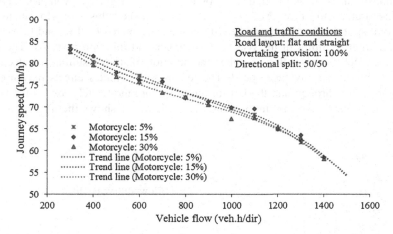

Fig. 9. Simulation results for speed/flow relationships for different percentages of motorcycle at overtaking section

2.6 Potential Effects of Priority T-Junctions on Journey Speed

The journey speeds simulated average through cars over the road section's 4 km long were attained for each set of conditions shown in Table 3. Figure 11 displays the journey speed's disparity, main road flow, and turning flow percentage with numerous traditional junctions per kilometer road. In terms of clarity, the major road flows outcomes are equivalent to 600 veh/h/dir were removed from the Figure. The results' trend for the main flow 600 veh/h/dir is identical to the results' trends for main road flows equivalent to 400 and 800 veh/h/dir.

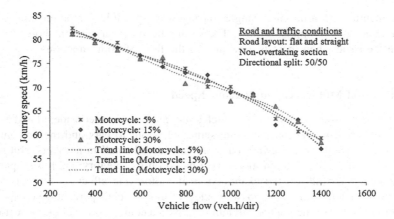

Fig. 10. Simulation results for speed/flow relationships for different percentages of motorcycle at non-overtaking section

Instinctively, a simple junction with no special right-turning lane made available on the main, the number and period of stops made by the right-turn vehicles relying on opposing traffic's the flow. McCoy et al. [5] established this scenario where 50/50 directional split that is considered heavily in this case increases flow and turns flow at every junction resulting in the rise in the number and duration of stops. The effects being combined increases flow, number and duration of stops resulting in a decrease in the through vehicles' average speed. The left turning vehicles effects may not be as significant if the through and the left turning flows are moderately low as the left turn vehicles movement does not involve stopping. Figure 11 shows the next facts:

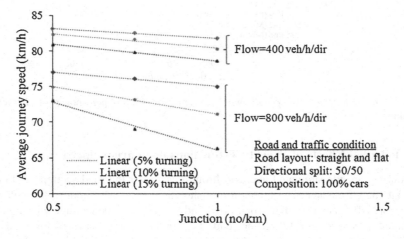

Fig. 11. Simulation results for variation of journey speed, major road flow, and percentage turning flow with the number of traditional junctions

- There is no or little effect by a junction on an average journey speed if there is no turning movement at the respective junction
- Every main road flow and turning flow percentage which is greater than 0%, the average journey speed falls with the rise of the number of traditional junction
- The average journey speed lessens with the increase in turning flow percentage at each junction per kilometer and every main road flow
- The average journey speed reduces with the major road flows

The speed, major road flow, and percentage turning flow differences with numerous modern junctions are revealed in Fig. 12. Moreover, for clarity purposes, the major road flow plots equivalents to 600 veh/h/dir are removed from the Figure. Lee and Brocklebank [3] recommended designed links' junctions, which possibly include recurrent ghost islands' provision for right turns and tapered entrances, having minimum influence on speed. The simulation outcomes for cases where special turning lanes were offered on all junctions seem to be supportive of this recommendation. Regarding traditional junctions, the journey speed does not show that is was affected by existing junctions if there are no turning movements at the specific junctions.

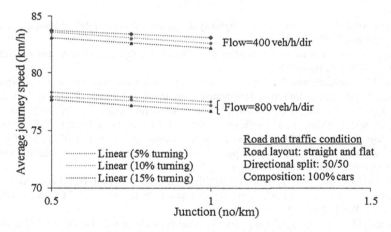

Fig. 12. Simulation results for variation of journey speed, major road flow, and percentage turning flow with the number of modern junctions

The indicator by the simulation results for a constant turning flow, there is no variation affecting major road flow. As predicted, the reduced speed rises slowly as with the increase of the turning flow for each major road flow. Instinctively, the reduced rate is dependent on the turning lane's length that play the role in determining the number of vehicles the lane can accommodate before the passage of through traffic is obstructed.

3   Conclusion

The simulation results similarly high point the possible usage of the model to evaluate the possible advantages in changing the traditional junctions into the modern type. More inclusive simulation runs that cover all potential road and traffic conditions aspects are needed. This was not taken into consideration in these applications attributable to time restriction. Nevertheless, for each considered road and traffic conditions, the results were based on several of the model's runs. For road and traffic conditions, the combination of all simulation runs delivered reliable output parameters/values. Consequently, the values averages of the applicable traffic parameters were attained with confidence.

Acknowledgments. The authors would like to thank Universiti Malaysia Sarawak (UNIMAS) and Universiti Teknologi Malaysia (UTM) for providing facilities and support for the accomplishment of this study.

References

1. Transportation Research Board: Highway Capacity Manual. TRB, National Academies, Washington, D.C. (2010)
2. Department of Transport: Design Manual for Roads and Bridges. Departmental Standard TD 9/93, HMSO, London (1996)
3. Lee, B.H., Brocklebank, P.J.: Speed/flow/geometry relationships for rural single carriageway roads. TRRL Contractor report 319, Transport Research Laboratory, Crowthorne, UK (1993)
4. Bujang, Z., Che Puan, O.: Simulation model of traffic operations on single carriageway roads: model calibration and validation. ARPN J. Eng. Appl. Sci. **12**(4), 945–950 (2017)
5. McCoy, P.T., Ballard, J.L., Wijaya, Y.H.: Operational Effects of Two-Way Left-Turn Lanes on Two-Way Two-Lane Streets, pp. 79–84. Transportation Research Record 869, TRB, National Research Council, Washington, D.C. (1982)
6. Ballard, J.L., McCoy, P.T.: Operational Effects of Two-Way Left-Turn Lanes on Two-Way, Four-Lane Streets, pp. 54–57. Transportation Research Record 869, TRB, National Research Council, Washington, D.C. (1983)
7. Ballard, J.L., McCoy, P.T.: Computer Simulation Study of the Operational Effects of Two-Way Left-Turn Lanes on Urban Four-Lane Roadways, pp. 54–57. Transportation Research Record 869, TRB, National Research Council, Washington, D.C. (1988)
8. Lane, R.: Introduction to traffic engineering – 4. Road Capacit. Traffic Eng. Control **9**(9), 440–443 (1968)
9. Wright, C.C., Hyde, T.: The measurement and interpretation of speed-flow relationships. Traffic Eng. Control **13**(11/12), 507–525 (1972)
10. Duncan, N.C.: Rural speed/flow relations. TRRL Laboratory Report 651, Transport and Road Research Laboratory, Crowthorne, UK (1974)
11. Duncan, N.C.: A note on speed/flow/concentration relations. Traffic Eng. Control **17**(1), 34–35 (1976)
12. Duncan, N.C.: A further look at speed/flow/concentration. Traffic Eng. Control **20**(10), 482–483 (1979)

13. Department of the Environment, Transport and the Regions: National road traffic forecasts (Great Britain) 1997: Working Paper No. 4, London (1997)
14. Transportation Research Board: Highway Capacity Manual, Special Report 209, 3rd edn. TRB, National Research Council, Washington, D.C. (1994)

Simulation Model of Traffic Operations on Single Carriageway Roads: The Development Process

Zamri Bujang[1(✉)] and Othman Che Puan[2]

[1] Department of Civil Engineering, Faculty of Engineering,
Universiti Malaysia Sarawak, Kota Samarahan, Sarawak, Malaysia
bzamri@unimas.my
[2] Department of Geotechnics and Transportation, Faculty of Civil Engineering,
Universiti Teknologi Malaysia, Johor Bahru, Johor, Malaysia

Abstract. The needs to develop the traffic simulation model for evaluating the effects of various road layout and road traffic characteristics on traffic operations are required as traffic simulation models are becoming an attractive option in evaluating traffic matters. The present traffic operations simulation models on single carriageway roads similarly suffering from a comparable fault. Consequently, it is necessary for a complete traffic simulation model to be developed to accomplish this task. It is crucial for re-development of the procedure to be incorporated with the Malaysian traffic conditions and characteristics for precise valuation and investigation. Such a model must have the capability to simulate traffic behavior for a variety of geometry and road layout, evaluate the effect of turning vehicles at unsignalised intersections and compositions of traffic which also include motorcycles on single carriageway roads.

Keywords: Simulation model · Model development · Traffic characteristic · Traffic behaviour · Traffic operation · Speed

1 Introduction

The trend in Malaysia shows that the increment number of vehicles on the road every year (Highway Planning Division, Ministry of Works Malaysia, [1]). This scenario will have a significant effect on the capacity of the road and the level of service especially the single carriageway roads. In order to be able to evaluate the traffic operations at single carriageway roads, a model that is capable to examine the effects of road layout and traffic characteristics should be developed. Traffic simulation modeling is becoming more attractive and effective tools in studying traffic issues. This enables traffic engineers and transportation planners to investigate the effect of changes in the network geometry, capacity analysis and traffic control strategies on traffic performance. The development of this simulation was carried out in this study aspect of traffic operations of single carriageway road at or near the road's capacity.

The initial part of the development process of simulation model in the modeling phases is indicated in Fig. 1. This modeling stage is important as it will give an insight

© Springer Nature Singapore Pte Ltd. 2017
M.S. Mohamed Ali et al. (Eds.): AsiaSim 2017, Part II, CCIS 752, pp. 620–632, 2017.
DOI: 10.1007/978-981-10-6502-6_53

understanding of the whole development process of the simulation model. The main components as shown in Fig. 2 will help to elucidate the overview of this simulation.

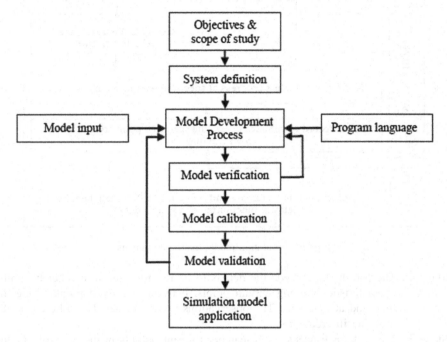

Fig. 1. The model's development process framework

This simulation model is separated into five main stages and described as follows:

Stage 1: This stage needs the road input data to be read by the researcher and junction's geometry; traffic characteristics; vehicle characteristics and junction turning movements.

Stage 2: The second stage needs the researcher to generate traffic streams from all travel directions with arbitrary arrival times, plain desired speeds, directional movements and all vehicle characteristics chosen from itemized probability distribution.

Stage 3: The third stage needs the researcher to simulate the traffic progress along the road and at the individual junctions where the individual vehicle progress at a constant time interval is studied. The procedure shows suitable speed changes, acceleration or deceleration, and the manoeuvre current type for example car following, overtaking, lane changing, turning and queuing. The decision rules for catching up, car following, close following, overtaking, lane changing, turning and other manoeuvres are decided from vehicle features, road geometry and junction layout.

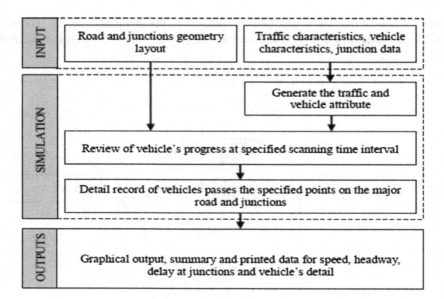

Fig. 2. Simulation model main components

Stage 4: The fourth stage needs the details to be recorded the researcher by traffic characteristics passing certain points, between identified points along the road and at junctions. The observations types and details are based on the user specific requirement.

Stage 5: The last stage needs the researcher to print outputs in the form of graphic display, output file comprising observations summary and numerous traffic parameters statistical tabulations itemized by the user.

2   Development Process

To have a clear understanding of the model's development process, the concept was centered on a states and events framework. The 'state' signifies whichever driving situations type or types of manoeuvres a driver tried or assumed at a specific instant of time while the 'event' signifying a state altered or speed modified or accelerated.

Table 1 shows each states used in determining a vehicle status at any given time. In considering traffic movements at junctions, a turning vehicle is not associated with any of the states as manifested in State Model 1 through 7. This is because a turning vehicle needs to reduce its speed in order to negotiate the turning radius when it approaches a junction into which it will turn. As shown in Table 1, the additional state, i.e., state 8, is used in an attempt to differentiate between the turning vehicles from the through vehicles at a specified junction. Apart from that, these states are also meant for vehicles approaching the stop line from the minor road. In the simulation, the turning vehicles that are travelling under these states are processed by different sets of program logic which describes the junction model.

Table 1. Categories of state engaged in the simulation model

State model	State category	Explanation
1	Freemoving	Vehicle moves easily on the major road
2	Normal following	Vehicle follows an obstructing vehicle with no intent to overtake
3	Close following	Vehicle follows narrowly an obstructing vehicle with intent to overtake
4	Performance limited	Vehicle speed is inhibited by its performance capability
5	Overtaking abortion	Vehicle is aborting an overtaking or lane changing manoeuvre
6	Overtaking	Vehicle is overtaking another vehicle on an overtaking section
7	Lane changing	Vehicle is overtaking another vehicle on an auxiliary section
8	Turning manoeuvre	Vehicle is making a turning manoeuvre to or from the junctions

2.1 Program Language

Microsoft Visual Studio and FORTRAN programming language are chosen and used in carrying out the study when writing the simulation model. This because it is evidently powerful and best suited for scientific and engineering applications Additionally, as the model depends on upon the NAGWARE library routines for random numbers and statistical distributions, the linkage between the Microsoft Visual Studio, FORTRAN and the library is made to put up the library usage.

2.2 Scanning Time Procedure

Another approach selected for this simulation model is the utilization of a scanning time procedure where all events in the study are updated at 0.5 s time interval. It is believed that the process is suitable for the time interval size utilized earlier by various researchers for example, Yousif [2], Miyahara [3], Chik [4] and Parker [5]; to provide a sensible accuracy of a microscopic model.

2.3 Model Input

The input data file includes information concerning traffic, vehicle and road characteristics that need to be simulated and also information concerning traffic measurements that is required for the output file. The input data file obtained can be created using XML text editor. There are two types of input data generally required in a traffic simulation model as follows; (a) the physical characteristics of the system and, (b) the characteristics of the traffic. It is further explained in Table 2 where it summarises some of the common information used as an input to most simulation of single carriageway roads.

Table 2. Usage of common input data in most traffic models summary

Type of data	Information required
Physical characteristics: Single carriageway roads	• Length of the simulation section, widths and number of lanes, and changes in geometry such as horizontal and vertical alignments, road marking and sight distance • Number of approaches and traffic control type • Location
Traffic characteristics: Driver's data Vehicular data	• Desired speeds and critical merging gaps • Vehicle types and associated parameters such as performance and size • Directional flow and headway distribution • Traffic composition and turning proportion at individual junctions

2.4 Model Output

On the other hand, for the model output, there are two different forms of output generated from this model; the graphical output and the traffic performance analysis. When the model is run to analyze traffic performance, the characteristic output for traffic volumes identified levels will be made of information showing several traffic variables measurements as follows:

- alongside profiles for spot speed points in addition to at respective major road exit points,
- journey speed and journey time,
- individual junctions traffic delay,
- major road headway exit point,
- major road overtaking data between points,
- end of the road section composition of desired speed, total flows.

3 Organization of the Simulated Road System

As shown in Fig. 3, this section illustrated the different segments of simulated road length. With the aim of doing so, the model road segment are made of three main segments for each major traffic direction, i.e., a warm-up segment, analyzed segment and a cool-off segment and these preparations could be seen clearly in Fig. 3 below.

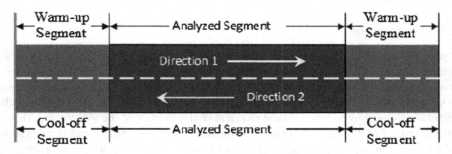

Fig. 3. Different segments of simulated road length in the model

3.1   Warm-Up Segment and Warm-Up Period

Another part of the simulated road system; a period where the model is permitted to run earlier before simulated traffic properties measurements are taken is known as a warm-up period. Related to warm-up segment is the adoption of the warm-up period. Nevertheless, a bias result may happen if the arbitrary time in which simulation starts, with no indication the situation is being simulated. Consequently, with the intention of eluding bias result, it is mentioned to comprise the similar characteristics warm-up segment previous to the analyzed segment and run on the model until some equilibrium condition is reached. The time taken for the equilibrium to be reached is called as the warm-up period. In this model, with the intention of achieving both warm-up segment and warm-up period appropriate length, the performance variation measured with distance; observation from the vehicle entry point into the system with the simulation time is a must.

3.2   Analyzed Segment

In this section, it entails the analyzed segment that depicts the part of the road where the traffic behavior will be analyzed. The part of the road that needs to be analyzed consists of several segments as defined according to their characteristics. However, the length of the analyzed segment may be varied from 1 km to 10 km and if required, priority T-junctions are included within this segment.

3.3   Cool-Off Segment

In addition to the above, a segment adjoining the simulated section at the end of the major road is called the cool-off segment where it simulates the vehicles that have exited the analyzed segment. The cool-off segment is considered straight and level. In cool-off segment as part of the study, a removal of vehicle is from the system exiting this segment. Although the vehicle is removed, the cool-off segment length used in the model is measured satisfactory to ensure the vehicles behavior in the analyzed segment as this removal process does not affect anything.

4   Road and Traffic Characteristics

In this part of the simulation model, the major aspects of the road and traffic characteristics will be highlighted and discussed. As seen in Fig. 4, it shows an example of the road system arrangement that includes junctions. If these junctions are excluded in the analysis, such a layout could be simplified to make a stretch of major road. The figure comprised the vehicle's entry/exit point sequences, the lines origin and destination. Information concerning the position in the simulation and each junction orientation is centered on the route of traffic as of point of entry indicated with 0 to the point indicated with 1. Consequently, in lieu of sign settlements, the traffic route as of points 0 to 1 and on or after points 1 to 1 on the major road are allocated respectively as Direction 1 and Direction 2.

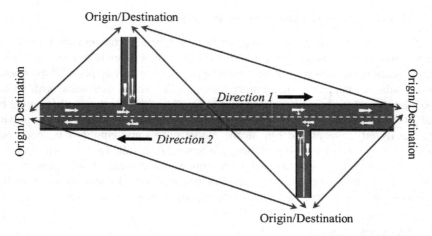

Fig. 4. Road system example made up of junctions, entry/exit points and origin/destination lines

4.1 Major Road

In this section, a few elements in this simulation model such as the road geometry such as horizontal alignment, vertical alignment, sight distance, auxiliary lanes and road marking in accordance with overtaking prohibition are looked into. When examining the details of road geometry, it could be seen that the road sections are divided into several sections according to its characteristics. There are two primary data compulsory for respective section; the position from which the section starts and the parameters important to that section. In order to obtain all the distance measurements, they should be measured from the entry point of the major road.

(a) Horizontal alignment

When specifying and determining the changes in horizontal alignment, it is not necessary to obtain both directions as one of the travelling directions is similar to the other opposite direction. With the intention having an equilibrium result in this study, the researcher's assumption is categorizing road curves as circular, with right- curved sectors having positive sign, and - left- curved - as negative. Mahdi [6] mentioned a measurement of a sector defined by a curve greater than 2000 m affects speed. In such situation, standardizing the study's result, the model is assumed to have a radius-defining curve lesser than 2000 m. For the other successive sectors with specific radius larger than 2000 m, they may be combined as one section.

(b) Vertical alignment

Mahdi [6] mentioned that grades lesser than 1 percent (absolute value) and other grades that is shorter than 200 m long have minimum influence on speed, where the successive sections may be definite as level road. Subsequently, in the vertical alignment, the each section is defined precisely by a grade and signed as a result (specifically affirmative meant for upgrade in addition to undesirable used for downgrade). Nevertheless, only one travel direction adequate for the description compulsory for the vertical alignment sections. In the resulting simulation procedure, local grade determination at location X is via the Eq. (1) (St. John and Kobett [7]; Mahdi [6]).

$$G_x = G(i) + \alpha\left(X - X_{G(i)}\right) \tag{1}$$

where:

$G(i)$ = section i at $X_{G(i)}$ percent evaluation

α = grade change rate, percent/m

X = position, specifically measured distance lengthwise the replicated road in travel direction for applicable grade (sign).

(a) Road marking

The changes that could be seen in the sections that describe the road markings are based on the overtaking prohibition. In describing this, it is divided into two sections; flag 1 is used to determine a section within which overtaking is permitted and flag 2 is used to determine a section within which overtaking is prohibited.

(b) Sight distance

In relation to road markings, a forward sight distance is used in the simulation for overtaking and also lane changing manoeuvres. These two are inter-related in terms of number of sections where they need to be at least equal for both sections; such as in the aspect of road characteristics and direction of travel for road markings. Therefore, it is important to specify relatively accurate both sight distances at the start and at the end of each section, as the parameter would affect the result of overtaking. For the simulation described above, the overtaking sight distance at X, within a sight distance section, is calculated using (St. John and Kobett [7]; Mahdi [6]).

$$S_x = S(i) + S_I\left(X - X_{S(i)}\right) \tag{2}$$

Where:

$S(i)$ = forward sight distance at the start of section i at $X_{S(i)}$, m,

S_I = rate of change of sight distance with position, m/m

X = position, specifically the measurement of distance along the direction of travel for road simulated for sight distance.

(c) Auxiliary lane

Auxiliary lane is the additional lane that helps to enhance traffic flow. The additional lane creates different types of traffic direction and for each of this direction, the number of sections with this aspect of road characteristics will be determined based on lane numbers. This auxiliary lane starts at the mid-point of the tapered entry and ends at the mid-point of the tapered exit.

4.2   Priority T-Junctions

Priority T-junctions inclusion in a simulation process is recognized with the specification the total of junctions that should be equivalent to or greater than 0. This could be clarified as such; if the identified total of junctions is superior than 0, individual junction would be numbered consecutively on or after upstream towards direction 1 downstream beginning with number 3 as Fig. 4 illustrated. The succeeding information must then be identified for respective junction.

(a) Location and orientation
      Each junction location should be measured beginning from direction 1 entry point of the travel to the minor road's center line projected to the major road. Additionally, the minor road orientation, namely in cases where the direction 1 of travel is on the right or left side, it must also be itemized for respective junction. Use flag 1 if the minor road is on the right-hand side and flag 0 if it is otherwise.
(b) Type of control
      On the other hand, flag 0 is also used to specify the type of junction control to represent a stop-controlled type, where flag 1 is used to specify the give-way type.
(c) Length and gradient of the minor road
      In this model, a short length of minor road is only considered at the separate junctions, specifically ranging from 100 to 200 m dependent of the length of the limited turning lane as this will be integrated in the model for simplicity. Each minor road gradient needs to be identified.

4.3   Traffic Characteristics

Another part of the simulation model that needs to be discussed is the traffic characteristics. There are a few elements required in the traffic data with the purpose of running the model includes the following:

- Headway distribution, volume (veh/h), cars percentage, HGVs percentage, motorcycles percentage, numbers of vehicle types in car, HGV and motorcycle categories, and composition (in fractions),
- Vehicles characteristics are vehicle types centered, contain power/weight ratio (W/kg), length (m) and particular standard deviations, besides a signal if respective vehicle type decreases speed downhill (flagged TRUE definite affecting vehicle types and flagged FALSE describes vehicle types not affected), and
- Drivers desired speeds for cars, HGVs, motorcycles, in addition to the particular standard deviations.

Another factor taken into account is the extra mandatory data if the simulation incorporates the junctions in. These extra information contain:

- O-D data Road to road. The O-D data must be specified infractions.
- Driver's critical gaps for respective turning manoeuvres at a T-junction. The driver's critical gaps (in sec) must be stated for major roads left- and right-turning vehicles from the minor road and for the right-turning vehicles.

- The move-up time. The inter-departure time between successive vehicles leaving the stop or yield line move-up time (in sec) is, commencing a queuing location, in utilizing the inconsistent traffic stream huge gap in.

O-D matrix figures containing fractions of traffic interchanges in the middle of entry points. O-D table road system was tabulated in Table 3 as presented in Fig. 4.

It could be determined as exemplified in Table 3, 80% vehicles that entered the system at point 1 will certainly end at point 2, and 20% at point 3. From the table, it could be expected that the traffic distributions from other entry points will produce a similar reading.

Table 3. A sample of tabulated O-D matrix

O	D			
	1	2	3	4
1	0	0.8	0.2	0
2	0.8	0	0.2	0
3	0	0	0	0
4	0.5	0.5	0	0

5 Vehicles Generation Process

Vehicles generation procedure linked to vehicles going into the system either from the end of the major road and also from junctions positioned at numerous points beside the road. This agrees that traffic volumes and the stated arrival configurations in the input. In this model, the course of journey taken by some of these vehicles will be either:

- navigating whole length of the road
- traversing the road's portion and leaving at any junctions or at the major road's end

When arriving at the road, the probabilistically determination of each course taken by the vehicle is in line with input data's turning percentages. Model-generated vehicles are in each travel direction in two different ways according to the required analysis type, namely intended for precise equal flow analysis, and to assess maximum flow.

Generally, a typical single carriageway road maximum flow ought to be stretched as soon as input flow surpasses 1800 veh/h/dir. Self-terminating model is as soon as the average speed drops under 30 km/h.

5.1 Basic Desired Speed

Utilizing a random number generated from standardized normal distribution shortened at ± 3 times the standard deviations and the consistent values quantified in the input data file, the individual driver's desired speed could be computed. In situations where the desired speed is not stated, the model will calculate the cars, HGVs and motorcycles mean basic desired speeds via the COBA speed/flow/geometry formulae for single carriageway roads (DTp [8]). The calculations include only the effects of carriageway width (CWID), widths of hard strip (SWID) and verge (VWID), and visibility or forward sight distance (VISI). Thus, the mean basic desired speeds for cars (VL), HGVs (VH) are given by

$$V_L = 72.1 + (2.0 \times CWID) + SWID \left(\frac{1.6}{SWID} + 1.1 \right) + (0.3 \times VWID) + (0.005 \times VISI)$$

(3)

$$V_H = 78.2 + (0.3 \times VWID) + (0.007 \times VISI) \tag{4}$$

The equations above show input variables that ought to be quantified in the input data file. In circumstances where there is no statement on visibility (VISI) in the above equations, it would be assessed by means of the following equation (DTp [8]):

$$LOG_{10} VISI = 2.26 + \frac{VWID}{25} - \frac{BEND}{400} \tag{5}$$

Where average bendiness is BEND in deg/km.

As Mahdi [6] stipulated, as it happened, there is no specification of the desired speeds standard deviations, the model would utilize the standard deviations equivalent to cars at 14 percent mean desired speed and 16 percent of cars and HGVs mean values.

5.2   Speed Based on Leader-Follower Interaction

In 2004, Che Puan [9] performed a comprehensive driver following behavior study for Malaysia's single carriageway roads. He established four categories of car following distance models as follows:

$$\text{Car following car :} \quad H_{CC} = 1.19V + 1.26 \tag{6}$$

$$\text{Car following HGV :} \quad H_{CH} = 1.12V + 4.04 \tag{7}$$

$$\text{HGV following HGV :} \quad H_{HH} = 1.21V + 9.33 \tag{8}$$

$$\text{HGV following car :} \quad H_{HC} = 1.19V + 5.17 \tag{9}$$

The above displays distance measurement in meters from front to front where V is speed in m/s. It is evident that models do not specify vehicle separation at zero speed even though there are consistency with Daou [10], Mahdi [6] and Hunt [11] proposal.

In brief, to evidently define drivers' car following distance attained from the studies, it is plotted and presented in Fig. 5. In addition, it could be seen that all vehicles safe car following distances are based on Daou [10], Smeed and Bennet (Lane [12]), the British Highway Code (Macpherson [13]) and Che Puan [9] is also plotted for comparison purposes.

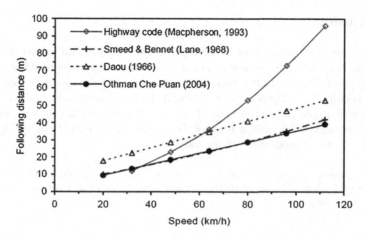

Fig. 5. Comparison of following distance (all vehicles)

5.3   Traffic Operations at Priority Junctions

The junction model employed in this study is based on the assumption that all drivers have an identical critical gap for each turning manoeuvre. In addition to the assumption that there is an identical critical gap to all drivers for an identical manoeuvre, the simulation of the vehicle at junctions also requires to follow the following rules:

- The vehicles are processed based on a first-in, first-out (i.e. FIFO) basis.
- The move-up time of the vehicles from stop situations is constant for all drivers. The replaceable default value is set at 3 s.
- Vehicles that move from stationary situations will use normal acceleration rates, i.e., 1.5 m/s^2 for cars and 0.75 m/s^2 for HGVs (Benekohal and Treiterer [14]).
- The speed of a vehicle negotiating the turning radius will not be faster than 20 km/h (McCoy et al. [15]). Vehicles are assumed safe from skidding with this speed although there is no firm evidence regarding the speed of a vehicle while negotiating the turning radius at a junction.
- There is no pedestrian traffic.
- In general, drivers are required to comply with all traffic rules which include the priority conventions.

In the model, it is assumed that when a turning driver has reached to a certain point at the upstream of the junction, he begins to decelerate in order to negotiate the turning radius or to stop (at the stop bar). A normal deceleration rate (i.e. 1.5 m/s^2) in this model as Homburger et al. [16] proposed is utilized with the theory that the driver has the advance knowledge that he will make a turn at a definite junction.

6 Conclusion

This study develop a research investigating and simulating traffic behaviour on single carriageway roads and the aim was examining the effects of various road layout, HGVs, overtaking provisions and traffic directional split on capacity and journey speed, and the effects of priority T-junctions on journey speed. The microscopic simulation model has been established. The simulation model has the ability to represent traffic operations on single carriageway roads and at priority T-junctions at or near capacity for a varied range of road layouts and traffic characteristics.

Acknowledgments. The authors would like to thank Universiti Malaysia Sarawak (UNIMAS) and Universiti Teknologi Malaysia (UTM) for providing facilities and support for the accomplishment of this study.

References

1. Highway Planning Unit. Road Traffic Volume 2013. Ministry of Works Malaysia (2014)
2. Yousif, S.Y.: Effect of lane changing on traffic operation for dual carriageway roads with roadworks. Ph.D. thesis, University of Wales College of Cardiff, UK (1993)
3. Miyahara, T.: The modelling of motorway traffic flow. Universities Transport Studies Group, Leed University, UK, pp. 1–12 (1994)
4. Chik, A.A.: The operation of midblock signaled pedestrian crossings. Ph.D. thesis, University of Wales College of Cardiff, Wales, UK (1996)
5. Parker, M.T.: A simulation model to study the effect of HGVs on capacity at motorway roadwork sites. Ph.D. thesis, University of Wales College of Cardiff, UK (1997)
6. Mahdi, T.A.: The effect of overtaking provision on the operating characteristics of single carriageway roads. Ph.D. thesis, University of Wales College of Cardiff, Wales, UK (1991)
7. St. John, A.D., Kobett, D.R.: Grade effects on traffic flow stability and capacity. NCHRP Report 185, TRB, National Research Council, Washington, D.C. (1978)
8. Department of Transport: Design Manual for Roads and Bridges, vol. 6. Departmental Standard TD 9/39, HMSO, London (1996)
9. Che Puan, O.: Driver's car following headway on single carriageway roads. Jurnal Kejuruteraan Awam **16**(2), 15–27 (2004)
10. Daou, A.: On flow within platoons. Aust. Road Res. **2**(7), 4–13 (1966)
11. Hunt, J.G.: Level of service on single carriageway roads – a study of following headways. Report to TRL Scotland, February 1997 (1997)
12. Lane, R.: Introduction to traffic engineering – 4 road capacity. Traffic Eng. Control **9**(9), 440–443 (1968)
13. Macpherson, G.: Highway and Transportation Engineering and Planning. Longman Scientific & Technical, Harlow (1993)
14. Benekohal, R.J., Treiterer, J.: CARSIM: Car-Following Model for Simulation of Traffic in Normal and Stop-and-Go Conditions. Transportation Research Record 1194, TRB, National Research Council, Washington, D.C. (1988)
15. McCoy, P.T., Ballard, J.L., Wijaya, Y.H.: Operational Effects of Two-Way Left-Turn Lanes on Two-Way Two-Lane Streets. Transportation Research Record 1194, TRB, National Research Council, Washington, D.C. (1982)
16. Homburger, W.S.: Transportation and Traffic Engineering Handbook, 2nd edn. Institute of Traffic Engineers, Prentice-Hall, Englewood Cliffs (1982)

Elliptical Curve Cryptography-Kerberos Authentication Model for Keystone in Open Stack

Veeramani Shamugam[1(✉)], Iain Murray[2], and Amandeep S. Sidhu[3]

[1] Department of Electrical and Computer Engineering,
Faculty of Engineering and Sciences, Curtin University, Miri, Malaysia
s.veeramani@curtin.edu.my
[2] Department of Electrical and Computer Engineering,
Faculty of Science and Engineering, Curtin University,
Bentley, Perth, WA 6102, Australia
[3] Curtin Malaysia Research Institute, Curtin University, Miri, Malaysia

Abstract. Cloud computing is a fastly developing technology, which will be a ubiquitous service in coming days. Cloud has additionally focalized numerous apparently unique components, for example, storage, compute, and so forth into a unified infrastructure. OpenStack is one of the eminent cloud computing programming in the cloud group. It is conveyed as Infrastructure as a Service, which implies and permits the clients to provision their own machines in cloud by utilizing its components, similar to computation, storage, and so on. Keeping in mind about the end goal to give such services, whereas OpenStack needs to verify its clients. The component in OpenStack that plays out this capacity is called Keystone. In Keystone, the present component has to give a token to the requesting clients, which is then given to different services from where the clients ask for particular services (e.g. storage, compute and so forth). In this paper, ECC-Kerberos based authentication model is examined and formulated for OpenStack. The key distribution of this examination is to increase the comprehension of the possibility of Kerberos in OpenStack with the end goal of authentication. A noteworthy advantage is that the authentication model in OpenStack can then be founded as an outstanding and very much high in standard. This proposed authentication model is implemented. The evaluation and demonstration of this implementation is also presented.

Keywords: Cloud computing · OpenStack · Key stone · Kerberos authentication · Elliptical curve cryptography

1 Introduction

OpenStack is an open source cloud working framework [1] that is involved with a few open source sub-services or projects which control the expansive pools of networking resources, storage and compute all through a datacenter, it has been oversaw through a dashboard that gives the managers control while enabling their clients to provision resources through a web interface. These services are given to make an Infrastructure

© Springer Nature Singapore Pte Ltd. 2017
M.S. Mohamed Ali et al. (Eds.): AsiaSim 2017, Part II, CCIS 752, pp. 633–644, 2017.
DOI: 10.1007/978-981-10-6502-6_54

Service cloud. All OpenStack services uncover a RESTful API [2, 9] for communication among them and also utilize the HTTP protocol [3, 4] for every information exchange. Moreover, by utilizing this kind of API, fault-tolerance and scalability is given to the model.

Notwithstanding, the genuine communication is given by workers, which are separate procedures devoted for specific molecules execution, perhaps running on different machines, associated by means of AMQP and utilizing a message transport which is RabbitMQ [2, 5, 9] by default. As for service information storage, each OpenStack benefit has its own particular SQL based database for storing the state data, yet to give throughput and versatility which is conceivable to execute recreated multi-master databases.

Therefore, to give every one of the resources expected to make an Infrastructure benefit cloud, which are accessible the accompanying services in OpenStack framework: Table 1: All Available Service in Open Stack [6].

Table 1. Available services in Open Stack

Name of service	Service type
Key Stone	Identity service
Nova	Compute service
Neutron	Networking service
Glance	Image service
Swift	Object Storage service
Cinder	Block Storage service
Heat	Orchestration service
Trove	Database service
Ironic	Bare Metal service
Sahara	Data processing service
Zaqar	Message service
Barbican	Key management service
Designate	DNS service
Manila	Shared File systems service
Magnum	Containers service
Murano	Application catalog
Congress	Governance service
Mistral	Workflow service
MagnetoDB	Key-value store as a service
Horizon	Dashboard
Ceilometer	Telemetry service

From the above list, the Table 1 describes about the requirements is important which are needed is Heat, Cinder, Nova, Keystone, Neutron, Celimeter, Glance and Horizon. And also, the following Fig. 1 represents the typical OpenStack Environment.

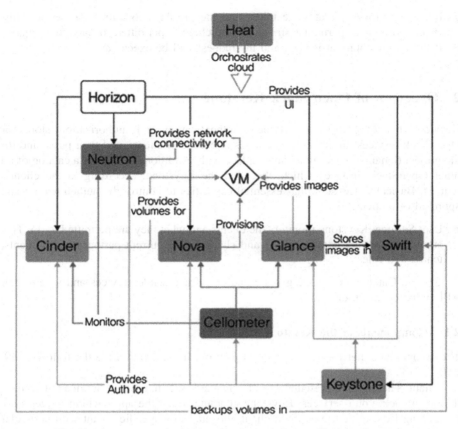

Fig. 1. The conceptual architecture of a typical OpenStack environment

OpenStack framework [7] takes after a basic procedure when a client is attempting to access to a service:

1. The client who is attempting to play out an activity to a service sends its qualifications to Keystone
2. Keystone sends a temporary token to the client and a rundown of tenants if any authentication is succeeding in the past by using these credentials.
3. The client sends the certifications to Keystone together with the desired tenant.
4. In the event, that the authentication of the accreditations and the desired tenant is right, Keystone sends a tenant token and a rundown of accessible service for this tenant.
5. The client decides the right endpoint relying upon the activity that should be performed and makes the request to the endpoint alongside the tenant token procured for authentication.
6. To stay away from connections from unauthorized substances, the Service ask for Keystone whether the received token is right and is permitted to utilize the Service.

7. If that keystone validates the token and the privilege to utilize the service, this checks to its own particular strategy if the client is permitted to make the request.
8. If the policy approval is right and the request will be executed.

2 Overview of Open Stack Keystone

Keystone benefit [8] gives a typical authentication and authorization store for OpenStack services. In which, Keystone is in charge of clients, and their parts, and for the project (tenants) where they have a place with. Additionally it gives a catalog of all other OpenStack Services which check on the Keystone, according to the client's request. Basically, Keystone has essential capacities to control the authentication and approval of a client:

- User Service: Keystone monitors the clients and what they are permitted to do. This errand is made by administrating and checking the current partner among clients, tenant and roles.

Service Catalog: Keystone gives a catalog of accessible services and where their API endpoints are found.

2.1 Components of the Keystone

The components that Keystone needs to play out its motivation are the following [9, 15]:

Client: The digital representations of a man are system, users or Service that utilizes the OpenStack cloud services. Keystone guarantees that the approaching requests are originating from a legitimate login client allocated to a specific tenant with particular role that can be relegated resource-access tokens.

Tenant: A tenant is a gathering in which, it is used to disconnect resources as well as clients. Groups can be mapped to clients, organization or projects

Role: A role incorporates an arrangement of relegated client rights and benefits for playing out a particular set of operations. A client token issued by Keystone incorporates a rundown of that client's roles. Therefore, benefits decide how to interpret those roles by their inward policies storing in each policy.json document.

Credentials: Credentials are information known just by a particular client who demonstrates his or her character.

Token: A token is a discretionary piece of content used to get to resources. Every token has a degree depicting the available resources which might be denied whenever and is substantial for a limited term.

Endpoint: A network accessible address is an endpoint, generally portrayed by URL, from which services are accessed.

3   Existing Authentication System in Open Stack

The group of Internal Services is given by keystone [10]. There are one or more endpoints to expose these services. Token, Policy Services, Identity and Catalog are provided by Keystone. The authentication system of Keystone [16] uses the Public key based method. By using the digital signature, the identity of the user is verified and the communication over the public networks is secured by allowing public key cryptography. The user is authenticated by an electronic signature called digital signature. In digital signature [17], the private key is used to sign the data by sender and to verify the signature by receiver using the public key of sender. With the specific public key, the identity of the user is guaranteed by Certificate Authority (CA) which plays a trusted role.

The role of a Certificate Authority (CA) in keystone [13, 14] is played by the Keystone manager utility in OpenStack or the third party can be used to do the same. For authentication, a keystone PKI token is used. A token which is signed by its keystone private key or signing is called as a PKI token. The PKI with Cryptographic Message Syntax (CMS) [18] is used by Keystone. The token which is often referred as CMS token, in which the expiration date, an issue and id of the token are contained by CMS token. The placing of the tenant information is followed by the information of the service catalog. The connection of the service done by obtaining specific services (Ex. Network service or compute) by means of the endpoints. The information of the user is list after the endpoints. The username, id and role of the user is showed by it. The id of the service is written in the CMS format is called as CMS data and the CMS token is the signed CMS data.

At the point, when a client signs into her machine with her username and password, keystone assembles the majority of the previously mentioned data and creates a CMS token and sends it to the client's workstation. The client's OpenStack [13] customer program Y in their workstation stores the token locally and utilize it for the later demands. At the point when the client later demands for a service utilizing her customer in the workstation, the customer send the token alongside the service request. The OpenStack benefit checks the client's signature and responds back with the token.

At the junction when customer needs any of the services like cinder, glance and nova and so on., it sends a request alongside the CMS token. The objective service gets the CMS token and checks the signature, and gives the requested service if the token is legitimate and the client is authorized.

Token Verification and Expiration: PKI token empowers services for disconnected verification. The three important things are for the verification, they are

- Verify Token Signature
- Token Expiration Date
- Revoked Tokens.

3.1   Process of Authentication for Keystone

Step 1: A request message REQ (username, password) sends to the Keystone from the Open Stack customer.

Step 2: The customer's username and password is verified by Key Stone. Furthermore, the CMS token is generated.

Step 3: Open Stack customer reserves the CMS token locally and it sends a service request with CMS token to the Open Stack Services.

Step 4: Open Stack Services separate the CMS from the request and it checks the signature of CMS, Revocation list and Expiration date.

Step 5: If the token is significant then Open Stack Services refresh the Request status else it sends an error message to the Open Stack customer

4 Proposed ECC-Kerberos Based Authentication System

The Kerberos protocol utilizes a focal KDC (key Distribution Center) [12] which goes about as a trusted outsider. In Kerberos, the KDC and alternate substances utilize a "secure" clock with the end goal of identifying the replay attacks and checking the validity of token. Kerberos utilizes the timestamp as an authenticator. However, the tickers are thought to be matched up with a little measure of known clock float. Therefore, OpenStack has different parts which are associated with each other, and there is additionally a keystone, authentication server, which gives authentication service to every component. Given a distributed set of Services, we trust Kerberos is a proper design for empowering between service and client to service authentication. In this proposed work, a public key and private key is produced by Elliptical Curve Public key cryptography [11].

4.1 Elliptical Curve Cryptography

In this phase, a public and private key is randomly selected from the key pool and exchanged between sending and receiving nodes. The key establishment phase uses an elliptic curve over prime field to generate a large key pool for node-verification purpose. An elliptic curve over prime field is an algebraic expression and is defined by the following equation:

$$y^2(mod\,p) = x^3 + Ax + B(mod\,p)$$

where, A and B are the coefficients and the variables x and y take the values only from the finite field within the range of prime field p. The given the values of these paclient Yeters, a large number of points on the curve can be generated by using basic elliptic curve operations, known as point addition and point doubling.

4.2 Kerberos Protocol with Elliptical Curve Cryptography

In the infrastructure of public key, each element needs both the keys (private and public). The certificate authority issues a declaration for each substance. In Kerberos [12], the KDC is considered as a certificate authority. The KDC has every one of the certificates and public key of each element, and every one of the substances have the certificate of KDC, with the goal that they can confirm the signature of KDC. And likewise, KDC has a secret key. Just KDC thinks about this key, and no other substance has the learning of it. Assume client X needs to communicate with another client Y. For speaking with client Y, client X needs to log at first into the workstation. The workstation will request TGT to KDC. In answer, KDC will send the TGT and session key. Here the TGT and a session key are encrypted with a key, which is created just for client X. KDC takes hash of this key, and signs it. At that point it encrypts the hash and the plaintext of the key with Client X's public key and sends it to Client X. At that point Client X's workstation gets the message. It decrypts the hash and the key. At that point it takes the hash of the key and checks it with the got hash. In the event that both the hashes coordinate with each other, then it utilizes the way to decrypt the TGT and the session key. Client X's workstation then reserves the TGT and session key locally (Table 2).

Table 2. List of Abbreviations used in this research work

List of Abbreviations	Abbreviations
TGT	Ticket Granting Ticket
KDC	Key Distribution Center
SKDC	Secret Key of KKDC
SK	Session Key
K_X	Key for Client X generated by KDC
K_Y	Key for ticket to Client Y by KDC
$SK_{keystone}$	Secret key for Keystone
SK_U	Session key for user and keystone
SK_{XY}	Session key for Client X and Client Y
E ("Client X", SK, SKDC)	Client X's workstations caches the ticket and session key locally.
$[h(K_Y)]_{KDC} \| K_Y \|$ Client Y$\|$ E ("Client X", SK_{XY}, K_Y)	Ticket to Client Y is given by this
E("user", SK_U, $SK_{keystone}$)	Keystone generates a session key for the user and sends the TGT and the key to client.
$\{ [h(K_{Nova})]_{Keystone} \| K_{Nova} \}$ Nova – E $\{$"User", User Metadata, SK_{UN}, $K_{Nova}\}$	Ticket to Nova

At the point when Client X needs to speak with Client Y, Client X's workstation sends a request that she needs to communicate with Client Y with TGT and an authenticator to KDC. KDC gets the request and checks the TGT and confirms the authenticator. KDC issues a ticket to Client Y and sends it to Client X. Ticket to Client Y contains a key, and K_Y created by KDC. KDC takes the hash of K_Y and signs it. At that point encrypts the hash and the plaintext of K_Y with Client Y's public key and places it in the ticket. Additionally, the ticket contains Client X's name, SK_{XY} (the session key for Client X and Client Y). Client X's name and SK_{XY} are encrypted with K_Y.

KDC encrypts the ticket to Client Y, Client Y's username and SK_{XY} with the Client X's session key SK_X and sends it to Client X. Client X's workstation decrypts the message and stores the ticket to Client Y and SK_{XY} locally. Client X sends the ticket to Client Y and an authenticator which is encrypted with SK_{XY}. Client X gets the ticket, checks the signature of KDC and recovers K_Y. Client X then decrypts SK_{XY} with K_Y and stores it locally. At last, Client Y confirms the authenticator and sends another authenticator to Client X as a response to her test. Client X confirms the authenticator and sets up a communication (Fig. 2).

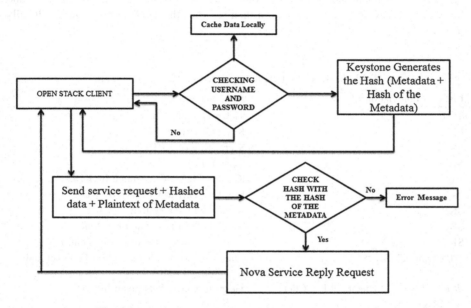

Fig. 2. Functioning of the proposed authentication model

Procedure for Kerberos with Elliptic Curve Public Key in Open Stack

1. An Open Stack client sends a request by using username and password to need a TGT.
2. Keystone generates a TGT and session key SK_C
3. Keystone issues the Session Key (SK_C) and TGT with the help of KDC.
4. Then the OpenStack verifies the signature and gets the key and TGT.
5. Again the Open Stack client send request ["Nova", TGT, Authenticator] to connect with Nova. And the authenticator sends request by E (timestamp, S_C)
6. Keystone provides the Ticket to Nova Service as {"Client", Client's Certificate, hash of user metadata}$_{KDC}$ and nova certificate = nova cert. E("Nova", Ticket to Nova, Nova Cert, S_A), user metadata.
7. Then OpenStack client send request to Nova [Ticket to Nova, Authenticator, user metadata] and authenticator send request as {timestamp}$_{Client}$.

8. Nova service verifies the signature of KDC and get client's certificate, and finally verifies the authenticator. Check for the revocation list and verifies the token. Then hash it and match with the received hash.
9. Nova service sends the response message with {authenticator}$_{Nova}$.
10. Again the Open Stack client verifies the Nova's signature and verifies the authenticator.

ECC-Kerberos with Public key cryptography can be utilized as a part of OpenStack. Here Keystone can go about as KDC and furthermore as a Certificate Authority. Keystone will have every one of the elements' certificate and public keys. Thus, every one of the elements has Keystone's public key. At the point when client sign into his workstation, the workstation sends a request to Keystone that client needs a TGT. Keystone creates a session key for the client and sends the TGT and the way to customer.

The OpenStack customer gets the message and decrypts SK_U and recovers the hash. It checks the hash with the hash of the SK_U. At that point it utilizes SK_U to decrypt TGT and SK_U and stores these locally. At the point when a Service is required from, says Nova, the client will send the TGT, alongside a request to keystone. Keystone will check the TGT and allow a ticket for Nova. At that point Keystone will send a ticket to the client.

The OpenStack customer sends the ticket to Nova and an authenticator to Nova. Nova checks the signature of Keystone and discovers K_{Nova} and the hash. It checks the hash with the hash of K_{Nova}. In the event that both match, Nova utilizes K_{Nova} to decrypt client metadata and session key SK_{UN}.

5 Proposed Authentication System Implementation in Open Stack and Evaluation

A timer is put to discover the distinction between the current model (which utilizes symmetric key cryptography in Keystone) and the proposed model (ECC-Kerberos Cryptography). The timer computes the token validation time and token generation time. In this way, in the recently proposed display, OpenStack Services, for example, Nova, are equipped for dealing with requests a great deal more effectively than the current OpenStack execution.

The below Fig. 3 represents to the token generation time for existing authentication model and proposed authentication model in Open Stack. Since the current model utilizes just digital signature for metadata, the time taken for token generation is lesser. On the opposite side, in the proposed model, client metadata is initially hashed and afterward it is marked by utilizing digital signature. So the time taken for the token generation is more noteworthy than the current model.

The Fig. 4 represents to the token validation time for existing model and proposed model. Hash is a littler string than the first metadata. So decrypting the hash information takes less time. Moreover, verifying the digital signature on the hashed information additionally takes essentially lesser measure of time.

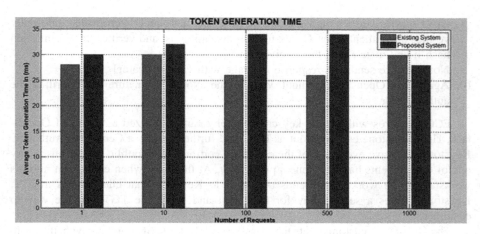

Fig. 3. Token generation time for proposed and existing system

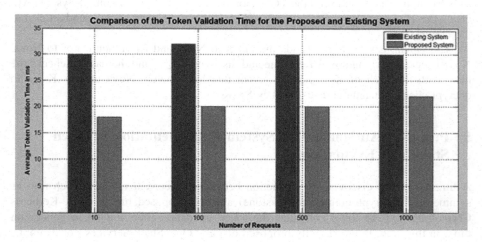

Fig. 4. Comparison of the token validation time for existing and proposed methodology

The Fig. 5 represents the reliability of the proposed authentication system and existing system. The proposed one is more reliable with also the increasing number of requests. So there must less time take for the execution of the process in the proposed system.

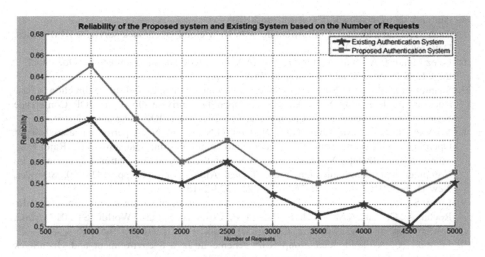

Fig. 5. Reliability of the existing and proposed system based on the number of requests in Open Stack

6 Conclusion

OpenStack is an eminent open-source programming for IaaS cloud. The use of this software is expanding step by step. So it is important to research the security engineering. We find that the current authentication model in OpenStack is unpredictable, and can set aside a lot of opportunity to authentication that what is perfect. Our hypothesis in this article was that the current model is time inefficient, but Kerberos is the time efficient authentication protocol for Open Stack. This new model is a time efficient framework without hampering any security issues.

OpenStack can be sent in a high volume server in genuine situations where its services may handle an extensive number of requests from various clients from a single and over numerous tenants. Thus, it will require a more effective and quick authentication framework. ECC-Kerberos can be a good exchange for the present protocol of OpenStack. ECC-Kerberos is intended for high volume servers and Kerberos additionally gives common authentication between the sender and recipient in distributed settings.

References

1. Petrillo, F., et al.: Towards a REST cloud computing lexicon. In: 7th International Conference on Cloud Computing and Services Science, CLOSER 2017 (2017)
2. Vyas, U.: Deploying multi-node cluster. In: Applied OpenStack Design Patterns, pp. 51–63. Apress (2016)
3. Chekam, T.T., et al.: On the synchronization bottleneck of openstack swift-like cloud storage systems. In: IEEE International Conference on Computer Communications, San Francisco, CA pp. 10–15, April 2016. IEEE Xplore® (2016)

4. Antonov, N.: OpenStack in Enterprise (2016)
5. Cash, S., et al.: Managed infrastructure with IBM cloud OpenStack services. IBM J. Res. Dev. **60**(2-3), 1–6 (2016)
6. Pérez Méndez, A., et al.: Integrating an AAA-based federation mechanism for OpenStack—the CLASSe view. Concurr. Comput.: Pract. Exp. (2017)
7. Shanmugam, V., et al.: Software defined networking challenges and future direction: a case study of implementing SDN features on OpenStack private cloud. In: IOP Conference Series: Materials Science and Engineering, vol. 121, no. 1. IOP Publishing (2016)
8. Vo Van, N., Chi, L.M., Long, N.Q., Nguyen, G.N., Le, D.-N.: A performance analysis of OpenStack open-source solution for IaaS cloud computing. In: Satapathy, S.C., Raju, K.S., Mandal, J.K., Bhateja, V. (eds.) Proceedings of the Second International Conference on Computer and Communication Technologies. AISC, vol. 380, pp. 141–150. Springer, New Delhi (2016). doi:10.1007/978-81-322-2523-2_13
9. Lima, S., Rocha, A.: A view of OpenStack: toward an open-source solution for cloud. In: Rocha, Á., Correia, A.M., Adeli, H., Reis, L.P., Costanzo, S. (eds.) WorldCIST 2017. AISC, vol. 569, pp. 481–491. Springer, Cham (2017). doi:10.1007/978-3-319-56535-4_49
10. Jakóbik, A.: A cloud-aided group RSA scheme in Java 8 environment and OpenStack software. J. Telecommun. Inf. Technol. **2**, 53 (2016)
11. Sabapathi, V., Visu, P., Varun kumar, K.A.: A hybrid cloud architecture for secure service—measures against poodle vulnerability. In: Suresh, L.P., Panigrahi, B.K. (eds.) Proceedings of the International Conference on Soft Computing Systems. AISC, vol. 398, pp. 707–713. Springer, New Delhi (2016). doi:10.1007/978-81-322-2674-1_67
12. Symeonidis, H.: Cloud Computing security for efficient Big Data delivery (2016)
13. Anisetti, M., et al.: Toward security and performance certification of open stack. In: 2015 IEEE 8th International Conference on Cloud Computing (CLOUD). IEEE (2015)
14. Kamboj, R., Arya, A.: OpenStack: open source cloud computing IaaS platform. Int. J. Adv. Res. Comput. Sci. Softw. Eng. **4**(5) (2014)
15. Sefraoui, O., Aissaoui, M., Eleuldj, M.: OpenStack: toward an open-source solution for cloud computing. Int. J. Comput. Appl. **55**(3) (2012)
16. Khan, R.H., Ylitalo, J., Ahmed, A.S.: OpenID authentication as a service in OpenStack. In: 2011 7th International Conference on Information Assurance and Security (IAS). IEEE (2011)
17. Jayaram, K.R., Milenkoski, A., Kounev, S.: Software architectures for self-protection in IaaS clouds. In: Kounev, S., Kephart, J., Milenkoski, A., Zhu, X. (eds.) Self-Aware Computing Systems, pp. 611–631. Springer, Cham (2017). doi:10.1007/978-3-319-47474-8_21
18. Markelov, A.: Certified OpenStack Administrator Study Guide (2016)

Real-Time Rendering Blood Flow Visualisation Using Particle Based Technique

Mohd Khalid Mokhtar$^{(\boxtimes)}$, Farhan Mohamed, and Mohd Shahrizal Sunar

UTM-IRDA Digital Media Centre, Media and Games Innovation Centre,
Universiti Teknologi Malaysia, 81310 Skudai, Johor, Malaysia
khalmokh@me.com
http://www.magicx.my

Abstract. The use of scientific visualization technique in real-time rendering environment has great potential to enhance user interaction in visualizing blood flow; therefore the integration algorithm of chosen scientific visualization technique and real-time algorithm should be developed and implemented in virtual environment. It is a basic fact that the effectiveness of blood flow visualization are reliant on two fundamental issues. First is how to present an improved visualization of cardiovascular flow, and the second is how to interactively visualize the fluidic blood flow in gaining insight into the cardiovascular physiology. This research proposed a framework on based on idea from previous research that improve visualization of blood flow by integrates with particle based simulation method in order to allow more user interaction. Despite the variety and number of existing method, there are still demands for new improved visualization technique with a mission to provide better information. Good understanding on blood flow pattern will aid clinician, engineer and researcher during the diagnosis and prognosis of pathology as well as the assessment of risk and follow-up finding.

Keywords: Scientific visualization · Blood flow · Physic-based animation · Position-based dynamic

1   Introduction

Recently, physical-based animation is actively popular used in industry like computer games, movies, education and training. Increase of computing power of CPU and GPU has empowered real-time simulation to produce plausible physical effect. Many simulation method are introduced to solve many simulation issues such as fluids, rigid bodies, cloth and fracture. Every year many new technique is released to allow more faster solution with more increased realism and also to reduce the gap with computational fluid dynamics (CFD).

Rendering physical phenomena are required base knowledge and theories from physical, mathematical and engineering field [2]. These field has reach impressive accomplishment in investigating natural phenomena such as motion

© Springer Nature Singapore Pte Ltd. 2017
M.S. Mohamed Ali et al. (Eds.): AsiaSim 2017, Part II, CCIS 752, pp. 645–655, 2017.
DOI: 10.1007/978-981-10-6502-6_55

of fluid. However, in physical-based animation these knowledges are sometimes not useful. These are because the main reason of computer animation is to produce images with high visual detail, high performance and low memory consumption [2]. In contrast to physically-based animation, CFD is more focus on to predict long-term behaviour and high precision without concern much on visual details. For interactive application, robustness of the application is key element that any physics-based animation must be fulfilled [4,16].

Strong demand of physics-based animation in interactive application especially in medical training and education allow many computer graphics models have been designed using physics theories for surgical training use [3,8,9,29]. Generally, in medical visualization involves standard pipeline including visualisation, image processing, and graphics rendering [8,29]. The latest publication in visualising medical data in 3D is by combining MRI flow data with physics based animation [7].

Blood flow plays main part in pathological vessel development that is why visualization and simulation of cardiovascular data become so important in understanding of the cardiovascular system and their pathological variations [27]. Flow visualization techniques such as color-coded streamlines, probe plane, isosurfaces and glyphs are commonly implemented by biomedical researchers [25]. Current trends of cardiovascular flow visualization implemented medical research and application describes in [26]. In advance medical training, the usage of computer graphics technique to enhance realism of medical simulator to explore disease has been implemented widely using physical-based animation.

The main propose of study is to produce a real-time interactive visualization system framework that integrate scientific visualisation and physical-based simulation technique for blood flow visualization in small vascular tree structure from large arteries to show complex correlation between vessel geometry and blood flow visualization technique for robust interactive application. This paper also described the current progress of this research.

In order to arrive to this research goal, there are three main objectives these framework needed to be achieved, which are:

1. To convert visualization data of blood flow from scientific visualization software into virtual reality environment
2. To introduce vector field technique in tubular structure of vascular tree to control animation of blood flow in virtual reality environment
3. To integrate visualization technique and physical-based simulation technique in order to produce real-time interactive visualization system of blood flow.

2   Background

Visualizing blood flow information from medical images data is interesting topic to be highlighted by recent researcher especially four-dimensional phase-contrast magnetic resonance imaging (4D PC-MRI) [10,24,26]. Limitations of human to access massive clinical data that growing time to time allows data visualisation and simulation field is significant to be explored. Visualisation is a process where the hidden data to be extracted and some important information unseen within medical data such as computerized tomography (CT) and magnetic resonance imaging (MRI) images. Integral curve is the common ways to depict flow through two main approaches: streamlines and pathlines [28]. Recently, particle system is quite popular to be explored by other researcher [7,11]. In 4D blood flow field visualizations, many researcher still find new solution for visual cluttering [13].

Physics based animation is among popular topic in real-time computer graphics. Physics based animation can be described as field in computer graphics to produce physically simulation in interactive rate with plausible effect. In medical visualisation, physics based animation has been implemented widely for example OpenTissue toolkit that integrate physics based animation with medical visualisation under one toolkit [1]. Every year new techniques are emerged with more robust and more high-detail effect produced. Fluid simulation is a active topic in computer graphics. In context of medical visualisation, many researcher has been utilized and update the new technique in physical based animation with consider the applicability of techniques. Refer to Table 1 to investigate the previous research that has implemented physics based animation into their project.

Table 1. Physics based animation implemented in real-time medical simulation.

Researcher	Phenomena	Area	Vessel region	Method
[19]	Blood stream, injured arterial vessel	Simple blood vessel	Straight	Smoothed Particle Hydrodynamics
[22]	Bleeding	Simple blood vessel	Straight	Smoothed particle hydrodynamics
[20]	Tubular flow, Bifurcation	Simple blood vessel	Straight, Bifurcations	Smoothed particle hydrodynamics
[29]	Propagation, Bifurcation	Vascular tree	Branching, Bifurcations	Smoothed particle hydrodynamics
[8]	Vessel rupture	Simple blood vessel	Aneurysm	Smoothed particle hydrodynamics
[11]	Heart chamber	Left ventricle	-	Smoothed particle hydrodynamics

Fundamentally, the characteristics of blood, as a fluid and vessel as surfaces to interact. Simulating fluid phenomena and deformable object are developed using numerical methods and algorithm that derived from Computational Fluid Dynamic (CFD). Navier-Stokes equations is well-known equation which is basis the most of CFD problems which formulated by Claude Navier and George Stoke [19]. The equation described the dynamics and conservation of momentum to simulate fluids. Many types of methods have been proposed in simulating fluid in CFD studies such as Smoothed Particle Hydrodynamics (SPH). SPH is mesh-free method which is firstly introduced to simulate astrophysical phenomena such as fission and star by Lucy (1997) and Gingold Monaghan (1977). SPH is also one of the most popular particle based fluid simulation vastly used in interactive system such as computer games and computational fluid dynamic. The implementation of SPH in various fields can be seen in [14]. Using SPH method for cardiac flow visualization is not new but rarely explored by researcher. Based on work done by [29], SPH is proven to simulate pulsatile flow in cardiovascular system with good reliability. It was first attempt to verify the capability of smoothed particle hydrodynamics. In real-time medical simulation several paper has used SPH method in their framework of the system [8,15].

In area of computer graphics and visualization, new fluid simulation techniques has been actively introduced until today. Advancement of computer technology is the biggest influences that encourages more advance simulation techniques emerged to be used in real-time. Stam and Fiume were pioneered the use of SPH method in computer graphics area [12]. The SPH method was utilized to depict fire and other gaseous phenomena. In 2004, blood flow simulation using SPH was first time introduced by Muller et al. [19]. The SPH simulated the blood flow of blood vessel in real-time for virtual surgery. Later, with introduction dedicated hardware such as PPU and programmable graphic processing unit (GPU) contributed other researchers to use improved SPH computational processes for blood flow simulation for fast development in training and virtual surgery [8,15,21,22]. Newest publications are more on focus on boundary management to manage interaction of blood flow with deformable wall of blood vessel and heart [9,20]. Macklin and Muller has published new improvement to particle based fluid simulation of SPH by introducing an iterative density solver integrated into the Position Based Dynamics framework (PBD). Latest update on particle-based system by using unified particle physics for real-time applications by Macklin open new opportunity for real-time application to improve rendering performance [5].

Based on latest survey done by [10] on blood flow simulation using 4D PC-MRI data for data assimilation and verification. Assimilation of measured data used to increase understanding and improve visual analysis of hemodynamics [7]. Simulated CFD and measured result verified to show the significant difference between both. Measured data coincide well mainly caused by limited spatial resolution.

De Hoon et al. is the first researcher successfully integrate MRI flow data with physics based fluid animation [7] that allow make good use of temporal resolution for 4D flow imaging. Physics based fluid allow less computational cost to represent the actual physics of fluid flow and provide high resolution and noise free model of the fluid dynamics. His works has inspired this work to use the velocity data to initialise the physical parameter to physics-based fluid method in vascular tree. New improvement for previous researcher work in simulating fluid in vascular tree with new solver to manage fluid-object interaction and able to maintain realism while increase the performance [20, 29].

Visualising vascular tree structure such coronary arteries in 3D from medical images is significant and establish topic within the wider field of visualizing medical images-based data [6, 23]. This field has proven applicability for diagnosis, therapy planning and educational purposes. For example in angioplasty procedure, vascular surgeon use 3D visualisation to interactive plan a stent implementation or bypass surgery. With new technology in medical devices, new insight and knowledge are possible to be revealed and interpreted that allow clinicians to understand more about patient and the cause of diseases using 3D visualisation.

3   Methodology

In this section describes the methodology and procedures that conducted to fulfil the objectives of this paper. Systematic and efficient development of this proposed framework is performed depend on approaches taken in this section. The research approach is illustrated in Fig. 1. Based on previous section, an integration method of scientific visualization technique and physics based algorithm will be developed to manage blood flow in vascular tree for interactive application.

In the first phase, the research will analyse all the fundamental approaches and techniques in blood flow visualisation and physics based animation. Latest survey on blood flow visualization can referred to [24, 28]. Three common method have been implemented to simulate blood flow such as Eulerian, Lattice-Boltzmann, and Lagrangian method [18]. Lagrangian method that represented by particle are chosen in this studied because this is best approach to simulate blood flow in real-time application. Several type medical image data are studied and such MRI and CT-Scan using common DICOM viewer software. Based on previous activities, suitable real patient medical image data is screened and chosen. For MRI images, phase-contract images will be processed to get the velocity data for large artery that contribute to small vascular network. These data will be segmented and reconstructed as a 3D volumetric cardiovascular model. Centreline reconstruction is then performed to get data about bifurcation information and reconstruction cross section. This process will be done by SimVascular. New particle-based simulation with boundary management solution is proposed to reduce the computational cost in preventing fluid particle passing through solid vessel boundaries. The technique will be synergy with the common blood flow simulation method.

This framework is introduced to integrate scientific visualisation and physical-based simulation technique for blood flow visualization in small vascular tree structure from large arteries to show complex correlation between vessel geometry and blood flow visualization technique for robust interactive application. In this activity, centreline and cross section of vascular will help fluid simulation to be more optimized. In the next stage, the blood flow physical information are simulated and decomposed into particle-based flow. These particles will allow to simulating coronary artery blood flow rendering. This particle-based fluid simulation method will also allow the simulation done in real-time.

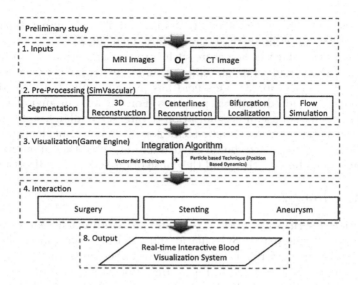

Fig. 1. Framework of the research.

3.1 3D Modeling and Centreline Generation

The MRI or CT images is used to generate 3D coronary mesh data were generated with the latest SimVascular. SimVascular is a complete pipeline from medical image data segmentation to patient specific blood flow simulation and analysis. Three types of vessel are chosen, a branched vessel and without branch vessel. Figure 2 shows the blood vessels used in our experiment that generated using SimVascular. The detail of 3D meshes then increased by performing Catmull-Clark subdivision surfaces before can be started to be used. Centreline reconstruction is by manually hand-selecting each point. The path then smoothed by SimVascular with sevaral parameter as depicted on Fig. 3.

3.2 Visualize Vector Data in Virtual Environment

MegaFlow is a package that allow you to use Vector Fields data to control the movement of objects or particle systems in Unity [30]. Vector field data are a 2D or 3D grids of values that describe the direction and magnitude of velocities for that point in space. The Vector Field is data generated by SimVascular. Figure 4 shows the sample visualization of vector data using MegaFlow package. This system will be customized in order to produce an integrate algorithm for vector field data and physic-based animation technique.

3.3 Position Based Dynamics for Vessel Interaction

The particle based physics using position based dynamics is a mesh-free method for solving deformable objects in many interactive graphic application. Based

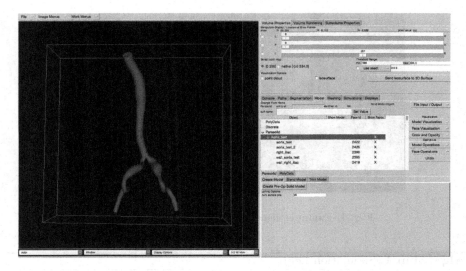

Fig. 2. Vascular model process by SimVascular.

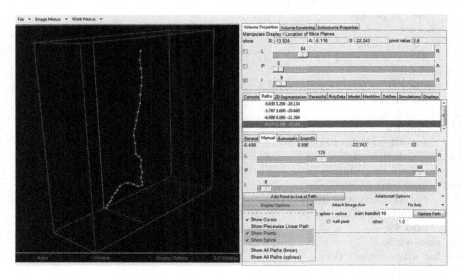

Fig. 3. Centreline construction data using path planing by SimVascular

on worked done by [16,17], algorithm of position based dynamics is shown in Algorithm 1. Each constraint is solved independently in a Jacobi fashion, rather than using sequential Gauss-Seidel iteration [16]. Previous work done by [7] will be reference how assimilation of measurement data and simulation data coupled to improve visualization of blood flow. In that studied, Fluid Implicit-Particle (FLIP) use a grid for the pressure solve and transfer changes back to particles [16].

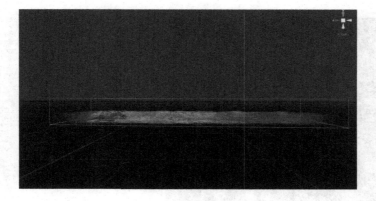

Fig. 4. Example visualisation vector data for Unity

Algorithm 1. Simulation Loop

1: **for all** particles i **do**
2:     apply forces $v_i \Leftarrow v_i + \Delta t F_{ext}(x_i)$
3:     predict position v_i^*
4: **end for**
5: **for all** particles i **do**
6:     find neighbouring particles $N_i(x_i^*)$
7: **end for**
8: **while** $iter < solverIterations$ **do**
9:     **for all** particles i **do**
10:         calculate λ_i
11:     **end for**
12:     **for all** particles i **do**
13:         calculate Δp_i
14:         perform collusion detection and response
15:     **end for**
16:     **for all** particles i **do**
17:         update position $x_i \Leftarrow X_i^* + \Delta p_i$
18:     **end for**
19: **end while**
20: **for all** particles i **do**
21:     update velocity $v_i \Leftarrow \frac{1}{\Delta t}(x_i^* - x_i)$
22:     apply vorticity confinement and XPSH viscosity
23:     update position $x_i \Leftarrow x_i^*$
24: **end for**

3.4   Boundary Handling

The most challenging problem in particle based technique is boundary management [11]. The problem is how to avoid vector from passing through solid boundaries with using of fluid to object interaction solver. In our implementation, interaction between fluid particles and blood vessel implemented by converting 3D mesh of extracted vessel into soft body object that represent by particle representation. Soft body objects is created by load Wavefront Object(.obj) file directly that originally created by SimVascular. By converting it into particle based representation, the blood vessel are now deformable objects. This particle representation is based from paper With coupling interaction model done by [5], the vessel is enabled performed two interactions with the simulated fluid simulation of blood. In this modal we must note this requires sampling the vessel surface with enough particles to prevent tunnelling effect.

Figure 5 shows initial visualization of blood flood tested on abdominal aorta arteries. The 3D mesh of blood vessels were represented by cloth object that automatically generated by position bases dynamic as it loaded into the program. At that figure, the stream of blood will be represented by vector field technique. Initial representation of rigid object of blood vessel using position-based dynamics shown in Fig. 5. This position-based dynamics implementation based on work done by [17].

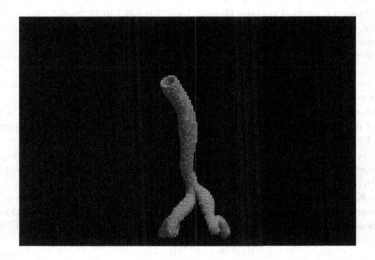

Fig. 5. Representation of solid object of blood vessel with particle-based technique.

4 Discussion and Conclusion

The framework of this paper will contribute to the visualization and also simulation of blood flow in real-time. By using particle based physics to provide opportunity to develop interactive blood flow visualization in vascular tree in easier implementation. The proposed position based dynamics technique is implemented to the interaction of physically blood flow visualization in vascular tree. The process involves several processes: reconstruction of CT images into 3D, boundary management and position based fluid flow solver with integrated coupling solver method for fluid-object interaction. Modelling the geometry of vessel requires us to select region of interest to be used with generated centreline as guided for 3D vascular tree model. Suitable physics based algorithms will introduce help to reduce the computational cost to visualize of blood flow in vascular tree network. However, the result of the research still not be achieved especially assimilation algorithm with measurement data. Future works include development of medical-related simulation system such as pre-surgery evaluation, stent installation simulation and also serious gaming for training purpose.

References

1. Erleben, K., Sporring, J., Dohlmann, H.: OpenTissue - An Open Source Toolkit for Physics-Based Animation (2005)
2. Erleben, K., Sporring, J., Henriksen, K., Dohlman, K.: Physics-Based Animation, Graphics series edn. Charles River Media Inc., Hingham (2005)
3. Etheredge, C., Kunst, E., Sanders, A.: Harnessing the GPU for real-time haptic tissue simulation. J. Comput. Graph. Tech. (JCGT) **2**(2), 28–54 (2013)
4. Foster, N., Metaxas, D.: Realistic animation of liquids. Graph. Models Image Process. **58**(5), 471–483 (1996)
5. Gerszewski, D., Bargteil, A.W.: Physics-based animation of large-scale splashing liquids. ACM Trans. Graph. **32**(6), 1–6 (2013)
6. Hansen, C.D., Johnson, C.R.: The Visualization Handbook. Butterworth-Heinemann, Oxford (2005)
7. de Hoon, N., van Pelt, R., Jalba, A., Vilanova, A.: 4D MRI flow coupled to physics-based fluid simulation for blood-flow visualization. Comput. Graph. Forum **33**(3), 121–130 (2014)
8. Jing, Q., Yim-Pan, C., Wai-Man, P., Choi, K.S., Pheng-Ann, H.: Learning blood management in orthopedic surgery through gameplay. IEEE Comput. Graph. Appl. **30**(2), 45–57 (2010)
9. Kim, K.H., Kang, D., Kang, N., Kim, J.Y., Lee, H.E., Kim, J.K.: Patient-specific coronary artery blood flow simulation using myocardial volume partitioning. In: Medical Imaging 2013: Computer-Aided Diagnosis, vol. 8670, pp. 867019–867019-5. doi:10.1117/12.2007898
10. Kohler, B., Born, S., van Pelt, R.F.P., Hennemuth, A., Preim, U., Preim, B.: A survey of cardiac 4D PC-MRI data processing. Comput. Graph. Forum, n/a–n/a (2016)
11. Kulp, S., Gao, M., Zhang, S., Qian, Z., Voros, S., Metaxas, D., Axel, L.: Practical patient-specific cardiac blood flow simulations using SPH. In: The IEEE International Symposium on Biomedical Imaging (ISBI 2013) (2013)
12. van der Laan, W.J., Green, S., Sainz, M.: Screen space fluid rendering with curvature flow (2009)
13. Lawonn, K., Glaßer, S., Vilanova, A., Preim, B.: Occlusion-free blood flow animation with wall thickness visualization. IEEE Trans. Visual. Comput. Graph. **22**(1), 728–737 (2016)
14. Liu, M.B., Liu, G.R.: Smoothed particle hydrodynamics (SPH): an overview and recent developments. Arch. Comput. Methods Eng. **17**(1), 25–76 (2010)

15. Maciel, A., Halic, T., Lu, Z., Nedel, L.P., De, S.: Using the physX engine for physics-based virtual surgery with force feedback. Int. J. Med. Robot. Comput. Assist. Surg. **5**(3), 341–353 (2009)
16. Macklin, M., Muller, M.: Position based fluids. ACM Trans. Graph. (TOG) **32**(4), 1–12 (2013). Conference SIGGRAPH 2013
17. Macklin, M., Muller, M., Chentanez, N., Kim, T.Y.: Unified particle physics for real-time applications. ACM Trans. Graph. **33**(4), 1–12 (2014)
18. Mokhtar, M.K., Mohamed, F., Zamri, M.N., Sunar, M.S., Chand, S.J.H.: A review on fluid simulation method for blood flow representation. In: Lai, K.W., Octorina Dewi, D.E. (eds.) Medical Imaging Technology. LNB, pp. 129–141. Springer, Singapore (2015). doi:10.1007/978-981-287-540-2_6
19. Muller, M., Schirm, S., Teschner, M.: Interactive blood simulation for virtual surgery based on smoothed particle hydrodynamics. J. Technol. Health Care **12**(1), 25–31 (2004)
20. Nobrega, T.H.C., Carvalho, D.D.B., van Wangenheim, A.: Simplified simulation and visualization of tubular flows with approximate centerline generation. In: 22nd IEEE International Symposium on Computer-Based Medical Systems, CBMS 2009, pp. 1–7 (2009)
21. Pang, W.-M., Qin, J., Chui, Y.-P., Heng, P.-A.: Fast prototyping of virtual reality based surgical simulators with PhysX-enabled GPU. In: Pan, Z., Cheok, A.D., Müller, W., Zhang, X., Wong, K. (eds.) Transactions on Edutainment IV. LNCS, vol. 6250, pp. 176–188. Springer, Heidelberg (2010). doi:10.1007/978-3-642-14484-4_15
22. Pang, W.-M., Qin, J., Chui, Y.-P., Wong, T.-T., Leung, K.-S., Heng, P.-A.: Orthopedics surgery trainer with PPU-accelerated blood and tissue simulation. In: Ayache, N., Ourselin, S., Maeder, A. (eds.) MICCAI 2007 Part II. LNCS, vol. 4792, pp. 842–849. Springer, Heidelberg (2007). doi:10.1007/978-3-540-75759-7_102
23. Preim, B., Oeltze, S.: 3D visualization of vasculature: an overview. In: Linsen, L., Hagen, H., Hamann, B. (eds.) Visualization in Medicine and Life Sciences, pp. 39–59. Springer, Heidelberg (2008). doi:10.1007/978-3-540-72630-2_3
24. van Roy, P.: Understanding blood-flow dynamics new challenges for visualization. Computer **46**(12), 60–67 (2013)
25. Schumann, C., Oeltze, S., Bade, R., Preim, B., Peitgen, H.O.: Model-free surface visualization of vascular trees. In: Proceedings of the 9th Joint Eurographics/IEEE VGTC Conference on Visualization, pp. 283–290. Eurographics Association (2007)
26. Sengupta, P.P., Pedrizzetti, G., Kilner, P.J., Kheradvar, A., Ebbers, T., Tonti, G., Fraser, A.G., Narula, J.: Emerging trends in CV flow visualization. JACC: Cardiovasc. Imaging **5**(3), 305–316 (2012)
27. Tanaka, N., Tanako, T.: Microscopic-scale simulation of blood flow using SPH method. Int. J. Comput. Methods **2**(4), 555–568 (2005)
28. Vilanova, A., Preim, B., Pelt, R., Gasteiger, R., Neugebauer, M., Wischgoll, T.: Visual exploration of simulated and measured blood flow. In: Hansen, C.D., Chen, M., Johnson, C.R., Kaufman, A.E., Hagen, H. (eds.) Scientific Visualization. MV, pp. 305–324. Springer, London (2014). doi:10.1007/978-1-4471-6497-5_25
29. Wang, Y.: Simulation of blood flow and contrast medium propagation for a vascular interventional radiology simulator. Ph.D. thesis (2009)
30. West, C.: Megaflow. http://www.west-racing.com/mf/?page_id=5892

A Debugging Framework for Parallel Discrete Event Simulation Application

Tianlin Li[1(✉)], Yuliang Zhao[2], Sirui Bao[1], and Yiping Yao[1]

[1] College of Information System and Management,
National University of Defense Technology, 137 Yanwachi,
Changsha, China
ltl@mail.ustc.edu.cn, {baosirui15,ypyao}@nudt.edu.cn
[2] AllSim Technology Inc., 658 LuGu Road, Changsha, China
zhaoyuliangyx@163.com

Abstract. Debugging is essential in parallel discrete event simulation (PDES) application development, directly determining the correctness of simulation application and the development efficiency. However, programmers prefer to add some debugging code into application code to speed up debugging. Besides, lots of debugging data generated from simulation execution need to be analyzed manually, resulting in debugging time-consuming and laborious. This paper proposes a debugging framework for PDES application named SUPE-Debug, which is built on the PDES engine SUPE. It provides automatic debugging code generation and debugging data visualization analysis function. Experimental results show that SUPE-Debug can automatically insert debugging code into the existing application code and provide a more intuitional way to display the debugging data for programmers to analyze. It is helpful for searching and locating errors, accelerating debugging progress and improving application development efficiency.

Keywords: PDES · Debugging code generation · Debugging data visualization

1 Introduction

Parallel discrete event simulation [1] is widely used to complex systems simulation, so PDES applications are usually very complex, consisting of many simulation entities and complex models. These conditions exacerbate the difficulty of application debugging, resulting in that debugging costs occupy a large part of application development [2]. In addition, simulation applications usually contain a large number of complex models. Since model developers' programming capabilities are uneven, resulting in that the overall quality of application code is poor and debugging becomes more challenging. To ensure the reliability of simulation application, it is necessary to ensure the correctness of simulation object state variable values generated from simulation execution, which requires artificial analysis to judge whether errors happen or not.

When programmers use the existing parallel discrete event simulation platform to develop simulation applications, they usually depends on the mature debugging tools to

M.S. Mohamed Ali et al. (Eds.): AsiaSim 2017, Part II, CCIS 752, pp. 656–665, 2017.
DOI: 10.1007/978-981-10-6502-6_56

debug, such as C/C++ language debugging tool in Microsoft Visual Studio, GDB in Linux and Java language debugging tool in JDK. These tools are very powerful, but complex to use. Besides, their data display function is not very intuitive. During actual debugging process, programmers usually prefer to add some debugging code into the application code facilitating debugging. The information generated from debugging code during application execution can be helpful for programmers to detect and locate errors. In view of this phenomenon, it is very meaningful to realize the automatic generation of debugging code. Another troublesome problem is debugging data visualization analysis, simulation object state variables will produce large amount of data during simulation execution. Through data analysis, programmers can find out whether the application occur errors. But analyzing such a lot of data manually will cost a lot and the efficiency is low. If these data can be processed and displayed in a more intuitional way automatically, it will greatly reduce the cost of data analysis and burden of programmers. Therefore, it is of great practical value to carry out automatic debugging code generation and debugging data visualization analysis technologies for PDES applications, aimed at accelerating debugging progress and improving application development efficiency.

The main contribution of this paper is that it proposed a debugging framework named SUPE-Debug for PDES application debugging, which is built on the PDES development engine SUPE. SUPE-Debug provides automatic debugging code generation and debugging data visualization analysis functions, aimed at improving application debugging efficiency. The framework mainly contains two modules, debugging code generator and debugging data visualization module. For simulation applications developed with SUPE engine, the framework can generate debugging code and insert them into application code files automatically. Besides, simulation object state variables will generate large amount of debugging data when executing simulation application, SUPE-Debug can process and display the debugging data in a more intuitional way, such as visualization and graphical display, to speed up detecting and locating errors. In addition, SUPE-Debug can also be used to analyze dynamic program slices and values of simulation object state variables, so the execution path and value change process of variables will be displayed explicitly for programmers to debug.

The remainder of this paper is organized as follows. Section 2 describes the background and related work. The third section presents the architecture and implementation mechanisms of SUPE-Debug. Section 4 is an experimental validation of the framework. In the fifth section we conclude the paper work.

2 Background and Related Work

There are some well-known parallel discrete simulation development platforms, such as SPEEDES [3, 4], GTW [5, 6], SUPE [7]. SPEEDES and SUPE both are parallel simulation development frameworks based on C++ language, while GTW is based on C language. So program debugging in these simulation platforms depends on existing C/C++ language debugging tools, like debugging tools in Visual Studio and GDB. Although these debugging tools are powerful, they are not easy to use and highly depend on programmers' capabilities. During actual debugging, programmers are more willing to add some code into the application code to facilitate debugging. Another question is that simulation state variables will generate large volume of data during simulation application execution. It is much difficult to find out errors from the massive data. What's worse, the existing data analysis tools cannot be directly used to process and analyze these data, because of complexity. All the above conditions have brought great challenges to debugging, resulting in PDES application debugging time-consuming and laborious.

The core idea of the program slices [8] is to decompose the program according to the variable value dependencies in the program. For a given tuple of variable and statement (v, s), calculating out all the statements in the program that may affect the value of variable v at statement s, then the achieved statements set is called slices. Program slices can be divided into static program slices and dynamic program slices. Static program slices are obtained by static analysis of the value dependencies among variables in the program code, containing all code statements which will have impact on the value of a specific variable. Dynamic program slices [9] refers to the program statements set which affect the value of the variable in actual program execution. The effect of static program slices on variables is consistent with the effect of the original program, but dynamic slices refer to the actual value dependencies of variables in the actual program execution. Therefore, the dynamic program slices can reflect the actual execution process of variables, helpful for variable debugging. According to the definition of slices, dynamic program slices consist of a series of static program slices subsets. Therefore, to obtain the dynamic program slices, we should obtain static program slices first.

Zeller proposed the incremental debugging [10], which has an important influence in the field of automatic debugging. The core idea is to compare the failing test cases with successful test cases to obtain difference between them, finding out the causes of faults. Automated incremental debugging has its technical characteristics, but drawbacks are obvious. Operating efficiency is low, and test cases are difficult to construct for complex PDES applications.

3   SUPE-Debug

SUPE-Debug mainly contains two modules, Debugging Code Generator and Debugging Data Visualization. By traversing simulation object code files and model header files, Debugging Code Generator can automatically insert debugging code into the appropriate location in simulation object code files to generate new simulation object code files. The inserted debugging code can help programmers to locate program statements where error occurs, obtain simulation object state variable values and dynamic program slices and write them into files which are called debugging data files. Therefore, when running the new simulation object code files on SUPE engine, debugging data files are generated, including variable value files and dynamic program slices files. Analyzing these data files manually will cost a lot. Debugging Data Visualization module is used to process these files and display them in an intuitive way such as graphical display. In addition, this module can display the dynamic program slices and values of simulation object state variables alternately, so the execution path and value change process of variables can be reconstructed explicitly. It becomes easy and comfortable for programmers to analyze debugging data files, finding out whether any errors occur and locating the corresponding program statements. Figure 1 illustrates the architecture of SUPE-Debug.

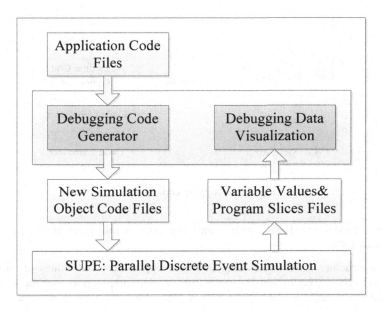

Fig. 1. SUPE-Debug architecture

3.1 Debugging Code Generator

Debugging Code Generator consists of two parts, a code analyzer and a code generator. The code analyzer contains a lexical analyzer and a parser, used to traverse simulation application code files to obtain code information automatically. The code generator contains code generation rules and an automatic code generator. According to the code information and code generation rules, Automatic code generator will generate appropriate debugging code and inserted them into the simulation application object code files, generating new simulation object code files.

In order to realize automatic generation of debugging code, it is necessary to realize automatic analysis and information extraction of application code, including simulation object code files and model header files. The automatic analysis and information extraction of the code is done by the code analyzer, and the information obtained will provide basis for debugging code generation.

The lexical analyzer is a lightweight C++ language lexical analyzer, because PDES applications based on SUPE are developed in C++ language. The parser receives results obtained by the lexical analyzer, recognizing the grammar and type of code statements. The main functions of the parser are to locate and extract all data structures in the application, locate model call statements and extract model information, obtain the declaration of state variables and their corresponding static program slices (Fig. 2).

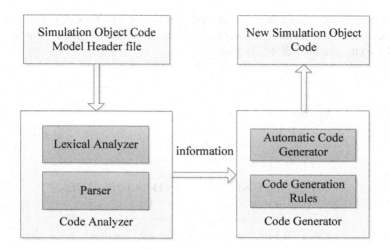

Fig. 2. Debugging code generator

As described above, the parser is mainly interested in four types of code statements. They are as follows:

(1) Data structure declaration code: In PDES application, the values of simulation object state variables usually come from model computation, and the simulation results are derived from these values. Therefore, the values of state variables should be recorded and stored. Data structure information can be used to generate debugging code which will write state variable values into files. So it is necessary to obtain the detail information of data structure declaration automatically.

(2) Simulation object state variables declaration code: In order to record state variable values, the names and data types of variables should be obtained first. Besides, state variable names are necessary to locate static program slices.

(3) State variables static program slices: Since dynamic program slices consist of a series of static program slices subsets, to obtain dynamic program slices, static program slices should be obtained first. By inserting some debugging code below static program slices, dynamic slices can be obtained while program executing. At this moment, the debugging code is used to write static slices into files.

(4) Model call interface code: In simulation application, variable values are usually derived from model computation. Besides, most of errors come from model code. Hence, model call interface code can point out the insertion position for debugging code.

When the parser scans to these four kinds of code, it will extract key information and pass the information to Code Generator. Then Code Generator generates corresponding debugging code according to the information and code generation rules, and inserts the generated code into application code to generate new simulation application code files.

Code Generator contains two parts, code generation rules and automatic code generator. Code generation rules determine what debugging code should be generated and where to insert them. Automatic code generator is responsible for generating debugging code and inserting them into application code files. Code generation rules can be divided into the following 2 kinds:

(1) For model interface code, the debugging code which can write state variable values into files should be generated and inserted just below the model interface code statements, because variable values will be updated after model execution. In addition, two additional lines of code statement can be inserted before and after model interface code statement, which are used to output some execution information log. When model runs crash, execution information log can help programmers locate which model occur errors as soon as possible.

(2) For each code statement of variable static program slices, a line of debugging code will be inserted just below it, like fprintf() function in C++ language, used to write the code statement into files. So when a code statement in static program slices participates in execution, the debugging code below it will write this code statement into files. So the dynamic program slices of each variable will be obtained.

When all simulation object code files are traversed and inserted with debug code, many debugging data files will be generated during application execution. Some of them are state variable value files, the rest of them are dynamic program slices files. In short, one state variable corresponds to a value file and a dynamic program slices file. The simulation application corresponds to one log file recording execution information.

3.2   Debugging Data Visualization

After inserted with debugging code, PDES application will generate large amount of state variable value files and program slices files. These data files are essential for application debugging. Considering the characteristics of PDES application, the contents of these files are usually complex, and existing data analysis tools cannot be directly used to process and analyze these files. It will cost a lot when just relying on manual analysis to analyze these files. In view of this problem, it is necessary to research debugging data visualization technology for PDES application, in other words a more intuitive data analysis tool will reduce the burden of programmers and speed up debugging progress. Debugging data visualization should contain the following functions:

The first function of debugging data analysis is data classification and quick search, making sure that programmers can quickly find the data which they are interested in. The most intuitive way is to classify the debugging data files according to their corresponding variables and simulation objects.

The second function is the graphical display of debugging data. For example, when a programmer is interested in an attribute of state variables, data analysis tool can draw a curve graph of the attribute values versus simulation time automatically. Graphical display is rather intuitive for programmers to analyze data.

The third function is debugging function. When the value of a variable is erroneous, programmers need to find out the code statements which result in the error. By displaying the state variable dynamic program slices and values alternately in simulation time order, programmers can clearly obtain the variable execution path and value change process. So it becomes rather easy to locate the wrong code statements (Fig. 3).

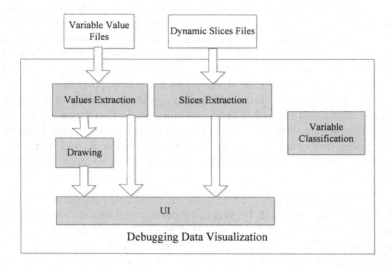

Fig. 3. Debugging data visualization

SUPE-Debug contains a debugging data visualization module which has the three debugging data analysis functions described above. This module mainly contains five sub-modules: value extraction module, program slices extraction module, drawing module, variable classification module and UI module. Value extraction and program slices extraction module are used to extract variable values and program slices from debugging data files and submit them to UI to display. Drawing module is used to draw a curve graph for the selected variable attribute values versus simulation time. The variable classification module can classify state variables automatically according to the simulation object which they belong to. The UI is used to display variable values, program slices and attribute value curve graph.

4   Validation

To validate the feasibility of SUPE-Debug, a small PDES application called souse was designed based on SUPE engine to test SUPE-Debug. The application described that a souse walked in the X-Y coordinate system, the probability of walking in four directions are all 0.25. The initial position is (0, 0), every 2S taking a step and the length of each step is 1. The total simulation time is 100 s. The simulation object contains a motion model used to calculate the next position according to current position. Figure 4 shows the comparison between origin simulation object code and new simulation object code inserted with debugging code. It shows that SUPE-Debug can generate specified debugging code. Figure 5 shows that debugging data visualization module can display dynamic program slices and values of selected state variable alternately, so the execution path and value changes can be reflected explicitly. Figure 6 demonstrates the curve graph of variable values versus simulation time.

```
void S_Souse::Init() {
        char stmp[100];
        PModel = new Model();
        pos = new position;
        pos->time = 0.0;
        pos->x = 0;
        pos->y = 0;
        PModel->Initialize(pos);
        SCHEDULE_StepEvent(0.0, SpGetObjHandle());
}
void S_Souse::Step() {
        double curtime = SpGetSimTime();
        PModel->ModelProcess(curtime);
        PModel->GetOutputData(pos);
        pos->time = SpGetSimTime();
        SCHEDULE_StepEvent( SpGetSimTime()+2.0,0);
}
```

```
void S_Souse::Init() {
        Slice = fopen("S_SouseCutLog.txt","w");
        m_fpw_pos = fopen("S_Souse_pos_0.txt", "w");
        ShowNameofStructposition(m_fpw_pos,&temp_pos);
        PModel = new Model();
        ...
        PModel->Initialize(pos);
        PrintStructposition(m_fpw_pos, pos);
        fprintf(S_SouseCutLog,"PModel->Initialize(pos);\n");
        SCHEDULE_StepEvent(0.0, SpGetObjHandle());
}
void S_Souse::Step() {
        ...
        PModel->GetOutputData(pos);
        PrintStructposition(m_fpw_pos, pos);
        fprintf(Slice,"PModel->GetOutputData(pos);\n");
        SCHEDULE_StepEvent( SpGetSimTime()+2.0, 0);
}

void S_Souse::PrintStructposition(FILE *fpw,position *p){
        fprintf(fpw, "%f %d %d\n" , p->time,p->x, p->y);
}
```

Fig. 4. Before and after debugging code generation

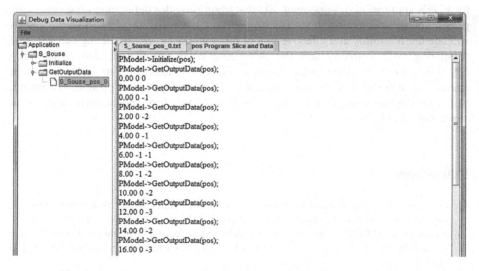

Fig. 5. Variable values and dynamic program slices displayed alternately

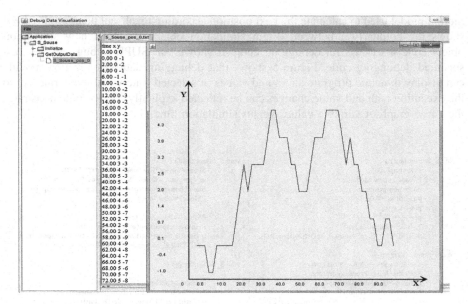

Fig. 6. Graphical display for variable attribute values versus time

5 Conclusion

In order to reduce programmers' burden of inserting debugging code into simulation application code and analyzing debugging data manually, this paper proposes a debugging framework named SUPE-Debug, which is built on the PDES engine SUPE for PDES application development. SUPE-Debug provides debugging code automatic generation and debugging data visualization analysis functions. Experimental results validate the feasibility and effectiveness of this framework. SUPE-Debug can generate debugging code correctly and the debugging code can play a role in auxiliary debugging. Besides, SUPE-Debug provides a more intuitional way to analyze the large amount of debugging data files generated from application execution. Therefore, SUPE-Debug can effectively accelerate debugging progress and improve application development efficiency.

References

1. Fujimoto, R.M.: Parallel and Distributed Simulation Systems. Wiley, Hoboken (2000)
2. Myers, G.J.: The Art of Software Testing, pp. 12–15. Wiley, New York (1979)
3. Steinman, J.: SPEEDES: synchronous parallel environment for emulation and discrete event simulation. In: Proceedings of Advances in Parallel and Distributed Simulation, pp. 95–103 (1991)
4. Chris, B., Robert, M., Steinman, J., Jennifer, W.: SPEEDES: a brief overview. In: Proceedings of SPIE, Enabling Technologies for Simulation Science V, pp. 190–201 (2001)

5. Perumalla, K.S., Fujimoto, R.M.: GTW++: an object oriented interface in C++ to the Georgia tech time warp system. Georgia Institute of Technology (1996)
6. Fujimoto, R.M., Das, S.R., Panesar, K.S.: Georgia tech time warp programmer's manual. Technical report, College of Computing, Georgia Institute of Technology, Atlanta, GA, July 1994
7. Yao, Y., Zhang, Y.: Solution for analytic simulation based on parallel processing. J. Syst. Simul. **20**(24), 6617–6621 (2008)
8. Weiser, M.: Program slicing. In: Proceedings of the 5th International Conference on Software Engineering, pp. 439–449 (1981)
9. Agrawal, H., Horgan, J.R.: Dynamic program slicing. In: Proceedings of the ACM SIGPLAN 1990 Conference on Programming Language Design and Implementation (PLDI 1990), pp. 246–256. ACM, New York (1990)
10. Zeller, A.: Why Programs Fail-A Guide to Systematic Debugging. Morgan Kaufmann Publishers, Burlington (2005)

A Hybrid Multiprocessor Scheduling Approach for Weakly Hard Real-Time Tasks

Habibah Ismail[(✉)] and Dayang N.A. Jawawi

Department of Software Engineering, Faculty of Computing,
Universiti Teknologi Malaysia, Johor, Malaysia
habibahisma@gmail.com, dayang@utm.my

Abstract. There are two major strategies to schedule real-time tasks in multi-processor systems; partitioning and global scheduling. The partitioning approach has acceptable overhead but cannot guarantee to be optimal. The global approach can provide this guarantee but it has considerable overhead. Thus, a multiprocessor real-time scheduling approach for weakly hard real-time tasks is proposed that employs hybrid scheduling. Studies have shown that current multiprocessor scheduling of weakly hard real-time tasks used imprecise computation model based on iterative algorithms. This algorithm decomposed into two parts; mandatory and optional, unfortunately, the result analysis is precise only if its mandatory and optional parts are both executed. Even, the use of hierarchical scheduling algorithm, such as two-level scheduling under PFair algorithm may cause high overhead due to frequent preemptions and migrations. In this paper, an alternative scheduling approach will be proposed, which is, its combines elements of the two well-known multiprocessor scheduling approaches. It aims to employs benefits and advantages of the partitioning and global scheduling. Accordingly, the proposed hybrid multiprocessor real-time scheduling is use the best algorithm of each of partitioning and global approaches, R-BOUND-MP-NFRNS and RM-US $(m/3m-2)$ with multiprocessor response time test. Schedulability experiments and simulation results using Matlab show the proposed hybrid multiprocessor scheduling approach to be effective for weakly hard real-time tasks.

Keywords: Hybrid scheduling approach · Multiprocessor real-time systems · Weakly hard real-time tasks · Partitioning and global scheduling

1 Introduction

The majority of real-time systems are not made up of hard tasks only, but also coexists with soft tasks. In this paper, the weakly hard real-time tasks whereas the occasional deadline misses are acceptable and a violation of the complete deadline meet does not cause significant failures, are considered. For weakly hard real-time tasks, the objective of scheduling process is to guarantee the temporal constraints of the hard ones will be always satisfied and to specify the number of deadlines missed of the soft ones precisely [1].

© Springer Nature Singapore Pte Ltd. 2017
M.S. Mohamed Ali et al. (Eds.): AsiaSim 2017, Part II, CCIS 752, pp. 666–678, 2017.
DOI: 10.1007/978-981-10-6502-6_57

Thus, schedulability analysis is used to determine whether there exists a schedule where the tasks can missed their deadlines by a bounded value when scheduled according to the adopted scheduling algorithm.

In multiprocessor, schedulability analysis is more challenges than uniprocessor because it consists of more than one processor in the system. Also, multiprocessor scheduling is not a simple extension of uniprocessor scheduling because its need some extensions for the techniques used for solving scheduling problem. There are two types of multiprocessor scheduling, *partitioning* and *global* scheduling approaches [2].

For partitioned scheduling, it start by partitioning tasks among processors and no migration is permitted on different processors. Partitioning multiprocessor real-time scheduling approach is simpler and easier to implement, and has an acceptable overhead for the underlying multiprocessor system but it cannot guarantee to provide an optimal schedule. The reason is that, due to its static task assignment and disability of tasks migration. Besides, the partitioning approach simplifies the multiprocessor real-time scheduling problem to the uniprocessor ones (in example, using the optimal uniprocessor real-time scheduling algorithms such as Rate Monotonic Algorithm (RMA) or Earliest Deadline First (EDF)).

While, for global scheduling, tasks migration on different processors during execution are permitted. In global approach, optimality of the scheduling via employing task migration can be expected. However, the most important deficit of the global multiprocessor real-time scheduling approach is its considerable overhead for the underlying system.

To handle these deficits of two existing approaches, a hybrid multiprocessor real-time scheduling approach is proposed by combine's elements of both partitioning and global scheduling approaches. The benefit from partitioning approach is, it has minimum overhead due to the tasks must be allocate to a specific processor. Meanwhile, the advantage from global approach is, it have optimal scheduling due to the migration capability. Many approaches have been proposed to schedule weakly hard real-time tasks for uniprocessor, there has been considerably less work on multiprocessor systems. Therefore, an alternative scheduling approach is presented in this paper to overcome the drawbacks of the existing algorithms.

The objective of the proposed hybrid scheduling approach is to achieve optimal schedulability by finding an optimal assignment of tasks to processor as well as have low overhead by limit the number of task migrations. Due to weakly hard real-time allow system not having to meet every deadline as long as lost deadline are precisely bounded, hence to satisfy the deadline satisfaction ratio as much as possible is include in our scheduling goals.

This paper is organized as follows. In Sect. 2, the related previous work are given. In Sect. 3, the proposed hybrid scheduling approach is presented. The experimental results with case study are given in Sect. 4. The experimental performance for another case study is presented in Sect. 5. Finally, our work of this paper is summarized and discussed as conclusions in the last section including the remaining an ongoing work.

2 Related Work

Research efforts on scheduling weakly hard real-time tasks on multiprocessor are relatively promising area of research. A complete theory of weakly hard real-time scheduling for multiprocessor systems is still to come.

To our knowledge, weakly hard real-time systems on multiprocessor was first considered by Wu and Jin [3]. They proposed the classical weakly hard real-time scheduling algorithms, namely Distance Based Priority (DBP) to apply into multi-processor applications, called Multiprocessor Distance Based Priority (MPDBPs) to guarantee QoS of both hard real-time tasks and multimedia streams even under overload conditions. In fact, the DBP algorithm originally was introduced by Hamdaoui and Ramanathan on uniprocessor system [4]. Another work is done by Kong and Cho [5] wherein they design new dynamic scheduling algorithm known as the Guaranteed Multiprocessor Real-Time Scheduling (GMRTS-MK) algorithm for (m,k)-firm constrained tasks on homogenous multiprocessors. Later, the same authors, Kong and Cho [6] propose an Energy-constrained Multiprocessor Real-Time Scheduling (EMRTS-MK) algorithms for weakly hard real-time for (m,k)-firm deadline constrained tasks running on multiprocessor.

Several hybrid scheduling approaches have been proposed, however all these previous works are focused on hard and soft real-time tasks. Practically, not much attention has been devoted to multiprocessor weakly hard real-time scheduling. Calandrino et al. [7] proposed a hybrid approach, called H-EDF for scheduling real-time tasks on large-scale multicore platforms with hierarchical shared caches. Shin et al. [8] develop techniques to support such cluster-based scheduling algorithms, and also consider properties that minimize processor utilization of individual clusters towards achieving improved utilization bounds. Afterwards, Tan et al. [9] proposed a hybrid scheduling method uses a two level scheduling scheme for real-time systems on the homogeneous multicore architecture. Safaei et al. [10] proposed the hybrid approach, named PFGN to satisfy two major goals of the combinations; optimality and lightweightness. Sanati and Cheng in [11] propose a novel semi-partitioning approach with an online choice of two approximation algorithms, Greedy and Load-Balancing, to schedule periodic soft real-time tasks in homogeneous multiprocessor systems with the objective to enhance the QoS by minimizing the deadline misses.

3 The Proposed Hybrid Scheduling Approach

Recently, the scheduling approach for the periodic task set on multiprocessor system is developed by extending the existing approach presented for uniprocessor system.

Our proposed approach use the partitioning as the base of the combination while using the global capabilities to complete it and improve system performance. Accordingly, base of the hybrid multiprocessor real-time scheduling approach is the partitioning approach, in which it has the minimum overhead and whenever needed, the global approach can be used to improve system utilization and to be near optimal via task migration in order to make use of processors empty capacity for execution of tasks.

Accordingly, the best algorithm of each of the partitioning and global approaches, named R-BOUND-MP-NFRNS and RM-US (m/3m−2) with multiprocessor response time test are employed. The reason for the need of response time calculations is the fact that weakly hard real-time tasks tolerates a bounded and predictable number of deadline misses using μ-pattern [1]. This pattern is applied to the scheduling approaches in order to make the hybrid multiprocessor scheduling approach resilient with exceptions. The proposed hybrid multiprocessor real-time scheduling approach consists of the following steps:

1. Partitioning approach phase:
    i. In order to prevent mixing task priorities between different task types, and to make it much easier to understand and use task sets in the system, highest priority is always set to hard tasks and then soft tasks would have the lowest priority.
    ii. All of the tasks in the task system are assigned and bound to the specific processors using the bin-packing heuristic, named next-fit.
    iii. Each processor schedules the tasks waiting in its waiting queue with the RMA policy. RMA priority assignment is optimal for weakly hard real-time tasks.
    iv. These will be continued until the situation in which no more task can be assigned to any of the processors.
    v. A task set was claimed schedulable under R-BOUND-MP-NFRNS if it could be successfully partitioned using the heuristic.
    vi. We determine whether a set of tasks allocated to a processor is schedulable given a particular fixed priority assignment by checking whether the worst case response time for each task is less than or equal to its relative deadline.
    vii. If the task does not satisfies the schedulability condition in the worst case, the number of deadline missed and met are then checking by the weakly hard constraint and μ-pattern (a met deadline is denoted by a 1 and a missed by 0) due to the concept of weakly hard real-time tasks is allow tasks to miss their deadlines but must be in a bounded and predictable way.

2. Global approach phase:
    i. The remained tasks in the task system are considered as tasks that must be scheduled on set of processors using global Rate Monotonic with Utilization Separation (RM-US), one of optimal scheduling algorithms for static priority global scheduling.
    ii. If the task set is schedulable, then calculate the measurement parameters (in example, deadline satisfaction ratio) to evaluate the performance of experiment.

3.1   R-BOUND-MP-NFRNS

All real-time tasks partitioning approach are based on heuristics of bin packing problems. Each task having its own dedicated processor, due to the partition method divides tasks into partitions. In order to determine a given task can be allocate to a given processor or not, we use the bin-packing heuristics. The following equation is to use as knowledge in schedulability test:

$$\sum_{i=1}^{n_p} \frac{C_i}{T_i} \leq B(r_p, n_p) \tag{1}$$

This condition uses information of the periods of the task set to achieve a high utilization. p is defined by the number of task assigned to processor p which denote by n_p. The fraction between the maximum and the minimum period among the tasks assigned to processor p is denoted by r_p. r denotes the set of all n tasks and it holds that $\forall_p : 1 \leq r_p < 3$. Let:

$$B(r_p, n_p) = np(r_p^{1/n_p} - 1) + 2/r_p - 1 \tag{2}$$

The algorithm R-BOUND-MP-NFRNS (R-BOUND-MP with next-fit-ring noscaling) by Andersson [12] is used to partition the scheduling algorithm which derives from the multiprocessor scheduling algorithm, R-BOUND-MP (combined R-BOUND with a first-fit-bin packing algorithm), that exploits R-BOUND [13]. R-BOUND is a uniprocessor scheduling algorithm for partitioned scheduling. The benefit of the R-BOUND is, it takes not only the number of tasks but also the relationship among periods into consideration. Meanwhile, next-fit bin-packing heuristic is a simple approach to distribute tasks among processors.

3.2 RM-US (m/3m−2)

For static priority multiprocessor scheduling with a periodic task set $\{T_1, T_2, T_3, \ldots, T_N\}$, where each task's deadline is equal to its period, to be allow to migrate and schedulable on m processors with RM algorithm, it need to satisfy the following properties [14]:

$$\sum_{i=1}^{N} \frac{C_i}{T_i} \leq \frac{m2}{3m - 2} \tag{3}$$

and,

$$\frac{C_i}{T_i} \leq \frac{m}{3m - 2}, \text{ for } 1 \leq i \leq N \tag{4}$$

If all individuals are less than $\frac{m}{3m-2}$ and the total utilizations are less than $\frac{m2}{3m-2}$, then the task set is schedulable and can migrate on m processors using global RM.

3.3 Multiprocessor Response Time Analysis (RTA)

Schedulability analysis of fixed priority scheduled systems can be performed by calculating the worst-case response time of the involved processes. Response time analysis (RTA) is an effective technique that has been widely used to derive schedulability tests and properties for various different models of task systems scheduled on uniprocessor [15]. The advantage of using scheduling bounds is that it does not require as much calculations. Response time analysis for multiprocessors uses the same principle as the uniprocessor case, where the response time, R_i for a task τ_i consists of [16]:

C_i The task's uninterrupted execution time (WCET)
I_i The interference from higher-priority tasks

$$R_i = C_i + I_i \tag{5}$$

However, the difference is that the calculation of interference has to account for the fact that higher-priority tasks can execute in parallel on the processors. The worst case interference term is:

$$I_i = \frac{1}{m} \sum_{\forall j \in hp(i)} \left(\left\lceil \frac{R_i}{T_j} \right\rceil . C_j + C_j \right) \tag{6}$$

Where $hp(i)$ is the set of tasks with higher priority than τ_i. The worst case response time for a task τ_i, is thus:

$$R_i = C_i + \frac{1}{m} \sum_{\forall j \in hp(i)} \left(\left\lceil \frac{R_i}{T_j} \right\rceil . C_j + C_j \right) \tag{7}$$

The system is deemed schedulable if the calculated response time for each process is less than its corresponding deadline. Here is a sufficient condition for static priority scheduling on multiprocessors:

$$\forall_i : R_i \leq D_i \tag{8}$$

4   Experimental Results

Selecting appropriate approaches for scheduling activities is one of the most important considerations in the design of a real-time system. In this approach, the R-BOUND-MP-NFRNS algorithm is used for allocating the tasks to each of the processors and the RM-US (m/3m−2) as real-time scheduling algorithm for each of the processors. Multiprocessor RTA must be calculate in order to decide whether a task will meet its deadline or not.

Selected case study namely Videophone application was originally derived from Shin et al. [17] to generate task sets are given as input for our experiment. The cases analysed by Bernat et al. [1] show that soft real-time systems are not that soft as it is generally required to specify upper bounds on the number and pattern of deadlines missed during a period of time.

As seen in the Table 1, *VSELP speech encoding* has the highest priority because the task priority was decreasing in each processor. Consider four tasks with four parameters in table below, where these tasks needed to be scheduled using 2 processors with

R-BOUND-MP-NFRNS. Each task τ_i is characterised by a triple $\{C_i, D_i, T_i\}$. The worst case execution time C_i includes various overheads. The deadline D_i is the time within of task execution must complete with respect to the beginning of the period. The deadlines are assumed to be equal of period. The period T_i is the minimum time interval between two successive invocations of τ_i. The utilization bound u_i, of task τ_i, is given by C_i/T_i.

Furthermore, the algorithm is responsible to sort the task periods in ascending order. On this analysis, processor 1 is the current one with the tasks has been assigned in order. Moreover, *VSELP speech encoding* has been selected and assigned into processor 1. Afterwards, *VSELP speech decoding* has been tried to assign into processor 1, which is successful due to the $T_2/T_1 = 1.0$ and $n_1 = 2$ gives the utilization sum for these two tasks is 0.8. The task named *MPEG-4 video encoding* is attempted to be assigned into Processor 1 where it fails due to the max (T_1,T_2,T_3)/min $(T_1,T_2,T_3) = 1.65$ and $n_2 = 3$ the utilization sum of these three tasks is 1.4 which resulting the task is assigned into processor 2. Next, processor 2 is identified as the current processor. Afterwards, the processor 2 has been assigned with task named *MPEG-4 video decoding* which the task assign is success due to the $T_4/T_3 = 1.0$ and $n_2 = 2$ gives the utilization sum of the tasks is 1.1.

The experimental results from Table 1 are as illustrated in Fig. 1 as the timing diagram of partition each of the tasks to each of the processors based on scheduling algorithm.

Table 1. Task parameters of the task set and processors.

Task	T_i	C_i	U_i	P_i
VSELP speech encoding (T_1)	40	20	0.5	1
VSELP speech decoding (T_2)	40	10	0.3	1
MPEG-4 video encoding (T_3)	66	40	0.6	2
MPEG-4 video decoding (T_4)	66	30	0.5	2

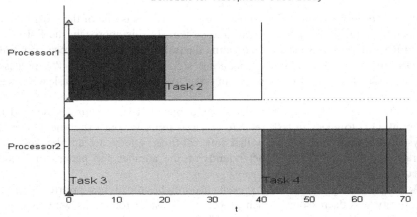

Fig. 1. Timing diagram for videophone application case study using R-BOUND-MP-NFRNS.

From the figure, the reader should realize that Task 4 unsuccessfully schedule to a dedicated processor. In order to make that task schedulable and optimal at the same time without risking deadline misses, thus the remained task must be allocated to empty processor. The worst case response time for that task must be calculate in order to ensure the task will pass the condition test.

From worst case response time test as depicted in Table 2, the results show that the response time, R_i for task *video decoding* (Task 4) is greater than its deadline. Eventhough it does not meet its deadline in the worst case, but by applying the weakly hard concept, the unschedulable tasks sets, in fact be schedulable with an acceptable bound of deadline misses using the weakly hard constraint and μ-pattern.

Table 2. Task set of videophone application.

Task	T_i	C_i	R_i	h_i	a_i
VSELP speech encoding (T_1)	40	20	20	40	1
VSELP speech decoding (T_2)	40	10	28	40	1
MPEG-4 video encoding (T_3)	66	40	39	1320	20
MPEG-4 video decoding (T_4)	66	30	90	1320	20

As can be seen from the result in Table 2, by using hyperperiod analysis, even though task *video decoding* (Task 4) missed its deadline in the worst case, the number of missed deadlines can be specified for that task and the response times for invocation of a task in the hyperperiod are bounded and predictable.

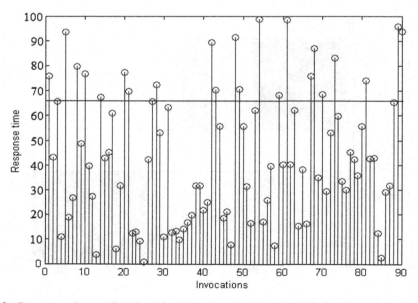

Fig. 2. Response times of task *video decoding* having $D_4 = 66$ for invocations in the hyperperiod.

Table 3. The exact distribution of the task video decoding.

Task video decoding	
Invocations	μ-pattern
1–30:	01010 11010 11101 11110 01111 10011
31–60:	11111 11111 10011 11001 11101 11101
61–90:	01111 10010 11011 11111 01111 11100

As shown in the parameters, the higher order period or the hyperperiod, h_i consist the number of invocations of a task in the hyperperiod at level i, $a_i = h_i/r_i$ [1]. The least common multiple (LCM) tool is using in order to get values of the hyperperiod [1]:

$$h_i = lcm\{Tj|\tau_i \in hep(\tau_i)\} \tag{9}$$

The Fig. 2 shows the worst case response time at each invocation within the hyperperiod at priority level 4. Each vertical line represents the worst case response time of the task. The deadline of the task is $D_4 = 66$. The hyperperiod $h_4 = 1320$. This means that the task is invoked $\alpha_4 = 90$ times within its hyperperiod at level 4.

The following Table 3 shows the exact distribution of the missed and met deadlines for invocations 1 to 90 of task *video decoding* (Task 4). The pattern is repeated cyclically every α_4 invocations. Checking Task 4's weakly hard constraint $\binom{2}{5}$ shows that it is satisfied, despite the miss.

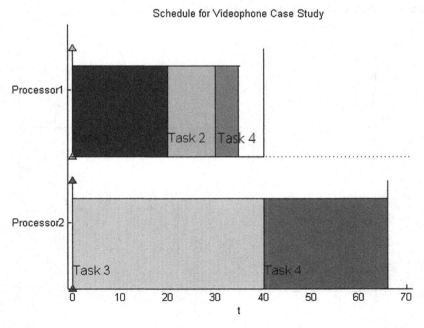

Fig. 3. Timing diagram for videophone application case study using the proposed hybrid scheduling approach.

Later, the unassigned task with 4 time units still can migrate from processor 2 to processor 1, scheduled with RM-US (m/3m−2). Figure 3 illustrates the timing diagram of videophone case study after scheduled using the proposed hybrid scheduling approach.

5   Performance Evaluation

Performance evaluation is one of the most important stages for designing and analyzing real-time systems. In this section, we give the Inertial Navigation System (INS) case study based on the one described by Borger [18] as benchmark. This system does not modelled as soft nor hard, but somewhere in between called weakly hard. This case study contains hard and soft functionalities. Thus, loosening constraints for certain tasks is acceptable. All parameters of tasks of INS system are listed in Table 4.

Table 4. Task set of INS case study.

Task	T_i	C_i	U_i	P_i	R_i	h_i	a_i
Attitude updater (T_1)	10	1	0.1	1	1	10	1
Velocity updater (T_2)	15	4	0.3	1	3	30	2
Attitude sender (T_3)	20	10	0.5	2	12	60	3
Navigation sender (T_4)	50	20	0.4	2	28	300	6
Status display (T_5)	50	25	0.5	1	50	300	6
Position updater (T_6)	60	32	0.5	1	75	300	5

In Fig. 4, we shows a timing diagram that task *Position Updater* (Task 6) preempt and migrate from Processor 1 to processor 2 by 2 time units in order to ensure a task set schedulable. The reference for the diagram as depicted in Fig. 5.

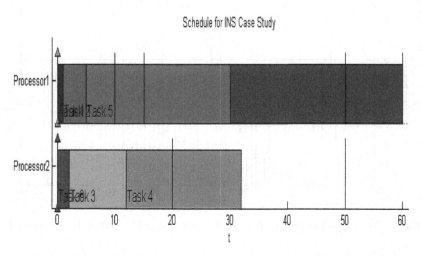

Fig. 4. Timing diagram for INS case study using the proposed hybrid scheduling approach.

The response time at each invocation within the hyperperiod at priority level 6 and as depicts in Fig. 6, the task is invoked $\alpha_6 = 75$ times within the hyperperiod at level 6. Despite the miss, the weakly hard constraint $\begin{pmatrix} 2 \\ 5 \end{pmatrix}$ for Task 6 is satisfied. The following Table 5 shows the exact distribution of the missed and met deadlines for invocations 1 to 75 of task *Position Updater*.

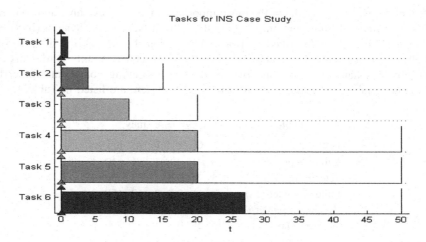

Fig. 5. Each task for INS case study.

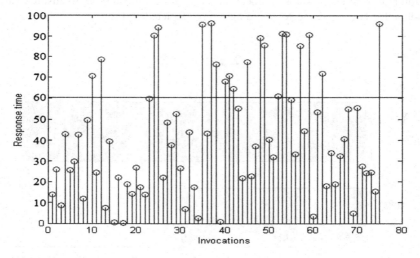

Fig. 6. Response times of task *Position Updater* having $D_6 = 60$ in the hyperperiod.

Table 5. The exact distribution of the task Position Updater.

Task position updater	
Invocations	μ-pattern
1–25:	11111 11110 10111 11111 11100
26–50:	11111 11110 10010 00110 11001
51–75:	10001 10101 10111 11111 11110

We use the metric or in other words, performance measurement parameters in order to quantitatively evaluate system performance through simulation experiments. The deadline satisfaction ratio is the fraction of all generated task sets that are schedulable with respect to an algorithm.

6 Conclusion and Future Work

In conclusion, after another case study, named INS has been used for schedulability tests; the result obtained is, the number of deadlines missed for videophone application is greater than INS for invocations 1 to 75. Also, from simulation experiment shows that deadline satisfaction ratio for videophone application is lesser than INS about 67%, while INS is around 75%, means that INS has higher success ratio than videophone. This is due to the fact that the task set of videophone application is softer than INS in term of the toleration of missed deadline. However, both case studies satisfied weakly hard constraint $\binom{2}{5}$.

The results analyses were investigated through an experiment with the videophone application and INS case studies. From the tests results, although the task set in systems with R-BOUND-MP-NFRNS would be unsuccessfully partition and unschedulable at multiprocessor response time test, they still can be bounded and predictable using weakly hard constraint and μ-pattern. Even, later on, the remaining unassigned task has ability to migrate to different processor using RM-US (m/3m−2) in order to ensure the system is schedulable.

From simulation results showed that most deadlines are indeed met using exact schedulability analysis. Most importantly, the proposed scheduling approach presented here can guarantee that both deadlines and timing constraints of the systems are successfully satisfied. At the same time, it can provide an optimal scheduling approach with minimal overhead. Thus, the proposed approach achieves our objective/aim and provide a solution to the problem stated in this paper.

For future work, we aim to do evaluation of comparing the hybrid scheduling approach proposed in this paper with other existing scheduling approaches, partitioning and global in terms of the performance of the experiment using the necessary metrics.

Acknowledgments. The authors would like to express profound gratitude to the GUP fund and Universiti Teknologi Malaysia (UTM) for their financial support and not forgotten, the Software Engineering Research Group (SERG) and EReTSEL lab members for their help.

References

1. Bernat, G., Burns, A., Llamosi, A.: Weakly hard real-time systems. IEEE Trans. Comput. **50** (4), 308–321 (2001)
2. Baker, T.P., Baruah, S.: Schedulability analysis of multiprocessor sporadic task systems. In: Handbook of Real-Time and Embedded Systems. Chapman Hall/CRC Press, Boca Raton (2007)
3. Wu, T., Jin, S.: Weakly hard real-time scheduling algorithm for multimedia embedded system on multiprocessor platform. In: 1st IEEE International Conference on Ubi-Media Computing, Lanzhou, pp. 320–325 (2008)
4. Hamdaoui, M., Ramanathan, P.: A dynamic priority assignment technique for streams with (m, k)-firm deadlines. IEEE Trans. Comput. **44**(12), 1443–1451 (1995)
5. Kong, Y., Cho, H.: Guaranteed scheduling for (m,k)-firm deadlines-constrained real-time tasks on multiprocessors. In: 12th International Conference on Parallel and Distributed Computing, Applications and Technologies, pp. 18–23 (2011)
6. Kong, Y., Cho, H.: Energy-constrained scheduling for weakly-hard real-time tasks on multiprocessors. In: Park, J.J.H., Chao, H.-C., Obaidat, M.S., Kim, J. (eds.) Computer Science and Convergence. LNEE, vol. 114, pp. 335–347. Springer, Dordrecht (2012). doi:10.1007/978-94-007-2792-2_32
7. Calandrino, J.M., Anderson, J.H., Baumberger, D.P.: A hybrid real-time scheduling approach for large-scale multicore platforms. In: 19th Euromicro Conference on Real-Time Systems (2007)
8. Shin, I., Lee, I., Easwaran, A.: Hierarchical scheduling framework for virtual clustering on multiprocessor. In: Euromicro Conference on Real-Time Systems (2008)
9. Tan, P., Shu, J., Wu, Z.: A hybrid real-time scheduling approach on multi-core architectures. J. Softw. **5**(9), 958–965 (2010)
10. Safaei, A.A., Haghjoo, M.S., Abdi, F.: *PFGN*: a hybrid multiprocessor real-time scheduling algorithm for data stream management systems. In: Cherifi, H., Zain, J.M., El-Qawasmeh, E. (eds.) DICTAP 2011. CCIS, vol. 167, pp. 180–192. Springer, Heidelberg (2011). doi:10. 1007/978-3-642-22027-2_16
11. Sanati, B., Cheng, A.M.K.: Online semi-partitioned multiprocessor scheduling of soft real-time periodic tasks for QoS optimization. In: IEEE Real-Time Embedded Technology and Applications Symposium (2016)
12. Anderson, B.: Static-priority scheduling on multiprocessors. Ph.D. thesis, Department of Computer Engineering, Chalmers University of Technology, Göteberg, Sweden (2003)
13. Lauzac, S., Melhem, R., Mosse, D.: An efficient RMS admission control and its application to multiprocessor scheduling. In: Proceedings of the IEEE International Parallel Processing Symposium, Orlando, Florida, pp. 511–518 (1998)
14. Guan, N., Gu, Z., Lv, M., Deng, Q., Yu, G.: Schedulability analysis of global fixed-priority or EDF multiprocessor scheduling with symbolic model-checking. In: 11th IEEE Symposium on Object Oriented Real-Time Distributed Computing, pp. 556–560 (2008)
15. Bertogna, M.: Real-time scheduling analysis for multiprocessor platforms. Ph.D. thesis, Scuola Superiore Sant'Anna, Pisa, Italy (2007)
16. Gujarati, A., Cerqueira, F., Brandenburg, B.B.: Multiprocessor real-time scheduling with arbitrary processor affinities: from practice to theory. Real-Time Syst. **51**(4), 440–483 (2014)
17. Shin, D., Kim, J., Lee, S.: Intra-task voltage scheduling for low-energy hard real-time applications. IEEE Des. Test Comput. **18**(2), 20–30 (2001)
18. Borger, M.W.: VAXELN experimentation: programming a real-time periodic task dispatcher using VAXELN Ada 1.1. Technical report CMU/SEI-87-TR-032 ESD-TR-87-195, November 1987

Simulation of Square Ring Microstrip Patch Antenna Performance Based on Effects of Various Dielectric Substrates

Abdul Rashid O. Mumin$^{(\boxtimes)}$, Rozlan Alias, Jiwa Abdullah,
Samsul Haimi Dahlan, Raed Abdulkareem Abdulhasan,
and Jawad Ali

Department of Communication Engineering,
Faculty of Electrical and Electronic Engineering,
Universiti Tun Hussein Onn Malaysia (UTHM),
86400 Parit Raja, Batu Pahat, Johor, Malaysia
abdulrashidomar3@gmail.com

Abstract. This paper presents the impact of dielectric substrates with different relative permittivity used in designing a square ring patch antenna. Choice of suitable substrate material is essential while configuring the square ring microstrip patch antenna, since dielectric constant of a substrate is a basic parameter over regulating return loss, gain, bandwidth, voltage standing wave ratio (VSWR), and effectiveness of radiation pattern. Two fundamental properties of substrate material is considered in this research i.e. dietetic constant and loss tangent. Therefore, increasing the permittivity of substrate material permits compact size of antenna, but return loss, gain and directivity of antenna diminishing with admiration to the increment of dielectric substrate. The proposed geometric antennas have been designed utilising Computer Simulated Technology (CST) Microwave and MATLAB as a tool for the application, the antenna is acknowledged utilising a square ring patch simulated with different dielectric constant and contains radiating patch and ground plane. It has been considered several of dielectric material whose permittivity ranges from 1.96 to 6.15 relying on demand of GSM at desired frequency 1.8 GHz.

Keywords: Patch antenna · Square ring · Slots · Substrate permittivity · Directivity

1 Introduction

Microstrip patch antennas are favoured in today's wireless communication applications which broadly utilizes due to their compactness for mobile, aircraft, satellites, radars. Therefore, microstrip antennas are in interest because of light weight, low profile, comfort of merger with devices, simple to fabricate [1]. Different approaches have been engaged to advance thick and smaller compact patch antennas [2]. However, establishing a concession between the design difficulty and achievement is still not to be achieved.

Moreover, permittivity and tangent loss are considerable critical parameters in design configuration of patch antenna. The greatest disadvantages reported for

M.S. Mohamed Ali et al. (Eds.): AsiaSim 2017, Part II, CCIS 752, pp. 679–694, 2017.
DOI: 10.1007/978-981-10-6502-6_58

microstrip antennas are their limited bandwidth and small gain [3]. Consequently, a suitable and proper selection for substrate permittivity lessens the measure about surface wave losses and subsequently, it enhances the antenna accomplishment particularly, impedance bandwidth, gain, and radiation efficiency [4]. The greater part regularly utilized dielectric constant to print microstrip patch antennas need a permittivity in the range from 2.2 to 12 relying on applications demand [5]. The particularized study defined by the past researchers specified that the nature impact degenerate the accomplishment of antennas. Even though, it is referred to the distinctive impact about the dielectric stacking with respect to patch antenna includes resonant frequency, and transmitting effectiveness reduction, then these impacts can be excluded by fine tuning. Impact of natural circumstances to which the antenna might be presented for use at the appropriate course of time, if it is to be under taken for the record throughout the proposed geometrical phase of antenna. The impact of resonant frequency of a square microstrip antenna with permittivity is studied, three primary parameters, which of the following are considered for antenna design such as a resonant frequency and height dielectric properties of material. It is important to determine the dimensions of the design from antenna arrangements [7–19].

Therefore, the work in this paper evaluates the impact of dielectric substrate with various permittivity on the antenna performance features, and the outcomes for return loss (S11), directivity, VSWR, impedance, gain, and radiation pattern, are also investigated. The impacts of substrate are defined in terms of dielectric properties on the patch antennas and its results are evaluated by using Computer Simulated Technology (CST) Microwave Studio. A square ring microtsirp patch antenna have been proposed in this study for the design purpose and its performance have been analysed and evaluated.

2   Square Ring Microstrip Antenna Design

The proposed geometry comprises of claiming metalized example for a light substrate. Once again, back surface of the substrate is recognized as ground plane, the substrate relative dielectric constant (ε_r) lies between 2.2 to 12. Furthermore, a viable dielectric constant (ε_{reff}) must chance to be acquired so as to represent the fringing and the wave of proliferation in the offering. To guarantee the radiation of square ring patch antenna of the fancied frequency. The suggested antenna setup will be designed using a square ring printed with respect to a dielectric constant, furthermore ground plane as illustrated in Fig. 1. Whereas Table 1 demonstrates the design parameters. A square model slotted is inserted at the focal point of the square patch diminishment.

It is significant to regulate the dimensions of the proposed configuration of square ring patch which includes the length and the width of the determined rectangular patch antenna and is altered by [6].

$$L_0 = W_0 = 0.46 \frac{\lambda}{\sqrt{\varepsilon_r}} \tag{1}$$

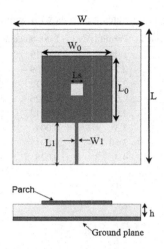

Fig. 1. The configuration structure of the suggested patch antenna

Table 1. The proposed geometry parameters utilized for square ring patch antenna.

Parameter	Symbols	Dimension (mm)
Width	W_0	18.41
Length	L_0	18.41
Effective dielectric	ε_{reff}	3.85
Length extension	ΔL_0	0.25
Feed of length	L_f	11.5
Feed line width	W_1	2.6
Wavelength	λ	0.166
Substrate high	H	1.6
Length of square ring	L_s	5

2.1 Model and Material Simulation

The proposed design of square ring microstrip patch antenna is configured and optimized using Computer Simulated Technology (CST) Microwave Software. The main purpose of this design is to investigate and evaluate the impact of substrate with different dielectric constant over the patch radiator. Several dielectric materials has been considered whose permittivity ranges from 1.96 to 6.15 relying on application demand which are listed in Table 2.

2.2 Program Code

The parameters such as length, width, effective dielectric constant and effective length used to design antenna can be calculated using MATLAB based program in which the dielectric constant, resonant frequency in GHz and substrate height is used as input to get the desired parameters mentioned earlier. The program is as follows:

Table 2. Validation of different substrates materials with width of square ring patch antenna

Material	Resonant frequency (GHz)	Permittivity ε_r	Loss tangent	Width of patch W_0 (mm)
RT5880LZ	1.8	1.96	0.0019	28.64
RT5880	1.8	2.2	0.0009	27.14
RT5870	1.8	2.33	0.0012	26.26
R04725JXR	1.8	2.55	0.0026	25.15
RT6002	1.8	2.94	0.0012	23.13
R04450B	1.8	3.3	0.004	22.12
R03035	1.8	3.50	0.0015	21.75
FR-4	1.8	4.3	0.025	19.10
TMM4	1.8	4.5	0.002	18.75
R03008	1.8	6.15	0.002	16.2

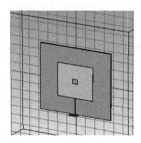

Fig. 2. Geometrical setup of square ring patch antenna using CST model

```
eo=8.854*10^-12; %Absolute Permittivity
uo=1.256*10^-6;  %Absolute Permeability

er=input('Dielectric Constant = ');
F=input('Resonant Frequency(GHz) = ');
H=input('Substrate height(cm) = ');
fr=F*10^9; %Conversion of resonant frequency to GHz
h=H*10^-2; %Conversion of substrate height to cm
W=(1/(2*fr*sqrt(uo*eo)))*sqrt(2/(er+1)); % Formulae for
%Width Calculation
w=W*10^2;
ereff=((er+1)/2)+((er-1)/2)*(1+12*(h/W))^(-1/2);
%Effective Dielectric Constant
deltaL=h*0.412*((ereff+0.3)*(W/h+0.264))/((ereff-
0.258)*(W/h+0.8)); %Extension in Length
deltal=deltaL*10^2;
L=(1/(2*fr*sqrt(ereff)*sqrt(uo*eo)))-2*deltaL;
l=L*10^2; % Formulae for length calculation
Leff=L+2*deltaL; %Effective Length
leff=Leff*10^2;
display(w,'W(cm)') %Displaying all the values
display(ereff)
display(deltal,'deltaL(cm)')
display (l,'L(cm)')
```

3   Results and Discussion

This paper has proposed square ring path antenna employing the Computer Simulated Technology (CST) Microwave Studio. Therefore, antennas are simulated for various dielectric substrate materials at frequency 1.8 GHz for GSM uses. In order to find out the dielectric specifications by the conventional method, it is needed to carry out data such as substrate height, dielectric constant etc. Meanwhile, patch antenna has established physical characteristics on a dielectric substrate having active electrical and magnetic properties of which a correct choice is very significant. Moreover, it is observed that change in substrate material usually disturbs antenna's performance as it concerns the output parameters. In fact, thickness of substrates are required for excellent performance of antenna, but they have dielectric constant in the lower end of the range due to larger bandwidth. This of course yields to better efficiency and loosely bound fields for radiation into space, resulting in large element size.

Similarly, with an increase in frequency, lower permittivity and thicker substrate, the radiation will increase. Furthermore, the cost, power loss and performance are trade-off considerations in choosing the substrate material as there are those with dielectric constant more than 10. In comparison, the patch size is smaller for higher dielectric constant which also reduces bandwidth and radiation frequency. Finally, it concludes that selecting the needed substrate material is an important part of antenna design procedure which is outlined in Table 3 showing significant role in performance parameters such as return loss (S11), VSWR, gain and directivity for each model at 1.8 GHz respectively. Figure 3 demonstrates the return loss, VSWR, gain and directivity of the proposed square rind antenna when it is simulated using RT5880LZ as a dielectric substrate. These results showed a significant values of gain around 6 dB.

Table 3.   Summarization of the results for different dielectric constant of substrates.

Material	Return loss (dB)	VSWR	Gain (dB)	Directivity (dBi)
RT5880LZ	−26.295	1.096	6.07	7.99
RT5880	−27.033	1.093	6.04	7.74
RT5870	−24.677	1.124	5.8	7.6
R04725JXR	−25.88	1.104	5.14	7.42
RT6002	−16.875	1.332	5.62	7.11
R04450B	−18.401	1.271	4.18	6.95
R03035	−13.409	1.5431	4.95	6.88
FR-4	−44.795	1.011	1.2	6.46
TMM4	−12.804	1.593	4.69	6.43
R03008	−12.409	1.630	4.07	4.09

In the similar manner Fig. 4 shows the return loss, VSWR, gain and directivity of the proposed square rind antenna when it is simulated using RT5880 as a dielectric substrate.

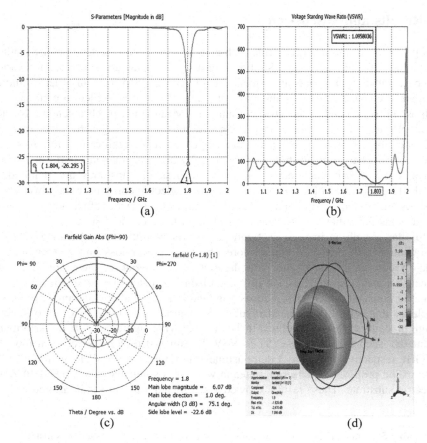

Fig. 3. Results using RT5880LZ substrate; *(a)* Return loss; *(b)* VSWR; *(c)* Gain; *(d)* Directivity

Similarly, Fig. 5 shows the return loss, VSWR, gain and directivity of the proposed square rind antenna when it is simulated using RT5870 as a dielectric substrate. From the figure it can be seen clearly that results at 1.8 GHz are still considerable.

Figure 6 then shows the return loss, VSWR, gain and directivity of the proposed square rind antenna when it is simulated using R04725JXR as a dielectric substrate.

In the same way Figs. 7, 8, 9, 10, 11 and 12 shows the results of the square ring simulation based on RT6002, R04450B, R03035, FR-4, TMM4, R03008 as a dielectric substrate and the results obtained after the simulation of each design shows the gain and directivity significant at 1.8 GHz which is the targeted frequency.

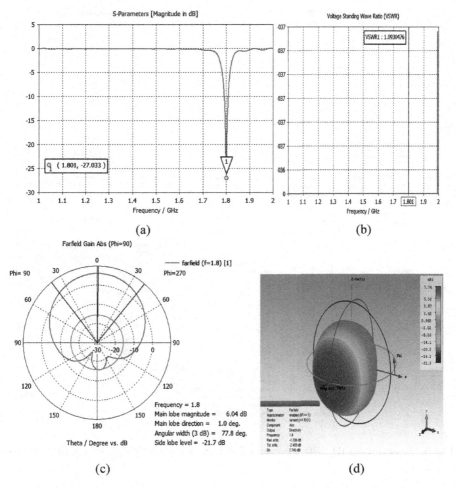

Fig. 4. Return loss *(a)* VSWR *(b)* Gain *(c)* and *(d)* Directivity using RT5880 substrate

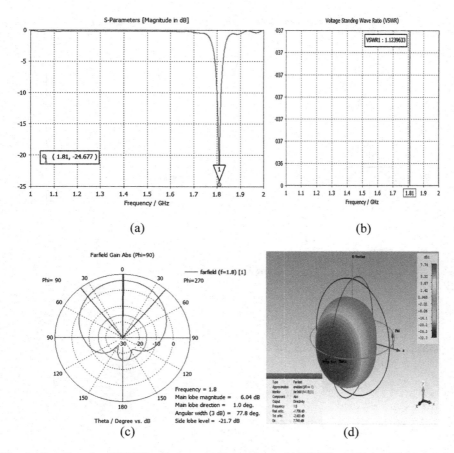

Fig. 5. Results using RT5870 substrate; *(a)* Return loss; *(b)* VSWR; *(c)* Gain; *(d)* Directivity

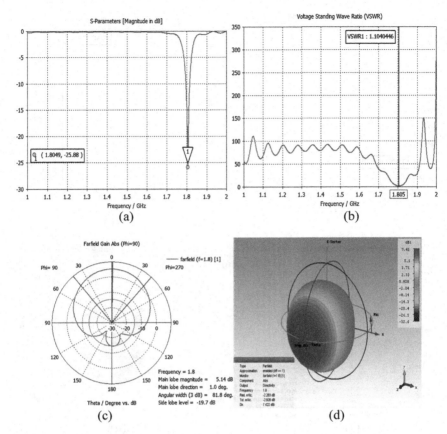

Fig. 6. Results using R04725JXR substrate; *(a)* Return loss; *(b)* VSWR; *(c)* Gain; *(d)* Directivity

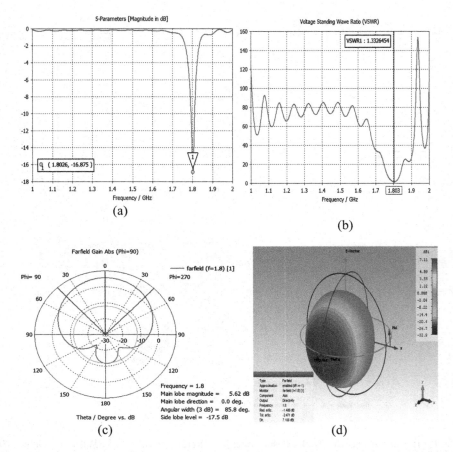

Fig. 7. Results using RT6002 substrate; *(a)* Return loss; *(b)* VSWR; *(c)* Gain; *(d)* Directivity

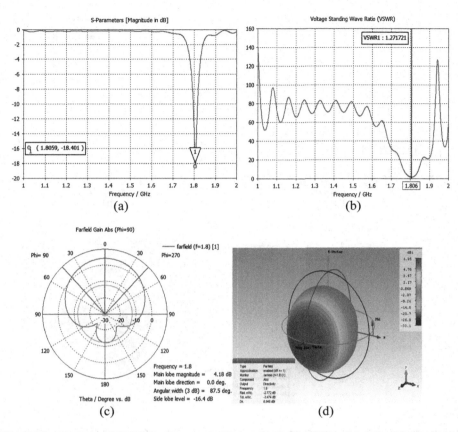

Fig. 8. Results using R04450B substrate; *(a)* Return loss; *(b)* VSWR; *(c)* Gain; *(d)* Directivity

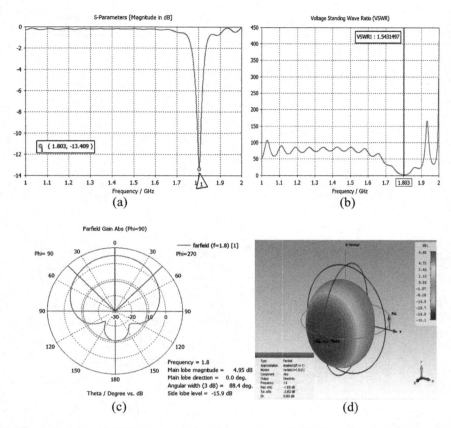

Fig. 9. Results using RT03035 substrate; *(a)* Return loss; *(b)* VSWR; *(c)* Gain; *(d)* Directivity

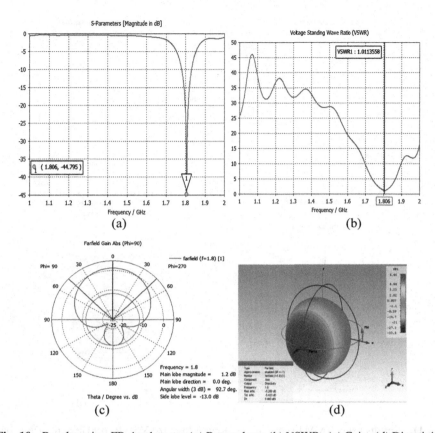

Fig. 10. Results using FR-4 substrate; *(a)* Return loss; *(b)* VSWR; *(c)* Gain; *(d)* Directivity

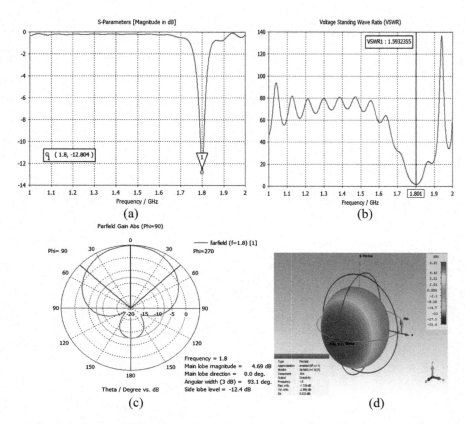

Fig. 11. Results using TMM4 substrate; *(a)* Return loss; *(b)* VSWR; *(c)* Gain; *(d)* Directivity

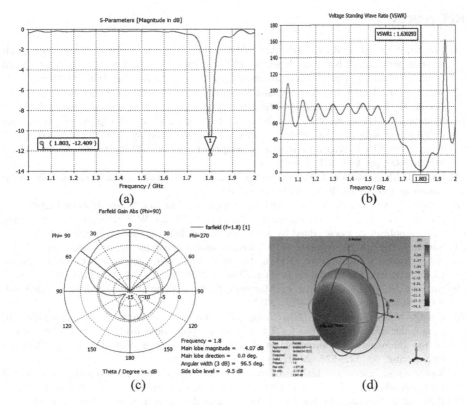

Fig. 12. Results using RT03008 substrate; *(a)* Return loss; *(b)* VSWR; *(c)* Gain; *(d)* Directivity

4 Conclusions

This paper has investigated the impacts of dielectric substrate on a microstrip patch antenna. A square ring microstrip patch antenna has been designed and simulated successfully using Computer Simulated Technology (CST) Microwave Studio. However, it has been observed that increment in the dielectric constant of the material, permits the compactness in antenna size. The results obtained from simulation revealed that the gain and directivity of square ring patch antenna increases by the decrease in dielectric constant of substrate. Introducing some slots on patch can investigate the performance of antenna such as return loss, gain, bandwidth and directivity.

Acknowledgments. The authors would like to thank office for research, innovation fund, commercialization and consultancy management (ORICC) of University Tun Hussein Onn Malaysia (UTHM) for sponsoring this work under grant (GPPS) Code U585.

References

1. Mumin, A.O., Alias, R., Awaleh, A.A., Abdulhasan, R.A.: Assessment of microstrip patch antenna performance based on dielectric substrate. Paper Presented at the 2015 International Conference on Computer, Communications, and Control Technology (I4CT) (2015)
2. Wong, K.-L.: Compact and Broadband Microstrip Antennas. Wiley, Hoboken (2002)
3. Girish, K., Ray, K.P.: Broadband Microstrip Antennas. Artech House, Norwood (2003)
4. Sharma, A., Dwivedi, V.K., Singh, G.: THz rectangular microstrip patch antenna on multilayered substrate for advance wireless communication systems. In: Proceedings of Progress in Electromagnetics Research Symposium, PIERS 2009, Beijing, China, 23–27 March 2009, pp. 627–631 (2009)
5. Pozar, D.M., Schaubert, D.H.: Microstrip Antennas: The Analysis and Design of Microstrip Antennas and Arrays. Wiley, Hoboken (1995)
6. Balanis, C.A.: Antenna Theory, Analysis and Design, 3rd edn. Wiley, Hoboken (2005)
7. Zhang, M.T., Jiao, Y.C., Koyuturk, M., Zhang, F.S., Wang, W.T.: Design of Antennas for RFID Application. Book edited by: C. Turcu, 554 p. InTech, Vienna, February 2009
8. Surjati, I., Yuli, K.N., Astasari, A.: Microstrip patch antenna fed by inset microstrip line for radio frequency identifcation (RFID). In: 2010 Asia-Pacific International Symposium on Electromagnetic Compatibility, Beijing, China, 12–16 April 2010, pp. 1351–1353 (2010)
9. Iftissane, M., Bri, S., Zenkouar, L., Mamouni, A.: Conception of patch antenna at wide band. Int. J. Emerg. Sci. 1(3), 400–417 (2011)
10. Gadag, M.M., Kamshetty, D.S., Yogi, S.L.: Design of different feeding techniques of rectangular microstrip antenna for 2.4 GHz RFID applications using IE3D. In: Proceedings of the International Conference on Advances in Computer, Electronics and Electrical Engineering, pp. 522–525 (2012)
11. Rajput, G.S.: Design and analysis of rectangular microstrip patch antenna using metamaterial for better efficiency. Int. J. Adv. Technol. Eng. Res. (IJATER) 2(6), 51–58 (2012)
12. Babu, R.S., Sampath, P.: Design of 4X4 rectangular microstrip phased array antenna for GSM applications. Int. J. Latest Res. Sci. Technol. 1(4), 403–407 (2012)
13. Nornikman, H., Malek, F., Saudin, N., Zainuddin, N.A., Shukor, M.M., Abd Aziz, M.Z.A., Ahmad, B.H., Othman, M.A.: Dual layer rectangular microstrip patch antenna with H-slot for 2.4 GHz range applications. In: IEEE Conference Publications: 3rd International Conference on Instrumentation, Communications, Information Technology, and Biomedical Engineering, pp. 44–48, November 2013
14. Prabhu, P., Poongodi, C., Sarwesh, P., Shanmugam, A.: Design a low profile printed monopole antenna for RFID applications. Int. J. Innov. Res. Sci. Eng. Technol. 2(2), 454–459 (2013)
15. Hamad, E.K.I.: Design and implementation of dual band micro strip antennas for RFID reader applications. Ciência e Técnica Vitivinícola (CIENC TEC VITIVINIC) J. 29, 1–10 (2014)
16. Kumar, S., Saurabh, A.K., Beniwal, N.S.: Dual band H shaped rectangular microstrip patch antenna for WLAN/WiMAX/bluetooth applications. Int. J. Adv. Res. Electr. Electron. Instrum. Eng. 3(3), 8220–8227 (2014)
17. Kiruthiga, V., Thamarairubini, K., Sowbakkiyam, S., Ramaya, K., Ashwin, K., Suresh Kumar, S.: Design and comparative study of meander antenna and micro strip patch antenna. Int. J. Adv. Res. Electron. Commun. Eng. (IJARECE) 3, 1526–1528 (2014)
18 Manchanda, S., Hatwar, M., Abhishek, B.: Design of meander line antenna for operating frequency of 2.5 GHz. Int. J. Comput. Appl. 93(19), 33–36 (2014)
19. ELHamraoui, A., Abdelmounim, E., Zbitou, J., Tajmouati, A., EL Abdellaoui, L., Errkik, A., Latrach, M.: Compact CPW-fed dual-band uniplanar antenna for RFID applications. In: IEEE Conference Publications: Third International Workshop on RFID and Adaptive Wireless Sensor Networks (RAWSN), pp. 73–77 (2015)

Ultra–Wideband Antenna Enhancement with Reconfiguration and Notching Techniques Evaluation

Raed Abdulkareem Abdulhasan[(✉)], Rozlan Alias,
Khairun Nidzam Ramli, Lukman Audah, Abdulrashid O. Mumin,
and Yasir Amer Jawhar

Department of Communication Engineering,
Faculty of Electrical and Electronic Engineering,
Universiti Tun Hussein Onn Malaysia,
86400 Parit Raja, Batu Pahat, Johor, Malaysia
raadabd39@gmail.com

Abstract. Many researchers have proposed notches and strips for band enhancement or interference reduction of ultra–wideband (UWB) antenna. Previous studies illustrated the advantage of using slot technologies and strips to change the antenna impedance matching. This study presents a comprehensive overview of the performances of reconfiguration techniques on UWB antennas based on filtering and matching band. Several studies are considered, and the performance of antennas designs that applied slot, strips, parasitic stubs, and spiral loop resonators are compared. Unwanted bands, such as WLAN and WiMAX systems, are interfered with UWB communications. The notches are used for either band rejection or bandwidth enhancement. Moreover, a hexagonal UWB patch antenna with the coplanar waveguide is demonstrated in this paper. The improvement of the UWB antenna bandwidth is realised by incising the patch size. Loading two L-shape strips on the radiation patch achieved band rejection at 5.15 GHz. The simulated parametric study represents different results achieved with different side–patch lengths. The best achievements of the proposed design are the UWB bandwidth from 2.8 GHz to 11.5 GHz, and the radiation gain of 4 dB at 5.8 GHz. Good omnidirectional radiation patterns observe on E-plane by bidirectional patterns provide on H-plane. Finally, the performance and implementing the studied UWB antennas are discussed in details.

Keywords: Slot · Strip · Band–rejection · Impedance matching · UWB antenna

1 Introduction

In recent years, ultra–wideband (UWB) technology has been a subject of interest in communication applications research. In 2002, the Federal Communication Commission authorised UWB with a spectrum of 3.1 GHz to 10.6 GHz. The total bandwidth for UWB with a bandwidth of 8 GHz is approximately 110% [1]. Several purposes,

© Springer Nature Singapore Pte Ltd. 2017
M.S. Mohamed Ali et al. (Eds.): AsiaSim 2017, Part II, CCIS 752, pp. 695–709, 2017.
DOI: 10.1007/978-981-10-6502-6_59

such as remote sensing, satellite connections, medical testing, radar, and military data transfers, have been developed to work on UWB spectrum [2]. The most challenging part of any communication system is antenna design. UWB antenna designs ensure ease of fabrication, fast data transfer rates, and omnidirectional radiation patterns. However, as the UWB works on a broad range of frequencies or allocates the spectrum frequency with several narrow bands, the operation of the system is interfered by the desired local bands. These narrow bands include the WiMAX (3.4 GHz) [3], WLAN (5.5 GHz) [4], HIPERLAN, and C–band. Over the last decade, many researchers proposed some techniques to overcome these interference problems. The current studies present insight into and analyses the performances of reconfiguration patch antenna techniques proposed in previous research. Adding a T–shaped stub on the ground plane to produce a band rejection of 5.5 GHz and a bandwidth of 7% was proposed in [5]. Including terminated stubs on the elliptical patch that provides a band rejection of 5.6 GHz [6]. Loading two inverted L–shaped slots on a coplanar waveguide (CPW) feed line that produces band rejection at 5.5 GHz [7]. Furthermore, a G–shaped slot antenna achieved dual resonance bands at WLAN and WiMAX [8].

This study presents a comprehensive review and analysis on UWB systems that employed common notching techniques, such as strips on a square patch and stubs behind the patch for bandwidth enhancement, butterfly–shaped parasitic stubs, and dual–band notch filters. Multi–states with dual–bands filter using U– and J–shaped notches. The ground plane effect is reduced by cutting a half–ring slot and adding an inverted L–shaped strip. A spiral loop resonator (SLR) is discussed for band–notched at 5.8 GHz. Multiple–input multiple–output (MIMO) two square patch antennas with a T–shaped stub and a dual I–shaped strip. An elliptical patch antenna with CPW–fed, and a U–shaped slot and two inverted L–shaped strips are introduced. Bandwidth improvement and band rejection are compared to identify which method performs better.

2   Study on Reconfigurations UWB Antennas

2.1   Strips for Bandwidth Enhancement

The design of the slot antenna for UWB applications initially has a simple rectangular slot antenna. A conductor strip is placed in the rectangular slot to achieve a broad bandwidth [9]. Two rectangular stubs are used in this research. The stubs are pasted on both sides of the ground plane to improve the antenna bandwidth of the UWB. Figure 1 illustrates the geometry of the proposed antenna in [9]. The bandwidth of the tested antenna reaches 120.41%. This bandwidth is calculated from a lower resonant frequency (3.06 GHz) to an upper resonant frequency (12.31 GHz). This frequency range operates based on a standard bandwidth of 802.15a. A single band is rejected when a stub is loaded on the left side of the square patch. This process achieves a WLAN band rejection of S11 = −1.8 dB at a centre frequency of 5.5 GHz. By optimizing the total length of stub Ls1, Ls2, and Ls3 (see Fig. 1), the centre notching frequency shifts to an upper or a lower frequency.

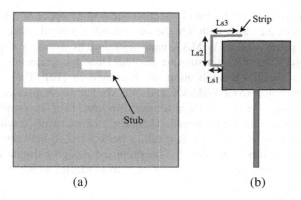

Fig. 1. The proposed antenna damnations with a strip and a stub [9]

2.2 Dual–Band Notches with Butterfly–Shaped Parasitic Stubs

In this study, the authors present two rejection bands, the WiMAX and WLAN bands, on a small rectangular antenna patch for UWB systems [10]. The total bandwidth of the proposed antenna after fabrication is ranged from 2.35 to 13 GHz. These bands are achieved the total bandwidth after reconfiguring the structure of the proposed antenna. The rejection bandwidth of the WiMAX starts from 3.25 GHz to 3.85 GHz, and the rejection bandwidth of the WLAN begins from 4.9 GHz to 6.2 GHz [10].

Figure 2 shows the total dimensions for the rectangular patch and its size reduction after cutting triangular steps at the lower edge. These steps are improved the impedance matching and to achieve the UWB bandwidth. The return loss is improved by applying two rectangular strips on the ground plane for the antenna. This reconfiguration significantly enhances the bandwidth and achieves a tested bandwidth of 155%. Moreover, this bandwidth covers a range beyond that of the UWB. On the one hand, the first band rejection is achieved by loading a U–shaped slot on the desired antenna patch to reject the WLAN band with a voltage standard wave ratio (VSWR) of 7.

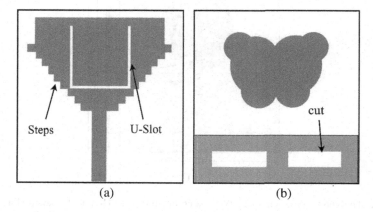

Fig. 2. The geometry of the antenna for UWB systems [10]

The centre frequency of this band rejection shifts to an upper or a lower frequency with the changes in the slot length. On the other hand, a butterfly–shaped is set on the backside of the patch achieve WiMAX band rejection, as shown in Fig. 2.

The reconfiguration characteristics are studied. Dual–band rejection and bandwidth enhancement for the UWB application are proposed in [10]. These improvements reduce the interference from WiMAX and WLAN bands. A perfect match can be achieved by choosing the best location for the strip line [11]. The proposed antenna is fabricated, and the results are measured. Then, the measurements results are validated with the simulation results. From this result, a perfect match between the simulation and measurement results is observed. The proposed design exhibits a great performance, simple structure, small size, and is easy to fabricate, which is very useful for UWB applications.

2.3   Multi–states with Dual–Band Filters

A circular patch with a microstrip–fed line is manufactured, presented, and printed on a square FR4 substrate to achieve the UWB characteristics [12]. Several parameters are studied, and the significant effect of the parameters of the antenna is summarised as follows: the length of ground plane Lg, the width of feed line Wf, and the width of substrate W. These effects can achieve impedance matching and reach the UWB bandwidth (3.1 GHz to 10.6 GHz). The authors in [12] are attempted to reduce the interference in the UWB frequency range in both the WiMAX and WLAN. To solve this problem, researchers are introduced U– and J–shaped notch filters, which are posted on the front side of the circular patch as shown in Fig. 3. The demonstrated dimensions are calculated and simulated by using the CST Microwave Studio software, which is compatible.

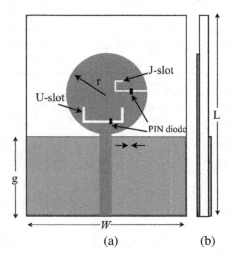

Fig. 3. The geometry of circular UWB patch antenna with U– and J–shaped slots [13]

The locations of these two slots were tested and optimised. Results display that the highest value of VSWR is achieved when the slot is set near the edge of the micro-strip–fed line. The highest current is distributed around the brink of the slot at the rejection frequency. The total length of the J–shaped slot enables filtering at a quarter guided wavelength of the centre notching frequency. The J–shaped slot rejects a WiMAX frequency ranging from 3.15 GHz to 3.7 GHz. The length of the U–shaped slot has inversely proportional to a half–guided wavelength of the notching frequency. The proposed antenna achieves the WLAN rejection bandwidth ranging from 5.15 GHz to 5.85 GHz.

The authors of [13] proposed a reconfigurable UWB antenna. Loading two copper stubs on the slots can control the slots' operational states. The stubs work as ideal PIN diode (ON or OFF) switch states. This condition proves that slot length significantly affects band rejection. This study also employs four operational modes for band rejection (see Fig. 4). Each state is calculated, simulated, and measured after fabricating four prototypes. The measurements are compatible with the simulation results of the band rejection. The reflection coefficient and radiation pattern results for all the four modes are measured.

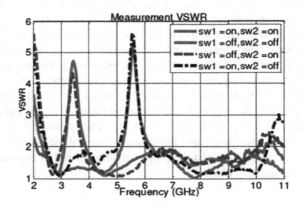

Fig. 4. Measurement of the VSWR for the reconfigurable UWB antenna [13]

2.4   Reduced Ground Plane Effect

A rectangular UWB antenna patch with the microstrip–fed line was tested for UWB applications. A notch was cutting from the square radiated area to decrease the effect of the ground plane [14]. Results show that the current arrangement is focused on the edge of the notch at the dismissal band. Two corners are cut from the lower side of the radiation part. In addition, the dimensions of the ground plane optimised for improving the impedance matching. At this point, the impedance is enhanced at the upper frequency. The results demonstrate the lower resonant frequency starts from 3 GHz. This frequency is reached by moving the connection point between the feed line and the radiation part to the left corner as shown in Fig. 5.

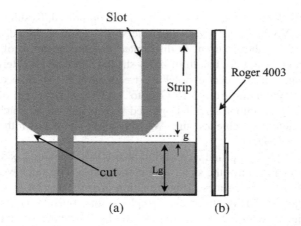

Fig. 5. The geometry of the UWB antenna with a strip [14]

As a result, the highest current is distributed on the right side of the patch with an additional strip line (L = 33 mm). When L is the longest path of the current flow, the proposed antenna has a lower resonant frequency that is equal to a half-guided wavelength. Several parameters in this design are studied and optimised to enhance the impedance matching. The antenna performance impacted by adjacent the feed line position, the gap below the radiated part, and modification the two corners of the patch.

The dimensions of the antenna are not symmetrical because of a notch and strip attach on the right side. Furthermore, the feed line is not connected to the centre of the radiated area. Therefore, the ground plane has current density higher than the current on the radiation part at a lower frequency of 3 GHz. The parametric study records the reflection coefficient for the notch, and the strip are changed the antenna properties. The Orbit MiDAS system is used to test the proposed antenna and to measure the radiation patterns at 3, 4, 5, and 10 GHz.

2.5   Cutting Ground Plane Slot and Strip

In [15] the authors are demonstrated a UWB antenna has a half–circular and half–square radiated ring. The microstrip–feed line of the antenna is calculated to reach the best matching. The ground plane is placed on the lower side of the substrate with an entire area is computed as ($g \times w$). The highest current is distributed along the edge of the ring. This hybrid geometry of the antenna has the largest patch dimension (L), which represents a half–guided wavelength of a lower resonant frequency. The outer circumference of the half–circular ring is equal to $R + d$ (see Fig. 6). The return loss for this design is less than -10 dB and has good impedance matching for all UWB ranges. The quality of the suggested antenna is developed by cutting a half–circular slot on the ground plane below the radiated patch. This ring cutting has a centre at the same location of the emitted ring. The notching obtains a VSWR $\leq$ 2 for UWB fractional bandwidth of 110%.

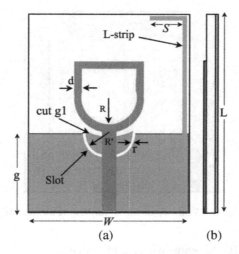

Fig. 6. Half–ring slot and L–shaped strip on the ground plane [15]

After this process, the brink of the ground plane has a longer path closer to the brink of the half radiation ring. Therefore, the current influxes of the ground area will increase. The half–ring notch has an entire circumference $(r + R')$. This ring notch enhances the inductance impact and advances the impedance matching of the UWB. The improved UWB antenna is reduced the Q factor. A parasitic stub is attached to the ground plane. This stub had an entire length of (Ls) and a width of (t) to improve the overall return loss. Eventually, the length of the ground plane is optimised to 11 mm, which can help in obtaining a good reflection coefficient and an omnidirectional radiation pattern. The proposed design achieves a peak gain of 3.5 dB and simulated VSWR of 1.4.

2.6   Band Notch by Using Spiral Loop Resonators

A modern technique is developed in [16] that rejects a band on the UWB antenna. This type of filter is called a spiral loop resonator (SLR). SLR is formed from two loop strips loaded on both sides of the radiation patch. The space between the radiated part and the SLR affects significantly on the antenna impedance. The SRL impedance is related to the current distribution on the SLR and the generated electromagnetic field around the SLR. The band rejection blocks the current distribution on the radiated part, and it depends on the SLR equivalent capacitance and inductance values. The design of the complementary split ring resonators (CSRR) adopts the same procedure with that of SLR. Figure 7 demonstrates all the dimensions of the SLR unit, as follows: $(L1)$ is the circumference of the SLR cell, (t) is the line width of SLR, and (c) is the gap between the loops. The analysis and simulation are revealed that these parameters for the SLR cell is achieved a band rejection performance of S11 = −3 dB at 6 GHz. The stop band of the filter is achieved by adding two SLRs beside the antenna patch. This technique has a low cost, a small size, and a simple design for ease of fabrication for UWB applications.

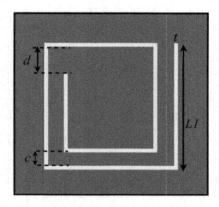

Fig. 7. Geometry of the spiral loop resonator [16]

2.7 Compact MIMO Antenna with Band Notch

The UWB MIMO band notch antenna is demonstrated in [17]. The antenna has a compact size of only 22 × 36 mm². The overall efficiency of 7%, which is achieved by loading I–shaped strips are connected to the ground plane. The I–shaped strips operate as band notch filters at 5.5 GHz. Two square patches with two ports represent a MIMO UWB antenna (see Fig. 8). The suggested design has various properties for all UWB ranges. The strips reject the WLAN band ranging from 5.15 GHz to 5.85 GHz. This MIMO antenna is achieved the UWB characteristics starting from a frequency of 3.1 GHz. The big dimension of the radiated part is adjusted to realise a lower resonant frequency. Nowadays, reducing the antenna dimension is the primary consideration in this field of research.

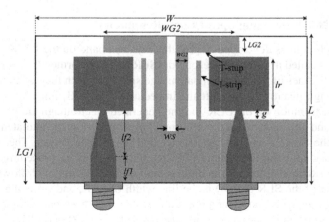

Fig. 8. Geometry of the proposed antenna [17]

Achieving a frequency of 3.1 GHz for the UWB antenna has been considered a difficult task. Different methods to reach an overall UWB bandwidth of 8 GHz range. The space between the ground plane and the lower side of the radiated part can be optimised by notching a slot on the ground area below the feed line. Equation (1) gives an estimation of the resonant frequency of the UWB antenna [17]:

$$f_r = \frac{144}{L_1 + L_2 + g + \frac{A_1}{2\pi L_1 \sqrt{\varepsilon_{re}}} + \frac{A_2}{2\pi L_2 \sqrt{\varepsilon_{re}}}} \tag{1}$$

where (L1 and L2) show the ground and the length of radiated patch, respectively, and (A1 and A2) are the areas of the ground and the radiation part, sequentially. All of these parameters are measured in millimetres. The effective dielectric constant (ε_{eff}) is determined by using the equation $\varepsilon_{eff} = (\varepsilon_r + 1)/2$. A T–shaped stub is loaded between the two square patches. This T–stub improves the impedance matching of UWB antenna.

A long slot is then cut at the centre of the T–shaped ground stub. The cut is used to separate the performances between the two antenna. The quarter wavelength is achieved by using the resonant reaction of the two ground strips. The band is notched to reduce the interference of the UWB bandwidth. The two microstrip–fed line ports achieve similar impedance matching because the two-MIMO antennas are symmetrically constructed. The antenna is kept packed by adding the T–shaped stub. This process reflects the radiated signal to separate the two MIMO cells. The authors further take one unit cell of the introduced MIMO antenna with a T–stub; the dimensions of the T–shaped stub are displayed in Fig. 8. The simulated S11 = −1.8 has a frequency of 5.5 GHz, which is consistent with the measurement [17].

When $l1 = L$, $l2 = lr$, $g = lf1 + lf2 - LG1$, $A2/l2 = lr$,

$$A_1 = (L_{G1}W_{G1})/2 + (L_{G2}W_{G2})/2 + [L - L_G - L_{G2} \times (W_{G1} + W_S/2)] \tag{2}$$

2.8   Elliptical Patch with Reconfiguration Notch

The resonating elements integrated with micro–electro–mechanical system (MEMS) switches are investigated in [6]. The authors are suggested a reconfigurable band–notch characteristic at a WLAN bandwidth ranging from 5.15 to 5.8 GHz, which will enhance the proposed elliptical patch for the UWB antenna. The elliptical radiation patch is introduced with a CPW–fed line. First, a U–shaped slot is loaded on the elliptical–radiated patch, which has an average length that is resonant to a half wavelength of the notching frequency.

This slot has a reconfigurable operation in which the MEMS switch posted on the slot activates and cancels the U–shaped slot operation. When the switch is activated, a short circuit will be formed between the two sides of the U–shaped slot. The switch will make the antenna work without notching mechanism. Thus, the slot will not reject any band. Secondly, two L–shaped strips are stacked on the left and right sides of the elliptical radiating part as shown in Fig. 9. Two MEMS switches are soldered on the two strips to activate or cancel the reconfigurable function for the suggested strips. These two strips are set to enhance the impedance matching for the elliptical radiation part at 8 GHz. When the switches deactivate and operate in OFF state, the open circuits will separate the strips from the elliptical patch. Therefore, the return loss of the suggested antenna is significantly improved when the switches operate in the ON state. The tested antenna is matched with a UWB range. The MEMS switches do not have any DC power, but the RF receives a signal rectifier, which will activate the reconfigurable switches. This new proposed technique is useful for energy harvesting, and it becomes more complicated during the antenna fabrication. When the authors have tested the proposed antenna, no significant difference is observed between the radiations patterns of the tested antenna at 8 GHz for both reconfiguration states. The mathematical formulation, transmission line models, and the final measurement results proved that the suggested antenna has an excellent achievement.

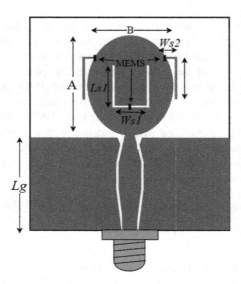

Fig. 9. Geometry of the elliptical patch for UWB applications [6]

3   Design and Simulation Results of Wideband Antenna

In this paper, a hexagonal patch UWB antenna is proposed. CPW feeding provides a wide bandwidth, and unique plane antenna structure. Therefore, the suggested antenna is employed the CPW feeding technique to realise a bandwidth. Figure 10 is presented the design geometry of the both side and top view. Both the hexagonal copper patch and CPW are printed on the top side of FR4 substrate. Conversely, the substrate has a clear bottom side. The strip line length (Lf) and width (Wf) are calculated to achieve 50-Ω impedance. The hexagonal patch has a calculated side length (S) is studied based

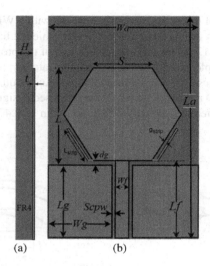

(a)   (b)

Fig. 10. (a) The side view and (b) top view of the proposed antenna geometry

on Eq. (3). The equivalent patch has an effective radius (r), length (L), feed line length (ρ) all in (cm), and lower frequency (F_L) [18]. The effective dielectric constant has a factor (k) of 1.15. Table 1 provides the physical design parameters.

$$F_L = c/\lambda = 7.2/[(L + r + \rho) \times k] \qquad (3)$$

Table 1. Parameters of the demonstrated antenna

Parameter	S	t	Wf	Lf	W_g	L_g	$Scpw$	Wa	La	H	εr	L_{strip}	g_{strip}
Value (mm)	10.8	0.035	2.54	15	12.43	14.3	0.3	28	43	1.6	4.3	7.8	0.5

The proposed hexagonal patch is simulated with different side length (S) by using CST microwave studio. Increasing the parameter S is increased the radiation area height (L). Therefore, the total tested antenna bandwidth can be improved. Figure 11 shows the return loss (S11) of the tested UWB antenna with increasing the patch sides S from 4 mm to 14 mm. On the one hand, the lower resonance frequency is achieved at 4.75 GHz by setting S of 4 mm. On the other hand, the lower resonance frequency is achieved at 2.56 GHz by setting S of 14 mm. the parametric study increased the tested UWB bandwidth of 2.2 GHz by incising S of 14 mm.

Figure 11 is presented a comprehensive managing to the UWB antenna. The hexagonal patch with CPW feeding technique is used to demonstrate UWB antenna parameters performances. Finally, incising patch height can be realised a broad bandwidth of UWB antenna at the lower resonance frequency.

The proposed design is simulated with the parameters, which are listed in Table 1. The demonstrated antenna achieved a broad UWB bandwidth from 2.8 to 11.5 GHz. Figure 12 (a) shows the proposed antenna return loss with sitting $S = 10.8$ mm. It can see that the return loss of the design less than −10 dB with UWB bandwidth. However, loading couple L-stripes on the radiation patch are achieved band rejection at WLAN band 5.15 GHz. Figure 12 (a) displays the return loss of the proposed antenna with two L-shape strips. The couple L-strips are achieved mismatching with S11 of -5 dB at the WLAN band. Indeed, these strips have entire length equals a quarter guided wavelength of notched band. The 3D radiation pattern of the proposed design is displayed in Fig. 12 b. The demonstrated antenna realised the radiation gain of 2.47 dB at 3.35 GHz.

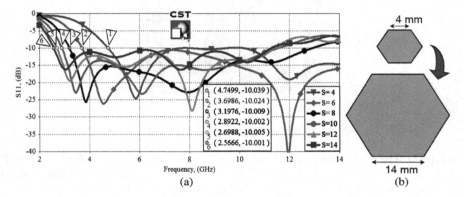

Fig. 11. (a) The simulated S11 with different S length (b) the patch configuration

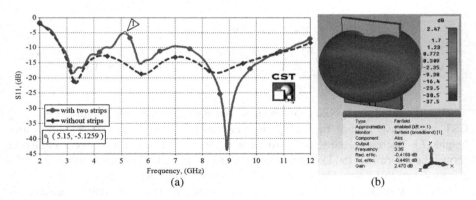

Fig. 12. (a) The simulated S11 of the proposed antenna (b) 3D radiation at 3.35 GHz

The polar radiation patterns of the demonstrated antenna are plotted in Fig. 13. The best three resonance frequencies are selected 3.35, 5.8, and 8.5 GHz. It can observe that the suggested antenna has omnidirectional radiation pattern for E-plane. However, the simulated results show a bidirectional radiation pattern for H-plane. Indeed, the highest radiation gain of 4 dB is achieved at 5.8 GHz with 170° of the H-plane. Therefore, the suggested antenna has an acceptable radiated gain, good performance, and broad bandwidth.

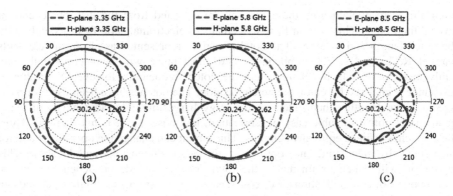

Fig. 13. The simulated radiation pattern (a) at 3.35, (b) at 5.8 and (c) at 8.5 GHz

4 Discussion

An inventive UWB antennas system is shown in this study. The modern study focuses on regular slots, cut, strips, and stubs. Many types of notches are developed for different objectives. These types of notches include U–, V–, T–, and J–, and ring–shaped slots on the patch. In addition, many types of strips validate in Table 2, such as L–shaped strips, I–shaped strips, and the SLR. These slots and strips could be placed in different positions, such as on the patch, ground plane, feed line, and substrates. The

Table 2. Antennas validation

Antenna type	Techniques	Band effect
Square patch with a microstrip–fed line	Strip and parasitic stub	Rejection at 5.5 GHz and bandwidth enhancement
Rectangular patch with a microstrip–fed line	Butterfly–shaped parasitic stub and U–shaped slot	Rejection at 3.4 GHz and 5.5 GHz and bandwidth enhancement
Circular patch with a microstrip–fed line	U– and J–shaped slots	Rejection at 3.4 GHz and 5.5 GHz
Rectangular patch with a shifted microstrip–fed line	Rectangular notch and strip	Impedance matching
Hybrid ring patches with a microstrip–fed line	Half–ring slot and L–shaped strip on ground plane	Impedance matching
Circular patch with CPW	SLR	Rejection at 5.8 GHz
MIMO two square patches with a microstrip–fed line	T–shaped ground stub and two I–shaped strips	Impedance matching and rejection at 5.5 GHz
Elliptical patch with CPW	Inverted U–shaped slot and two L–shaped strips	Impedance matching at 8 GHz and rejection at 5.5 GHz
Hexagonal patch with CPW	Increasing the patch size and loading couple L-strips	Lower frequency at 2.8 GHz and rejection at 5.15 GHz

main aim is to explain how these notches are operated from the distributed current around their edge. This current flow will create an electromagnetic field depending on the notch length and location. The notches can be represented as electronic elements parallel R, L, and C. The impedance and capacitance will connect to gather an equivalent circuit, which will represent the notch frequency. However, the value of resistance is changed based on the notch location. The notches have been used for band rejection, bandwidth enhancement, and energy harvesting. The advantages of using geometrical notches enable easy of fabrication, low cost, and it is not damage. Thus, these notches achieve equivalent circuits. This circuit can change the operating band for each notch by calculating and optimising the notch dimensions and location. This regulation will match or mismatch the total antenna impedance depending on the requirements of the applications. Moreover, each notch can reject a single band and can work as a filter. Two symmetric notches, however, they have similar diminutions and can reject a single band. One hybrid notch can reject multiple bands depending on the reconfiguration of the design.

5 Conclusion

This study comprehensively analyses on the performance of reconfiguration techniques for UWB system. The investigation focused on the performance of notching techniques that are used for band stop filtering, bandwidth enhancement, and impedance matching. The discussions are revealed how notches are operated from the current flow around their edge. This current will create an electromagnetic field depending on the notch length and location. Some researchers proposed several methods used to compare techniques for solving interference problems on UWB systems. These techniques have been classified into four categories: strips, slots, parasitic stubs, and SLRs. This study is contributed by improving the UWB antenna bandwidth. Increasing the radiated patch height is significantly effected on the lower resonance frequency of the UWB antenna. The radiation pattern performance of the antenna will test on the future works.

Acknowledgments. The authors would like to thank the Universiti Tun Hussein Onn Malaysia for the generous financial support under the Contract Grant (U550).

References

1. Rao, J.C., Rao, N.V.: CPW-fed compact ultra wideband MIMO antenna for portable devices. Indian J. Sci. Technol. **9**(17), 1–9 (2016)
2. Jahanbakht, M., Neyestanak, A.A.L.: A survey on recent approaches in the design of band notching UWB antennas. J. Electromagn. Anal. Appl. **4**(2), 77–85 (2012)
3. Prabhu, P., Elamaran, E., Desai, S.L.: Design of self–similarity multi–fractal antenna for WiMAX application. Indian J. Sci. Technol. **9**(15), 1–6 (2016)
4. Sudhakar, A., Satyanarayana, M., Prakash, M.S., Sharma, S.K.: Frequency notched UWB printed monopole antenna with protruding strips inside rectangular slot. Indian J. Sci. Technol. **8**(29), 1–6 (2015)

5. Ojaroudi, N., Ghadimi, N.: UWB small slot antenna with WLAN frequency band-stop function. Electron. Lett. **49**(21), 1317–1318 (2013)
6. Nikolaou, S., Kingsley, N.D., Ponchak, G.E., Papapolymerou, J., Tentzeris, M.M.: UWB elliptical monopoles with a reconfigurable band notch using MEMS switches actuated without bias lines. IEEE Trans. Antennas Propag. **57**(8), 2242–2251 (2009)
7. Reddy, S.M., Rao, P.M., Madhav, B.: Enhancement of CPW-fed inverted L-shaped UWB antenna performance characteristics using partial substrate removal technique. In: 3rd International Conference on Signal Processing and Integrated Networks (SPIN), Noida, India, pp. 454–459. IEEE (2016)
8. Marzudi, W., Abidin, Z.: Dual-wideband G-shaped slotted printed monopole antenna for WLAN and WiMAX applications. In: 2013 IEEE International RF and Microwave Conference (RFM), pp. 225–227. IEEE (2013)
9. Archevapanich, T., Rakluea, P., Anantrasirichai, N., Purahong, B., Chutchavong, V.: Rectangular slot antenna with asymmetrical conductor strip for bandwidth enhancement coverage UWB standard. In: Tanaka, S., Hasegawa, K., Xu, R., Sakamoto, N., Turner, S. J. (eds.) AsiaSim 2014. CCIS, vol. 474, pp. 105–115. Springer, Heidelberg (2014). doi:10. 1007/978-3-662-45289-9_10
10. Beigi, P., Nourinia, J., Mohammadi, B., Valizade, A.: Bandwidth enhancement of small square monopole antenna with dual band notch characteristics using U-shaped slot and butterfly shape parasitic element on backplane for UWB applications. Appl. Comput. Electromagnet. Soc. J. **30**(1), 78–85 (2015)
11. Alias, R.: Simulation of radiation performance for mobile antennas using a hybrid FEM-FDTD computational technique. In: 4th International Conference on Modeling, Simulation and Applied Optimization (ICMSAO), Kuala Lumpur, Malaysia, pp. 1–5. IEEE (2011)
12. Abdulhasan, R.A., Alias, R., Awaleh, A., Mumin, A.: Design of circular patch microstrip ultra wideband antenna with two notch filters. In: (I4CT) 2015 International Conference on Computer, Communications, and Control Technology, Kuching, Malaysia, pp. 464–467. IEEE (2015)
13. Abdulhasan, R.A., Attiah, M.L., Alias, R., Awaleh, A., Mumin, A.: Multi-state UWB circular patch antenna based on WiMAX and WLAN notch filters operation. J. Eng. Appl. Sci. ARPN **10**(19), 8907–8911 (2015)
14. Chen, Z.N., See, T.S., Qing, X.: Small printed ultrawideband antenna with reduced ground plane effect. IEEE Trans. Antennas Propag. **55**(2), 383–388 (2007)
15. Alsath, M.G.N., Kanagasabai, M.: Compact UWB monopole antenna for automotive communications. IEEE Trans. Antennas Propag. **63**(9), 4204–4208 (2015)
16. Kim, D.-O., Jo, N.-I., Choi, D.-M., Kim, C.-Y.: Design of the novel band notched UWB antenna with the spiral loop resonators. PIERS Online **6**(2), 173–176 (2010)
17. Liu, L., Cheung, S., Yuk, T.: Compact MIMO antenna for portable UWB applications with band-notched characteristic. IEEE Trans. Antennas Propag. **63**(5), 1917–1924 (2015)
18. Ray, K., Tiwari, S.: Ultra wideband printed hexagonal monopole antennas. IET Microwaves Antennas Propag. **4**(4), 437–445 (2010)

Research on Synthetic Natural Environment Data Cube Based on XML B+ Tree Structure

Chao Lin[✉], JiangYun Wang, and Liang Han

BeiHang University, Beijing 100191, China
linchao921017@163.com

Abstract. Because the synthetic natural environment data has many characteristics of multi-source, heterogeneous and massive, the data cube technology which can handle multi-dimensional data is applied to the synthetic natural environment data management system. While the traditional data cube technology has the problem of low construction and query efficiency. This paper presents a data cube based on XML B+ tree structure. The data cube leads into XML data files. By dividing the source data dimensionively, the B+ tree is constructed layer by layer, and binary coding is established for each hierarchy node to preserve the association and inheritance relationship between the dimensions. At the same time, the construction and query algorithm is given.

Keywords: Data cube · XML · Synthetic natural environment · B+ tree · Dimension

1 Introduction

With the continuous development of simulation technology, the scale of simulation system is increasing, and the information management of simulation data becomes more and more important. The extraction of synthetic natural environment information is a hot topic in the field of combat simulation and modeling. As the synthetic natural environment data has the characteristics of many sources, heterogeneous, massive, and thus it has brought great difficulty for the integration of synthetic natural environment information. It is the main goal of data management informationization to realize the multi-dimensional real-time acquisition and storage of synthetic natural environment data, the integration of information grid and the comprehensive application of knowledge.

The traditional relational database has the weakness of low efficiency of query, lack of ability to deal with multi-dimensional relationship, and thus it can not meet the above requirements. And the emergence and development of data warehouse technology is a good solution to this problem. The core technology of data warehouse is online analytical processing (OLAP). This is a software technology for online data access and analysis for specific issues. The technology enables users to perform a variety of query analysis operations on the data, while the results of the query analysis can be fed back to the user for further decision analysis. The Data Cube is the logical model of OLAP. Because OLAP improves the speed of query analysis by calculating a

© Springer Nature Singapore Pte Ltd. 2017
M.S. Mohamed Ali et al. (Eds.): AsiaSim 2017, Part II, CCIS 752, pp. 710–718, 2017.
DOI: 10.1007/978-981-10-6502-6_60

large number of aggregation operations in advance, the construction of the Data Cube is critical to the speed of the query response.

The traditional data cube construction technology has the following problems: the first is the lack of the description of the relationship between dimension and the level; the second is the lower efficiency of the update; the third is the redundancy of storage space. The emergence of XML is a good solution to the above problems. XML (Extensible Markup Language) is a meta markup language that provides a format for describing semi structured data. It is a method for putting structured data in a text file. XML documents are self describing so that both human and machine can understand it [1]. Therefore, the online analysis of XML data directly is a question worthy of study. Most of the current XML-based data warehouses are based on star models. Use the key-value to construct the cube by directly associating the fact file with the dimension file. Some scholars have proposed XCUBE data cube model, which consists of three files, respectively XCubeSchema, XCubeDimension and XCubeFact. The XCubeSchema file contains the schema structure of the data cube, the structure of the dimension file, and the inheritance relationship of the hierarchy at the same dimension as described in the dimension file. XCubeDimension is the XCube's dimension file that stores all the dimensions of the data cube, the dimension hierarchy, and the mutual inheritance between the different levels of the same dimension. XCubeFact stores all the fact nodes in the XCube.

In the above structure, the constructed data cube has a problem that the construction time is long and the update efficiency is not high. In this paper, we will first analyze the characteristics of the synthetic natural environment data. For the characteristics of synthetic natural environment data, we will improve the structure of XCube. In the study, we used a B+ tree to optimize XCube to describe the relationship between multiple dimensions, and to optimize the routing problem in the query and update process.

2   Related Work

2.1   Analysis of the Characteristics of Synthetic Natural Environment Data

The synthetic natural environment refers to the description of the physical world in which all military system models exist and interact. It includes terrain, atmosphere, ocean and space four areas [2]. Due to the wide range involved, the data is very large, with massive characteristics. Moreover, with the simulation of the process of increasing the number of entities, synthetic natural environment data will show exponential growth. The environmental data will change as the position changes, and will change over time. Thus the environmental data has Space-time characteristics. At the same time, the synthetic natural environment data source is very widespread, and the type is also very diverse, including environmental survey, observation, testing, special investigation, satellite remote sensing, other special survey data, as well as international exchange of information. The quality and accuracy and other related technical data and information of these materials are different, including monitoring methods, data extraction methods and models, technical indicators, instrument name and parameters, identification analysis and testing methods, correction and correction methods and related technical standards involved. And Environmental data also has the characteristics of multi-resolution. For example, different entities have different resolution requirements for terrain. Infantry tanks generally require a few meters to tens of meters of terrain resolution, and the aircraft will need a few hundred meters to one kilometer terrain resolution. As the resolution increases, the amount of data will increase rapidly. Not only that, when the simulation of the user use synthetic natural environment data, it often involves cross-attributes. For example, in a simulation, when the aircraft and the ship are in the confrontation, it will have to include longitude, latitude, time and other common attributes. In analyzing these properties, we usually need to distinguish between the atmosphere and the ocean theme. Thus, the attributes have a crossed relationship.

2.2   XML-Based Data Cube

As a self-describing markup language, XML can flexibly represent a variety of information in heterogeneous data sources depending on the application, including data exchange between applications, structured and semi-structured documents, and the output of data in the database [3]. Because XML allows users to customize the label, users can freely add labels, define their own rules to form a description of the data for the specific markup language. In addition, XML can use XML Schema to constrain XML documents, thereby enhancing the XML document standards, reducing the potential of the error. And the structure of the XML tree is very suitable for modification, there are international standard DOM can be used to access and manipulate the document. There are also XPath standards that can be queried in a more intuitive language. It can reduce the burden of data processing. At present, XML-based data warehouse has been a certain research, and its main ideas are basically the same. There are three points indispensable: the first is the XML description of the facts file; the second is the XML description of the dimension file; third is the XML description of dimension relation and inheritance relationship file. And for the three specific forms of XML need to be different for different backgrounds to improve.

And in the meantime, how to combine XML and data warehouse, which is an efficient tool for supporting decision-making, is becoming the hot spot in current computer science. There is obvious difference between XML data, which can describe semi-structured, even unstructured data conveniently because of its flexibility, and relational data. And how to construct data warehouse with XML brings the challenge in this area [4].

3   XML B+ Tree Structure

Data cube is the basis for data query aggregation. Because of the complex relationship of the synthetic natural environment data, a reliable structure is needed to connect different topics, different dimensions, different levels, and different levels. The data cube determines the interconnection between attributes and determines the way the entire data system is running and maintained. This paper will use the B+ tree way to build the data cube.

3.1 B+ Data Cube Related Concepts

For a n dimensional space, the multidimensional hierarchical B+ tree is constructed by the corresponding n dimension hierarchies. Under normal circumstances, the dimension is on the above which has least number of leaf nodes. Where each dimension hierarchy is composed of one or more B+ trees, and the number of B+ trees per dimension is equal to the number of keywords in all B+ leaf nodes in the previous dimension hierarchy.

Correspondingly, we can binary-coded each non-leaf node of each dimension, encoded as follows:

$$B^{m_j^i} = \begin{cases} B^{(m_j^i)}_{ord(father(m_j^i))} & j = 1 \\ B^{father(m_j^i)} * B^{m_j^i}_{ord(father(m_j^i))} & j \neq 1 \end{cases} \qquad (1)$$

Among them, $father\left(m_j^i\right)$ represents the parent of m_j^i. $ord\left(father\left(m_j^i\right)\right)$ represents the m_j^i dictionary location in its parent. $B^{m_j^i}_{ord(father(m_j^i))}$ represents the binary encoding of the m_j^i at this level. The coding length of $B^{m_j^i}_{ord(father(m_j^i))}$ - l_j^i is the maximum number of dimension members of layer j. $l_j^i = \left| lb\max\left\{ cardinality\left(children\left(m_{j-1}^i\right)\right)\right\}\right|$ [5].

The combination of dimension hierarchy encoding is encoded by the most fine-grained hierarchical coding of each dimension, which is used to uniquely represent tuples. $B^D = B^{m_{h_1}^1} \cdot B^{m_{h_2}^2} \cdot B^{m_{h_3}^3} \cdots\cdots\cdots B^{m_{h_n}^n}$, where h_i represents the finest granularity of the i-th dimension. For the dimension level, the use of binary coding without the use of integer coding has many advantages: the first is to speed up the query; the second is to save the storage space, not causing space redundancy.

3.2 XML B+ Tree Structure

For XML-based data cube, the content stored in the XML file usually contains the following 3 points:

(1) the contents of the fact node.
(2) the content of the dimension.
(3) the relationship between the relationship between inheritance and inheritance.

And many researchers make that the three contents are stored in three XML files. The three files are XCubeSchema,XCubeDimension, and XCubeFact, respectively. The dimension structure of this model is more complex, which leads to a reduction in the construction time efficiency. While the XML file based on the B+ tree hierarchy can simplifie the storage of the dimension structure. Since we have coded the dimension hierarchy, the B+ tree structure formed by the hierarchical coding will simplify the processing of the XML file. The leaf node of the B+ tree represents the fact node, and only the leaf node holds the fact value. Because of the presence of coded indexes, the relationships and inheritance relationships between dimensions will be reflected in the binary code, so that only an XML dimension file with binary encoding will be required to complete the work of the XCubeSchema and XCubeDimension files.

Therefore, this paper proposes an improved XML data cube scheme. We use two XML files to describe the structure and content of the data cube. The first file is XB+ TreeFact, which is used to describe the leaf nodes of each B+ tree, that is, the corresponding fact node for each dimension. The second file is XB+ TreeSchema, which is used to describe the structure of the multi-dimensional hierarchy B+ tree.

For example, we use the marine environment temperature as the theme to establish a data cube, the star model is as follows (Fig. 1):

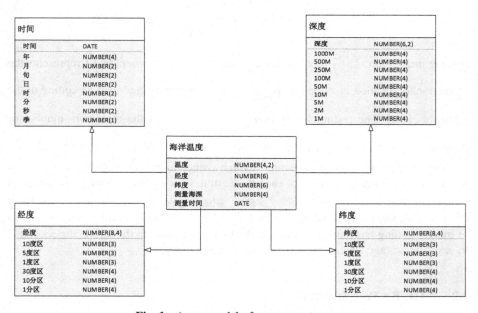

Fig. 1. A star model of ocean temperature

The diagram depicts the star model of marine ambient temperature. Marine environment temperature as the theme, but also contains time, longitude, dimension, depth of the four dimensions. Each dimension is divided into different levels according to the granularity.

XML based data cubes abstract several table and fact tables into a XML representation model that conforms to the XML Schema specification, as shown in the following figure (Fig. 2):

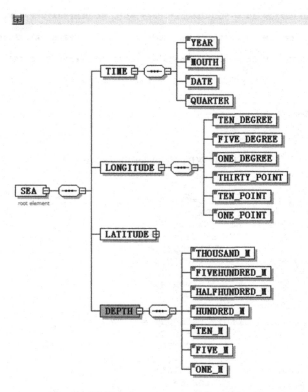

Fig. 2. XML schema constraint specification

According to the star model above, we can build XB+ TreeFact and XB+ Tree-Schema files. The XB+ TreeFact file structure is shown below (Fig. 3):

The picture shows the XB+ TreeFact file, which records the fact that the actual value and the current fact value correspond to the smallest granularity in each dimension, that is, the lowest level member

The XB+ TreeSchema file structure is shown below (Fig. 4):

This picture shows the structure of XB+ TreeSchema files. It is a tree structure. Each layer corresponds to a dimension hierarchy, and each node has a binary code that records the location of the node in the B+ tree, that is, it stores the dimension or the hierarchy of association and inheritance of relationship. The way of coding has been mentioned below.

```
1     <XB+TREE_FACT)
2
3    ⊟<CELL>
4
5         (DIMENSION id = "TIME" node ="{OCEANTEMPERATURE/TIME}"/>
6
7         (DIMENSION id = "LONGITUDE" node ="{OCEANTEMPERATURE/LONGITUDE}"/>
8
9         (DIMENSION id = "LATITUDE" node =" {OCEANTEMPERATURE/LATITUDE}"/>
10
11        (DIMENSION id = "DEPTH" node =" {OCEANTEMPERATURE/DEPTH}"/>
12
13
14   └</CELL>
15
16   </XB+TREE_FACT>
17
18
```

Fig. 3. XB+ TreeFact file structure

```
1     <?xml version="1.0" encoding="UTF-8" ?>
2    ⊟<XB+TREESCHEMA>
3    ⊟<ROOT BCOde = " ">
4    ⊟    <TIME BCOde = " ">
5    ⊟        <YEAR BCOde = " ">
6    ⊟            <MONTH BCOde = " ">
7                    ......
8                    </MONTH>
9                </YEAR>
10           </TIME>
11   ⊟    <LONGITUDE BCOde = " ">
12   ⊟        <DEGREE BCOde = " ">
13   ⊟            <POINT BCOde = " ">
14                   ......
15                   </POINT>
16               </DEGREE>
17           </LONGITUDE>
18   ⊟    <LATITUDE BCOde = " ">
19   ⊟        <DEGREE BCOde = " ">
20   ⊟            <POINT BCOde = " ">
21                   ......
22                   </POINT>
23               </DEGREE>
24           </LATITUDE>
25   ⊟    <DEPTH BCOde = " ">
26   ⊟        <METER BCOde = " ">
27   ⊟            <POINT BCOde = " ">
28                   ......
29                   </POINT>
30               </METER>
31           </DEPTH>
32   -</ROOT>
33   └< /XTREESCHEMA >
```

Fig. 4. XB+ TreeSchema file structure

4 Algorithm of Data Cube Based on XML B+ Tree

The structure of the XML B+ tree has been described above. This section describes the construction of the data cube based on the XML B+ tree structure.

4.1 XB+ TreeSchema Construction Algorithm and Process

XB+ TreeSchema is a process of creating a hierarchical decomposition of source data content. The root node of the tree is root. The hierarchical relationship of the tree is distinguished by the binary coding of each node. This paper uses the structure of the B+ tree.For the tree structure, we can use the recursive way to build the data cube to improve the efficiency of the construction.

This paper assumes that the data source is S and the hierarchy is H, and the algorithm steps are as follows:

Step 1: Analyze the format of the source data S and loop through all the source data to get all dimension levels $H_1, H_2, H_3, \cdots\cdots, H_n$;

Step 2: Traversing the source data S again, obtaining the source data S_i of the corresponding hierarchy H_i, and hierarchically dividing each H_i to generate a hierarchical subtree;

Step 3: Binary code is encoded for each node, with a value of $B^{m_j^i}$;

Step 4: Determine whether the node value S_i is a fact node that conforms to the XB+ TreeFact file structure,If it is, output the value, otherwise S_i and H_i as the new source data S, return to Step 1;

The detailed algorithm pseudocode is as follows:

```
Program XB+TreeSchema (Data source S, Hierarchy H)
(1) begin
(2) Traverse S to get all of hierarchy H₁,H₂, H₃,······,Hₙ
(3) for Hᵢ = H₁ to Hₙ
(4) begin
(5)     output <H id = Hᵢ>
(6)         Traverse S to get Sᵢ,meets the condition Hᵢ
(7)         For each node to be encoded Bᵐʲⁱ
(8)         if Sᵢ is the fact node
(9)             output Sᵢ
(10)        else
(11)            XB+TreeSchema (Sᵢ, H′)
(12)        end if
(13)    output </H>
(14) end
(15) end
```

4.2   Query Algorithm for Data Cube Based on XML B+ Tree

After building the XB+ TreeSchema and XB+ TreeFact files, the data cube based on the XML B+ Tree is built. For data cube, the main purpose is to query the data. This section describes the query algorithm for data cube based on XML B+ tree.

The data cube based on the xml B+ tree is divided according to the dimension hierarchy and stored in the xml file as a B+ tree. Each hierarchy corresponds to a dimension. And because we use the structure of the B+ tree, we can search through the binary code index. Binary indexes reflect hierarchical association and inheritance relationships. We only need to follow the user needs to query the dimension from the root node through the index to search by hierarchy. In the case of data query, the first node of the root node of the tree is traversed first, that is, the first hierarchy. After finding the node attribute value matching the query condition, the node will output the subtree with the node as the root node as the range of the next query. So the scope of the next query than the entire source file has a large degree of reduction. And finally find the desired result.

5   Analysis and Conclusion

This paper discusses the problem of low efficiency of traditional data cubic construction and query. At the same time, the characteristics of comprehensive natural environment data are analyzed, and the data cube technology is applied to the information management system of synthetic natural environment data. By dividing the source data into hierarchical hierarchies, binary coding is performed for each node at each hierarchy, and the B+ tree is constructed layer by layer. At the same time we use XML itself for the tree structure of the data file format to save dimension, binary index and the fact node into the file. Realize the rapid construction of data cube and quick query. But this article is only given a simple example, the follow-up will also be applied to the processing of large-scale data.

References

1. Parimala, N., Pahwa, P.: From XML schema to cube. Int. J. Comput. Theory Eng. **1**, 236–243 (2009)
2. Liqing, S., Hangren, W.: Research on the development of synthetic natural environment database. J. Syst. Simul. **19**(16), 3688–3692 (2007)
3. Chou, L., Zhao, Q.: Data warehouse system based on XML. Appl. Comput. Syst. **13**(2), 12–14 (2004)
4. Zhou, Y., Zhao, Y., Ma, T.: XML data cube based on tree structure. J. Converg. Inf. Technol. **8**(4), 423–430 (2013)
5. Zhao, Q., Chen, S., Hu, K.: Multidimensional hierarchical cube extensible storage structure. J. Appl. Sci. **25**(2), 166–170 (2007)

Adaptive Packet Relocator in Wireless Network-on-Chip (WiNoC)

Mohd Shahrizal Rusli[1]([✉]), Asrani Lit[1], Muhammad Nadzir Marsono[1], and Maurizio Palesi[2]

[1] Universiti Teknologi Malaysia, 81310 Skudai, Johor, Malaysia
{shahrizal,asrani2,mnadzir}@utm.my
[2] DIEEI, University of Catania, V. A. Doria 6, 95125 Catania, Italy
maurizio.palesi@unikore.it

Abstract. In wireless Network-on-Chip (WiNoC), radio frequency (RF) transceivers account for a significant power consumption, particularly its transmitter, out of its total communication energy. In current WiNoC architectures, high transmission power consumption with constant maximum power suffers from significant energy and load imbalance among RF modules which leads to hotspot formation, thus affecting the reliability requirement of the network system. This paper proposes an energy-aware adaptive packet relocator mechanism, in which, based on transmission energy consumption and predefined energy threshold, packets are routed to adjacent transmitter for communication with receiver radio hub, aiming an optimized energy distribution in WiNoC. The proposed strategy alone achieves total communication energy savings of about 8%.

Keywords: Wireless Network-on-Chip · Energy-aware mechanism · Energy threshold · Energy imbalance

1 Introduction

The Network-on-Chip (NoC) [2] emerged as the communication backbone integrating high density processing cores is one of the best candidates to replace bus-interconnects system on a single die. However, as the number of cores in the network size increases, the scalability limitations of conventional planar metal interconnect NoC such as high latency and power consumption become significant. Several improved NoC architectures have been proposed such as 3D NoCs [13,22], photonic NoC [14–16] and wireless NoC (WiNoC) [4,6,19] to mitigate the problem.

WiNoC introduces long-range and high bandwidth radio frequency (RF) interconnects that can possibly reduce the multi-hop communication of the planar metal interconnects in conventional NoC platforms. Implementing WiNoC architecture improves about 20% performance and 30% energy savings over the fully wired NoC links [4,5]. However, high transmission power consumption with constant maximum power makes WiNoC suffers from significant energy and load

© Springer Nature Singapore Pte Ltd. 2017
M.S. Mohamed Ali et al. (Eds.): AsiaSim 2017, Part II, CCIS 752, pp. 719–735, 2017.
DOI: 10.1007/978-981-10-6502-6_61

imbalance among RF modules which leads to hotspot formation, thus affecting the reliability requirement of the network system. Computation and communication loads vary over time depending on various intrinsic and extrinsic factors such as power saving mode specification, data streaming and long duration of data transmission. These features necessitate extra computation and communication run-time efforts causing load imbalance and potential hotspot formation.

The communication density grows higher as distant cores communicate, inextricably linked to heavy resource utilization and eventually cause high energy consumption. A task migration scheme based on predictive task allocation to balance the energy distribution in WiNoC has been proposed through thermal management in [12]. However, both wired and wireless links must be considered in this scheme which results in complexity in terms of implementation. Consequently, characteristics such as dynamic energy management on WiNoC platform which can offer improvement in energy distribution while satisfying system reliability constraint must be considered in the search of the power and energy optimization in WiNoC system.

In this paper, a scheme that dynamically distributes energy dissipation at the upper layer network of WiNoC architectures is presented. The adaptive packet relocator technique is aimed at balancing the transmission power on WiNoC platforms. The idea is that when an energy threshold is reached at a radio hub, an adaptive packet relocator block inside the transmitter transfers the packets to the nearest radio hub through a dedicated physical link for data communication with packets destination radio hub. It has been proven that for efficient energy wireless communication, the path length should be more than three hops [10].

The rest of the paper is organized as follow. Firstly, the literature review on the energy dissipation for WiNoC is presented in Sect. 2. Next, the proposed design is presented in Sect. 3. The experimental setup and results analysis are discussed in Sects. 4 and 5, respectively. Finally, the conclusion and recommendation for future work are presented in Sect. 6.

2   Related Works

The communication latency among the cores becomes the bottleneck in NoC-based system due to multi-hop nature of the system. Several wireless NoC architectures that propose introduction of radio frequency (RF) transceivers as a communication medium have been introduced [3,8]. This is motivated by the previously recognized antenna designs that operate in high frequency at deep submicron level [7]. Some guidelines on designing RF modules that operate in sub-terahertz frequencies have been discussed in [4]. Hybrid architecture of electrical link and wireless link NoC has been introduced in [5]. Cluster-based WiNoC architectures connect each RF module to a group of neighboring processing cores [5,18]. A proposed architecture applies small world property that integrates traditional NoC topologies communicating with different topologies via radio hubs considering long range communication [17]. WiNoC introduces areas and power overheads because the wireless communication require transceiver and antenna components.

Most WiNoC architectures employ a non-coherent OOK based transceiver due to its simple implementation although consuming higher power than the other schemes. The OOK modulation has been widely applied on many platforms such as McWiNoC [18], iWise [5] and mSWNoC [6]. Traditionally, low-power techniques have focused on minimizing power. mm-wave OOK wireless power gated transceiver has been investigated [11]. In [5], runtime traffic-driven adaptive transceiver is adopted by segregating static and dynamic networks. A dynamic voltage and frequency scaling technique based on predictive core switching rate has been proposed by Ganguly et al. [6]. However, Mineo et al. [9] proposed a reconfigurable transmitter that selects transmitting power. The design drives a power amplifier (PA) to configure real output power based on power level provided by variable gain amplifier (VGA) module at runtime. Dynamic power tuning has been an established technique in the context of radio communication such as mobile phones and wireless sensor network.

In the context of WiNoC, dynamic power management requires specific controller and implementation policy in CMOS technology. The main problem of this scheme is that such optimal transmitting power must be characterized offline by using time-consuming field solver simulator and the accuracy has not yet been calibrated for on-chip antennas. However, these approaches alone cannot achieve optimal energy balancing, because they do not consider energy distribution on WiNoC platform such as the switching activities that occur at respective radio hubs, for instance.

Although communication energy at wired and wireless link layers consume about 20%–30% of the total WiNoC energy, if a particular RF transmitter propagates data for a long period when other transmitters are less utilized, imbalanced energy density distribution may occur, causing hotspot formation in the particular fraction of area. In traditional 2D NoC [1], task migration involves dynamic task rescheduling and remapping of originally assigned core-task execution to available cores within the cluster partition. Data need to be rescheduled because of limited memory capacity and multihop natures of 2D NoC. Recently, Murray et al. [12] proposes a task migration technique based on predictive task allocation. However, this method requires implementation on both wired and wireless links of WiNoC, thus introducing high complexity and affects the performance gain. Hence, the above-mentioned WiNoC are not fully capable of balancing the energy distribution. For this reason, this paper presents an energy aware scheme that applies a mechanism which dynamically reroutes the transmitting packets based on normalized energy constraint. The energy-aware scheme is different with its traditional counterpart due to the large bandwidth capacity the transceivers can transmit.

3 Adaptive Packet Relocator

In this section, a scheme that dynamically reconfigures the transmission energy dissipation at the upper layer network of WiNoC architectures is introduced. In the first subsection, the design algorithm of the strategy is discussed. The proposed architecture and its components are detailed out in the following subsection.

3.1   Adaptive Scheme

Figure 1 illustrates a finite state machine implementing the adaptive packet relocator manager. Distributed power manager adopts two modes of operations which are Reconfiguration Period (RP) and Reconfiguration State (RS). During RP period, each WiNoC transmitter collects the periodic energy dissipation for packets transmitted via wireless link. The energy dissipation is calculated based on the buffer occupancy by packets stored in the radio hub transmitter buffer and the router-to-radio hub buffers of a particular cluster accessing the radio hub for communication with destination radio hub. The transmission access in WiNoC follows the most commonly used scheme in conventional NoC that is the wormhole routing scheme. Therefore, the wireless energy dissipation is formulated by considering total number of bits in these buffers being transmitted through wireless links.

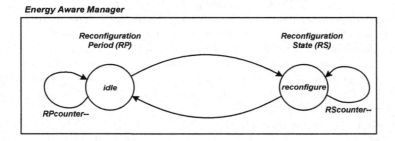

Fig. 1. Finite state machine implementing the proposed scheme

As soon as the adaptive module notifies excessive packet energy dissipation beyond an energy threshold, it activates an energy aware mechanism that transmits incoming packets via overhead wired links, entering the Reconfiguration State (RS). Based on the energy management strategy, next incoming packets are directed to the closest radio hub via a look-up table in each radio hub until the original transmitter energy value decrements below the allowable quantity. The packets are piggybacked on the adjacent radio hub for communication with destination radio hub based on the packet header information.

The management strategy can be formalized as in Algorithm 1. A source radio hub, i, transmits packets to a destination radio hub, j, via antenna of the source transmitter. Each transmitter, T, consists of a dedicated module, $PC[T]$, that counts the number of transmitted packets passing through the internal $FIFO$ radio hub buffer of a transmitter during wireless transmission. The radio hub buffer has larger buffer size than the conventional NoC, which is 8 flits per buffer per wireless channel. Following the wormhole routing technique, after the first group of packets in this buffer are transmitted, the packets stored in router-to-radio hub buffer follow the same channel passing through the radio hub buffer for wireless transmission. Therefore, by calculating the bits switching activity of packets inside the radio hub buffer provides the wireless transmitted energy. It is used to determine the allowable energy threshold of the radio hub.

Algorithm 1. The proposed adaptive packet relocator scheme

---

1 **Input** : PC, $energy\_threshold$
2 **while** true **do**
3   $PC \leftarrow k$
4   **if** $(E_{current} > E_{threshold})$ **then**
5   **if** $(en\_token = 1)$ **then**
6   **for** $(i = k; i > 0; i\text{-}\text{-})$ **do**
7         $SendCmdRelocate(T, Tadj)$
8         $PC \leftarrow k - 1$
9   **end for**
10   **else**
11       $BufferPacket(T)$
12   **else**
13     $SendCmdTransmitWireless(T, R)$
14 **end while**

The period RP varies up to maximum 1000 cycles so that the energy dissipation of a particular transmitter is regulated. Packet routing decision is made during this period by either adopting regular wireless data transmission or adaptive packet relocation scheme. $PC[T]$ is decremented each time i transmits packets to j. Although $PC[T]$ is a local variable to each router, it is driven upon activation by the control switch of the radio hub, that is regulated by the network control mechanism. Since the proposed architecture is a one-way communication, all transmitted bits are considered to be received by the neighbour radio hub. It is assumed that there is a good energy detection module, attached to each radio hub, providing accurate packet transmission energy information. At present, there has been no energy detection model in WiNoC buffer has been developed yet. Thus, the energy detection module is designed as mentioned in the previous paragraphs. The mechanism senses and computes the energy of incoming packets in the radio transmitter $FIFO$ buffer before the end of period $PC[T]$. Signal $energy\_current$ determines run-time energy consumption within the period $PC[T]$. When RP ends and no excessive energy consumption as limited by $energy\_threshold$ is reported at transmitter radio hub T_{src}, signal $energy\_current$ is not asserted. If the current energy dissipation is below the threshold as predefined by the user requirement, the adaptive packet relocator module transmits the packets via normal operation using wireless link.

The algorithm is activated as soon as the signal $energy\_current$ is asserted due to over consumption of packet transmitted energy. If the total computed energy of transmitted packets is greater than the energy threshold denoted by $energy\_threshold$, radio transmitter T forward the next incoming packets to T_{adj} through an overhead wire link. The $energy\_threshold$ value is predetermined before the execution of RP to guarantee reliability. An internal updown counter, k inside the adaptive manager counts the number of cycles which packets are routed to T_{adj} via wired link when the energy aware mechanism is activated for optimized energy distribution all over the WiNoC platform. k is initially configured to a user defined value and is decremented each cycle when triggered.

3.2 Architecture

The core architecture of this approach is the adaptive packet relocator. The module features a dynamic packet relocation scheme that senses the transmitted packets energy dissipation inside the transmitter buffer across a finite window cycle and adapts the systems most suitable energy aware decision. The energy aware scheme routes incoming packets to adjacent radio hub via either wired links introduced at the upper layer network or regular wireless transmission when necessary.

The adaptive packet relocator consists of a strategy that regulates the transmission energy from source T to destination R as well as a lookup table consisting of pair $<T_{src}, T_{adj}>$ employed for energy management strategy as shown in Fig. 1. During the period RP, packets are received by transmitter module for wireless communication via an 8-bit input TX_PKT_i after the serializer module. If the accumulated energy of the transmitter buffer that stores the packets is less than the energy threshold, the packets are transmitted via an 8-bit TX_ANTENNA output port. However, if the energy is equal or greater than the normalized threshold, TX_WIRE is used to route packets to T_{adj} for communication with destination radio hub.

As soon as the energy aware mechanism is activated, packets from T_{src} are received by input TX_PKT_{i-1} of T_{adj}. Based on the destination field of the received packets, T_{adj} broadcasts the data via its antenna, $TX\_ANTENNA$ output port. If the transmitted packet is destined for T_{adj}, RX_i output port passes down the packet to IP core for computational process. The commands cmd_in and cmd_out are used by the module to obtain the proprietary control in administering its energy aware mechanism (Figs. 2 and 3).

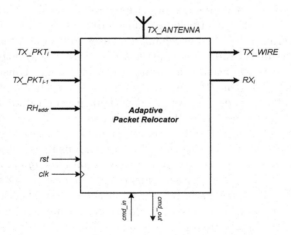

Fig. 2. Adaptive packet relocator module

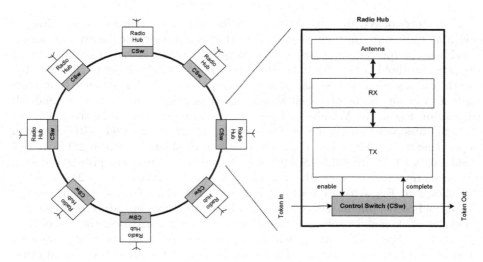

Fig. 3. Radio hubs in ring topology

4 Experimental Setup

We implement the proposed technique in an extended version of Noxim [20] supporting wireless communications. It has been applied on two WiNoC architectures: WCube64 [21] and iWiSe64 [5]. We apply transmission power with a single transmitting power and vary the number of radio hubs to prove scalability of the proposed design. The proposed design has been modeled in VHDL and synthesized using Synopsys Design Compiler and mapped on 28 nm CMOS standard cell-library from TSMC operating at 1 GHz. Benchmarking has been done with SPLASH-2 and PARSEC application files. The transmitter power is set to 794 μW (-1 dBm) which corresponds to 1.4 pJ/bit. The attenuation map has been obtained from the Ansoft HFSS (High Frequency Structural Simulator) modeled with zigzag antenna.

5 Experimental Results

This section discusses the experimental results and analysis of the proposed scheme. The results are discussed by looking into the effects of energy threshold (E_{th}), relocation period (RP), packet injection rate (PIR) and the performance of benchmark suites used. Throughout the analysis, seven various application files from SPLASH-2 and PARSEC benchmark suites are used in the experiment.

5.1 Effects of Energy Thresholds, E_{th}

The proposed adaptive packet relocator scheme is applied on WCube and iWise WiNoC architectures. The experimental results are compared with the baseline architectures of WCube and iWise that utilize constant power for communication with all radio hubs on their platforms. In this experiment, the energy dissipation and latency metrics are observed as energy threshold is varied to normalized energy threshold of between 0.2 to 0.8. The relocation delay is set to 10 cycles due to the optimal energy dissipation the scheme provides, PIR is set such that a low latency output can be obtained and no power management scheme is employed. Based on Fig. 4, the WCube architecture with the proposed adaptive relocator scheme dissipates energy below the baseline architecture (2.95×10^{-8} J) when operating at E_{th} 0.2, 0.3 and 0.4. The energy is dissipated between 2.98×10^{-8} J and 3.09×10^{-8} J from 0.5 until 0.8. Different from WCube, the proposed design gives energy overheads for all E_{th} beyond the baseline iWise energy 2.65×10^{-8} J as shown in Fig. 4(b). Figures 4(c) and (d) show the effect of varying energy threshold on communication latency. Both architectures introduce between 2 to 3 cycles of average latency overheads over the baseline architectures latency.

A low threshold value provides greater system's responsiveness towards energy management strategy. This condition provides more frequent alternative paths to route packets as well as achieving more balanced energy dissipation in WiNoC architectures. The low energy threshold provides a good benefit to highly imbalanced energy distributions network by adopting more frequent packet relocation activity. Inversely, a high energy threshold results in a less regulated packet relocation in WiNoC. Hence, packets are transmitted more frequently via regular wired and wireless transmission path. The latency fluctuations are due to benchmark suites with different application domains which are unpredictable. However, the fluctuations vary between 2 and 3 cycles overhead from the baseline architectures. Due to the stringent energy consumption of WiNoC, energy dissipation increases as the energy threshold increases. The trend is observed when the design is implemented on WCube and iWise architectures with 16 radio hubs each (Fig. 5). It can be observed, on average, the implementation of the proposed design on iWise results in average 6% energy overhead. On the other hand, only 1% average energy overhead is observed for WCube. The energy overheads shown in both architectures indicate the power consumptions to relocate the packets via inter-radio hub wired links when the energy threshold is reached as well as the wireless transmission energy to reach destinations.

5.2   Effects of Relocation Period (RP)

The relocation period is varied to observe the effect on system performance. Relocation period is the number of periods when packets are relocated to the adjacent radio hub via upper subnet layer wired link. In this experiment, the energy dissipation and latency metrics are observed as the relocation period is varied to 10, 20, 30, 40 and 50 cycles. E_{th} is set to 0.5 to represent the mean energy overheads employed by the proposed scheme, PIR is set such that a low latency output can be obtained and no power management scheme is employed. Based on Figs. 6(a) and (b), both architectures with the proposed scheme dissipate energy beyond their baseline energy for all relocation delay values under

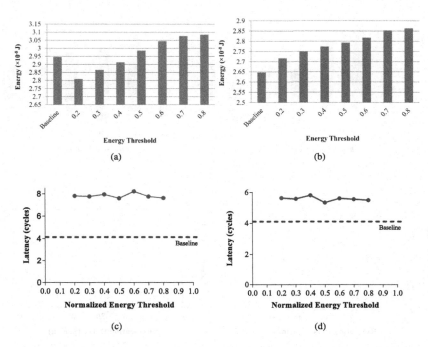

Fig. 4. Energy threshold in terms of energy dissipation for (a) WCube (b) iWise and latency impacts for (c) WCube (d) iWise with the adaptive packet relocator design verified using seven application files in the SPLASH-2 and PARSEC benchmark suites.

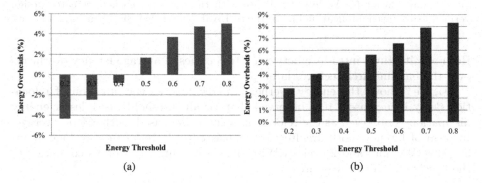

Fig. 5. Performance analysis in terms of energy threshold impact on WiNoC architectures with the adaptive packet relocator design verified using seven application files in the SPLASH-2 and PARSEC benchmark suites: (a) WCube (b) iWise.

investigation. The energy is dissipated between 2.95×10^{-8} J and 3.09×10^{-8} J for WCube whereas between 2.73×10^{-8} J and 2.86×10^{-8} J for iWise. Figures 6(c) and (d) show the effect of varying relocation periods on communication latency.

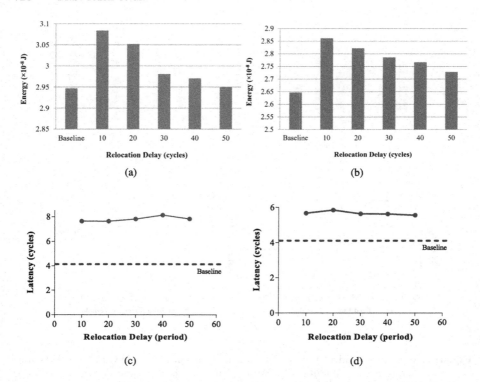

Fig. 6. Relocation periods in terms of energy dissipation for (a) WCube (b) iWise and latency impacts for (c) WCube (d) iWise with the adaptive packet relocator design verified using seven application files in the SPLASH-2 and PARSEC benchmark suites.

Both architectures introduce between 2 to 3 cycles of average latency overheads over the baseline architectures latency.

Figure 7 shows the energy overheads percentage as the duration of relocation delay is increased. It is observed that for all threshold cases, lesser energy dissipation is observed as the relocation delay is increased, with 8% on average. In term of latency, both architectures consistently introduce on average about 3 cycles (WCube) and 2 cycles (iWise) longer execution period as compared to the baseline architectures latency.

5.3   Effects of Packet Injection Rates (PIR)

The previous analyses are carried out based on low injection rate. Different packet injection rates are explored on the proposed scheme to observe how it impacts the energy savings as well as the latency. Eventhough only a single injection rate point is taken, the latency trend represents the entire category. In this experiment, the energy dissipation and latency metrics are observed as the PIR is varied to three different categories which are low, medium and high. The relocation period is set to 10 cycles, E_{th} is set to 0.5 to represent the mean

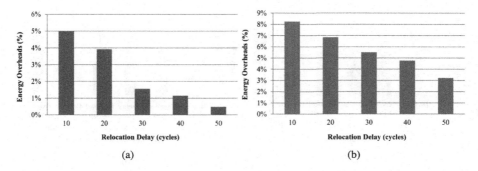

Fig. 7. Performance analysis in terms of energy overheads on WCube and iWise architectures with the adaptive packet relocator design as compared to their baseline architectures: (a) WCube (b) iWise.

energy overheads employed by the proposed scheme and no power management scheme is employed. In the low injection rate case, the latency starts at about 4 cycles with PIR of 0.00001 flits/cycle/node. The medium injection rate of 0.0001 flits/cycle/node returns average packet latency of about 30 cycles. Packet latency of 100 cycles and above is defined as high when PIR is 0.0005.

Based on Figs. 8(a) and (b), both architectures with the proposed scheme dissipate energy beyond their baseline energy for all PIR categories. However, the energy dissipation gap between the baseline and the proposed scheme is not significantly large even for medium and high PIR categories. Figures 8(c) and (d) show the effect of varying the injection rates on communication latency. The proposed design applied on WCube architecture introduces small latency overhead as compared to its baseline latency when all three PIR categories are utilized. As the proposed architecture is implemented on both WCube and iWise, they perform better than the baseline architectures in high PIR category. However, both low and medium PIR categories show small latency gap between the proposed scheme and its baseline.

Referring to Fig. 9, both WiNoC architectures illustrate energy dissipation pattern when the injection rates are increased. As higher rates are injected into the network, the transceivers characterize more significant energy dissipation and hence invoking the action of transmitter energy management. However, due to the network congestion, packets latency rises exponentially thus less number of packets arrived at the receiver. This affects the characterization of the transmission energy as well as the effectiveness of the proposed adaptive packet relocator scheme. Despite this factor, on average the proposed scheme performs about 6% energy overheads as compared to the baseline architectures.

Packet latency increases as the PIR increases. The percentages of increased latency when the proposed scheme is employed on WCube and iWise architectures are within acceptable range. In the low injection rate case, the latency increases between 2 and 3 cycles from the baseline architectures, as discussed in the previous analysis. This is considerably low where the platforms operate

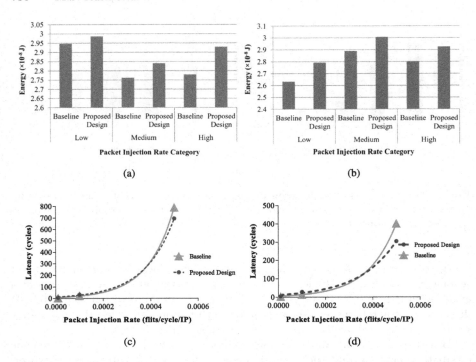

Fig. 8. Packet injection rates in terms of energy dissipation for (a) WCube (b) iWise and latency for (c) WCube (d) iWise with the adaptive packet relocator design verified using seven application files in the SPLASH-2 and PARSEC benchmark suites.

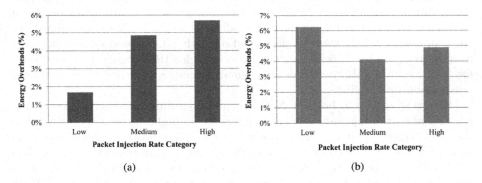

Fig. 9. Performance analysis in terms of energy overheads on WiNoC architectures with the adaptive packet relocator design verified using seven application files in the SPLASH-2 and PARSEC benchmark suites: (a) WCube (b) iWise.

in the optimized performance. As higher number of packets are injected during medium injection rate, the average latency is about 10 cycles higher than the baseline architectures as shown in Figs. 8(c) and (d). The higher the rate of packet injection for transmission, the higher the occurrences of energy threshold is reached. Hence, packets relocation via radio hub wired links take place more frequently, causing busy network. As more transmitters achieve energy constraint frequently, the latency increases due to the migrated packets waiting for transmission as well as packet retransmission. As the packet injection rate increases, the proposed architecture implemented on iWise and WCube offer reduced latency compared to the baseline architectures. High injection rate on both platforms that implement the proposed design results in exponentially high latency. However, there is an average reduced latency of about 100 cycles for both architectures. This occurs due to the alternative paths that are provided by the packet relocator module, offering better performance during high traffic in the network. Table 1 shows the individual benchmark suites reduced latency achieved when high PIR is applied on the adaptive packet relocator scheme.

Overall, this technique introduces latency and fluctuated energy overheads because the source transceivers that relocate packets are developed without the scheme of learning the information about adjacent radio hubs energy status. Thus, packets are relocated even when other trasmitters reach the energy constraint requirement, causing packet saturation at adjacent radio hubs. Therefore, a neighbour-energy-status-aware scheme can be considered for future work to achieve a more balanced energy and better performance WiNoC.

Table 1. Individual reduced latency of SPLASH-2 and PARSEC benchmark suites when the adaptive packet relocator is applied on WCube and iWise WiNoC architectures for high PIR

Program	WiNoC	Baseline latency (cycles)	High PIR latency (cycles)	Reduced latency (cycles)
Barnes	WCube	886.238	829.509	56.729
	iWise	475.537	357.839	117.698
Blackscholes	WCube	829.249	766.055	63.194
	iWise	448.915	353.143	95.773
Fluidanimate	WCube	886.238	829.509	56.729
	iWise	475.537	357.839	117.698
Freqmine	WCube	991.282	632.578	358.704
	iWise	410.252	319.949	90.304
Streamcluster	WCube	886.238	829.509	56.729
	iWise	475.537	357.839	117.698
Swaptions	WCube	307.821	227.328	80.493
	iWise	139.209	89.534	49.675
Vips	WCube	743.84	745.507	$(-)1.667$
	iWise	385.572	294.485	91.087

5.4   Performance of SPLASH-2 and PARSEC Benchmark Suites

From the experimental results discussed previously, it is observed that 0.5 gives an optimized E_{th} value (near 8%) since the performance degradation difference is minimum on WCube architecture. The analysis has been carried out considering a relocation delay of 10 clock cycles. Observing the SPLASH-2 and PARSEC benchmark suites performance, Tables 2 and 3 show the energy dissipation and latency for the proposed design as well as the baseline WiNoC, respectively. E_{th} 0.2, 0.5 and 0.8 are used for analysis purpose to show the energy dissipation pattern which differs from one application file to another. While there are a few SPLASH-2 and PARSEC applications that introduce energy overheads, several applications introduce significant energy savings as shown in Fig. 10(a) and (b).

Table 2. SPLASH-2 and PARSEC benchmark suites energy dissipation comparison applied on WCube and iWise WiNoC architectures.

Program	WiNoC	Baseline energy ($\times 10^{-18}$ J)	E_{th} 0.2 ($\times 10^{-18}$ J)	E_{th} 0.5 ($\times 10^{-18}$ J)	E_{th} 0.8 ($\times 10^{-18}$ J)
Barnes	WCube	2.868	2.895	3.032	3.094
	iWise	2.434	2.267	2.738	2.789
Blackscholes	WCube	3.182	2.545	2.788	2.923
	iWise	2.721	2.603	2.704	2.769
Fluidanimate	WCube	2.868	2.895	3.233	3.320
	iWise	2.434	2.727	2.638	2.694
Freqmine	WCube	2.840	3.034	3.196	3.268
	iWise	2.602	2.748	2.812	2.922
Streamcluster	WCube	2.868	2.895	3.133	3.300
	iWise	2.434	2.587	2.683	2.753
Swaptions	WCube	3.012	2.856	2.835	2.923
	iWise	2.658	2.663	2.824	2.903
Vips	WCube	2.991	2.546	2.685	2.763
	iWise	3.048	3.018	3.148	3.209

As the energy threshold specification is applied to all transceivers on the entire platform, the average energy distribution pattern can be achieved. For WCube architecture implementing the proposed design, the energy distribution are lower than its baseline energy dissipation between 0.2 and 0.4 threshold while more energy is dissipated for 0.5 and above. However, iWise architecture dissipated energy overheads for all threshold probably due to the higher transmission frequency at intra- and inter- cluster level since it adopts multi-channel transmission. The higher the number of wireless channel are utilized, the higher the energy overheads may be obtained apart of the distributed transmission energy.

Table 3. SPLASH-2 and PARSEC benchmark suites latency comparison applied on WCube and iWise WiNoC architectures.

Program	WiNoC	Baseline latency (cycles)	E_{th} 0.2 latency (cycles)	E_{th} 0.5 latency (cycles)	E_{th} 0.8 latency (cycles)
Barnes	WCube	4.174	7.940	7.760	7.938
	iWise	4.072	5.655	5.155	5.463
Blackscholes	WCube	4.173	8.021	7.225	7.137
	iWise	4.067	5.672	5.597	5.615
Fluidanimate	WCube	4.174	7.940	7.760	7.938
	iWise	4.071	5.655	5.155	5.463
Freqmine	WCube	4.141	7.944	6.700	8.007
	iWise	4.072	5.743	5.290	5.479
Streamcluster	WCube	4.174	7.940	7.760	7.938
	iWise	4.071	5.655	5.155	5.463
Swaptions	WCube	4.088	7.463	7.479	6.136
	iWise	4.071	5.368	5.164	5.511
Vips	WCube	4.128	7.484	8.565	8.296
	iWise	4.091	5.732	5.893	5.526

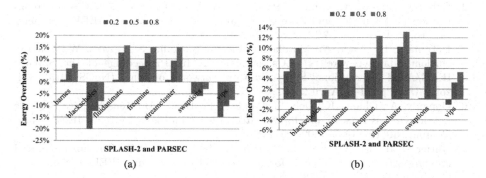

(a)   (b)

Fig. 10. Performance analysis of SPLASH-2 and PARSEC benchmark suites in terms of energy overheads

6 Conclusion and Future Work

In this paper, an energy aware management scheme for distributing WiNoC energy at the radio hub layer has been proposed. Based on the experimental results, the energy overheads and latency present as the trade off in this scheme. The radio-hubs in a WiNoC architecture are one of the main contributors of the total communication energy. In particular, the receiver and the buffers into a radio-hub account for a significant fraction of its total energy consumption. Thus, reducing the energy consumption of such power-hungry elements is mandatory in the context of energy efficient WiNoC architectures. The proposed strategy achieves total communication energy savings of about 8%.

Overall, this technique introduces latency and fluctuated energy overheads because the source transceivers that relocate packets are developed without the scheme of learning the information about adjacent radio hubs energy status. Thus, packets are relocated even when other trasmitters reach the energy constraint requirement, causing packet saturation at adjacent radio hubs. Therefore, a neighbour-energy-status-aware scheme can be considered for future work to achieve a more balanced energy and better performance WiNoC.

References

1. Al Faruque, M., Jahn, J., Henkel, J.: Runtime thermal management using software agents for multi-and many-core architectures. IEEE Des. Test Comput. **27**(6), 58–68 (2010)
2. Benini, L., De Micheli, G.: Networks on chips: a new SoC paradigm. IEEE Comput. **35**(1), 70–78 (2002)
3. Deb, S., Chang, K., Ganguly, A., Yu, X., Teuscher, C., Pande, P., Heo, D., Belzer, B.: Design of an efficient NoC architecture using millimeter-wave wireless links. In: Proceedings of the 13th IEEE International Symposium on Quality Electronic Design (ISQED 2012), California, USA, pp. 165–172, March 2012
4. Deb, S., Ganguly, A., Pande, P.P., Belzer, B., Heo, D.: Wireless NoC as interconnection backbone for multicore chips: promises and challenges. IEEE J. Emerg. Sel. Topics Circ. Syst. **2**(2), 228–239 (2012)
5. DiTomaso, D., Kodi, A., Matolak, D., Kaya, S., Laha, S., Rayess, W.: Energy-efficient adaptive wireless NoCs architecture. In: Proceedings of the Seventh IEEE/ACM International Symposium on Networks on Chip (NoCS 2013), Arizona, USA, pp. 1–8, April 2013
6. Ganguly, A., Chang, K., Deb, S., Pande, P.P., Belzer, B., Teuscher, C.: Scalable hybrid wireless network-on-chip architectures for multicore systems. IEEE Trans. Comput. **60**(10), 1485–1502 (2011)
7. Gutierrez Jr., F., Agarwal, S., Parrish, K., Rappaport, T.S.: On-chip integrated antenna structures in CMOS for 60 GHz WPAN systems. IEEE J. Sel. Areas Commun. **27**(8), 1367–1378 (2009)
8. Hu, W.H., Wang, C., Bagherzadeh, N.: Design and analysis of a mesh-based wireless network-on-chip. In: Proceedings of the 20th IEEE Euromicro International Conference on Parallel, Distributed and Network-Based Processing (PDP 2012), Garching, Germany, pp. 483–490, February 2012
9. Mineo, A., Palesi, M., Ascia, G., Catania, V.: An adaptive transmitting power technique for energy efficient mm-wave wireless NoCs. In: Proceedings of IEEE Design, Automation and Test in Europe Conference and Exhibition (DATE 2014), Dresden, Germany, pp. 1–6, March 2014
10. Mineo, A., Palesi, M., Ascia, G., Catania, V.: Exploiting antenna directivity in wireless NoC architectures. Microprocess. Microsyst. **43**, 59–66 (2016)
11. Mondal, H.K., Deb, S.: Energy efficient on-chip wireless interconnects with sleepy transceivers. In: Proceedings of the 8th IEEE International Design and Test Symposium (IDT 2013), Marrakesh, Morocco, pp. 1–6, December 2013

12. Murray, J., Wettin, P., Pande, P., Shirazi, B., Nerurkar, N., Ganguly, A.: Evaluating effects of thermal management in wireless NoC-enabled multicore architectures. In: Proceedings of the IEEE International Green Computing Conference (IGCC 2013), Virginia, USA, pp. 1–8, June 2013
13. Pavlidis, V.F., Friedman, E.G.: 3-D topologies for networks-on-chip. IEEE Trans. Very Large Scale Integr. VLSI Syst. **15**(10), 1081–1090 (2007)
14. Shacham, A., Bergman, K., Carloni, L.P.: Photonic networks-on-chip for future generations of chip multiprocessors. IEEE Trans. Comput. **57**(9), 1246–1260 (2008)
15. Vantrease, D., Schreiber, R., Monchiero, M., McLaren, M., Jouppi, N.P., Fiorentino, M., Davis, A., Binkert, N., Beausoleil, R.G., Ahn, J.H.: Corona: system implications of emerging nanophotonic technology. In: Proceedings of the 35th International Symposium on Computer Architecture (ISCA 2008), Beijing, China, pp. 153–164, June 2008
16. Pan, Y., Kumar, P., Kim, J., Memik, G., Zhang, Y., Choudhary, A.: Firefly: illuminating future network-on-chip with nanophotonics. In: Proceedings of the 36th Annual International Symposium on Computer Architecture, Texas, USA, pp. 429–440, June 2009
17. Yu, X., Sah, S.P., Deb, S., Pande, P.P., Belzer, B., Heo, D.: A wideband body-enabled millimeter-wave transceiver for wireless network-on-chip. In: Proceedings of the IEEE 54th International Midwest Symposium on Circuits and Systems (MWSCAS), Seoul, Korea, pp. 1–4, August 2011
18. Zhao, D., Wang, Y., Li, J., Kikkawa, T.: Design of multi-channel wireless NoC to improve on-chip communication capacity. In: Proceedings of the Fifth ACM/IEEE International Symposium on Networks-on-Chip (NoCS 2011), Pennsylvania, USA, pp. 177–184, May 2011
19. DiTomaso, D., Kodi, A., Kaya, S., Matolak, D.: iWISE: inter-router wireless scalable express channels for network-on-chips (NoCs) architecture. In: Proceedings of the IEEE 19th Annual Symposium on High Performance Interconnects (HOTI), California, USA, pp. 11–18, August 2011
20. Catania, V., Mineo, A., Monteleone, S., Palesi, M., Patti, D.: Noxim: an open, extensible and cycle-accurate network on chip simulator. In: Proceedings of the IEEE 26th International Conference on Application-specific Systems, Architectures and Processors (ASAP 2015), Ontario, Canada, pp. 162–163, July 2015
21. Lee, S.-B., Tam, S.-W., Pefkianakis, I., Lu, S., Chang, M.F., Guo, C., Reinman, G., Peng, C., Naik, M., Zhang, L., et al.: A scalable micro wireless interconnect structure for CMPs. In: Proceedings of the 15th Annual International Conference on Mobile Computing and Networking (MobiCom 2009), Beijing, China, pp. 217–228 (2009)
22. Feero, B.S., Pande, P.P.: Networks-on-chip in a threedimensional environment: a performance evaluation. IEEE Trans. Comput. **58**(1), 32–45 (2009)

Highly Efficient Power Amplifier
for Microwave Transmitter

Farid Zubir[✉] and Reuban Rao Radhakrishnan

Department of Communication Engineering, Faculty of Electrical Engineering,
Universiti Teknologi Malaysia, Johor Bahru, Malaysia
faridzubir@utm.my, reubanrao93@gmail.com

Abstract. Sustainability is currently becoming a trend in technologies such as telecommunications. The goal is to reduce power consumption and increase the battery life of mobile nodes. The highest power consumer in the telecommunication module, the power amplifiers were designed using inefficient configurations as the older emphasize is only to achieve highest linearity possible at the output. This work proposes designs for Class E power amplifiers operating at 2.4 GHz based on nonlinear SPICE FET models using two different Sokal's empirical equations. One emphasizes considerations of output power with quality factor, the other does not. Clear differences can be observed through simulation results as the newer Sokal's equation proved to be more efficient. This analytical solution can be used to design future power amplifiers where efficiency is the prime concern.

Keywords: Class E · SPICE models · Field effect transistors

1 Introduction

With the world moving towards the era of 5G networks where the means of communication can soon extend between 50 billion devices, technological trends are now looking into better coverage, low power consumption and more connected devices [1]. In concurrent to this future, power wastages are tackled vigorously and key components in the communication modules which are heavily power dependent are introduced with new types of highly efficient configurations. From these modules, the highest power consumer is the power transistor in the power amplifier [2]. Qin et al. in [3] stated that power amplifiers that are highly efficient always sought for because of these devices tend to have longer battery life, reduced power dissipation and are generally smaller in size. Conventional classes of power amplifiers are used in current generation RF and microwave systems. This conventional designs however wastes most of its input power in forms of energy dissipation of heat which cannot be avoided due to the very nature of power components used to drive amplification models [4]. Highly efficient switching mode amplifier such as the Class E has potential to provide a solution to the above as it has a theoretical efficiency of 100%. This would reduce the power wastage compared to conventional power amplifiers. The main focus or drive of this work is to look into aspects of switching mode power amplifiers which is theoretically able to achieve 100% efficiency. In comparison, commercial power amplifiers

© Springer Nature Singapore Pte Ltd. 2017
M.S. Mohamed Ali et al. (Eds.): AsiaSim 2017, Part II, CCIS 752, pp. 736–745, 2017.
DOI: 10.1007/978-981-10-6502-6_62

used in the current designs only can operate with the highest achievable power added efficiency, (PAE) of merely 50%. The subject of measurement for power amplifiers has always been vague and argued amongst circuit designers and academicians but for this dissertation the PAE will be used as decisive measurement for power efficiency. Switching mode amplifiers such as Class E or Class F are not preferred by RF circuit designers due to its highly non-linearity. However, this disadvantage can be solved by using linearization techniques such as pre-distortion or feedback/feed forward techniques. In practicality, there is always tradeoffs between achieving high PAE and output power which will be proved in this paper. Besides that, investigations towards intermodulation distortion, (IMD) will be conducted across power amplifier configurations. It would be such a waste to discard a power amplifier that has very high potential in conserving energy such as the switching mode amplifier.

2   Analytical Solutions

2.1   Class E Power Amplifier Background

The general approach designing a Class E amplifier is by looking into the works of Nathan O. Sokal, one of the key founders of the Class E configuration. Nathan has introduced several empirical equation which has been fine-tuned over the years to achieve a much more reliable and accurate result. These equations gives the value of passive components in $\left(R_{load}, L_s, C_s \text{ and } C_p\right)$ which induces a non-overlapping current and voltage waveforms, vital to sustain a high PAE [2]. Figure 1 illustrates the general schematic of the Class E amplifier.

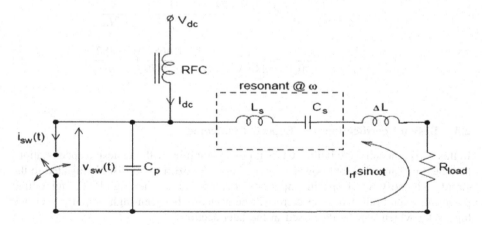

Fig. 1. Basic arrangement of a Class E power amplifier. RFC is the DC block. $\mathbf{L_s}, \mathbf{C_s}$ are the resonator circuit elements. $\mathbf{C_p}$ is the shunt capacitor which charges during transistor ON period and discharges during transistor OFF period. ΔL is only required if there is need to shift waveforms for a better non-overlapping waveform.

2.2 Passive Element Design

Udin [5], has designed the passive components based on older version of Sokal's empirical equation listed below as Eqs. (1) to (3). All values of passive components can be calculated except for R_{load}. By practicality, designer would prefer to choose $R_{load} = 50\,\Omega$. Sokal and Sokal [2] claimed, output power deteriorates between 10% to 38% of expected values for values of Q_L between 1.7678 to 5 using the equations prior to his. In the newer formula, the values of Q_L should be chosen above 1.7678 to avoid zero division for resonator capacitor, C_S.

$$C_P = \frac{1}{2\pi f R \left(\frac{\pi^2}{4} + 1\right)\left(\frac{\pi}{2}\right)}. \tag{1}$$

$$C_S = C_P \left(\frac{5.447}{Q_L}\right)\left(1 + \frac{1.153}{Q_L - 1.153}\right). \tag{2}$$

$$L_S = \frac{Q_L R}{\omega}. \tag{3}$$

Sokal's new equations put heavy consideration to output power with correlation to quality factor to produce a much accurate result. However, the equation to calculate L_S is similar.

$$R_{LOAD} = 0.5786 \left(\frac{V_{DD}}{P_{OUT}}\right)\left(1 - \frac{0.451759}{Q_L} - \frac{0.402444}{Q_L^2}\right). \tag{4}$$

$$C_P = \frac{1}{5.44668\omega R}\left(1 + \frac{0.91424}{Q_L} - \frac{1.03175}{Q_L^2}\right) + \frac{1}{\omega^2 L_S}. \tag{5}$$

$$C_S = \frac{1}{\omega R}\left(\frac{1}{Q_L - 0.104823}\right)\left(1 + \frac{1.101468}{Q_L - 1.7879}\right) - \frac{0.2}{\omega^2 L_S}. \tag{6}$$

2.3 Design Specification and Expected Outcome

In this work, the aim is to build a Class E power amplifier with the design specifications tabulated in Table 1. Input power ranging from −20 dBm to 50 dBm is injected to the circuit to identify which specific input power can produce either high PAE, high output power, or even both. However there will be tradeoffs between high output power and high PAE which will be discussed in the later sections.

The values for passive components are calculated using Eqs. (1) to (6) as shown in Table 2. As discussed in the previous section, the value for the passive component.

R_{load} is chosen as 50 Ω and the resonator inductor, L_s are same for both equations. By rule of thumb is RFC should be at least 30 times more than the resonator inductor, L_s [6].

Table 1. Design specifications for Class E amplifiers. These designs are to operate at 2.4 GHz and with the expected PAE of over 70%.

Parameters	Proposed Class E circuit specifications
Operating frequency	2.4 GHz
FET models	STAZ, CURTICE2, TQ_MATRK
Minimum PAE	70%
Loaded quality factor	7
Input power	−20 dBm to 50 dBm

Table 2. Calculated passive component values based on prior and newer version.

Passive component values	Passive component values based on Eqs. (1)–(3)	Passive component values based on Eqs. (4)–(6)
R_{load}	50 Ω	50 Ω
L_s,	23.21 nH	23.21 nH
C_s	0.2433 pF	0.2701 pF
C_p	0.22685 pF	0.23299 pF

To control the harmonics, the resonator circuits denoted by L_s and C_s provide a condition of circuit where it is short at the fundamental frequency and open at all the harmonics. As a comparison, a Class B configuration requires to be short circuited at all the harmonics [7, 8]. Based on Fig. 1 there is a requirement for selecting a switching type of device. We have decided to use the field effect transistor (FET) as the switching device of choice because of ease of use and high ratio of ON and OFF state resistance [3]. Power amplifiers generally are designed with FETs thus it best in this dissertation the FET is used as the switching device to understand how suitable is this element in a Class E configuration. To determine whether a configuration is operating in Class E, we can look at the output waveform as a conclusive factor besides a high PAE. Due to the switching nature of Class E power amplifier, there can be no coexisting current and voltage at any instantaneous time resulting in the theoretically efficiency of 100%. The circuit should either conducts maximum current swing during the transistor ON period with voltage almost zero, charging the parallel capacitor, C_s. After presumably 50% duty cycle, transistor goes to OFF state where capacitor, C_s discharges to the load resulting in maximum voltage swing, with current almost zero. One important criteria worth mentioning is the simplicity of the Class E design compared to other switching power amplifiers such as the Class F or Class F^{-1}. The small number of reactive capacitance of Class E amplifier can be easily absorbed as part of the output matching network. Figure 2 shows the typical output waveform of a Class E amplifier which shows no over-lapping between voltages and currents waveforms. Thus there is no product of power (P = VI) which results in no power dissipation hence efficiencies reach 100%, theoretically.

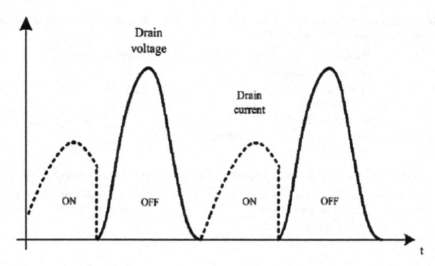

Fig. 2. Class E output waveforms. Current conducts during transistor ON period, while voltage is produced during transistor OFF period. This results in non-overlapping waveforms.

3 Simulation and Analysis

In this dissertation, three types of SPICE FET models used are the STAZ, CURTICE2 (Curtice Quadratic), and TQ_MATRK (TriQuint TXModified Materka) available in the AWR MWO library.

3.1 Simulator Circuit Design

By rule of thumb, the FET must be driven in the saturation region to function in switching mode. V_{GS} is chosen at the saturation level on the load line with highest V_{DS} curve to achieve maximum output voltage and current swings. However, it is important to make sure V_{GS} value chosen is not too low (below threshold voltage) which causes the FET to not even turn on. Each of the FET stated above have their own specific V_{GS} and V_{DS} with swept input power (−20 dbm to 50 dBm) and operating at 2.4 GHz matched with Class E passive elements calculated (Table 2). Figure 3 illustrates the STAZ Class E power amplifier designed using the AWR MWO simulator. An HBTuner is used to replace the input matching network for ease and simplicity. Values of passive component calculated in Sect. 2.3 are loaded as the output matching network (OMN).

A reference model without the passive elements shown in Fig. 4 is also designed as a comparison with the prior. All three circuits will be compared for their performances which are the circuit designed based on older equations, the circuit designed based on Sokal's newer equation and the reference circuit with no OMN.

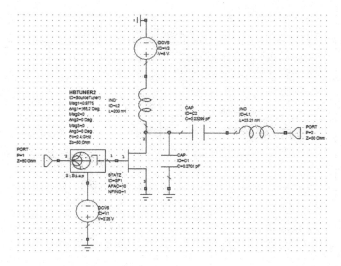

Fig. 3. STAZ Class E design utilizing HBTUNER2 with matched values of magnitude and angle for maximum power transfer across ports (S11 matching).

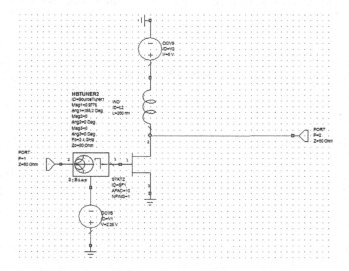

Fig. 4. STAZ Class E reference circuit design without passive components of Table 2 as OMN.

3.2 Simulation Results

Figure 5 shows the PAE with swept input power for the STAZ FET circuit for all three types of configurations. This circuit is able to achieve PAE as high as 97.2% for the input power (Pin) of 30 dBm at 2.4 GHz utilizing Sokal's newer equations. Non-overlapping current waveforms can also be observed on the FET's output as shown in Fig. 6. Current swing for the STAZ amplifier peaks at 144.6 mA and voltage swing

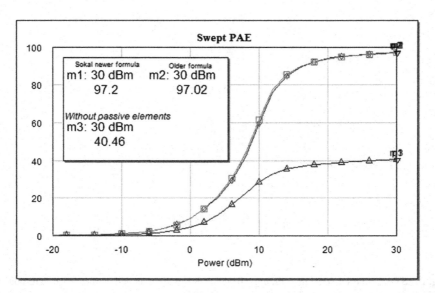

Fig. 5. PAE for STAZ model for all three circuits. Blue line is the reference Class E circuit. Pink is Class E circuit with OMN based on Sokal's newer equation while brown line is the older equation. (Color figure online)

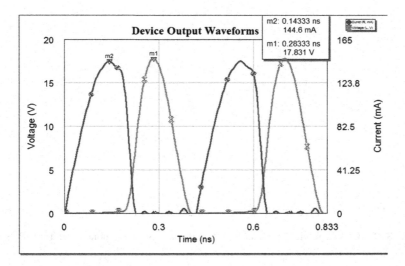

Fig. 6. STAZ non-overlapping waveform output. This is the expected non-overlapping waveforms similar to Fig. 2.

peaks at 17.831 V with little overlapping. In all three FET Class E designs, the newer Sokal's equations produces the highest PAE. However, performance varies across the other FET models. Table 3. displays comparisons between the three models. The CURTICE 2 circuit has a PAE of 81.09% as its highest providing injection power is set at 26 dBm.

Table 3. PAE comparison between FET models in AWR MWO library.

Passive component values	STAZ Pin = 30 dBm	CURTICE2 Pin = 26 dBm	TQ_MATRK Pin = 4 dBm
Reference circuit PAE	40.46%	11.28%	23.51%
Sokal's older equation PAE	97.02%	75.05%	71.16%
Sokal's newer equation PAE	97.2%	81.09%	72.99%
Output power	48.07 dBm	28.4 dBm	25.02 dBm
Amplifier gain	18.07 dB	2.4 dB	21.02 dB

The TQ_MATRK requires a much lower input power of 4 dBm for the device to operate at its highest PAE of 72.99%. This FET may be suitable to be used as a Low Noise Amplifier (LNA) at the receiver side which usually receives very low input power. On the contrary, even though TQ_MTRK has the lowest PAE among all three FETs, it has the highest gain of all the FETs which is 21.03 dB. An important consideration that might be vital during a power amplifier design.

There is always a tradeoff between PAE and output power for a FET. We can achieve a high PAE but not without adverse effect to the output power. Not all FET can produce a high PAE and output power simultaneously. Table 4 shows the highest output power achievable across all three models with its effect on their PAEs. Note that all FET models in this section are simulated from circuits designed from Sokal's newer formula. Just like in achieving highest PAE in the previous section, each FET model requires its own specific input power shown in Table 4. The STAZ configuration suffers a PAE deterioration by 11.14% from its maximum PAE if the circuit is driven to produce a high output power of 54.07 dBm. CURTICE 2 suffers the most with PAE deteriorating by 58.19% for a mere amplification output of 32.4 dBm. CURTICE 2 has only a 2.4 dB gain which may be a problem in some design specifications as there may

Table 4. PAE and output power comparison across FET devices.

Passive component values	STAZ Pin = 36 dBm	CURTICE2 Pin = 30 dBm	TQ_MATRK Pin = 8.304 dBm
Highest output power	54.07 dBm	32.4 dBm	29.325 dBm
Amplifier gain	18.07 dB	2.4 dB	21.021 dB
Instantaneous PAE	85.88%	22.9%	27.571%
PAE deterioration	11.14%	58.19%	45.419%

be insufficient amplification. On the contrary, once again the TQ_MATRK device shows its capability of producing a very high gain of 21.0121 dB. With the input power of 8.304 dBm (lowest among the 3 FET models), TQ_MTRK is able to produce output power of 29.325 dBm but with cost of PAE to drop by 45.419%.

Another interesting criteria to look into is the IMD existing at the output gate of FETs. IMD or simply known as neighboring distortion occurs due to non-linear characteristic that exist at the FET gate node. This causes other nearby frequencies besides than the fundamental to have unwanted powers and gains, reducing overall performance since the goal is to operate at one frequency band solely which is at 2.4 GHz. However, IMD is not necessarily bad. It really depends on what type of operation that this circuit was designed to achieve; either wideband or narrowband. For narrowband operations, IMD is catastrophic as it introduces unwanted noises which leads to higher bit error rate due to intersymbol interference. But for wideband, IMD is rather a lucrative as the FET can operate in a much higher bandwidth giving way for usage of wideband techniques such as orthogonal frequency-division multiple access, OFDMA which is widely being discussed to be implemented in upcoming 5G systems [3]. Table 5 displays the frequencies range for the three types of FET models. STAZ has the widest band amongst the three with a leeway of 200 MHz and CURTICE 2 has the narrowest band with only 50 MHz gap.

Table 5. Intermodulation ranges comparison between FET devices.

FET types	STAZ	CURTICE2	TQ_MATRK
Frequency range	2.3–2.5 GHz	2.4–2.45 GHz	2.35–2.5 GHz

4 Conclusion

In this contribution, high efficiencies can be achieved using SPICE FET models using Sokal's equations. Simulations results were compared to prove validity that Sokal's newer equations is able to achieve higher efficiency. However considerations must be taken between tradeoffs that exist between PAE and output power. These Class E circuits can be used as either PAs or LNAs depending on the bandwidth, PAE or output power considerations and functionality of FET in Class E configuration. Future works can look into harmonic terminations for Class E PAs which may improve performance.

Acknowledgement. This work was supported by Ministry of Higher Education (MOHE), Faculty of Electrical Engineering, Research Management Centre, Universiti Teknologi Malaysia (UTM) under Potential Academic Staff Grant (Cost Center No: Q.J130000.2723.02K57).

References

1. Ashtom, T.: Lauching of UTM Ericsson Innovation Centre for 5G. Universiti Teknologi Malaysia, Kuala Lumpur (2016). Hisham, D.A.
2. Sokal, N., Sokal, A.: Class E-A new class of high-efficiency tuned single-ended switching power amplifiers. IEEE J. Solid-State Circuits **10**(3), 168–176 (1975)

3. Qin, Y., Gao, S., Sambell, A., Korolkiewicz, E.: Design of low-cost broadband class-E power amplifier using low-voltage supply. Microw. Opt. Technol. Lett. **44**(2), 103–106 (2004)
4. Norouzian, F.: Dual-Band and Switched-Band Highly Efficient Power Amplifiers (2014)
5. Udin, M.: RF LDMOS Power Amplifier Class E for Wireless Communication. Universiti Teknologi Malaysia, Skudai (2006). pp. 52-55
6. Cripps, S.: RF Power Amplifiers for Wireless Communications, 1st edn. Artech House, Norwood (2006). pp. 192-196
7. Zubir, F., Gardner, P.: A new power combiner using aperture coupling technique for push-pull class B power amplifier. pp. 1–4. IEEE (2013)
8. Zubir, F., Gardner, P.: Differentially fed multilayer antennas with harmonic filtering for push-pull class B power amplifier integration. pp. 96–99. IET (2013)

An Optimized Reduction Technique via Firefly Algorithm and Gravitational Search Algorithm

Norul Ashikin Norzain and Shafishuhaza Sahlan[(✉)]

Faculty of Electrical Engineering, Universiti Teknologi Malaysia,
UTM Skudai, Johor Bahru, Malaysia
shafis@fke.utm.my

Abstract. To improve effluent quality of a wastewater treatment plant (WWTP), an optimized model order reduction (MOR) for the high order WWTP system is proposed. A high order model may lead to inefficient analysis of the system and can be computationally expensive. Hence, an accurate and suitable reduced order model needs to be obtained. In this research, an optimized MOR algorithm is proposed by the combination of Frequency Domain Gramian based Model Reduction (FDIG) and Singular Perturbation Approximation (SPA). To reduce the high order model to lower order model with minimum reduction error, optimization techniques of Firefly Algorithm (FFA) and Gravitational Search Algorithm (GSA) is applied. To show the effectiveness of the proposed technique, a case study on WWTP is utilized. From the results obtained, the optimized reduced order models obtained is a 9th order system which yield the lowest reduction error while preserving the stability of the original system.

Keywords: Reduction technique · Singular perturbation approximation · Frequency domain interval gramian · Firefly algorithm · Gravitational search algorithm

1 Introduction

In process engineering industry, the processes involved are designed to improve certain standards in fulfilling current customers' requirement. Hence, to realize this requirement, an accurate system model is a necessity. A good representation of a process plant can be observed from the high order system obtained. However, due to steep computational costs incurred, a high order system is not desirable in the industry. Hence, model order reduction technique (MOR) is introduced. MOR, as the name suggest, is a technique for reducing the computational complexity of mathematical model in numerical solution. The purpose of MOR is to replace a large number of dynamical systems to smaller scale while preserving the input and output dynamic, representing the original system accurately.

A number of model order reduction techniques have been proposed in the literature, such as hankel norm approximation, balanced truncation and singular perturbation approximation (SPA) [1]. For all the mentioned techniques, the stability of original system is preserved. SPA in particular, is a model reduction method where the stability of the original system is preserved [2–4]. Ideally, a reduction method should minimize

© Springer Nature Singapore Pte Ltd. 2017
M.S. Mohamed Ali et al. (Eds.): AsiaSim 2017, Part II, CCIS 752, pp. 746–759, 2017.
DOI: 10.1007/978-981-10-6502-6_63

the reduction error at the whole frequency range which is often not feasible to achieve. However, for some systems, the minimization of reduction error is more important over certain frequency interval than other frequencies such as in controller reduction application [3, 5, 6]. This motivated the author to apply frequency weighted in model order reduction.

Enns [7] was the first to implemented frequency weighted in model order reduction technique. In general, this technique include frequency weighting in the balanced truncation technique, and known as frequency weighted balanced truncation method. This method may use input weighting, output weighting or both. However, Enn's method only yields stability of the reduced order model with single weighting present. To overcome the drawback of instability of the reduced order model, several other technique have been proposed such as Gawronski and Juang's method [8]. This technique is emphasizing on reduction in specified frequency known as frequency domain interval gramian based model reduction technique (FDIG), utilizing frequency interval gramian. In literature, promising results on FDIG are obtained.

For an accurate reduced order model, the reduction error which is the difference between the reduced model and the estimated model must be very small, in order to represent the system accurately. It is an important element utilized in model order reduction technique as a way to select an accurate reduced order model. in this work, the reduction errors are considered for the whole frequency range of the original system.To improve the efficiency of the proposed model order reduction technique, optimization technique will be utilized in this research. In order to obtain a lower reduction error, an accurate frequency interval is required. The main goal of optimization in a system is to obtain an optimized frequency interval in order to reduce the original system with the minimum error. The FFA and GSA estimation is based on calculation of minimum objective function by using integral square error (*ISE*).

Currently, the well-known optimization techniques are inspired by swarm intelligence. The advantages of this technique over traditional techniques are observed through its robustness and flexibility which can deal with complex problems [9]. Therefore, this paper will focus on model order reduction by combination of SPA and Gawronski and Juang method (FD-SPA) with the implementation of Firefly Algorithm (FFA) and Gravitational searching Algorithm (GSA) as the optimization technique. FFA and GSA is proposed in this work due to their robustness, versatility and easy to implement which requires a small number of parameters to run.

2 Activated Sludge Process

In biological stage of wastewater treatment plant, activated sludge process is the most common proses used. This research is focused more on the secondary treatment, which is the activated sludge process (ASP). The activated sludge process is capable to improve the effluent quality. In addition to that, activated sludge process is a highly reliable and flexible which is it can be implemented with any type of wastewater [10]. The conventional activated sludge process utilized reactors which consist of anoxic tank and aerobic tank. The number of tanks depend on the size of the distributed area.

An overview of activated sludge process for the case study, i.e. Bunus Regional Sewage Treatment (RSTP) is presented in the following sections.

2.1   Overview of Bunus Regional Sewage Treatment (RSTP)

In Fig. 1, block diagram of activated sludge for Bunus RSTP is presented. From [11], there are four reactors which consists two anoxic tanks and two aerobic tanks and a secondary clarifier in Bunus's activated sludge process.

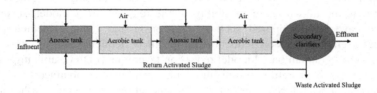

Fig. 1. Bunus's activated sludge process [11]

From the plant, four inputs data are obtained, which are Biochemical Oxygen Demand (BOD), Chemical Oxygen Demand (COD), Suspended Solids (SS) and Ammonium (NH4) whereas the output is *pH* of water. Based on previous research [11], the researcher focuses on modelling of single input single output (SISO) system, where the input is Suspended Solids and output is *pH*. A mathematical model of 20th order is obtained through System Identification via Linear ARX model in a state space form.

3   Proposed Algorithm, FD-SPA

In general, model order reduction technique is aimed at approximating a complex system to a simpler system while preserving the characteristic of the original system. In this section, the combination of singular perturbation approximation and frequency domain interval gramian based model reduction (FD-SPA) is presented. Consider the original system which is represented as state-space form in Eq. (1).

$$\dot{x} = Ax + Bu$$
$$y = Cx + Du \tag{1}$$

where u is the input and y is the output respectively. The frequency domain interval controllability gramian P and the observability gramian Q are respectively defined by

$$P(\omega) = \frac{1}{2\pi} \int_{-\infty}^{+\infty} R(\omega) BB^T R^*(\omega) d\omega \tag{2}$$

$$Q(\omega) = \frac{1}{2\pi} \int_{-\infty}^{+\infty} R^*(\omega)C^T CR(\omega)d\omega \tag{3}$$

where $R(\omega) = (j\omega - A)^{-1}$ and $R^*(\omega) = (-j\omega - A^*)^{-1}$. When the system is stable, the controllability gramian P and observability gramian Q, is equal and diagonal. The gramian P and Q are obtained by satisfying the following Lyapunov equations.

$$AP + PA^T = -BB^T$$
$$A^T Q + QA = -C^T C \tag{4}$$

P_Ω and Q_Ω respectively defined by Eq. (5).

$$P_\Omega = P(\omega_2) - P(\omega_1)$$
$$Q_\Omega = Q(\omega_2) - Q(\omega_1) \tag{5}$$

and $\Omega = (\omega_1, \omega_2)$ is the frequency interval of the system. Initially, the predefined frequency interval is based on trial and error focusing on the irregularities of the system since it is the most disturbed part of the system. With the implementation of FDIG technique in this equation, the predefined frequency interval is specified. Hence, by focussing at the predetermined frequency range, the proposed algorithm is able to significantly follow the most disturbed part of the system. Thus, the effectiveness of the proposed algorithm is highlighted. The equation of gramian $P(\omega)$ and $Q(\omega)$ are presented in Eqs. (6) and (7) respectively.

$$P(\omega) = \frac{1}{2\pi} \int_{-\infty}^{+\infty} R(\omega)BB^T R^*(\omega)d\omega \tag{6}$$

$$Q(\omega) = \frac{1}{2\pi} \int_{-\infty}^{+\infty} R^*(\omega)C^T R(\omega)d\omega \tag{7}$$

and $\Omega = [-\infty, \infty]$ the gramian $P = P_\Omega$ and $Q = Q_\Omega$. Alternatively, the limited frequency interval gramian P_Ω and Q_Ω in (5) are obtained from the Lyapunov equation as given in (8)

$$AP_\Omega + P_\Omega A^T + W_C(\Omega) = 0$$
$$A^T Q_\Omega + Q_\Omega A + W_O(\Omega) = 0 \tag{8}$$

where $W_C(\Omega) = W_C(\omega_2 - \omega_1)$ and $W_O(\Omega) = W_O(\omega_2 - \omega_1)$ and W_C and W_O are positive definite which act as low pass filters for the signal. Since WWTP is a fast response system [12], the technique offers a good advantage to the system. The equation then yield

$$P(\omega) = PS^*(\omega) + S(\omega)P$$
$$Q(\omega) = S^*(\omega)Q + QS(\omega)$$

(9)

and

$$W_C(\omega) = S(\omega)BB^T + BB^T S^*(\omega)$$
$$W_O(\omega) = S(\omega)C^T C + C^T C S^*(\omega)$$

(10)

where, $S^*(\omega)$ is the conjugate transpose of $S(\omega)$

$$S(\omega) = \frac{1}{2\pi} \int_{-\infty}^{+\infty} R(\omega)d\omega$$
$$= \frac{1}{2\pi} \ln(j\omega I - A)(-j\omega I + A)^{-1}$$

(11)

From the obtained frequency domain frequency interval gramian P_Ω and Q_Ω, the transformation T is obtained to transform the original system into a balanced realized system. Transformation T is obtained from the factorization of frequency domain interval gramian in (12)

$$P_\Omega = Q_\Omega = USV^T$$

(12)

where U and V are unitary matrices while S is a positive definite diagonal matrix. A balanced system is obtained by the following Eq. (13).

$$A_{bal} = T^{-1}AT$$
$$B_{bal} = T^{-1}B$$
$$C_{bal} = CT$$

(13)

From the balanced realized system, the controllable and observable state will be truncated by the SPA equation. Hence, the reduced system G_r obtained is stable and balanced as in Eq. (14). The best reduced model of the system is then chosen based on the minimum reduction error while preserving the characteristic of the original system. The reduced order model is given by $G_r = (A_{SP}, B_{SP}, C_{SP}, D_{SP})$ or in the matrix form,

$$G_r = \left[\begin{array}{c|c} A_{SP} & B_{SP} \\ \hline C_{SP} & D_{SP} \end{array}\right]$$

(14)

where

$$A_{SP} = A_{bal,11} - A_{bal,12}A_{bal,22}^{-1}A_{bal,21}$$
$$B_{SP} = B_{bal,1} - A_{bal,12}A_{bal,22}^{-1}B_{bal,2}$$
$$C_{SP} = C_{bal,1} - A_{bal,12}A_{bal,22}^{-1}C_{bal,2}$$
$$D_{SP} = D - C_{bal,2}A_{bal,22}^{-1}B_{bal,2}$$

(15)

To improve the effectiveness of the proposed MOR, swarm optimization technique is applied. As mentioned previously, the early predefined frequency interval is based on trial and error. Through the proposed optimization technique, an optimized frequency interval can be obtained. Optimization technique used in this research is swarm intelligence optimization which are Firefly Algorithm (FFA) and Gravitational Search Algorithm (GSA). The estimation of FFA and GSA techniques is based on the minimum value of the Integral Square Error (ISE) as shown in Eq. (16).

$$ISE = \int_0^\infty e^2(t)dt \tag{16}$$

where e is the error between the error between the estimated system G and the reduced system G_r which is $e = G_0(s) - G_r(s)$. Finally, an optimized reduced order model is obtained in Eq. (17) as shown below.

$$G_{OPT} = (A_{OPT}, B_{OPT}, C_{OPT}, D_{OPT}) \tag{17}$$

4   Swarm Intelligence Optimization

Currently, well-known optimization techniques are inspired by swarm intelligence. They are characterized by a decentralized way of working that mimics the behavior of social insects such as ants, bees and termites as well as other animal societies such as ant colonies, fish schooling, bird flocking and bird herding. The advantages of this technique over traditional techniques are observed through its robustness and flexibility which can deal with complex problems [9].

4.1   Firefly Algorithm (FFA)

The optimization technique proposed in this work is firefly algorithm (FFA). FFA is inspired by flashing pattern of behavior of fireflies in nature [13]. Their flashing light is produced by biochemical process of bioluminescence. The purpose of firefly flash is a signal system to attract other fireflies. The parameter setting for FFA technique is presented in Table 1. In literature [14], number of fireflies used for most application is

Table 1. The parameter setting for FFA technique.

Initialization	
No. of fireflies	30
No. of iteration	1000
Alpha, α	0.25
Beta, β	0.20
Gamma, γ	1
No. of fireflies	30

15 to 100, though the best range number of fireflies is between 25 and 40. For the parameter of alpha, beta and gamma, a default setting is used.

4.2 Gravitational Search Algorithm (GSA)

Another swarm intelligent technique is GSA, which is constructed based on the law of gravity and mass interactions. This algorithm uses the theory of Newtonian physic and its searcher agent are collection of masses [15]. In GSA, the masses are isolated. Every mass in the system can see the situation of other mass by using gravitational force. Therefore, gravitational mass is a way of transferring information between different masses [15]. In Table 2, the parameter setting for GSA technique is shown. The selection of parameter is important in optimization tuning. In this optimization technique, parameter alpha used is 25 in order to decrease the computational time.

Table 2. The parameter setting for GSA technique.

Initialization	
No. of agents	50
No. of iteration	1000
Alpha, α	25
G constant	100
No. of agents	50
No. of iteration	1000

5   Results and Discussion

To reduce the high order system to a lower order system, model order reduction technique of the proposed MOR, FD-SPA are applied to the case study. A good reduced order model is chosen based on the lowest reduction error while preserving the characteristics of the original system. In this work, the proposed technique focuses on low frequency intervals which is less than 1 rad/s [16]. Due to the operational cost of real plant, the required model order system applicable to plant operation is ranged between 1st and 10th. The results obtained are represented in Sigma plot as well as in numerical values.

5.1   Analysis on Raw Data from Bunus Regional Sewage Treatment Plant (RSTP)

The purpose of this analysis is to show that the proposed algorithm is applicable to a single-input-single-output (SISO) linear system. In the proposed technique, the predefined frequency interval is between 0.22 rad/s to 1.4 rad/s. By utilizing, FD-SPA, Table 3 shows the numerical reduction error of the reduced order model of 1st to 10th order using the proposed FD-SPA technique. The reduction errors are considered for

Table 3. Reduction error of FD-SPA MOR technique for 1st to 10th order system.

Order	Reduction error
10th	0.0422
9th	0.0025
8th	0.0029
7th	0.0107
6th	0.0026
5th	0.0129
4th	0.0087
3rd	0.0108
2nd	0.0106
1st	0.1058

the whole of the original system. The reduction errors are considered for the whole of the original system. From the behaviour of the reduced order models and the numerical reduction error, it can be concluded that the reduced order of models 6th, 8th and 9th order are considered as the best reduced order models with the proposed FD-SPA technique.

To show the effectiveness of the proposed technique, the reduced 9th order system is emphasized. As previously mentioned, the predefined frequency interval is between 0.22 rad/s and 1.4 rad/s. Based on Fig. 2, it is observed that the reduced 9th order system follows the original system closely, especially at low frequencies as well as the predefined frequency interval between 0.22 rad/s to 10.5 rad/s.

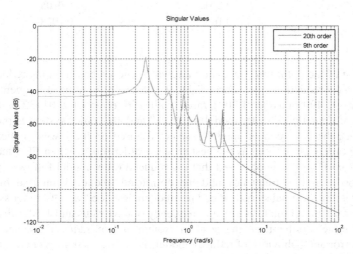

Fig. 2. Sigma plot of the reduced order model using FD-SPA technique for 9th order system

5.1.1 Analysis of Optimization Using FFA

In order to improve the effectiveness of the model order reduction, FFA technique is implemented. In the early stage of the research, the range of predefined frequency interval was determined based on trial and error. The predefined frequency interval is 0.22 rad/s to 1.4 rad/s. Thus, in order to find an accurate optimized frequency interval three different range of frequency intervals along the irregularities of the system are chosen. Then, in order to find the optimized frequency interval, several iterations of optimization tuning simulation is performed. Once the optimized frequency range is obtained, these values are applied to the proposed FD-SPA technique, and optimized reduction error is obtained. Table 4, the numerical reduction error of reduced order model from 1st to 10th order of the chosen optimized frequency interval is presented.

Table 4. The reduction error from 1st to 10th order reduced model using FFA technique.

Order/optimized frequency interval (rad/s)	Reduction error		
	0.0499–1.3106	0.1501–1.3017	0.2499–1.3001
10th	0.0024	0.0024	0.0024
9th	0.0025	0.0025	0.0025
8th	0.0036	0.0031	0.0028
7th	0.0028	0.0029	0.0026
6th	0.0027	0.0026	0.0025
5th	0.0181	0.0171	0.0140
4th	0.0088	0.0087	0.0086
3rd	0.0174	0.0140	0.0145
2nd	0.0108	0.0107	0.0105
1st	0.1063	0.1059	0.1058

The best of the optimized frequency interval is chosen based on the reduced model with the lowest reduction error. Form Table 4, the best of optimized frequency interval is between 0.2499 rad/s to 1.3001 rad/s with *ISE* error of 6.01632×10^{-6}. The behaviour of the reduced order model of 6th, 9th and 10th order system is presented in Fig. 3. Since the best reduced model is selected based on the lowest reduction error, these three orders are chosen as the best reduced order model when FFA technique is utilized. From Fig. 3, it is observed that the reduced order model follows the original system closely at low frequency and the optimized frequency interval but slightly deviates from the original system at certain frequencies. A 6th and 9th order system start to deviate from the original system at a frequency of 0.81 rad/s and 1.50 rad/s while the 10th order system differ from the original system at 1.66 rad/s. Thus, depending on reduction error and behaviour of reduced model, 10th order system is chosen as the best reduced models.

From Fig. 4, the convergence curve shows how the fitness changes during optimization process. In Fig. 4, it can be observed that the FFA technique converges at around 142nd iteration.

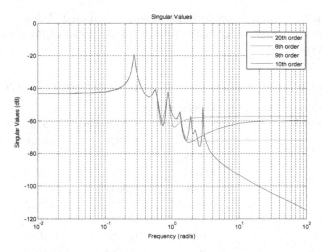

Fig. 3. Sigma plot of the reduced order model between frequencies 0.2499 rad/s to 1.3001 rad/s for of 6th, 9th, and 10th order system

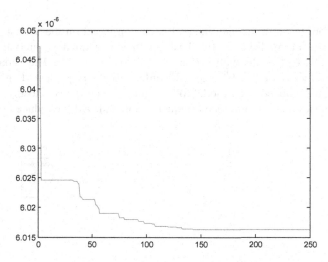

Fig. 4. The convergence curve of optimization for the optimized frequency interval using FFA technique

5.1.2   Analysis of Optimization Using GSA

Another swarm optimization technique discussed in this work is the utilization of gravitational search algorithm (GSA) with the proposed FD-SPA MOR technique. As the optimization process is similar, three different ranges of frequency intervals along the irregularities of the system are chosen. In order to obtain an optimized frequency interval, several iterations of optimization tuning is acquired. Table 5, the numerical reduction error of reduced order model from 1st to 10th order of the chosen optimized frequency interval.

Table 5. The reduction error from 1st to 10th order reduced model using GSA technique.

Order/optimized frequency interval (rad/s)	Reduction error		
	0.4432–0.6743	0.4499–0.6597	0.5389–0.6580
10th	0.0026	0.0026	0.0026
9th	0.0025	0.0026	0.0036
8th	0.0027	0.0027	0.0055
7th	0.0046	0.0048	0.0295
6th	0.0734	0.0740	0.0822
5th	0.0737	0.0746	0.0992
4th	0.1056	0.1056	0.1057
3rd	0.1063	0.1063	0.1057
2nd	0.1063	0.1063	0.1065
1st	0.1064	0.1064	0.1066

The best optimized frequency interval is chosen based on the lowest or minimum reduction error. From Table 5, the best optimized frequency interval is between 0.4432 rad/s to 0.6743 rad/s with *ISE* error of 3.90494×10^{-7}. The behaviour of the reduced order model of 8th, 9th and 10th order system is presented in Fig. 5. It is observed that the reduced order model follows the original system closely, significantly at low frequencies and the optimized frequency interval. All the reduced order models

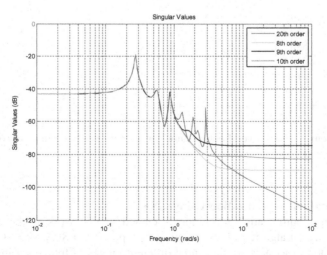

Fig. 5. Sigma plot of the reduced order between frequencies 0.4432 rad/s to 0.6743 rad/s for 8th, 9th and 10th order system

deviate from the original system at a frequency of 1.05 rad/s. It can be observed that the behaviour of the three reduced order models are quite similar. Hence, based on the lowest reduction error, it can be concluded that the 9th order system is the optimized reduced order model when GSA technique is applied.

From Fig. 6, the change of fitness during optimization process can be monitored. It is observed form Fig. 6 that the GSA technique converges at early stage which is at the 127th iteration.

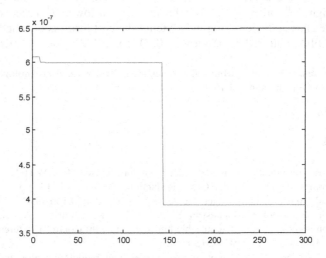

Fig. 6. The convergence curve of optimization for the optimized frequency interval using GSA technique

5.1.3 Summary

Table 6 shows the reduced order model and the reduction error from the predefined frequency interval and optimization techniques. It is observed that FFA and GSA technique present a different range of frequency intervals. By utilizing the proposed FD-SPA technique, a reduced model of 9th order provides the lowest reduction error compared to GSA and the trial and error technique. However, the difference between

Table 6. The comparison of the reduction error between predefined frequency interval and the optimized frequency interval.

Frequency interval (rad/s)	Best reduce model	Reduction error
Predefined (0.22–1.40)	9th	0.0025
FFA (0.2499–1.3001)	10th	0.0024
GSA (0.4432–0.6743)	9th	0.0025

the trial and error reduction error and optimized reduction error is too small, hence both techniques can be considered as the best optimization technique for the proposed algorithm.

6   Conclusion

In this paper, a new model order reduction technique which emphasizes on low frequency range is proposed. Based on the results obtained, FD-SPA technique is able to reduce the high 20th order of the WWTP model to a lower 9th order system while preserving the characteristic of original system. The best result is obtained through the utilization of FFA, with reduction error of 0.0024 and *ISE* value of 6.01632×10^{-6}.

Acknowledgments. The author would like to acknowledge Universiti Teknologi Malaysia for Geran Universiti Penyelidikan (GUP) Tier 2 Vot Number 14J58.

References

1. Schilders, W.: Introduction to model order reduction. In: Schilders, W.H.A., van der Vorst, H.A., Rommes, J. (eds.) Model Order Reduction: Theory, vol. 13, pp. 3–32. Research Aspects and Applications. Springer, Heidelberg (2008). doi:10.1007/978-3-540-78841-6_1
2. Ishizakiy, T., Sandberg, H., Johansson, K.H., Kashima, K., Imura, J.I., Aihara, K.: Singular perturbation approximation of semistable linear systems. In: Control Conference (ECC), 17 July 2013, European, pp. 4508–4513 (2013)
3. Kumar, D., Nagar, S.K.: A new frequency weighted model reduction technique using balanced singular perturbation approximation. In: India Conference (INDICON), 13 December 2013. Annual IEEE, pp. 1–5 (2013)
4. Saragih, R.: Singular perturbation approximation of balanced infinite-dimensional systems. Int. J. Control Autom. **6**(5), 409–420 (2013)
5. Ghafoor, A., Sahlan, S., Sreeram, V.: A new frequency weighted model reduction technique and error bounds. In: 2007 International Conference on Mechatronics and Automation, 5 August 2007, pp. 1962–1967. IEEE (2007)
6. Kumar, D., Nagar, S.: Square-root frequency weighted balanced model reduction via singular perturbation approximation. In: Electrical Engineering Congress (iEECON International), 14 March 2014. IEEE, pp. 1–4 (2014)
7. Enns, D.F.: Model reduction with balanced realizations: an error bound and a frequency weighted generalization. In: The 23rd IEEE Conference on Decision and Control, 12 December 1984. IEEE, pp. 127–132 (1984)
8. Gawronski, W., Juang, J.-N.: Model reduction in limited time and frequency intervals. Int. J. Syst. Sci. **21**(2), 349–376 (1990)
9. Blum, C., Li, X.: Swarm intelligence in optimization. In: Blum, C., Merkle, D. (eds.) Swarm intelligence. Natural Computing Series, pp. 43–85. Springer, Heidelberg (2008). doi:10. 1007/978-3-540-74089-6_2
10. Mulas, M.: Modelling and control of activated sludge processes. University Degli Studi di Cagliari (2006)
11. Halim, F.A.: Empirical Modelling Of Activated Sludge Process Via System Identification. Universiti Teknologi Malaysia, Johor Bahru (2014). Bachelor of Engineering

12. Eek, R.T.P., Sahlan, S., Wahab, N.A.: Modeling of waste water treatment plant via system id & model reduction technique. In: 2012 IEEE Conference on Control, Systems & Industrial Informatics (ICCSII), 23 September 2012, pp. 131–136 (2012)
13. Yang, X.-S.: Firefly algorithm. Nature-inspired metaheuristic algorithms. **20**, 79–90 (2008)
14. Yang, X.-S.: Firefly algorithms for multimodal optimization. In: International Symposium on Stochastic Algorithms, pp. 169–178 (2009)
15. Rashedi, E., Nezamabadi-Pour, H., Saryazdi, S.: GSA: a gravitational search algorithm. Inf. Sci. **179**(13), 2232–2248 (2009)
16. Lee, T., Wang, F., Newell, R.: Robust model-order reduction of complex biological processes. J. Process Control **12**(7), 807–821 (2002)

Dynamic Planning of Infrastructure and Logistics Resources in Distribution Centers

Mauricio Becerra Fernández[1][✉]
and Olga Rosana Romero Quiroga[2][✉]

[1] Engineering Faculty, Catholic University of Colombia, Bogotá, Colombia
mbecerra@ucatolica.edu.co
[2] Technical Management, Suppla S.A., Bogotá, Colombia
olga.romero@suppla.com

Abstract. Logistics operators face the dilemma about how to increase the efficiency of logistics networks in high demand volatility environments, reaching the best possible cost, especially in distribution centers in the supply chain which significantly absorbs capital of the organizations. This work is based on a Colombian logistic operator. The article approaches the contrast of scenarios for the development of infrastructures at the level of heights and lease contract time of the warehouse from a dynamic perspective using systems dynamics modelling, as a support tool for financial and contractual decisions as well as for the allocation of resources as collaborators and logistics equipment which, by integrating market variability, provides a strategic vision in different planning horizons for the evaluation of performance measures, depending on the use of resources, demand served, lower operating costs and growth in financial results.

Keywords: System dynamics simulation · Distribution centers · Infrastructure · Resource allocation · System capacity · Logistic operator

1 Introduction

Transformations in value chains, lead to changes in the management of logistics networks, demanding greater efficiency and effectiveness. In this environment, the efforts of logistic experts are based on designing robust planning and control systems, along with performance measurement tools, pursuing a better allocation of resources. The main challenge, then, is to balance the variability of demand conditions using capacity models to facilitate and reduce uncertainty in decision-making.

Dynamic market conditions are especially relevant for companies specializing in the management of logistics networks, companies which continually seek strategies to improve the performance of value chains and the ability to integrate the actors competing in the market, however those companies have the opportunity to cooperate in their logistics processes, with an integral vision to cope with the growing and evolving complexity of systems. According to the annual study of logistics operators carried out by Capgemini [1], in the particular case of Colombia, growth rates in the logistics

© Springer Nature Singapore Pte Ltd. 2017
M.S. Mohamed Ali et al. (Eds.): AsiaSim 2017, Part II, CCIS 752, pp. 760–773, 2017.
DOI: 10.1007/978-981-10-6502-6_64

sector have grown between 11% and 22% in the last 6 years, showing a clear tendency towards outsourcing. However, despite this growth, the levels are far removed from those in reference to countries such as the United States and some European countries.

Logistic operators arise as specialized experts in the optimization of supply chains that should promote strategies. According to Armstrong [2], 88% of the first 100 "Fortune 500" companies hire third-party logistics services (3PLs) and the lasts 100, only hire 21%. In addition, outsourcing logistics operations can reduce costs by up to 15% and logistics companies achieve between 10% and 25% savings in the time of the product delivery cycle.

The search for efficiencies by the side of these operators, must entail the increase of competitiveness, reflected in aspects such as costs, opportunity and innovation, that is to say, a greater capacity of the process to attend increasingly dynamic markets, with variable demands, short product life cycles, atomization of the final destination, direct delivery to the consumer, service associated with the product, traceability and visibility of supply chain flow.

Considering the aspects mentioned above, it becomes more important to think about a common connector of logistics processes, such as distribution centers, locations which, in addition to guaranteeing the preservation of merchandise, should also act as central axis of planning in the supply chain and aggregation product value, hence it is also important to have infrastructures that increase the efficiency of logistical flows, generating benefits for the operators that can later be perceived by their customers and consumers.

The above creates an adequate space to develop models that facilitate the understanding of the implications of infrastructure design and resource allocation, such as the relevance of investments to be made, productivity of the equipment and impact on logistics costs, through the dynamic evaluation of the performance of distribution centers, area in which increasing limitations as the availability of land, plus the variability of the demand faced by logistics operators, challenge the decision makers, who under controlled environments, must analyse with a medium and long term perspective the effect of the leverage points of business growth and the increase of competitiveness.

The planning of operational capacities has been approached by various authors such as Heizer and Render [3], Hopp and Spearman [4], Krajewski and Ritzman [5], Sipper and Bulfin [6], Chase et al. [7], Collier and Evans [8]. Chopra and Meindl [9], Krajewski and Ritzman [5], define aggregate planning as a process for determining required resource levels related to aggregate decisions rather than decisions at the unit level. Heizer and Render [3], Hillier and Liberman [10] and Burkard et al. [11], propose allocation models in order to minimize costs. Authors as Gu et al. [12], Buil and Piera [13], Zevgolis [14], Gray et al. [15], Suk and Sung [16], Men and Zhou [17], Rao and Rao [18], Xu and An [19], Berg and Zijm [20], Geng et al. [21] develop models for the design of distribution centers focusing on logistics equipment and layout.

According to the literature review, there is no evidence of research addressing the logistics infrastructure in warehouses based on the dynamic behaviour of the market and its continuous feedback, the variability of demand and the impact that this can generate in the adequate definition of the specifications of the locations, all this associated to variables such as height, impact of lease contract times, necessary investments and the continuous planning in the allocation of resources, which together allow to respond aptly to the service levels and the profitability and growth of a company.

An adequate combination of the variables of height and time of contract of lease of the distribution center are determining factors in the logistic model to be implemented, due to their direct incident on the level of investments and financial corporate stress, which in turn define in a direct way the continuity of the companies and added to the situations of the environment, such as the growth exceeded of the mega-cities, shortage of physical spaces and high costs of the land, generate a major challenge before the search state of the decrease of the logistic costs and where precisely the activities of the distribution center represent 38% of the total of these costs [22].

This article deals with the planning of logistics capabilities from a strategic perspective that facilitates the decision making in the development of locations of the logistics network to achieve sustained growth and profitability of the business and in a tactical level, it provides a dynamic model for proper administration of resources in an environment of uncertainty and constant change.

2 Simulation Model

The study is approached using system dynamics methodology for analysing the causal relations and the feedback of the system, and through the effects of its variables and the behaviour in the time. The stages considered in the modelling process are illustrated below (See Fig. 1).

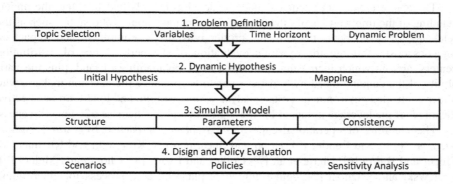

Fig. 1. Phases in the construction of the system dynamics model for the selection of infrastructure and allocation of resources.

2.1 Subscripts, Parameters and Variables of the Model

For the development of the model using system dynamics, elements such as subscripts, parameters and variables were defined. Tables 1 and 2 present the most relevant.

Table 1. Model subscripts.

Subscript	Description	Iteration	Units
i	Simulation Time	(1, 2, 3,..., 60)	Months
l	Height	(1 = 8, 2 = 12, 3 = 18)	Meters
k	Installation contract time	(1 = 60; 2 = 120)	Months

Table 2. Elements of the model.

Type	Name
Parameters of the model	• Workforce performance • Equipment performance • Performance of positions per square meter • Growth Policy • Delay in equipment assignment • Delay in equipment deallocation • Financing rate • Gross margin target • Market price • Contract time • Delay in the allocation of workforce • Delay in workforce deallocation
Stock variables	• Served Demand • Non-Served • Square Meters • Equipment in the system • Workforce • Total Cost • Total Revenues • Revenue not Collected • Accumulated Gross Margin
Flow variables	• Expected Demand • Served Demand • Square Meters Assigned • De-assigned square meters • Assigned Equipment • De-assigned Equipment • Assigned workforce • De-assigned workforce • Perceived Revenue • Revenue not Collected • Total Cost • Gross Margin • Capacity used
Auxiliary variables	• Available position capacity • Available Equipment Capacity • Available workforce capacity • Capacity for equipment assignment • Capacity for workers assignment • Capacity for allocation of square meters • System capacity • Projected demand • Discrepancy of demand • Occupancy index of installed positions • Occupancy index of system's capacity • Growth module • Capacity required • Equipment required • Workforce required • Security cost • Cost of utilities • Depreciations • Maintenance cost • Other costs • Cost per square meter • Cost per equipment mobilization • Cost per worker • Renting cost • Cost of equipment mobilization • Workforce cost • Cost per position • Margin discrepancy • Price discrepancy • Gross Margin per Month • Price per position

The stock and flow diagram that relates the mentioned elements of the model is shown in the Fig. 2.

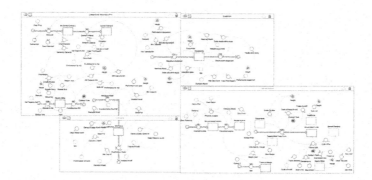

Fig. 2. Stock and flow diagram

2.2   Sectors of the Model

To analyse the model, four sectors were developed to collect the behaviour of the system and allow the generation of performance measures, as shown in Fig. 3 and explained below (the blue line describe the material flow and the red line describe the information flow).

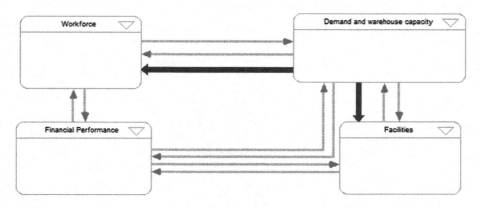

Fig. 3. Sectors of the dynamic model.

Demand and Capacity Sector

For the projection of aggregate demand and volumetric capacity required to meet the necessary logistic positions, performance measures were used as the aggregate demand satisfied (which includes the total demand served, from the grouping of the needs of two or more clients of the logistics provider), the capacity used, the capacity required and the occupancy rate, which are subject to the height of the distribution center and the lease time of the facility, resulting in logistical costs which make part of the gross margin of the year and that constraint the growth of the collaborative warehouse in terms of square meters assigned.

Mobilization Equipment Sector
In the allocation of mobilization equipment, based on the height analysed, the performance of the equipment is determined according to the productivity achieved in terms of its characteristics, which allows to calculate the need to assign or to dis-assign equipment, the previous is associated to the installed capacity of positions as a result of projected aggregate demand.

Workforce Sector
For the workforce allocation sector, the height of the distribution center and the consolidated capacity to be served defined by the projection of aggregate demand, affects the collaborative allocation or dis-assignment of workforce, which depends on compliance with corporate policies, such as the target of gross margin, affected by logistical costs, which among other elements is subject to the contract time of the installation, thus affecting the total demand of the system.

Financial Performance Sector
With the calculation of the capacity of the system, dependent on the three sectors: volume space, mobilization equipment and workforce, the demand to be served as a result of available resources is determined, which generates costs associated with other resources, such as surveillance, utilities, maintenance and depreciation. The sum of the costs associated with all resources, determines the cost of the service and thus, the selling price. With these elements, it is possible to calculate the performance of each scenario, where the objective is to increase the gross margin and the demand served as a result of the logistic operation.

3 Simulation and Discussion

The simulation is developed through the different strategies that allow determining the allocation of resources (area, workers and equipment) to obtain the best financial margin and income of the analysed period, with a run of 60 months. As performance measures, the utilization of capacity, demand served and gross margin as a result of the operation are calculated. Finally, we analyse the convergence of the capacity utilization and the margin of the operation in order to contrast them with the dynamic hypothesis: A logistic operator when planning its infrastructure in distribution centers considering heights and contract time, can improve logistic performance measures at the financial level, demand growth and resource utilization.

For this, within the model the contrast of different strategies for the design of infrastructure is performed by combining the heights in the distribution center and the contract times as shown in Table 3. As for the height of the distribution center, it is evaluated considering the current national regulations and policies on maximum construction spaces according to geographical location and contract times are subject to

Table 3. Heights at the distribution center and installation lease contract times.

Model variations			
Height in meters (A)	8	12	18
Contract time in months (C)	60	120	

market conditions, where by type Infrastructure and the value of investments and their return, times are managed between 60 and 120 months.

The analysis of the results is based on the evaluation of six strategies to determine the best combination of distribution center height and lease time (see Table 4).

Table 4. Variations in the model for the analysis of strategies.

Strategy	Storage height	Contract time
Strategy 1	8	60
Strategy 2	8	120
Strategy 3	12	60
Strategy 4	12	120
Strategy 5	18	60
Strategy 6	18	120

3.1 Behaviour of the Model's Input Data

In the analysis of the input variables of the model, the variable demand of aggregated logistic positions was used for the total of selected clients. Projected demand is affected by changes in the system at warehouse in terms of height and time of lease of the facilities, which affects financial performance with market impact, affecting either positively or negatively the demand. The projected demand is reduced as the height of the warehouse is lower, obtaining the highest demands for cases in which the height of the warehouse is 18 m and 12 m with contract times of 120 months (see Fig. 4).

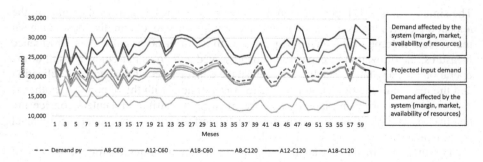

Fig. 4. Behaviour of demand.

3.2   Total Costs Behaviour

The costs of the system as a result of the allocation of resources (area, work force and equipment), allow determining the cost per position occupied, associated with the demand served. The behaviour of these costs is reflected in Fig. 5, with the best average cost in the warehouse of 12 m and contract time of 120 months, compared to the lowest performance in the warehouse of 8 m and contract time of 60 Months.

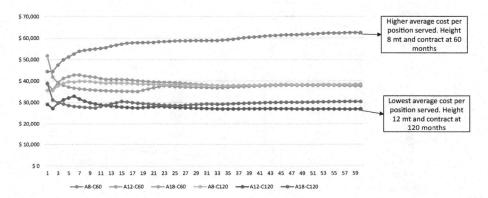

Fig. 5. Behaviour of total costs per occupied logistics position.

3.3   Occupation Rate

The highest occupancy rate of the system's capacity is obtained in the warehouse of 12 m high and 120 months of contract, with an average occupancy of 90.5% versus the warehouse of 8 m and 60 months of contract with an average occupation of 63.3% (see Fig. 6).

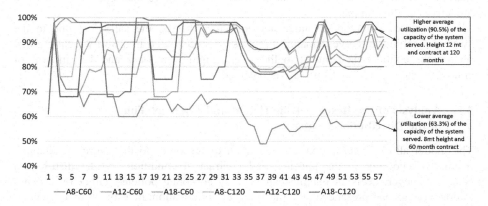

Fig. 6. Occupation rate of the capacity of the system.

3.4   Financial Performance

The performance of the system is analysed through the result of the accumulated operating margin in the simulated period, the revenues received and the revenues not received by the non-served demand (see Fig. 7).

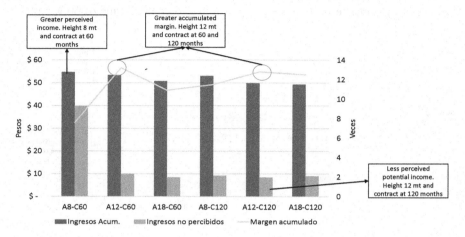

Fig. 7. Ratio of net interest income, accumulated income and non-perceived income.

The largest accumulated financial margin is obtained in a distribution center with 12 m of height with 60 and 120 months of lease, equivalent to 13.2 times and 12.8 times, correspondingly. Significantly away from financial performance in low-height distribution centers.

Regarding perceived revenues, the best performing strategy is the equivalent of a distribution center at 8 m high and a contract to 60 months, however, its financial margin is 7.6 times, implying that at the level of financial results, this is not the most attractive for the company.

In terms of potential revenues not collected, that is, the sales lost due to the system's inability to serve demand, it is mostly concentrated in a 8-m warehouse and 60 months contract, in contrast to the 12-m height warehouse and 120 months of contract, where the lowest lost sale is obtained.

3.5   Analysis of the Results of the Height and Contract Time of the Distribution Center

The model allows determining the allocation of resources to the aggregate demand planning, according to the physical and contractual conditions of the distribution center, however, decision making can vary by corporate policies, either by a penetration strategy and presence in the market, cost optimization, investment management, innovation and sales increase.

For this case study, the measures of performance and behaviour of the system variables are evaluated through the financial margin obtained and the demand served, as fundamental aspects that determine the sustainability of the business and positioning in the market, seen as the greater capture of demand to an adequate margin, improving the allocation of resources associated with the provision of the service (see Fig. 8).

Fig. 8. Elements for the evaluation of the strategy.

Accordingly, a weighting of the results obtained at the level of financial margin and demand served by the different strategies is made, considering that the shareholders of the business are more interested in the result at the margin level, but with a relevant participation in the market that allows positioning. According to this, we consider the financial margin with a weight of 0.6 and the demand served in 0.4 (see Tables 5 and 6).

Table 5. Accumulated margin and demand served for each strategy.

Strategy	Accumulated margin (times)	Demand served (10 thousands)
A8-C60	7.6	77.1
A12-C60	13.2	110.6
A18-C60	11.1	108.7
A8-C120	11.5	112.0
A12-C120	12.8	145.0
A18-C120	10.7	129.2

Table 6. Weighting results.

Strategy	Accumulated margin (0,6)	Demand served (0,4)	Total weighted
A8-C60	35%	21%	56%
A12-C60	60%	31%	91%
A18-C60	50%	30%	80%
A8-C120	52%	31%	83%
A12-C120	58%	40%	**98%**
A18-C120	49%	36%	84%

According to the data obtained, the strategy that allows to obtain the best combination between the financial margin and demand served is through the distribution center of 12 m in height with contract to 120 months (see Fig. 9).

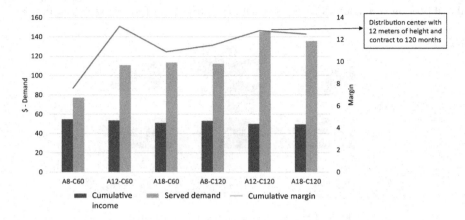

Fig. 9. Contrast of accumulated financial margin vs. demand served and income received.

Although the accumulated revenues are not the highest, the demand served is increased as a result of the allocation and use of resources, which impacts on costs and prices of the most competitive service, generating an attractive financial margin for the business

3.6   Hypothesis Testing

It is interesting to verify that factors such as the height and time of lease affect the financial margin and the demand served in the proposed model. Using the F test (Fisher) in the Eqs. (1) and (2) to analyse the following hypothesis.

Height and contract time of the distribution center and its effect over the financial margin

- H_0: The height and time of lease of the distribution center do not influence the financial margin.
- H_1: The height and time of lease of the distribution center influence the financial margin.
- Significance level $\alpha = 0.05$

$$F \sim F_{0.05;2;348} = 3.021 < F_c = 3.377 \tag{1}$$

- Decision: Reject the null hypothesis.
- Conclusion: The sample data make it possible to determine that the height and time of the lease contract of the distribution center influence the financial margin.

Height and time of contract of the distribution center and its effect over the demand served

- H_0: The height and time of lease of the distribution center do not influence the demand served.
- H_1: The height and time of lease of the distribution center influence the demand served.
- Significance level $\alpha = 0.05$

$$F \sim F_{0.05;2;348} = 3.021 < F_c = 5.605 \tag{2}$$

- Decision: Reject the null hypothesis.
- Conclusion: The sample data allow us to determine that the height and time of the lease of the distribution center, influence the demand served.

4 Conclusions and Future Work

The variability of the markets generates the need to approach logistic designs from a dynamic perspective, especially when their performance is directly linked to the competitiveness of organizations in an environment of uncertainty.

This work succeeds in representing the system through an integral model, which combines aspects of a strategic and tactical nature, as well as physical and financial resources, which together generate a broad picture for decision-making that directly affects the logistic services, but that also cascades to customers and consumers, to improve logistic performance across.

Likewise, the development of this model, as a continuous simulation technique, facilitates the operationalization of corporate strategies of the logistic operator, which is the object of the case study, for the implementation of an efficient network, involving the allocation of investments associated with the type of infrastructure, conditions contractual and dynamic capacity planning.

For the case study, the model allows to evaluate the infrastructure of the distribution center, which although intuitively may indicate that greater use should be made of the volumetric space, for example, warehouses over 18 m high, however under the conditions studied in terms of level of investment, contract times, costs of necessary resources and leasing costs, results show that the option that best option representing the interests of the logistics operator, in terms of encouraging the growth of demand, greater use of resources and improvement of the logistical cost, is a distribution center of 12.2 m of free storage height.

Given the above, this work is presented as a contribution to logistic operators, aligned with market expectations, thanks to its prospective approach and that under the analysis of conventional methods, would not allow the dynamic integration of elements that are within the reach of this work, such as times of delay, causal relationships not evident and the affectation of corporate policies.

For future research, we propose to analyse collaborative processes between customers competing in the market but who can take advantage of synergies, due to the consolidated and specialized action of the logistics operator, with a view not only to the corporate impact, but also to increase competitiveness for the environment in general, as well as the integration of new technologies that can increase operational efficiency in a sustainable way.

References

1. Langley, J., Capgemini (2014). http://www.capgemini.com/, http://www.capgemini.com/resource-file-access/resource/pdf/3pl_study_report_web_version.pdf. Último acceso: Agosto 2014
2. Armstrong & Associates: Agosto 2014. http://www.3plogistics.com/3PLmarketGlobal.htm. Último acceso: Agosto 2014
3. Heizer, J., Render, B.: Principios de adminsitración de operaciones. Prentice Hall, Méxio (2009)
4. Hopp, W.J., Spearman, M.L.: Factory Physics: Foundations of Manufacturing Management, p. 216. McGraw-Hill, New York (2001)
5. Krajewski, L.J., Ritzman, L.J.: Administración de operaciones, estrategia y análisis, pp. 9, 300. Pearson education, México (2000)
6. Sipper, D., Bulfin Jr., R.L.: Planeación y Control de la Producción, Primera edición, p. 177. McGraw-Hill, México (1998)
7. Chase, R.B., Jacobs, F.R., Aquílano, N.J.: Administración de la producción y operaciones para una ventaja competitiva, pp. 243, 275, 276, 279, 432, 444. McGraw-Hill, México (2005)
8. Collier, D.A., Evans, J.R.: The Service/Quality Solution: Using service management to gain competitive advantage, pp. 11, 16. Thompson Ediciones, Burr Ridge (1994)
9. Chopra, S., Meindl, P.: Administración de la cadena de suministro. Prentice Hall, México (2008)
10. Hillier, F.S., Liberman, G.J.: Introducción a la Investigación de Operaciones. McGraw-Hill, México (2002)
11. Burkard, R., Dell'Amico, M., Martello, S.: Assignment Problems, p. 2. Society for Industrial and Applied Mathematics, USA (2009)
12. Gu, J., Goetschalckx, M., McGinnis, L.F.: Research on warehouse design and performance evaluation: a comprehensive review. Eur. J. Oper. Res. **203**, 539–549 (2010)
13. Buil, R., Piera, M.A.: Warehouse redesign to satisfy tight supply chain management constraints. WSEAS Trans. Inf. Sci. Appl. **5**, 286–291 (2008)
14. Zevgolis, I.: Building underground: special techniques for a storage facility. In: Construction Research Congress 2005: Broadening Perspectives, pp. 1079–1088 (2005)
15. Gray, A., Karmakar, U., Seidmann, A.: Design and operation of an order-consolidation warehouse: Models and application. Eur. J. Oper. Res. **58**(1), 14–36 (1992)
16. Suk, H., Sung, G.: A performance evaluation model for order picking warehouse design. Comput. Ind. Eng. **51**(2), 335–342 (2006)
17. Men, J., Zhou, H.: Modeling and simulation for warehouse design based on witness. J. Syst. Simul. 420–424 (2011)
18. Rao, A., Rao, M.: Solution procedures for sizing of warehouses. Eur. J. Oper. Res. **108**(1), 16–25 (1998)
19. Xu, H., An, L.: Warehousing planning and design of specialty resources in Shangzhi logistics park. In: Logistics Engineering and Intelligent Transportation Systems (2010)

20. Berg, J.V.D., Zijm, W.: Models for warehouse management: classification and examples. Int. J. Prod. Econ. **59**(1), 519–528 (1999)
21. Geng, J., Lu, Y., Yang, H., Chen, D.: The design of stereoscopic warehouse stacker' motion and control system. In: Lee, G. (ed.) Advances in Automation and Robotics, Vol. 2. Lecture Notes in Electrical Engineering, vol. 123. Springer, Heidelberg (2011). doi:10.1007/978-3-642-25646-2_18
22. Guasch, J.L.: Inter-American Development Bank (2011). http://www.iadb.org/wmsfiles/products/publications/documents/36610117.pdf. Último acceso: 12 2014

Author Index

Printed in the United States
By Bookmasters